WHERE TO GO WHEN
ITALY

WHERE TO GO WHEN
ITALY

FOREWORD BY FRANCES MAYES

DK

LONDON, NEW YORK, MELBOURNE, MUNICH, AND DELHI

CONTRIBUTORS Annalisa Pomilio, Elisa Checchi, Rino Parlapiano, William dello Russo, Adrian Woodford
TRANSLATORS Jennifer Radice, Fiona Wild
LIST MANAGERS Julie Oughton, Christine Stroyan
DESIGN MANAGERS Mabel Chan, Sunita Gahir
SENIOR EDITOR Sadie Smith
EDITORS Fay Franklin, Hugh Thompson
ART EDITOR Tracy Smith
DTP DESIGNER Jamie McNeill
PRODUCTION CONTROLLER Rebecca Short
PROOFREADER Debra Wolter
INDEX Helen Peters
AMERICANIZER Helen Morford
PUBLISHER Douglas Amrine

Reproduced by Adda Officine Grafiche Spa, Filago (Bergamo, Italy)
Printed and bound in Singapore by Star Standard PTE

First published in the United States by Dorling Kindersley Publishing Inc., 375 Hudson Street, New York 10014
First American Edition 2010
10 11 12 13 10 9 8 7 6 5 4 3 2 1

A CATALOG IN PUBLICATION RECORDS IS AVAILABLE FROM THE LIBRARY OF CONGRESS.

ISBN 978-0-7566-6905-8

www.traveldk.com

Every effort has been made to ensure that this book is as up-to-date as possible at the time of going to press. Some details, however, such as telephone numbers, opening hours, prices, and travel information are liable to change. The publishers cannot accept responsibility for any consequences arising from the use of this book, nor for any material on third-party websites, and cannot guarantee that any website address in this book will be a suitable source of travel information. We value the views and suggestions of our readers very highly. Please write to: Publisher, DK Travel Guides, Dorling Kindersley, 80 Strand, London, WC2R 0RL, Great Britain.

HALF TITLE IMAGE: The Leaning Tower of Pisa, Tuscany
TITLE PAGE IMAGE: The Colosseum, Rome, Lazio
FOREWORD IMAGE: The Puez-Odle Massif, Parco Nazionale Puez-Odle, Trentino-Alto Adige

CONTENTS

JULY

AUGUST

SEPTEMBER

OCTOBER

NOVEMBER

DECEMBER

FOREWORD

People often ask me, "When is the best time to go to Italy?" I pretend to contemplate for a moment, then reply, "January through December." My answer is true – anytime is good for a trip to Italy; all the months have their unique qualities. My favorite time happens to be winter, when Italy totally belongs to itself. Fewer travelers are about, so that a stranger in the piazza is suddenly an object of curiosity, not just another tourist, as in summer. Rome is utterly delicious after the winter holidays. All the less-visited museums are empty and the restaurants more intimate. Since winter has cooled the ardor of the motorcyclists and Vespas, crossing the street is no longer a death-defying act. Winter, really, is not so serious in Rome; I've dined outside on New Year's Eve. I have a dream of going to Capri in winter. Probably most of the hotels are closed, but surely there's a perched, white B & B, surrounded by lemon trees and overlooking that bluest of seas. For hikers, Capri is so alluring. Though there are steep ups and precipitous downs, views at every turn dazzle the eye. And, ah! There is a real Capri away from the *centro*, a landscape of lanes, secret gardens, and gates. Before each one, I long to take a big black key from my pocket and enter.

As I'm paging through the destinations described in this book, I barely can keep from hauling my suitcase out of the attic. For each month, around fifty enticing trips are proposed. I've lived part of the year in Italy for twenty years. This irresistible book reminds me that there's more – much more – to see than I have seen. Scicli, Stilo, Rivisondoli, Atri, Cervinia, Angera – these winter recommendations pull me like strong magnets.

Now I take back what I said about preferring winter – fall is as sublime as Keats's *Ode to Autumn*. The noble town of Mantua is perfect for a September jaunt. And spring is simply ideal. The poppy-strewn hills invite walking, and at the spa town of Bagno Vignoni you can soak your feet in hot springs. What to choose in April? Handsome Bergamo or the villages on Elba, where Napoleon cooled off? And Italy in summer, when the collective energy of the country zings. The cool air of Sarnano in Le Marche, the jazz festival in Perugia, Alpine adventures in Valle D'Aosta – what will it be? I'm drawn to water: Sardinia seems paradisiacal. Yes, summer is best.

There, I'm back to my recommendation – January through December. No other country has the infinite variety of Italy, from the tip of a Dolomite mountain to the southernmost wave on Pantelleria. When I travel to other countries I'm often secretly asking myself, "why am I here, when I could be in Italy?"

Frances Mayes

JANUARY

Where to Go: **January**

On January weekends, winter sports fans head for the major ski resorts, such as Pila, where as well as classic downhill ski runs there are specially built snowparks for snowboarders' tricks; serious ice fans might want to tackle climbing one of the spectacular frozen waterfalls at Val di Susa, one of the most beautiful mountain resorts in Europe. Winter can also be good for nature-lovers – try the Parco Nazionale della Majella for exhilarating experiences such as the Wolf Weekend, two days following the tracks of wolves on the hunt. But January is not all about the great outdoors – it's a perfect month for visiting beautiful cities that are filled with great art and architecture, such as Rome, Florence, Bologna, and Orvieto. Each of these

FESTIVALS AND CULTURE

UNFORGETTABLE JOURNEYS

NATURAL WONDERS

ORVIETO The exterior of the Duomo clad in black and white stripes

CASTEL DEL MONTE The extraordinary castle in the Alta Murgia

PARCO DELLA MAJELLA Wolves thriving in the Abruzzo hills and woods

HERCULANEUM
CAMPANIA

The city buried by lava

After a tour of the excavations at Herculaneum, the city destroyed by the eruption of Vesuvius in AD 79, climb up to the summit of the volcano to admire the impressive crater.

See pp24–5

"The sumptuous Villa dei Papiri alone is of immense value, yielding 1,826 rolls of carbonized papyrus with ancient, mainly Greek, texts."

ORVIETO
UMBRIA

A lofty town whose striped cathedral is visible from afar

Explore this extraordinary town of art, which stands on a rocky spur. Its 14th-century cathedral is a masterpiece of Italian Gothic.

See pp22–3

TRICARICO
BASILICATA

An ancient carnival

Head to Tricarico, in the heart of the Basilicata region, for a lively carnival where the masks recall the tradition of transhumance, when flocks were moved to new pasture.

www.aptbasilicata.it

PIACENZA
EMILIA-ROMAGNA

City of palazzi along the Po

On the banks of the Po River, Piacenza is a lively city with an excellent theater season and a venerable historic center.

www.provincia.piacenza.it/turismo

FLORENCE
TUSCANY

Heart of the Renaissance

Florence is full of art treasures dating back to the Middle Ages and the Renaissance, when it was culturally one of the most important cities in Europe.

See pp12–13

CASTEL DEL MONTE
PUGLIA

Mystery of the octagonal castle

Castel del Monte, built by the emperor Frederick II, is an impressive work of architecture revealing extensive knowledge of mathematics and astronomy.

See pp20–21

SCICLI
SICILY

A Baroque voyage

A terrible earthquake in 1693 devastated eastern Sicily. From the ruins rose a sequence of sumptuous Baroque towns, from Noto to the lesser-known Scicli.

www.comune.scicli.rg.it

BOLOGNA
EMILIA-ROMAGNA

A lively, welcoming city

Explore this friendly metropolis. The seat of the oldest university in Europe is filled with splendid monuments and home to world famous gastronomical dishes.

See pp18–19

MONTEFALCO
UMBRIA

In the footsteps of a saint

Follow Francis of Assisi across Umbria, passing countless sites connected with Italy's national saint; including Assisi, Cannara, and the stunning walled city of Montefalco.

www.bellaumbria.net

SANTA MARGHERITA DI BELICE
SICILY

Finding Italy's greatest novel

Lampedusa's novel, *The Leopard*, vividly describes 19th century Sicily. A "literary park" traces his life from Margherita di Belice to Palermo.

www.sicilyontour.com/eng

PARCO DELLA MAJELLA
ABRUZZO

Experience the thrill of tracking an Apennine wolf

Head out into the wilderness to track down this elusive animal that has become a symbol of the Abruzzo – it's a thrilling weekend.

See pp30–31

PIETRAROJA
CAMPANIA

Welcome to Jurassic Park

Pietraroja is home to Paleolab, an important geo-paleontological park, where the first fossil of a new dinosaur was discovered in Italy. Find your own fossils here.

www.geologi.it/pietraroja

"It is possible to follow a wolf's tracks, work out its hunting trails, listen to the howling of its pack, and even observe, from a safe and respectful distance."

SESSA AURUNCA
CAMPANIA

An open-air museum

Located within the chestnut woods of the regional park Roccamonfina-Foce Garigliano, Sessa Aurunca has a 2nd-century BC Roman theater and a lovely medieval cathedral.

www.parcodiroccamonfina.it

SANTA CATERINA VALFURVA
LOMBARDY

Hike on snowshoes through the pristine forests of the Alta Valtellina

A snowshoe hike across the Parco dello Stelvio will reward you with stunning alpine vistas.

www.alta-valtellina.it

PORTO SELVAGGIO
PUGLIA

A green, gold, and blue oasis

Porto Selvaggio lies on a stunning stretch of the Mediterranean. Marshlands and cliffs accessible only on foot harbor rare birds and rarer lemon trees.

www.turismo.regione.puglia.it

Previous page: Detail of the ceiling of the Sistine Chapel, Rome

cities has its own unmistakable character, and buildings that reveal the fascinating story of a great past. There are even older stories from ancient cities such as Herculaneum, the Roman metropolis buried under lava in AD 79, and Volterra, with its 9th-century BC Etruscan origins. Although it is deep midwinter, January in southern Italy can be unexpectedly mild, with gentle warm days and bright sunlight. Days like these would be perfect for exploring Taormina, which nestles into the Sicilian coast around a spectacular ancient Greek theater, or Castel del Monte, the castle of mysterious numbers built by Frederick II, which stands proud among gently rolling hills covered with vines and olives, in an area famous for its delicious wines and olive oil.

LUXURY AND ROMANCE

TAORMINA A town held in the warm embrace of the Mediterranean

TAORMINA
Sicily

The most dramatically sited Greek theater in Sicily

In a location of great natural beauty, Taormina has a Greek theater, built overlooking the sea, an Arabian necropolis, and a Byzantine Madonna.

See pp16–17

VOLTERRA
TUSCANY

On the trail of the Etruscans

Famous for the skillful working of alabaster, Volterra has a notable historic center of Etruscan origin, filled with fascinating Roman ruins and medieval buildings.

See pp32–3

"A hilltop town in the heart of Tuscany, Volterra resembles a quirky catalog of Italian history."

STILO
CALABRIA

A Byzantine pearl

Seek out the heart of Calabria, and discover this charming village. Set on the side of a mountain, Stilo was an important center for Orthodox Christianity in the Middle Ages.

www.vacanzaincalabria.it

FERMO
LE MARCHE

An ancient, elegant town in the heart of Le Marche

At the foot of Monti Sibillini, Fermo is centered around Piazza del Popolo and its many monuments include a Romanesque-Gothic cathedral.

www.le-marche.com

CORTINA D'AMPEZZO
VENETO

Skiing in style

Ski resorts are rarely known for their looks, but Cortina d'Ampezzo boasts spectacular scenery, fine restaurants, and the best shopping the other side of Milan.

www.dolomiti.org/dengl/cortINA

ACTIVE ADVENTURES

PILA A fabulous ski resort in the beautiful Valle d'Aosta

ORTISEI
TRENTINO-ALTO ADIGE

The fun of downhill skiing

Ortisei is one of the main centers for winter sports in Val Gardena. It is part of a skiing circuit that links more than 310 miles (500 km) of ski runs in the Dolomites.

www.ortisei.it

VAL DI SUSA
PIEDMONT

The ultimate ice challenge

Test your climbing skills on the dramatic frozen waterfalls in a lovely alpine valley dominated by the charming medieval Abbazia di Sacra di San Michele.

See pp14–15

LIVIGNO
LOMBARDY

Slopes for all tastes

Livigno is extremely well equipped for winter sports, with pistes for downhill skiing, cross-country skiing, and for snowboarding.

www.livigno.eu
www.alta-valtellina.it

PILA
VALLE D'AOSTA

Snowboarding tricks

Show off your skills in Pila's Snowpark, in a skiing resort reachable in just a few minutes from Aosta thanks to an up-to-the-minute cable car.

See pp26–7

VAL DI SOLE
TRENTINO-ALTO ADIGE

A ski circuit in the pretty Dolomite mountains

From Folgarida to Marilleva, the Val di Sole offers a skiing circuit of 75 miles (120 km) as well as ice skating, dog sledding, and snowshoeing.

www.valdisole.net

FAMILY GETAWAYS

ROME The ruins of the Circus of Maxentius seen from the Via Appia outside Rome

RIVISONDOLI
ABRUZZO

Three kings come to town

Nestled beneath Monte Calvario, Rivisondoli hosts a splendid re-enactment of the Epiphany, with the arrival of the Three Kings.

www.abruzzo2000.com/abruzzo/laquila/rivisondoli

BORMIO
LOMBARDY

Enjoy skiing and relaxing

Set within the Parco Nazionale dello Stelvio, Bormio has excellent ski facilities, and great aprés ski. It has also been known since antiquity for its relaxing spa waters.

www.bormio.com

ROME
LAZIO

The most famous ancient city and the seat of Christianity

Enjoy the great embrace of Piazza San Pietro, and visit the Vatican Museums, home to the Sistine Chapel and its marvelous frescoes.

See pp28–9

COLLODI
TUSCANY

Pinocchio and butterflies

Collodi has a delightful garden dedicated to Pinocchio and his creator, Carlo Lorenzini, as well as a butterfly house filled with pretty, fluttering specimens.

www.pinocchio.it

"The Sistine Chapel is the culmination of a visit to the Vatican Museums, one of the greatest art collections in the world."

GEMONA DEL FRIULI
FRIULI-VENEZIA GIULIA

Keeping traditions alive

In the village of Gemona, the feast of Epiphany is celebrated with the unusual "Befana del Tallero" festival, with processions and events in medieval costume.

www.turismofvg.it

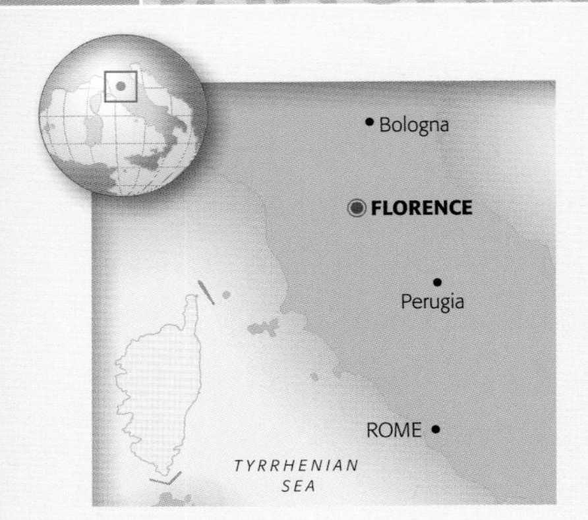

GETTING THERE
Florence airport is 3 miles (5 km) from the city; a shuttle bus runs every 30 minutes. Frequent train and bus services link Santa Maria Novella station in central Florence with Pisa International Airport.

GETTING AROUND
The historic center of Florence is easy to get around, and delightful to explore on foot.

WEATHER
Winter temperatures average 41°F (5°C). Sunny days are not unusual.

ACCOMMODATIONS
L'Albergotto, a small Renaissance palazzo, offers enchanting views over the city; doubles from US$140; www.albergotto.com

Villa Liana is a 19th-century former British consulate furnished with antiques and set in a lovely garden; doubles from US$140; www.hotelliana.com

The 4-star Monna Lisa, housed in an ancient convent building, is steeped in old-world charm; doubles from US$225; www.monnalisa.it

EATING OUT
Whether you dine at an exclusive restaurant or a humble *osteria*, it is impossible to be disappointed by Tuscan food. Elegant Enoteca Pinchiorri is known worldwide for the quality of its food (dinner from US$310), and has one of the finest wine cellars in Europe; www.enotecapinchiorri.com

PRICE FOR TWO
US$300 per day including accommodations, food, and admissions. If dining at Enoteca Pinchiorri, triple the budget for that day.

FURTHER INFORMATION
www.firenzeturismo.it

Michelangelo's David

The world's most famous sculpture was executed by Michelangelo between 1501 and 1504, the year in which it was placed in front of Palazzo Vecchio. It took four days to transport the enormous figure, protected inside a wooden cage that was slid along on greased beams. It was moved again in 1872 when, to protect it from extreme weather, it was taken to the Galleria dell'Accademia, where it can still be seen today. The statue on display in Piazza della Signoria is a copy.

Left (left to right): *Bistec alla Fiorentina* – Florentine style steak; façade of the church of Santa Maria Novella; interior of the sacristy of San Lorenzo

Right: Harmonious central nave of the 15th-century church of San Lorenzo, with its magnificent paneled ceiling

Main: The magnificent dome and Neo-Gothic façade of Florence's cathedral, Santa Maria del Fiore, an architectural masterpiece

CRUCIBLE OF CULTURE

IN TWO FLORENTINE CITY SQUARES, just a few hundred paces apart, visitors are drawn back to a time when political and religious powers vied with one another, resulting in an explosion of cultural creativity that still resonates today. Piazza della Signoria and Piazza del Duomo are the heart of Medici Florence, brimming with extraordinary works of art and tracing in their architecture the city's history from the Middle Ages to the Renaissance. The oldest building on Piazza del Duomo is the Baptistry, started in 1059 and completed in 1128, containing marvellous 13th-century mosaics, Lorenzo Ghiberti's breathtaking bronze doors, and an exterior lavishly clad in white and green marble. The motif of multicolored marble is repeated in the cathedral, flanked by Giotto's splendid bell tower and topped by Brunelleschi's great dome, lending a wonderful chromatic harmony to the square. Not far away is Piazza della Signoria, one of the most beautiful public spaces in Italy and effectively an open-air museum. Dominated by the 14th-century bulk of Palazzo Vecchio, the piazza is graced by magnificent sculptures. Of these, Michelangelo's *David* is the most famous,

Above: *Orpheus* by Baccio Bandinelli (1493–1560) in the courtyard of Palazzo Medici Riccardi

Below: Night view of the Palazzo Vecchio

but other masterpieces include the bronze sculpture of *Judith and Holofernes* by Donatello; Cellini's *Perseus*; Ammannati's *Fountain of Neptune*; and *The Rape of the Sabine Women* by Giambologna.

Florence's unequaled blend of medieval and Renaissance elements can also be seen in many of the city's monuments. The church of Santa Croce, which reflects a fusion of Romanesque and Florentine Gothic styles, houses frescoes by Giotto in the Capella Peruzzi; the celebrated *Crucifix* by Cimabue, created in 1288; works by the great masters of the Renaissance, such as Donatello's *Annunciation*; the tomb of Michelangelo; and Brunelleschi's Capella dei Pazzi, completed in 1461. In Santa Maria Novella, the city's most Gothic church, visitors can admire the *Crucifix* by Giotto alongside Masaccio's *Trinity*, a masterpiece of perspective, and frescoes by Domenico Ghirlandaio and Fra Filippo Lippi. San Marco, a Dominican convent modified by Michelozzo in the 15th century, houses paintings by Fra Angelico, a key link in the transition from medieval to Renaissance art. And, while San Lorenzo, the church of the powerful Medici family, was lavished with their worldly wealth, the cultural wealth of Florence lies throughout the city for every visitor, rich or poor, to enjoy.

FLORENTINE DIARY

From the 13th to the 15th century Florence was the undisputed capital of European culture and art. Five days is enough time to discover its wealth of architectural and artistic treasures, but also to enjoy all the other delights of a charming and lively Tuscan city, famed for its cuisine and its style as well as its art *(see also pp154–5)*.

Five Days of Cultural Wonders

DAY 1

Start your visit in Piazza del Duomo: a visit to the interior of the Baptistry is a must and, if you can face the 463 steps, climb up to the top of the cathedral dome to admire the views. Move on to Piazza della Signoria and wander among its many sculptures. For the most part these are copies (the originals are scattered in various museums), but the effect is spectacular nonetheless.

DAY 2

You cannot say you have seen Florence without a visit to the Uffizi, one of the most important art galleries in the world, housed in a 16th-century building. Spend the day exploring this cultural treasure-house.

DAY 3

Visit the church of Santa Croce, celebrated for the tombs of famous men such as Michelangelo, Machiavelli, and Galileo. Afterward, walk to the Conventi di San Marco; on the way, visit the Ospedale degli Innocenti (Hospital of the Innocents), the Florentine orphanage opened in 1444 and designed by Brunelleschi. At San Marco, see the museum's extraordinary collection of works by Fra Angelico.

DAY 4

A tour of Renaissance Florence must include a visit to Brunelleschi's church of San Lorenzo, with the funerary chapel of the Medici family. Nearby is the Palazzo Medici Riccardi, whose museum provides an overview of the Renaissance and Baroque periods. From here, go to Santa Maria Novella and admire its Gothic form; don't miss the frescoes in the cloisters to the left of the church.

DAY 5

A short distance south of the oldest part of Florence, the church of San Miniato al Monte is among the magical sites in the city. It is one of the oldest and most harmonious examples of Tuscan Romanesque architecture, and the views from here are superb.

Dos and Don'ts

- ✓ Take a break from art to explore the shops in the streets of the center: Florence is one of Italy's capitals of fashion.
- ✗ Don't go to the Uffizi gallery without having pre-booked: there are always really long lines. You can buy tickets online at www.firenzemusei.it; this site also sells tickets for other Florentine museums.
- ✓ Visit one of Florence's historic *caffès*, such as Giubbe Rosse, a famous literary haunt, or Giacosa, where the Negroni cocktail was created.

Below: Fra Angelico's *Annunciation* (c.1445) in San Marco

GETTING THERE
Situated in the northwest of the Piedmont region, Val di Susa can be reached by car from Turin's Caselle airport, via the A32 freeway. This also links Turin to Bardonecchia for the Frejus alpine tunnel from France. There are also good train and bus links.

GETTING AROUND
A network of secondary roads link the towns in Val di Susa. To get between the skiing resorts of Via Lattea, it is enough to don skis: there are 250 miles (400 km) of connected pistes.

WEATHER
Expect typical alpine winter weather – spells of heavy snowfall alternating with crisp, sunny days.

ACCOMMODATIONS
Chalet Faure, situated in the historic center of Sauze d'Oulx, is a delightful small hotel housed in an old alpine chalet; doubles from US$170; www.faure.it

In Sestriere, right by the pistes of the resort, Hotel Duchi d'Aosta and Hotel Torre are both perfect bases for a skiing holiday; full board for two around US$325 per day; www.clubmed.it

EATING OUT
Mountain huts at higher altitudes offer robust and flavorful mountain cuisine at less than US$20 a head. Expect hearty pasta and potato dishes featuring cheese, mushrooms, and cured ham.

In the evening, dine in one of the many typical restaurants serving Val di Susa specialties. Try Mamma Lia in Sestriere (from US$30) or 'L Gran Bouc in Claviere (US$40–55; www.granbouc.it).

PRICE FOR TWO
US$400 per day, including meals, accommodations, and Via Lattea ski pass, valid throughout the valley.

FURTHER INFORMATION
www.turismotorino.org
www.valsusainfo.it

Pioneer of the Pistes

Skiing as a sport in Italy began in Val di Susa, thanks to Adolf Kind, a Swiss engineer living in Turin in the 1890s. He sent for a pair of ash-wood skis from Norway, the first ever seen in Italy. His daring exploits scared the locals, but converted friends in Turin, who founded the Club Alpino Italiano. The CAI opened the first Italian "alpine station" at Oulx in 1906. He may have shocked residents of Val di Susa at the time, but Kind is now something of a local hero for launching the area as a winter sport destination.

Above (left to right): Sunrise above the clouds; detail, School of Marquetry and Woodworking in Melezet; ascending to the pistes by chair-lift
Main: Ice-climber tackling a frozen waterfall

EXHILARATION ON ICE

It is ancient, enduring alpine country, Val di Susa. As is so often the case in these high mountain ranges (the Rocciamelone peak reaches 11,608 ft/3,538 m), the region welcomes the traveler wholeheartedly. The dramatic Sacra di San Michele is a perfect symbol for a valley which, thanks to its relatively accessible Alpine slopes, has for centuries been a point of both contact and strife between various peoples. This extraordinary Benedictine abbey, founded at the end of the year 1000 on the site of an ancient Roman military outpost, was established to provide refuge for travelers and the local population in the face of frequently recurring invasions. Today, Val di Susa is a place where Provençal and Piedmontese cultures have overlapped and harmonized to create a unique local identity. Its strong character is reflected in the robust nature of the regional food: Susa mountain cheeses (Brus and Reblochon are typical) have an intense aroma, and the cured meats are strongly flavored, well suited to the powerful local wines.

Val di Susa attracts those who feel a deep passion for nature and landscapes, who relish peaks conquered step-by-step, appreciate the white sea of a fresh fall of snow, and enjoy the warmth of a glowing fire that rewards a tired visitor on arrival at any of its mountain refuges, such as Sigot 9,580 ft (2,920 m) near the lake and glacier of Galambra, or the Blais hut 9,375 ft (2,858 m). Adventurous visitors will find Val di Susa a paradise for ice-climbing. With many challenging *couloirs* (narrow gorges or crevasses) and spectacular frozen waterfalls, there are at least 20 sites to excite keen climbers, especially around Oulx, Bardonecchia, and Cesana, although some ascents should only be tackled by those with a lot of experience and a local guide. Still, with the resorts of its Via Lattea ("Milky Way") combining cross-country and downhill skiing, high-altitude hiking, climbing, and breathtaking panoramas, Val di Susa offers plenty of exhilaration for everyone.

Val di Susa attracts those who feel a deep passion for nature and landscapes, who relish peaks conquered step-by-step, appreciate the white sea of a fresh fall of snow...

Inset: Skiers relax in the sun between one descent and the next
Below (left to right): Sacra di San Michele Abbey, perched on Monte Pirchiriano; market stall displaying many varieties of potato, a key regional staple

MOUNTAIN DIARY

According to experts, Val di Susa has more ice-climbing sites than anywhere else in the Alps. But there is much more to see and do, from pistes suitable for every level of skier to important historical sites. A three-day break is the perfect introduction to the many facets of this beautiful, exciting, and hospitable region.

Three Days of Thrills

DAY 1

On the road that leads to the main ski resorts of the Via Lattea, almost at the mouth of Val di Susa, lies the Sacra di San Michele, an imposing centuries-old abbey, built on the peak of Monte Pirchiriano. For a good view of the abbey, pause at the terrace in front of the entrance.
It is also well worth the effort of climbing up the Scalone dei Morti ("Staircase of the Dead") as far as the Porta dello Zodiaco ("Zodiac Gate") to visit the interior of the complex and view the lovely 1505 fresco of the Annunciation in the church.

DAY 2

Spend the day ice-climbing. In the Alta ("high") Val di Susa, there are many great opportunities to try this: Grand Hoche in Oulx; Cima delle Blave and Testa dei Ban in Bardonecchia; and Testa Brusà in Sestriere, to mention just a few. Hire an experienced guide and prepare to be challenged.

DAY 3

Fans of skiing can find plenty to enjoy in the Via Lattea, which combines the facilities of Sestriere, Cesana, Claviere, San Sicario, Sauze d'Oulx, and Montgenèvre in France, and offers 211 linked pistes, served by 91 ski lifts. Spend the day exploring just some of them, then round off a long day on the slopes with a hearty meal of alpine specialties in Claviere at 'L Gran Bouc.

Dos and Don'ts

- ✗ Don't attempt to climb on ice without the necessary physical and technical preparation and without the right equipment: this is a dangerous extreme sport.
- ✓ Those keen on cross-country skiing should try the circuits of Pragelato and Thures. The latter is adapted for the blind.
- ✓ If you are in Val di Susa at the beginning of the new year, go to the Festa della Befana, held in Susa on January 6. This is the last event in a series of celebrations taking place throughout the Christmas period.
- ✓ Go downhill skiing at night on the floodlit pistes of Sestriere.
- ✓ Buy something made from carved wood, a typical local craft.

Below: Monumental Porta Savoia in the town of Susa, Val di Susa

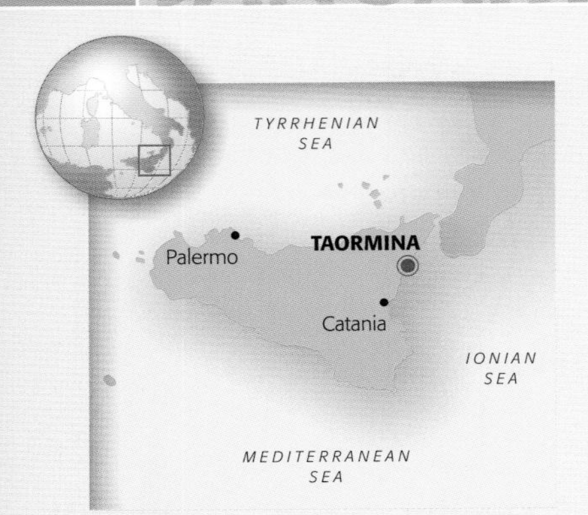

GETTING THERE
Taormina is 37 miles (60 km) from Catania's Fontanarossa Airport on the A18. Hourly buses link Catania and Taormina.

GETTING AROUND
Taormina is best explored on foot. A cable car links the town with the seaside below at Mazzarò, and buses run to Castelmola and Giardini Naxos.

WEATHER
Even in winter, temperatures never dip below 50°F (10°C).

ACCOMMODATIONS
For luxury and charm, choose the San Domenico Palace, housed in a converted 15th-century Dominican monastery; doubles from US$495; http://sandomenicopalace.hotelsinsicily.it

Villa Sant'Andrea is an aristocratic residence converted into an exclusive hotel. Set in luxuriant gardens, and with its own private beach, it dominates the bay of Mazzarò; doubles from US$335; www.framonhotelgroup.com

EATING OUT
Elegant Casa Grugno offers dishes made from local ingredients, interpreted in new ways, such as a platter of raw fish with a sorbet of citrus and ginger (dinner from US$70); http://casagrugno.it

For genuine Sicilian cooking in a traditional setting, Al Duomo is a good choice – meals from US$40; www.ristorantealduomo.it

PRICE FOR TWO
US$640 per day including accommodations, meals, local travel, and admissions.

FURTHER INFORMATION
www.taormina.it

Giardini Naxos

A small seaside resort just a short distance from Taormina, Giardini Naxos is the site of the first Greek colony in Sicily. According to legend, the Phoenicians had spread a rumor that Sicily was populated with monsters in order to deter Greek settlement on the island. When the Athenian Theocles was shipwrecked along the coast, he discovered that the story was untrue and returned to found the town of Naxos in 735 BC. Ruins of the town walls and a temple can still be seen, set among lemon trees in lovely countryside, and a museum exhibits finds from the site.

BETWEEN ETNA AND THE SEA

On one side looms the great bulk of Mount Etna, complete with its menacing crater; on the other stretches glorious blue sea: this is how Taormina first appears to visitors. Constructed on terraces clinging to the slopes of Monte Tauro, Taormina has a fascination all of its own, and has long been one of Sicily's most celebrated tourist destinations. It is enough simply to sit on one of the steps of the Greek theater to feel immediately captivated – in a "coup de theater" worthy of the genius of the greatest set designer, the backdrop to the stage is split by a wide cleft that makes a perfect frame for the spectacular panorama of Etna and the bay beyond. The Greek theater may be the most famous monument in Taormina, but equally renowned is the *passeggiata*, or stroll, along Corso Umberto I, the narrow street that crosses the full width of the town. Shopping is the main pursuit here: Taormina is

Main: Mount Etna and the Ionian Sea, viewed from the ancient Greek theater in Taormina

Above left (top to bottom): Dramatic castle of Monte Tauro; stone details on a Taormina house; prickly pear in Villa Comunale

Left: Breathtaking panorama from a terrace in Taormina

Right (left to right): Typical local ceramics; coastline below Taormina, with Isola Bella on the left; fruit stall selling aromatic Sicilian lemons

well-known for its antiques and handicrafts, but there are also chic boutiques galore, as well as delicatessens crammed with delicious local produce. Retail therapy can here be combined with some of the most splendid vistas in the world, from the terrace of Piazza IX Aprile, for example.

Other delights include architectural treasures such as the church of San Giuseppe, built in pure Rococo form, and the Palazzo dei Duchi di Santo Stefano, in Arab-Norman style. Just a short distance from the center a peaceful atmosphere prevails, at, for example, the Villa Comunale, a glorious garden created at the end of the 19th century by Lady Florence Trevelyan Cacciola, which offers tranquil green corners and lovely views over the bay below. The bay is splendid whatever the season, thanks to Taormina's mild climate. Take the cable car down to the sea for magnificent walks along the coast, to the cove dominated by the tiny Isola Bella, today a World Wide Fund for Nature reserve, or to Spisone, with its lovely sandy beach. Taormina is undoubtedly a jewel of the Ionian coast, and its many facets dazzle visitors like the sunlight on its clear blue waters.

ISLAND DIARY

Taormina is wonderful in every season, but perhaps in winter, when the flow of tourists slows, it holds a more discreet allure. Four days will allow you time to discover not only the chic and artistic side of this beautiful town, but also the historic and natural treasures to be found in the area.

JAN

Four Days of Discovery

DAY 1

The most spectacular and striking sight in Taormina is the site of the Greek theater, constructed in the 3rd century BC. From here you can walk to Corso Umberto I to stroll, shop, and dine. Stop to admire the view from the terrace in Piazza IX Aprile and visit the ancient churches in the town, such as the cathedral and San Giuseppe. For another wonderful view of the town, follow the steps up to the medieval castle at the top of Monte Tauro – it is well worth the climb.

DAY 2

The easiest way to reach Taormina's beach is by cable car, but you can also walk down the long flight of steps from the center. Continue on as far as the cove of Isola Bella; at low tide it is possible to reach the island on foot, otherwise rowing boats are available for rent for a closer look at the island and its wildlife, which includes hoopoes, kingfishers, and rare lizards.

DAY 3

Visit Villa Comunale, filled with luxuriant vegetation and blessed with wonderful panoramic views. Don't miss the unusual pagoda-like towers, follies decorated with pumice stone, built by Florence Trevelyan Cacciola, a passionate ornithologist, for bird-watching. After lunch visit the excavations and museum at Giardini Naxos, the earliest Greek settlement in Sicily.

DAY 4

Take a bus out to Castelmola, an enchanting, car-free village a short distance from Taormina, dominated by a medieval castle. There are lovely views of the Ionian coastline from the belvedere in the village square. Have lunch at the quaint and charming Bar Turrisi and sample a glass or two of the local almond wine.

Dos and Don'ts

- ⊗ Taormina is a paradise for shopping but don't expect low prices; items for sale are almost always of excellent quality, but are quite expensive.
- ✓ For a combination of great views and the best people-watching during the evening *passeggiata*, choose a café table on Piazza IX Aprile.
- ✓ Try the local sweet, aromatic almond wine. The variety made in Castelmola has a particularly good reputation.

FEB MAR APR MAY JUN JUL AUG SEP OCT NOV DEC

Below: Corso Umberto I, one of the most picturesque streets in old Taormina

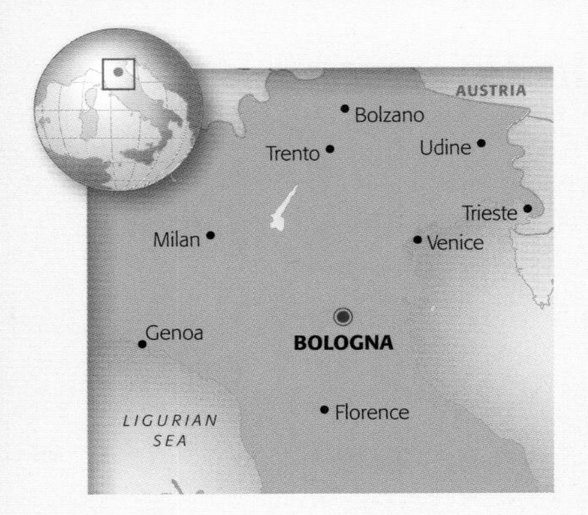

GETTING THERE
The capital of Emilia-Romagna, Bologna is well connected by freeway to other major Italian cities, being close to the A1 (Milan–Naples), the A13 (Bologna–Padua), and the A14 (Bologna–Taranto). A shuttle bus links Bologna's Guglielmo Marconi Airport with the city center 4 miles (6 km) away.

GETTING AROUND
Explore Bologna on foot or make use of the good bus network; alternatively, rent a bike.

WEATHER
The maximum daytime temperature is only around 43°F (6°C). The wind can be brisk at this time of year, but there are still many sunny days. Fortify yourself against the cold with hearty Emilian cooking.

ACCOMMODATIONS
The charming Commercianti is in part of the former town hall, while the Novecento is a designer hotel in 1930s style; both are part of the Bologna Art Hotels chain; doubles from US$235; www.bolognarthotels.it

For sheer luxury, opt for the Grand Hotel Baglioni. The restaurant has frescoes by the Carracci brothers; doubles from US$305; www.baglionihotels.com

A more economical option is the delightful B&B Le Vele; doubles from US$85; www.beblevele.it

EATING OUT
There are countless good restaurants in which to try traditional dishes, often creatively reworked. Among them are Cantina Bentivoglio (dinner from US$35); Osteria de'Poeti (US$55); and Battibecco (US$120).

PRICE FOR TWO
US$335 per day, including meals, accommodations, admissions, local travel, and a City Pass.

FURTHER INFORMATION
http://iat.comune.bologna.it

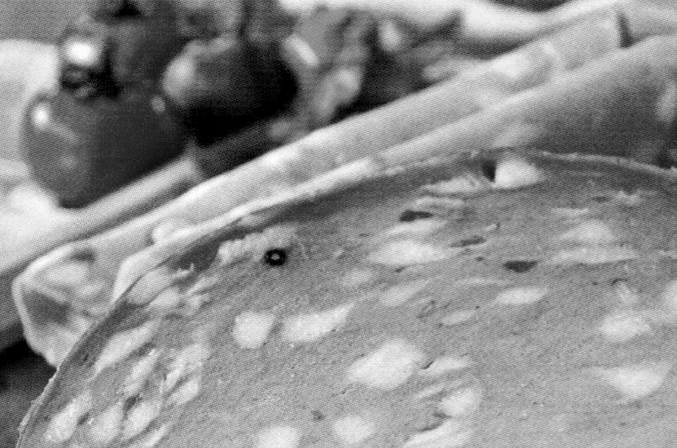

The Capital of Italian Cuisine

One of the nicknames for Bologna is *La Grassa* ("the Fat"), and its cuisine is universally celebrated. Some of its dishes, such as pasta with *ragù* (a meat-based sauce), are almost synonymous with Italian food worldwide. But there are two truly authentic symbols of Bologna's gastronomy. One is mortadella, a delicious spiced and lightly smoked pork sausage. The other is tortellini, little twists of stuffed pasta which, according to legend, were devised by an Emilian innkeeper and modeled on the navel of Venus.

Above (left ro right): Elegant open space of Piazza Maggiore; aerial view of Bologna and the Torre Prendiparte
Main: Torre degli Asinelli and, behind it, Torre Garisenda, twin symbols of the city

CULTURE AND CUISINE

Bologna has three nicknames: *La Dotta* ("the learned"); *La Grassa* ("the fat"); and *La Rossa* ("the red") – and it lives up to them all. Site of the oldest university in Europe, founded in 1088 on an even older studium (place of learning), Bologna has a vibrancy common to most university towns. This lively atmosphere pervades its streets, flanked by porticoes – over 25 miles (40 km) of attractive arcades run throughout the city center – under which it is always a pleasure to stop and chat, and its squares, lined with ancient churches and magnificent palaces.

Bologna is a city that seems to wrap itself around you like a warm embrace. Perhaps this is partly due to the deep red color of its buildings, which confers a cozy warmth, even in the monumental areas such as Piazza Maggiore and Piazza del Nettuno, at the heart of the city. The two squares stand adjacent, bordered by buildings that date back to medieval Bologna, when this was one of the most powerful cities in central Italy. At that time the city bristled with around 200 towers, built by the more important families, initially for military reasons but later also as a symbol of prestige. Today, only around 15 of them remain, but these are enough to make the city's skyline unmistakeable. Indeed, two of the towers, Torre degli Asinelli and Torre Garisenda, have become the symbol of Bologna.

San Petronio is a favorite church of the Bolognese. Begun in 1390, it was to be bigger than St. Peter's in Rome but, when Bologna joined the Papal States, Pope Pius IV halted the project. Although its façade is unfinished, it does have a superb doorway, the work of Jacopo della Quercia. San Petronio stands in the heart of the Quadrilateral, the oldest part of Bologna, and is a perfect starting point for a tour of this welcoming city. Explore on foot, enjoying the cordiality of its citizens, the pleasant shelter offered by the porticoes, and the inviting smells from the *osterias* in what is rightly deemed the capital of Italian food.

Bologna is a city that seems to wrap itself around you like a warm embrace.

Inset: Beautiful hallway in the Archiginnasio, now the city library
Below (left to right): Courtyard of one of Bologna's lovely palaces; *Ecstasy of St. Cecilia* by Raphael, in the Pinacoteca Nazionale

BOLOGNESE DIARY

Bologna grew up on an important crossroads of the Roman road network, so it has always been a center of culture and commerce. In four days there is ample time to visit its fine monuments and museums, browse the many smart shops (January is sale time) and relax each evening over a dinner of the remarkable cuisine for which it is renowned.

Four Days in La Dotta

DAY 1
Begin your visit in the heart of the city. Piazza Maggiore is surrounded by medieval palaces and home to the church of San Petronio. A passage leads to Piazza del Nettuno, dominated by its monumental 16th-century fountain. The nearby streets, sheltered by porticoes, are perfect for strolling, dining, and a bit of shopping.

DAY 2
To admire wide-ranging views of Bologna, climb up the Torre degli Asinelli (bear in mind that there are 498 steps, however). Close by is the complex of Santo Stefano, one of the most charming places in the city, which consists of four churches. The oldest, dedicated to the martyrs Vitale and Agricola, dates from AD 392.

DAY 3
A visit to the university is a must. Archiginnasio, the oldest part of the university, was built in 1563 to bring together the various schools under one roof. Palazzo Poggi, the current seat, houses some of the university's 19 museums, including a naval museum, a military museum and a museum of astronomy. It stands on the arcade-lined Via Zamboni, the heart of Bologna's university life.

DAY 4
Devote a whole day to the Pinacoteca Nazionale art gallery, one of the most important museums in Italy. It opened in 1796, during the Napoleonic era, when the Bologna senate gathered together works of art from churches and monasteries to prevent them from being taken to France. Highlights include Raphael's *Ecstasy of St. Cecilia* and Perugino's *Madonna in Glory*.

Dos and Don'ts

- ✓ At the Palazzo del Podestà, in Piazza Maggiore, stand two people at opposite corners of the Voltone del Podestà, the open arcade formed by the pilasters supporting the tower. Its acoustics mean that, if one whispers, the other will be able to hear perfectly well what is said.
- ✗ If you are a student, do not climb to the top of Torre degli Asinelli: according to Bologna legend, whoever gets to the top will not get a degree.
- ✓ Bicycles are the preferred method of transportation with the locals, and there are plenty of rental shops around the city. For a less energetic way of getting around, buy an inexpensive City Pass of ten bus tickets.

Below: Tagliatelle with *ragù*, the classic bolognese meat sauce

GETTING THERE
Castel del Monte is in the Alta Murgia of Puglia, 30 miles (48 km) from Bari airport, where car rental is available. Take the A14, exit Andria-Barletta, then the SS170.

GETTING AROUND
The SS16 follows the coast to Trani and Barletta. Head inland on the SP238 to Ruvo di Puglia.

WEATHER
January is the coldest month in Puglia, but the average daytime temperature is still 55°F (13°C).

ACCOMMODATIONS
Pino Grande is an authentic Puglian farmhouse *(masseria)*, close to Castel del Monte; doubles from US$110; www.ilpinogrande.it

Part of Palazzo Filiso in the center of Trani, Hotel Regia has elegant rooms and a panoramic terrace; doubles from US$170; www.hotelregia.it

Trani's Palazzo Telesio houses the Maré Resort Spa, combining old-world charm with chic modern decor; doubles from US$280; www.mareresort.it

EATING OUT
Corte in Fiore restaurant in Trani serves excellent Mediterranean cuisine (dinner from US$50) in a romantic setting; www.corteinfiore.it

Osteria Antichi Sapori in Montegrosso, in the hills near Castel del Monte, features authentic regional cooking (from US$50); www.antichisapori.biz

PRICE FOR TWO
US$415 per day including accommodations, meals, car rental, and admissions.

FURTHER INFORMATION
www.casteldelmonte.beniculturali.it

Stone and Water

The octagonal structure of the castle is repeated in the internal courtyard. At one time there was a basin at the center of the courtyard, also octagonal, beneath which there was a large cistern. The interior is divided into two levels, each consisting of eight trapezoid rooms. The upper story is reached by spiral staircases housed in three towers. The other towers contain bathrooms, each with a washbasin, an unusual feature that demonstrates Frederick's forward-thinking approach to hygiene.

CASTLE OF ENIGMAS

EIGHT SIDES, EIGHT OCTAGONAL TOWERS, 16 rooms (eight on each floor), and as many windows: these are just some of the strange symmetries found at Castel del Monte, which, with its multiplicity of enigmas, continues to exert a fascination on astronomers, architects, historians, and anyone intrigued by a mystery. And the mysteries surrounding this place are legion. For intance, why was it built? We know that it was built in the 13th century for Emperor Frederick II (1194–1250), who may also have designed it. He was himself a multi-faceted character, capable of combining great political flair with an open-minded interest in every form of art and science. His castle is set on a rocky ridge, atop a 1,770-ft (540-m) hill, and is visible from a considerable distance. It dominates the surrounding countryside, its huge, pale form standing out like a geometric rock of calcareous stone, its color shifting from white to pink in the changing light.

Main: Façade of Castel del Monte showing four of its eight towers

Above left: Frescoed panel from the famous Tomb of the Dancers, discovered in Ruvo di Puglia in 1833 (now in the Museo Archeologico Nazionale in Naples); gargoyle on the façade of the cathedral in Ruvo di Puglia

Left: Basilica di Santa Maria Maggiore in Barletta

Right (left to right): Typical ancient Murgian olive grove; Trani's Duomo, built at the water's edge

Yet, unlike Frederick's other forts, it is without strategic importance. In fact, it is not a fortress at all; it is not surrounded by a ditch, and there are no arrow slits. It is known that it was seldom used, apart from occasional celebrations such as the marriage of Violante, Frederick's daughter, in 1246. Some hypothesize that it was built as a hunting lodge, but there are no stables or other facilities needed for such a purpose.

The structure of the building is unique, every aspect demonstrating an obsession with mathematics and astrology. The octagon itself is a shape imbued with significance – for medieval man it represented the intermediate stage between the Earth (symbolized by the square) and the heavens (symbolized by the circle). It is no coincidence that the cup of the Holy Grail was octagonal, and legend has it that at one time the chalice was kept here. However, the entire construction is full of pre-Christian astrological meaning. For example, at the solstice and the equinox, the shadows thrown by its walls exactly match the length of the internal courtyard. This is indeed a magical and mysterious place, and anyone with imagination will be spellbound by the power and harmony emanating from its walls.

DISCOVERER'S DIARY

Castel del Monte is the jewel in the crown of the Alta Murgia, a region of rolling hills sweeping down to the sea. A land renowned for oils, wines, and food, it is equally rich in history and extraordinary art treasures. Four days allows time not only to wonder over the mysteries of the castle itself, but to sample many other unique regional delights.

Four Days in Magical Murgia

DAY 1

Spend your first day puzzling over the enigmatic castle, then take a leisurely drive to Trani. The road crosses the last spurs of the Alta Murgia, a gently undulating landscape carpeted with vines and olives. Excellent extra-virgin olive oil and quality wines are produced here. Along the way, pause at some of the *masserie*, large fortified farms typical of the area, and vineyards, many of which offer tastings and opportunities to buy.

DAY 2

In Trani, visit the 13th-century cathedral, which stands in an isolated position by the port. Imposing from the outside, its interior is also unusual. It is composed of three levels, each a newer one on top of an older: the Hypogeum of San Leucio, the church of Santa Maria at street level, and a 13th-century campanile above. Castello Svevo, facing the sea, is one of the many castles built by Frederick II, part of a network of fortifications that served to defend the territory.

DAY 3

Drive up the coast to Barletta. Here, too, two imposing buildings dominate the town: the cathedral, begun in 1140, and the castle, also built for Frederick II. This massive fortress, at one time surrounded by the sea (the old moat has been made into a green space), is today the symbol of Barletta.

DAY 4

Spend the day in Ruvo di Puglia. Visit the delightful Romanesque cathedral, built above existing buildings, and the Archeological Museum housed in the Neo-Classical Palazzo Jatta, which includes a fine collection of Greek and pre-Roman Puglian vases.

Dos and Don'ts

- ✗ Don't struggle with public transportation to get to Castel del Monte. Although there are buses from Trani, they are infrequent. It is best to get there by car.
- ✓ Buy Castel del Monte olive oil: it is a DOP (*Denominazione di Origine Protetta* or protected designation of origin) oil, gleaming yellow and with exquisite flavor and fragrance. Try it with rustic Altamonte bread dipped in as an appetizer.
- ✓ Sample excellent Castel del Monte red and rosé wines, and the rare, sparkling Moscato di Trani.
- ✗ Don't underestimate winters in inland Puglia. Even though this is the south, take warm clothing for a visit in January.

Below: Traditional, long-lasting Murgian bread

GETTING THERE
The nearest airport to Orvieto, in southwest Umbria, is at Perugia 48 miles (78km), which is linked by road. There are regular train and bus services to Orvieto from Perugia itself.

GETTING AROUND
It is a pleasure to explore Orvieto on foot. The easiest way to reach the historic center is by funicular from Piazzale Cahen.

WEATHER
Expect some chilly and windy days. The maximum temperature averages 43°F (6°C).

ACCOMMODATIONS
In the Umbrian countryside, 7 miles (12 km) northwest of Orvieto, the *agriturismo* (rural farm bed-and-breakfast) Borgo San Faustino is a lovingly restored group of ancient farm buildings with pool and restaurant; doubles from US$55; www.agriturismoborgosanfaustino.it

Palazzo Piccolomini, in the town itself, is a papal residence dating from the 16th century, offering 4-star comfort in very pleasant surroundings; doubles from US$215; www.hotelpiccolomini.it

EATING OUT
I Sette Consoli, a restaurant housed in the medieval sacristy of the adjacent church of Sant'Angelo, serves traditional cuisine (dinner from US$70), with the emphasis on seasonal ingredients; www.isetteconsoli.it

PRICE FOR TWO
US$350 per day including accommodations, meals, local travel, and admissions.

FURTHER INFORMATION
www.orvietoturismo.it

Pozzo di San Patrizio

In 1527 Pope Clement VII, fleeing from the Sack of Rome, sought refuge in Orvieto. He decided that the town needed tanks and wells so that a water supply could be maintained in the event of a siege. This led to the construction of the Well of San Patrizio, on the site of the Rocca d'Albornoz fortress. It is 203 ft (62 m) deep, with access by means of two independent spiral staircases, one for ascent and one for descent, linked by a wooden bridge; each staircase has 248 steps. The well is lit by 70 large openings.

Above (left to right): Gargoyle on Orvieto's Duomo; sheep's milk cheese with truffle, an Umbrian specialty; striking striped cathedral walls
Main: Façade of Orvieto's 14th-centruy Duomo with its central triangular mosaic, *Coronation of the Virgin*

TOWN OF POWER AND PEACE

To see it from a distance, Orvieto looks like an immense fortress. This effect is emphasized by the great wall of volcanic rock on which the town stands: a great bastion that is an integral part of Orvieto's history. From its platform of stone, Orvieto has dominated the surrounding countryside since the Etruscan era, when it was called Velzna and was a town of great strategic and economic importance. Orvieto is symbolized by its cathedral. Its construction, begun in 1290, lasted nearly three centuries and involved contributions from the major Italian artists of the time: from Lorenzo Maitani, responsible for the design of the Latin cross plan and the façade with three gables, to Andrea Orcagna, designer of the splendid rose window that decorates the façade; from Fra Angelico and Luca Signorelli, who worked on the Capella di San Brizio, to Ugolino di Prete Ilario, whose hand can be detected in various frescoes. The result is an astonishing ensemble. First, the dazzling exterior, striped alternately in white and grey-blue, with its majestic façade and great rose window, rich assembly of bas reliefs and superb mosaics. Then, the elegant and lofty interior that is home to countless art treasures by Gothic and Renaissance Masters. It only requires stepping outside again to realize that Orvieto has even more to offer. From the 11th century until as late as 1860, it was part of the Papal States, and powerful popes held sway here in the Middle Ages. They have left important monuments, such as the three 13th-century Palazzi Papali built for Urban IV, Gregory X, and Martin IV, as well as Palazzo Soliano, built for Boniface VIII, a fortress erected in the 14th century by Cardinal Albornoz, and the church of Sant'Andrea, where Pope Innocent III declared the Fourth Crusade. Orvieto today is very much a town where life is carried on at "walking pace." Stroll its ancient streets, browse in its shops, and finish the day with a fine meal of Umbrian cuisine, accompanied by a glass or two of Orvieto, the delicious white wine made from ancient vines grown on the hillsides around this historic town.

From its platform of stone, Orvieto has dominated the surrounding countryside since the Etruscan era...

Inset: Detail from Signorelli's *The Last Judgement* in the cathedral's Capella di San Brizio
Below (left to right): Quiet Orvieto street at night; central nave of the cathedral

SMALL-TOWN DIARY

Orvieto takes great pride in its history. An extraordinary repository of art, it is also a pleasant place to wander at leisure, relaxing in the gentle pace of a small town. In three days you can see all the sights without having to rush, pausing when you wish to enjoy delicious local food and the region's famous wine.

Three Days Steeped in History

DAY 1

A visit to the cathedral is essential. Gaze at the façade and admire the sober composure of the interior, then go in search of its treasures: frescoes by Ugolino di Prete Ilario in the Tribune and in the Cappella del Corporale, and frescoes by Fra Angelico and Luca Signorelli in the Cappella di San Brizio. Make your way to the historic center for lunch, then explore its medieval streets, and walk as far as the Rocca d'Albornoz to see the striking Pozzi di San Patrizio.

DAY 2

The Museo Claudio Faina is well worth a visit. Housed in the Palazzi Papali (Papal Palaces), it holds important finds from Etruscan necropolises in the area. Not far away is the underground Mill of Santa Chiara, carved out of the rock. There are also many churches of note in the town. Don't miss Sant'Andrea, flanked by its 12-sided tower, or San Domenico, with a lovely series of frescoes dating from the 16th century.

DAY 3

Take a tour of Underground Orvieto: a fascinating labyrinth of caves, tunnels, and subterranean passages carved out by the inhabitants since prehistoric times. After lunch, tour the area around the town to see Etruscan necropolises at ancient settlements, such as Crocifisso del Tufo and Cannicella. Before the end of the day, head to the abbey of Santi Severo e Martirio, which dates from the Middle Ages and is in a glorious setting. It is now a luxury hotel, so sip an *aperitivo* on the terrace and watch the sunset.

Dos and Don'ts

- ✓ Sample the wines of the region. Orvieto stands at the center of one of Italy's most important wine-producing areas. Orvieto is a famous dry white, but try the reds as well.
- ✓ Get a Carta Orvieto Unica from the tourist office. This entitles you to entry to all the monuments and museums in the town, as well as travel on the bus and funicular.
- ✗ You cannot visit Underground Orvieto without having pre-booked a guided tour; you can do this online at www.orvietounderground.it or when you are there.
- ✓ Book tickets in advance for one of the Umbria Jazz Winter concerts; these take place every year in late December and early January in Orvieto.

Below: Tower of the abbey of Santi Severo e Martirio

GETTING THERE
Naples' Capodichino airport is 6 miles (10 km) from Herculaneum. Take the Circumvesuviana train to Ercolano Scavi station or, by car, the A3 freeway to the site.

GETTING AROUND
Visit the excavations on foot. A bus runs to within 220 yards (200 m) of the summit of Vesuvius; from there, continue on foot.

WEATHER
The weather in January is changeable. Temperatures vary from 39–55°F (4–13°C).

ACCOMMODATIONS
One of the loveliest Vesuvian villas, Villa Aprile, has been converted into a chic modern hotel, the Miglio d'Oro Park Hotel; doubles from US$170; www.migliodoroparkhotel.it.

The elegant Villa San Gennariello offers delightful bed and breakfast accommodation in Portici; doubles from US$110; www.villasangennariello.com

Casa nel Verde is a welcoming B&B beside the ruins; doubles from US$100; www.lacasanelverde.com

EATING OUT
As a change from the ubiquitous (albeit delicious) pizza Napoli and calzone, Osteria Viva lo Re, situated close to the ruins, serves outstanding seafood and classic Italian cuisine with a modern, elegant twist (dinner from US$35); www.vivalore.it

PRICE FOR TWO
US$250 per day for accommodations, meals, local travel, and admissions.

FURTHER INFORMATION
www.ercolanonline.it
www.parconazionaledelvesuvio.it

The Summit of Vesuvius

From a distance, with its blunt profile dominating the Bay of Naples, Vesuvius does not look particulaly threatening. Neither is it impressively high, at little more than 3,940 ft (1,200 m) – at the time of the eruption in AD 79 it is thought to have been almost double that. However, on arrival at the summit, after ascending the final incline on foot, it is impossible not to be awestruck. Visitors may walk around the exterior of the old outer cone, now inactive, and look into the impressive crater which, although smaller, is still active and accessible only to trained volcanologists.

IN THE SHADOW OF VESUVIUS

An avalanche of lava, boiling mud, and choking ash, smothering everything in its path to a depth of 49–65 ft (15–20 m) and then solidifying into a rock-hard tomb – that should have been the last the world ever saw of Herculaneum, the Roman town destroyed in AD 79 by an erupting Vesuvius. By the end of the eruption, every trace of the charming little seaside town had vanished. A new town, Ercolano, grew above the old, and over the course of time, all memory of its ancient incarnation was lost. Then, in the early 18th century, an Austrian prince passionate about antiquity unearthed marble and other traces of an ancient building while constructing a villa at Portici. The first series of excavations took place between 1738 and 1765, commissioned by the Bourbon king Charles V. To avoid disruption to Ercolano, archeologists created a system of subterranean tunnels, which were closed up once any finds had been removed. They reached as far

Main: View along a paved street in Herculaneum, lined with remarkably intact houses and shops

Left: *Polyphemus Receives Galatea's Letter*, a fresco now preserved in the Museo Archeologico Nazionale in Naples

Right: Tomato frittata, a tasty and easy dish to make; remarkably preserved colonnade, evidence of the splendour of ancient Herculaneum; craftsman in Torre del Greco, carving coral for jewelry

as several temples and the Villa dei Papiri. Excavation work was resumed in the 19th century and then again in 1927, bringing to light around a third of the ancient settlement.

The most recent excavations, carried out in 1980, concentrated on the beach and revealed the fate of the town's inhabitants. They had fled there in the hope of escape, but were caught by the river of lava. It left them perfectly preserved, with their clothes, jewels, and the valuables they were taking with them. Most of ancient Herculaneum is still buried today; however, sufficient buildings have been uncovered to make this an archeological site of global importance. The sumptuous Villa dei Papiri alone is of immense value, yielding 1,826 rolls of carbonized papyrus with ancient, mainly Greek, texts. The great fresco of marine life in the men's *frigidarium* of the Baths; the fine mosaics in the Casa del Mosaico di Nettuno e Anfitrite and the shop to its side that still had goods on the counter; the wooden furniture in the Casa del Mobilio Carbonizzato; the shady terraces of the Casa dei Cervi – each one brings Herculaneum and its people to life, as if these places are still part of a vibrant town, just around the corner, out of sight.

Above: Herculaneum's *thermopolium*, where its citizens could buy prepared dishes and drinks

Below: White façade of Villa Campolieto, built in 1775, a masterpiece by the architect Luigi Vanvitelli

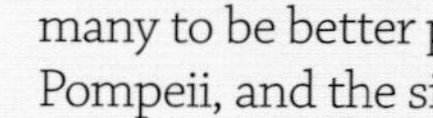

VOLCANO DIARY

The ruins at Herculaneum are considered by many to be better preserved than those of Pompeii, and the site is a more manageable size, meaning that it can be explored in a single day. This allows you time to visit some of the lovely "Vesuvian Villas" and make the must-do ascent to the summit of Mount Vesuvius, all in the space of a three-day visit.

Three Days in the Past

DAY 1

Spend the day in the excavations at Herculaneum. The visitor route takes you through various quarters of the town, passing through an area of elegant houses, often decorated with frescoes or mosaics and in some cases with terraces overlooking the Bay of Naples; along the *Decumanus Maximus* (main east–west street), lined with shops and taverns; and to the Baths, decorated with frescoes and mosaics on an aquatic theme.

DAY 2

Visit Portici, just a short walk from the ruins. In 1738 the Bourbon king Charles V built a sumptuous royal palace here. Many noble Neapolitans imitated him and this part of the Bay of Naples has been known as the Miglio d'Oro ("golden mile") ever since, because of its splendid villas. Among the finest is the Rococo-style Villa Signorini, next to the royal residence, with a magnificent garden overlooking the sea. At Ercolano itself are Villa Campolieto, with a splendid elliptical colonnade, Villa Favorita, in late-Baroque style, and Villa Ruggiero, on the slopes of Vesuvius.

DAY 3

Spend the day in the Parco Nazionale del Vesuvio. The road from Ercolano is stunning, and the rich volcanic soil means that it is lush and productive. Farms along the way sell local produce such as wine, including the famous Lachryma Christi ("Tears of Christ"). On the slopes of Vesuvius, visit the Crèator Vesevo, an open-air sculpture gallery, and the Observatory, with its fascinating museum, before making the ascent to the summit.

Dos and Don'ts

- ✗ Don't make the ascent of Vesuvius if the weather is bad. Check the forecast to be sure of a clear day on which to appreciate the stunning views from the summit.
- ✓ Wear sturdy walking shoes or boots, both for walking around the excavations and for the visit to Vesuvius.
- ✓ If you have time, visit the Museo Archeologico Nazionale in Naples to see the treasures unearthed during the excavations at Herculaneum and taken there for safe keeping.
- ✓ Buy a coral cameo. This is a traditional craft in the Ercolano area, practised particularly in the suburb of Torre del Greco, where there is a small museum dedicated to the trade.

Below: Opulent atrium of a house in Herculaneum

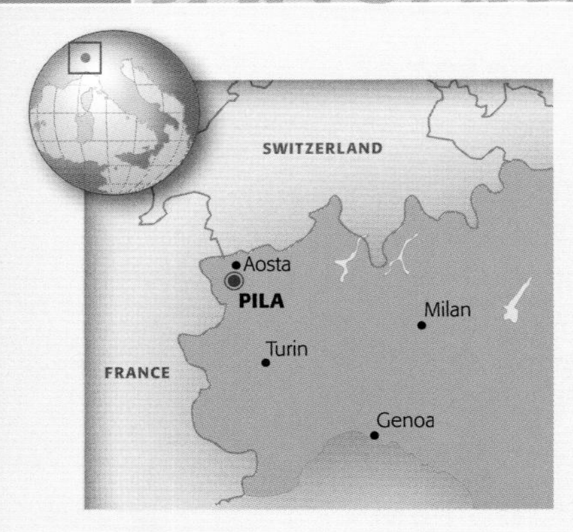

GETTING THERE
Pila lies in Valle d'Aosta. The nearest airport is Turin's Caselle 70 miles (115 km) and there is a shuttle bus connection to Aosta. From there, the best way of getting to Pila is by gondola lift (*telecabina*), which takes 18 mins. A substitute bus service runs when the lift is closed.

GETTING AROUND
Ski-lifts and hotels are linked by pistes, enabling visitors to travel around on skis. A good bus service connects all the villages.

WEATHER
January never disappoints dedicated skiers: snow is guaranteed. Sunny days are not unknown, although they can be very chilly.

ACCOMMODATIONS
Au Petit Chevrot, just outside Aosta, has elegant, comfortably furnished apartments; two-room apartment with twin beds from US$110 per day; www.aosta-appartamenti.com

Family-run hotels Della Nouva (doubles from US$100; www.hoteldellanouva.it) and Chacaril (doubles from US$100, www.aostahotel.com) in Pila have cozy, traditional rooms and great views.

EATING OUT
Try traditional dishes at high-altitude mountain huts: polenta with mushrooms or melted cheese; *sorsa*, vegetable stew with *salamelle* (sausage); *raclette* (melted cheese with potatoes); or *braserade* (thin slices of meat cooked on a brazier). They are often open in the evening; transport by snowmobile can be arranged (average cost US$35 per person).

PRICE FOR TWO
US$265 per day including accommodations, meals, and lift passes, but not equipment rental.

FURTHER INFORMATION
www.pilaturismo.it

The Fiera di Sant'Orso

Every year at the end of January, local craftsmen gather in Aosta for a fair that has taken place for hundreds of years – the Fiera di Sant'Orso. They converge from every corner of the valley to show their wares: wood-carvings; pieces made from local *ollare* stone; wrought iron and leather goods; local *drap* (rough-woven sheep's wool cloth); pillow lace; wickerwork and more. The night of January 30, known in local dialect as the *veillà*, is celebrated with folk music, torchlit processions, and a feast of local food.

Main: Talented snowboarder making a spectacular leap in Pila's Snowpark
Left (top to bottom): Enjoying a sudden snowfall; typical local house with an impressive woodpile; polenta with *fonduta* (melted cheese), a local specialty

WINTER WONDERLAND

Until a few decades ago the slopes around Pila were just mountain pasture, dotted with cows and chalets, and all that could be seen here in winter was undisturbed snow and majestic peaks. Today, however, Pila is one of the most advanced ski resorts in the world, at an altitude of nearly 5,900 ft (1,800 m). The pistes are easily reached: a 3-mile (5-km) gondola lift links Pila with the town of Aosta and, at a brisk pace of over 20 mph (30 kph), it can whisk 2,400 passengers up the mountain every hour. The lift, which came into operation in December 2008, is in its own way a small marvel in the alpine world: in just eight months workers managed to dismantle the old installation, set up the new one and put it into operation, a record for any mountainous area. Work proceeded with speed because Pila's ethos is one of "total ski," the concept being to link all the resort facilities, hotels, and services by ski trails, so that skis are the only form of transport needed. This is just one of the aspects that make Pila a

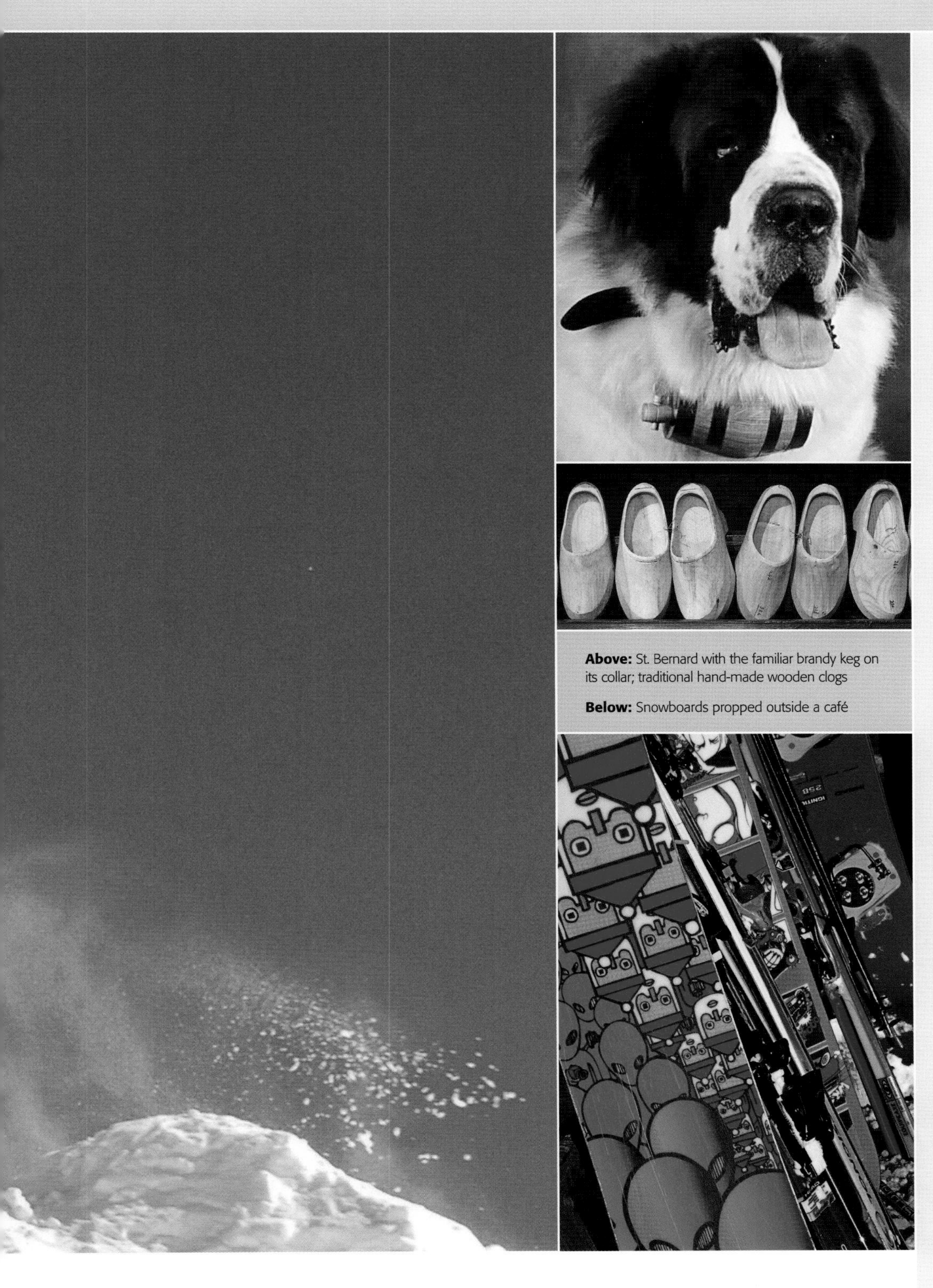

Above: St. Bernard with the familiar brandy keg on its collar; traditional hand-made wooden clogs

Below: Snowboards propped outside a café

destination of choice for skiers – the resort also includes a slalom run for the advanced skier, including a timed route with barrier, gates, and photo sensor at the finish, as well as gentler runs for the less adventurous. There are lovely, marked snowshoe trails for the positively sedate.

The snows of Pila are also an unequaled playground for keen snowboarders, with a Snowpark that extends over nearly 765 yards (700 m) on a natural terrace facing the Alps. Numerous circuits and facilities cater for every level of expertise, from lessons for the beginner to a Freestyle Area, with a Pipe Zone and a Slopestyle Zone, for the dedicated professional. The halfpipe is especially popular: a channel 49 ft (15 m) wide and 394 ft (120 m) long, carved out of deep snow, along which to race or perform tricks with the board. On arrival at the far end, boarders can take it easy while a chair-lift takes them back to the top of the park, refreshed and ready for the next descent. Yet Pila remains something of a secret beyond Italy, so its well-groomed pistes are seldom crowded and its lift lines rarely long – it's an ice paradise just waiting to be discovered.

ALPINE DIARY

Pila is a paradise just made for skiing and boarding, but there are other activities away from the slopes, and great options for après-ski, as well. Essentially, though, the whole place is a Snowpark and a sheer delight for winter sports fans. A four-day break will give you a taste of everything Pila has to offer, but you are sure to return.

Four Days on the Pistes

DAY 1

Spend the day at Pila's official Snowpark, which lies just to the left of the Nouva chair-lift arrival. Keen snowboarders will enjoy a genuine jibbing course with natural obstacles, and there is also a spectacular halfpipe and a huge jump. For first-timers, there is a beginners' area where you can start off in complete safety, with instructors on hand.

DAY 2

Assess your skill on any of the four alpine skiing routes at Pila, or simply savor the pleasure of skiing any of the 25 pistes. Covering a distance of 44 miles (70 km) in total, there is plenty of choice for every level of skier. At lunchtime, if you are feeling a bit rusty, book a lesson for the afternoon to get your ski-legs back.

DAY 3

Check that the weather is suited to a day off-piste. Pila runs organized freeriding day trips accompanied by an instructor or guide, along routes through amazing scenery. In the evening, after a long day of challenging skiing, relax over a hearty traditional dinner high in the mountains, at one of the refuge-hut restaurants close to the pistes. No need to stretch those tired legs – you can be transported there and back by snowmobile.

DAY 4

If you can bear to leave the skis or board behind, rent some snowshoes and take to the marked trails. It is also possible to go on an organized night hike on snowshoes. This is a magical experience, especially on the long clear nights typical of a Valle d'Aosta winter.

Dos and Don'ts

- ⊗ Don't attempt skiing or freeriding without first having taken lessons, and don't go off on your own if you are a novice. Don't head off-piste without having first checked the weather and avalanche forecasts.
- ✓ Always carry an ARVA (Appareil de Recherche de Victimes d'Avalanche, or avalanche transceiver) with you.
- ⊗ Don't start out on a day's skiing without a good breakfast, and take some energy bars with you as a snack.
- ✓ In the evening, sample a restorative *vin brûlé*, a Valle d'Aosta specialty of hot, spiced wine.

Below: Skiing in the sunshine on a gentle piste in the Valle d'Aosta

GETTING THERE
Rome's Leonardo da Vinci Airport at Fiumicino 16 miles (26 km) is linked by a shuttle train service, the Leonardo Express, to Termini station in the city center, a 30-minute ride. Shuttle bus services and taxis also run to and from the city.

GETTING AROUND
Rome is lovely to walk around; use public transportation for longer distances.

WEATHER
The weather in January can be wintry but it is rare for temperatures to drop below freezing.

ACCOMMODATIONS
Hotel Regno is ideal for families, with good-sized rooms, sleeping up to four, from US$300; www.hotelregno.com

The Hotel Rex offers younger guests play areas, books, DVDs, and playstations; family suites from US$335; www.hotelrex.net

EATING OUT
There are hundreds of restaurants and trattorias in the city, to suit all tastes and all budgets. But if you want to try authentic Roman cooking, head for the restaurants of the Testaccio district (site of the old slaughterhouse) and the Jewish quarter. Classic dishes include *coda alla vaccinara* (braised oxtail), *bucatini all'amatriciana* (hollow, spaghetti-like pasta with a spicy tomato and pancetta sauce), and *carciofi alla giudia* (deep-fried artichokes).

PRICE FOR A FAMILY OF FOUR
US$530 per day, including accommodations, meals, local travel, and admissions.

FURTHER INFORMATION
www.turismoroma.it
www.vatican.va

Vatican Treasures

The Vatican Museums house several superb collections, built up over 500 years. Among the most important is the Pio-Clementine Museum, with its nucleus of Greek and Roman sculptures. The muscular sculpture group *Laocoön*, which dates from the 1st century AD, was the Museums' first acquisition. Others include Roman copies of Greek statues such as *Apoxyomenos* (an athlete drying off after a race) and the *Apollo del Belvedere (above, center)*. More recent statues also figure, such as *The Pugilists* and *Perseus Triumphant*, both works by Antonio Canova, produced in the late 18th and early 19th centuries.

Left: *Croccante*, a sweet made with nuts and fruit, much loved by children

Right (left to right): Ruins of the Circus of Maxentius on Via Appia Antica; Mausoleum of Casal Rotondo, the largest of the tombs lining the Via Appia Antica; helicoidal staircase at the entrance to the Vatican Museums

Inset: Aerial view of St. Peter's Square in Vatican City

Main: The celebrated *Creation of Adam*, painted by Michelangelo on the ceiling of the Sistine Chapel

THE ETERNAL CITY

THE SISTINE CHAPEL IS, FOR MANY, the heart within the heart of Rome, built in the 15th century, and decorated by Michelangelo with one of the most beautiful fresco cycles ever created. Old Testament stories are depicted in succession on the vault and along the walls, in scenes full of life, such as the *Creation of Adam*, painted around 1511. No one could fail to feel the impact of this work, or fail to feel the spark of life that the Creator is about to pass to Man. It is certainly a work of genius, even though Adam's extended hand was repainted by pupils after the death of the great artist, while another pupil, nicknamed Braghettone ("breeches-painter") was charged with painting loincloths (later removed during restoration) onto Adam and other nude figures, in a move designed to placate the ire of several scandalized cardinals. The Sistine Chapel is the culmination of a visit to the Vatican Museums, one of the greatest art collections in the world. The museum's history began in 1506, when a statue was discovered in vineyards in Rome's suburbs. Pope

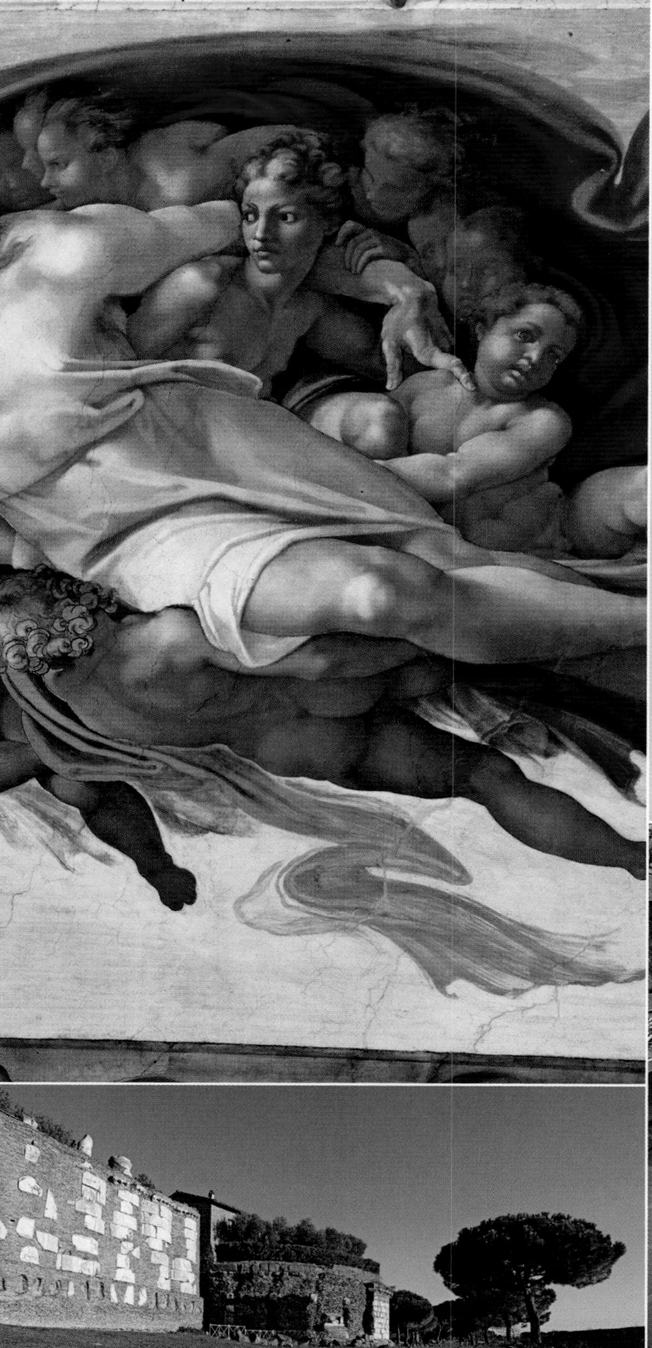

In St. Peter's Square you cannot fail to appreciate the harmonious lines of this extraordinary amphitheater, embraced by the curves of Bernini's colonnade, which welcomes visitors and pilgrims with open arms.

Julius II, a keen patron of the arts, dispatched Michelangelo to look at the piece, and he recommended its purchase. This was the *Laocoön*, and its acquisition marked the beginning of the magnificent collection.

Outside, in St. Peter's Square, it's easy to appreciate the harmonious lines of this extraordinary amphitheater, embraced by the curves of Bernini's colonnade, which welcomes visitors and pilgrims with open arms but, at the same time, preserves and protects the sacred aura of the site.

From here, a road leads straight to the Tiber River and to Castel Sant'Angelo, the mausoleum built for Emperor Hadrian in AD 125. It was named by Pope Gregory I who, during a plague epidemic in 590, had a vision of the archangel Michael sheathing his sword upon the summit. To commemorate the apparition, a statue of the angel was placed on the top of the castle. Made of wood, it soon disintegrated. A replacement, made of marble, was destroyed during a siege. The next, of marble with bronze wings, shattered in 1497 when a bolt of lightning struck the castle's gunpowder store. Two more statues took their turn before the bronze one seen today. To put it another way, while even angels may come and go, Rome remains eternal.

CAPITAL CITY DIARY

For millennia, Rome has attracted artists and architects who have enriched the place with many masterpieces, making this one of the most beautiful cities in the world. Four days affords a perfect introduction – any more would be overwhelming. But you will certainly want to return time and again *(see also pp236–7; pp287–8)*.

Four Days of Art and History

JAN

DAY 1

On your first day, head straight to magnificent St. Peter's Square, and of course visit St. Peter's Basilica itself to see some of its priceless works of art, such as Michelangelo's *Pietà*. After lunch, walk down to Castel Sant'Angelo, built as a funerary monument for Emperor Hadrian. In front the lovely bridge of Ponte Sant'Angelo, lined with statues carved by Bernini and his pupils, straddles the Tiber.

DAY 2

Devote the day to visiting the Vatican Museums, an immense collection of valuable paintings and sculptures. It is impossible to see everything in one day so choose one of the suggested itineraries, which all finish in the spectacular Sistine Chapel. There are four routes, marked by different colors, all of which start at the Quattro Cancelli (Four Gates) at the northern end of the complex.

DAY 3

In the morning, visit the church of San Giovanni in Laterano, the first Christian basilica built in Rome. Next to the church is a baptistry founded in the 5th century, and Palazzo del Laterano, the papal residence until 1309. In the Palazzo is the chapel known as the Sancta Sanctorum, which leads to the Scala Santa ("Holy Stair"). According to Christian tradition, this was the staircase climbed by Jesus to reach the room where he met Pontius Pilate. Spend the afternoon exploring the imposing Roman Baths of Caracalla and the leafy Aventine Hill, with its splendid city views.

DAY 4

Today, head out to the Via Appia Antica, the Roman road that once linked the city to Brindisi on the coast of Puglia. Here there are ancient catacombs where Christians, in the era of persecution, met to pray and bury their dead. Among the most interesting is the Catacomb of San Callisto, whose tunnels stretch for 12 miles (20 km) underneath the city of Rome.

Dos and Don'ts

- ✓ Take a boat trip on the Tiber River, an alternative and fascinating way to see the city.
- ✗ Don't be tempted to drive in Rome. Parking is scarce and expensive, and the Roman driving style is terrifying.
- ✓ Visit Via Appia Antica by bus or metro on Sundays or public holidays when access to the site is prohibited to vehicles and you can savor the peace and tranquility.

Below: Magnificent Castel Sant'Angelo, viewed from the Ponte Sant'Angelo

FEB
MAR
APR
MAY
JUN
JUL
AUG
SEP
OCT
NOV
DEC

GETTING THERE
The Majella is in the heart of Abruzzo. The nearest airport is at Pescara 30 miles (50 km). By car, take the A25 freeway, then the exit for either Pratola Peligna, Bussi, Torre de' Passeri, or Alanno-Scafa. Continue on minor roads to the villages in the park. Buses and trains also link Pescara with the villages of the Majella.

GETTING AROUND
You will be on foot, snowshoes, or skis much of the time. To get from village to village, a car is advisable.

WEATHER
Daytime temperatures in L'Aquila average 47°F (8°C), and it is often sunny, but it will feel much colder in the park with snow on the ground, and there is the chance of further snowfall at any time. It can drop below freezing at night.

ACCOMMODATIONS
Il Majo mountain hut, with seven beds, is the base for the Wolf Weekend. Food is included in the price (US$280 per person including transportation, guide, and insurance); www.rifugioilmajo.com

The *agriturismo* Capriccio di Giove in Cansano is a typical Abruzzo rural farmhouse offering bed and breakfast; doubles from US$90; www.ruraltourism.it

EATING OUT
Try regional specialties, such as polenta with wild boar sauce, in the mountain huts, restaurants, and *agriturismi* in the park; you will dine well for less than US$35 per person.

PRICE FOR TWO
US$315 per day, including the Wolf Weekend, other accommodations, food, car rental, and Majella Cards.

FURTHER INFORMATION
www.parcomajella.it

The Marsican Bear

Hunted by man since time immemorial, the Marsican brown bear is now a threatened species. A museum dedicated to the bear has been established at Palena, in an area of the park traditionally associated with its presence. The museum's role is also to educate people about bears and to encourage visitors to show interest in, and show respect for, these animals. To this end, a visit to the museum can be combined with a guided walk along one of the bear paths, to observe the bears' natural surroundings and look for signs of their presence.

Above: River Aventino gushing over rocks near Taranta Peligna; eagle owl, present in numbers in the Majella; wolves roaming free in the Park
Main: The symbol of the Park: a splendid Apennine wolf

THE KINGDOM OF THE WOLF

THE ONLY MASSIF IN ITALY TO FEATURE IN AN OATH (*mannaggia alla Majella*, "damn it to Majella," is an old Abruzzo saying), the Majella lives up to its reputation. It may be an imposing, utterly beautiful mountainous area, its slopes covered in dense forest and its majestic peaks blanketed with snow, but it is also a harsh environment for the people who live there. Solemn and impressive from all angles, Majella is made up of a highly compressed calcareous massif, rising to a series of towering peaks (the highest, Monte Amaro, is 9,170 ft/2,795 m high) and vast, high-altitude plateaus, and features deep valleys carved out over millennia by the rivers coursing down its slopes.

The Parco della Majella is a protected area and a nature preserve, more than half of it on land over 6,560 ft (2,000 m) high, and is home to plants and animals that have all but vanished elsewhere. For example, the Apennine wolf, the symbol of the park, has been considered threatened with extinction since the 1970s, but today is present here in significant numbers once again. You may even meet one – well, not exactly meet, but it is possible to follow a wolf's tracks, work out its hunting trails, listen to the howling of its pack, and even observe them, from a safe, respectful distance. All you need is a spirit of adventure and a love and respect for the environment. The Wolf Weekend hikes organized by the Parco della Majella help you to achieve just this, offering a safe way of getting closer to wolves and other park animals (wild boar, Abruzzi chamois, as well as the smaller mammals that are the usual prey of wolves), to observe them and study their behavior in their natural habitat. These trips last two days, and aim to interfere as little as possible with the surrounding landscape, a natural environment made even more atmospheric and majestic in the cushioned silence of a blanket of snow. It takes only minutes to forget the rest of the world and feel transported into a unique and magical atmosphere. All that remains is to wait for the wolf...

It is possible to follow a
volf's tracks, work out its
unting trails, listen to the
howling of its pack, and
ven observe them, from a
e and respectful distance.

Inset: Party of cross-country skiers on a trail in the Park
Below (left to right): Aerial view of the Parco della Majella rising through the clouds; *Scamorza* cheese, a specialty of Abruzzo

WILDLIFE DIARY

Described by the Roman scholar Pliny the Elder as "the father of mountains," Majella has protected status as a national park. The landscape is harsh, but rich in history and beauty; wild, but with traces of man's presence. You could visit just for the Wolf Weekend, but six days allows you to get to know the park and all its wildlife to the full.

Six Days on the Trail

Drive through the park to Cansano, the main center for mountain hikes in the Parco della Majella. It is from here that you will depart for the start of your Wolf Weekend, based at Il Majo mountain hut.	**DAY 1**
After your first night in the cozy hut, the Wolf Weekend begins in earnest with hikes to find traces of wolves, their prey, and other forest mammals. Return at sunset for a hearty supper, then go for a short walk to hear the howling of the wolves. There are more hikes the next day before it is time to return to Cansano.	**DAYS 2–3**
Follow one of the many cross-country ski trails in the park. One of the loveliest begins at Tavola Rotonda (accessible via chair-lift from Campo di Giove), crosses the Majella gorge, goes as far as Macchia di Sécina, and then returns to Campo di Giove.	**DAY 4**
Drive to Palena to visit the Marsican bear museum, then continue to Lama dei Peligni, where there is a special reserve for rare Abruzzi chamois. The species had been lost from the Majella at the beginning of the 20th century, but it has been reintroduced and is now thriving.	**DAY 5**
Cross the park to Guardiagrele, a pretty village known as the Gateway to the Majella, thanks to its position, clinging to the eastern slopes. It dates from the Middle Ages, and still has many interesting buildings, among them the church of Santa Maria Maggiore, with a splendid 14th-century doorway, and the monumental Palazzo Vitacolonna, from the 18th century. Enjoy the view from the Belvedere, called the "terrace of the Abruzzo," from which you can see the Adriatic Sea.	**DAY 6**

Dos and Don'ts

- ✓ If you go hiking in the Parco della Majella, remember to take drinking water, food, and a basic first aid kit.
- ✗ In the park, don't leave the marked paths; this is not only forbidden, it can also be dangerous.
- ✗ Don't collect flowers, mosses, rocks, or anything else within the park: it is prohibited.
- ✓ Buy a Majella Card: this entitles you to discounts not only on entry to the park, but also in hotels, and shops. An individual card, valid for a week, costs around US$7.50.

Below: Abruzzi chamois on a rocky slope in the park

JAN FEB MAR APR MAY JUN JUL AUG SEP OCT NOV DEC

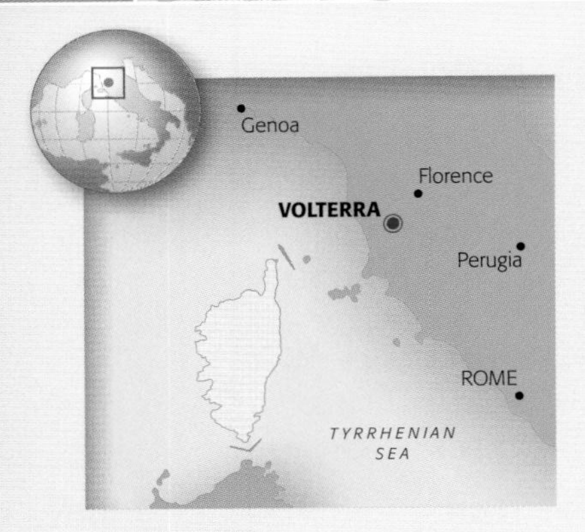

GETTING THERE
Volterra is in western Tuscany. From Pisa (Galileo Galilei Airport) take the A12 south; leave at Rosignano Marittimo exit and take the Via Aurelia, then turn off at Cecina for the SS68 to Volterra. From Florence (Amerigo Vespucci Airport) take the SGC Florence to Siena road, leave at Colle Val d'Elsa Nord exit, then take the SS68.

GETTING AROUND
Volterra is best explored on foot.

WEATHER
Winters are generally dry and the temperature averages between 37°F and 45°F (3–7°C).

ACCOMMODATIONS
The Park Hotel Le Fonti, close to the center of Volterra, has two swimming pools, a spa, and a terrace. Standard doubles from US$125; www.parkhotellefonti.com

The San Lorenzo farm, 1 mile (2 km) from Volterra, is a charming complex of houses built around a small 18th-century church; rooms from US$60; www.agriturismo-volterra.it

EATING OUT
In the historic center, the restaurant and wine bar Del Duca offers traditional dishes with a creative touch. It has a pleasant garden and well-stocked wine cellar. About US$60 for a meal; www.enoteca-delduca-ristorante.it

Try the Etruria restaurant for local dishes based on game, mushrooms, and truffles, costing US$30–42; tel. 0588 86064.

PRICE FOR TWO
About US$265 for a night's stay, meals, and entrance to the Museo Etrusco Guarnacci.

FURTHER INFORMATION
www.turismo.intoscana.it

The Art of Alabaster

Volterra alabaster is a pale, translucent stone. Its soft consistency makes it much easier than marble to sculpt and work, so it is ideal for designs that are rich in detail. The Etruscans used the stone for making sarcophagi and funerary urns – sometimes even covering it with gold leaf. The stone went out of favor during the Middle Ages and it was not until the end of the 18th century that there was renewed large-scale demand for the stone with its unique glow and luminance. Today there are still many traditional alabaster craftsmen in Volterra.

Volterra resembles a quirky catalog of Italian history put together by someone with no respect for dates.

Main: Volterra's Duomo and ancient center bathed in the evening sun
Above (top to bottom): The Porta dell'Arco, originally built by the Etruscans; the abbey of San Salvatore perched on top of Volterra's impressive crags

THE ANCIENT HEART OF TUSCANY

A HILLTOP TOWN IN THE ANCIENT HEART OF TUSCANY, Volterra resembles a quirky catalog of Italian history put together by someone with no respect for dates. Etruscan tombs fight for space with Renaissance buildings and Roman remains stand in the shade of medieval towers. The city walls actually date back to the 5th century BC and include two highly prized examples of Etruscan architecture: the Porta dell'Arco, built with blocks of volcanic rock; and the Porta Diana, which led to a vast necropolis on the outskirts of the town. There are at least 10 such gates from the medieval period, as well as many columns and archways. But Volterra is not merely "the city of gates," it also boasts beautiful monuments, such as the Roman theater, the cathedral and baptistry of San Giovanni del Duecento, and the Rocca Nuova, the fortress that Lorenzo de' Medici built in the 15th century. The street names – Vicolo degli Abbandonati (Alley of the Abandoned), Piazzetta dell'Ortino (Little Market Garden

Left (left to right): The nave of Santa Maria Assunta, Volterra's Duomo; a minestrone of fresh vegetables and beans, delicious with typical Tuscan bread and olive oil; an aerial view of the Roman theater; the Palazzo dei Priori, the oldest town hall in Tuscany

Square) – conjure up a colorful history, but for a more tangible evocation of the past explore the rich collection of ancient Etruscan finds at the Museo Etrusco Guarnacci. Marvel at the touching sentiment of the Urn of the Married Couple and the extraordinary, spindly bronze votive statuette Evening Shadow, which would not look out of place in a modern art gallery.

Volterra is also the world capital of alabaster, the headquarters of a special craftsmanship that dates as far back as the Etruscans, who used it for funerary urns many centuries before Christ. This magical stone, with its hidden veins of color and subtle transparency, lends itself to intricate and delicate carving and drew curious tourists here in the 18th century. And today, Volterra's craftsmen jealously guard the secrets of a tradition that has never been forgotten. In their tiny workshops and galleries, these artisans work their magic, almost bringing the stone to life as they create extremely delicate bas-reliefs, extraordinary decorations, and exquisite ornaments, somehow combining the sensibilities of the modern world with the evocative power of ancient times.

ALABASTER DIARY

Far from concealing its age, Volterra displays its 3,000 years of history proudly. And with good reason: in the 5th century BC the town was one of the greatest Etruscan centers, keeping its prestige through the Roman era and into the age of medieval city-republics. Spend two days discovering the city's charming mix of historic buildings.

A Weekend in Volterra

DAY 1

A visit to the town must start with the Etruscan excavations, near the ancient acropolis now occupied by the Medicean fortress, where remains of temples and frescoes have come to light. The Museo Etrusco Guarnacci, one of the most important in Italy, is also not to be missed. It houses famous finds such as the *Urna degli Sposi* (Urn of the Married Couple), a sepulchral monument of the 2nd century BC and the votive statuette *Ombra della Sera* (Evening Shadow), named by the poet Gabriele D'Annunzio. If you're still in the mood for museums, take a look at the Ecomuseo dell'Alabastro (Alabaster Eco-museum) to learn all about this special stone of Volterra.

DAY 2

Explore the medieval aspect of the city by starting at the Piazza dei Priori, one of Italy's most spectacular medieval squares, harking back to a time when Volterra was an independent city, free from the influence of Florence. The oldest building is the Palazzo dei Priori, built in the first half of the 13th century. Walk down the surrounding streets, characterized by the spectacular tower-houses, to reach the Romanesque cathedral and the baptistry. It was built in 1283 but underwent modifications until the 16th century – the dome is said to have been designed by Brunelleschi. A little farther on stands the theater and bath complex dating all the way back to the Roman Empire, testimony to another golden age in Volterra's history.

Dos and Don'ts

✓ If you want to buy alabaster products, buy from the traditional workshops and make sure the piece you buy has the trademark "Alabastro in Volterra" inscribed on it.

✗ Don't try to visit the Medicean fortress – it has always been used as a jail and is currently a maximum security prison.

✓ If you can, make sure you visit the Farmers' Market (Mercato e gusto) on the first Saturday in every month. Here, local food producers sell their products direct to customers.

✗ Don't go to the Museo Etrusco Guarnacci in the afternoon: in winter it's open only in the morning.

Below: Urn of the Married Couple in the Museo Etrusco Guarnacci

FEBRUARY

Where to Go: **February**

February is synonymous with Carnevale (Carnival) so where should you go if not to Venice, to see the most famous masks in Italy (and, of course, to visit one of the most fascinating cities in the world)? But this is also the month for Milan Fashion Week, with the chance to go shopping in the chic capital of Italian design, to seek out the city's artistic treasures, or to feel the magic of looking out over the city from between the spires on the cathedral roof terrace. Then again, in February, the days start to lengthen, you're aware of the scent of spring in the air – this is the perfect time to visit the elegant cities of the south, places rich in monuments and ancient splendors such as Palermo, Lecce, and Noto. Or, step back into to the 4th century, with the splendid

FESTIVALS AND CULTURE

AQUILEIA The ancient ruins of the Roman gate

ATRI
ABRUZZO

An ancient village with a splendid cathedral

Atri is a fascinating place with a maze of streets and alleys and a beautiful Romanesque cathedral.

www.regione.abruzzo.it/turismo/en/index.html

SANREMO
LIGURIA

Wonder at the City of Flowers during the Music Festival

Known for its mild climate, colorful flowers, and blue sea and skies, this delightful seaside city is the setting for the Sanremo Music Festival.

www.sanremoguide.it/en

REGGIO CALABRIA
CALABRIA

View exquisite works of art from classical antiquity

The museum of Reggio Calabria is home to the Riace Bronzes, two of the finest examples of classical Greek sculpture.

http://turismo.reggiocal.it

AQUILEIA
FRIULI-VENEZIA GIULIA

One of the most important Christian buildings in Italy

Once a prosperous Roman colony, Aquileia boasts important historic ruins, as well as a splendid basilica complex with 4th-century mosaics.

See pp48–9

MONDOVÌ
PIEDMONT

A lovely town of art among the mountains of Piedmont

The old heart of Mondovì is a harmonious ensemble of churches and palazzi, including the splendid Chiesa di San Francesco Saverio.

www.turismoinlanga.it

UNFORGETTABLE JOURNEYS

PALERMO & MONREALE The elegant gardens of the Palazzina Cinese

AGRIGENTO
SICILY

Ancient Greek temples among flowering almond trees

The best-preserved Greek temples outside Greece are set just outside a delightful city, overlooking the sea on the beautiful Sicilian coast.

See pp46–7

GAETA
LAZIO

A place of travelers, ancient and modern

Sandwiched between mountain and sea, Gaeta boasts an impressive visitors' book, from Aeneas and Ulysses to St. Philip Neri.

www.goitaly.about.com

PALERMO & MONREALE
SICILY

A blend of diverse cultures

Visit and learn about the history of the Normans, Arabs, the Byzantines, and the Greeks – all have left their mark on Palermo.

See pp40–41

"Seen from a distance, San Leo appears to sit within a Renaissance painting, surrounded by gentle folds of rolling hills..."

SAN LEO
LE MARCHE

A mighty hilltop fortress

The fortress of San Leo, with Roman origins, was used as a top-security prison in medieval times; its impressive presence still dominates the surrounding hills.

See pp58–9

METAPONTO
BASILICATA

In search of ancient Greece

Southern Italy was once known as Magna Graecia; traces of Greek civilization lie all along the Ionian coast, from Policoro to the superb excavations at Metaponto

www.aptbasilicata.it

NATURAL WONDERS

SCILLA Rughudi Vecchio in the Parco Nazionale dell'Aspromonte

VAL TREBBIA
EMILIA-ROMAGNA

A steep valley, with high cliffs and dense vegetation

Val Trebbia combines natural beauty with lovely old towns such as Marsaglia, on the confluence of the Trebbia and Aveto rivers.

www.altavaltrebbia.net

PARCO REGIONALE DELLE PICCOLE DOLOMITI LUCANE
BASILICATA

In the green heart of Basilicata

The Lucania Dolomites offer wild and spectacular landscapes with woods of oak trees and rare plants.

www.parcogallipolicognato.it

MACUGNAGA
PIEDMONT

A window on the snowy slopes of Monte Rosa

At the heart of the ancient Walser culture, Macugnaga is a famous ski resort in a spectacular position beneath magnificent Monte Rosa.

www.piemontefeel.org

SCILLA
CALABRIA

Seat of many myths, Scilla is a fascinating coastal town

A long sandy beach, a sheer cliff with an ancient castle on top – this is Scilla, on the Costa Viola, backed by the Parco dell'Aspromonte.

See pp54–5

"...Scilla is a beauty – one of the most picturesque towns on the Calabrian coast."

PESCASSEROLI
ABRUZZO

Explore the wilderness of the Parco Nazionale d'Abruzzo

Pescasseroli predates the Roman Empire and is an entrance point to the Abruzzo National Park, and the departure point for many hikes.

www.pescasseroli.net

Previous page: Piazzo San Marco, with the impressive Palazzo Ducale in the foreground

mosaics of Aquileia, full of movement and color, or with the mighty fortress of San Leo, in Le Marche, perched high on a rocky outcrop like a tall ship at sea. Perhaps you'll want to travel even farther back in time among the ancient Greek temples of Agrigento, surrounded by blossoming almond trees. The sea, too, now at the end of winter, is starting to return to a warm blue, whether it is at Portofino in Liguria, the little harbor crowded by pastel-colored houses, or at the extreme tip of Italy's "boot," in Scilla, the place that Homer filled with monsters, but which, today, offers a marvelously long, sandy, and sheltered beach. And for thrill-seekers, here is an idea from Aosta: a flight in a hot-air balloon over the snow-covered Alps. What more could you want?

LUXURY AND ROMANCE

PORTOFINO A lovely village in a small cove, surrounded by greenery

PORTOFINO
LIGURIA

A picture-postcard village hidden in luxuriant nature

Truly charming, Portofino has painted houses huddled by the harbor and the ancient abbey of San Fruttuoso, on the beautiful Ligurian coastline.

See pp50–51

MILAN
LOMBARDY

At the heart of the Italian capital of fashion and design

Shop in the "Golden Quadrilateral" of fashion – Milan's four main streets – but don't forget to climb up to the cathedral terrace to admire the lovely city views.

See pp56–7

NOTO
SICILY

An over-the-top Baroque jewel

A town of pre-Greek origins, Noto was razed to the ground by an earthquake in 1693 and rebuilt in Baroque style out of glowing honey-colored tufa stone.

See pp52–3

"Milan is a modern city with an ancient heart. As the fashion capital of the world, it's a paradise for those who live to shop."

CERVINIA
VALLE D'AOSTA

Ski and climb the mountains in one of the liveliest alpine towns

Synonymous with mountain climbing and skiing on the slopes of the Matterhorn, Cervinia is also the place for shopping, relaxation, and fun.

www.cervinia.it

LUCCA
TUSCANY

Once one of the most powerful city states in Italy

Be charmed by Lucca, with its green walls-cum-gardens and lovely piazzas. Visit the glorious aristocratic villas built in the surrounding countryside.

See pp42–3

ACTIVE ADVENTURES

AOSTA Heli-skiing – a demanding sport for adrenaline junkies

CAVALESE
TRENTINO-ALTO ADIGE

Skiing for all tastes at the heart of the Val di Fiemme

Cavalese is the most important town in the Val di Fiemme and one of Italy's capitals of winter sports, with 60 miles (100 km) of ski runs.

www.visitfiemme.it

PARCO NAZIONALE DEL CIRCEO
LAZIO

Trekking in the coastal park

The Parco Nazionale del Circeo, on the coast of southern Lazio, contains a particularly rich ecosystem, to be explored along its many paths.

www.parcocirceo.it

AOSTA
VALLE D'AOSTA

A ride in a hot-air balloon over the Alps

Experience the thrill of admiring magnificent alpine peaks from a unique angle – on-board a hot-air balloon from the town of Aosta.

See pp38–9

LIMONE PIEMONTE
PIEDMONT

Winter sports on "the mountain of the two coasts"

At the very heart of the maritime Alps, Limone Piemonte is a well-equipped ski resort on a mountain pass joining the "two coasts."

www.limonepiemonte.it

PORTO TOLLE
VENETO

Bird-watching in the Po delta

The *golene* (flood plains) of Ca' Pisani and Ca' Gornera, close to Porto Tolle, are perfect spots for observing the many different bird species that populate the Po delta.

www.deltaportotolle.it

FAMILY GETAWAYS

VENICE One of the splendid masks worn during Venice Carnevale

"The Grand Canal may display Venice's most showy face; but simply by strolling around the alleyways of the districts, you'll discover the city's more subtle charms."

VENICE
VENETO

There's an air of drama in this city of a thousand bridges

Venice is thronging with boisterous mask-wearers, bringing the Carnival alive, against the stunning backdrop of this waterborne city.

See pp44–5

STRA
VENETO

A maze, mysterious gardens, and a spectacular villa

Perhaps the most magical of all the houses lining the Brenta canal, the Villa Pisani in Stra has a fiendish maze to keep the whole family enthralled.

www.villapisani.beniculturali.it

SCIACCA
SICILY

Mardi Gras for all the family

The pre-Lent carnival of floats and gaudy figures, not to mention the beaches and spas, make Sciacca the best family getaway in beautiful Sicily.

www.whatsonwhen.com

ANGERA
LOMBARDY

See the Rocca di Angera dating from the 12th century

Angera, by the enchanting Lake Maggiore, is dominated by a well-preserved fortress, now home to an interesting doll museum.

www.lagomaggiore.net

CREMONA
LOMBARDY

Renaissance and Baroque music and architecture

Cremona, which has a lovely medieval center for families to explore, is also well known for the craft of violin-making.

www.italiantourism.com/discov3.html

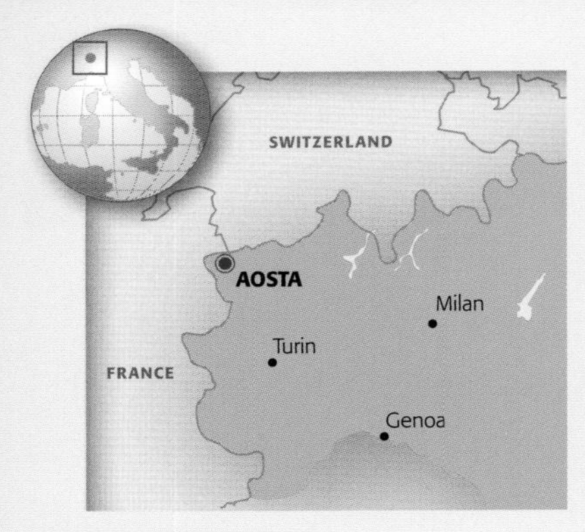

GETTING THERE
In the north of Italy, the Valle d'Aosta, the country's smallest region, nestles in the western arc of the Alps. The nearest airport is Turin Caselle, an hour away on the A5 freeway. If you are not taking a car, there are plenty of trains and buses from Turin. If you are coming from the French side by car, go through the Mont Blanc Tunnel and take the SS26.

GETTING AROUND
Aosta is a small town and pleasant to explore on foot. To reach the surrounding valleys, it is best to rent a car or to use the efficient bus service.

WEATHER
As you'd expect, the weather can be harsh, alternating between great days of sunshine and heavy snowfalls.

ACCOMMODATIONS
The Hotel Cecchin, a few steps from Aosta's Arco di Augusto, offers comfortable rooms in traditional style, from US$120; www.hotelcecchin.com

Set in the hills, the Ambrosia B&B has a fine garden, rooms from US$85; www.bedbreakfastaosta.com

In Courmayeur, the traditional Hotel Emile Rey has kept its rural alpine charm with doubles from US$80; www.hotel-rey-courmayeur.com

EATING OUT
The Praetoria restaurant is a favorite with locals and tourists, serving Valle d'Aosta cuisine for US$28–35; tel. 0165 44356. Restaurant and wine bar Ad Forum offers a local menu for US$42; tel. 0165 40011.

The Cadran Solaire in Courmayeur is a cozy, rustic bistro – dine for around US$40; tel. 0165 844 609.

PRICE FOR TWO
About US$210 per day for meals and accommodations. A hot-air balloon flight will cost around US$250 each.

FURTHER INFORMATION
www.regione.vda.it/turismo; www.mongolfiere.it

Left (from bottom): Enchanting alpine scenery at Courmayeur; the Romanesque cloister of the Collegiata di Santi Pietro e Orso, Aosta; *tegole* (from the Italian for roof tile), traditional nutty biscuits; the Roman Arco di Augusto (Arch of Augustus) dating back to 25 BC

Right (left to right): Fabulous alpine view from the cable car up to Punta Helbronner at 11,360 ft (3,462 m); traditionally decorated cowbells; 12th-century carved capital in the cloister of the Collegiata di Santi Pietro e Orso

Main: A hot-air balloon floating above the clouds amid the beautiful Alpine peaks

Heli-Skiing Off-Piste

Expert skiers can now add one more exciting experience to their list of must-do activities: heli-skiing – combining a mountain helicopter trip with the thrill of an off-piste descent. The helicopter whisks you off to seldom visited and precipitous summits, so you can get away from the crowds and ski in stunning surroundings on untouched deep powder snow. But be warned: it's expensive and you must always go with an experienced guide, with knowledge of the local avalanche danger spots.

THE SKY'S THE LIMIT

Few things can beat sipping a chilled glass of delicious Champagne. Except, of course, the scintillating experience of enjoying the same glass of champagne while gracefully floating in a balloon over the Italian Alps, home to some of the highest mountains in Europe. Up there, it's so silent you can almost hear the bubbles fizzing in your glass. And the view, once you've cleared the cotton-wool clouds, is stupendous – you're eye-to-peak with the spectacular serrated peaks of the mountains, robed in all their dazzling icy finery.

The place to do this is Aosta – a European ballooning capital, so it's extremely easy to organize. Simply contact the Aosta Club Aerostatico and book your flight – any reason will do: a birthday, a romantic jaunt, a wedding anniversary. But the best reason, if a reason be needed, is that a comparable thrill is hard to find. The Aosta pilots are genuine aeronautic professionals, mountain experts, and extremely good hosts. While flying in the balloon you

can not only drink a toast but also enjoy a gourmet dinner – a romantic meal eaten at 10,000 ft (3,000 m) over the Alps certainly beats a table for two at most restaurants. You can have the whole experience made into a movie, but the best thing about the trip is that you get such a fantastic view of the great mountain chains. To the west looms the majestic Mont Blanc at an astonishing height of 15,781 ft (4,810 m) and, almost as massive, Grand Paradiso, to the south; then as you float east you can make out the distinctive granite pyramid of the Matterhorn at 14,692 ft (4,478 m).

In the magic of the moment, a turreted castle in the valley below looks like it has come straight out of a fairy-tale and the alpine villages look fresh off a chocolate box. Drifting silently over a national mountain park, you'll be be advised to keep an eye out for the usually shy local residents – the chamois, ibex, and mighty golden eagle. An adventure with Aosta's pilots may start in the town center but once you're up and flying – the sky's the limit.

BALLOONING DIARY

A flight in a hot-air balloon is the perfect way to appreciate a town's relationship with the mountains. Three days allows you to enjoy the balloon experience and also explore the town and the surrounding mountains – Aosta is the goal of winter sports aficionados, yet boasts monuments from two thousand years of history.

Three Days in Aosta

DAY 1

Explore Roman Aosta. Start from the triumphal Arco di Augusto (Arch of Augustus), built in 25 BC on the right bank of the Buthier River. Then cross by the Roman bridge and enter the town through the fortified, square gateway, Porta Pretoria. A little farther on, admire the impressive façade of the Teatro Romano – like a 72-ft (22-m) cheese grater – and the amphitheater, partly incorporated into the Convento di San Giuseppe. Then press on to the Piazza Giovanni XXIII, above the ancient forum; here you can still see the cryptoporticus, an ancient covered walkway.

DAY 2

Today is the day of your hot-air balloon flight. It will take about three hours in total. In the afternoon, visit the ancient symbol of the town, dating back to the medieval era, the Gothic Collegiata di Santi Pietro e Orso. The complex of buildings was started in the early Middle Ages, although the present configuration dates from the 15th century. Don't miss the 11th-century ceiling frescoes and the splendid capitals in the Romanesque cloister. Aosta's cathedral is also worth a visit – behind the Neo-Classical façade there is a Gothic interior with more exquisite 11th-century frescoes.

DAY 3

Head over to Courmayeur at the foot of the monumental Mont Blanc, the highest mountain in Europe. Ride the cable car up to the vertiginous Torino refuge at 11,075 ft (3,375 m) and enjoy the wonderful views from its terrace of the spectacular *Dent du Geant* pinnacle 13,165 ft (4,015 m) and the whole Mont Blanc massif.

Dos and Don'ts

- ✗ Don't overdo it with Valle d'Aosta coffee: it is flavored with lemon zest and reinforced with a generous amount of local brandy. You drink it from a *grolla* (a special wooden cup with several spouts) and it can be very alcoholic!
- ✓ Buy a *drap*, a sheep's wool cloth, woven on traditional hand-looms. These were traditionally limited in color to grey, blue, black, or red but nowadays they are also made in some extremely vivid hues and with geometric patterns. Tough, durable, and warm, they make great furnishing fabric.
- ✓ If you go up in a hot-air balloon, wrap up warmly: it is cold at high altitude and there can be an icy wind.
- ✗ Don't be tempted by heli-skiing unless you are physically fit and an experienced skier in deep snow.

Below: An elegant boutique shop window in Courmayeur

JAN
FEB
MAR
APR
MAY
JUN
JUL
AUG
SEP
OCT
NOV
DEC

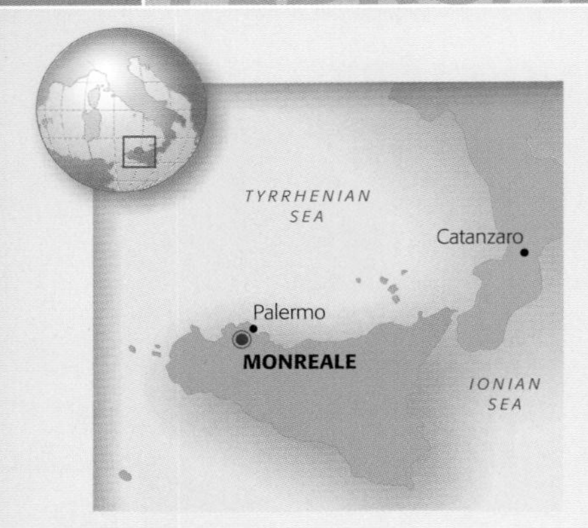

GETTING THERE
Palermo, the regional capital, is in north-western Sicily, on the coast. The 19-mile (30-km) trip from the airport can be made by car or shuttle bus via the A29, or by train on the Trinacria Express (45 minutes). Monreale is only 3 miles (5 km) from Palermo and can be easily reached by car or bus.

GETTING AROUND
Both cities are best explored on foot. For longer journeys, use a car or taxi.

WEATHER
Even in winter, there are pleasant sunny days and the weather is never too harsh.

ACCOMMODATIONS
In Monreale, an old mill has been converted into a charming hotel, the Baglio Conca d'Oro; rooms from US$235; www.hotelbaglioconcadoro.com

In Palermo, the 19th-century *belle époque* Villa Igiea is one of Sicily's most prestigious hotels with doubles from US$350; www.villa-igiea-palermo.com

The Art Nouveau Hotel Joli, is also very charming, with rooms from US$120; www.hoteljoli.com

EATING OUT
In Palermo's center, the Bellotero offers traditional cuisine with an original touch; tel. 091 582 158. For a romantic dinner nearer the sea, try the Charleston le Terrazze; tel. 091 450 606, or Bye Bye Blues; tel. 091 684 4623. Meals cost from US$55.

PRICE FOR TWO
Between US$400 and US$500 per day for meals and accommodations.

FURTHER INFORMATION
www.palermotourism.com

Sicilian Marionette Theater

The Sicilian marionette theater is a tradition that goes back three centuries. The wooden marionettes are called "pupi" and are over 3 ft (1 m) high, although their style and size varies according to their origin. The puppets tell the epic tale of the Holy Roman Emperor Charlemagne's knights. The story is not always told in one performance; the events continue in a series of episodes, sometimes taking several days. The Museo Internazionale delle Marionette was created in Palermo to keep the tradition alive and it holds a rich collection of *pupi* and exhibits from all over the world.

Above (left and right): The elegant gardens of the Palazzina Cinese (1799), on the edge of the Parco della Favorita, the largest green space in Palermo; *sfinciuni*, a delicious spicy Sicilian version of the pizza

NORMAN TREASURES

It comes as no surprise that, in Italy, an enlightened sovereign who was reluctant to collect taxes should have been called "Good." But Guglielmo II of Sicily (1153–89) more than deserved his nickname, not just for his fiscal largesse but also because he built the wonderful Duomo of Monreale in 1176. Stories about him emphasize the holy character of the sovereign, telling how the Madonna appeared to him indicating where a huge amount of treasure was hidden. Guglielmo went on to retrieve the gold and used it for the Duomo (instead of taxing the people). A visit to Monreale confirms that this is one of the most magnificent and fascinating monuments in Italy's vast heritage.

Different civilizations have clearly left their mark on Sicily's art and culture through the years, each one borrowing from its predecessor and combining it with their own to create a harmonious blend. The exterior of Monreale's Duomo reveals its Norman influences, especially in the arches and use of black and white stones (alternating limestone and lava), while the apses evoke Arab influences with their pointed arches and geometric and polychromatic decorations. But it is inside that the building really comes to life. The three aisles, 295 ft (90 m) long, have a cross-vaulted ceiling in the Byzantine style, but are divided by columns surmounted by the pointed arches that again recall the classic Arab style. The vast golden gleaming mosaics that cover the walls – said to contain 4,850 lb (2,200 kg) of gold leaf – are classic Byzantine while the side chapels are splendid examples of Sicilian Baroque. This layering and interweaving of different styles and eras is also a characteristic of the monuments in nearby Palermo, where a similarly varied set of architectural styles has been wonderfully blended together. See how well it works at the Duomo, built on the site of an Arab mosque and displaying Arab-Norman, Gothic, and Baroque elements. Other examples in Palermo include La Martorana, a splendid church with dazzling Byzantine mosaics; the Palazzo dei Normanni, started by the Muslims and finished by the Normans, and the nearby Capella Palatina built by King Ruggero II in 1130 and decorated with elegant and eye-catching mosaics.

Main: The gold-covered interior of the Duomo of Monreale, one of the finest examples of Norman architecture in Italy
Below (left and right): Palermo's Duomo, built in various styles between the 12th and 18th centuries; aerial view of Monreale's splendid Duomo and cloister

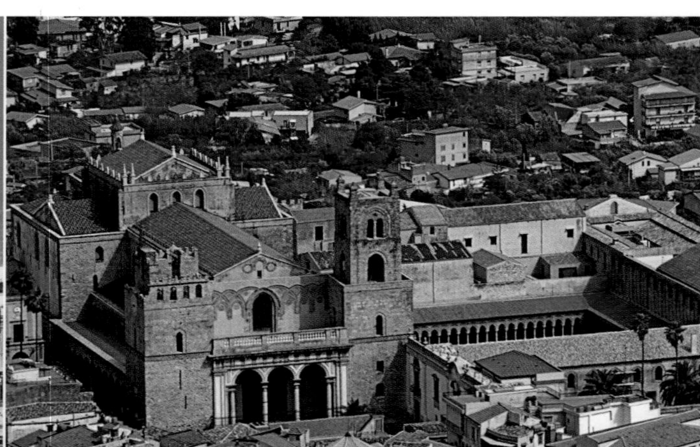

SICILIAN DIARY

Palermo has twice been the capital of Sicily, first under the Arabs, then under Norman rule. Two periods of peace, prosperity, and power enabled the city to concentrate on its art and architecture. Spend one day admiring Monreale's Duomo and two more in Palermo, exploring the city's many architectural masterpieces.

Three Golden Days

DAY 1

Spend the first day in Monreale, visiting the Norman Duomo. Stroll among the adjoining cloisters whose columns are decorated with a variety of glorious motifs. Return to Palermo in the evening and walk up to Monte Pellegrino, the promontory that marks the northern end of the bay, giving one of the best views of the city.

DAY 2

In Palermo, discover the monuments of the Norman period: the Palazzo dei Normanni, built by the Arabs in the 9th century and converted by the Normans into a splendid palace; the Capella Palatina, just next door, where Arab, Byzantine and Norman motifs blend together. Then tour the Duomo, which combines the architectural features of a mosque with more typically Christian designs. Those with strong stomachs could then visit the catacombs at Piazza Cappuccini, with the preserved bodies of 8,000 people. Afterward, head back toward the bay for an evening stroll and a drink beside the sea.

DAY 3

On your second day in Palermo, make sure you visit La Martorana. This church, built in 1143 and decorated with mosaics, is another fine piece of Norman architecture. There are two more splendid churches around the same square, Piazza Pretoria, worth seeing. Santa Caterina, considered by some to be the most beautiful Baroque church in Palermo; another is San Giuseppe dei Teatini, topped by a large dome and richly decorated inside. Look out, too, for the 16th-century Fontana Pretoria that stands out front – the nude statues on this fountain scandalized the faithful churchgoers. From here, go and look around the Mercato della Vucciria, Palermo's most famous general market.

Dos and Don'ts

- ✓ Be patient and resign yourself to joining the line (not always disciplined) to visit the Palazzo dei Normanni and, next door, the Capella Palatine. They are well worth the wait.
- ✓ Go and see a performance of the Sicilian marionettes – several theaters in Palermo stage the puppet shows as does the Museo Internazionale delle Marionette.
- ✓ For a quick snack, try *sfinciuni*. This is a type of spicy pizza available all over the city and made with tomatoes, onions, and *caciocavallo*, a Sicilian cheese.
- ✗ Don't take any notice of the illegal "parking attendants," who will try to sell you tickets for what are actually free parking spaces.

Below: A typical Palermo alleyway close to the Duomo

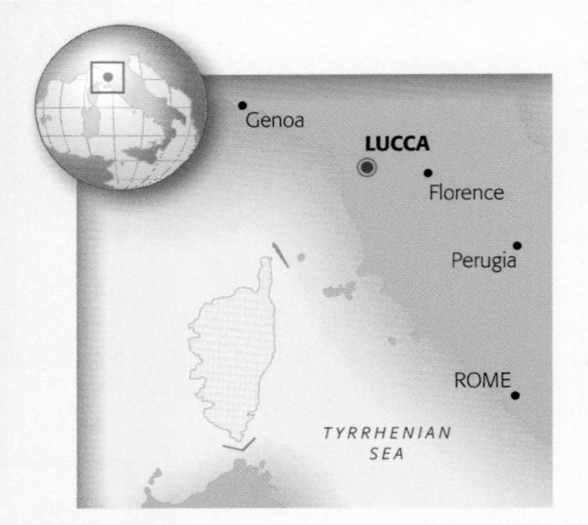

GETTING THERE
Lucca, in northern Tuscany, can be reached by car from Florence (Amerigo Vespucci Airport) using the A11, or by taking the SS12 from Pisa's Galileo Galilei Airport, which is closer. Lucca is connected to Pisa and Florence by train and also by a good bus service.

GETTING AROUND
Lucca is easy to explore on foot (or bicycle), but to visit the surrounding area it is best to go by car.

WEATHER
The average temperature is between 37°F and 54°F (3–12°C), but there are often mild and sunny days.

ACCOMMODATIONS
Elegant La Romea is located on the first floor of a 14th-century palace in the town center – the suite is sumptious; rooms from US$140; www.laromea.com

South of Lucca, in San Lorenzo a Vaccoli, there are two lovely hotels. Locanda l'Elisa has a quiet country location, rooms from US$140; www.locandalelisa.it

The 19th-century Villa Marta also promises a relaxing stay, from US$320; www.albergovillamarta.it

EATING OUT
Try the local cuisine at central Buca di San'Antonio, from US$40; www.bucadisantantonio.com

Antica Locanda dell'Angelo, also in the historic center, offers meals from US$40; www.locandadellangelo.it

North of Lucca, at Ponte a Moriano, La Mora cooks traditional dishes such as *maiale di cinta al cavolo nero*, a Sienese pork dish with black cabbage; meals from US$75; www.ristorantelamora.com

PRICE FOR TWO
From US$305 to US$445 per day including meals, accommodations, and the Lucca Card.

FURTHER INFORMATION
www.luccatourist.it

Fountains and Beer

Built in the 17th century by wealthy merchants from Lucca, Palazzo Pfanner is surrounded by a splendid Italianate garden, graced with statues and fountains. It was acquired in the 19th century by the Austrian brewer Felice Pfanner, who had been invited by Duke Carlo Felice of Bourbon to establish the first brewery in the region. The brewery was set up in the cellar of the palace, and the gardens, complete with a pergola and bar for serving guests, soon became a favorite meeting place for everyone who likes spending a few hours with a tankard or two of beer.

TUSCANY'S BEST-KEPT SECRET

The quickest way to appreciate Lucca's picturesque charm, though not the easiest for your thighs, is to tackle the 230 steps up to the top of the Torre dei Guinigi with its crown of holm oaks. Up on the terrace, 144 ft (44 m) above the ground, under the unexpected shade of the trees, you will be able to witness the magical sight of a completely intact fortified town – looking much as it did hundreds of years ago. Or get to know Lucca the slow way, examining the historic buildings one by one, as you walk a circuit of the town along the extraordinary promenade created on top of the massive walls. Whichever you do, you will inevitably fall under the spell of a town that has preserved the rhythms and ambience of times past. Wander through the center, along Via Fillungo and the nearby streets packed with towers and medieval palaces that now overlook fashionable boutiques, lively bars, and restaurants

Main: Piazza dell'Anfiteatro, built on the site of a former Roman amphitheater

Left: A stretch of Lucca's ancient city walls

Right (left to right): *Buccellato*, a ring-shaped Luccan cake flavored with aniseed; items of interest from Giacomo Puccini's house, still filled with the composer's possessions; detail of the sarcophagus of Ilaria del Carretto, a masterpiece by 15th-century sculptor Jacopo della Quercia

Right of main (top to bottom): Tiled rooftops in Lucca's historic center; the Duomo in Piazza San Martino with its striking colonnades and multi-tiered loggias

serving the best of Tuscan gastronomy. As you stroll it is impossible not to be bowled over by the beauty of the piazzas. Each one has its own unmistakable character: Piazza Anfiteatro, one of the most lively and romantic places in Lucca, was created in the Middle Ages on top of a 2nd-century Roman arena – the houses built next to each other follow the original elliptical shape; Piazza San Frediano, towered over by the basilica decorated with fine 13th-century mosaics; Piazza San Martino, dominated by its impressive Duomo whose Romanesque façade, with tiers of arcaded loggias, resembles an elaborate wedding cake; and Piazza San Michele whose basilica perfectly fuses the Romanesque and Gothic styles. There are also surprises to be found in Lucca's beautiful surrounding countryside: you must spend at least a day exploring the lush fertile landscapes, dotted with the magnificent 16th-century villas of the nobility. There are more than 300 of these exquisite Tuscan gems, set in large and carefully tended gardens, just waiting for you to discover them.

PIAZZA DIARY

Everything in Lucca reminds the visitor of its past history as a proud and independent city – it has a 16th-century encircling wall; the historic center still shows traces of its Roman past from the layout of the streets and the shape of the squares; and the fine Romanesque churches, streets, and houses evoke the glory days of the Middle Ages.

Three Days in Lucca

DAY 1

The best way to explore the center of Lucca is to walk around the city walls: it's a 2-mile (4-km) circuit but it gives you the opportunity to admire the town's major historic buildings. Cycling is popular here so it is very easy to rent some bikes and cycle around. Relax afterward at the Piazza Anfiteatro: these days this market square is a fashionable meeting spot with lots of bars with outdoor tables where you can enjoy a glass or two of the local wine.

DAY 2

Explore the center of Lucca farther; stop and admire its lovely churches. Wander around the pretty boutiques on Via Fillungo and the adjacent streets, and admire the Art Nouveau windows of many of the shops. Don't miss the composer Giacomo Puccini's house, a 15th-century building that contains many of his personal possessions as well as the piano on which he wrote *Turandot*. For a breathtaking panorama, climb to the top of the Torre dei Guinigi or the slightly lower Torre dell'Orologio (Clock Tower); from here you'll have a spectacular 360° view of the city, as far as the Apennines.

DAY 3

There are many aristocratic villas in the countryside, within easy striking distance from Lucca. Among the finest are the Villa Reale di Marlia, a sumptuous residence acquired in 1806 by Elisa, Napoleon's sister, then the Princess of Lucca and Piombino; the Villa Torrigiani di Camigliano, one of the best examples of Baroque in Tuscany; and Villa Mansi, with a garden designed by architect Filippo Juvara (1678–1736).

Dos and Don'ts

- ✓ Buy the Lucca Card, which gives you free entry to many of the town's historic buildings and museums (US$17).
- ✗ Don't miss the exquisite tomb of Ilaria del Carretto in the Duomo, and the Volto Santo, a much-revered wooden crucifix that is carried around the city every year on September 13.
- ✗ Don't go to the villas outside Lucca without booking the visit in advance: not all of them are open to the public. For more information, visit www.villelucchesi.net
- ✓ Go and see Lucca's Museo Nazionale del Fumetto e dell'Immagine (National Comics and Illustrations Museum). It is filled with fabulous displays about the great 20th-century artists and illustrators and their most famous creations.

Below: Fountain in the gardens of the Villa Reale di Marlia

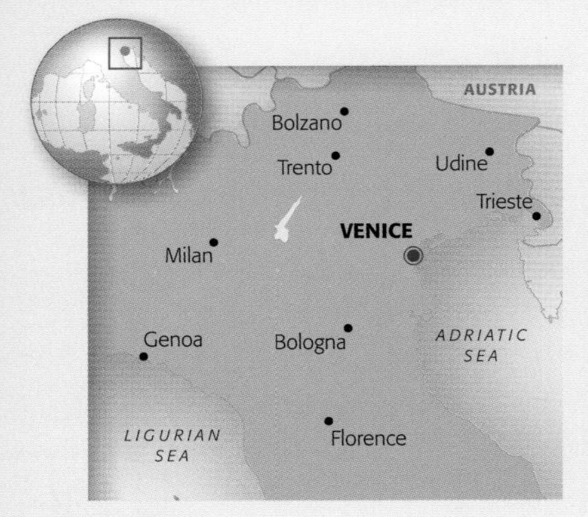

GETTING THERE
From Marco Polo Airport you can take a shuttle bus or taxi that will carry you to the Piazzale Roma in 20 minutes. From there continue to the center on foot or by *vaporetto*. You can also opt for the Linea Alilaguna water bus – it can be more convenient than a taxi – which connects the airport to Venice, stopping at important parts of the city.

GETTING AROUND
On foot and by *vaporetto*.

WEATHER
February is generally a cold month, but Carnival fever heats up the city!

ACCOMMODATIONS
Your children will be well looked after at the elegant Hotel Flora (www.hotelflora.it), often for free or discounted stays, and you'll have everything you need from cot to diapers. From US$475 during Carnival (down to US$265 at other times).

The Hemingway apartments are ideal for families, as are the Frari apartments of Houses in Venice; rooms from US$165 per day; www.housesinvenice.com

EATING OUT
Try polenta, served with *carni in umido* (meat stew) or dried salt cod or cuttlefish, and Venetian-style liver with onions. Dishes like these are served in restaurants such as Vini da Gigio, from US$50 (www.vinidagigio.com); Osteria Antico Dolo, from US$70 (www.anticodolo.it) and Al Graspo de Ua, from US$85 (tel. 041 520 0150).

PRICE FOR A FAMILY OF FOUR
From around US$495 to US$820 for meals, accommodations, and the Venice Card.

FURTHER INFORMATION
www.turismovenezia.it; www.carnevale.venezia.it

Carnival Masks

The *mascherari*, the artisans who made the Carnival masks, had a special status in Venice and established their own guild as far back as 1436. They were fêted as artists and were assigned helpers who were called *targheri*. The mask, however, was not used solely at Carnival, but on many occasions throughout the year. There were various models: the *bauta*, generally for men, was made out of a cloak (*tabarro*) and a three-cornered hat, beneath which was worn the *lavra*, a white mask; and the *moretta*, which was a much smaller oval mask, often decorated with lace and veils, and generally used by women.

Above (left to right): The stately Baroque façade of the 17th-century Ca' Pesaro on the banks of the Grand Canal; historic gondola on display on the first floor of the Ca' Rezzonico, home to the Museum of 18th-century Venice

CARNIVAL ON WATER

THE VENETIAN CARNIVAL IS AN ANCIENT FESTIVAL: the document with which the Senate of the Republic declared the last day before Lent to be a feast day dates back to 1296. Since then, the Carnival has been a festive symbol of the city: a yearly party like no other, still retaining many traditional features: the historic procession in costume along the Grand Canal, lead by the doge and his wife, the dogaressa; the "flight of the angel," in which a woman in an angel costume "flies" down from Piazza San Marco's Campanile to join the crowds below; the Marie Parade, when the fairest lady is chosen as Carnival Queen; and on the final day, the swim in the icy waters of the lagoon and the prize for the most beautiful mask.

This extraordinary, magical floating museum of a city forms the framework for this frenetic party. And to discover it, you must start off on the water by traveling along the Grand Canal, Venice's "main road," which wends its way through the heart of the city. The Grand Canal is 3 miles (4 km) long and flows past the most beautiful of Venice's palaces, constructed over more than five centuries by the city's richest and most powerful families and forming an extraordinary physical compendium of architecture. Admire the decorous Ca' da Mosto, one of the oldest of the palaces and built in Venetian-Byzantine style, then compare it with the Ca' d'Oro, whose intricate façade is like fine lace and best represents Venetian-Gothic architecture. Ca' Foscari is decorated with a complex pattern of pointed arches and motifs in contrast to the classic Renaissance Ca' Corner, all pillars and round arches. Then there's the masterly 17th-century Ca' Rezzonico, whose façade moves from dark to light through its use of bays, balconies, and pillars, and the well-proportioned Baroque Ca' Pesaro and Neo-Classical Palazzo Grassi, both now used for art exhibitions.

The Grand Canal may display Venice's most showy face; but simply by strolling around the districts, up the little alleyways, over humped bridges, and through tiny squares, you'll discover the city's more subtle charms. Away from the center and the crowds, you'll find you can hear the gentle lapping of the water and you'll see Venetians doing the ordinary things such as walking the dog, chatting on cell phones, and eating out, in this most extraordinary of cities.

Main: A colorful character poses by the Grand Canal during the Carnival at Venice
Below (left to right): Biblioteca Nazionale Marciana, a library repository for valuable and ancient manuscripts; the Rialto bridge, one of the focal points of the city, lit up at night

RENAISSANCE DIARY

Built on 117 small islands and criss-crossed by 150 canals, Venice rises from the water like a mirage. Its six districts or *quartieri* are packed with art treasures, palazzi, and exquisite churches. Six days will be enough time to enjoy the festival, see Venice's highlights, and also visit a couple of other islands in the lagoon *(see also pp222–3)*.

JAN

FEB

Six Days Among the Canals

Take the *vaporetto* – or, better still, a classic romantic gondola – and tour the Grand Canal to properly appreciate the impressive sequence of palaces that lines its banks.	**DAY 1**
Climb Piazza San Marco's Campanile for superb views of the square below and the city. Then explore the other historic buildings in the square, the Basilica and the Palazzo Ducale. Finish the day with a wander through the nearby alleyways.	**DAY 2**
Visit the Rialto, the commercial center of the city and cross the famous bridge to explore the district. Don't miss two very lively markets: the Erberia, where fruit and vegetables from the countryside are unloaded every day from barges, and the Pescheria, bringing the important supply of fish to the city.	**DAY 3**
Immerse yourself in the art treasures of the city's churches. There is an embarrassment of riches: visit San Giorgio Maggiore, one of Palladio's finest buildings or Chiesa dei Frari, with masterpieces by Titian and Bellini and Canova's tomb; the Scuola Grande di San Rocco with works by Tintoretto and the Basilica dei Santi Giovanni e Paulo, with the tombs of 25 doges.	**DAY 4**
Start the day with a tour of the Museum of 18th-century Venice in the Ca' Rezzonico, to see what the interior of a palazzo would have been like at the height of Venetian splendor. Spend the afternoon visiting some of the farther off islands, such as Torcello with its Byzantine Duomo, or colorful Burano.	**DAY 5**
Visit the Venetian ghetto, created in 1516, when the Jews were assembled on a small island in Cannaregio where there was a foundry or *gheto*, hence the name. In the afternoon, explore the long seaside stretch of the Lido on bicycles.	**DAY 6**

Dos and Don'ts

- ✓ Get a Venice Card to have the city at your disposal: it allows unlimited use of public transportation, access to the city's main cultural sites, and various other concessions. A card for 7 days costs US$135 for an adult and US$120 for a child.
- ✗ Don't be put off by the crowds that pack Venice during Carnival: they are part of the spectacle. Just don a mask and surrender yourself to the mischievous atmosphere.
- ✓ Visit the Palazzo Venier dei Leoni. Built in 1748, it was bought in 1948 by Peggy Guggenheim, businesswoman and patron of the arts. She filled it with 20th-century art and turned it into the Guggenheim Museum, one of the most important in Venice.

Below: Tintoretto's *Theft of the Body of St. Mark* in the Gallerie dell'Accademia

MAR
APR
MAY
JUN
JUL
AUG
SEP
OCT
NOV
DEC

GETTING THERE
Take the A29 from Palermo airport (100 miles/ 160 km), then follow National Roads to Agrigento. From Catania airport take the A19 towards Palermo, then the SS640 to Agrigento (100 miles/160 km). There are direct buses from both airports.

GETTING AROUND
Many local buses go from Agrigento to the Valley of the Temples, leaving from Piazzale Rosselli. It is best to rent a car if you are visiting sights outside Agrigento.

WEATHER
Agrigento has a pleasantly mild climate; the mean temperature does not fall below 50°F (10°C).

ACCOMMODATIONS
The delightful Baglio della Luna hotel is in a 13th-century building that overlooks the Valley of the Temples and has a luxuriant Mediterranean garden. Doubles from US$280; www.bagliodellaluna.com

Domus Aurea is an 18th-century country villa in Gothic-Moorish style, converted into a luxury hotel; rooms from US$250; www.hoteldomusaurea.it

EATING OUT
The Dehors – Baglio della Luna's smart restaurant – will delight you with its creative and stylish menu based on fish and local produce; meals from US$50.

The rustic Trattoria dei Templi offers typical Sicilian cuisine. Enjoy dishes such as marinated raw fish medley or Sicilian orange salad with crayfish and *bottarga* (dried and salted roes of grey mullet). Meals around US$40; www.trattoriadeitempli.com

PRICE FOR TWO
Around US$400 per day including accommodations, food, and the cost of visiting the Valley of the Temples.

FURTHER INFORMATION
www.lavalledeitempli.it

The Almond Blossom Festival

Agrigento's mild climate means that spring comes very early, covering the area's many almond trees with blossom by February. With the ancient temples as a breathtaking backdrop, the *Festa del Fiore del Mandorlo* (almond blossom festival) celebrates this yearly flowering with singing, dancing, processions, and fireworks. The festival is dedicated to the theme of peace and friendship between peoples; its most important and exciting moments are the lighting of the torch of friendship in front of the Temple of Concordia and the Sunday procession of traditional folkloric groups and Sicilian painted carts.

Left (left to right): The rui of Eraclea Minoa overlookin the gorgeous Sicilian coastlir almonds, a key product of Agrigento; Temple of Conco built on a rocky massif in the 5th century BC

Right (left to right): The v clay "steps" of the Scala dei Turchi descending into the s ceramic tiles displaying Sicili motifs and colors; the impressive columns of the Temple of Hercules, Agriger

Main: Almond tree in blossom in front of the Temple of Concordia, Valley of the Temples, Agrigento

MAGNA GRAECIA IN BLOOM

FROM A DISTANCE THE HILLSIDE appears to be dotted with white balls of cotton; as you get close enough to see that these are actually almond trees in blossom, you're struck by the outline of five Greek temples against an intensely blue sky; this is the wonderful view of the Valley of the Temples seen from the coastal road in February. A sight that still recalls the time when Agrigento was the magnificent city of Akragas in Magna Graecia – a city so splendid that the ancient poet Pindar called it "the most beautiful city of all those inhabited by mortals." Despite the name, the five temples are actually not in a valley but set high on a ridge, visible from all around. The temples, all in the Doric style, are made from local limestone – and they may even have originally been faced with marble. Their size is impressive: in fact, the Temple of Olympian Zeus, started around 480 BC, would have been one of the largest of the ancient world if its construction had not been interrupted by the Carthaginians attacking and sacking the city.

Above (top to bottom): Agrigento Duomo, built by the Normans in the 11th century; olive trees growing in the fertile land around the city

Today, only its ruins remain, but they still give an idea of the vast size of the project – one of the supporting statues of Atlas is nearly 26 ft (8 m) high. The other temples are in a better state of preservation: the Temple of Hera Licinia still has 24 of its original columns standing; the Temple of Concordia is the best preserved, because it was converted into a basilica in the 4th century AD; the Temple of Hercules, built in the 6th century BC, is the oldest, and the Temple of Castor and Pollux (or Dioscuri) was destroyed by an earthquake and partially rebuilt in the 19th century.

Medieval Agrigento has a different sort of charm: perched on a rocky buttress where its citizens took refuge to defend themselves from the Saracens' raids in the 9th century, it welcomes visitors with its bright colors. At its heart lies a dense maze of narrow streets with steep flights of steps leading up to churches often built on the sites of pagan temples. The two best examples of this are Agrigento Duomo, built over the temple of Zeus, and the church of Santa Maria dei Greci, built on the site of the temple of Athene.

TEMPLE DIARY

Welcome to Magna Graecia: Agrigento, with its Valley of the Temples, was a major center of one of the greatest civilizations of ancient times. Greek sophistication influenced the Romans, who in turn helped shape Europe and most of the Western world. Three days will give you time to explore the area and fully appreciate the achievements and grand architecture of the ancient Greeks.

Three Days of Early Spring

DAY 1

Spend the morning visiting the Valley of the Temples. As well as exploring the five Doric temples, a visit to the excavations of the nearby Greco-Roman town is also worthwhile. You can still see the rectilinear street pattern and the excellent archeological museum has kept the finds from the excavations, including vases and Greek sculptures. In the afternoon, explore Agrigento's medieval quarter and soak up its special atmosphere. Don't miss the Monastero di Santo Spirito, reached via a long winding flight of steps, with its wonderful stucco ceiling and 14th-century cloisters.

DAY 2

Visit the coastal ruins of Eraclea Minoa, a short distance west of Agrigento. This ancient Greek city looks out over the sea and is surrounded by beautiful, unspoiled countryside. The floor of the excavation is covered with shards of pottery. Then head on to Capo Bianco below, one of Sicily's best and most spectacular beaches where the crystal clear waters lap against stark white cliffs.

DAY 3

Still farther to the west, on the coast, you'll find Selinunte. The ruins here are among the most atmospheric in the Mediterranean. Excavations have brought to light various temples, a mighty system of fortifications, and an acropolis, all enjoying a delightful coastal setting.

Dos and Don'ts

- ⊗ Don't reveal any embarrassing secrets when you are visiting Agrigento's Duomo: an unusual acoustic phenomenon means that anyone standing near the main altar can hear the quietest whisper from near the entrance. Try it and see!
- ✓ Take a boat trip along the Agrigento coast and admire the beauties of the shoreline, such as the Scala dei Turchi, a spectacular white rocky buttress that juts out into the sea.
- ⊗ Do not entrust yourself to the numerous unauthorized guides who will offer to take you round the Valley of the Temples (instead, apply to the Association of Agrigento Tour Guides: www.associazioneguideagrigento.com).
- ✓ Do try the specialties of Agrigento's cuisine – particularly the desserts, such as *cuscusu*, an Arab-influenced dish made with couscous, almonds, and pistachio nuts.

Below: Medieval detail above a door in the historic center, Agrigento

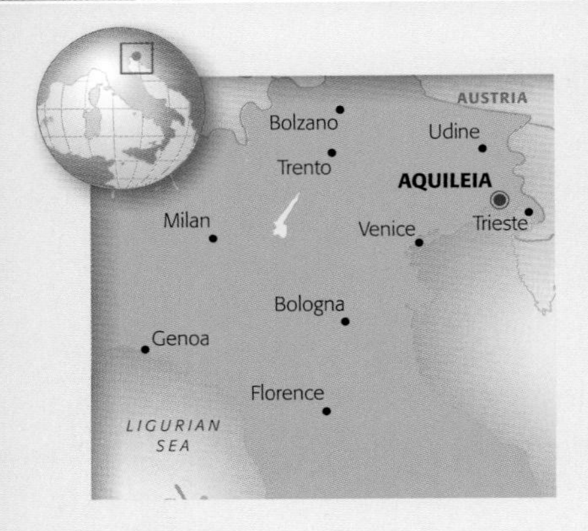

Above (left to right): Exterior of the Patriarchal Basilica di Aquileia, built in 1031; typical house in the historic center of Grado

GETTING THERE
Aquileia is on the Friuli coast, in the province of Udine. The regional airport Friuli-Venezia Giulia di Ronchi dei Legionari is only 9 miles (14 km) from the city and is connected to it by a regular bus service.

GETTING AROUND
Aquileia is easily explored on foot, and there is a good network of trains and buses for farther afield. Visitors will, however, enjoy the freedom of touring in a car.

WEATHER
The temperature in winter ranges between 32°F and 50°F (0–10°C).

ACCOMMODATIONS
Hotel Patriarchi, just steps from the basilica, offers spacious rooms from US$122; www.hotelpatriarchi.it

In Grado, the Hotel Marea offers B&B with a double room for US$112 on the seafront; www.hotelmarea.it

The elegant Hotel Hannover in Grado has double rooms from US$195; www.hotelhannover.com

EATING OUT
On the outskirts of town, La Colombara restaurant serves regional dishes and homemade desserts, www.lacolombara.it; at Al Ponte you can enjoy typical Friuli cuisine, www.ristorantealponte.com; meals at both restaurants cost around US$35–40.

Fish plays a leading part in the menu at the Tavernetta all'Androna di Grado. Try the seafood soup and the scampi risotto; www.androna.it

PRICE FOR TWO
You will spend about US$295 per day on local travel, meals, and accommodations.

FURTHER INFORMATION
www.aquileia.net; www.grado.it

The Marano Lagoon

South of Aquileia, along the line of the coast, a string of small sandy islands effectively create the Marano lagoon out of a bay. The edge of the lagoon is indented with canals and irrigation ditches, and reed beds and inflowing freshwater rivers make the brackish water attractive to migrating birds on the way to or from northern Europe. Today, the lagoon is part of two nature reserves with a wetlands center, whose staff can organize boat trips for visitors to spot the wildlife.

MOSAIC TALES

SPREAD OUT LIKE AN ENORMOUS CARPET on the floor of the basilica, the largest ancient mosaic in the world (8,073 sq ft/750 sq m) is divided into nine panels that depict wondrous stories like a picture-book: Jonah and the Whale, in a sea that is filled with fantastic creatures; the Four Seasons; the Parable of the Good Shepherd; and general scenes of animals and birds. The mosaic is in the Basilica di Aquileia, one of the greatest historic buildings of Christianity. The current structure is the last in a succession of churches; the first was built in AD 313, the same year that Christians ceased to be persecuted in the Roman Empire, but it suffered serious damage during the invasion of Italy by Attila the Hun (AD 452). It was the patriarch Poppo who rebuilt the basilica in the 11th century, in approximately the form we see it today; it was altered again after an earthquake in 1348 and the interior decorations were added in the 15th century, under Venetian rule.

Despite all the different architects, the church is majestic in the purity of its execution. The simple Romanesque-Gothic exterior is unadorned, with a slender bell tower and a façade connected by a portico to the next-door Chiesa dei Pagani and the remains of a 5th-century baptistry. But the interior is magnificent and airy, lined with Gothic arcades and adorned by the huge 4th-century mosaic. But that's not all. The two crypts are also truly exquisite: La Cripta degli Scavi, covered with fine mosaics, and La Cripta degli Affreschi, with a cycle of paintings from the 12th century.

The Basilica was an important church, constructed in one of the most important cities in Roman times, thanks to its location on a major trading route between the Adriatic and the Danube basin. Aquileia still retains many features from the Roman era, such as the ruins of the port, which at one time connected it to the sea, and the forum; but, above all, it has the valuable collections in the Museo Archeologico Nazionale, one of the best in northern Italy. The town is no longer an important commercial and strategic center; instead Aquileia is in the heart of a region renowned for its white wines and scented by Adriatic breezes; a territory shaped for millennia by humankind, yet still with large areas of rugged and solitary charm.

Main: Detail showing the vibrant colors of the mosaics in the Basilica di Aquileia
Below (left to right): Another detail of the mosaic showing the artist's skillful use of color; the remains of the Roman forum in Aquileia; a dish of golden fried *sardoni* (sardines)

MOSAIC DIARY

At the time of the Roman Empire, Aquileia was one of the richest cities in Italy. Today it welcomes visitors with a fantastic early Christian complex, adorned with astonishing art. Four days will also allow you to visit Grado beside the beautiful lagoon and explore the glorious Friuli countryside, shaped by centuries of wine production.

Four Days by the Lagoon

DAY 1

Start with a visit to the Basilica di Aquileia and admire the mosaic floor, protected today with a clear plastic cover. Don't miss the two splendid crypts, too. Then go to the ruins of the forum and the river port and set aside time to visit the Museo Archeologico Nazionale and explore its valuable collections.

DAY 2

Spend the morning on the islands in the lagoon, visiting the wildlife center and looking for marsh harriers and little egrets. In the afternoon, get to know the beautiful Friuli countryside – and the local wine – touring the *frasche* (branches), the characteristic wine-growers' bars, so named because their emblem is a little sprig hung on a door. By visiting these bars, often in large farmhouses, you'll be able to get a real taste of rural culture.

DAY 3

Dedicate this day to a visit to Grado, which looks out to sea from one edge of the lagoon. The town has a fine medieval center with a network of narrow lanes and a picturesque canal port, flanked with brightly colored houses. Don't miss the Basilica di Sant'Eufemia, with its octagonal baptistry, and the Basilica di Santa Maria delle Grazie, which also has some fine mosaic floors.

DAY 4

Take a trip to Palmanova, a fortified city that still retains the plan of a nine-pointed star. It was built by the Venetians in 1593, with strong wide ramparts joined to the large hexagonal central square by straight avenues, like spokes of a bicycle wheel. Palmanova's perfect geometry is truly amazing.

Dos and Don'ts

- ✓ If you have the chance, take a boat from Grado to do a bit of island hopping and see the quaint *casoni* – wooden huts thatched with straw and used by fishermen as shelters.
- ✗ Don't set off for a trip on the lagoon without booking in advance with the Reserve Wardens (www.riservenaturali.maranolagunare.com).
- ✓ Try the *boreto a la grasiana*, a delicious fish soup served with white polenta; this is one of the characteristic dishes of the Friulian lagoon.

Below: The ancient ruins of the Roman port at Aquileia

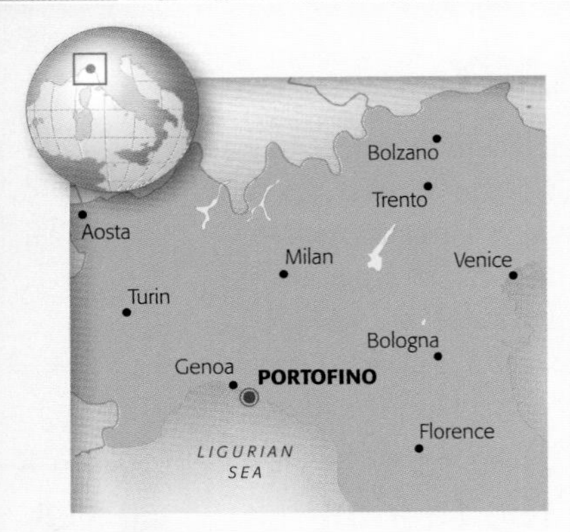

GETTING THERE
On the Ligurian Riviera in the Gulf of Tigullio, Portofino can be reached from Genoa (Cristoforo Colombo Airport) by the A12 freeway, leaving at the Rapallo exit, or by the Via Aurelia. However, parking is not easy, so it is better to take the bus, or the ferry from Rapallo or Santa Margherita.

GETTING AROUND
Forget the car, Portofino is best explored on foot. To visit other places on the coast, there's decent public transportation (ferries, trains, or buses).

WEATHER
The sea ensures that winter temperatures never fall very low and there are plenty of sunny days.

ACCOMMODATIONS
At the Portofino Kulm Hotel, luxurious doubles start at US$295; www.portofinokulm.it

Try the sumptuous Excelsior Palace di Rapallo del Thi Collection; doubles from US$280; www.thi.it

For slightly better value, the elegant seaside Lido Palace Hotel in Santa Margherita has doubles from US$195; www.lidopalacehotel.it

EATING OUT
In Portofino, try the Delfino restaurant, on the Piazzetta, for a romantic dinner (US$110), www.delfino-portofino.it; for simpler local cuisine in a cozy atmosphere, visit Batti (US$85); tel. 0185 269 379.

In the larger town of Santa Margherita, the Trattoria dei Pescatori serves fine Ligurian cuisine. Meals cost US$50–55; www.trattoriapescatori.it

PRICE FOR TWO
You will spend about US$335–530 per day on meals and accommodations.

FURTHER INFORMATION
www.portofinocoast.it

Christ of the Depths

In 1954 a huge bronze statue of Christ the Redeemer by the sculptor Guido Galletti was lowered into the sea near San Fruttuoso. Placed at a depth of 56 ft (17 m), the statue symbolizes the link between the local people and the sea. Every year in July a laurel crown is laid at its feet in memory of those who have perished at sea. The statue can be glimpsed from the surface when the sea is calm and is a popular destination for scuba divers. Two more statues from the same mold were later sunk at St. George, in the Caribbean and Key Largo, USA.

HOLIDAY ROMANCE

A PRETTY CLUSTER OF PASTEL-COLORED HOUSES circling a small harbor and fringed by green woods, Portofino had enough charm to win over even the Wehrmacht. When ordered to destroy the town during World War II, the German army spared it at the insistence of the Baroness von Mumm who had always loved the place. Thanks to her, we can still enjoy some of the most famous views in Italy – Portofino perched on a promontory overlooking the azure sea; the typical Ligurian coastal village unchanged by time; the picture-postcard harbor bobbing gently with gaily colored boats; a coastline of dense chestnut woods cloaking mountains that run to the sea and tumble down into the water.

Portofino offers something for everyone: shopaholics and high rollers should not miss the Piazzetta, lined with boutiques, cozy restaurants, delicious gelaterias, and shaded bar terraces. Admire the charming

Main: A pretty balcony overlooking Portofino's famous Piazzetta

Left: One of Portofino's luxurious villas in a spectacular cliffside location

Right (left to right): Pastel houses lining Portofino's shoreline; *cappon magro*, a traditional dish of seafood, vegetables, and *salsa verde*; pretty enamel tiles used for road signs

Right of main (top to bottom): Old-fashioned fishing boat in Portofino harbor; the same harbor seen from above, filled with more modern craft

architecture of the churches of San Martino, tucked away behind the square, and San Giorgio, up high on the promontory. While you're up there, take a look around the mighty bastion of Castello Brown, bought by the British Consul in 1870 and visited by such luminaries as Guy de Maupassant, Kandinsky, Freud, and Hemingway. And there's more – who can resist the shimmering blue seas? Take a stroll along the coastline to discover a myriad delightful little coves. If the exploring bug takes you, walk to another gem – San Fruttuoso, an ancient Benedictine abbey in a tiny fishing hamlet. It was built in the 13th century on an earlier chapel and nestles into the cliffs beside the sea amid a luxuriant covering of aromatic maquis. Romantic types should consider taking the 20-minute walk to the lighthouse on the southern side of Portofino mountain to watch the magical sunset.

Boutiques, elegant hotels, excellent restaurants, walks in verdant surroundings, ancient abbeys, beaches washed by gentle seas, romantic sunsets: these are the many aspects of this delightful place, famous worldwide for its natural beauty and simple pleasures.

RIVIERA DIARY

Portofino is not just a delightful village with elegant boutiques and smart restaurants, it is also a place of primitive, almost spiritual beauty, ideal for a romantic and relaxing break. Five days will allow you to relax a bit in Portofino and also have time to explore the delightful villages and secluded bays of the Ligurian Riviera at your own pace.

JAN
FEB

Five Days by the Sea

DAY 1 Arrive in Portofino and explore the village: walk up to the Piazzetta from the small harbor, with its rows of pink and yellow houses that appear to rise from the water; wander around the boutiques and little shops that stretch along the street; then climb up to the splendid church of San Giorgio and admire the wonderful view.

DAY 2 Visit the Castello Brown, an ancient fortress that became the residence of British diplomat Montague Yeats Brown in 1870 and later passed to the Mumm dynasty (of Champagne fame) who helped save the town during World War II. From here, walk to the lighthouse and enjoy the colors and fragrance of the Mediterranean maquis.

DAY 3 Take an early morning walk to San Fruttuoso – it should take about 2–2½ hours (but you can make the journey by ferry). The abbey is worth the effort because of its delightful countryside setting and coastal location.

DAY 4 Visit Santa Margherita, at the heart of the Gulf of Tigullio. Don't miss the port – it still has the colored houses that recall its past as a fishing village. More accessible than Portofino, it has grown considerably and is now one of the most fashionable tourist spots in Liguria.

DAY 5 To round off your tour of the Gulf of Tigullio, set aside a day to explore Rapallo. This has grown even more than Santa Margherita and has been an upmarket resort since the middle of the 19th century. It has a fine seafront lined with Art Nouveau buildings and overlooked by castle ruins.

Dos and Don'ts

- ✗ Don't try to go by car to Portofino: it's reached by a narrow road full of hairpin bends and often choked with traffic. It is also difficult to find a parking place when you get there.
- ✓ Try diving. The waters around Portofino are rich in sea life: a marine nature reserve was created in 1999 and has become a real underwater paradise for scuba divers.
- ✓ Buy a handmade *pizzo a tombolo* or lace cushion, a traditional form of artwork kept alive by the women of Santa Margherita Ligure and Rapallo.
- ✓ Take a boat trip along the coast to enjoy the beautiful view of Portofino's harbor from the sea.

MAR
APR
MAY
JUN
JUL
AUG
SEP
OCT
NOV
DEC

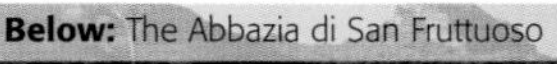

Below: The Abbazia di San Fruttuoso

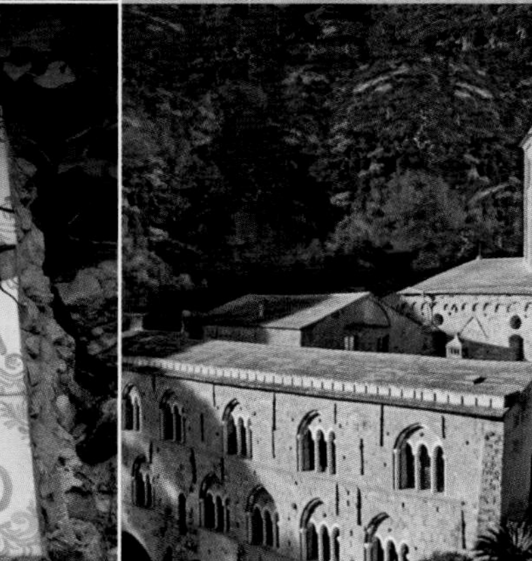

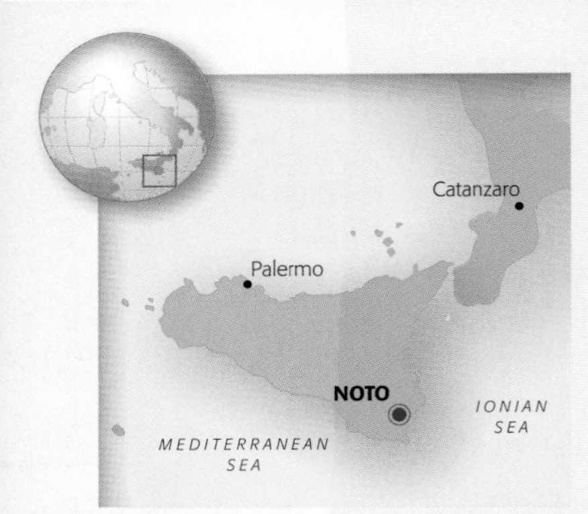

GETTING THERE
Noto is in southern Sicily, a short distance inland. From Catania, the nearest airport, take the SS114 as far as Syracuse, then the A18 freeway to Noto.

GETTING AROUND
The town is best explored on foot, but a car is essential for visiting places outside Noto.

WEATHER
Despite it being winter, the weather is quite mild with a mean temperature of 54°F (12°C).

ACCOMMODATIONS
The Monteluce Country House is surrounded by fragrant Mediterranean maquis and looks out over the Gulf of Noto; it offers various lodging options, from a single room B&B or a cottage suite with kitchen, garden, and terrace, to a splendid separate villa. Rooms from US$180; www.monteluce.com

The Corte del Sole, near the Vendicari Reserve, is a 19th-century farmhouse that has been superbly restored using original materials. You'll love its authentic old-style atmosphere, with doubles from US$110; www.lacortedelsole.it

EATING OUT
Enjoy the local cuisine in a welcoming atmosphere at the Camine, from US$28; tel. 0931 838 705.

The *agriturismo* Al Casale dei Mori offers traditional home cooking – rustic and romantic. Meals from US$35–40; www.fattoriavillarosa.com

PRICE FOR TWO
Allow around US$250 per day for meals and accommodations.

FURTHER INFORMATION
www.infioratadinoto.it

The Oasis of Vendicari

A series of large brackish pools separated from the sea by a strip of maquis and a long thin sandy beach: this is the Vendicari Reserve, once an area of significant salt production. In this wild oasis of salt marsh, thousands of migrating birds and swamp turtles find shelter. The landscape is dotted with the remains of ancient fortifications and criss-crossed by a network of channels, from when the saltworks were active. There are walking paths around the area and hides for bird-watching – look out, too, for disused 18th-century tuna-fishing nets.

Inset: A typical farmhouse complex on the outskirts of Noto

Left: View up Via Nicolaci to the monastery of Montevergine

Right (left to right): The Palazzo Ducezio seen from the rooftops of Noto; Sicilian *cassata*, a sponge and cream cheese concoction; clear waters off the island of Capo Passero; the 18th-century Fountain of Hercules in front of the church of San Domenico, Noto

Main: The grand façade of Noto's Duomo, one of the city's Baroque masterpieces

BORN-AGAIN BAROQUE

IT ALL STARTED WITH AN EARTHQUAKE. On January 11, 1693 a dreadful tremor hit southeastern Sicily, causing the total destruction of most of the villages and towns in the area and killing tens of thousands of people. But out of disaster was created one of the world's unique treasures: the town of Noto was reborn 9 miles (15 km) from its old center. It is one of the most beautiful towns in Sicily, noted for the homogenous design of its buildings – an imaginative yet orderly Baroque style that gracefully combines playful ornamentation with serious architecture.

The task of rebuilding Noto was entrusted, a mere week after the earthquake, to Giuseppe Lanza, the Duke of Camastra, who engaged a team of architects including the Flemish military engineer Carlos de Grunenberg and Vincenzo Sinatra, Rosario Gagliardi, and Paolo Labisi to work on the project. With them he created an exemplary model of urban planning: a town with two focal points – the residential quarter and the quarter intended for

...the sense of visual harmony is enhanced by the warm pink stone, perfectly suited to the Baroque style.

BAROQUE DIARY

Noto is Italy's Baroque jewel and the once-destroyed town is now more splendid than it ever was. Three days gives time to enjoy the town's charm and explore its surroundings. Beyond Noto, you'll find a landscape thick with olive, almond, and citrus trees, more reconstructed towns, and the irresistible Sicilian coastline.

Three Days in the Pink

DAY 1

Spend the day exploring the town. Start from the Piazza Municipio, with a broad flight of steps that draw the eye to the spectacular cathedral. See the fine pink-stone palaces, such as the Palazzo Ducezio and the Palazzo Landolina. From here, walk to the Piazza XVI Maggio and admire the church of San Domenico and the nearby convent of the Dominican Fathers, both designed by Rosario Gagliardi. Climb up the nearby church of San Carlo for the magnificent view of Noto from its bell tower. Don't forget to relax for a moment with a sweet treat, some Sicilian *cassata*, washed down with a glass of Moscato di Noto, a distinctive local sweet wine.

DAY 2

Visit the coastal town of Avola, famous for its almonds and red grapes. It was also reconstructed after the 1693 earthquake, but on a hexagonal plan centered on Piazza Umberto I. Do not miss two more fine examples of Sicilian Baroque, the Annunziata and Madre churches.

DAY 3

Spend a day enjoying the beauty of Sicily's eastern coastline – rent a car and visit the small bays and beaches south along the coast, as far as Portopalo, a small and pretty fishing village that holds a fish market at the harbor every evening. A short distance from the shore lies the island of Capo Passero with a 14th-century fortress – take a boat trip to explore the island's delightful caves and admire the glorious pink sunsets.

Dos and Don'ts

- ✓ Try Nero d'Avola, a robust red wine produced in the Noto area. It is best drunk with hearty meat dishes and strong cheeses.
- ✗ If you are using public transportation, don't go by train, but take the bus (from Catania and Syracuse) – the train station is a fair distance from the center of Noto.
- ✓ Try to be there for the town festival on February 19, the feast day of San Corrado Confalconieri. A spectacular procession files along the streets carrying the urn containing the saint's remains and followed by the faithful – and often barefoot – followers.

administration, politics, and religious observance. These are linked by a gridded network of streets and impressive squares – architectural set pieces, such as the Piazza Municipio. On one side of the piazza, at the top of a long flight of steps, stands the San Nicolò Cathedral, its façade flanked by two bell towers; opposite it is the Palazzo Ducezio, with its Classical arched portico. Nearby, the Palazzo Nicolaci di Villadorata, with an exterior graced by carved stone lions, gryphons, gargoyles, and winged horses, and an interior decorated with brocade-covered walls and frescoed ceilings, recalls the splendor of the Sicilian nobility of centuries past.

There are architectural delights throughout Noto and the sense of visual harmony is enhanced by the warm pink stone, perfectly suited to the Baroque style. Note the elegant curved façade of the church of San Domenico, Gagliardi's masterpiece, and the Palazzo Trigona, whose stately front is enhanced by a series of undulating balconies. It's impossible not to surrender to the beauty of this town and admire the genius of the men who created this masterpiece in just a few years.

Below: Finely crafted gargoyle from the façade of the Palazzo Nicolaci di Villadorata

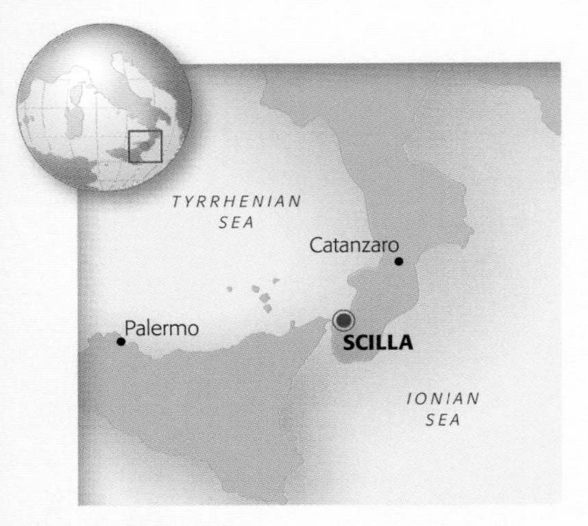

GETTING THERE
The busiest international airport in Calabria is the Lamezia Terme. To get to Scilla, which is on the Strait of Messina, take the A3 freeway and leave at the Scilla exit.

GETTING AROUND
Explore Scilla on foot. To visit the surrounding areas it is better to go by car, as there is not a good network of rural public transportation in the area.

WEATHER
The winter is short and mild, with temperatures ranging between 46°F and 59°F (8–15°C).

ACCOMMODATIONS
The Piccole Grotte B&B is an authentic 19th-century fisherman's house on the seafront in Chianalea, Scilla, with rooms from US$100; www.lepiccolegrotte.it

Also in Chianalea, the oldest part of Scilla, the Glauco B&B has rooms from US$70; www.bbglauco.it

Further north, a short distance from Tropea, the Luxury B&B's exposed beams and brickwork, terracotta floors, and roof terrace will ensure a pleasant stay. Rooms from US$70; www.bbluxury.eu

EATING OUT
The small Bleu de Toi restaurant in Chianalea, run by a fishing family, offers plenty of local fish dishes, with dinner around US$40–50; www.bleudetoi.it

In Tropea, on the cliffs above the sea, Pimm's restaurant serves excellent fish dishes with sea views. Meals cost around US$50–70; tel. 0963 666 105.

PRICE FOR TWO
Around US$225 for meals and accommodations.

FURTHER INFORMATION
www.vacanzaincalabria.it

The Mighty Swordfish

Large numbers of this great fish – in the Mediterranean a fully grown swordfish can be as much as 10 ft (3 m) long – migrate south each year to breed in warm waters. During these migrations, on routes that remain unchanged from one year to the next, the fish pass through the Straits of Messina. Here they are caught with methods that have also changed little over the years – by a harpoon thrown by a fisherman from a thin gangplank sticking out from the prow. The majestic swordfish is one of the glories of Calabrian gastronomy and features in many local recipes.

BEAUTY, BUT NO BEAST

SCYLLA MAY BE THE GREEK NAME of the legendary six-headed beast who attacked ships as they passed through the Strait of Messina in *The Odyssey* but, in real life, the Italian Scilla is a beauty – one of the most picturesque towns on the Calabrian coast. It's an ancient settlement, perched on both sides of a promontory that projects into the sea like a great eagle with open wings. On the south side of the headland there is a long sandy beach, backed by steep cliffs with fine views of the Baroque façade of the church of Spirito Santo; on the northern side is Chianalea, the oldest part of the town, consisting of a small harbor between rows of tight-packed houses rising from the sea. Between the two, on the rocky outcrop, the Castello Ruffo occupies a spectacular position. In the 16th century, this ancient and impregnable fortification became the residence of the Ruffo family, one of the most

Main: View of Scilla, strategically located on the Strait of Messina

powerful dynasties in the southern half of Italy. This castle reminds visitors of the rest of the ancient Greek myth. If they managed to get past Scylla, sailors then had to watch out for Charybdis, the mythical monster who lived in nearby caves and swallowed and spewed out vast quantities of seawater three times a day, creating enormous, deadly whirlpools. You need only visit the fortress to understand the origin of the myth as you listen to the noise of the sea – roaring, crashing, and gurgling – as it surges back and forth into the caves below.

Today, Scilla may be one of the most popular places for exploring the Costa Viola, the stretch of the Calabrian coastline named for the intense colors of the sea, but it maintains a strong seafaring tradition. The town is one of the centers for catching swordfish in the old-fashioned way – using a harpoon. And it is precisely this ability to combine ancient myths and traditions with the requirements of present-day tourism, together with extraordinary landscapes and pretty clifftop villages, that help to create the magical charm of the town of Scilla.

Left of main (top to bottom): The delightful sandy beach of Tropea; fishing boats in the harbor at Chianalea; dried Calabrian chili peppers, a common ingredient of many local dishes

Left: A view of Roghudi Vecchio, a small town spectacularly perched on the Aspromonte massif

Right (left to right): A narrow alleyway in Chianalea; view from the battlements of Castello Ruffo

COSTA VIOLA DIARY

Ravishing inlets and secluded coves, where the shifting light transforms the colors of the sea into shades of intense purplish blue; a dramatic craggy outcrop facing out toward Sicily; an unspoiled fishing town. These are the ingredients of the spell cast by Scilla and four days is the perfect length of time to explore all its charms.

A Four-Day Odyssey

DAY 1

Devote the day to Scilla: wander through its streets and follow the narrow Via Chianalea between the traditional houses along the seashore. Climb up to the Castello Ruffo and enjoy the fine views of the sea, here and there colored incredible shades of purplish blue. Then relax for a while on the Marina Grande Beach – it is sheltered and often pleasantly warm, even out of season.

DAY 2

Inland from Scilla you'll find the Parco Nazionale dell'Aspromonte, the largest in Calabria, which helps maintain the unspoiled beauty of the mountainside. Covered in forest and riddled with canyons and *fiumare* – mountain torrents that dry up in summer, the park offers numerous interesting walks where you will see plenty of flora and fauna, and traditional Calabrian villages.

DAY 3

Return to the coast and admire the marvelous views and remarkable colors of the Costa Viola. Stop in Tropea, a medieval village built on sandstone above a jagged coastline with beaches separated by rocky outcrops. In summer, this is the most popular tourist destination in Calabria – so it can get busy.

DAY 4

Explore Capo Vaticano, one of the most exciting and undeveloped parts of the Tyrrhenian coast, with a string of sandy white beaches washed by turquoise waters and enclosed by high granite cliffs and impressive rock stacks.

Dos and Don'ts

- ✓ Try local specialties – *zibibbo* raisins, made from the grapes of a special, very sweet variety of Muscat grape, and the small, aromatic, and much-loved *verdelli* lemons.
- ✗ Don't venture into the Parco Nazionale dell'Aspromonte without a guide: the park is filled with wildlife and has a good network of paths but is wild and relatively unfrequented. Farthermore, it is criss-crossed by *fiumare* – watercourses that are dry for much of the year but prone to flash floods after rain.
- ✓ Go bird-watching at Capo Vaticano: the Strait of Messina is one of the best places for seeing resident and migratory birds such as storks, falcons, buzzards, and even vultures.

Below: Ancient houses of Tropea built into the cliff face

GETTING THERE
Linate airport is 4 miles (7 km) from Milan and Malpensa airport 31 miles (50 km). From Linate, you can take the urban bus service to the city center. The handy Malpensa Express train will take you to the city center in 40 minutes, while the Malpensa shuttle bus connects both airports and Milan Central train station.

GETTING AROUND
Using a car is not recommended; it is better to walk and use public transportation.

WEATHER
It will be fairly cold, though there should be quite a few mild sunny days.

ACCOMMODATIONS
For a truly luxurious stay, try the Grand Hotel et de Milan, from US$620; www.grandhoteletdemilan.it

The Bulgari Hotel is central yet surrounded by gardens and restored by architects Antonio Cittero; doubles from US$875; www.bulgarihotels.com

The Four Seasons Hotel, converted from a 14th-century convent, has a magnificent cloister; doubles from US$865; wwwfourseasons.com

EATING OUT
You will find all types of cuisine in Milan; try Cracco for a unique gastronomic experience – www.ristorantecracco.it; enjoy classic cuisine at historic Savini – www.savinimilano.it; dine on traditional *osso buco* (succulent braised veal) and risotto at *belle époque* restaurant Boeucc, www.boeucc.it. All serve meals from US$85.

PRICE FOR TWO
Allow about US$1,060 for luxury accommodations and meals.

FURTHER INFORMATION
www.turismo.comune.milano.it

Happy Hour

Go out in Milan early in the evening during the week and you'll find the bars have tables laden with all kinds of nibbles and snacks, to be enjoyed free with your glass of wine or a cocktail. The interlude between the end of the working day and returning home is called "happy hour" – a Milanese-style apéritif. Less grand and formal than dinner, but more than just a quick drink at the bar, this has now become a feature of Milan night life. The period between 6:30 and 9:30pm is a time to meet up and enjoy a snack, a drink, and a chat with friends or new acquaintances.

Main: Ancient and modern, the buttresses of Milan's Duomo and the silhouette of the Velasca Tower
Above (top to bottom): Piero del Pollaiolo's *Portrait of a Woman (c.1470)*, one of the prized pieces of the Museo Poldi Pezzoli; model at Milan Fashion Week

THE HEIGHT OF FASHION

HIGH ABOVE MILAN FROM THE TOP of the magnificent Duomo, the beautiful gold statue of the Madonnina looks out over the city's rooftops. She is kept company by another 135 statues delicately balanced on fragile-looking pinnacles and spires. If it's a clear evening and the wind has blown the clouds and city haze away, then you should join her, to enjoy the famous city views: the great piazza in front of the cathedral, the vast expanse of rooftops, here and there enlivened by the green splashes of penthouse gardens and, on the distant horizon, the majestic Alps, their white peaks gradually turning to pink in the gentle rays of the setting sun.

Milan's Duomo is a vast pyramid of a church, an extraordinary blend of 14th- and 15th-century north European Gothic shapes, diffused and softened by the filigree work of later Renaissance architecture. Visitors can climb up to the roof terraces to find themselves in this magical world where time seems to have stopped, suspended between heaven

Above: The Galleria Vittorio Emanuele II in Milan, a covered arcade designed in 1861 and filled with boutiques and smart cafés and restaurants

Below: The Naviglio Grande (Grand Canal), originally used to bring in the marble to build the cathedral, now lined with shops, artists' studios, and nightclubs

and earth yet close to the center of a bustling city. These remarkable terraces are faced with the same pale pink marble as the rest of the structure and extend over an area of 86,000 sq ft (8,000 sq m).

Time won't stand still forever, however, and you need only go down to street level to find yourself in a totally different world: crowded streets, hustle and bustle, and, above all, shopping to die for. It is in the shadow of the cathedral that you will find the so-called "fashion quadrilateral," the heart of a city that prides itself on being one of the world's capitals of design and haute couture. The area is bounded by streets with names that are legendary in the world of high fashion (Via Montenapoleone, Via della Spiga, Via Bagutta), where you will find all the badges and brands of the most famous couturiers. Twice a year, in February and September, Fashion Week comes to Milan in a sumptuous flurry of fashion shows, catwalks, and events attended by the most famous names in international fashion. Your visit to Milan is the perfect opportunity to splash out on your own fashion extravaganza, if on a smaller, more personal scale – all under the watchful eye of Madonnina.

SHOPPING DIARY

Milan is a modern city with an ancient heart. As one of the fashion capitals of the world, it's a paradise for those who live to shop. The city moves at a frenetic pace, but there's still time to relax with an apéritif and find places where you can get away from it all. Four days is ample time to explore, shop, and chill out, Milan-style *(see also pp304–5)*.

Four Days of Fashion and Culture

DAY 1

Spend the morning touring Milan's magnificent Duomo, the third largest church in the world. The façade, completed at the beginning of the 19th century, is not so impressive but the interior, with its five aisles, is magnificent. It can hold about 40,000 people – the entire population of the city when construction work started at the end of the 14th century. Don't miss the roof terraces for a close-up view of some of the 3,400 statues and stunning citywide panoramas. Have lunch and then use the afternoon to wander around the Galleria Vittorio Emanuele II; note its elegant metal and glass vaulting and its prestigious boutiques and restaurants.

DAY 2

Enjoy a shopping trip in the "fashion quadrilateral": a labyrinth of streets whose shop windows are graced by the most famous names of the fashion world. In Via Manzoni, visit the Museo Poldi Pezzoli: enjoy its fine collection of paintings and sculpture displayed within the splendid interior of a 19th-century aristocratic residence.

DAY 3

Stroll along Via Dante, an elegant pedestrian precinct lined with shops and pleasant bars, and enjoy the striking view of Castello Sforzesco. This palace was built by Gian Galeazzo Visconti and, in the 15th century, became the seat of Ludovico Sforza's court, one of the most flamboyant in Europe.

DAY 4

Visit the basilica of San Lorenzo Maggiore; in front of it stand 16 columns from a 2nd-century Roman temple. The basilica, one of the oldest round churches in the western Christian world, was built between the end of the 4th century and the beginning of the 5th, although what can be seen today is mainly 16th century. Then explore the Navigli quarter, one of the most lively in the city and full of bars, restaurants, and shops. In the past it was part of an extensive network of canals but, today, all but a small stretch has been filled in.

Dos and Don'ts

✓ Be at the cutting edge of fashion: opposite the cathedral is the center for the most elegant and up-to-date shopping in the city, with all the prestigious brand names from clothing to gifts and fancy goods for the home.

✗ Don't try driving into the city center: parking spaces are scarce and expensive. It's better to use the Milan metro.

✓ A must for the gourmand is a visit to Peck, the city's best food and wine shop, selling the finest Milanese gastronomy – oils, wines, chocolates, cheeses, and pretty jars of preserved fruits.

Below: Details of the Castello Sforzesco

GETTING THERE
San Leo is in the northern part of Le Marche, near the Republic of San Marino. If you are coming by car from Rimini's Federico Fellini Airport, take the SS258; otherwise, take a regular bus to Pietracuta (runs three times a day), then change for San Leo.

GETTING AROUND
Explore San Leo on foot (the center is pedestrian only), but rent a car to visit places outside the town.

WEATHER
Expect typical winter temperatures between 34°F and 48°F (1–9°C).

ACCOMMODATIONS
In the heart of San Leo, the family-run Castello hotel is in a converted historic building. Rooms from US$75; www.hotelristorantecastellosanleo.com

In Montemaggio, in the hills east of San Leo, the Poggio Duca *agriturismo's* two modern farmhouses promise a pleasant stay – with tennis courts and bike rentals. From US$85; www.poggioduca.it

EATING OUT
The La Rocca inn has panoramic views and serves traditional recipes based on local produce but adapted to modern tastes. Among its specialties are local cheeses and salamis, salt-marsh lamb with thyme and *passatelli* (a type of noodle) with truffles. Meals cost US$35–42; www.laroccasanleo.it

Relive the atmosphere of a bygone era in the Osteria La Corte, converted from a 15th-century palace in the center of San Leo. It serves traditional cuisine; meals from US$42; www.osterialacorte.it

PRICE FOR TWO
US$195 per day for meals and accommodations.

FURTHER INFORMATION
www.le-marche.com

Cheese from the Pit

Formaggio di fossa, or cheese from the pit, is the pride of Talamello, a village west of San Leo. The process starts in August, when the cheese, made of sheep's or goat's milk, is wrapped in cotton sacks and put into a rock pit that has been disinfected with fire and lined with straw. Finally the pit is sealed and not reopened until November, for the final maturing. The resulting cheese is firm and creamy, straw-colored and without a crust, but with an unmistakable aroma. The story goes that the technique developed in medieval times when the village was forced to hide its cheeses when threatened by attack.

Seen from a distance, San Leo appears to sit within a Renaissance painting, surrounded by gentle rolling hills.

Main: The massive fortress of San Leo, dominating the surrounding countryside
Inset: Rare Eleanor's falcon, inhabitant of rocky crags

VIEW FROM THE TOP

Seen from a distance, San Leo appears to sit within a Renaissance painting, surrounded by gentle rolling hills leading up to a craggy spur topped by a great fortress that looks to have sprung from the very mountain itself. The fortress's novel design – two massive towers below high walls that taper to a point like the prow of a ship – was the creation of Francesco di Giorgio Martini, who built it for the lord of the region Federico da Montefeltro. The architect modified an existing medieval fort, transforming it, according to Venetian scholar and poet Pietro Bembo into a "miraculous implement of war." Such was the fame of the fortress that it was considered the ultimate prison – Cagliostro, the mysterious Palermo adventurer, self-styled miracle-worker and escape artist, was confined there until his death.

San Leo is not only one of the most beautiful fortresses in Italy, it is also a medieval village that has remained virtually unchanged through the centuries. It owes its name to the Dalmatian St. Leo, a visiting stonemason who,

Left (left to right): The parish church of Santa Maria Assunta, the oldest building in the part of Le Marche known as Montefeltro; the medieval town of Pennabilli; inside the fortress of San Leo; panoramic view from the fortress at San Leo

in the 4th century, chose the place to be the center for his missionary work. Its origins, however, go back farther still – the Romans built a temple up here dedicated to Jupiter, taker of the spoils of war, which grew into the settlement Mons Feretrius. Over the years, the area became known as Montefeltro, and gave its name to a powerful dynasty of warlords who, enriched by continuous warmongering, dominated the region until the end of the 15th century.

Today, to walk through San Leo is to step back through time. See the church of Santa Maria Assunta, an 11th-century basilica with an 8th-century altar canopy and a sanctuary supposedly built by St. Leo himself. Nearby, in the main piazza, stands the masterful Romanesque 12th-century cathedral and impressive Palazzo dei Conti Nardini, where St. Francis of Assisi once stayed. San Leo is a fascinating place to explore. Wander among the ancient houses and narrow alleyways before climbing up to the impressive fortress – from there you'll be able to truly appreciate the glorious views of the village huddled below, nestling in the folds of the surrounding hills.

FORTRESS DIARY

An impregnable fortress perched high on cliffs, a village that has retained its medieval layout in a countryside of gentle green hills, dotted with ancient hamlets: this is San Leo, one of the most delightful places in Le Marche. Four days will allow you to see San Leo and to explore the surrounding area and visit other interesting villages nearby.

Four Days of Art and Cuisine

DAY 1

Spend this day exploring San Leo. Start with the fortress – you can drive up to it if you have a car. The building is constructed on two levels: the long, boat-shaped keep above and the towers joined by a fragmented wall below. Spend the rest of the day in the center and enjoy a peaceful stroll in a preserved medieval village. Don't miss this chance to try the excellent local cuisine, with its traditional handmade pasta and *raviggiolo*, a delicious cheese made with fresh goat's or sheep's milk.

DAY 2

Take a meandering drive west to Sant'Agata Feltria, a pretty hamlet dominated by the Fregoso fortress. This is another masterpiece by Francesco di Giorgio Martini, who adapted an existing fortification, again for Federico da Montefeltro. Sant'Agata Feltria is also the white truffle capital of Le Marche, so be sure to try something flavored with truffle for lunch.

DAY 3

Visit Taramello, a short distance west, an ancient hamlet renowned for its *formaggio di fossa* (cheese from the pit). This gastronomic speciality, *Ambra di Talamello* (Talamello amber), is a DOC or Controlled Designation of Origin cheese. It is also worth visiting the Museum of Contemporary Arts dedicated to Fernando Gualtieri.

DAY 4

On your last day, spend some time in Pennabilli. This pretty town south of San Leo was created in 1350 by the alliance of two rival villages on adjacent rocks. It is a truly charming place with churches, a castle, and, for clever clogs, Mateureka, a museum of calculus. See, too, the Orto dei Frutti Dimenticati (Garden of Forgotten Fruit) – an open-air museum with beautiful art installations dotted among endangered varieties of fruit trees that once grew locally.

Dos and Don'ts

- ✓ When you visit the San Leo fortress, make sure you see the gloomy well-like prison cell where Cagliostro died in 1795.
- ✗ Don't go to Mateureka in February without pre-booking a visit – it is open daily in July and August. For more information, call 0541 928 659 or visit www.museialtavalmarecchia.it
- ✓ If you're looking for an original souvenir, buy a traditional ceramic apothecary's pot made by local craftsmen.

Below: The valuable white truffles or "white gold" of Sant'Agata Feltria

MARCH

Where to Go: **March**

It is the beginning of spring and March sees the first mild days of the year. It is the perfect time to witness Nature's reawakening, with woods and trees taking on spring's particularly vibrant shade of green. To appreciate the early days of spring to the full, take a stroll in a marvelous garden such as that at Villa Hanbury, on the Ligurian Riviera, where you can catch glimpses of the lovely sea in between the flowers and shrubs, or in the gardens of Il Vittoriale, on Lake Garda, once the home of Gabriele d'Annunzio, an important and controversial Italian poet. For the sporty, head for somewhere such as Baunei, in Sardinia, to hike the paths that snake along one of the Mediterranean's most beautiful coasts, or wrap up warm and hit the high ski slopes of northern Italy – Val

FESTIVALS AND CULTURE

TARANTO Fishing boats sheltering in a small harbor

FERRARA
EMILIA-ROMAGNA

A cultured capital with wide avenues and ancient walls

Largely rebuilt in the 16th century, thanks to urban planning by the Este family, Ferrara was one of the great centers of the Italian Renaissance.

See pp68–9

"Ferrara is the triumphal achievement of an incomparable urban civilization that created a city of symmetry and harmony."

CIVIDALE DEL FRIULI
FRIULI-VENEZIA GIULIA

A treasure chest of art

Capital of the first Lombard dukedom in Italy, Cividale has retained monuments spanning the years from its founding by the Celts to the Renaissance.

www.cividale.net

TRAPANI
SICILY

Holy Week processions

Holy Week in Trápani culminates in a procession of wooden figures, known as the Misteri, being carried through the streets.

www.italyheaven.co.uk/sicily/trapani.html

TARANTO
PUGLIA

Holy Week is celebrated with rituals unchanged for centuries

One of the more important centers of Magna Graecia, Taranto is a city of ancient traditions, especially the unique ceremonies of Holy Week.

See pp80–81

TREVISO
VENETO

A miniature Venice with a harmonious historic center

Famous for its *radicchio* chicory, Treviso has canals and waterways, and a medieval historic center with piazzas and painted houses.

http://turismo.provincia.treviso.it

UNFORGETTABLE JOURNEYS

POMPEII The tiers of the covered theater – Odeion – in Pompeii

POMPEII
CAMPANIA

Immerse yourself in the last seconds of a Roman city

Buried under a layer of ash and lava from the volcano Vesuvius in AD 79, Pompeii is a poignant open museum of Roman life and death.

See pp76–7

OGLIASTRO
BASILICATA

Road with a view

The SS18 is a spectacular coast road with precious few bus tours to spoil it. The road follows the curves of the Gulf of Policastro, peeping over dramatic coastlines.

www.cilento-travel.eu

CASELLA
LIGURIA

A dramatic panoramic route on a narrow-gauge railway

A glorious 15-mile (25-km) stretch of winding railway track, along the fringes of the Apennines with occasional glimpses of the sea.

www.travelplan.it/genoa_guide.htm

ANGUILLARA SABAZIA
LAZIO

Cycling past the charming lakes of northern Lazio

Cycle from Anguillara Sabazia to Orvieto, dining on lake fish and drinking great wine, past volcanic lakes set in beautiful countryside.

www.randotrek.com

MONTEFIASCONE
LAZIO

History through the soles of the feet

From the beautiful town of Montefiascone, you can walk the original road to Rome. In places, the road looks as good as new.

www.italia.it/en/regions/lazio.html

NATURAL WONDERS

VAL VIGEZZO A pristine natural mountain wilderness, rich in wildlife

COMACCHIO
EMILIA-ROMAGNA

The Mississippi Delta, but with better food

When the Po River finally finishes its journey at Comacchio, it has splintered into a 100 branches, creating lagoons and wetlands.

www.adriacoast.com

BAGNOREGIO
LAZIO

A city reclaimed by nature

The so-called "dying city" of Bagnoregio stands precariously upon a fast-disappearing cliff in one of the strangest landscapes in the whole of Europe.

www.infoviterbo.it

VALLE PELLICE
PIEDMONT

A natural alpine valley, home to the Waldensian community

See the fabulous natural patrimony of mountains, forests, and lakes populated by the Waldense, an eco-friendly religious community.

www.torinopiupiemonte.com

PARCO REGIONALE DELLE ALPI APUANE
TUSCANY

Mountains of marble

Famed for the beauty of their white marble, the Api Apuane are wild and rugged mountains with numerous marked trails.

www.parks.it/parco.alpi.apuane

"This is a magical valley, sheltered by the surrounding peaks, unhurried by the pace of modern life, dotted with pretty alpine hamlets."

VAL VIGEZZO
PIEDMONT

Cross-country skiing in an unspoiled natural landscape

Known as the "Artists' Valley" for its beauty, Val Vigezzo is also popular with fans of winter sports, especially for its cross-country skiing trails.

See pp66–7

Previous page: The snow-topped summit of Monte Rosa in the Aosta Valley, at sunset

Vigezzo, for example – which are still holding on to their snow. Spring also brings Easter, a festival greeted everywhere with rituals going back many centuries, such as the bizarre hooded processions in Taranto which take place at the end of Holy Week. March is also a good time to go in search of the great historical treasures to be found in Italy's regions: walk through the medieval heart of Glorenza, marvel at the unmistakable Baroque of Lecce, the evidence of courtly power in Ferrara, the tragedy of Pompeii, the city buried by the eruption of Vesuvius. Or, take a quiet moment to appreciate the emotional power of a monument such as the Sacrario di Redipuglia, a shrine dedicated to more than 100,000 young men and women, who died during World War I.

LUXURY AND ROMANCE

VILLA HANBURY Verdant paradise on the headland of La Mortola

ACTIVE ADVENTURES

BAUNEI The aquamarine waters and white sands of Cala Mariolu

FAMILY GETAWAYS

GLORENZA The Ortles mountains, covered in deep snow

VILLA HANBURY
LIGURIA

A botanical jewel overlooking the Ligurian coastline

In the luxuriant gardens at Villa Hanbury, thousands of tropical and subtropical botanical species mingle with local shrubs.

See pp78–9

ACQUAPPESA
CALABRIA

Weekend in the Terme Luigiane, the oldest spa resort in Calabria

Known in Roman times, the Terme Luigiane resort lies in the picturesque valley formed by the River Bagni, not far from some lovely beaches.

www.termeluigiane.it

LECCE
PUGLIA

See Lecce's Baroque splendor – the "Florence of the South"

Capital of Puglia in the 16th century, Lecce is graced with splendid monuments that make it one of the most beautiful Italian cities of art.

See pp70–71

FIESOLE
TUSCANY

An Etruscan town of delights with views over Florence

Fiesole has always been a popular destination with visitors because of its Roman remains and splendid villas surrounded by verdant gardens.

www.fiesole.com

SOAVE
VENETO

Imposing walls among the vineyards

Set in the heart of the wine growing area, Soave is bottled up in a winding circle of walls which climbs the hill and surrounds the town.

www.tourism.verona.it

VALLO DELLA LUCANIA
CAMPANIA

Go horseback-riding in the Parco Nazionale del Cilento

This is a densely wooded mountain area rich in wildlife – a trip to the sanctuary on Monte Gelbison (also known as Monte Sacro) is a must.

www.parks.it/parco.nazionale.cilento

"The emotional impact of the monumental war memorial at Redipuglia is immense."

FOGLIANO REDIPUGLIA
FRIULI-VENEZIA GIULIA

Hike in beautiful hills where fierce battles were once fought

In Redipuglia, on the Slovenian border amid glorious countryside, there is a poignant memorial to those who died here in WWI.

See pp82–3

MAGLIOLO
LIGURIA

Enjoy sea views on the Alta Via in the Ligurian mountains

A departure point for lovely walks, Magliolo lies on a section of the panoramic and wild mountain path, the Alta Via dei Monti Liguri.

www.parks.it/grandi.itinerari/altavia

BORGO PACE
LE MARCHE

Explore the dense forests of the Valle del Metauro

Discover the wilderness of Valle del Metauro – and don't miss the fascinating old Benedictine abbey in the village of Lamoli.

www.paradisepossible.com

BAUNEI
SARDINIA

A route of extraordinary beauty between land and sea

Hike in one of the most captivating stretches of Italian coastline, close to the Gennargentu massif and rich with traces of ancient Nuraghic civilization.

See pp64–5

PASTRENGO
LOMBARDY

African animals meet dinosaurs

The "Parco Natura Vivo," near Lake Garda, is an excellent safari park boasting cheetahs and lions. It also has a wonderful Dinosaur Park and an arboretum.

www.parconaturaviva.it/

PARCO FAUNISTICO LE CORNELLE
LOMBARDY

An animal park for the kids

Bergamo has an idyllic location, but kids will love the city cable car and getting up close to the animals in nearby Parco Faunistico le Cornelle.

www.turismo.bergamo.it

GLORENZA
TRENTINO-ALTO ADIGE

A pretty town where time seems to have stood still

The walls of Glorenza, the "Smallest Town in the Alps," enclose streets lined with arcades and houses painted in South Tyrolean style.

See pp72–3

"...wander Glorenza's nooks and crannies, peeping into courtyards and browsing in its quaint shops."

IL VITTORIALE
LOMBARDY

The extraordinary home of Gabriele d'Annunzio

In a superb location on Lake Garda, Il Vittoriale was built by controversial poet d'Annunzio as a fascinating museum for his deeds and work.

See pp74–5

LA THUILE
VALLE D'AOSTA

Skiing and sport for all tastes

A great favorite with skiers, La Thuile has 90 miles (150 km) of stunning ski runs, as well as entertainment and sporting activities for all ages.

www.lathuile.it

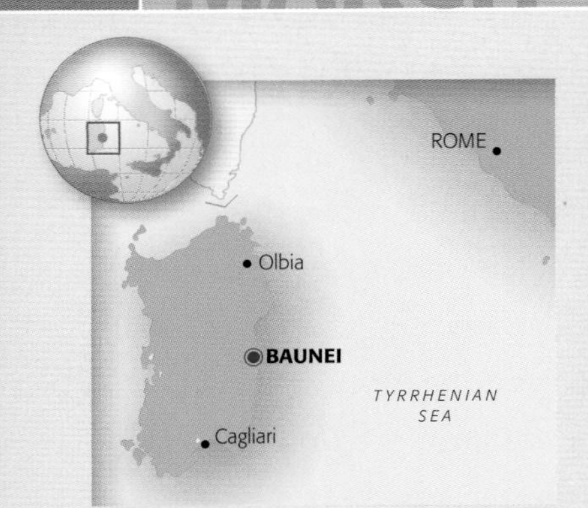

GETTING THERE
Baunei is located close to the eastern coast of Sardinia, in the province of Ogliastra. The SS125 runs down through this province, following the coastline, and connects Baunei with the main airports at Olbia, in the north, and Cagliari, in the south.

GETTING AROUND
It all depends on what you want to do. There are a great many excursions to be undertaken on foot, horseback, or mountain bike. For something a little less active, consider a trip in a 4WD vehicle or rent a boat from the Marina di Baunei-Santa Maria Navarrese.

WEATHER
Expect mild weather, around 63°F (17°C) rising to 79°F (26°C). Ideal for just relaxing or taking an excursion.

ACCOMMODATIONS
The Cooperativa Goloritzé, in Golgo in the heart of Baunei, is ideally located for excursions. It has six bedrooms (doubles from US$75) and pitches for tents (US$8 per person). It can also organize walks, horseback-riding, and mountain bike trips; www.coopgoloritze.com

Close to Baunei, but on the coast, Casa di Tina in Santa Maria Navarrese is a small, elegant B&B with a view of the sea. Rooms from US$70; www.lacasaditina.it

EATING OUT
The Cooperativa Goloritzé's restaurant offers typical Baunei cuisine. Meals cost about US$35.

At the Golgo restaurant, set in an idyllic olive grove, you can enjoy salamis, local cheeses, roast pork, goat, and home-made desserts. Meals cost around US$35; www.golgotrekking.com

PRICE FOR TWO
Around US$190 per day for meals and accommodations.

FURTHER INFORMATION
www.turismo.ogliastra.it

The King of the Mountain

The only surviving wild sheep in Europe, the mouflon is particularly common in the wild areas of Sardinia, Corsica and other Mediterranean islands. Able to survive on even the most leathery plants, the mouflon is well-adapted to arid regions. The mouflon's most striking feature is its large horns, spiralling out from the side of its head – only the males have these and they can each reach a length of over 2 ft (60–70 cm). This agile creature is regarded as the symbolic animal of Gennargentu, the vast mountainous massif that looms up behind Baunei, the haunt of vultures, eagles, and the Sardinian wildcat.

Left (from top to bottom): The impressive Punta Longa, a craggy pinnacle of Baunei's limestone massif, rising from the sea; sheep, the hardy livestock of local farmers; the remains of a *nuraghe* (megalithic home) in Ogliastra

Right (left and right): A chunk of crumbly aged pecorino, an excellent Sardinian cheese; crystal-clear sea and white sands at delightful Cala Mariolu (Mariolu Cove)

Main: Dramatic skies over Sardinia's rugged and wild coastline

BETWEEN SEA AND MOUNTAIN

Poised between sea and mountain, the small town of Baunei nestles between the turquoise blue of one of the most beautiful coastlines in the Mediterranean and a stunning amphitheater of hills and mountains, topped by the high peaks of the Gennargentu massif. Over many thousands of years, water running off the mountains has carved out deep gorges and cave systems from the rugged limestone mountains – here you'll find the Grotta del Fico, and the Grotta di Goloritzé and the terrifying pothole, called *Su Sterru* in Sardinian dialect, the deepest in Europe at 968 ft (295 m). This is perfect territory for hardy outdoor types – hikers, cavers, and rock climbers. But closer to the sea, the terrain becomes more gentle, maquis-covered scrubland sloping down to the vivid blue water. It is here that you'll find the primary attraction of the area – the gorgeous isolated bays and inlets. These tiny patches of paradise, characterized by tall rocky pinnacles, white sand, and cool translucent water, dot

the 25 miles (40 km) of pristine chalk cliffs. The crowds are kept away as it's not always easy to reach them – it's a two-hour hike to Cala Goloritzé (Goloritzé Cove) from Baunei, although you can get there by boat from Santa Maria Navarrese. But the effort of a hike is rewarded with a sea of a thousand shades of blue, warm talcum-soft sand, and spectacular rock formations.

But that's not all the region has to offer. The landscape is littered with evidence that the area around Baunei has been settled since prehistoric times. There are many interesting relics from the Nuraghic civilization that inhabited Sardinia between the Bronze Age and the 2nd century AD – more than 7,000 of their distinctive stone dwellings (*nuraghe*) remain over the whole of the island. In Baunei, Nuraghic architecture developed its own distinct style, which can be seen in the ruins of the villages at Orgoduri and Coe Serra. These ancient Sardinian tribes also left behind the playful *betilo* next to the church of San Pietro in Golgo – a standing stone monolith uniquely carved with a human face – and the stone funerary monuments at Triei, the Tombe dei Giganti (Tomb of the Giants).

MULTICOLOR DIARY

The intense green of the Mediterranean maquis; the sun-baked gold of the plateau interior; the deep blue of the sea, fading from turquoise into green: these are the colors of Baunei. Three days will allow you time to explore the rich natural beauty of the area as well as discover some of relics left behind by the Nuraghic civilization.

Four Days Among the Nuraghe

DAY 1

To fully appreciate the area's marvelous countryside, take a trek along the path from Baunei that crosses the Golgo plateau, famous for its deep gorge and shady holm oaks. From here you can carry on to Cala Goloritzé. This route takes you past the Coe Serra *nuraghe*, the church of San Pietro in Golgo and the *betilo* (Nuraghic monolith) close to the church. See it all from a different perspective (and rest the legs) by returning by boat along the coast.

DAY 2

Take a trip to Santa Maria Navarrese, one of Baunei's hamlets and a maritime center, constructed around the little church of the same name. Legend has it that the daughter of the king of Navarre had the village built in the 11th century as a thanksgiving for having survived a shipwreck. The town has a fine beach sheltered by a grove of pines and a harbor where you can take a boat to one of many small coves for the day.

DAY 3

In the morning, take a short walk inland to the Tombe dei Giganti (Tomb of the Giants) in Triei, close to Baunei; it is one of the oldest prehistoric monuments in Sardinia. Later, if you've still got some energy left, hire a bike and go cycling along the paths once used by charcoal-burners and shepherds. Otherwise, simply chill out at the beach.

DAY 4

For your final day, relax beside the sea again. You can enjoy a relatively easy walk to the beach at Luna, where a long white beach awaits you, or take a boat to the beaches at Cala Sisine (you can also go on foot, but it's a long walk) and Cala Mariolu, which has a marvelous beach with smooth white marble pebbles.

Dos and Don'ts

- ✓ Take plenty of drinking water with you on treks: the routes go through uninhabited areas, where water is hard to obtain.
- ✗ Do not go trekking around Baunei unless you are physically fit: although there are not many large steep hills, the routes are often demanding. Always use local guides.

Below: The cone roof inside a *nuraghe* near Baunei

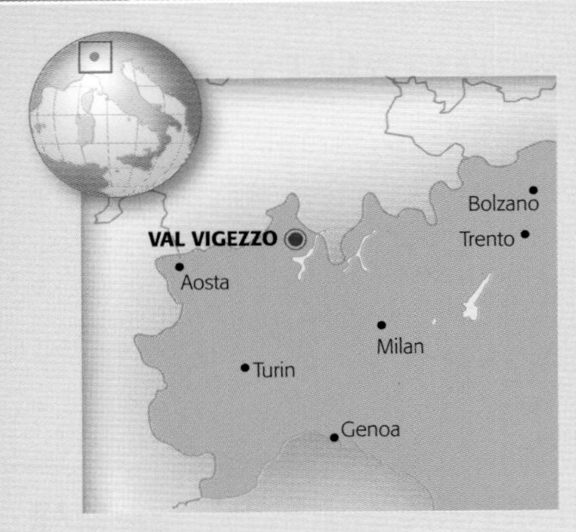

GETTING THERE
Val Vigezzo runs through the far north of Piedmont to the Swiss frontier. Distances from the nearest airports are: Milan Malpensa 60 miles (100 km); Milan Linate 80 miles (130 km); and Turin Caselle 110 miles (165 km). It's easy to reach by car: from Turin, take the A4 freeway and continue on the A26; from Milan, take the A8 and then the A26. In either case, take the Masera-val Vigezzo exit.

GETTING AROUND
You can get around Val Vigezzo by car or a regular scheduled bus service. A narrow-gauge train also serves the entire valley, from Domodossola to Locarno. Cable cars run from several of the valley towns up to the pistes of Piana di Vigezzo.

WEATHER
While it remains typical, snowy winter weather in March, the days are getting longer, allowing more time on the slopes or for exploring the valley.

ACCOMMODATIONS
In Santa Maria Maggiore the hotel Miramonti offers comfortable bedrooms furnished in alpine style; doubles from US$140; www.almiramonti.com

In the historic center of Malesco, the small B&B Leon d'Oro is a restored 15th-century palace. They serve an excellent breakfast in "Vigezzo" style with local salami and other regional products; doubles from US$85; www.leondoro.eu

EATING OUT
There are numerous *agriturismi* (farm restaurants), trattorias, and alpine huts where you can enjoy a meal of typical local dishes for around US$35 a head. These include *pasta rustica* (pasta with potato, bacon, and onions); risotto with porcini mushrooms; onion and nettle soup; and roast kid. To finish, try a slice of *fiacia*, a type of jam tart.

PRICE FOR TWO
US$265 per day to include accommodations, car rental, meals, train tickets, and admission to the park. If skiing, add US$70 per day for lift passes.

FURTHER INFORMATION
www.vallevigezzo.vb.it

The Centovalli Train

A different and fascinating way to see Val Vigezzo is to take the narrow-gauge train that runs all the way from Domodossola to Locarno. Inaugurated in 1923, the railway snakes along 33 miles (52 km) of lovely scenery, past shimmering cascades, along or across deep gorges, over 83 bridges, and through 31 tunnels. It is possible to break the journey to explore one of the picturesque mountain villages served by the train, but the journey in itself is well worth the price of a ticket.

Above: Monte Gridone dominates Piana di Vigezzo; alpine chamois, frequently spotted in these mountains

ALPINE DELIGHTS

VAL VIGEZZO IS A MAGNIFICENT NATURAL BALCONY OPENING TO THE WEST below the impressive profile of Monte Rosa, and encircled by the summits, not as high but equally rugged and romantic, of the Lepontine Alps. This is a magical valley, sheltered by the surrounding peaks, unhurried by the pace of modern life, dotted with pretty alpine hamlets nestling in pastures and woodland.

Winter sports enthusiasts will be in their element here: the upper slopes and the surrounding mountains offer downhill skiing at Piana di Vigezzo, as well as cross-country routes that pass through forest, clearings, and snow-dusted pine groves amid unspoiled and ravishing scenery. If the spring arrives early and the lower slopes are beginning to thaw, the pistes of Val Loana will still be thick with good snow thanks to its higher altitude. But Val Vigezzo has other delights in store for lovers of mountain scenery, nature, and rural life. Hikers will relish the pleasure of walking here, from the gentle contours of the valley floor, to the higher altitudes of larch, beech, and fir forest and, higher still, to the edge of the treeline, with its endless vistas of snowcovered summits and rocky peaks. For nature-lovers, Parco Val Grande is 58 sq miles (150 sq km) of the most rugged landscapes in the Alpine arc, a territory almost entirely devoid of human habitation, but richly forested and home to many rare species of flora and fauna.

The region had preserved its traditions and its way of life despite the arrival of small-scale tourism. Its gastronomic specialties, ideally suited to the alpine lifestyle, are centuries old: bread with walnuts, raisins, and figs; preserved and cured meats, such as liver mortadella, air-dried mountain ham, and "violin" – salted and spiced leg of goat or chamois; as well as a wide variety of cheeses, from *toma* at various stages of ripening to *züfi*, a type of ricotta. Val Vigezzo's other name is "The Valley of the Painters," not just for the landscape that so appeals to artists, but also for the lovely paintings to be found on the external walls of many of its village houses. This is just one more example of the delightful and surprising nature of this place, and one more reason why it charms everyone who comes here.

Main: Boarder cutting a course through fresh powder snow on the immaculate slopes of Piana di Vigezzo
Below (left to right): Local specialty *runditt*, or *stinchett*, a buttery flatbread; cross-country skiers enjoying some late winter sunshine

WINTER SPORTS DIARY

Val Vigezzo is an extensive and beautiful plateau, 2,600 ft (800 m) above sea level. When the snow covers its pastures, it becomes a paradise for skiers and boarders, but over the course of three days you can combine a day or two on the slopes with an exploration of some of the other charms of a region unspoiled by the passage of time.

Three Days Amid the Peaks

DAY 1

There are several options for a day of winter sports. Santa Maria Maggiore is the start of a cross-country skiing piste that links up with Druogno and Malesco in a beautiful circular route. At certain times of year, part of the route is floodlit for nocturnal competitions. Those who love downhill skiing can take the cable car that departs from Prestinone for the alpine resort of Piana di Vigezzo, 5,660 ft (1,725m) above sea level. For high-altitude skiing, head up to Val Loana, which is reached from Malesco. There, the piste (3 miles/5 km long), is open even in low season. At lunchtime, fortify yourself with hearty local dishes at one of the mountain chalet-restaurants.

DAY 2

For a relaxing day, visit the hamlets in the valley. They include charming Malesco, famed for its mineral water springs; Santa Maria Maggiore, whose curious Museo Dello Spazzacamino is devoted to chimney sweeps, a traditional trade in the valley (sweeps from here worked all over Europe); and Craveggia, whose parish church contains "The Treasures of the King of France," including the wedding gown of Marie Antoinette, Louis XIV's funeral blanket, and other precious items.

DAY 3

Spend the day in Parco Val Grande. There are marked hiking trails, but to get the most from your visit, go with a guide who can point out flora and fauna that you might otherwise miss, such as chamois and golden eagles. Pack a picnic of local produce to bring with you, but be sure not to leave any garbage behind when you leave.

Dos and Don'ts

- ✓ Look out for the pictures painted on the walls of houses in the country or preserved in the numerous chapels scattered about the villages and along the mountain paths.
- ✓ Decide in advance what you want to do in Parco Val Grande by visiting the website: www.parcovalgrande.it
- ✗ Never leave the marked paths in Parco Val Grande unless accompanied by an authorized guide.
- ✓ Always check the weather forecast and snow conditions information before venturing on to the slopes. In spring the risk of an avalanche, as the sun warms the snow, is higher.

Below: Cable car ascending to the Piana di Vigezzo

GETTING THERE
Ferrara is in northeastern Emilia-Romagna. Bologna's Guglielmo Marconi Airport is 25 miles (40 km) via the A13 freeway and the SS64. A shuttle train runs from the airport to Bologna station, from where Ferrara is 30 minutes by train.

GETTING AROUND
Ferrara is a small city, easily explored on foot. Alternatively, bicycle rental is readily available. You will need a car to visit the Parco Delta del Po, which is around 18 miles (30 km) from Ferrara.

WEATHER
The average daytime temperature in March is a pleasantly mild 61°F (16°C).

ACCOMMODATIONS
Treat yourself to a princely stay at the Hotel Duchessa Isabella, a 16th-century palace with frescoed ceilings; doubles from US$420. Less expensive is the hotel's romantic annexe, the Locanda della Duchessina; doubles from US$132; www.duchessaisabella.com

The Hotel de Prati is a charming small, central hotel; doubles from US$110; www.hoteldeprati.com

EATING OUT
Il Don Giovanni serves elegant cuisine using local produce (dinner from US$55). Its Il Dolce wine bar is more informal (pasta dishes from US$16; mains from US$24); www.ildongiovanni.com

La Provvidenza specializes in local cuisine such as *cappellacci alla zucca* (pasta parcels stuffed with pumpkin); *pasticcio alla ferrarese* (a pie with a macaroni filling); and *salama da sugo* (a type of sausage with mashed potato); dinner from US$42; www.laprovvidenza.com

PRICE FOR TWO
US$315–470 including meals, accommodations, local travel, and one day's car rental.

FURTHER INFORMATION
http://www.ferrarraterraeacqua.it

Ferrara's Special Bread

Ferrara's *a coppia* bread is a specialty made of two pieces of dough, joined in the middle and twisted to form four crisp horns. Unique to the city, its origins date back at least as far as the Carnival of 1536, when it was first recorded as being served during a dinner in honor of Ercoli II d'Este, Duke of Ferrara at the time.

JEWEL OF THE RENAISSANCE

It is hard to judge whether Ferrara is an medieval city or a modern one. It is true that its historic center goes back to the 14th century but, when the d'Este dynasty reworked it in the 16th century, they made it into Europe's first truly modern city, an example of urban planning that still has merit today. This city on the fringes of the Po Delta was also the seat of a court that attracted the most illustrious painters of the Renaissance, from Piero della Francesca to Andrea Mantegna, from Titian to Pisanello. It was here that the astronomer Copernicus and the pharmacologist Paracelsus received their degrees; here that Ludovico Ariosto and Torquato Tasso lived and wrote.

One of the many pearls of the city is the Palazzo Schifanoia, the delightful residence where the d'Este's spent their leisure time, and whose appealing name appropriately means "escaping boredom." You can feel the lively Renaissance spirit everywhere you turn. It has left its legacy in the form of a

Main: One of the beautiful frescoes in the Salone dei Mesi of the Palazzo Schifanoia

city center of wonderful cohesion and beauty that is a magnificent feast for the eyes. It is encircled by 6 miles (9 km) of city walls that have remained intact since the Renaissance (the only other examples of this in Italy are at Bergamo, Lucca, and Grosseto).

From the buttresses you can see the city laid out before you, including the dominant forms of Castello Estense and the town hall, linked by a raised corridor that Alfonso d'Este filled with works of art, and the crowning glory of the cathedral, Basilica di San Giorgio Martire, whose grandiose façade is dazzling in its richness of style. From the cathedral it is a short step to the Quadrivio degli Angeli, the crossing of two important medieval roads around which were built many lovely palaces. The finest of the these is the Palazzo dei Diamanti (Palace of Diamonds), designed by Biaggio Rossetti and so-named because of the 8,500 diamond-shaped bricks used in its construction, which is now home to the Pinacoteca Nazionale gallery of art.

All in all, Ferrara is the triumphal achievement of an incomparable urban civilization that created a city of symmetry and harmony that has remained intact up to the present day.

Above: Ornate portal of Ferrara's magnificent Basilica di San Giorgio Martire

Below (left to right): Cloister of San Romano, now the Museo della Cattedrale (Cathedral Museum); brickwork detail of the Palazzo dei Diamanti; walls of Castello Estense reflected in its moat; fishing boats in the Po Delta; façade of the medieval Loggia dei Merciai

FERRARESE DIARY

The center of Ferrara combines buildings from different periods into a perfect amalgam of the medieval with the Renaissance, and so a visit to Ferrara is truly a journey into the past. A weekend would be enough time to explore the marvels of the city's art and architecture, but an extra day allows you to venture beyond its walls and get back to nature in the Po Delta.

Three Days of the d'Estes

DAY 1

In the morning, take a tour of the city walls, then descend to the oldest part of Ferrara, the area around the Duomo, parts of which can be dated back to 1135. The cathedral has a very fine and unusual façade, Romanesque in the lower section and Gothic in the upper, plus a Renaissance bell tower. To its right is the 15th-century Loggia dei Merciai (Haberdashers' Gallery), which still houses numerous workshops. A little further on is Castello Estense, a 14th-century fortress that was transformed by the dukes of Ferrara into a residence after 1477 and became one of the most important centers of the Renaissance. Continue on to Palazzo Schifanoia; be sure to see in particular the 15th-century frescoes in the Salon dei Mesi (Salon of the Months), a masterpiece of the Ferrara school of painting.

DAY 2

Today, explore the area to the north of Castello Estense, near the crossroads of the Corso Ercole I and the Corso Porta Mare. This area was extended in 1492 and is full of beautiful palaces, including the Palazzo dei Diamanti. Then continue to the house of Ludovico Ariosto, author of *Orlando Furioso* (1516).

DAY 3

Drive out to the Parco Delta del Po for the day. Head northeast to Mesola, where the d'Este summer residence is now a visitor center for the delta, or southeast to the lagoon town of Comacchio. Both afford wonderful opportunities for wildlife-watching tours of the delta. In the north you can spot rare red deer among the pines; in the south you may see flamingoes on the lagoon.

Dos and Don'ts

- ✓ Sample Ferrara's delicious little *pampetano* cakes. Flavored with spices, nuts, and candied fruits, and covered with bitter chocolate, they are delicious with a mid-morning cappuccino.
- ✓ Buy a *ceramica graffita* vase, a specialty of Ferrara: the pottery is engraved with a sharp iron tool and then coated with strong colors that are dissolved by the firing process, with unusual chromatic effects.
- ✗ Don't visit the delta of the Po without insect repellent. The humidity of the region makes it an essential.
- ✓ For an unusual souvenir, buy something made of *paviera*, a reed typical of the Po Delta.

Below: View of the inner courtyard of Castello Estense

GETTING THERE
Lecce is in southern Puglia, on the Adriatic Sea. The nearest airport is at Brindisi 30 miles (50 km), from where there is a direct bus service to Lecce. By car, take the SS613.

GETTING AROUND
Cars and buses are not allowed in the city center, making it a pleasure to explore on foot.

WEATHER
March is a fairly mild month in the south, with temperatures of 45–59°F (7–15°C).

ACCOMMODATIONS
The Patria Palace is the most luxurious hotel in Lecce. The 18th-century palace has been restored by master craftsmen using superior materials, and its frescoes are by Italian and international artists; doubles from US$225; www.patriapalacelecce.com

The elegant Orangerie d'Epoque is situated in the city center, in a 19th-century building of great charm set in a luxuriant orange grove; doubles from US$112; www.lorangeriedepoque.com

EATING OUT
Salentine cuisine features many delicious dishes, made with simple ingredients but full of flavor, including *ciceri e tria* (tagliatelle with chick peas); *orecchiette con le cime di rape* (pasta with turnip tops); *involtini di agnello alle erbe* (boned, rolled lamb with herbs); and desserts made with honey.

Try the local cuisine at Cucina Casereccia (tel. 0832 245178) or the Osteria degli Spiriti (www.osteriadeglispiriti.it). Both about US$35–42.

PRICE FOR TWO
Between US$225 and US$335 per day including accommodations, meals, and local travel.

FURTHER INFORMATION
www.comune.lecce.it

The Basilica of Galatina

Galatina, a short distance south of Lecce, was an important Greek colony in the Middle Ages. The most special treasure in its beautiful walled historic center is the Basilica di Santa Caterina d'Alessandria. Its construction began in 1384 at the wish of the local lord, Raimondello Orsini del Balzo, who wanted to preserve there a finger of Saint Catherine which, legend says, he miraculously acquired during a pilgrimage to Mount Sinai. The basilica has an ornately carved exterior, a fine rose window, and its walls are covered with wonderful 15th-century frescoes.

Above (left to right): Façade of Palazzo Marrese; shrine in the cloister of Santa Maria di Cerrate

FLORENCE OF THE SOUTH

LECCE'S HISTORIC HEART IS NOTHING SHORT OF A MASTERPIECE IN STONE. Nestled amid the olive groves of the Salentine peninsula – the "heel" of Italy – it was an important center in Greek and Roman times, and was of great importance under the Republic of Veneto, but owes its most famous flowering to Charles V, who made it the capital of Puglia in 1539. This began a long period of prosperity, in the course of which the town acquired the magnificent historic buildings that have justified its sobriquet as "Florence of the South."

Lecce Baroque is something special, and owes much to the soft, pale local stone with its spellbinding golden glints; a type of malleable limestone that can be transformed by outstanding craftsmen into festoons, imaginative tracery, graceful lacy motifs, and statues clad in sumptuous drapery. To fall in love with Lecce Baroque, you need only go to the impressive and harmonious Piazza del Duomo. An enclosed square (tradition has it that the people of Lecce sheltered here from enemy attacks in medieval times) it contains some of the finest buildings in the town: the Palazzo Vescovile, the palace of the Seminary, and the Duomo. The latter has two façades: the main one, less visible, is serious and dignified, but the lateral one, visible as you enter the square, has extravagant and opulent decorations. The Piazza del Duomo may be striking in its theatrical style, but the building that best expresses Lecce Baroque is the Basilica di Santa Croce. Built over nearly 200 years with contributions from illustrious local artists, it is a riot of decorative motifs – flowers, animals, gargoyles, cherubs – depicted in stone, with such a subtle feel for chiaroscuro that, at sunset, the slanting rays of sunshine seem to bring the whole façade to life.

Lecce has other marvelous testimonies to her past, as well: some that had remained hidden for centuries were brought to light at the beginning of the 20th century and are now part of the very fabric of the city. For example, in Piazza Sant'Oronzo, near the remains of the 2nd-century AD amphitheater (it could seat 20,000 spectators), the lovely 16th-century church of Santa Maria della Grazie looks on to a Roman column that once marked the end of the Appian Way, which is in turn surmounted by an 18th-century statue of Sant'Oronzo, the patron saint of Lecce. Diverse indeed, and yet, as with the rest of the city, these elements blend together to form a remarkable and harmonious ensemble typical of Lecce, one of Italy's most beautiful cities.

Main: Beguiling sirens sculpted on an external capital of the Basilica di Santa Croce
Below (left to right): Richly decorated interior of Lecce's Duomo; tiered seating around the Roman amphitheater arena

BAROQUE DIARY

Built in a richly exuberant Baroque style, Lecce's palaces, convents, and churches glow golden in the evening sun, making it a very special city. This a place in which to linger but, with five days at your disposal, you can also venture out into the lovely surrounding Salentine countryside to discover more of the region's architectural and natural beauty.

Five Golden Days

DAY 1

Begin by visiting the Piazza del Duomo to admire its unusual "closed square" layout. Visit the Duomo, the work of Giuseppe Zimbalo, who also built the nearby campanile. Inside, don't miss the 16th-century stone nativity scene, which expresses an artistic and devotional tradition widespread in southern Italy. After lunch, make your way to the 16th-century Castello, a massive structure with four corner bastions, built for Charles V.

DAY 2

Discover Lecce's churches: the Basilica di Santa Croce, with a magnificent façade and airy interior whose special features are the coffered ceiling and columns with finely chiselled capitals; Sant'Irene, for its opulent Baroque altars; and San Matteo, with its original façade enlivened by concave and convex features.

DAY 3

In the morning visit the remains of Roman Lecce: the vast amphitheater of the Piazza Sant'Oronzo, carved out of limestone rock, and the smaller theater nearby. The statues and reliefs that once decorated them are now in the Sigismondo Castromediano museum of art and archeology, so pay a visit here after lunch to see them.

DAY 4

Head 12 miles (20 km) south to Galatina, a wine-producing town with Greek origins and a lovely basilica.

DAY 5

Visit the abbey of Santa Maria di Cerrate, a medieval jewel within the lovely wildlife preserve, Parco di Rauccio, a short distance north of Lecce. There are remarkable frescoes inside and a romantic 13th-century cloister. Also pay a visit to the Museum of Folk Traditions, next door.

Dos and Don'ts

- ✓ For a cheap and delicious snack lunch, try the Lecce specialty of *rustici*. These are small, round, filo-pastry pies filled with things like mozzarella and tomato, served hot.
- ✓ Buy something made of papier-mâché. Lecce has an ancient tradition of working this material, which is used by local artisans to make the sacred figures seen in local churches.
- ✗ Don't book a hotel outside the center of Lecce: quite apart from the inconvenience, the town's outskirts are uninspiring.
- ✓ Spend a pleasant evening people-watching along the Via Imperatore Augusto, a place where the city's large student population likes to hang out.

Below: Orecchiette, a Puglian pasta often served garnished with turnip tops

GETTING THERE
Glorenza is in the Alta Val Venosta, in the northern part of Trentino-Alto Adige. The nearest international airport is Verona. From here, take the A22 leaving at the Bolzano Sud exit on to the main road to Merano and then the SS38 to Glorenza-Val Venosta.

GETTING AROUND
The SS38 is the main road running through the glorious Val Venosta. Most of the valley towns are well connected by an efficient bus service.

WEATHER
The weather is still wintry in March, with maximum temperatures around 43°F (6°C) and minimum temperatures dropping below 32°F (0°C).

ACCOMMODATIONS
In the town center, the Gasthof Grüner Baum offers modern rooms with simple furnishings in a recently restored historic palace. Rooms are US$72 per person per night, including breakfast, with discounts for children; www.gasthofgruenerbaum.it

Hotel Watles is on the outskirts of Malles at an altitude of 5,740 ft (1,750 m) and has a magnificent view of Val Venosta and the Ortler mountains. The Alpine-style rooms cost from US$52 per person for B&B – discounts for children; www.watles.com

EATING OUT
The Stambecco restaurant, in the center of Glorenza, offers typical Alto-Adige dishes such as *canederli* (dumplings), barley soup, and shin of roast pork with cabbage. Meals from US$35 (tel. 0473 831 495).

PRICE FOR A FAMILY OF FOUR
Expect to pay about US$350 to US$420 per day for meals and accommodations. For two days of skiing, add about US$168 for the ski passes.

FURTHER INFORMATION
www.suedtirol.info
www.glurns.suedtirol.com

The Apples of Val Venosta

The apple is without question the pride of Val Venosta. Apples are cultivated on the sunny slopes of the valley – it has the lowest rainfall in the Alps – and exported all over Europe. Harvest time is a festival for numerous students, who flock to the region to augment their income. The apple also plays a major part in the local Tyrolean cooking: it is the main ingredient not only in strudel, the traditional dessert, but also in jams and sauces that are served with the local game in a delicious contrast of flavors.

ALPINE FAIRY TALE

Enclosed within intact city walls, with narrow cobblestone streets, sheltered porticoes, town hall, and churches, Glorenza has changed little in over 500 years. But look beyond the town at its stunning Alpine surroundings, the mountains still dusted with snow looming over the fertile glacial valley, and you're seeing something that has changed little in over 50,000 years; still breathtaking and still unspoiled.

Tiny Glorenza prospered during the Middle Ages due to its position at the entrance to the Val Venosta, on the route to Rome from Switzerland and Austria. However, the town was drawn into the bitter wars of the period and was destroyed by Swiss troops in 1499. The Holy Roman Emperor Maximilian I entrusted its rebuilding to the military architect Jörg Kölderer, who widened the city wall with a rampart walk (still there today) and fortified it with many embrasures and towers. The walls were not completed until 1555.

Main: Providing shelter from the cold and snow, 16th-century porticoes in Glorenza

Pass through the main gate and surrender yourself to the town's charms – discover its nooks and crannies, peep into courtyards, and browse in its quaint shops. If at any time you tire of this, try a restorative snack, a strudel with cream, perhaps, and a coffee, and resume your tour. Visit Castel Glorenza, an aristocratic 18th-century residence built into the city wall, and Casa Frölich, with its delightful sundial, bow window, and Renaissance fresco – an allegory of the Seven Deadly Sins – on its façade. Or stroll out of town to see the Chiesa di San Pancrazio and wonderful Alpine views.

If you feel the urge to explore further afield, there are other jewels in the valley. Don't miss Castel Coira, in Sluderno, an austere 13th-century fortress that was transformed during the Renaissance era into a smart aristocratic residence; or the Chiesa di San Benedetto in Malles, commissioned by Charlemagne and decorated with a beautiful series of Carolingian frescoes that date back as early as the 9th century. And, if you need to make more room for strudel, then you can burn off some calories in the mountains by walking in the pristine Parco Nazionale dello Stelvio or skiing its snowy slopes.

Above: The late 15th-century Chiesa di San Pancrazio – the Baroque onion dome was added in 1664

Below (left to right): The impressive Castel Coira, home to excellent displays of weapons and a substantial art collection; *canederli*, large savory or sweet dumplings, are a delight of Trentino-Alto Adige; view of the Ortler mountains, which reach 12,810 ft (3,905 m); one of Glorenza's picturesque porticoed streets

MEDIEVAL DIARY

In the very heart of the Alps, Glorenza – also known as Glurns to the Austrians – still looks every inch the medieval fortified town, set amid the beautiful scenery of a most attractive mountain valley. Four days will give you a day in town, two days of fabulous skiing, and a day exploring the other towns and sights in the valley.

Four Days in the Alpine Valleys

DAY 1

Dedicate the first day entirely to exploring Glorenza, wandering the little streets, admiring the houses and their late-medieval appearance, keeping the cold at bay with the hearty local cuisine, and browsing through the many traditional carved-wood souvenirs. If you have time, pay a visit to the museum in the Porta di Tubre, and do not miss the view of the town from the Chiesa di San Pancrazio, just outside the center.

DAYS 2–3

Spend a couple of days taking advantage of the Parco Nazionale dello Stelvio, one of the largest protected areas in Italy and a favorite destination for winter sports enthusiasts. From Glorenza, you can easily reach the ski slopes of Watles – only 15 minutes away by car. If you wish to travel farther, you can ski at San Valentino, Belpiano, Valle Lunga, Trafoi, and Solda all'Ortles, or the slopes at the bottom of Slingia. The skiing is excellent and the slopes will be quiet.

DAY 4

For your last day, it's time for some more sightseeing along the valley. Sluderno, with its fine Castel Coira, is a little way south east and Malles, a bit farther north, has a fine early medieval church with Carolingian frescoes. Don't miss the nearby abbey of Monte Maria, a complex that dates back to the 12th century (but was restructured in the Baroque era) whose massive white bulk nestles into the woods – it has an impressive Baroque interior.

Dos and Don'ts

- ✓ Buy an Ortler Skiarena ski pass: you can use this at many of the local ski stations. For more information, visit www.ortlerskiarena.com
- ✗ Don't be rowdy in the public bars – the locals in Glorenza like peace and quiet.
- ✓ Remember that a free shuttle bus goes every day from Glorenza to Watles.
- ✓ For a truly romantic outing, take a ride on a horse-drawn sleigh through the snowy woods of Val Venosta.

Below: Peregrine falcon, a common bird of prey in the Alta Val Venosta

GETTING THERE
Il Vittoriale is in the Gardone Riviera, in Lombardy, on the western shore of Lake Garda. The villa is about 20 miles (30 km) from Brescia airport, on the main road to Salò. Or, take the train to Desenzano del Garda and then a scheduled bus to Il Vittoriale.

GETTING AROUND
A car would be useful for touring around Lake Garda, if you're contemplating a longer stay, but the bus service is good enough for a weekend.

WEATHER
Expect average temperatures around 55°F (13°C).

ACCOMMODATIONS
The exclusive Villa Fiordaliso, on the lakeside, was once owned by D'Annunzio. Its luxury period atmosphere guarantees a delightful stay – suites from US$780 per day; www.villafiordaliso.it

Le Tre Gatte B&B is in the center of the Gardone Riviera, a short distance from the lake. It has two attractive double rooms and a small garden; US$42 per person; www.letregatte.com

EATING OUT
The Locanda agli Angeli restaurant, opposite Il Vittoriale, offers a welcoming atmosphere and very fine cuisine, from US$50; www.agliangeli.com

On the lake shore, the Ristorante du Lac serves a typical Lake Garda menu, with dishes such as grilled whitefish. Average price US$42.

PRICE FOR TWO
About US$420 per day for accommodations, food, and entry to the museum and gardens of Il Vittoriale (or about US$1,035 per day if you stay at the Villa Fiordaliso).

FURTHER INFORMATION
www.vittoriale.it

D'Annunzio's Ladies

D'Annunzio's first wife was Maria Hardouin, whom he married in 1883 and had three children with. But the most important woman in his life was the actress Eleonora Duse *(above)*, with whom he started a relationship in 1897. She was tormented by the poet's infidelities yet, when Duse was dying, she is alleged to have said: "I forgive him for exploiting, ruining, and humiliating me. I forgive him everything, because I love him." In his study, D'Annunzio kept a bust of Duse covered with a veil, so as not to feel pain in seeing the woman to whom he caused much suffering.

Main: The richly furnished dining room inside Il Vittoriale degli Italiani

POMP AND ECCENTRICITY

Poet, journalist, aviator, soldier, politician, and life and soul of early 20th-century Italian drawing rooms, Gabriele D'Annunzio also had the time to build a monument to himself – Il Vittoriale degli Italiani. Located in the Gardone Riviera, the complex is a park, villa, monument, and museum, all in one. Despite its quiet leafy gardens, this is no monument to peace; in fact, it is more a celebration of Italian history and bravery in the face of more powerful enemies. The prow of the ship *Puglia*, a gift from the Italian Navy, is mounted on a slope by the lake. There's also memorabilia from D'Annunzio's two most famous adventures: a torpedo boat from the *Beffa di Buccari* (the Buccari Joke), a raid carried out on February 10, 1918, when a group of Italian boats, with D'Annunzio on board, managed to penetrate the Austro-Hungarian coastal defenses and launch six torpedoes at their ships at anchor; and the airplane in which he flew over Vienna on August 9, 1918 to drop leaflets over the capital of the

Above: Garda olive oil, a specialty of the region

Far left (above and below): Balcony view over the calm waters of Lake Garda; the elegant 1892 Villa Feltrinelli at Gargnano, now converted into a lakeside hotel

Below: The Piazzetta Dalmata inside Il Vittoriale

Austro-Hungarian Empire with declarations ("We could drop bombs by the ton, but we only drop a tricolor salutation – the three colors of liberty") written by the aviator-poet himself.

But the heart of the extraordinary complex remains his residence, called La Priora, cluttered with furniture from every period and every culture, and infused with D'Annunzio's unmistakable, if sometimes badly misguided, spirit. See the creative meditation room, with the striking-looking bed that could be either a cradle or a coffin, and his study, whose low doorway forces the visitor to bow on entry in reverence to intellectual effort – this was the only room that D'Annunzio, who suffered from photophobia, did not keep in permanent semi-darkness.

Gabriele D'Annunzio started building Vittoriale, whose lush green expanse covers around 10,000 sq ft (90,000 sq m), in 1921, but the expense proved too much for him. Mussolini became prime minister of Italy in 1922 and decided to help fund Annunzio's building project, perhaps to keep him quiet. It still was not finished at the time of D'Annunzio's death on March 1, 1938.

LAKESIDE DIARY

Il Vittoriale is a lovely villa complex with leafy gardens and a fascinating history, but its star feature is its location by Lake Garda. It can take a whole day to see the villa complex, so spend the following day exploring the beautiful lake by boat and pay a visit to the incomparable Isola del Garda with its splendid villa and gardens.

A Weekend on Lake Garda

DAY 1

Devote the whole day to visiting Il Vittoriale. More like a town than a residence, it extends over a large area and includes buildings, squares, avenues, and fountains. The eccentric personality of D'Annunzio is present in everything here. The place is a monument to the man and his life: tour La Priora, his gloriously over-the-top residence filled with extraordinary objets d'art. Look out for the ship *Puglia*, perched on the side of a hill and the torpedo boat with which he carried out the *Beffa di Buccari* in 1918. There are also vintage cars, an open-air Greco-Roman theater – which puts on plays in summer – and a war museum. In the evening, enjoy a lakeside supper, watching the lights twinkle along the shore.

DAY 2

Today is a day to explore the lake, starting with a trip to the old town of Salò, with it famous long promenade. It was also the seat of the Fascist government (the Republic of Salò) between 1943 and 1945. From here take a boat along the shoreline as far as Limone sul Garda, one of the most northerly places in the world to cultivate lemons. Return to the Gardone Riviera for lunch and then take another boat to the jewel that is the Isola del Garda – a magical island with a spectacular Neo-Gothic villa and lush Italianate gardens set in the sparkling blue waters of the lake.

Dos and Don'ts

- ✗ Do not go to Il Vittoriale without booking in advance; visits are possible only with a guide. Wear comfortable shoes as there's a lot of walking to do. For information on opening hours, visit www.vittoriale.it
- ✓ Make sure you try the local produce: olive oil and citrus desserts – especially the small lemon chocolates. Lemon trees can grow here due to the warming effect of the lake.
- ✓ Go for a boat trip on the lake: use private boats for short cruises or hop from town to town on the regular navigation services. For information, visit www.navigazionelaghi.it
- ✓ Spend some time in the Andre Heller Botanical Garden (until recently the Hruska Botanical Garden), a spectacular garden and floral collection with artwork set among the plants.

Below: D'Annunzio's aircraft suspended in the cupola of Il Vittoriale

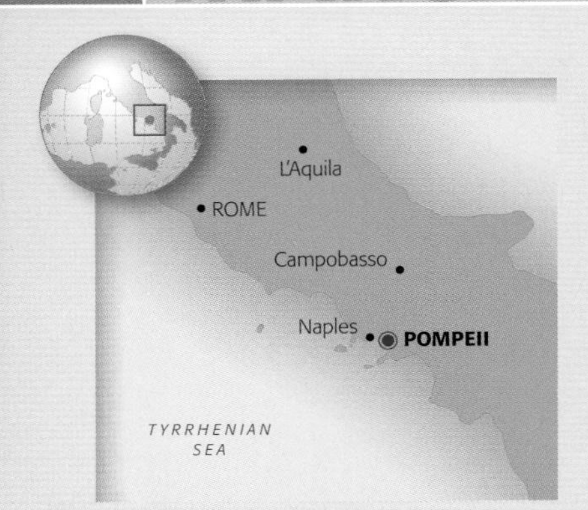

GETTING THERE
Pompeii is 19 miles (30 km) south of Naples and Capodichino Airport. From here, it's possible to take the Circumvesuviana train to the archeological site. By car, take the A3 freeway, leave at the Pompeii exit, and follow signs for the excavations.

GETTING AROUND
Pompeii itself is best explored on foot. There are good train and bus connections between Naples and the Amalfi Coast; to reach the coast by car, take the A3 and leave at the Vietri sul Mare exit.

WEATHER
The spring weather is perfect for visiting the site and there are fewer visitors in March.

ACCOMMODATIONS
The Hotel Amleto is in the historic center, a few steps from the ruins. Its rooms have touches of Roman Pompeii with mosaics and polychrome marble and there is a lovely roof garden. Doubles from US$112; www.hotelamleto.it

The modern, central Hotel Forum has comfortable rooms; doubles from US$125; www.hotelforum.it

EATING OUT
Il Principe restaurant has an elegant ambience and its menu includes some dishes from ancient Rome – modified for contemporary tastes. One of its specialties is vermicelli with *garum* (a popular Roman condiment). Meals cost between US$70 and US$98; www.ilprincipe.com

Pizza-lovers should try spacious Zí Caterina, with meals around US$28–35; www.zicaterinapompei.it

PRICE FOR TWO
About US$280 per day for accommodations, meals, and entrance to the ruins.

FURTHER INFORMATION
www.pompeiisites.org
www.costadiamalfi.it

Ancient Delicacies

The food remains found in the ruins of Pompeii help to answer the question, what did the ancient Romans eat? Their everyday diet was based on grain – as a porridge or in the form of bread – vegetables, cheeses, and fruit. Important condiments included *garum*, made from salted fish left to ferment in the sun (Asian fish sauces are made in the same way) and, of course, olive oil. The most popular drink was wine, flavored with honey and spices. Poorer people drank *posca*, made of soured wine or vinegar flavoured with herbs and diluted with water.

Above (left to right): A southern Italian dish, *Penne alla pummarola* (penne pasta with fresh tomato sauce); the Porta Nocera, Pompeii; fresco from a villa in Stabiae, a town 3 miles (5 km) from Pompeii
Main: Detail of the frescoes in the Villa dei Misteri

A ROMAN TRAGEDY

A BLACK CLOUD APPEARS AT DAYBREAK ON THE HORIZON. Then there's an enormous explosion and the sun is blotted out by dust, toxic fumes, and a deluge of red-hot stones and pumice. That is how, with the eruption of Vesuvius in AD 79, life came to an end in Pompeii, a city that dated back over 700 years. The tragedy was immense; at least 2,000 of the 10,000 inhabitants died immediately, suffocated by clouds of toxic gas or crushed in the collapsing buildings. The remainder fled, terrified, as molten lava covered their homes. The spectre of a curse hung over the site – Pompeii had been destroyed 15 years before by an earthquake, but it was rebuilt. This time the people did not return and over the years even the memory of the city was lost. When some buildings were discovered in the 17th century, during the digging of a canal, nobody could identify the town.

Much of what we know about Pompeii – what the buildings were used for and to whom they belonged – comes from the frescoes that adorn many of the houses, their rich colors looking as though they had been applied just yesterday. Many Roman nobles had villas and estates there, or else they came to enjoy the wine – and the favors of Greek or African slaves employed in the many *lupanari* or brothels, identified by their erotic frescoes. Pompeii's main street, Via dell'Abbondanza, its cobbled surface rutted with marks from cartwheels, is lined with villas full of frescoes that depict the activities of artisans and merchants, the owners having worked themselves up into the middle-classes. Pompeii was a place for relaxation, a comfortable city near the coast, filled with holiday homes, bath houses, and theaters, and surrounded by a countryside rich in olive groves and vineyards.

However, despite the beauty of it all, anyone who visits the site will come away remembering the poignant forms of the inhabitants overtaken by the disaster. Men and women, mothers still hugging their children, slaves next to their masters, even domestic animals, stopped in their tracks two millennia ago and dramatically transformed in an instant into statues.

ompeii was a place for relaxation, a mfortable city near ne coast, filled with oliday homes, bath uses, and theaters...

Inset: A victim of the eruption of Vesuvius, Pompeii
Below: The archeological site of Pompeii; pretty Positano, clinging to the cliffs on the Amalfi coastline

VESUVIUS DIARY

Pompeii is a window to an ancient world that disappeared in just a few hours. Four days will also allow you to see Herculaneum (see pp24–5), and climb up the once deadly volcano. You should also spend a couple of days exploring the delights of the Amalfi Coast – after all, its what attracted most Pompeiians here 2,000 years ago.

Four Days Under the Volcano

DAY 1

A visit to Pompeii starts at the Porta Marina. Walk along the Via Porta Marina, flanked by important ruins: the Temple of Venus and, a bit farther on, the Forum, where justice was administered. Carry on to the temples of Apollo and Jupiter and the *macellum* – the food market. All of these are surrounded by a great labyrinth of side streets. Other sites of particular interest include the Stabian Baths, the sumptuous House of the Faun, with its famous mosaic of Alexander the Great, the House of the Vetti, adorned with striking paintings, and, a little outside the city, the Villa dei Misteri, with a famous cycle of frescoes linked to the cult of Dionysus.

DAY 2

Catch a bus from Pompeii to Herculaneum, another Roman city destroyed by the eruption. Smaller than Pompeii and nearer to the volcano, Herculaneum is even better preserved as it was quickly covered by boiling mud. After exploring the ruins, grab a bite to eat and catch a shuttle bus up Mount Vesuvius – or walk if you have the energy. The volcano is currently dormant, and the views over the coastline are superb.

DAYS 3-4

Spend two days on a jaunt to the Amalfi Coast, one of the most famous and spectacular stretches of coastline in the Mediterranean. Start at Sorrento and round the cape on the winding coastal road, enjoying the outstanding scenery that comes into view at every curve. Positano is a real pearl of a village, perched above the sea. Carry on to Amalfi, famous for its cathedral at the top of a long and impressive flight of steps, and go as far as Ravello, in one of the finest positions on the coast. Don't miss the marvelous view that unfolds from the gardens of the Villa Rufolo, in the middle of the village.

Dos and Don'ts

- ⊗ Don't use unauthorized guides to explore the excavations. The official ones have the appropriate identity badge. Ask about guides at the ticket office.
- ✓ Don't miss the "electoral propaganda" of the Roman politicians in Pompeii; it is still visible on the walls along the streets, written in large red and black letters, with various candidates' slogans.
- ⊗ Don't go to the Amalfi coastline on the weekend: the narrow roads become very congested. It's better to go midweek.

Below: One of the Roman theaters at Pompeii

GETTING THERE
To reach Villa Hanbury in Ventimiglia, near the French border in western Liguria, take the train from Genoa, which is served by Cristoforo Colombo Airport. If driving, take the A10 freeway, leaving at the Ventimiglia exit.

GETTING AROUND
The A10 freeway is the main road for the Riviera dei Fiori: the freeway runs parallel to the SS1, or the old Via Aurelia, which follows the coast. The minor roads are scenic but winding and slow. There is a good local network of trains and buses.

WEATHER
The climate is Mediterranean and mild, with mean maximum temperatures around 59°F (15°C).

ACCOMMODATIONS
The Baia Beniamin inn is a gem of a hotel, on a promontory and looking out to sea. It has five charming bedrooms and is famed for its epicurean cuisine. Doubles from US$390; www.baiabeniamin.it

B&B Casa Lorenzina is in a converted convent, surrounded by lush vegetation and with a view of the sea. Rooms from US$85; www.casalorenzina.it

EATING OUT
The Baia Beniamin restaurant offers high-class cooking in an elegant ambience by the sea. Meals cost around US$85; www.baiabeniamin.it

Balzi Rossi, on the cliffs above the sea, serves excellent meals in a smart setting. Fixed-price menu about US$98; www.ristorantebalzirossi.com

PRICE FOR TWO
Between US$310 and US$615 per day including entrance to Villa Hanbury and its gardens.

FURTHER INFORMATION
www.amicihanbury.com/menu_english.html

THE ENCHANTED GARDEN

PALM TREES FROM MAURITIUS, subtropical flowers from Kenya, succulents from Chile, eucalyptus and tree ferns from Australia: exotic plants from all parts of the world thrive in the botanic gardens at Villa Hanbury. Perched on the Mortola promontory, which juts out into the sea between Ventimiglia and the French border, this is a little piece of paradise created with enthusiasm and loving care by Sir Thomas Hanbury, a wealthy Englishman who made his fortune importing tea from China. He fell in love with the area during a visit in 1867 and decided to create a botanic garden here, devoting the rest of his life to the project. The work was continued after his death by his son Cecil and Cecil's wife Dorothy, who brought her artistic sensitivities to bear on the project, thinning out some of the botanical collections, creating pergolas and flowerbeds, and opening up vistas. The result is an exceptionally beautiful garden, best

Main: Terrace overlooking the lush gardens and coast at Villa Hanbury

The Bridge at Dolceacqua

Inland from Ventimiglia, Dolceacqua is a picturesque medieval village, divided in two by the Nervia River. The older part, known as Terra, is linked by a graceful medieval humpback bridge to the more modern Borgo. The village climbs up the slopes of a hill in a series of concentric semicircles. At the top stand the ruins of Castello Doria, an ancient fortress that was transformed over time into a nobleman's residence. The village was much loved by Monet, who depicted it in a famous painting, *Bridge at Dolceacqua,* in 1884.

enjoyed simply by strolling along the paths and stopping to admire the views that open up between the plants. Walking in the garden you'll see succulents, rare agaves, water lilies, and the most northerly growing papyrus plants in the world. You'll also be able to enjoy the aromas of ancient varieties of citrus trees and the Australian forest, full of luxuriant eucalyptus trees.

This array of rare and exotic species in the garden is impressive enough, but the non-botanist will also be captivated by the romantic corners that open up at every step: beds of pretty cyclamens that flower at the end of winter, the little 18th-century temple in the middle of the succulents, and the elegant belvedere in front of the villa, with views out to sea. And there's more – visitors can explore the delightful *giardinetti,* or small gardens, devoted to the aromatic plants loved by Dorothy and view the little Moorish kiosk, containing the remains of Sir Thomas and his wife Katherine. In short, this is a "garden of dreams" where the botanic species are looked after not only out of scientific interest but also to celebrate the beauty and artistry of nature.

Above: *The Slave*, an elegant marble statue in the gardens, thought to be from the school of Antonio Canova

Below (left to right): The *zucchina trombetta* (trumpet courgette), a typical regional product; the cathedral of Santa Maria Assunta overlooking the city of Ventimiglia; the bright flowers of *Carpobrotus acinaciformis*, also known as "Fig of the Hottentots"; the exclusive beach at Balzi Rossi

FLOWER DIARY

Villa Hanbury's gardens form part of the pretty Riviera dei Fiori (Riviera of Flowers). A weekend is just about long enough to appreciate the Riviera's natural beauty, to explore Ventimiglia with its cathedral and exotic garden, to head inland to medieval Dolceacqua and travel along the coast to the beach and museum at Balzi Rossi.

A Weekend in Ventimiglia

DAY 1

Today explore Ventimiglia, the last important center in Italy before the French frontier. Spend the morning exploring the medieval area west of the Roia River that divides the city in two, visiting the Romanesque cathedral, Santa Maria Assunta, with its 13th-century baptistry.

In the afternoon, walk out to the lush gardens of Villa Hanbury. They're in a wonderful location, not far from the town center, on a promontory that extends into the sea. Admire the delightful views that unfold as you stroll along the shady paths past colorful and exotic species.

Dinner will give you the chance to explore the specialties of Ligurian cuisine: the most typical regional dishes are *torta verde* (green tart, made with locally grown vegetables); *pisciadela* (focaccia bread with tomatoes, onions, olives, and anchovies), and *barbagiuai* (fried ravioli filled with pumpkin and cheese).

DAY 2

In the morning, drive inland up along the Nervia valley to the quaint village of Dolceacqua, famous for its medieval bridge, castle ruins, and pretty vegetable gardens. Enjoy a rural lunch before heading back to the coast.

In the afternoon, head along the Riviera dei Fiori to Balzi Rossi, a short distance from the French border. It's not just an exclusive and pretty beach, it's also an important prehistoric site. There is a series of caves facing the sea that were inhabited in Palaeolithic times and used for burials that date back to the last phase of the Wurm Glaciation (between 29,000 and 8,500 years ago). Visit the small museum nearby, which houses many of the objects that were discovered in the caves.

In the evening, enjoy a spectacular meal at Balzi Rossi's excellent eponymous restaurant, while looking out to sea.

Dos and Don'ts

- ✓ When in the village of Dolceacqua, make sure you try the local Rossese wine, one of the most esteemed in Italy.
- ✗ Don't go to Villa Hanbury without checking the opening hours, which vary according to the time of year. You can call 0184 229 507 or visit www.amicihanbury.com
- ✓ Spend some time in the excavations at Albintimilium, the most important Roman monument in Liguria, on the eastern fringe of Ventimiglia; there you will see the ruins of the ancient Roman city with baths, theater, and grand houses.

Below: Villa Hanbury on the Mortola promontory

GETTING THERE
Taranto is in Puglia on the Ionian coast. The nearest international airports are Brindisi 43 miles (69 km) and Bari 60 miles (97 km). If you are coming by car, take the SS7 from Brindisi or the A4 from Bari, leaving at the Taranto exit.

GETTING AROUND
A car is useful to get around, or use the rail network that links many of the towns inland to the coast.

WEATHER
The Gulf of Taranto has a typical Mediterranean climate. March is mild, with temperatures between 45°F and 59°F (7–15°C).

ACCOMMODATIONS
The modern Grand Hotel Delfino faces on to the seafront. It has spacious, comfortable rooms, a good restaurant, a swimming pool, and a fitness center. Doubles from US$195; www.grandhoteldelfino.it

The light and airy hotel and restaurant Al Faro is set in an 18th-century farm near the sea. Doubles from US$168; www.alfarotaranto.it

In the old town center, the small Buonanotte Margherita B&B offers comfortable rooms at US$85 per night; www.buonanottemargherita.it

EATING OUT
At Gesù Cristo you can expect the very freshest fish brought directly from the adjacent fish market. Meals cost around US$42 (tel. 099 452 6466).

The Vecchie Cantine farm offers traditional cuisine, based on local produce. Meals cost between US$35 and US$55 (tel. 099 777 2589).

PRICE FOR TWO
Expect to pay between US$240 and US$350 per day for meals, accommodations, and local travel.

FURTHER INFORMATION
www.tarantoturismo.it

Rudolph Valentino

Rodolfo Alfonso Pietro Filiberto Raffaello Guglielmi, better known as Rudolph Valentino, was born in Castellaneta, not far from Taranto, in 1895. He emigrated to Paris in 1912 and in the following year to America, where he became famous as the archetypal Latin lover in films that have become legendary: *Four Horsemen of the Apocalypse*; *The Sheik; Blood and Sand*. A museum dedicated to him has been opened in Castellaneta, a special treat for his fans.

Above (left to right): The Villa Peripato gardens, a green oasis at the heart of Taranto; mussels, one of the region's typical seafoods; characteristic Baroque architectural details in the historic center of Martina Franca, near Taranto
Main: The *perdune*, brothers of the church of Carmine di Taranto, in traditional habit during Holy Week

MYSTERIES OF TARANTO

BAREFOOT AND DRESSED IN WHITE COWLS with two tiny holes for eyes, the mysterious *perdune* (penitents) walk slowly along the city streets, swaying hypnotically from side to side, accompanied by the sounds of a funeral march and a crowd of thousands. This is Taranto during Holy Week. The Procession of Our Lady of Sorrows starts out just after midnight on Good Friday from the church of San Domenico Maggiore and returns the following afternoon; crowds also follow the Procession of the Mysteries, which leaves on Good Friday afternoon from the church of Carmine di Taranto and returns on Saturday morning to pray until bells at midnight announce that Christ has risen. This is an ancient ritual, kept alive in a city that is deeply attached to its historic traditions.

Taranto is set in a wide gulf that forms a safe haven for boats. The oldest part of the city sits on an island at the entrance to a natural harbor, known as the Little Sea. In Roman times, when maritime trade was of paramount importance, the town's location helped it become the largest city in Magna Graecia – the area of southern Italy colonized by Greeks – with 300,000 inhabitants and a boundary wall over 9 miles (15 km) long. The fascinating remains from this magnificent period can be seen in the Museo Archeologico Nazionale.

he mysterious *perdune* walk slowly along the city streets, swaying pnotically from side to le, accompanied by the nds of a funeral march...

Taranto's Old Town retains its medieval atmosphere thanks to its intricate network of alleyways. See the squat, muscular 16th-century fort, Castello Aragonese; the cathedral of San Cataldo, with a simple Romanesque interior behind its more elaborate Baroque façade; and the 14th-century Chiesa di San Domenico. On the peninsula to the east, joined to the island by the famous swing bridge, lies the 19th-century Città Nuova (New Town), developed after the unification of Italy. During this period, Taranto underwent major development because of its strategic, industrial, and military importance. As a result, this part of the city is graced with wider streets in a structured grid and lined with houses, shops, and the pleasant gardens of the Villa Peripato, looking out over the Little Sea.

Inset: Cupolas of the cathedral in Grottaglie
Below (left and right): Grottaglie wine jars are a prized product of the Salento region – the "heel" of Italy; fishing boats on the Gulf of Taranto

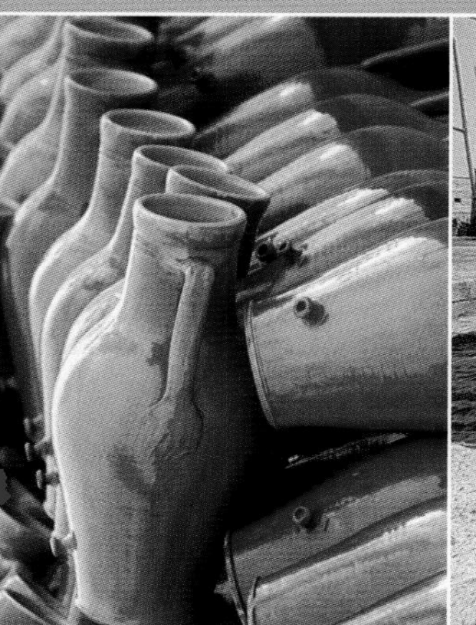

HARBOR DIARY

Despite major industrial development in recent years, Taranto has still managed to preserve the beauty of a Mediterranean coastal city in and around its ancient island center. Four days here will allow two days to appreciate its charm and two days to see something of the glorious Ionian coast and interesting and historic inland towns.

Four Days in the Gulf of Taranto

DAY 1

Start from the Castello Aragonese and explore the island center. Zig-zag through the alleyways to the cathedral of San Cataldo. Don't be deceived by the Baroque façade – this is one of the oldest churches in Puglia and inside it you will find a simple Romanesque design incorporating ancient Greek columns. Continue to San Domenico, the church built by Federico II in the 14th century. On your tour of the city, be sure to stop for lunch, maybe to enjoy local specialties: *tarantella* (a spicy sausage made with tuna) served with *scattiata* (sweet peppers).

DAY 2

See Taranto's ancient Greek legacy at the excellent Museo Archeologico Nazionale, which has a remarkable collection of Greek vases. There's a lot to see, so don't try to rush it. After all that time indoors, get some fresh air in the leafy gardens of the Villa Peripato. Then press on to the Concattedrale, a modern church with an extraordinary perforated façade, built by Giò Ponti and completed in 1971. If you enjoyed the vases at the archeological museum, consider a trip to nearby Grottaglie, famous for its ceramics.

DAY 3

Relax by the wonderful coast of the Gulf of Taranto: a succession of beaches flanked by pine groves. Drive to the Stornara nature reserve to the south, a large pine forest bordering the sea. Follow the coastal road all around the gulf to some of the best beaches at Torretta.

DAY 4

Take a trip to picturesque Martina Franca – its old town center has winding alleyways, whitewashed houses, and Baroque extravagance. See, too, Massafra, famed for its settlements built into the rocky gorge. Explore the caves and rock-cut churches, and admire the Byzantine frescoes.

Dos and Don'ts

- ✗ Don't set off for Taranto without having booked in advance: accommodation is booked up early for Holy Week.
- ✓ Buy some pottery from Grottaglie, not far from Taranto, famous in ancient times for its vases, plates, and other objects decorated with traditional designs.
- ✗ Be subtle when photographing or filming the Holy Week processions: remember that it is a serious religious event.
- ✓ Pay a visit to the town's Museum of Oceanography, which will give you an opportunity to see the marine fauna of the gulf.

Below: The crypt of San Leonardo, cut into the rock at Massafra

JAN FEB MAR APR MAY JUN JUL AUG SEP OCT NOV DEC

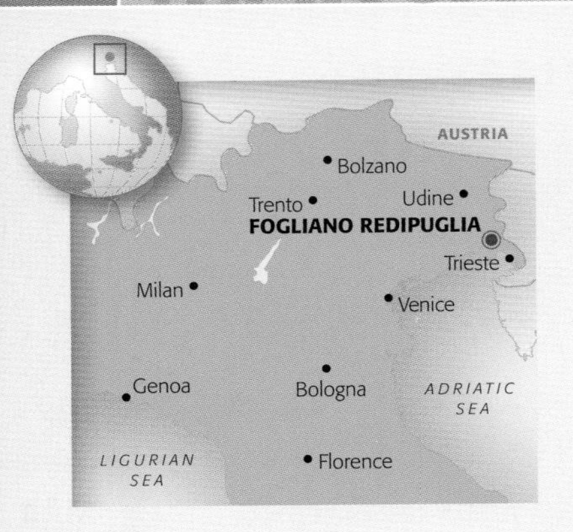

GETTING THERE
Fogliano Redipuglia is in the southeastern corner of Friuli-Venezia Giulia. The airport is 3 miles (5 km) from Fogliano Redipuglia, linked by local buses.

GETTING AROUND
The most convenient way of getting around is by car. From Redipuglia there is a well-marked road to Sacrario, about 1 mile (2 km) away.

WEATHER
March temperatures only reach around 52°F (11°C), but the chill easterly wind (the Bora) is on the wane, and it's also a fairly dry month.

ACCOMMODATIONS
The traditional farmhouse L'Ensoleillèe has a sauna, garden, swimming pool, and three elegant rooms, from US$98; www.lasoleggiata.it

Villa al Bosco is a comfortable B&B in Jamiano, about 4 miles (6 km) south of Gorizia, with rooms from US$42 per person; www.villa-albosco.it

La Transalpina, in Gorizia, is located in one of the most exclusive parts of the town. Double rooms from US$100; www.transalpina.com

EATING OUT
The *agriturismo* La Tradizione offers typical Friulian cuisine with a farm shop attached. Meals cost around US$35–42; www.agriturismolatradizione.it

Expect creative cooking – traditional food with a twist – using seasonal produce at L'Arcimboldo. Meals from US$35–42; www.arcimboldo.go.it

PRICE FOR TWO
About US$210 per day for meals and accommodations.

FURTHER INFORMATION
www.turismofvg.it

The Battle of Caporetto

It was at Caporetto in the Friulian mountains, just a short distance from Redipuglia, that the Italian army suffered one of the worst defeats in its history at the hands of the Austro-Hungarian and German army. The battle, which lasted for just over a day between October 24 and 25, 1917, cost Italy 11,000 dead, with 19,000 wounded and 300,000 taken prisoner. Today, Caporetto is no longer part of Italy: it is called Kobarid and belongs to Slovenia.

MONUMENTS AND MEMORIES

CUT INTO THE GREEN SLOPE OF A PRETTY Friuli mountainside like a large and brutal scar, the monumental flight of 22 steps is a stark reminder of the bravery of young men and the terrible price of war. Based on a design by the architect Giovanni Greppi and the sculptor Giannino Castiglioni, the Sacrario di Redipuglia marks the burial place of 39,857 known and 60,330 unknown Italian soldiers. It is presided over by a single block of porphyry weighing 75 tonnes, the tomb of Emanuele Filiberto, Duke of Aosta and commander of the Third Italian Army, surrounded by the five tombs of his generals. A chapel keeps vigil over the memories of the fallen, and two adjacent rooms house an exhibition of the personal possessions of the soldiers, both Italian and Austro-Hungarian – a moving display that gives a human dimension to those who fought and died. World War I resulted

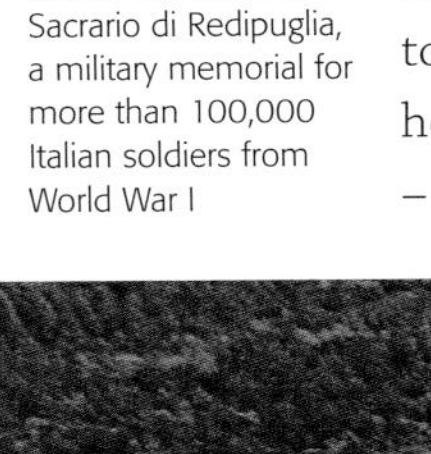

Main: The massive Sacrario di Redipuglia, a military memorial for more than 100,000 Italian soldiers from World War I

Left: One of a network of trails that criss-cross the Julian Alps, affording wonderful trekking

Right (left and right): Detail of the Sacrario di Redipuglia, the monumental flight of steps in Carso stone; an Italian WWI trench on the Carso plateau, near Gorizia

in losses of an unbelievable magnitude: there were more than 8.5 million military and more than 6.5 million civilian deaths. But climb to the top of the Sacrario di Redipuglia and gaze on the surrounding countryside, so peaceful and serene that it seems almost impossible that here, on the slopes of Monte Sei Busi, some of the bitterest battles of that terrible war were fought.

As well as the beautiful hills and mountains, which are perfect for walking through, there are interesting towns to explore. Cormons, in the beautiful Collio hills, is famous for its soft white and red wines, and has a medieval center graced by many fine 17th- and 18th-century buildings constructed under the Habsburg Empire. Right on the Slovenian border, Gorizia is an ancient fortress town with plenty to see – the Castello di Gorizia, Gothic and Baroque churches, military museums, and elegant palazzi filled with beautiful artwork. All around, the peaceful rolling hills are cloaked in lush green vineyards and dotted with pretty wine-producing villages.

Above: Traditional Friulian *gubana*, a cake dating back to the 15th century, made of a buttery brioche dough swirled with grappa, raisins, and walnuts

Below (top and bottom): The 14th-century Gothic Chiesa di Santo Spirito in Gorizia; the now peaceful Carso plateau, once the scene of terrible fighting

MEMORIAL DIARY

It's impossible not to be moved by the memorial – more so because the brutal conflict was fought in a place of such beauty, on a rocky plateau among the limestone hills of the Carso. Spend a day visiting the war memorial and then hiking in the nearby countryside. The next day, explore a couple of other towns nearby, enjoying the fruits of peace – fine architecture, food, and wine.

JAN FEB **MAR**

A Weekend in the Carso

DAY 1

Climbing up the Sacrario can be a very moving experience. The monument ascends the slopes of Monte Sei Busi, which saw bitter fighting in the first phase of a conflict that killed many soldiers on both sides. To understand the conditions in which these battles were fought, visit the Sacrario Museum, which has photographs, weapons, reconstructions of trenches, and equipment. Not far away there is a path that leads to the Monte San Michele, from where there is a splendid view of the war theater. Spend the rest of the day exploring the hills and working up an appetite for some Friuli ham and cheeses followed by *gubana*, a traditional cake, all washed down with local Oslavia wine.

DAY 2

Visit Gorizia, known as the "Nice of the Habsburg Empire"; its medieval Castello di Gorizia reflects a time when it presided over the surrounding area. Around the castle there are Habsburg villas, palazzi, and parks – fine examples of elegant architecture. The castle houses a collection of furniture, ornaments, and frescoes from the Middle Ages to the 19th century. The Musei Provinciali di Gorizia is also worth a visit; its exhibits include mementos and records of the fierce fighting that took place in this region. Visit Palazzo Atems with its frescoes and fine halls, and special exhibition of the month. A visit to Gorizia must end up in a restaurant: the city is famous for its excellent Friuli cuisine.

Dos and Don'ts

- ✓ Go for a trek in the Carso, the limestone karst has been eroded into interesting hollows, caves, and strangely shaped rocks. For information, visit www.turismofvg.it
- ✓ If you have time, take a trip to the Collio hills, near Gorizia. Some of Italy's most prized wines come from here.
- ✓ Go to see a traditional folkloric show with medieval dances accompanied by period instruments; these shows take place in the Castello di Gorizia every year on the last Sunday in March.
- ✗ Don't set off for a long walk without taking appropriate equipment – boots, comfortable clothes, and a cagoule.

APR MAY JUN JUL AUG SEP OCT NOV DEC

Below: Symbol of the city, Castello di Gorizia, founded in the 11th century

APRIL

Where to Go: **April**

It is in the clear days of April, when the breezes blow away the clouds, that Naples offers its most splendid panoramas: those famous scenes of the city with Vesuvius looming menacingly in the background, above the deep blue water of the bay. These are also the perfect climatic conditions for long bracing walks over the beautiful island of Elba, or a bike ride along the Valle Aurina, below the stunning Trentino peaks, to the border with Austria. For anyone who loves the mountains, but does not want to hike or cycle, there is the "Trenino Rosso" – Little Red Train – which departs from Tirano and crosses the breathtaking Bernina pass, among glorious mountain peaks, to glitzy St. Moritz. For a relaxing walk in lush green countryside head for Lake Maggiore, where at

FESTIVALS AND CULTURE

MODENA A vintage car going through its paces before the Mille Miglia

SARZANA
LIGURIA

History and hazelnuts

Sarzana is rich with noble palazzi, piazzas, and churches. During the "Fiera delle Nocciole," the Hazelnut Fair, it becomes a colorful bazaar, with goods of all kinds on sale.

www.turismoprovincia.laspezia.it/en

ABBAZIA DI PIONA
LOMBARDY

A splendid abbey that seems to rise up from the water

The medieval abbey at Piona, on Lake Como, dates from the 7th century and is set in a beautiful landscape on a small peninsula.

www.cistercensi.info/piona

NARNI
UMBRIA

Medieval jousting

Narni is an ancient town perched on a crag high above the Nera Valley. Each April it hosts a grand jousting tournament, the "Corsa all'Anello."

www.argoweb.it/narni/narni.uk.html

"There are three main reasons to visit Modena: art, gastronomy, and fast cars."

MODENA
EMILIA-ROMAGNA

A city that combines the best of Italian art, cars, and food

Modena is known for its great art and architecture, famous for its sleek and fast cars, and revered for its fantastic cuisine.

See pp96–7

PRATO
TUSCANY

A city with an ancient heart, and a history of textile manufacture

Dating back to the Etruscan era and famous for the production of cloth, Prato is full of ancient monuments, and has a fine Museum of Textiles.

www.pratoturismo.it

UNFORGETTABLE JOURNEYS

NAPLES Reggia di Capodimonte, a royal palazzo now housing a museum

NAPLES
CAMPANIA

See the Angevin monuments that dominate this great city

Enjoy a tour around Il Vomero, the large hill overlooking Naples, and admire the views, from grand Castel Sant'Elmo and from Villa Floridiana.

See pp102–3

BERGAMO
LOMBARDY

A city with two souls

Bergamo Alta is full of magnificent medieval and Renaissance art, but the "Borgo" (lower town) also has interesting palazzi and churches just waiting to be discovered.

See pp104–5

ELBA
TUSCANY

Unspoiled nature on the island of Napoleon's exile

Elba is the most important island in the Tuscan archipelago: six wild fragments of land surrounded by an intensely blue sea.

See pp106–7

POPULONIA
TUSCANY

Sea, history, and nature around an old Etruscan town

Baratti-Populonia, between the headland of Piombino and the bay of Baratti, contains Etruscan trails and offers lovely views.

www.costadeglietruschi.it

ASSISI
UMBRIA

Journey to one of Italy's spiritual capitals

Everything in this town relates to its most famous son, St. Francis. The church dedicated to him here is a masterpiece of Italian art.

See pp90–1

NATURAL WONDERS

CINQUE TERRE Manarola, with its Ligurian pastel-colored tower-houses

ISOLA DI CAPO RIZZUTO
CALABRIA

A protected marine reserve on the coast of the Ionian sea

Take a glass-bottomed boat to inspect the seabed, or visit the creatures in the aquarium instead.

www.ampcaporizzuto.it

GUIGLIA
EMILIA-ROMAGNA

At the heart of the Apennines, a landscape of pinnacles

Look for spring flowers, peregrine falcons, and foxes in the wild, wooded, and rocky Parco Regionale dei Sassi di Roccamalatina.

www.parks.it/parco.sassi.roccamalatina

PRALORMO
PIEDMONT

Tip-toe through the tulips in the gardens of Castello di Pralormo

In April, when the tulips are in flower, the festival known as "Messer Tulipano" (Mr. Tulip) is held in the magical castle gardens.

www.piemontefeel.org

CINQUE TERRE
LIGURIA

Fall in love in the glorious Riviera di Levante

The cliffside paths linking the villages of the Cinque Terre are so romantic that one section is known as the Via dell'Amore.

See pp94–5

VAL DI NON
TRENTINO-ALTO ADIGE

A natural paradise of canyons, lakes, caves, and apple trees

In spring, when all the apple trees are in flower, spectacular, scented white clouds cover the slopes of the Val di Non like balls of cotton.

www.valledinon.tn.it

Previous page: Detail of an ornate window grill at Palazzo Borromeo, Isola Bella on Lake Maggiore

this time of year the gorgeous gardens of the villas of Pallanza explode with color. Or head to Liguria, to the rightly celebrated Cinque Terre, and stroll along cliffside paths overlooking the sea and linking some of the most romantic places in Italy. Then, of course, there are the magnificent cities of art, with their long history and great architecture – Modena, with its splendid Romanesque cathedral; Bergamo, with its *città alta* or walled upper town; and Ragusa, divided by a ravine into Upper and Lower Ragusa, but joined by four bridges. And then there is the heady spirituality of towns like Assisi, the birthplace of St. Francis, Italy's revered patron saint, or the Abbazia di Montecassino, founded by St. Benedict and rebuilt after the devastations of World War II.

LUXURY AND ROMANCE

RAGUSA An architectural detail of the sumptuous castle of Donnafugata

ISCHIA
CAMPANIA

A volcanic island of enchanting beauty covered with myrtle

Sea, nature, and famous warm-water spa facilities make Ischia, the largest island in the Bay of Naples, a much sought-after tourist destination.

www.infoischiaprocida.it

"A cascade of ornate buildings, tumbling down the slopes of two adjacent hills, austere yet radiant in the bright sunshine... this is Ragusa."

RAGUSA
SICILY

In the heart of Sicily, a major city of grand Baroque art

Destroyed by an earthquake in 1693, Ragusa was rebuilt on two sites that were eventually joined together by four bridges.

See pp108–9

SCANNO
ABRUZZO

A lovely hilltop village close to a small and pretty lake

Old stone houses, ancient mansions, steep flights of steps, and paved alleys make Scanno ,one of the most enchanting villages in the Abruzzo.

www.scanno.org

FRASCATI
LAZIO

Historic Roman hill-town

Frascati has long been a traditional vacation spot for the Roman aristocracy, as can be seen from the beautiful villas in the area.

www.italyheaven.co.uk/frascati.html

BAGNO VIGNONI
TUSCANY

A luxurious spa weekend in the Tuscan hills

Bagno Vignoni is famous for its Piazza delle Sorgenti, where a spring (*sorgente*) of water of volcanic origin bubbles up, feeding the spa facilities of the town.

www.ctnet.it/vignoni

ACTIVE ADVENTURES

VALLI DI TURES E AURINA Cyclists enjoying the great outdoors

PARCO NAZIONALE DEL GRAN SASSO E MONTI DELLA LAGA
ABRUZZO

Free climbing in Abruzzo

Go climbing on the cliffs of the Corno Grande and Monte Camicia, the highest peaks in the Apennines.

www.parks.it/indice/ParcNat.php

ZOAGLI
LIGURIA

Diving in the Ligurian sea

Zoagli has plenty of scuba diving schools that offer the chance to dive with expert instructors, in search of the many marvels that lie underneath the water.

www.turismoinliguria.it

PARCO DEL TICINO
PIEDMONT

A river park in a rural setting

Explore the Parco del Ticino, along the many paths, bike trails, and country roads that wind along the river, among ancient abbeys, quaint little villages, and castles.

www.parks.it/indice/ParcReg.php

VALLI DI TURES E AURINA
TRENTINO-ALTO ADIGE

On a mountain bike in an unspoiled landscape

Below the peaks of Trentino, pedal along a route of great beauty on a 30-mile (50-km) bike path.

See pp92–3

CORBARA
UMBRIA

An ideal destination for keen fishermen and cavers

Not far from Corbara, in a protected preserve, you can fish in the wilds of the Parco Fluviale del Tevere or explore the caves and canyons.

www.parks.it/parco.fluviale.tevere

FAMILY GETAWAYS

PALLANZA A sea of tulips at Villa Taranto

PACENTRO
ABRUZZO

A hot-air balloon floats over a beautiful Abruzzo village

The medieval village of Pacentro comes alive for the Feast of San Marco with the ceremonial launch of a hot-air balloon.

www.borghitalia.it

MONTECASSINO
LAZIO

Climb up to the mighty abbey founded by St. Benedict

Although it was destroyed in World War II, Montecassino, one of the most important abbeys in antiquity, was rebuilt stone by stone.

See pp100–1

TIRANO
LOMBARDY

On board the Bernina Express

Travel by train from the Valtellina to St. Moritz in Switzerland, along one of the most breathtakingly beautiful routes in the world. Be sure to stop off in the spa town of Bormio.

See pp98–9

VASTO
ABRUZZO

Nature on the Adriatic coast with glorious, unspoiled beaches

In the Vasto area lies the Riserva Naturale di Punta Aderci – where nature thrives beside the sea with something for the whole family.

www.abruzzo-turismo.com

"The vegetation thrives throughout the season, but in spring there are carpets of flowers to augment the delightful views over the lake."

PALLANZA
PIEDMONT

See the flower-filled gardens of the villas on Lake Maggiore

The banks of Lake Maggiore are home to many sumptuous villas with wonderful lakeside gardens that are open to the public.

See pp88–9

GARDENS OF DELIGHT

A PERGOLA IS GARLANDED WITH TRESSES OF BLUE AND YELLOW WISTERIA; a dazzling sea of tulips sways gently in the warm spring breeze; and limpid lakes are covered with the wide leaves and elegant blooms of water lilies and lotus flowers. There are terraced gardens, sparkling with small waterfalls; a majestic avenue of conifers down which to stroll; cherub-bedecked fountains and vibrant Japanese maples ... all these and much more make up the marvelous gardens of Villa Taranto.

The villa stands on the shore of Lake Maggiore at Pallanza, on a peninsula that affords wonderful views of the lake and the verdant shores on the other side. It has a fascinating history. Built in 1880 as La Crocetta for the Conte d'Orsetti, with pretty, if unremarkable, grounds, the property was acquired in 1931 by Captain Neil McEacharn, a Scotsman and a Royal Archer, who was passionately interested in

Main: Villa Taranto in Pallanza, looking on to a swathe of tulips

GETTING THERE
Pallanza is on the western shore of Lake Maggiore. Milan's Malpensa Airport is 43 miles (70 km) away, with a bus service to the lake (book in advance from SAF: tel. 0323 552172). By car, take the A26 and leave at the Verbania exit.

GETTING AROUND
Pallanza and its surroundings are easily explored on foot or by using public transportation.

WEATHER
Spring in the Italian lakes brings frequent sunny days with temperatures around 65°F (18°C).

ACCOMMODATIONS
The 4-star Hotel Pallanza is a lovely Art Deco mansion with a lakeside terrace; rooms for four people from US$355; www.pallanzahotels.com

The 3-star Belvedere-San Gottardo is also on the lake, and has spacious rooms sleeping up to four people; from US$280; www.pallanzahotels.com

EATING OUT
Try home-made ravioli or grilled fish (dinner from US$42) at elegant little Il Torchio; tel. 0323 503352.

La Latteria ("The Dairy") features local produce, including lake perch, in its dishes (from US$35); tel. 0323 53447.

In Suna, 15 minutes' walk from central Pallanza, the Hostaria Damatraa gives traditional cuisine a new twist (from US$35); www.damatraa.com

PRICE FOR A FAMILY OF FOUR
US$350–510 per day including accommodations, meals, local travel, and admission fees.

FURTHER INFORMATION
www.villataranto.it
www.verbania-turismo.it

Lovely Lake Mergozzo

A small, teardrop-shaped lake, bounded on one side by steep mountain slopes, Lake Mergozzo was once the western end of Lake Maggiore. Over centuries, alluvial deposits from the River Toce formed into a spit of land that now separates the two. Secluded and peaceful, Mergozzo is known for its clear, clean waters, which are among the least-polluted in Italy. Motorboats are forbidden here, and fishing is carefully regulated. The little village of Mergozzo itself is a cluster of multi-colored houses lining the lake shore, dominated by the slender steeple of its 17th-century church.

Left (left and right): The Chariot of Venus in the garden of Villa San Remigio; lake perch, one of the region's signature dishes

Right (left and right): Vast water lily pads on a lake at Villa Taranto; path through the blooms at Villa Taranto

botany. He renamed the villa in honor of one of his ancestors, who was created duke of Taranto by Napoleon, and set about transforming the grounds into the glorious gardens that we see today. It became his life's work, and his mausoleum is set within the gardens that he loved.

Nearby, Villa San Remigio was built at the beginning of the 20th century by the Marquis Silvio della Valle di Casanova and his wife, the Irish painter Sofia Browne. The grounds were conceived as a succession of picturesque corners, each portraying a particular sentiment: thus you pass from the Garden of Hours, in memory of a happy childhood, to those of Joy, Memories, Sadness, and Sighs. The interior of the villa is equally delightful, and this romantic spot is justly popular as a wedding venue.

With its splendid vistas and fine medieval center, Pallanza has always been a preferred holiday spot for the northern Italian aristocracy. Just off its shoreline, the tiny island of San Giovanni was conductor Arturo Toscanini's favorite residence for many years. Its timeless atmosphere, mild climate, and verdant lakeside setting make Pallanza the perfect spring destination for anyone who appreciates tranquil charm.

VILLA DIARY

Pallanza is a place of peaceful beauty. In spring, the blooms and blossom add to its appeal, and the clear air makes for fantastic views all the way to Switzerland. Four days is an ideal length of time in which to get to know it, strolling along the lovely lake shore, wandering its historic streets, and exploring in the gardens of its historic villas.

Four Days Amid the Flowers

DAY 1

Spend the day at Villa Taranto. The house itself cannot be visited, but its gardens are open to the public from spring to fall and are not to be missed, both for the variety and rarity of the botanical species that have become acclimatized here and for the wonderful vistas of its lovely plantings set against a backdrop of one of the most romantic corners of Lake Maggiore.

DAY 2

Visit the Villa San Remigio. Built by two young, artistic lovers, it has a façade in Lombardian Baroque style and is approached by a long flight of steps. You can enjoy a splendid view over the lake from the balcony; while the gardens, equally gorgeous, are designed to create delightfully romantic hideaways where other buildings are nestled, such as the porter's lodge in 18th-century style, the medieval-looking artist's studio, and the little chapel, built on a cliff with more lovely lake views.

DAY 3

Spend the morning strolling along the lake shore at Pallanza. Visit the Villa Giulia, its façade embellished with loggias and columns; then go to the Palazzo Dugnani, now an art gallery. From here a path leads to the Madonna di Campagna church, rebuilt in the 16th century but retaining its Romanesque campanile. After lunch, take a bus over to Lake Mergozzo.

DAY 4

Visit Cannero, north of Pallanza. The village stands on a promontory opposite two small islands on which are located the Castelli di Cannero, the sturdy remains of medieval fortresses. The lake shore here is a peaceful oasis closed to traffic.

Dos and Don'ts

- ✓ Try the king of Maggiore's lake fish – *perisco*, or perch. *Perisco alla mandorle* is a local favorite in which filets of perch are fried in butter with flaked almonds.
- ✗ Don't bother to bring a car to Lake Maggiore; parking is difficult in the little villages and traffic slow on the narrow roads. Instead, make use of the efficient ferry services.
- ✓ Camellias are plentiful on Lake Maggiore. Pallanza, Cannero, and other towns along the shore stage shows dedicated to this lovely flower each spring. Inquire at tourist offices for details.
- ✗ Don't just turn up at Villa San Remigio. Visits are by 2-hour guided tour only, booked in advance (tel. 0323 503249).

Below: Mergozzo village, reflected in the calm waters of its lake

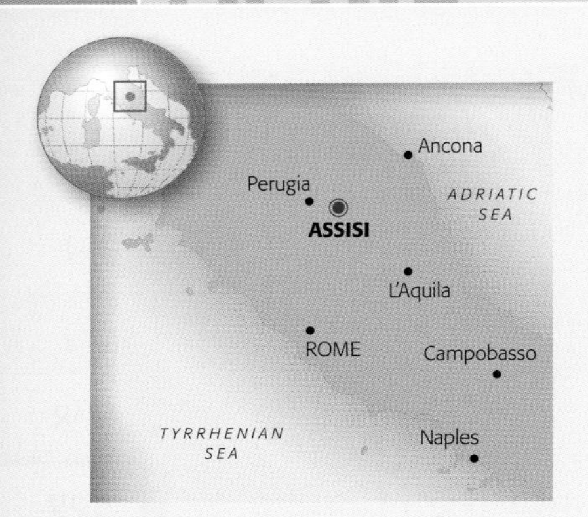

GETTING THERE
Assisi, in northern Umbria, is only about 7 miles (11 km) from Sant'Egidio Airport in Perugia. It is less than half an hour to Assisi by taxi or rental car.

GETTING AROUND
It is best to leave the car outside the city walls and explore the center on foot.

WEATHER
April is a pleasant month: the weather is mild, the trees are in blossom, and the days are getting longer.

ACCOMMODATIONS
The Hotel Umbra, in the historic center, has a garden and terrace, and offers spacious and pleasant rooms from US$112; www.hotelumbra.it

The Romantik Hotel Le Silve is a magnificent farmhouse in the Parco del Monte Subasio, a few miles from Assisi. The building dates back to the 10th century. Double rooms from US$225; www.lesilve.it

East of Assisi, Le Case *agriturismo* offers a warm welcome, swimming pool, good local food, and homemade beer! Doubles from US$50; www.agriturismo.it/lecaseresidenzadicampagna

EATING OUT
You can enjoy delicious, authentic Umbrian cuisine in many restaurants in Assisi and its surroundings; barbecued meat, mushrooms, and truffles are particularly good. Try La Pallotta (www.pallottaassisi.it) and La Buca di San Francesco (tel. 075 812 204); both serve meals from around US$42.

PRICE FOR TWO
From US$230 to US$405 per day for accommodations, meals, and car rental.

FURTHER INFORMATION
www.assisi.com
www.assisionline.com

St. Francis's Hermitage

Tucked away on the forested slopes of Monte Subasio, a few minutes drive east from Assisi, lies the peaceful Eremo delle Carceri (Hermitage of the Prisons). Not a prison, it is rather somewhere St. Francis would withdraw with his followers to pray. The hermitage was enlarged in the 15th century with the construction of the church and a small convent. See the cave where the saint slept and prayed, and the mossy, ancient oak where, according to tradition, the birds would come and perch to listen to his words and then scatter in all directions – symbolizing the missionary work of the Franciscans in the years to come.

CLOSER TO HEAVEN

Assisi sits on the peaceful slopes of Monte Subasio, permeated with a powerful spirituality. You need only take a short stroll through the narrow, winding streets to feel yourself transported back to the 13th century, to the time when St. Francis, the patron saint of Italy, brought about a revolutionary change in Western monasticism, and St. Clare, who followed in his footsteps, founded the Order of Poor Clares. Visit during Holy Week for the ultimate time-travel experience. Religious fervor envelops the town the week before Easter, as it celebrates with rituals that have remained unchanged for centuries. The Deposition from the Cross (*Scavigliazione*) is a 13th-century Holy Thursday tradition when a statue of Jesus is freed from the cross in the cathedral of San Rufino to be carried the next day to the Basilica di San Francesco and back in a picturesque torchlit procession. The religiosity radiates from the pink stone houses of this medieval city, its walls and fortresses, and, of course, its majestic soaring churches, and inspires its inhabitants and visitors alike.

Below (top and bottom): Parco Monte del Subasio, an area of limestone hills, perfect for exploring on foot; a narrow passage in the town of Assisi

The town of Assisi may boast a long history, indeed its origins go back to Roman times, but it was actually shaped in the Middle Ages. The Old Town has well-preserved walls with eight fortified gates and is overlooked by two forts, one of which was built on a Roman fortification. However, it was St. Francis and his works that gave the town its most important historic building – the Basilica di San Francesco. The construction of this magnificent structure – somewhat at odds with his preachings about the necessity of leading a simple life – started in 1226, a year after the saint's death. It consists of two churches, one on top of the other. The lower basilica is small and simple, with a crypt containing the sepulchre of St. Francis, which wasn't discovered until 1818. The upper basilica, built in the Italian Gothic style is light and airy with a large nave leading to the altar. The frescoes in the basilicas are extraordinary and include works by the most important painters of the period: Giotto, Cimabue, Lorenzetti, and Simone Martini. The result is one of the greatest cycles of frescoes in the history of Western art, almost an anthology of Italian painting between the 13th and 14th centuries, in a church that is a spiritual point of reference for the whole Christian world.

Main: Detail of a Pietro Lorenzetti fresco in the Basilica di San Francesco: *The Entry of Jesus into Jerusalem* (c.1315–30)

Above (top and bottom): View of Assisi's rooftops, the Torre del Popolo and the Rocca Maggiore; a detail of the upper Basilica di San Francesco

Below: Soup made with spelt (a traditional variety of wheat) – a local specialty

SPIRITUAL DIARY

Assisi is one of Italy's key spiritual centers, home to the country's patron, St. Francis. However, it's also a splendid town that has kept its medieval structure intact and is the custodian of some outstanding artistic masterpieces. Spend two or three days appreciating Assisi and a couple more days exploring the other towns nearby.

Five Days in the Pink City

DAY 1

Spend the day in the Basilica di San Francesco. There's a lot to see in the two Italian Gothic-style churches. The body of the saint was moved to the crypt in 1230, but was only discovered in 1818. The wall paintings are marvelous, from Cimabue's portrait of the saint to Lorenzetti's bold, almost luminous compositions. Don't miss the cycle of frescoes – 28 panels – depicting the life of St. Francis, painted by Giotto. Look out, too, for the Cappella di San Martino with frescoes by Simone Martini.

DAYS 2-3

For the next two days, see what else Assisi has to offer. Start from the Piazza del Comune, flanked by the 1st-century BC Tempio Minerva and press on to the fortress, with fine views of Assisi and the countryside. Wander through the alleys, visiting the churches that form a key part of Assisi's attractions: Santa Chiara, with the gentle interplay of alternate pink and white stone; the Duomo (San Rufino), with its fine Romanesque façade; and Santa Maria Maggiore, the town's oldest cathedral, built in the 11th century. Spend an afternoon hiking through the woods to the Eremo delle Carceri (Hermitage of the Prisons).

DAYS 4-5

Spend two days exploring the nearby towns – San Damiano is where the St. Francis began his work of reforming the Church and wrote the *Canticle of Creatures*. Bettona is an atmospheric town with Etruscan walls and some great art in its churches. Cannara is a small farming community, famous for its onions and for being one of the places where St. Francis preached to the birds. Spend some time in the Parco del Monte Subasio, either walking or visiting the local vineyards.

Dos and Don'ts

- ✓ Visit the antique show and market that takes place in Assisi in April and May. It is famous for the quality of its antiques.
- ✗ Don't drive around in the city; it is better to leave your car near the walls, in one of the large parking lots linked to the center by a bus service.
- ✓ Go trekking, following the numerous paths that cross the Parco del Monte Subasio, a short way from Assisi.
- ✓ Do try the DOC wine from Assisi as well as the more local Grechetto. Visit vineyards on the Strada de Vini del Cantico – see www.stradadeivinidelcantico.it for details.

Below: The Basilica di Santa Chiara at Assisi, a 13th-century masterpiece

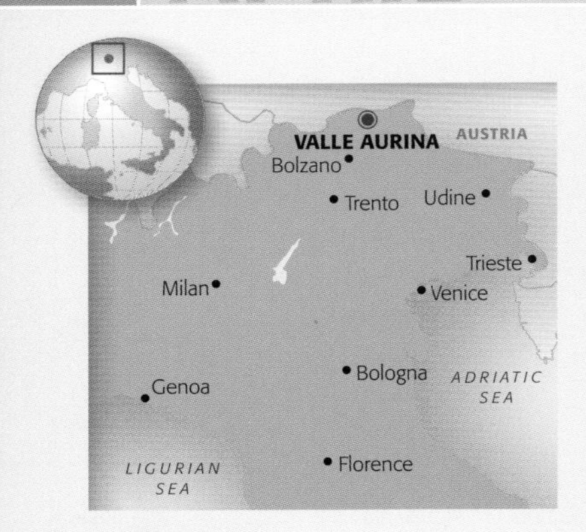

GETTING THERE
The valleys of Tures and Aurina are in Trentino-Alto Adige, north of Brunico, close to the Austrian border. The best way of getting there is by car or taxi. From Verona airport, take the A22 freeway, leaving at the Bressanone exit, then the SS49 to Brunico followed by the SS621 to Brunico.

GETTING AROUND
By bike, of course! Although there is also a bus system along the valley.

WEATHER
The summits will still be capped with snow, but spring is coming to some places in the valley; the snows are retreating, the temperatures are rising, and the days are getting longer.

ACCOMMODATIONS
There are many good-quality B&Bs, apartments, and *agriturismi* in the area offering a Tyrolean welcome at good prices. Make use of the services and equipment at designated mountain bike hotels, such as the Innerhofer at Gais, just north of Brunico. Rooms from US$62; www.hotel-innerhofer.com

Or try the Rainerhof apartments near Cadipietra, from US$55 per night; www.rainerhof.info

EATING OUT
You can "refuel" in restaurants for about US$35 per person, enjoying specialty Tyrolean dishes such as bacon with black bread, dumplings, barley soup, and shin of pork with sweet strudel for dessert.

PRICE FOR TWO
About US$170 for meals and accommodations. If you rent mountain bikes by the day, add about US$20 per person.

FURTHER INFORMATION
www.tures-aurina.com
www.suedTyrolerland.it

The Waterfalls of Riva

The whole length of the Riva valley is awash with water, and wherever you go you'll be able to see foaming rivers and frothing cascades that have carved out channels through the mountains. Head from Riva di Tures to see the spectacular Cascata di Riva, a series of cascades of the River Riva as it rushes down the rocky mountain walls. Riva di Tures is also an ideal starting point for walks and climbs in the Parco Naturale Vedrètte di Ries-Aurina. In winter, there are fantastic opportunities to go climbing on the glacier.

Above (left to right): Mountain cheese, one of the region's best products; typical Tyrolean farmhouse in Trentino-Alto Adige; walking in the unspoiled Valle Aurina
Main: An intrepid cyclist fords a cascading mountain river

PEAK ACTIVITY

WHAT IS IT ABOUT MOUNTAINS that drives people to activity? It's not enough to simply sit back and admire their grandeur and beauty, you need to walk, climb, or cycle up them; and ski, raft, and cycle down. Whatever the reason, the valleys of Tures and Aurina are excellent places to join in. Here, you're beneath the gaze of an incredible 14 summits over 10,000 ft (3,000 m) – the mountains reign supreme on all sides. A good way to get around the valleys is by bike – start from Brunico and head north where the valley floor is wide and full of wonderful views that captivate both eye and soul. Then the valley splits in two at Campo Tures, guarded by a formidable castle. To the east, the mountains have closed in, creating the spectacular waterfalls and cascades on the way to Riva di Tures. Or, continue straight on for the gentler Valle Aurina, which extends like a finger to the Austrian border. The valley is only about 30 miles (50 km) long, so the distances aren't far, and if you keep to the valley floor there are no hilly sections – you should still have plenty of energy left for other activities.

Mountains ... it's not enough to simply sit back and admire their grandeur and beauty, you need to walk, climb, or cycle up them; and ski, raft, and cycle down.

Perhaps you would like to try white-water rafting – descending the mountains in a flimsy inflatable boat, the shocking spray of icy water in your face as you bounce between the rocks. But don't worry, the tours are run by professionals. And no visitor should miss out on the chance to explore the unspoiled nature preserve of the Parco Naturale Vedrette di Ries-Aurina, part of the largest protected area in Europe, extending deep into Austria. Here the mountains are draped in gleaming white glaciers and dotted with sparkling blue lakes, while the green hillsides are cloaked in larch and pine trees and home to foxes, chamois, marmots, peregrine falcons, and eagle owls. And if this isn't reward enough for the hard work – you've also burned off enough calories to justify filling up on hearty smoked meat and dumpling casseroles and excellent mountain cheeses, all washed down with local wines.

Inset: The beautiful Parco Naturale Vedrette di Ries-Aurina
Below (left and right): Castello di Tures; cycling through unspoiled countryside

CYCLING DIARY

Enjoying the valleys of the South Tyrol is not something you should rush. Six days will allow you to tour the pretty Alpine villages by bicycle and still have time for other activities such as walking or rafting, and even a day simply relaxing and taking in the beautiful mountain scenery. You can rent bicycles from Brunico.

Six Days in the Saddle

DAY 1

Start your visit at Brunico and explore the pretty medieval center, with its network of alleyways and 13th-century castle. Buy any last-minute supplies and fill up on the local cuisine – you'll need the energy!

DAYS 2–3

For the first day of cycling, head to Campo Tures, stopping for lunch at Gais, which has one of the oldest churches in the South Tyrol. At Campo Tures, take time to walk up to the 13th-century castle, in the north of the village.

Stay the night and spend day three white-water rafting or take a side trip to Riva di Tures to see the stunning waterfalls and visit one of the highest villages in the Tyrol. You could also consider walking into the Parco Naturale Vedrette di Ries-Aurina from Riva.

DAYS 4–6

Set off along Valle Aurina, cycling at your own pace. Stop in Lutago and relax in its pretty town center with plenty of shops and bars. A few miles farther on, in Cadipietra, there's an interesting mining museum – copper was once an important local resource.

Pack a picnic and spend a day hiking up to stunning Lake Chiusetta at 7,055 ft (2,150 m) or simply explore the pristine Parco Naturale Vedrette di Ries-Aurina. And don't forget to treat any aching limbs to a rejuvenating sauna and spa visit – most of the hotels along the way will have facilities. Another interesting stop is Predoi, which has two small museums on farming and mining.

The cycle route finishes in Casere, a famous center for mountain sports. Don't miss the fine 15th-century church of Santo Spirito. From here it is possible to take a bus back to Brunico (with the bike as luggage).

Dos and Don'ts

- ✓ Buy a cushion embroidered with lace; this traditional craft is practiced in the valleys of Tures and Aurina. In Casere, you can watch a demonstration of this highly prized lace being made.
- ✗ Don't overestimate your fitness – unless you have been training, keep the distances short to start with and don't try any ascents. The altitude will make it seem harder than usual.
- ✓ Try the local cheeses, which have a flavor of herbs from high Alpine meadows, and the *strauben*, fritters served with jam.
- ✗ Don't go trekking without suitable clothing and checking the weather forecast; it can still be very cold in April.

Below: Relaxing by Lake Chiusetta

COASTAL ROMANCE

FIVE GORGEOUS CLUSTERS OF PASTEL-COLORED HOUSES, built on rocky spurs, and overlooking a sparkling blue sea: these are the Cinque Terre, or Five Lands, one of the most scenic parts of Liguria. Strung along the scrub-covered coastline, these villages were home to hardy fishermen and farmers who, like their ancestors before them, lived off the sea and cultivated vines on the steep, rocky terraces with patience and skill. Surprisingly, in this harsh environment, the vines that grip so tenaciously to the cliffs have always produced excellent wine. The villages have changed remarkably little over the years – until the 20th century, they were virtually cut off from the rest of the world, accessible only by boat or via tortuous mule tracks.

Although the five villages of the Cinque Terre have much in common, each has its own special character and layout. Monterosso is divided into two districts: next to the old village is the sandy and

Main: Sculpture on the Via d'Amore in Manarola representing two lovers kissing

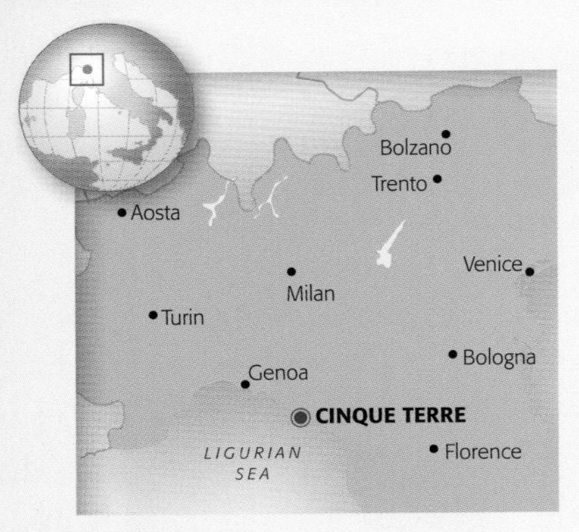

GETTING THERE
It is inadvisable to drive to the Cinque Terre, on the Ligurian Riviera. Parking is expensive and once here, you will not need the car. The best way to get here is by train: the service runs every hour along the coast between Genoa (the nearest airport) and La Spezia, stopping at stations in Cinque Terre.

GETTING AROUND
Explore the Cinque Terre by walking the Sentiero Azzurro (Blue Path) that connects the villages (total walking time 5 hours). If you do not wish to walk you can take the train, or even a ferry.

WEATHER
April is ideal for walks and warm enough to be on the beach, although the sea will still be cold.

ACCOMMODATIONS
There are numerous guesthouses and B&Bs: you can stay in a welcoming family atmosphere in places that are generally simple but clean and comfortable and provide good value for money (from US$70).

EATING OUT
One of the pleasures of the coast is the local cuisine of fresh fish and seafood, especially anchovies prepared in the local way in *tegame alla Vernazzana* (oven-cooked with potatoes, cherry tomatoes, and spices). Expect, too, soups and pasta, served with pesto or walnut sauce.

In Vernazza, try Gianni Franzi or Gambero Rosso; in Riomaggiore, La Lanterna; in Monterosso, Ciak or Carugio. All of these restaurants serve excellent regional cuisine – the average price for a meal is US$35–42.

PRICE FOR TWO
About US$200 per day for food, accommodations, and the Cinque Terre Train Card.

FURTHER INFORMATION
www.cinqueterre.it; www.cinqueterre.com

Portovenere

If you can spare one more day, spend it at Portovenere, south of the villages of the Cinque Terre. It stands on a promontory looking out to sea toward three islands – Palmaria, Tino, and Tinetto. You will be enchanted by the pretty houses scattered around the little harbor and the late 13th-century church of San Pietro. Perched on the tip of castle fortifications, the church is faced with the black and white stone stripes that are typical of Ligurian architecture. It also incorporates an older chapel built in black Palmaria marble, with a small loggia facing the sea.

upscale beach of Fegina, the longest on this stretch of the coast. Vernazza is a genuine fishing village, situated on an inlet where the village square borders the harbor. Corniglia is a traditional agricultural hill village, connected to the sea and the train station by nearly 400 steps. Its wines have been celebrated since ancient times (amphorae were found in Pompeii with "Cornelia" written on them). Manarola, clinging to a black rock on a cliff above the sea, was once enclosed within the boundaries of an ancient castle, now in ruins. Riomaggiore was built on the banks of a steep mountain torrent (now covered) and so its houses are all tall and narrow and accessible at different levels.

The five villages are linked by the 7-mile (12-km) Sentiero Azzurro, which runs along the coast between Monterosso and Riomaggiore. This path offers stunning views as it winds through terraced slopes, with vines and olive groves on one side and the sea on the other. The most famous section is the Via dell'Amore (Walk of Love), which joins Riomaggiore and Manarola. Part carved out of the cliffs and part suspended above the sea, this short and easy walkway is perfect for a romantic evening stroll.

Top left (anticlockwise): Vernazza's little harbor, with its characteristic fishing boats; signs marking the different routes in the Cinque Terre; a view of Corniglia, high on a cliff above the vivid blue sea; aerial view of Vernazza and its harbor; the famous Monterosso anchovies, used in numerous delicious local dishes

CLIFFTOP DIARY

The Cinque Terre is one of the most romantic places in Italy. For centuries its inhabitants have lived on the cliffs between the sea on one side and the steep yet fertile mountainous landscape on the other. Four days is enough time to tour this astonishingly beautiful coast, studded with charming little villages.

Four Spellbinding Days

DAY 1

The first part of the Cinque Terre that you reach when traveling from Genoa is Monterosso. Explore the ancient village and see the parish church of San Giovanni Battista with its fine façade of horizontal stripes, and enjoy a few hours of sunshine on the glamorous beach at Fegina. At night, there's a view of the other four villages, their lights twinkling on the sea.

DAY 2

Walk to Vernazza, a village with a slower pace of life. Don't miss the church of Santa Margherita d'Antiochia with its impressive 131-ft (40-m) belfry. Enjoy a long lunch by the harbor, watching the people passing by. Move on to Corniglia, more of a hill village than a fishing port, accessed by its steep *lardarina* (staircase).

DAY 3

Next it's Manarola – a compact village that huddles on a promontory above the sea. Enjoy the fine views from the church of San Lorenzo, or go swimming off the harbor – if you don't mind the cool water. To reach Riomaggiore, take the Via d'Amore, the path carved out of cliffs with some of the most stunning views in Liguria.

DAY 4

In Riomaggiore, the last of the Cinque Terre villages, take the scenic walk up to the castle ruins and then head up to the church of the Madonna of Montenero, set in a breathtaking position overlooking a huge stretch of the coastline. Look, too, for the murals of fishermen, grape growers, and farmers, painted by Argentine artist Silvio Benedetto (b.1938).

Dos and Don'ts

- ✓ Buy the Cinque Terre Train Card (a card for three days will cost about US$27); it gives you access to the Sentiero Azzurro, use of the Park's mini-buses, and unlimited use of the trains on the Levanto–La Spezia railway line.
- ✗ Do not walk along the Sentiero Azzurro unless you have suitable footwear – sneakers will be fine.
- ✓ Taste Cinque Terre's superb wines. The most famous is Sciacchetrà, a sweet raisin wine – the name means "press it and forget about it for a long time."
- ✓ Try one of the many walks suggested by the national park, which protects and develops this remarkable territory. Information from www.parconazionale5terre.it

Below: Manarola with typical pastel-colored Ligurian "tower houses"

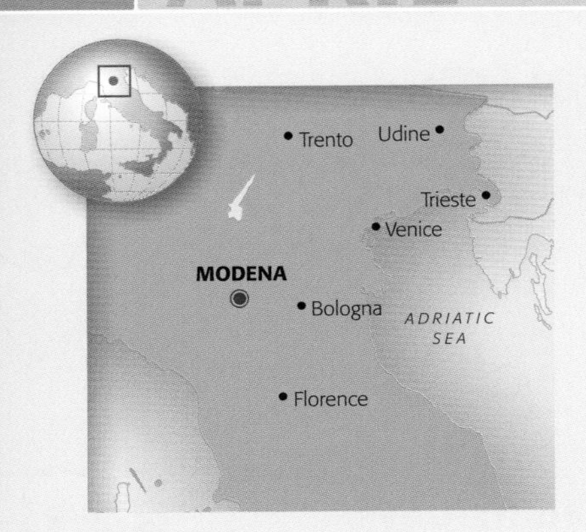

GETTING THERE
Modena is in the heart of Emilia-Romagna, about 30 miles (50 km) from Bologna; a shuttle bus runs from Bologna's Marconi Airport to Modena (US$28 return). Modena is near the junction of the A1 and A22 freeways and is easily reached by car.

GETTING AROUND
Explore the town on foot, enjoy a slow stroll and discover the hidden corners.

WEATHER
Spring is the best time to visit the Po Valley, as it can get cold in winter and oppressively hot in summer.

ACCOMMODATIONS
The Canalgrande Hotel, set in an ancient park, was once a convent and then a grand villa, and still retains a dignified historic atmosphere, doubles from US$250; www.canalgrandehotel.it

The Angolino di Riposo is a pleasant and quiet B&B, with rooms from US$110; www.angolinodiriposo.com

The 3-star Hotel Estense, modern and comfortable, is close to the city center and has good transport links; rooms from US$182; www.hotelestense.com

EATING OUT
Try the famous classic Fini restaurant (tel. 059 223 314) for a sumptuous dinner of traditional local specialties. Or, for modern molecular gastronomy, try Massimo Bottura's innovative cuisine at the Osteria Francescana; www.osteriafrancescana.it. Meals from US$98 per person.

The Oreste (tel. 059 243 324) is less costly, but nevertheless excellent, serving rich, traditional food in a family atmosphere for US$50–56.

PRICE FOR TWO
From US$250 to 390 per day, depending on choice of accommodations; more for luxury dining.

FURTHER INFORMATION
http://turismo.comune.modena.it

Home of the Prancing Horse

That the citizens of Modena love their cars is well-known and this passion gets even more intense each April with the Modena Terra di Motori (Modena, land of motor cars) fair. For a few days, the city becomes an open-air museum dedicated to a century of motoring with exhibitions, events, and a popular vintage car rally. Naturally, local manufacturer Ferrari's cars are at home here and the most prestigious models from *Cavallino Rampante* (Ferrari's symbol, the Prancing Horse) drive through town for the occasion: a treat for all car lovers!

ART, GASTRONOMY, AND CARS

There are three main reasons to visit Modena: art, gastronomy, and cars. The art is found in the outstanding architecture of the Duomo, one of the masterpieces of Italian Romanesque, created in the 12th century by the architect Lanfranco and the sculptor Wiligelmus, and an army of master craftsmen and sculptors from northern Italy. Although there are several magnificent doors and a splendid façade dominated by a great rose window and graced by exquisite loggias, arches, and corbels, the Duomo's key artistic feature is the dynamic bas-relief frieze, carved on the exterior, which captures the essential spiritual world of the medieval age. Next to the Duomo, stands the Torre Ghirlandina, an impressive 280 ft (86 m) high. The tower was built by Arrigo da Campione in the 13th century and owes its name to the two *ghirlande* (garlands) or marble balustrades that adorn the spire.

Then there is gastronomy: Modena is one of the capitals of Italian cuisine. Balsamic vinegar, made from reduced grape juice and barrel-matured for up to 25 years, may well be the jewel in the

Below (top to bottom): Handmade tortellini, a classic local pasta variety; barrels used to produce the city's famous balsamic vinegar **Inset:** a detail of Modena's cathedral

The Duomo's key artistic feature is the dynamic bas-relief frieze ... which captures the essential spiritual world of the medieval age.

crown of Modena's culinary tradition, but the mainstay of local cuisine is pork. This versatile meat is prepared in every way possible from cured cold meats and salamis served with *gnocco frito,* a salty, fried puffed pastry, to delicate hand-folded tortellini and *zampone*, stuffed pig's trotters. All these delights, naturally, are washed down with a chilled glass or two of Lambrusco, the excellent local red wine that is as full-bodied and sparkling as Modena's citizens.

Finally, there is the motor car, which here means not only Ferrari and Maserati, acknowledged as the top names in the Italian car industry, but also Stanguellini, the superb small-engine racing cars that once competed so valiantly in the historic Mille Miglia, the 1,000-mile (1,609-km) road race from Brescia to Rome and back, between 1927 to 1957. And even though driving one of these rare and beautiful racing cars may be just a distant dream, you can admire the legends up close in the two museums dedicated to this modern passion of Modena: the Museo Stanguellini, which houses over 30 models from racing cars to sports coupés, and the vintage car museum of Umberto Panini, which has an almost priceless collection of Maseratis.

Main: Via Farini, in the heart of Modena, with the 17th-century Chiesa di San Giorgio

Above: A cherry tree in blossom in the countryside outside Modena, well-known for its cherries

Below: Clock tower of the Palazzo Ducale, seat of the Estense court from the 17th to the 19th century

GOURMET DIARY

Three days should be enough time to enjoy all the treats Modena has to offer: open piazzas, sumptuous palaces, and a beautiful Duomo. Viewing all this architecture can work up a serious appetite, so it's a good thing that the city is renowned for its cuisine. And, last but not least, there is the local passion for the motor car, as seen in the two fantastic motor museums.

Three Days in Modena

DAY 1

Start your tour in the spectacular Piazza Grande, with the shady colonnade of the Palazzo Comunale, the Torre dell'Orologio (clock tower), and the superb Romanesque Duomo and its soaring campanile. In the evening, treat yourself to a delicious meal from one of Modena's finest restaurants, washed down with a fabulous bottle of Lambrusco.

DAY 2

Visit the Palazzo Ducale, a grand Baroque 17th-century palace. Next, spend some time exploring the 18th-century Palazzo dei Musei, now a gallery displaying the paintings collected by the powerful dynasty d'Este over 500 years. Opera-lovers should not miss the Teatro Comunale, dedicated to the great Modena tenor, Luciano Pavarotti. By now you've probably seen enough architecture, so try something different with a tasting of the city's famous balsamic vinegar – the real stuff is just delicious!

DAY 3

As you're in Modena, you have to dedicate some time to the motor car, the grand passion of the locals. There are two major car museums in the city, each filled with modern mechanical masterpieces: the Umberto Panini museum, which has one of the best Maserati collections; and the Museo Stanguellini, which tells the history of this stylish and vintage brand.

Dos and Don'ts

- ✓ Browse around the stalls in the antique fair held in Modena on the last weekend of every month; especially if you're looking for that special souvenir. However, if you are looking for something specifically local, your best option is to visit the craft fair held in April.
- ✗ Don't go to the Palazzo Ducale without booking in advance; this really is obligatory (tel. 059 220 022).
- ✓ Buy a small bottle of genuine balsamic vinegar – much of what is sold outside Italy is not the real thing, but an imitation – but bear in mind that it is very expensive.
- ✗ Don't overdo things with Modenese cuisine; it may taste delicious but, when you get home, you could find that you've put on a few pounds!
- ✓ Find out where there's tastings of balsamic vinegar and lovely Lambrusco, Modena's local wine. For more information, visit http://turismo.comune.modena.it

Below: Modena delicatessen, a gastronomic treasury

GETTING THERE
The Bernina Express departs from Tirano in Alta Valtellina in northern Lombardy, on the border with Switzerland. The most convenient way of getting to Tirano is by train from Milan or Bergamo airports.

GETTING AROUND
On the Little Red Train *(Trenino Rosso)*, of course! To visit other towns in the Valtellina, such as Grosio and Bormio, use the efficient bus service.

WEATHER
Spring has arrived in the valleys, but there is still snow at high altitudes and the air can feel wintry, with temperatures as low as 32°F (0°C).

ACCOMMODATIONS
The Hotel Bernina, near the *Trenino Rosso* station, has rooms for four from US$195 (tel. 0342 902 424). The Piccolo Mondo has a pleasant garden and will cost about US$70 per person for B&B; www.albergopiccolomondo.it

Accommodation in St. Moritz is expensive, but try Hotel Chesa Rosatch in Celerina; doubles from US$88; www.rosatsch.ch

EATING OUT
You can enjoy the hearty Valtellina cuisine in most of the restaurants: try *pizzocheri* (a type of pasta), and *risotto allo Sforzato* (risotto with local wine). In Tirano, try the Antica Osteria dell'Angelo. A meal costs around US$35; www.osteriadellangelo.com

PRICE FOR A FAMILY OF FOUR
About US$390 per day for accommodations and meals, plus the cost of a second-class ticket for the Bernina Express (US$50 return per person; children under 6 travel free).

FURTHER INFORMATION
www.rhb.ch; www.tiranoonline.it

The King of Valtellina Wines

Ever since Roman times, vines have been cultivated in Valtellina by clever use of terracing, which makes full use of the sun's heat. As a result, the area has always produced wines of distinction. The king of local wines, however, is *Sforzato*, made from Nebbiolo grapes that are left to wither on the vine until January so that they dry out and develop a distinctive and potent bouquet. The result, after at least two years of maturing, is a wine to be savored and enjoyed by an open fire or as an accompaniment to the local meat dishes.

Panoramic carriages allow passengers to appreciate the views of azure blue Alpine lakes, thick pine forests, high Alpine pastures, and great icy glaciers.

Left (left to right): Pretty Sondalo in the heart of Alta Valtellina Bernina Express cross a dramatic mountain viaduct; a hearty dish Valtellina-style *pizzoc*

Right (left to right): of many spa hotels in area; a stunning lake mountain landscape the Bernina valley

Main: The Bernina Express, one of the most exciting railways in Europe
Inset: The little church of Santa Perpetua, above the town of Tirano

MOUNTAIN EXPRESS

There are not many trains that feature in UNESCO's World Heritage List, but the Bernina Express is one of them, and you need only enjoy a ride in one of its pillar-box red carriages – hence the nickname "Little Red Train" – to understand why. It's not because of the carriages, however, even though they were designed by Italian automotive expert Pininfarina. The marvel is the 90 miles (145 km) of extraordinary landscape that is covered in 4 hours and the ingenious engineering solutions that enable the train to connect Italy and Switzerland (Tirano to St. Moritz), climbing up over the 7,392-ft (2,253-m) Bernina Pass without the slightest problem, even in the severest snowy winters – and it can get very snowy around here.

Construction started on the railway in 1910 and the first journey was made in 1913. From then on this line has been admired as one of the most spectacular railway journeys in the world; it is also the highest altitude

transalpine railway in Europe. One of the highlights is reached just outside Brusio station. Children and adults will gasp with delight at the famous spiral viaduct that looks like part of a rollercoaster ride and enables the train to climb 98 ft (30 m) in a very small space. And then there is the breathtaking mountain scenery. The panoramic carriages with their tall, curving windows allow passengers to fully appreciate the views of azure blue Alpine lakes, thick pine forests, high Alpine pastures, and great icy glaciers, and they'll even be able to catch sight of the summit of Monte Bernina (13,280 ft/4,049 m) above them.

The train carries on past glamorous St. Moritz but you should get off here and see what this chic and cosmopolitan town has to offer. Spend a night and rub shoulders with the über-rich in one of the oldest – and sunniest – winter sports resorts. And if it snows, don't worry, you'll still be able to return to Tirano as nothing stops the Bernina Express. Day-in, day-out, powerful snowplough engines shuttle along the narrow-gauge track, clearing the way for the Little Red Train.

ALPINE DIARY

Tirano is the entry point to Alta Valtellina, the Lombardy valley famous for mountains, spas, and winter sports, but it is probably best known as the starting point for the Bernina Express. Three days will give you time to see Tirano, cross over to Swiss St. Moritz and enjoy a day by the lake before returning for a day in Alta Valtellina.

Three Days in Alta Valtellina

DAY 1

At Tirano, board the Bernina Express. The journey to St. Moritz takes about 3 hours along a route that crosses over the Bernina Pass, a climb of 7,392 ft (2,253 m) with inclines of up to 1 in 14 without using the usual mountain train solution – the rack-and-pinion system. It is worth making the journey in one of the panoramic carriages, which afford perfect views of the natural wonders along the route. Disembark in St. Moritz to catch your breath and stretch your legs. The town itself isn't especially pretty, but walk east along the lakeside and visit Celerina – it has a pleasant cobbled center and is next to the finish of the Cresta Run.

DAY 2

Spend the night in St. Moritz and then set off back to Tirano, getting off along the way at Diavolezza to admire the wonderful view of Bernina and Lake Bianco, and then taking the next train. Back in Tirano, explore the historic center of the village – there are some impressive houses and the sanctuary of the Madonna. At dinner, try the excellent Valtellina wines, especially the delicious *Sforzato,* made from grapes grown at high-altitude.

DAY 3

Today, explore Alta Valtellina. Visit charming Grosio and stroll through woods to see its famous prehistoric rock carvings. Don't miss, also, the Chiesa di San Giorgio decorated with a fine series of frescoes. Continue along the valley to Bormio, a renowned winter ski center, spa town, and a starting point for splendid mountain walks.

Dos and Don'ts

- ✓ Buy an example of local craftsmanship in Grosio, famous for products made of wrought iron, pewter, and copper.
- ✓ When exploring outside, always dress in layers and take warm, windproof clothing with you.
- ✗ Don't plan a trip on the Bernina Express without booking in advance; this is obligatory. For information, visit www.rhb.ch or www.treninorosso.it
- ✓ Visit Bormio's hot springs – it has been a spa town since the Middle Ages. There are two main establishments: the modern Bormio baths (www.bormioterme.it) and the Bagni Vecchi or old baths (www.bagnidibormio.it), just outside the village.

Below: A panoramic carriage in the Bernina Express

GETTING THERE
Montecassino is in the southern part of Lazio. The nearest airports are Rome 100 miles (160 km) and Naples 60 miles (100 km). From the A1 freeway between Rome and Naples take the exit to Cassino. If you come by train, you can take a bus or taxi from Cassino station to the abbey.

GETTING AROUND
The best way to tour the area is by car.

WEATHER
Expect variable spring weather, with some sunny and some rainy days and mean temperatures of between 43°F and 64°F (6–18°C).

ACCOMMODATIONS
The Rocca Hotel in Cassino is perfect for a family with children: it is located near a water park and has a miniclub and children's activities. It can also provide cots, high chairs, and children's menus. Four-bed rooms from US$160; www.hotelrocca.it

The farmhouse La Pisana, near the Abbazia di Fossanova, has delightful apartments in old restored farmhouses sleeping 4 from US$168 per night; www.agricolalapisana.it

EATING OUT
You can eat well for US$35 in many restaurants and farmhouses that serve delicious Lazio cuisine. One of the very best is the Antica Osteria Fanti in Priverno, near Fossanova (dinner about US$35); www.anticaosteriafanti.it

PRICE FOR A FAMILY OF FOUR
About US$350 per day for meals and accommodations.

FURTHER INFORMATION
www.montecassino.it; www.casamari.it

The First Pharmacists

Benedictine Rule imposes an obligation to care for the sick. Accordingly, the monks grew medicinal herbs and used the Arab methods of distillation to create potions, building special rooms to store them. Thus the *monacus infirmarius* came into existence, responsible for preparing and looking after the medicines. This ancient herbal wisdom is the origin of the medicines sold today at the Abbazia di Casamari and its 18th-century pharmacy.

Main: Renaissance cloister of the Abbazia di Montecassino, with delightful views over the surrounding countryside
Above (top to bottom): Interior of the church of the Abbazia di Casamari; the abbey's luxuriant garden

IN THE STEPS OF ST. BENEDICT

MONTECASSINO, AN IMPOSING WHITE EDIFICE visible for miles, stands on the summit of Monte Calvario. The Abbazia di Montecassino was founded in 529 by St. Benedict, who laid down the precepts of Benedictine Rule, obliging the monks to study and engage in manual labor. It developed into a center of learning throughout the Middle Ages, when a great many works of classical antiquity were translated and transcribed. In this way, the monks preserved a thousand years of erudition, dating back to the ancient Greeks, and created the famous Cassino collection of illuminated manuscripts kept in the abbey's libraries. It was also here that the first documents in early Italian dialect were created, from which the Italian language evolved. Over the centuries, many fine works of art came to Montecassino and the abbey was transformed into a grand Baroque building arranged around three large connecting cloisters. In February 1944, all this was destroyed by an Allied bombing raid during the battle of Monte Cassino. When the conflict was over, rebuilding

Left (left to right): Aerial view of the Polish memorial and cemetery at Montecassino; Abbazia di Montecassio on the summit of Monte Calvario; *Caciotta*, a delicious soft buffalo milk cheese typical of the region

work started at once and the original structure was faithfully restored. Vast cemeteries containing the remains of soldiers of the German and Allied forces are testament to the fierce fighting that took place here; one of the most moving memorials is the Polish cemetery, tended by the monks.

St. Benedict's teachings found a home in other great abbeys in Lazio. The Abbazia di Casamari was one of the most important monastic centers in central Italy. Its austere structure has been perfectly preserved: the cloister, the solemn Gothic church, and the abbot's house all still emanate a feeling of serenity. Similarly peaceful, the Cistercian Abbazia di Fossanova, consecrated in 1208, is arranged around a church and a cloister: this is where the monks led their lives, marked then as now by the rhythms of prayer and work in accordance with St. Benedict's Rule.

Leaving behind the monasteries infused with spirituality, burn off some energy along the delightful coastline. There is plenty to explore on walks in the area, along roads and paths which are also passable by bike, between the sea and the coastal lake at Sabaudia.

BENEDICTINE DIARY

It was at Montecassino that St. Benedict prescribed his Rule, but the deeply felt spiritual revival that he inspired gathered momentum in southern Lazio and led to the establishment of other abbeys, such as those at Casamari and Fossanova. Four days should be enough time to see and appreciate their beauty, peace, and tranquillity.

Four Days of Spirituality

DAY 1

An itinerary of Benedictine spirituality cannot start anywhere else but Montecassino. Visit the abbey's museum, which houses material and documents that relate its history as well as illuminated manuscripts and incunabula (hand printed books). Don't miss the Polish war memorial and cemetery, which contains the remains of 1,072 soldiers who died in the battle of Monte Cassino in 1944.

DAY 2

Travel 20 miles (30 km) northwest, to the Abbazia di Casamari and its Gothic 13th-century church and cloister, surrounded by a colonnade with finely carved capitals. The 18th-century pharmacy, where herbal remedies are still prepared using centuries-old recipes, is sure to fascinate children. Make sure you get a chance to enjoy the traditional Lazio cuisine, such as roast lamb and buffalo milk cheese.

DAY 3

Visit Abbazia di Fossanova. It was founded by Benedictine monks and includes an exquisite church and a very fine cloister that is Romanesque on three sides and Gothic on the fourth. Don't miss the refectory and the guest quarters where philosopher and theologian St. Thomas Aquinas died in 1274.

DAY 4

As an antidote to all this rich religious history, spend your final day on the coast, where the kids can burn off some excess energy and you can take in some restorative sea air. The headland where the well-known tourist resort of San Felice Circeo stands is very beautiful, with a long sandy beach stretching to the north, fringed by the coastal lake of Sabaudia. The area is perfect for relaxing walks or bicycle rides.

Dos and Don'ts

- ✓ If you have time, explore the war cemeteries in the area around Cassino. The most important ones are the Commonwealth War Graves in Cassino and Minturno and the German cemetery in Colle Marino, near Caira.
- ✗ Don't wear clothes that are low-cut, short, or revealing when you visit places of worship.
- ✓ To relax for a few hours, go to the thermal baths in Castelforte towards the coast from Cassino. Enjoy the hot springs for therapeutic cures and beauty treatments.

Below: View into a cloister at Abbazia di Montecassino

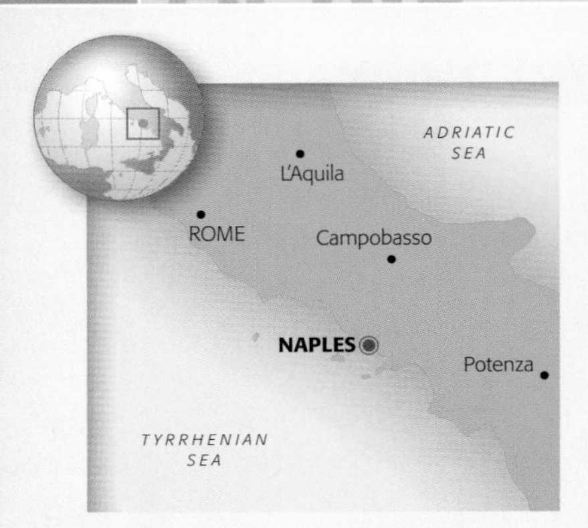

GETTING THERE
Naples is the capital of Campania, and a gateway to the south. From its Capodichino Airport a shuttle bus runs to the city, taking around 30 minutes.

GETTING AROUND
Explore the city center on foot and use public transportation for longer distances.

WEATHER
April is a perfect month to visit; daytime highs average 64°F (18°C) but it is sometimes even warm enough for a swim in the sea.

ACCOMMODATIONS
The Miseria e Nobiltà B&B is an elegant, historic apartment in the heart of the city; doubles from US$90; www.bbmiseriaenobilta.it

Relais Posillipo is in a quiet district with lovely views; doubles from US$125 (US$168 with balcony or terrace); www.relaisposillipo.it

Costantinopoli 104, a 19th-century villa in the city center, has a lovely garden and swimming pool; doubles from US$358; www.costantinopoli104.com

EATING OUT
Trattoria dall'Amico Gamberone, with a delightful garden, serves local specialties and great pizzas; dinner from US$35 (tel. 081 665344).

La Bersagliera offers traditional dishes (US$42) and has a terrace with bay views; www.labersagliera.it

PRICE FOR TWO
US$250–470 per day, depending on your choice of hotel, but including accommodations, meals, local travel, and admissions.

FURTHER INFORMATION
www.inaples.it

Regal Capodimonte

The Royal Porcelain Factory in Capodimonte was founded in 1743 by Charles VII of Naples, to emulate the German Meissen pieces that were part of the dowry of his wife, Maria Amalia of Saxony. Unable to replicate the hard paste of northern Europe, his potters developed a softer version, and it is this that gives Capodimonte the delicate and vibrant appearance for which its charming floral arrangements and elegant figurines are known. "True" Capodimonte was produced for less than 100 years; today the name is a blanket term for the style.

Main: View of the city and the Bay of Naples, with Vesuvius in the background
Above (top to bottom): Delightful Villa Floridiana; bustling Via Chiaia in the heart of the old city

A CITY THAT MUST BE SEEN

NAPLES' CLASSIC PICTURE-POSTCARD VIEW unfolds before your eyes from the ramparts of Castel Sant'Elmo, perched on the summit of Vomero, the highest part of the city. There before you is the royal palace, Castel dell'Ovo, the long trail of Via Roma, and, beyond, the teeming streets of the Spanish Quarter. There is the great sweep of sparkling blue sea that is the Bay of Naples and there, of course, the unmistakeable cone of Vesuvius in the distance.

Castel Sant'Elmo was built for King Robert of Naples at the beginning of the 14th century, in part by hollowing out the volcanic rock on which it stands. For centuries, its dungeons held one of the most fearsome prisons in Italy. An equally outstanding view can be seen from the monastery of San Martino, just a few steps further on. Built in the 14th century but considerably altered in subsequent centuries, it is now one of the most complete examples of Neapolitan Baroque: a treasure chest of frescoes, stucco, canvases, and other works by the most distinguished artists working in Naples in the 17th century.

Above (top to bottom): Pizza Margherita, an icon of Neapolitan cuisine; spectacular Salottino di Porcellana in the Capodimonte Palace Museum

Below: Montesanto funicular, connecting the Vomero district with the lower part of Naples

The monastery now houses one of the city's finest museums, the Museo Nazionale di San Martino. Perhaps its most charming exhibit is a Neapolitan nativity scene, made at the end of the 18th century by grand masters of an art that was a long-established and noble tradition in Naples.

Vomero is the smart residential area of Naples. Once a verdant and secluded area, in the 19th and 20th centuries it saw the arrival of many grand villas amidst its greenery. The most beautiful is the Villa Floridiana, whose gardens are today the "green lungs" of the district. It was restored in Neo-Classical style in the early 19th century by Lucia Migliaccio, wife of Bourbon king Ferdinand I of Naples, and is surrounded by parkland that slopes gently downhill to a pagoda with fine views.

The other major green space in a city badly in need of them is the park of Palazzo Capodimonte. Built as a hunting lodge for the Bourbons, it was enlarged by Charles VII to house his art collection. Today it is one of the most important museums in Italy. Together these former royal residences gaze down over the vibrant, chaotic, fascinating city that their former owners once ruled. "See Naples and die!" is a saying coined by the Bourbons – a little overdramatic, perhaps, but you certainly must see Naples.

NEAPOLITAN DIARY

Naples is a city in which periods of history seem to overlap and form an idiosyncratic whole containing many treasures for you to discover and enjoy. Bask in the warmth of its people; savor its rustic southern cuisine; and thrill to its bustling, noisy, urban charm. Five days allows time to do all of this and more *(see also pp250–1)*.

Five Days by the Bay

DAY 1

Ascend by funicular to the district of Vomero. At the monastery of San Martino, pause at the belvedere for a dramatic vista of the city. Visit the museum at the former monastery, with its collection of nativity scenes, then climb up to the ramparts of Castel Sant'Elmo for panoramic views. Finish the day at lovely Villa Floridiana, which houses an important ceramics museum.

DAY 2

Spend the day in the heart of the city. Begin at the Museo Archeologico Nazionale di Napoli, packed with treasures from Pompeii and Herculaneum, then wander narrow streets lined with ancient buildings and lovely churches to arrive at the spectacular cathedral of San Gennaro.

DAY 3

Take the bus to Capodimonte and visit the palace museum. As well as its famous collection of pictures, including a Botticelli *Madonna*, the ornate historic apartments are worth a visit. A curiosity is the Salottino di Porcellana (porcelain room) – its walls are entirely covered with Capodimonte porcelain.

DAY 4

Chiaia Riviera is Naples' most elegant quarter, with designer shops and the famous seafront, a long but pleasant walk, starting from Castel dell'Ovo, a fortress resembling a cliff of volcanic rock rising from the sea, and finishing in Mergellina, an ancient fishing village that is now the city's tourist port. Dine at a harborside restaurant as you watch the sun set over the bay.

DAY 5

Stroll along Via Posillipo, which follows the promontory just north of the city, offering marvelous views. There are many historic houses, such as Neo-Classical Villa Doria d'Angri, and other splendid private residences, many of which have their own path down to the beach.

Dos and Don'ts

- ✗ Don't be fooled into paying a huge sum for seemingly "authentic" Capodimonte. With so much porcelain now bearing the name (and often the factory's signature mark of a crowned letter N), this is a market best left to the experts.
- ✓ While pizza is a Neapolitan specialty not to be missed, you should also try the inimitable *sfogliatella*, buttery puff pastry filled with ricotta flavored with cinnamon and orange peel.
- ✓ Keep your valuables out of sight, and your bag firmly closed. Naples is notorious for pickpockets.

Below: Palazzo Capodimonte, viewed from its beautiful gardens

GETTING THERE
Bergamo is about 30 miles (50 km) northeast of Milan. Orio al Serio Airport, 3 miles (5 km) from Bergamo, is linked to the town by shuttle bus.

GETTING AROUND
Bergamo is a delightful city to explore on foot. Funicular railways connect Bergamo Alta with the Borgo, or lower town.

WEATHER
Spring has arrived in Lombardy, bringing pleasant daytime temperatures of around 61°F (16°C).

ACCOMMODATIONS
Beautiful La Valletta Relais in Bergamo Alta is surrounded by parkland – ideal for a peaceful stay; doubles from US$132; www.lavallettabergamo.it

Entro le Mura B&B is situated in a small, converted medieval palace with a courtyard and a garden; doubles from US$84; www.bedandbreakfast-elm.it

The 4-star Excelsior San Marco is modern and elegant, with a swimming pool and a spa; doubles from US$175; www.hotelsanmarco.com

EATING OUT
Trattoria Sant'Ambroeus, in a romantic corner of the Piazza Vecchia, offers fresh interpretations of Bergamo and Milanese cuisine (dinner from US$62); www.trattoriasantambroeus.it

The historic Vineria Cozzi has a romantic and informal atmosphere and gives a personal touch and unusual flavors to traditional recipes (from US$42); www.vineriacozzi.it

PRICE FOR TWO
US$280 per day including accommodations, meals, and local travel.

FURTHER INFORMATION
http://turismo.provincia.bergamo.it

Cappella Colleoni

Originally designed by Amadeo as a mausoleum for the mercenary leader Bartolomeo Colleoni (c.1395–1475) and his daughter Medea, the Cappella Colleoni was built between 1472 and 1476 on the site of the Santa Maria Maggiore sacristy. The cupola and ornate façade, covered in polychrome marble, make the chapel seem as large as the basilica. Inside is Colleoni's tomb, surmounted by a gilded wooden equestrian statue and embellished with bas-reliefs. Nearby is the sarcophagus of his favorite child, Medea, who died at the age of just 15. The beautiful ceiling frescoes are by Tiepolo.

Above (left to right): Statue on the church of Santa Maria Maggiore; *casoncelli alla bergamasca* (pasta stuffed with spiced, fruity meat); exterior of Santa Maria Maggiore; concert at the Bergamo Jazz Festival

BEAUTY HIGH AND LOW

Bergamo is not one city but two, set amid one of Italy's most fertile plains: the Borgo below, and Bergamo Alta on the hill. While it has plenty of noble palaces, a superb art gallery, and a fine 17th-centry theater, the Borgo presents the image of a modern, dynamic city with busy streets full of shops and restaurants; but Bergamo Alta has the fascination of a medieval town. It is a fortified citadel, its steep, narrow streets enclosed within 16th-century Venetian walls, where centuries of history have become stratified and preserved. To see these two faces for yourself, you need only walk around the city walls, which afford fine views of the Borgo and the plain to one side, and the maze of the upper city's buildings and streets on the other. Bergamo was ruled by Venice from the 15th to the late 18th century, and you are reminded of this as you enter the upper town through its Porta San Giacomo, which bears the Lion of Saint Mark, emblematic of that city.

Bergamo Alta's heart beats strongest in its squares, where medieval austerity gives way to the spacious monumentality of the Renaissance. In Piazza Vecchia, an airy Renaissance ensemble created in the 15th century by the demolition of medieval houses and workshops, you will find the 17th-century Palazzo Nuovo; the Palazzo della Ragione, from the period of the medieval city-republics; and the tower of the *campanone*, or big bell, which strikes 100 times every evening at 10pm (in the past this signified the nightly closing of the gates in the walls). Although the Piazza del Duomo is smaller, other outstanding historic buildings are crowded into it to form what resembles an asymmetrical stage set. Santa Maria Maggiore is a splendid Romanesque church completed in the 14th century. The exquisite stonework and bas-reliefs on its porches are by the same master craftsmen who were responsible for its magnificent octagonal baptistry. Here, too, is the Cappella Colleoni, a chapel built to hold the tomb of the *condottiere* Bartolomeo Colleoni and his daughter Medea, with splendid adornments in multicolored marble.

These two squares were the religious and civil heart of the city, but Bergamo Alta also played a role in the past as a fortified bastion of great military and strategic importance. Traces of this remain in two impressive fortifications: the fortress, a complex with an imposing keep, begun in 1331 and reinforced in subsequent centuries; and the 14th-century citadel, built to protect the western part of the city. The defensive role of these two buildings is long past, but they help retain the particular and fascinating atmosphere of a city still firmly anchored by its noble history.

Main: View of the Piazza Vecchia with the Contarini fountain at its center and the *campanone* behind
Below (left to right): Sunset over Bergamo Alta; *Mystic Marriage of Saint Catherine* by Lorenzo Lotto, in the Galleria dell'Accademia Carrara

CITADEL DIARY

Bergamo Alta, the upper part of the town, is full of lovely Renaissance and medieval buildings. It's a peaceful, almost other-worldly place, especially in contrast to the more modern lower town. With three days at your disposal you can explore both parts of Bergamo at leisure and, if your timing is right, enjoy some great jazz as well.

Three Days Above and Below

DAY 1

Begin your day on the Viale delle Mura and enjoy the lovely views of the city. Then enter Bergamo Alta and stroll through its ancient, twisting alleyways until you reach the Piazza Vecchia, the symbol of the city, and the nearby Piazza del Duomo. After lunch, walk around the exterior of Santa Maria Maggiore to admire the fine apsidal wall, then go inside to see the sumptuous interior. Be sure to see the tomb of Bergamo-born Gaetano Donizetti, the operatic composer. Then go next door to the Cappella Colleoni, a masterpiece of Lombardian Renaissance. Look upward to be dazzled by Tiepolo's marvelous frescoes.

DAY 2

Today, visit Bergamo Alta's two fortifications, the fortress and the citadel. From these you can enjoy fine views as far as the foothills of the Alps. In the afternoon, music-lovers should visit the Museo Donizetti, displaying manuscripts and memorabilia. If you haven't had your fill of views, climb the *campanone* (bell tower) for a truly bird's-eye view of Bergamo and beyond.

DAY 3

Dedicate the day to exploring the Borgo, the lower part of the town. The worldly heart of the city is the Sentierone, a fine avenue of trees lined with shops and boutiques. After some shopping and lunch, spend the afternoon at the Galleria dell'Accademia Carrara, which houses a superb collection of 15th- and 16th-century paintings from the main Italian and foreign schools, including works by Botticelli, Titian, Raphael, Tiepolo, Canaletto, Holbein, Breughel, and Velázquez.

Dos and Don'ts

- ✓ Be sure to try local specialties such as the sweet Moscato di Scanzo wine, said to taste of cinnamon, pepper, and rose. It is delicious with the local almond sponge cakes, topped with a chocolate bird, called *polenta e osei*.
- ✗ Don't miss the small but luxuriant botanic garden in the walls of Bergamo Alta, an oasis that shelters a wide range of plants in a location that commands the finest views of the city.
- ✓ Time your visit to coincide with the prestigious Jazz Festival, which enlivens theaters (including the lovely Teatro Donizetti), churches, galleries, streets, and squares each April.

Below: Venetian Porta San Giacomo, leading to the lower town

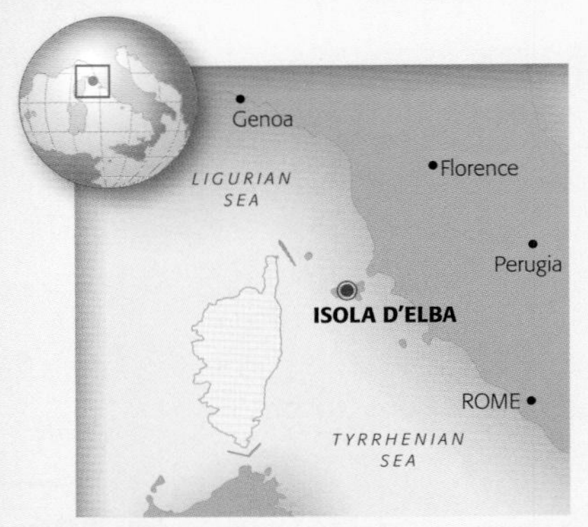

GETTING THERE
Elba lies 6 miles (10 km) off the Tuscan coast. The main embarcation port is Piombino, 53 miles (85 km) from the nearest airport, at Pisa. Ferries take about 1 hour to reach the ports of Portoferraio, Cavo, Rio Marina, and Porto Azzurro.

GETTING AROUND
Elba has an extensive road network; the easiest way to get around is by scooter or mountain bike. There is also a good public transportation system.

WEATHER
Daytime temperatures of around 68°F (20°C) are great for walking or relaxing on the beach, though the sea will still be rather cold.

ACCOMMODATIONS
The Cernia-Isola Botanica, on the cliff-edge at Capo Sant'Andrea, has stunning views, a swimming pool, and a gourmet restaurant; doubles from US$308; www.hotelcernia.it

Le Pitte, at Marina di Campo, has self-catering apartments with terraces in an attractive garden setting from US$70 per day; www.lepitte.it

EATING OUT
You can enjoy creative cooking based on local dishes at Capo Nord, on the seafront at Marciana Marittima; dinner from US$70 (tel. 0565 996983).

In Marina di Campo, the Al Moro restaurant serves classic Mediterranean food (from US$42) and you can dine outside in the lovely garden; www.almoro.it

PRICE FOR TWO
US$210–350 per day to include accommodations, meals, and local travel, including scooter hire.

FURTHER INFORMATION
www.aptelba.it

Birdwatcher's Paradise

The very rare red Corsican seagull, which glides effortlessly over the open sea; the lesser Mediterranean shearwater, which flies brushing the water with its wing tips; the heron, with its distinctive crest and markings; the cormorant, swimming under water in pursuit of a fish; gannets; egrets; falcons; kites – these are just a few of the species that you can expect to see on the islands of the Tuscan archipelago. This is a favored place for over-wintering species, and a resting-point during long migrations, thanks to a perfect natural environment that has remained unspoiled despite the influx of tourism. Be sure to bring your binoculars.

Main: Sunset over the coast of Elba
Above (top to bottom): One of the islands' many species of butterfly; view of the Cala Rossa on Capraia; *caciucco*, a delicious fish soup typical of the region

NAPOLEON'S ENCHANTED ISLE

THE MOST BEAUTIFUL VIEW OF THE ISLAND OF ELBA is to be had while suspended in one of the open "birdcages" of the cable car that ascends Monte Capanne, the granite massif whose peak is the highest point on the island. Spread before you is Elba's jagged coastline, the smaller islands of the Tuscan archipelago rising from the intensely blue sea, and, further still, on a clear day, the island of Corsica. This panorama is just one of the marvels of an island that blends the delights of a beautiful coastline, where white sandy beaches alternate with rocky coves, and an interior whose verdant vegetation is dotted with picturesque villages huddled on rocky cultivated terraces.

Until a few decades ago, Elba was known only as the place to which Napoleon Bonaparte was exiled in 1814. Today its visitors come willingly, but, fortunately, the island has managed to preserve its natural beauty largely as it was during his stay, thanks to the creation of the Parco Nazionale Arcipelago Toscano, the largest protected marine area in Europe.

Left (left to right): Coastline near the port of Cavo; lush vegetation typical of Elba; aerial view of the beautiful village of Capoliveri

This natural heritage is interwoven with fascinating reminders of the island's history. Elba is rich in mines that were worked from the Etruscan era until the 20th century, and some can still be visited. Then there are the fortifications built by the Medici family at Portoferraio in the 16th century; the fortresses of Porto Azzurro; and the villas where Napoleon lived – the Palazzina dei Mulini at Portoferraio and the villa at San Martino, his summer residence.

On Elba, it often feels as if you have stepped back into a Mediterranean landscape of long ago and, in the tiny villages, time seems to have stood still. Capoliveri, nestling among the vineyards on the slopes of Monte Calamita, is just one such place. Set on a peninsula that juts out into the sea at the extreme southeast of Elba, it's a perfect starting point for exploring the splendid beaches on this side of the island. But, more than that, this is a village typical of Elba's magical appeal, with enchanting narrow streets, a pleasant small square, and outstanding views, where you can savor the unchanged, unhurried lifestyle of an island steeped in history, legend, and ancient tradition.

ARCHIPELAGO DIARY

Elba captivates visitors with its crystal-clear sea, beaches and coves, quaint villages, and marvelous wildlife. This remarkable scenery is shared with the six other small islands forming the Tuscan archipelago, one of the most fascinating corners of Italy. Six days will give you plenty of time to discover the best of them.

Six Days of Island Wonders

DAY 1

Spend your first day in Portoferraio, Elba's main harbor, where you can visit the ancient fortifications and the Palazzina dei Mulini, the house occupied by Napoleon during his exile. After lunch, walk to the San Martino villa, his summer residence, and carry on to the Chiesa Della Reverenda Misericordia to see the emperor's death mask.

DAY 2

Today, go to Marciana, on the northern side of Monte Capanne. Take a ride up to the summit of the mountain in a cable car to admire the splendid views. Take a jacket, as it will be chilly at the top. Later, walk to Poggio, where there is a fine view of Marciana and the coast.

DAY 3

Head to Capoliveri, a delightful hill village, from which you can reach the wonderful beach at Naregno and the Cala dell'Innamorata ("Cove of the Loved One"). Then spend the afternoon in pretty, lively Porto Azzurro.

DAY 4

Go by boat to the island of Giglio. In spring the landscape is a mass of wild flowers, which you can enjoy on a walk up to the lovely fortified village of Giglio Castello.

DAY 5

Visit Capraia, the island closest to Corsica, and a nature preserve rich in fauna and flora. Take a boat trip around the island to appreciate its rugged volcanic beauty.

DAY 6

Take one more boat trip, this time to tiny, tranquil Giannutri. The island has a jagged coastline, full of natural caves favored by divers and snokelers. In spring the sight of thousands of seabirds nest-building on the cliffs is spectacular. Dine on freshly caught fish at the island's only restaurant, the Taverna del Gran Duca, on the harbor at Cala Maestra.

Dos and Don'ts

- ✗ Don't expect to visit all the islands in the Tuscan archipelago; the national park authorities in charge of them set specific visitor limits on some, for example Montecristo. For information, visit: www.islepark.it
- ✓ Elba's beauty is best appreciated at walking pace, so bring sensible shoes. Be sure, too, to pack a pair of binoculars and bird and plant identification books – you'll be glad you did.
- ✓ Visit Elba's aquarium, opened in 2000 at Marina di Campo. Dedicated to Mediterranean marine flora and fauna, it is one of the most comprehensive aquariums in the world.

Below: Crystal-clear waters off the coast of Montecristo

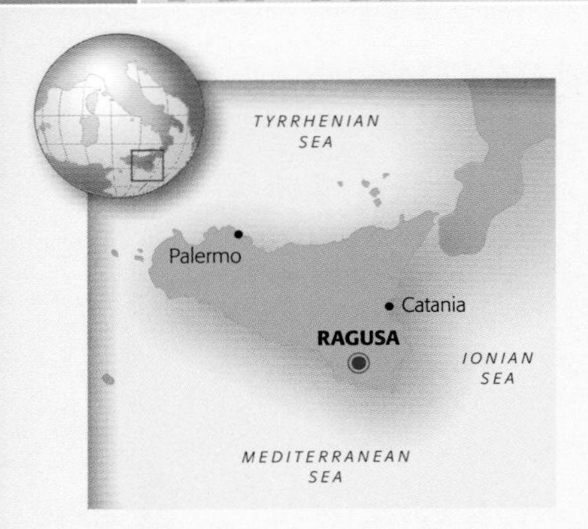

GETTING THERE
Ragusa is in the hinterland of southern Sicily. The nearest airport is Catania's Fontanarossa 52 miles (100 km), where car rental is available. Take the coastal SS114 to Siracusa, then the SS194 to Ragusa.

GETTING AROUND
It is best to get around Ragusa on foot and by public transportation, but a car is essential if you want to visit the surrounding area.

WEATHER
By April, spring is well under way in Sicily, with daytime temperatures around 68°F (20°C).

ACCOMMODATIONS
A stay in the beautiful 12th-century former monastery of Eremo della Giubiliana, just southwest of the town, is a unique experience. The luxurious bedrooms and suites have been converted from monks' cells; doubles from US$320; www.eremodellagiubiliana.it

The Locanda Don Serafino, a charming small hotel in the center of Ragusa, is an elegant combination of ancient and modern; doubles from US$205; www.locandadonserafino.it

EATING OUT
Ristorante Duomo, by the cathedral (dinner from US$98; www.ristoranteduomo.it) and Baglio, in an ancient farmhouse by the city gates (from US$55; www.baglio.it), both serve creative cuisine that reinterprets traditional flavors and ingredients.

PRICE FOR TWO
US$490 per day including accommodations, meals, and car rental.

FURTHER INFORMATION
www.ragusa.net

An Ancient Flavor

Ragusano is one of Sicily's most ancient cheeses, the lengthy and complicated production of which involves great craftsmanship. First, there are several stages of cooking and salting the curds, in which traditional wooden implements are used. Then the curds are pressed into the huge block shape that gives them their local name of *scaluni* ("step"). Finally, the cheeses are matured for six months, during which time they are rubbed with olive oil and vinegar. The result is a cheese of intensely delicious aroma and flavor, best accompanied by a glass of the region's spicy red wine.

A cascade of ornate houses, tumbling down the slopes of two adjacent hills, austere yet radiant in the bright sunshine ... this is Ragusa.

Main: View of Ragusa Ibla
Above: Delicious, tiny tomatoes that are the specialty of Pachino

REBORN FROM THE RUINS

A CASCADE OF ORNATE HOUSES, tumbling down the slopes of two adjacent hills, austere yet radiant in the bright sunshine of Italy's southernmost point, and surrounded by the green countryside of one of Sicily's richest and most fertile regions – this is Ragusa. To the first-time visitor, it appears as if it must have stood here for eternity. Yet this is a town that suffered a tremendous blow, in the form of the disastrous earthquake of 1693. It devastated the entire region and razed Ibla, the ancient inhabited center of Ragusa, to the ground.

As elsewhere in Sicily in the wake of such devastation, most of the population decided to start from scratch and build a new Ragusa on the plateau that overlooked the site of the old town. However, the Ragusan aristocracy refused to abandon their ancestral palaces, choosing instead to rebuild them amid the ruins, retaining the original town plan. And so, the reborn Ragusa grew up as a divided city. Today the two centers, Ragusa Superiore and Ragusa Ibla, coexist, linked

Left (left to right): Crenelated wall of the Castello di Donnafugata; narrow flight of steps known as the "ascent of the clock"; fountain in the Piazza del Duomo

Inset: Façade of the Duomo di San Giorgio

by a rocky ridge. Ibla has maintained the alluring austerity and aloofness of an ancient city that chose to withdraw from trade and bargaining in order to preserve its aura of nobility. Ragusa Superiore, meanwhile, as the "new" quarter is called today, boasts many splendid buildings in the ornate yet dignified Sicilian Baroque style that is the signature architectural feature of the entire region.

Sedate Ibla has some surprises in store, however. One is the Chiesa di Santa Maria dell'Idria, with its cupola clad in sky-blue majolica tiles. It comes dramatically into view at one of the many hairpin bends of Corso Mazzini, the road that links the two parts of the city. Then there are the numerous flights of steps. A functional feature in a city full of ups and downs, they lead you to such delights as the majestic façade of the Chiesa del Purgatorio; the Duomo di San Giorgio, a Baroque masterpiece by Rosario Gagliardi; and the lovely Giardini Iblei, exquisite gardens perched on the edge of the old city, containing the romantic ruins of three medieval churches. Follow the twists and turns of Ragusa's narrow stairways, and who knows what other treasures you may find.

HILLTOP DIARY

Ragusa is well off the beaten tourist trail, making this a gem that you can discover in peace. With four days at your disposal you can adopt the locals' unhurried approach to life as you wander (and climb) the ancient streets, and there's time to go and see some other magnificent sites in the lovely surrounding countryside as well.

Four Days of Exploration

DAY 1

For a breathtaking view of Ragusa Ibla, walk up the hairpin bends of Corso Mazzini. If you have the time and the energy, get there by means of the Salita Commendatore, an alleyway that is all steps and arched passageways, lined with fine churches and remarkable palaces. It is pleasant to wander about with no particular purpose, enjoying the town's romantic corners; but don't miss the Piazza del Duomo, dominated by the spectacular cathedral.

DAY 2

Visit Ragusa Superiore, starting at the archeological museum. As you leave, pause to take in the spectacular view of the valley that divides the town. Stop for lunch in the elegant square that faces the cathedral of San Giovanni Battista. Then wander the streets lined with magnificent Baroque palaces – look out for the gargoyles on the Palazzo Bertini's three windows.

DAY 3

Spend the morning at Castello di Donnafugata, an opulent 19th-century nobleman's residence 11 miles (18 km) southwest of Ragusa. Of its 120 rooms, 20 can be visited, including the Music Room with its trompe l'oeil frescoes. There is a challenging maze in the grounds. At lunchtime, head down to Marina di Ragusa on the coast and spend the afternoon there.

DAY 4

Drive to lovely Modica (passing over the vertigo-inducing Guerriere Bridge), 9 miles (15 km) south of Ragusa. It too was rebuilt after the 1693 earthquake and is another jewel of the Baroque, clinging to the sides of a steep gorge. It's famous for its chocolatiers, who create unusual flavors such as black pepper and chili, and hosts the Chocobarocco Festival each April.

Dos and Don'ts

- ✓ Try the delicious small tomatoes from Pachino. The warm climate and fertile soil here mean that they will be ripe and juicy even at this early point in the year.
- ✗ Don't plan to visit Castello di Donnafugata in the afternoon: it is only open in the morning.
- ✓ Chocoholics should try to time their visit to coincide with Modica's Chocobarocco Festival. For information, visit the website at www.chocobarocco.it

Below: Flower-decked balcony in Ragusa Ibla

MAY

Where to Go: **May**

May is the month when spring really comes to the fore, with an explosion of vegetation and bursts of sunshine that hold the promise of summer. There's an understandable longing to be near the coast, to explore places such as Isola di San Pietro, an island to the southwest of Sardinia, or Finale Ligure, where the most fearless climbers can test their skills by free climbing on rocky cliffs. But inland, Nature also reveals her glories at this time of the year in the pine woods and gently rolling hills of the Maremma – perfect for exploring on horseback with the *butteri* (cowboys), or the flower-filled gardens of Stresa on Lake Maggiore, with its jewel-like islands. And for the young (and not so young), there is the excitement of Gardaland, the biggest theme park in Italy,

FESTIVALS AND CULTURE

GUBBIO Set into the forested slopes of Mount Ingino

BRESCIA
LOMBARDY

An important city since Roman times at the foot of the Alps

Brescia's historic center is packed with churches and palazzi, around the Renaissance Piazza della Loggia and the monastic complex of Santa Giulia.

See pp128–9

CEFALÙ
SICILY

An impressive town of art on the northern coast of Sicily

Cefalù is famous for its cathedral, a jewel of Norman architecture, the art collection in the Museo Mandralisca, and its pretty harbor.

www.cefalu.it

"...a fascinating journey through time which retraces, monument by monument, every stage of a lengthy and fascinating history."

CERVIA
EMILIA-ROMAGNA

A "Wedding to the Sea"

Witness a ritual dating back to 1445, where Cervia renews her marriage vows with the sea. A ring thrown into the water has to be found by the fishermen for good luck.

www.turismo.comunecervia.it

GUBBIO
UMBRIA

A headlong run in a traditional festival without equal

Gubbio is the setting for the Festa dei Ceri, when figures of saints on "candles" are carried through the streets on the shoulders of men.

See pp124–5

SASSARI
SARDINIA

A colorful celebration of folk history and horsemanship

The Cavalcata Sarda is a fiesta where folk in regional dress from all over the island compete on horseback with traditional singing and dancing.

www.goingtosardinia.com

UNFORGETTABLE JOURNEYS

PIENZA A view of the Renaissance town, set in the Tuscan countryside

ST. BERNARD PASS
AOSTA

Over the Alps

For thousands of years, travelers have crossed the St. Bernard Pass into Italy. Monks with their famous dogs still greet travelers at the top.

www.absoluteastronomy.com/topics/Great_St._Bernard_pass

VICENZA
VENETO

See the grace and harmony of a city styled by Palladio

Spend a weekend in a city of art, to admire masterpieces by one of the most brilliant and influential architects of the Renaissance.

See pp118–19

TIVOLI
LAZIO

Relax in an environment fit for a Roman emperor

Tivoli was chosen by Emperor Hadrian as the site for his villa. Later, Renaissance residences were sited here, such as Villa d'Este.

See pp136–7

PIENZA
TUSCANY

Tour a town transformed in the 15th century for Pope Pius II

A humanist and patron of the arts, Pope Pius transformed his native village, according to Renaissance canons, into a historic gem.

See pp134–5

MACOMER
SARDINIA

Climb on the Trenino Verde from Macomer to Bosa Marina

Ride the winding railway all the way to the coast, through Sardinia's glorious and wild countryside, with splendid panoramas.

www.treninoverde.com

NATURAL WONDERS

ISOLA DI SAN PIETRO Cala Guidi, a beach of intoxicating beauty

MAREMMA
TUSCANY

Ride through the wilderness of the marshes of Maremma

The Parco della Maremma, home of the *butteri* (cowboys), gives protection to varied wildlife, with vast pine woods and a sandy coast.

See pp130–31

PROCIDA
CAMPANIA

A secluded and intimate island in the Bay of Naples

A wall of tall, pastel-colored houses, little coves perfect for bathing, panoramic boat tours: these are the joys of Procida.

www.capriweb.com/Procida

LAGO DI PILATO
LE MARCHE

Magical mountain lake

The specatular Lago di Pilato is set between the peaks of Pizzo del Diavolo and Monte Vettore, at 6,368 ft (1,941 m). It is one of the few Apennine lakes of glacial origin.

www.sibillinifoothills.com

ISOLA DI SAN PIETRO
SARDINIA

A little piece of Liguria in the splendid Sardinian sea

A short distance from the coast is an island populated by Ligurians who maintain the traditions and language of their place of origin.

See pp120–21

"San Pietro is particularly lovely in spring. The air is warm, the wild flowers are in bloom, and the sea is beautifully clear."

MONTE SANT'ANGELO
PUGLIA

A dazzling array of flowers

The Gargano Peninsula is an exceptionally rich area for botanists. The Arcadian landscape is punctuated by medieval towns such as Monte Sant'Angelo.

www.anitalyattraction.com

Previous page: The stunning coastline of Isola di San Pietro, Sardinia

overlooking the watery expanse of Lake Garda. The excitement of the season ripples through the country and manifests itself in the spirited spring festivals that enliven so many towns. Each May, Gubbio, for example, uses its medieval center as the setting both for the Festa dei Ceri, an exciting race where teams carry huge "candles" through the town, and for the traditional Palio della Balestra (crossbow tournament). May weekends are also the perfect time to discover the old cities of art: Brescia, with its Lombard heart; Padua, an important university city; Vicenza, with its Palladian masterpieces; Catania, at the foot of Mount Etna; Pienza, the Renaissance town built by Pope Pius II, and Tivoli, where the Roman Emperor Hadrian built the villa of his dreams.

LUXURY AND ROMANCE

CATANIA The volcanic stone statue of an elephant, emblem of the city

STRESA
PIEDMONT

Islands set like jewels into the waters of an enchanted lake

Stroll the lakeside promenade at Stresa, past elegant hotels and flower-filled gardens, with unforgettable views of the magical Borromean Islands.

See pp132–3

LEVICO TERME
TRENTINO-ALTO ADIGE

A weekend at a spa in the heart of Valsugana

Amid lakes, mountains, and wonderful scenery, Levico has a large thermal spa rich in exotic plants.

www.visitvalsugana.net

ALGHERO
SARDINIA

A town with a Catalan flavor close to beaches and caves

The heart of Alghero is a fascinating maze of winding alleys. Enjoy trips to the natural marvels of Capo Caccia and the Grotte di Nettuno.

www.algherosardinia.net

MONTAGNANA
VENETO

The most beautiful and complete medieval city walls in Europe

Montagnana is a step into the Middle Ages, with battlemented walls interrupted by the great Rocca degli Alberi and the Castello di San Zeno.

www.veneto-net.com

CATANIA
SICILY

The "City of the Elephant," built out of lava

Rebuilt to a modern urban plan in dark volcanic stone after the earthquake of 1693, Catania has a unique Baroque style.

See pp116–7

ACTIVE ADVENTURES

FINALE LIGURE Chiesa di San Lorenzo set high on a cliff

GROTTE DI STIFFE
ABRUZZO

The thrills of caving

Below a traditional-looking village on the slopes of a mountain, an underground river has carved out marvelous cave systems, with waterfalls and enchanting lakes.

www.abruzzoverdeblu.it

CASCATE DELLE MARMORE
UMBRIA

Whitewater delights in Umbria

Beneath the famous Cascate delle Marmore waterfalls, you can begin an adventure canoeing down the rapids of the River Nera.

www.raftingmarmore.com

SCOPELLO
PIEDMONT

For lovers of river sports

Valsesia is a top location for trying river sports such as kayaking, rafting, or canyoning, with a great many schools and specialist holiday resorts.

www.atlvalsesiavercelli.it

FINALE LIGURE
LIGURIA

Perfect cliffs for climbing on the glorious Ligurian coast

A delightful seaside town with a medieval core, Finale challenges climbers with its steep cliffs – and relaxes them on its sandy beaches

See pp126–7

SENIGALLIA
LE MARCHE

Kitesurfing and windsurfing tricks on the beach

An old mercantile port on the Adriatic coast, Senigallia is today a bathing resort and home to several windsurfing and kitesurfing schools.

www.kitesenigallia.com

FAMILY GETAWAYS

PADUA The splendid arcades and fountain of Piazza delle Erbe

"Along the way you are catapulted into spectacular scenes of swashbuckling fun, with fierce pirates, spooky shipwrecks, and even sea monsters."

CAPALBIO
TUSCANY

Sculptures overlooking the sea

Capalbio is a stunning village overlooking the Mediterranean. On a nearby hill, the extraordinary "Tarot Garden" features bizarre and colorful sculptures of Zodiac signs.

www.initaly.com/regions/kids/kid1.htm

GARDALAND
VENETO

Italy's largest theme park

A massive collection of exciting and innovative attractions that are enjoyed by three million visitors a year: Gardaland is the kingdom of entertainment for all ages.

See pp114–15

SANT'ALESSIO
LOMBARDY

A wild countryside walk a short step from sophisticated Milan

Stay in the metropolis of Milan, but head out to the wildlife preserve of Sant'Alessio to observe birds of prey, storks, and herons in the wild.

www.aboutmilan.com

CAMOGLI
LIGURIA

Be amazed by the enormous frying pan of Camogli

On the second Sunday in May, this Ligurian village hosts a fun Fish Festival, when a giant frying pan is used to cook fish for all.

www.prolococamogli.it

PADUA
VENETO

An elegant, lively city

An old university city, Padua is home to splendid works of medieval art such as the sublime frescoes by Giotto in the Cappella degli Scrovegni.

See pp122–3

GETTING THERE
Gardaland is in the Veneto, at Castelnuovo del Garda. The airports of Verona and Brescia are both 7 miles (12 km) away, and the park is just off the A4 freeway. From Peschiera station, a free shuttle bus runs to the park.

GETTING AROUND
In the park you will be on foot. Lake Garda itself is a pleasure to get around by ferry.

WEATHER
May sees plenty of warm sunshine and average daytime temperatures of 72°F (22°C).

ACCOMMODATIONS
Gardaland Hotel Resort is adjacent to the park; a free shuttle bus runs between the two. It has vast gardens with its own water park; family rooms for four from US$177; www.gardalandhotel.it

At Peschiera del Garda, the Hotel Bella Italia has a wide variety of family-friendly facilities, including swimming pools, entertainment, a play area, and babysitting services; rooms from US$82 per person, discounts for children; www.hotel-bellaitalia.it

EATING OUT
There are plenty of places to eat within the park (from US$14), ranging from kiosks and cafés to pizza houses and restaurants. Around the lake are many restaurants with waterside terraces where you can sample the delicious lake trout.

PRICE FOR A FAMILY OF FOUR
US$480 per day including accommodations, meals, admission to Gardaland, and local travel.

FURTHER INFORMATION
www.gardaland.it

Canevaworld

If one theme park is not enough for you (or, more likely, your kids), don't worry, there's another one just a few minutes up the lake. Would you like to dive into the waters of a Caribbean lagoon; enter the glamorous world of Hollywood movies, taking part in shows with cinema sets from famous films; or cheer on jousting knights while you feast at a medieval tournament? There is only one place in Italy where you can do all of these things, and that's Canevaworld, the entertainment park at Lazise. Established in the 1980s, the park's 121,000 sq yards (100,000 sq m) are full of attractions for all tastes, ages, and interests.

Above (left to right): Entrance to Fantasy Kingdom in Gardaland; Sirmione's lovely Roman Grotte di Catullo; impressive fortifications at Peschiera del Garda

LAKESIDE WONDERLAND

SEVEN HUNDRED THOUSAND SQUARE YARDS OF THRILLS and entertainment are not an everyday find. So, as soon as the spring weather starts showing the first signs of summer warmth, the young and the young-at-heart head for an otherwise quiet corner of the Veneto to revel in the magic of Gardaland, Italy's largest amusement park, which takes its name from the beautiful Lake Garda on which it stands.

Established in 1975, and regularly updated since then, Gardaland offers every kind of attraction for the entertainment of the nearly three million visitors it welcomes annually (making it the fifth most visited theme park in the world). A classic example of what's available is I Corsari ("The Buccaneers"), a "dark ride" opened to the public in 1992 (at least 30 companies were involved in its construction over the course of two years) which, following a long series of improvements, is still the principal attraction at Gardaland today, and one of the most impressive of its kind in Europe. The ride starts in the hold of a Spanish galleon and continues on boats that travel along an underground river. Along the way you are catapulted into spectacular scenes of swashbuckling fun, with fierce pirates, spooky shipwrecks, and even sea monsters.

There is plenty to admire at Gardaland, not only the magnificence and audacity of the rides, but also the careful attention paid to environmental concerns and care for the landscape of this lovely area on the shores of Lake Garda. Within these constraints the park has built many facilities unique to this part of the world, such as the first theme hotel to open in Italy and the largest 4-D cinema in Europe. There are endless opportunities to shed pent-up adrenaline – by shooting the rapids in a rubber dinghy; trying to escape from an earthquake-shaken Atlantis; taking part in an expedition to Siberia; or confronting the Blue Tornado, an inverted roller coaster with an exhilarating (some say terrifying) spiral race to the finish. Like so much at Gardaland, it is world class.

You are catapulted into spectacular scenes of swashbuckling fun, with fierce pirates, spooky shipwrecks, and even sea monsters.

Main: Blue Tornado roller coaster in action
Inset: Interior of the Gardaland theater
Below (left to right): Riding the Jungle Rapids; Prezzemolo, Gardaland's mascot, welcoming visitors on board the park train

GARDA DIARY

Gardaland is an Italian phenomemon, with myriad attractions suitable for all ages. But a visit here also offers the perfect opportunity to get to know this part of the Lake Garda shore, one of Italy's most enchanting places. A three-day break is an ideal introduction to the region – just as long as you are able to tear the kids away from the park.

Three Magical Days

DAY 1

Spend the whole day in Gardaland. Among its many attractions are Magic Mountain, an unforgettably thrilling experience for fans of roller coasters; Jungle Rapids, a ride down a river in full spate in a rubber dinghy; Space Vertigo, a plunge into the void from a 130-ft (40-m) tower; the Delfinario, one of the biggest dolphinariums in Italy; Ramses: The Awakening, an epic laser sword battle against aliens, set in the temple of Abu Simbel; and Fantasy Kingdom, a fairyland for young children.

DAY 2

For a complete change of pace, visit lovely Peschiera del Garda. The town stands where the River Mincio flows into the lake, and is surrounded by canals. It once had an important strategic role, hence its impressive 15th-century pentagonal fortress and the network of smaller forts around it.

DAY 3

Following the shore of Lake Garda west, or going by ferry from Pescheria, you will arrive at Sirmione, one of the most enchanting of the lakeside towns and known as "the Pearl of Garda." It extends along a slim spit of land that juts out into the lake, offering sublime views. At the entrance to the town is the magnificent 13th-century Rocca Scagliera fortress, while at the end of the peninsula is the Grotte di Catullo, the ruins of a great Roman villa reputely owned by the poet Catullus, from which there is a stunning panorama. Sirmione is also a spa town, so treat yourself to a mud bath or a massage while the children tuck into Garda's famed *gelati* (ice creams).

Dos and Don'ts

- ✓ Always carry drinking water with you: even though there are plenty of cafés and kiosks at Gardaland, they are not always close at hand and can get very crowded. Save your precious time for the entertainment and rides.
- ✗ Don't visit Gardaland on the weekend: you are likely to find very long lines for the most popular rides.
- ✓ Allow yourself a relaxing session at the Sirmione spa, which benefits from hot springs discovered in the 19th century.
- ✓ Go for a boat trip on Lake Garda; there are various options available in Sirmione harbor, from lake ferries to private boats for rent. Only from the water can you glimpse the lakeside villas of millionaires and celebrities.

Below: Beautiful harbor and castle at Sirmione

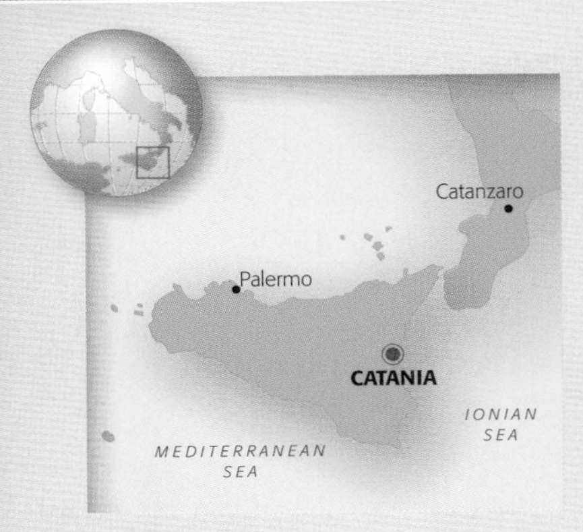

GETTING THERE
Catania lies on the eastern coast of Sicily, a 20-minute bus ride from its Fontanarossa airport.

GETTING AROUND
The city is easy to get around on foot, while buses run to Acireale.

WEATHER
May is perfect for visiting the city, with clear, sunny days and temperatures averaging 75°F (24°C).

ACCOMMODATIONS
On the seafront, surrounded by a large park, is the 5-star luxury Romano Palace; doubles from US$236; www.romano-palace.com

In the heart of the historic center, the Royal Hotel Catania is an 18th-century palazzo, luxuriously furnished and with a health club; doubles from US$162; www.hotelroyalcatania.it

Overlooking the sea in Acireale, the Santa Tecla Palace has a private beach, swimming pool, and spa; doubles from US$198; www.hotelsantatecla.it

EATING OUT
Osteria Antica Marina is close to the fish market of Sant'Agata from which it sources the finest seafood (dinner from US$48). Try *alga mauro* (red algae), which the locals dress with salt and lemon, or pasta with sea urchins; www.anticamarina.it

For a romantic dinner, Il Cuciniere serves traditional cuisine with a modern twist in elegant, intimate surroundings (from US$48); www.katanepalace.it

PRICE FOR TWO
US$360 per day for accommodations, meals, and local travel.

FURTHER INFORMATION
www.apt-catania.com

Every Day is Market Day

Catania's lively market presents a picturesque spectacle each day of the week, its stalls piled high with fish, meat, cheeses, boxes of vegetables, and fruit, all set out in the crowded alleyways close to the cathedral. In fact, it is not a single market but two: the superb fish market (A Piscaria) and a general produce market, which lie adjacent to one another. Whatever you want, you are sure to find it here, amid this riot of color, appetizing aromas, and animated conversation. Even if you're not buying, a stroll around the market is a very entertaining and enjoyable part of Catanian life.

Main: Elephant statue on the Fontana dell'Elephante in Piazza del Duomo

CITY OF LAVA

LYING BETWEEN THE IONIAN SEA AND THE SLOPES OF MOUNT ETNA, Catania's history is inextricably woven in with that of the volcano that overlooks the town. Not least, Etna is responsible for the somber color of the city's buildings, having supplied the dark volcanic rock from which they are built. Catania's story is a painful one, interrupted by eruptions and earthquakes, in common with many other towns in eastern Sicily.

After an eruption in 1669, the lava flow stretched as far as the coast and, although the town was spared, the surrounding countryside was devastated. An appalling famine ensued, bringing people in great numbers from the country to the town. In 1693, an earthquake razed Catania to the ground killing 20,000 people, according to estimates of the time. Reconstruction began at once, incorporating a radical overhaul of the city's layout, with broad streets and spacious squares entirely in Baroque style, albeit an austere and distinctive Baroque because of the dark volcanic stone

Left (left to right): Etna gazing down on the domes of Catania's Duomo; fertile green fields outside the city; *pasta alla Norma*, a traditional dish of Catania; detail of the Fontana dell'Amenano in Piazza del Duomo

Below (top to bottom): Stunning interior of Teatro Bellini; strange landscape of the slopes of Etna

used. The Piazza del Duomo was built at the heart of the new city, surrounded by fine palazzos and perhaps the best expression of Catania Baroque. Still elegant today, at its center stands the Fontana dell'Elephante and in the middle of the fountain is the Roman-era elephant that is the symbol of the city. Carved from a single block of lava, it carries on its back an Egyptian obelisk topped by a globe.

Before the fountain stands the cathedral of Sant'Agata, dedicated to the city's patron saint. Built in the 12th century, it was extensively rebuilt after the earthquake, with a new façade by the Baroque master Vaccarini. Castello Ursino, on the other hand, a powerful fortress built around 1250 for Frederick II, is still medieval in appearance. It originally stood on a promontory but, in the eruption of 1669, the lava flow reached it, filling in the moat and distancing it from the water. The Roman amphitheater, which held 16,000 spectators, dates from the 2nd century AD.

Thus, the many layers of Catania's history unfurl slowly before your eyes, like the petals of a dark rose, layer upon layer, epoch after epoch, to reveal the city as a quintessence of Sicilian history.

CATANIAN DIARY

Despite the ravages of earthquakes and eruptions, Catania retains many traces of its three millenia of history. While its striking dark Baroque dominates every vista, there is plenty more to be discovered here. Four days allows plenty of time to do that, as well as to travel along the Ionian coast for a visit to another masterpiece of the Baroque.

Four Baroque Days

DAY 1

Start your visit in Piazza del Duomo, with its Catania Baroque buildings, characterized by the contrast of dark volcanic stone and pale limestone. From here, pass through Porta Uzeda and head to Castello Ursino, to admire its massive size and visit the Catania civic museum within. Later, stroll along Via Etnea, an elegant street lined with lovely Baroque palazzi that leads to the foot of Etna and to the ruins of the amphitheater, one of the largest built in Roman times.

DAY 2

Today, go in search of places associated with Catania's most famous "sons": Bellini, Greco, and Verga. The musician Vincenzo Bellini died at the age of 34 in 1835. The Teatro Bellini, one of the largest theaters in Europe, is dedicated to him, and his birthplace is now a charming museum in his honor. In Piazza Bellini is a museum of the works of the 20th-century artist Emilio Greco. The house where the writer Giovanni Verga lived and died, in 1922, is also a museum displaying his belongings.

DAY 3

Spend the morning browsing the market, then, after lunch, take a stroll down Via dei Crociferi, flanked by fine examples of Catania Baroque, such as the arch of San Benedetto (completed in the course of a single night, according to legend) and the church of the same name, at the top of a long flight of steps. Here, too, is the church of San Giuliano, with a lovely convex façade.

DAY 4

Take a bus to Acireale, a jewel of Sicilian Baroque on the coast 10 miles (16 km) north of Catania. The Duomo, which dates from the end of the 16th century, has two bell towers covered in multicolored tiles.

Dos and Don'ts

- ✓ Watch a traditional Sicilian puppet show at Acireale's Teatro Stabile dell'Opera dei Pupi.
- ✓ Try *pasta alla Norma*, spaghetti with a sauce made with tomato, eggplants, ricotta, and basil, and named after the opera by Bellini.
- ✗ Be wary of young men zooming around on small motorbikes, not only when crossing the road but also when simply walking along. This is a notorious form of transportation for thieves, who can grab your bag and make a high-speed getaway.

Below: Ornate caryatids on the façade of Palazzo Biscari

GETTING THERE
Vicenza is linked by bus and train to Venice's Marco Polo Airport (37 miles/60 km) and Verona's Valerio Catullo Airport (27 miles/44 km). The town is just off the A4 freeway which links Turin, Milan, Venice, and Trieste.

GETTING AROUND
Vicenza is pleasant to explore on foot or by bicycle (there are plenty of bike rental shops). A bus service runs from the train station to La Rotonda.

WEATHER
A daytime temperature of 73°F (23°C) and many sunny days mean that May is an ideal time to visit.

ACCOMMODATIONS
The hotel Campo Marzio, in the historic center, is charming and cozy; doubles from US$130 (US$323 during trade fairs); www.hotelcampomarzio.it

Hotel Villa Michelangelo is an elegant 18th-century residence set in parkland 3 miles (5 km) to the south of the city center; doubles from US$330; www.hotelvillamichelangelo.com

EATING OUT
Vicenza's specialty is *baccalà* (dried salt cod with oil and garlic), delicious with polenta. This, and other delicacies, can be sampled at Agli Schioppi, a friendly restaurant in the city center (dinner from US$28); www.ristoranteaglischioppi.com

For dining with breathtaking views over the city, head to Da Biasio in the hills just south of town, where a fresh approach is taken to traditional dishes (from US$62); www.ristorantedabiasio.it

PRICE FOR TWO
US$425 per day to include accommodations, meals, local travel, and admissions.

FURTHER INFORMATION
www.vicenza.com

Vicenza's Gilded History

The tradition of working gold in Vicenza has ancient origins. Already a flourishing trade in the 14th century, it was practiced by highly skilled craftsmen who passed on their expertise from father to son. Objects of great beauty and elegance were made. The mastery of Vicenza goldsmiths was such that their fame quickly spread throughout Italy, and their work became an increasingly important element in the city's economy. Today Vicenza hosts one of the premier jewelry trade fairs, attracting exhibitors from all over the world.

A CITY GRACED BY GENIUS

HARMONIOUS AND ELEGANT, THE OLD CENTER OF VICENZA has been shaped by history: the street layout is Roman, its long Corso Palladio marking the classic *Decumanus Maximus* (the main east–west street), while the layout of its squares is medieval. These are now lined with elegant 16th-century palazzi, many of which reveal the hand of Andrea Palladio (1508–80), one of the greatest and most innovative architects of his time. His Classical style is unmistakable, and is immediately apparent in the basilica, the former Palazzo della Ragione. This was the first major work in which Palladio was involved in the city. Commissioned to look at ways of supporting the building, Palladio enclosed the old palazzo within a two-tier loggia of white stone, making it feel suddenly light and airy. The basilica dominates the civil and commercial center of Vicenza, the lively Piazza dei Signori, where another Palladian building, the Loggia del Capitaniato also stands.

Main: Interior of a Palladian masterpiece, the spectacular Teatro Olimpico

Above: Statue of Andrea Palladio in the old center of Vicenza, the work of Vincenzo Gajassi

Below: Rustic dishes of *baccalà alla vicentina* (dried cod cooked with milk, flour, and cheese)

Far right (top to bottom): Detail of a fresco by Giambattista and Giandomenico Tiepolo at Villa Valmarana ai Nani; Classical façade of Villa La Rotonda; aerial view of the city of Vicenza with its majestic basilica

Another civic masterpiece is the Teatro Olimpico. Built for the most part of wood and stucco painted to resemble marble, and completed after the architect's death by his pupil Vincenzo Scamozzi, the theater was built in the grounds of Castel San Pietro. Its structure echoes that of ancient theaters, with a semicircular, stepped auditorium and a *trompe l'oeil* ceiling, painted to give the impression of a roof open to the sky. The stage set, the only one to survive from the Renaissance, was designed by Scamozzi for the opening night in March 1584, and represents Thebes in accordance with Renaissance concepts of the ideal city.

Palladio also worked for noble Vicentine families, for whom he designed gems such as Palazzo Chiericati, its harmonious façade adorned with great loggias. La Rotonda, perched on a hilltop south of the city, was built as a residence for Count Paolo Almerico and is now regarded as Palladio's masterwork. It is designed to a perfectly symmetrical square plan, set within an imagined circle, with four entrances leading to a splendid central room crowned with a cupola. This miracle of harmony is celebrated as one of the most beautiful buildings of all time.

PALLADIAN DIARY

Located at the heart of the Venetian plain, at the foot of the Monti Berici, Vicenza is known as the "City of Palladio." The celebrated Renaissance architect lived and worked here and the city contains many examples of his genius. You can see the very best of them in just a short visit.

Two Days of Masterworks

DAY 1

Begin your visit to the city in Piazza dei Signori and admire the splendid porticoes of the basilica and the nearby Loggia del Capitaniato. The square is at the heart of Vicentine life, always lively and the site of a bustling market each Thursday. Stop for a coffee and watch the world go by. Next, make your way to Palazzo Valmarana and Palazzo Chiericati, passing by Casa Pigafetta, the former home of a Vicentine navigator who accompanied Magellan on his voyage around the world in 1519, and who was one of the few men on the expedition to return. After lunch, spend the afternoon at the Teatro Olimpico, one of the jewels of the city. The nearby church of Santa Corona is worth a visit too, for its frescoes by Veneto artists.

DAY 2

Take the bus out to La Rotonda, the country villa regarded as Palladio's consummate masterpiece, to admire its perfect structure, rich decoration, and the 17th- and 18th-century furnishings. A short walk away is Villa Valmarana, built in the 17th century. It is also known as the Villa ai Nani because of the statues of dwarves *(nani)* on the walls surrounding the house. The villa contains a lovely series of frescoes by Giambattista Tiepolo and his son. The nearby Da Vittorio restaurant serves what many consider to be the best pizzas in town.

Dos and Don'ts

- ✓ Make use of the inexpensive Biglietto Unico pass when visiting Vicenza. Valid for three days from first time of use, it gives you access to all the main museums in the city, as well as to the Teatro Olimpico (excluding performances).
- ✓ Visit the church of Santa Corona to see the tomb of Luigi da Porto, author of the tale *Giulietta e Romeo*, which inspired Shakespeare to write his own version, *Romeo and Juliet*.
- ✗ Don't overdo it with the *grappa*. This locally distilled spirit is perfumed and exquisite, but is extremely strong.
- ✓ Buy something made of gold: the goldsmiths of Vicenza are famous throughout the world, and each individual shop sells its own unique designs.

Below: Piazza dei Signori, the historic heart of Vicenza

GETTING THERE
San Pietro lies off the southwest coast of Sardinia. From Cagliari airport, Isla Sant'Antioco (linked to the mainland by a causeway) is 38 miles (60 km) by bus. From here it is a 30–40 minute ferry trip to Carloforte, San Pietro's only town.

GETTING AROUND
The best way of getting around the island is on two wheels. Bike and scooter rental is available.

WEATHER
May on San Pietro is warm but not muggy, with clear fresh days, fine for walking or time on the beach, though the sea will still be fairly cold.

ACCOMMODATIONS
On the seafront at Carloforte, Hotel Hieracon is a fine palazzo in Art Deco style; doubles from US$124; http://nuke.hotelhieracon.com

The friendly B&B Il Ghiro is a late 18th-century building with two rooms; doubles from US$75; www.carlofortebedandbreakfast.it

For those in search of peaceful surroundings, the Poecylia resort is ideal; doubles from US$247; www.poecyliaresort.it

EATING OUT
At Da Nicolo you can sample Sardinian cooking at the highest level (dinner from US$62–70); www.luigipomata.com

Authentic Carloforte cuisine can be found at Al Tonno di Corsa, where *tonno* (tuna) takes pride of place (from US$48–55); www.tonnodicorsa.it

PRICE FOR TWO
US$250–410 per day, including accommodations, meals, local travel, and scooter hire.

FURTHER INFORMATION
www.isoladisanpietro.eu

Ligurian–Maghreb Cuisine

San Pietro's unusual history could not fail to produce a unique gastronomic tradition: a fusion of Ligurian and North African cuisine, making use of excellent local produce. The results are outstanding: from *cashcà*, a variation on vegetable couscous, to *cassolla*, a rich fish and seafood broth; from *farinata*, a type of chick-pea flour pizza bread, to *cappunnadda*, thin, dried flatbread that is softened with water and dressed with oil and tomato, at one time an everyday dish for the island's sailors. Superb tuna dishes also feature strongly, thanks to San Pietro's traditional tuna traps.

AN ISLAND LOST IN TIME

THE LOVELY LITTLE ISOLA DI SAN PIETRO rises rockily from the azure waters off the coast of Sardinia. Of volcanic origin, the island extends over 20 sq miles (50 sq km), with 12 miles (18 km) of delightful coastline, wild and rocky to the north and west, where jagged cliffs falls dramatically into the sea, with dramatic overhangs and gulleys, but gentler towards the south, with sandy coves and lovely beaches.

The island is home to around 6,500 inhabitants, most of whom live in the town of Carloforte. These people are not Sards but come originally from Liguria, and theirs is a remarkable story. Their ancestors departed in 1542 from Pegli, not far from Genoa, bound for the island of Tabarka, off the Tunisian coast, where the sea was rich in coral from which they could make a living. Over time, however, Tabarka's coral stocks were depleted, and disagreements with the local populace became

Main: The idyllic bay of Cala Guidi near Carloforte

Above: Caletta, one of the most beautiful stretches of coastline on San Pietro

Below: Sunset over the lighthouse on Isla Sant'Antioco

increasingly bitter. So, nearly 200 years after their arrival in North Africa, a significant number of Tabarkans chose to accept the invitation of Charles Emmanuel III, king of Sardinia at the time, to colonize the uninhabited island of San Pietro. Their links to Liguria remained strong, however, and in 2004 Carloforte became an honorary municipality of the province of Genoa. These long-standing ties also permeate the local dialect – they still speak a form of Ligurian here – and the architecture, with tall pastel-colored, balconied houses looking on to narrow streets that closely resemble the *carrugi*, or alleyways, of Genoa.

Today, little San Pietro lures thousands of tourists each year, drawn to its crystal clear seas and its beautiful, varied coastline. Nor is the interior of the island any less appealing – large areas are still covered in scented Mediterranean maquis, with wide stands of Aleppo pine and holm oak. This harmony of land and sea and fusion of ancient and diverse cultures, make the Isola di San Pietro a place of genuine fascination and timeless charm.

ISLAND IDYLL DIARY

San Pietro is particularly lovely in spring. The air is warm, the wild flowers are in bloom, and the sea is beautifully clear. The summer visitors have yet to arrive, and you will have the place almost to yourself when you head off to explore. After four days of walks, boat trips, nature, history, and good food, you'll return home totally refreshed.

Four Tranquil Days

DAY 1

Spend your first day on Sant'Antioco, the largest island of the Sulcis archipelago. Inhabited since Phoenician times, there are still many traces of the past here, especially in the upper part of the eponymous main town on the island: the acropolis, the Punic necropolis, the Roman amphitheater, and the Phoenician–Punic *tophet*, which was both a place of worship and a burial site for children. Just before sunset, take the ferry over to San Pietro.

DAY 2

Any visit to Isola di San Pietro has to start in Carloforte, the island's only town. Explore the narrow streets and steps leading up from the sea front, and admire the old 19th-century palazzi. Visit the oratory of the Chiesa della Madonna dello Schiavo, where a rare, revered, and reputedly miraculous black Madonna is kept.

DAY 3

A boat tour around the island is a must. There are various options – you could be dropped off at the beach of your choice and then collected later, or simply scout out the best one to return to by bike or moped later in the day.

DAY 4

Walk out to the salt pans just a short distance from the town. They fell into disuse many years ago and, as a result, have become a habitat for numerous species of wading bird, such as avocets, black-winged stilts, egrets, and flamingoes. After lunch, head out westward to the Lipu oasis, in an area of great interest to naturalists, where Eleonora's and peregrine falcons nest.

Dos and Don'ts

- ✓ Visit Italy's westernmost lighthouse, at Capo Sandalo on Isola di San Pietro. It dates from 1864 and is still an extremely important point of reference for sailors.
- ✓ Try to time your visit to coincide with the annual tuna festival in late May, when chefs from around the world gather to compete in cooking the best tuna dish.
- ✗ Don't pick any plants or flowers, and don't leave any garbage on the paths or on the beach: this remarkably unspoiled landscape deserves your respect.
- ✓ Visit the tuna fishing nets. The best ones are at Punta around 4 miles (6 km) from Carloforte. However, if you are squeamish, avoid them during the *mattanza*, the annual major kill.

Below: View of San Pietro's salt pans

GETTING THERE
Padua is in the heart of the Veneto. The nearest airport is at Venice, with bus links to Padua, a journey of under an hour.

GETTING AROUND
The historic center of Padua is easily explored on foot. City Sightseeing runs bus tours of the town.

WEATHER
Although the Veneto is one of Italy's rainiest regions, May brings plenty of sunny days, with temperatures reaching 73°F (23°C).

ACCOMMODATIONS
The Hotel Grand Italia, an Art Deco building in a good position near the historic center, has large rooms and suites sleeping 3–4 from US$227; www.hotelgranditalia.it

Giardino Nascosto is a quiet, elegant B&B in the historic center. The upper room is arranged on two levels, with a double bed on a platform and twin beds below, from US$150; www.ilgiardinonascosto.it

EATING OUT
Caffè Pedrocchi is a Padua institution, where students and intellectuals have been dining since 1831 (dinner from US$35); www.caffepedrocchi.it

Boccadoro is a family-run restaurant serving regional cuisine (from US$62); www.boccadoro.it

PRICE FOR A FAMILY OF FOUR
US$330 per day for accommodations, meals, and a PadovaCard for local transportation and admissions.

FURTHER INFORMATION
www.turismopadova.it

City of Fairy Tales

Shows, workshops, games, entertainment – all these and more are part of Città in Fiaba, a traveling event for kids, which transforms Padua and other nearby towns into magical places each spring. It begins in Padua and then goes on the road, returning to Padua for the grand finale at the end of May. In June and July it resumes with an evening version: Città in Fiaba al Chiaro di Luna ("city of fairy tales by moonlight"). It's a great chance for children to invent stories, dress up, make things, and generally have fun in the company of other kids of all ages, from a wide range of countries as well as Italy.

Above (left to right): Detail of Mantegna's *Martyrdom of St. Christopher*; dish of *risi e bisi* (rice and peas), a specialty of the Veneto; view over Piazza dei Signori to Palazzo del Capitano; loggia of Palazzo della Ragione on Piazza delle Erbe
Main: Sumptuous interior of the Cappella degli Scrovegni

A TREASURE HOUSE OF ART

An ancient university town, Padua is rich in culture and history and a favored destination for art-lovers, but it is also a city that is cheerful, busy, and full of life, in which students, academics, pilgrims, and tourists rub shoulders happily at market stalls and sidewalk café tables.

We have Reginaldo degli Scrovegni (placed by Dante in the Seventh Circle of Hell in his *Divine Comedy*) to thank for the fact that we can admire here one of the most perfect expressions of Western art: the frescoes by Giotto in the Cappella degli Scrovegni, commissioned in 1303 by Scrovegni's son Enrico, to make amends for the misdeeds of his father. It is the most complete surviving cycle by the great artist, a series of scenes from the life of Christ whose realism and narrative power are a great introduction for young people to the marvels of Italian Renaissance painting. It's miraculous that it escaped the destruction wrought by World War II. Other major monuments in Padua were not so lucky. The Chiesa degli Eremitani is one example. Bombed to rubble in 1944, the church has been magnificently restored, but many frescoes from a 15th-century cycle by Mantegna in the Cappella Ovetari, of the lives of St. Christopher and St. Jacob, were lost. Just two scenes survived: the *Martyrdom* and the *Assumption of St. Christopher*, while the *Martyrdom of St. James* was reconstructed from tiny fragments.

Padua's piazzas are lively places, animated by the comings and goings of students, crowded with market stalls, and lined with elegant shops.

Despite the devastations of war, the medieval center of Padua is remarkably intact. At its heart is a group of squares, including Piazza dei Signori, dominated by the clock tower of Palazzo del Capitanio, and Piazza delle Erbe, graced by the elegant loggia of the Palazzo della Ragione. Nearby are the Duomo and baptistry, home to one of the most complete medieval fresco cycles in Italy, by Menabuoi. Padua's piazzas are lively places, animated by the constant comings and goings of students, crowded with traditional market stalls, and lined with elegant shops, making the city one of the most vibrant in Italy.

Inset: Anatomical theater at the University of Padua
Below (left to right): Façade of Palazzo della Ragione from Piazza delle Erbe; *The Kiss of Judas*, part of the Cappella degli Scrovegni frescoes

FRESCO DIARY

First and foremost you will want to see the art treasures that Padua has to offer, but there's so much more to enjoy here as well. Luckily the historic center is so compact that, over three days, you can intersperse the cultural thrills with the pleasures of the town's student café-culture, and spend time browsing market stalls and chic boutiques.

Three Cultural Days

DAY 1

A visit to the Cappella degli Scrovegni is the top priority today, to see Giotto's wonderful frescoes, followed by the nearby Chiesa degli Eremitani, with its paintings by Mantegna. Pause for a picnic lunch in its lovely grounds, then throw yourself into the fun of the bustling market, pausing to admire Palazzo della Ragione (have a look at the interior, where there are more marvelous frescoes). End the day with an apéritif at Caffè Pedrocchi, a historic 19th-century café that resembles a Classical temple.

DAY 2

Visit Palazzo del Bò, the oldest part of the university. Older children will be fascinated by the dais on which Galileo gave lectures in 1592, and the Anatomical Theater, dating from 1594, the first of its kind in Europe. Then head for Piazza Duomo, where the cathedral and Romanesque baptistry stand. The latter is decorated with a fine 14th-century fresco cycle by Giusto de' Menabuoi.

DAY 3

Visit the great Chiesa di Sant'Antonio, an important destination for pilgrims. Begun in 1232 to house the remains of the saint, it reflects the influence of Byzantine churches in the crown of domes that dominate it. The altar has magnificent reliefs by Donatello. After lunch, head for the leafy charms of the Orto Botanico, the oldest botanical gardens in Europe, first planted in 1545. Kids will especially love the large collection of carnivorous plants.

Dos and Don'ts

- ✗ Don't turn up at the Cappella degli Scrovegni without having made a reservation: you will not get in. You can book in advance online at: www.cappelladegliscrovegni.it
- ✓ Bear in mind that, prior to entering the chapel, you must wait in an acclimatization room, and visits are limited to 15 minutes only.
- ✓ Try the traditional local dessert, *pinza*. This is a rustic dish based on mixed maize and whole wheat flour, flavored with fennel seeds, currants, dried figs, and orange peel.
- ✓ Buy a PadovaCard. Valid for three days, it gives unlimited travel on the bus and tram network, a space in the town's main parking lot, entrance to numerous museums and monuments, including the Cappella degli Scrovegni, as well as other discounts and deals. It is valid for an adult and one child under 14.

Below: Bountiful market stall in Piazza delle Erbe

GETTING THERE
The closest airport to Gubbio, which is in northeast Umbria, is at Perugia, 25 miles (40 km) away. A bus service runs from Perugia train station to Gubbio.

GETTING AROUND
The best way to explore Gubbio is on foot, though a cable car can take you up to the cathedral. Rent a car for the day to get to the Parco del Monte Cucco.

WEATHER
The weather is very pleasant in May, with daytime temperatures reaching highs of 75°F (24°C).

ACCOMMODATIONS
In the town, the charming Park Hotel ai Cappuccini is a former monastery dating from the 1700s, set in attractive gardens; doubles from US$330; www.parkhotelaicappuccini.it

Locanda del Gallo is a 12th-century house in the Umbrian hills, 9 miles (15 km) southwest of Gubbio; doubles from US$165; www.locandadelgallo.it

Casa Branca is a traditional farmhouse set in tranquil woods, 7 miles (12 km) southeast of the town; doubles from US$124; www.casabranca.it

EATING OUT
Taverna del Lupo offers top-notch cooking (dinner from US$68). Try grilled meats or pasta, served with truffles or *formaggio di fossa* (a hearty local cheese, matured underground); www.mencarelligroup.com

Il Piatto d'Oro is a trattoria serving homemade traditional food from US$35 (tel. 075 9256238).

PRICE FOR TWO
US$275–480 including accommodations, meals, local travel, and one day's car rental.

FURTHER INFORMATION
www.comune.gubbio.pg.it

The Day of the Crossbow

On the last Sunday in May the Palio della Balestra, a crossbow tournament, is held in Piazza Grande. This event dates back to a time when the crossbow was a weapon capable of deciding battles and the societies of archers were powerful bodies. The Palio is a competition between the bowmen of Gubbio and a rival team from Sansepolcro in Tuscany, in which archers have to hit the center of a target from a distance of 120 ft (36 m). This battle of sharp eyes, steady hands, and strong arms is accompanied by a procession in historical costume, a colorful spectacle that brings the town to life.

Main: Raising the vast pedestals amid the crowds of onlookers at the Corsa dei Ceri

A RIOT OF COLOR

IN GUBBIO, THE EVE OF SANT'UBALDO is an occasion of great significance and celebration, and has been since the 12th century. On this day, May 15, the world-famous Corsa dei Ceri ("Race of the Candles") and its accompanying Festa, or festival, take place. Surprisingly, perhaps, the so-called "candles" are made of wood. They are actually the figures of three saints – Sant'Ubaldo, Sant'Antonio, and San Giorgio – mounted on tall, octagonal pedestals that resemble gigantic hourglasses. These are carried as fast as humanly possible through the steep streets and alleyways of the town as far as the basilica of Sant'Ubaldo, the protector of Gubbio, perched at the top of the mountain above the town.

It is a tough race (each statue weighs around 880 lb/400 kg), but it is not a real competition; the patron saint always has to arrive first. The skill and the challenge lie more in getting through, and climbing up, the narrow streets and alleyways of this still manifestly medieval town, without slipping, falling, tilting the statues, or knocking them

Left (left to right): Gubbio's terraced layers; green Umbrian hills surrounding the town; Fontana dei Matti in Largo del Bargello: *crescia con i ciccioli*, a local specialty of fat-enriched focaccia bread

Inset: Elegant tower of Palazzo dei Consoli

When the festival is over, Gubbio regains its composure and resumes its role as a calm and stately town, deep-set in the lovely Umbrian countryside.

against the buildings. All this takes place with the vociferous encouragement of an enthusiastic crowd of onlookers, who surround the *ceraioli* (candle-bearers) and eagerly participate at all stages of the race, filling the streets with a great hubbub of noise and color.

When the festival is over, Gubbio regains its composure and resumes its role as a calm and stately town, deep-set in the lovely Umbrian countryside. The town was flourishing even in ancient Roman times, as can be seen by the theater ruins which dominate the landscape, just beyond the medieval quarter. The 14th-century Palazzo dei Consoli looms over the town center, its imposing bulk visible from a distance, with elegant arcades and crenelated tower. The palazzo is faced by the magnificent Piazza Grande, the heart of medieval Gubbio and a terrace as much as a square, supported by walls and embankments, with broad vistas over the lower part of town and the surrounding hills. The view is one of the most charming aspects of Gubbio, one of the oldest towns in Umbria, where natural and artistic beauty blend to form a vision of complete harmony.

CORSA DIARY

Gubbio's long history is still very evident, not only in the harmony of its buildings, but also in traditions such as the exhilarating Corsa dei Ceri. This is a great time to visit a town which is almost a symbol of medieval Umbria. With three days at your disposal you can combine a day of uproarious fun with some relaxed exploration.

Three Contrasting Days

DAY 1

Begin the day in Piazza Grande, the heart of medieval Gubbio. After admiring the spectacular panorama that can be enjoyed from the terrace, visit the elegant Palazzo dei Consoli. Then make your way to Largo del Bargello, home to Palazzo del Bargello and with the little Fontana dei Matti ("fountain of the mad") in its center. According to tradition, someone who circles the fountain three times can be defined as *matto* or Eugubine (a citizen of Gubbio). Gubbio is, in fact, sometimes known as the "city of the mad" because of the unpredictable nature of its inhabitants. Don't miss Palazzo Ducale, with its elegant Renaissance form, or the nearby cathedral, which dates from the 12th century.

DAY 2

Fiesta day! If you don't want to be part of the crowd, take the Colle Eletto cable car that ascends to the church of Sant'Ubaldo, on top of Monte Igino. As well as giving you the chance to admire this 16th-century building, and watch the arrival of the Corsa, the cable car offers great views of the town and the surrounding countryside.

DAY 3

Just south of Gubbio, almost on the border with the neighboring region of Le Marche, is Monte Cucco, now protected by its status as a national park. Within the park, from the village of Sigillo, you can go on a variety of walks, seeking out natural geological features of great interest, such as the Grotta di Monte Cucco, one of the world's deepest cave systems. There are historical and art treasures here, too, such as the hermitage of San Girolamo and the abbey of Santa Maria di Sitria.

Dos and Don'ts

✓ Try *torta al testo*, a type of focaccia (the *testo* is the round pan in which it is cooked) with Pecorino cheese, typical of Umbria. There are numerous variations.

✓ Don't attempt to drive into Gubbio itself, as you risk getting stuck in its narrow streets, and most parking spaces in the town are reserved for local residents. Leave the car just outside the town and resign yourself to walking.

✗ During the Corsa dei Ceri, don't stand in the middle of the street: the *ceraioli* proceed at speed, followed by the crowds, and there is the risk of being swept away.

Below: Team banner on display during the Corsa dei Ceri

GETTING THERE
Finale Ligure lies 47 miles (75 km) west of Genoa airport on the Riviera di Ponente. By car, the SS1 follows the coast. There is also a fast train link.

GETTING AROUND
Explore Finale on foot. To travel to other resorts along the riviera, the options are car, train, or bus.

WEATHER
Average daytime highs of 68°F (20°C), clear skies, and spring flowers welcome the visitor in May.

ACCOMMODATIONS
Within the walls of Finalborgo, the B&B Letti al Castello is a 15th-century house full of charm, with a pretty garden. There is a storage area for climbing equipment, and maps and guides for the use of guests; doubles from US$82; www.lettialcastello.it

In the hills just above Finalborgo are two B&B farms (*agriturismi*) close to the rock climbing sites: Ai Cinque Campanili, with a pool in its gardens (doubles from US$96; www.agriturismo-liguria.com) and I Lamoi, an organic farm with simple rooms (doubles from US$48; www.ilamoi.it).

EATING OUT
For a quick snack (under US$14), visit one of the many *focaccerie-panetterie* that bake the famous focaccia of Liguria, served with cheese or dressed in various ways, *farinata* (pizza-like snacks made with chick-pea flour), and savory tarts.

For traditional Ligurian cooking, try the Ristorante Ai Torchi, housed in an old mill (dinner from US$62); tel. 019 690531.

PRICE FOR TWO
US$235 per day including accommodations, meals, car rental, and admissions.

FURTHER INFORMATION
www.comunefinaleligure.it

The Grotte di Toirano

Discovered in 1950, the caves of Toirano run beneath the limestone hills of Val Varatella, in the Ligurian hinterland. This is a vast cave system, with stalactites and stalagmites of every dimension, as well as aragonite "cave-flowers." The Grotta di Santa Lucia Inferiore is one of the most enchanting caves, with so many delicate concretions that it looks like the setting for a fairy tale. Neanderthal handprints, dating back 12,000 years can be seen on the walls here. The caves are also important for their prehistoric remains, among them rare traces of the cave bear *Ursus spelaeus*.

Above (left to right): Chiesa di San Lorenzo, set in lovely landscape; the tree-lined roads of Alassio, busy with visitors
Main: Climbers tackle one of the region's many rugged cliffs

BETWEEN SEA AND SKY

FINALE LIGURE WAS NOT ALWAYS ONE SINGLE TOWN, but three villages (Pia, Marina, and Borgo), separate entities until 1927, scattered along one of the most beautiful sections of the Ligurian coast. Today, it is not only a perfect location for a traditional seaside vacation, but also a major center for one of the most interesting rock-climbing areas in Italy; experts have identified at least 218 routes.

There are two kinds of rock-climbing to try here, inland and coastal, both of them fascinating. The most spectacular, however, has to be a cliff climb – in other words, scaling the cliffs and promontories overlooking the sea. Among the most stunning sites are Monte Sordo, Rocca di Corno, Rocca di Perti, and the cliffs of Rian Cornei, but every climb turns into a unique experience here, suspended between the deep blue of the sea and the light azure of the sky. The ascent up Rocca di Perti, in particular, is suitable even for those with minimal experience, and is a favorite of a wide range of climbers because beautiful panoramas are guaranteed without the necessity for high-level technical preparation.

Narrow medieval streets offer captivating glimpses of lovely views, and unexpected little squares are delightful places in which to people-watch as you dine.

The Finale area offers all kinds of other activities too. There are hikes and walks to suit all tastes and all levels of fitness. For example, a hike on the plateau from Varigotti to Noli passes the ancient Chiesa di San Lorenzo; or, in order to enjoy the breathtaking views from Capo Noli, walk the coast from Monte di Portofino to Capo Mele. Other sports available at Finale include paragliding and hang-gliding, making the most of local peaks and thermals and, especially, benefiting from the knowledge of experienced local instructors. Gliders can even land on the beach – a wonderful experience.

After all this activity, relax and recharge yourself in pretty Finalborgo, the upper town. Narrow medieval streets offer captivating glimpses of lovely views, and unexpected little squares are delightful places in which to people-watch as you dine on local treats such as *ravioli di boraggine* (herb-stuffed ravioli). By morning you will be raring to go once again.

Inset: Celebrated Muretto di Alassio ("Little Wall of Alassio"), a town monument
Below (left to right): View over Finalborgo; dish of *trofie liguri*, a local specialty using the region's famous pesto sauce

OUTDOORS DIARY

One of the favorite vacation destinations in this lovely coastal region, Finale is also eagerly sought out by climbers, keen to test themselves on the cliffs overhanging the sea. Over the course of three days you can try your hand at this and other activities, while also having time to go sightseeing, eat well, or simply relax on the beach in the sunshine.

Three Days on the Riviera

DAY 1

Devote the first day to exploring Finale. Don't miss the Chiesa di Santa Maria di Pia, rebuilt in the 18th century with a beautiful Rococo façade but retaining its 13th-century bell tower. Most importantly you must visit Finalborgo, set farther back from the coast. Almost entirely surrounded by 15th-century walls, the village is home to the lovely church of San Biasio, rebuilt in the Baroque era. Its slim bell tower is the symbol of the town.

DAY 2

Go on an excursion into the hinterland behind Finale, now a protected regional park. The area is characterized by plateaus offering beautiful views of the coast, interrupted by spectacular bastions of rock. This is the kingdom of the free-climber, who will find various routes with bolted climbs, but it is also perfect for hikers and keen mountain bikers, with a variety of paths and trails. To the southwest are the Grotte de Toirano, so visit them in the afternoon.

DAY 3

Spend your last day in Alassio, a jewel of this palm-fringed riviera on the Baia del Sole ("Bay of the Sun"), which has retained the appearance of a fishing village despite tourist development. Wander along Via XX Settembre – the Budello, or "gut," as it is known – a narrow street running parallel to the sea, lined with elegant shops. Stroll down Corso Dante, to see its famous Muretto. This wall is decorated with tiles bearing the signatures of famous celebrities, such as Ernest Hemingway, who visited Caffè Roma, an Alassio institution since the 1930s.

Dos and Don'ts

- ⊗ Unless you are an experienced climber, do not attempt to scale Finale's cliffs. Simply walking along the coastal paths will present you with unforgettable views.
- ✓ Try *trofi*, a rolled pasta unique to this region, usually served *liguri*-style with potatoes and green beans, dressed with a traditional basil-based pesto sauce.
- ✓ The hinterland of the Riviera del Ponente is one of the few places where chinotti (*Citrus aurantium*) are grown; buy sweets and syrups made from these small, scented citrus fruits.
- ✓ When visiting the Grotte di Toirano wear sturdy shoes and take a warm sweater. The obligatory guided tour lasts around 70 minutes and covers 0.75 miles (1.3 km) of rocky paths.

Below: Smart, uncrowded beach at Finalmarina, the lower part of Finale

GETTING THERE
Brescia's airport is about 12 miles (20 km) east of the city, which is in eastern Lombardy. A shuttle bus service links the airport with the Brescia train station, taking less than 30 minutes.

GETTING AROUND
In the town, get around by public transportation or on foot. For a trip to Franciacorta, the best means is by car, giving you the freedom to stop and explore.

WEATHER
May is a warm and sunny month, with average maximum temperatures of around 72°F (22°C).

ACCOMMODATIONS
A 4-star hotel close to the center, the Ambasciatori has good-sized, comfortable rooms; doubles from US$137; www.ambasciatori.net

Antica Villa is a small, charming hotel housed in an 18th-century residence, in the city's green oasis at the foot of the Ronchi hills, doubles from US$75; www.hotelanticavilla.it

EATING OUT
Trattoria Porteri is the place to try cuisine local to the area (dinner from US$42): homemade pasta, including the local specialty, *casoncelli* (meat-stuffed pasta), stuffed rabbit, and polenta; www.porteri.it

Osteria al Bianchi is one of the oldest restaurants in town (from US$35; www.osteriaalbianchi.it); Osteria la Grotta is another venerable institution; its specialties are platters of cured meats and cheeses, served with excellent wines (from US$42; www.osterialagrotta.it).

PRICE FOR TWO
US$205–270 per day, including accommodations, meals, local travel, and Brescia Musei Desiderio cards.

FURTHER INFORMATION
www.bresciaholiday.com

Race of a Thousand Miles

From 1927 to 1957, the Mille Miglia (literally, "A Thousand Miles") was one of the most important car rallies in the world. The route went from Brescia to Rome and back again, and was an exhilarating endurance race. Legendary feats were achieved, like the record set by the British racing driver Stirling Moss who, driving a Mercedes-Benz 300 SLR, completed the course in 10 hours and 8 minutes in 1955. To evoke memories of the race, the Mille Miglia Storica ("Historic Mille Miglia") has been held in Brescia each year since 1977. Vintage cars, dating from before 1957, follow a similar route to the original, at a somewhat gentler pace.

AN ANCIENT PRIDE

The history of Brescia can be seen in every corner of its historic center: from Roman Brixia to the era of the Lombards; from the town's days as a free commune in the late-19th century to Venetian rule; up until the time of Italian unification, in which it was one of the most important protagonists. A visit to the city is, as a result, a fascinating journey through time that retraces, monument by monument, every stage of a lengthy and fascinating history.

The oldest traces can be seen in Piazza del Foro, with its ruins of the Tempio Capitolino, a temple dating from AD 73, and of the Roman theater. This was the heart of Brixia, the ancient name for Brescia, an important center for iron-working in Roman times. From the Lombard era there is the monastery of San Salvatore-Santa Giulia, a complex founded in 753 by Queen Ansa, wife of Desiderio, the last of the Lombard kings. This was where Ermengarda, daughter of Desiderio, sought refuge and eventually died. She was the second wife of Emperor Charlemagne, but was repudiated when he decided to go

Above (top to bottom): Fine views of the city from Brescia's castle; Cloister of Santa Giulia, today a treasure house of art; ruined portico of the Tempio Capitolino

Main: Magnificent cupola of Duomo Nuovo

Below: Row of Franciacorta vines, with Castello di Passirano in the background

to war with Lombardy. She is a romantic figure, an impression reinforced by the writer Alessandro Manzoni in his tragic play *Adelchi*. Despite the modifications of subsequent centuries, the complex still maintains its medieval appearance, very much as Ermengarda would have known it.

Also dating from the Middle Ages is the cathedral of La Rotonda, built, as its name suggests, to a circular plan. The 13th-century Palazzo del Broletto and Torre del Popolo (Tower of the People), are reminders of the time when Brescia was a free commune, while Piazza della Loggia dates from the era of Venetian rule. Constructed in the 15th century, it is overlooked by Palazzo della Loggia, whose roof resembles the keel of a ship. There are traces in Brescia, too, of the Risorgimento, the movement that led to the unification of Italy, when, after defeat in the First War of Independence (1848), Brescia resisted Austrian troops for 10 days. The town's Risorgimento museum documents this epic stand, as a result of which Brescia became known as "The Lion of Italy." Today, this lion still takes pride in its noble history, its fine architecture, and its dynamic future – which makes the town a memorable place to visit.

HISTORY-LOVERS' DIARY

In Brescia, you stumble upon architectural and historical treasures simply while strolling the lively streets of its old center. The fact that these streets are lined with enticing shops makes for some great retail discoveries as well. In three days you can combine these two pleasures as you wish, and still have time to visit the superb vineyards nearby.

Three Days Steeped in the Past

DAY 1

Start your first day in Piazza della Loggia and, from here, following Via dei Musei, you will come to all the town's main monuments: Il Broletto, La Rotonda, the Tempio Capitolilo, and, at the end of the street, the monastic complex of San Salvatore and Santa Giulia, which includes the city's main museum and art gallery.

DAY 2

Devote the day to the castle and its museums: not only the one dedicated to the Risorgimento, but also the Luigi Marzoli Museo delle Armi Antiche. The armorers of Brescia have been world-renowned for centuries, and this museum of historic weaponry houses one of the finest collections of armor and weapons in Europe, tracing the "art of war" across the centuries. The castle complex itself is lovely, and there are marvelous views from the square close to Torre Mirabella tower.

DAY 3

Today, leave the city behind and take a leisurely tour of the surrounding countryside. Stretching westward from the outskirts of Brescia to the shores of Lake Garda and Lake Iseo is a landscape of gently rolling hillsides that yield some of Italy's most prestigious wines, including Franciacorta, a highly rated sparkling wine. Grapes have been cultivated here since Roman times, and many of the wineries are housed in beautiful historic buildings, at which you can stop for tastings of wines and other artisanal products, meet the winemakers, and buy wines at affordable prices that are hard to find elsewhere.

Dos and Don'ts

- ✓ Go for a tour along one of the wine routes easily accessible from Brescia. For detailed itineraries and maps, visit: www.stradadelfranciacorta.it
- ✗ Brescia Calcio football team has fiercely loyal fans, as do their local rival clubs. When a home match is being played, things can get quite lively in the bars around town. Should a scuffle break out, make a hasty exit.
- ✓ Buy a Brescia Musei Desiderio card (around US$27, valid for a year), which gives you entry to all the civic museums as well as various other benefits and discounts.
- ✗ Don't underestimate the weather: even in May there may be hot and humid days.

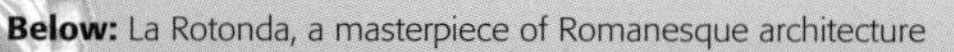

Below: La Rotonda, a masterpiece of Romanesque architecture

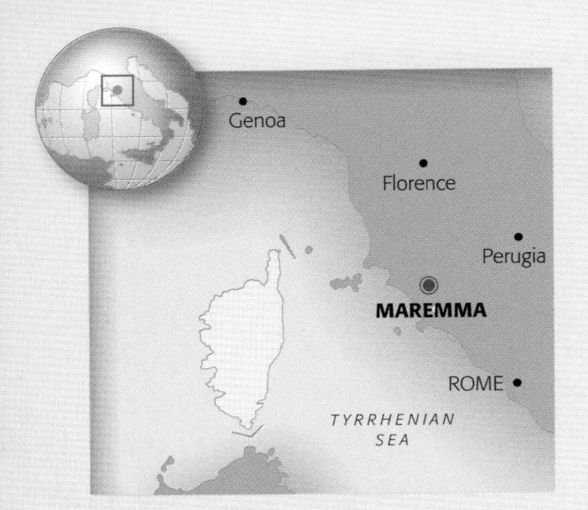

GETTING THERE
Florence and Pisa airports are around 100 miles (150 km) from Grosseto, the main town in the Maremma, southern Tuscany. From Florence, take the Florence-Siena freeway and then the SS223 to Grosseto; from Pisa, take the A12, then the SS1.

GETTING AROUND
Grosseto can be explored on foot. Visit the Parco Naturale della Maremma by car, or by using the trains and buses linking Grosseto and Alberese, which is home to the main visitor center.

WEATHER
May is sunny, pleasantly warm, and ideal for walking.

ACCOMMODATIONS
In Grosseto, Albergo San Lorenzo has large, pleasant rooms from US$94; www.albergogrosseto.com

Within the Parco Naturale della Maremma, the farm Il Duchesco offers local produce, horseback-riding, and comfortable rooms from US$90; www.ilduchesco.it

La Pulledraia del Podere Montegrappa offers great organic homegrown produce and double rooms with B&B from US$110; www.pulledraia.it

EATING OUT
There are many *agriturismo* farms and trattorias where you can try dishes such as *acquacotta* (Tuscan vegetable soup), *oca alla maremmana* (goose in red wine), and *finocchiona* (sausages flavored with fennel), for under US$35 a head.

PRICE FOR TWO
US$220 per day for food, accommodations, and entrance to the Parco Naturale della Maremma. Add US$250 for a day's riding with the Maremma cowboys.

FURTHER INFORMATION
www.lamaremmafabene.it; www.parco-maremma.it; www.cavallomaremmano.it

Saturnia Cascades

Saturnia is a lovely hilltop town, located a little way inland from Grosseto in glorious hill-walking countryside. However, Saturnia offers more than just pleasant walks – it also boasts a number of sulfur springs bubbling out at a toasty 99.5°F (37.5°C). The town's hot springs have attracted visitors since the Roman era – legend has it that Saturn's thunderbolt split open the earth, releasing the hot water. Choose between treatments at luxurious and expensive spa resorts or open-air public cascades where you sit under the warm water in the rolling Tuscan countryside.

RIDING WITH THE COWBOYS

THE SOUTHERNMOST PART OF THE TUSCAN COAST, the Maremma is bordered in the hinterland by a massive chain of hills which flattens out into marshland and pine forests as it reaches the coast. Once largely a no-go zone, the Maremma was an expanse of marshes populated by fearsome brigands and riddled with malaria-carrying mosquitoes. Man struggled to survive in this harsh environment until the 19th century when most of the marshes were reclaimed. The brigands were replaced by the *butteri*, the Maremma's famous cowboys who spend their days in the saddle, rounding up the wild cattle. As a result, the *butteri* are expert horsemen and the tough Maremmano horse is a symbol of the area.

Today, much of the Maremma is a regional park and nature preserve covering around 40 sq miles (100 sq km) with a variety of superb natural environments. The hill areas to the north and the south

Main: A Maremmano horse grazes in a field of flowers near Grosseto

Left: The Rocca Aldobrandesca on the rocky promontory of Talamone

Right (left to right): Statue of Leopoldo in the center of Piazza Dante in Grosseto; a pine-shaded road in the Parco Naturale della Maremma; pretty tassel hyacinth (*Muscari comosum*), known locally as *cipollaccio*

Far right (top and centre): A type of salami made from wild boar; the horse, still widely used in the Maremma

were home to the ancient Etruscans whose necropolises allow us a tantalizing glimpse of their civilization. Picturesque hill-towns dot the interior, while along the coast you'll see towers built to keep watch for Saracen pirates. At the region's heart, the River Ombrone spreads out to create a large wetland area supporting many bird species – an irresistible attraction for bird-watchers. Nearby, the Monti dell'Uccellina is a spectacular green line of hills that runs along the coast, where great tracts of fragrant pine forest shield tiny stony coves and long sandy beaches that are washed by crystal clear waves. Just south, the coastline turns into rocky cliffs that run all the way to Talamone, an ancient fishing village perched on a promontory, still looking out over the sea for pirates.

The Maremma is just perfect for exploring by foot or on a bike. However, the best method, and one that is in keeping with the history of the Maremma, is by horse. There's no better way to spend a day than riding with the *butteri,* rounding up the cattle like a real Maremma cowboy.

MARSHLAND DIARY

On the shores of the Tyrrhenian Sea, backed by a chain of wooded hills, the Maremma is still a wild landscape. Four days should allow you to tour the region's main town, Grosseto, and spend a few days exploring the interior of the Parco Naturale della Maremma and the coast, including a day's riding with the *butteri*.

Four Days in the Saddle

DAY 1

Explore Grosseto and wander around its 16th-century Medici walls, now transformed into gardens just perfect for a pleasant walk. The wide walls form a hexagonal shape and enclose the whole of the historic center of the city. Enjoy a Tuscan lunch before visiting the Romanesque cathedral – originally dating back to the 13th century, it was extensively remodeled in the 19th century. See, too, the smaller churches of San Francesco and San Pietro, which date from the medieval period.

DAY 2

Start the second day exploring the Parco Naturale della Maremma. Head to the visitor center at Alberese and follow one of the park's trails highlighting points of natural and historical interest along the way. In the afternoon, drive south to Talamone and spend some time at the coast, exploring the village, or relaxing on the splendid beach.

DAY 3

Today is the day to try your hand at living the life of the local cowboys – the *butteri*. There is a variety of excursions that enable you to get up close to the wild fauna in the Maremma. You'll also be fed large amounts of filling farmhouse food and the cowboys often put on a show of their skills in the evening.

DAY 4

On your last day, spend the morning soaking away the aches and pains of horseback-riding in the restorative thermal springs at Saturnia. Then, explore the Etruscan necropolis at Sovana and its *vie cave,* a road chiseled out of the tufa stone, in places over 30 ft (10 m) deep.

Alternatively, you can choose to simply take it easy, spending the day at Marina di Alberese, a splendid beach close to Grosseto.

Dos and Don'ts

- ✓ You can tour the Parco Naturale della Maremma by canoe, via the rivers Ombrone or Merse, if you don't fancy horseback-riding. Ask at the visitor centers in Alberese or Talamone.
- ✓ It is wise to wear walking boots for walks in the park. Take plenty of water, plus a weatherproof jacket and mosquito repellent.
- ✗ Do not stray from the marked paths. A shuttle bus takes visitors to the start of some of the trails.
- ✓ Do be aware that there are parts of Marina di Alberese beach that are for naturists only – that means no swimming trunks!

Below: The Merse River, Parco Naturale della Maremma

GETTING THERE
Stresa lies on the western side of Lake Maggiore. Milan's Malpensa Airport is 20 miles (32 km) away, with regular direct bus links to Stresa.

GETTING AROUND
A good ferry service operates around the lake, linking all the towns and the islands. The cable car up to Mottarone departs every 20 minutes.

WEATHER
May in the Italian lakes sees fine days and warm temperatures of around 77°F (23°C).

ACCOMMODATIONS
The luxurious Grand Hotel des Iles Borromées has been a favorite with celebrities since it opened in 1861; doubles from US$425; www.borromees.it

The Villa e Palazzo Aminta is a palatial hotel and spa with frescoed rooms; doubles from US$440; www.villa-aminta.it

EATING OUT
In the heart of Stresa, Piemontese serves regional food with a modern interpretation (dinner from US$62); tel. 0323 30235.

The gazebo restaurant I Mori (in Villa e Palazzo Aminta) is perfect for a romantic dinner in a lovely setting (set menu US$95); www.villa-aminta.it

PRICE FOR TWO
US$510–645 per day including meals, accommodations, local travel (including ferries and cable car), and admission fees.

FURTHER INFORMATION
www.stresa.org; www.borromeoturismo.it
www.stresa-mottarone.it

Music by the Water

In May, the splendid flower-filled gardens around Lake Maggiore become venues for a series of open-air concerts that take place on weekends in Stresa and other picturesque spots, combining the charm of lakeside locations with the perennial appeal of music. The Concerti di Primavera (Spring Concerts) are a prelude to a series of summer events – Settimane Musicali di Stresa e del Lago Maggiore (Stresa and Lake Maggiore Music Weeks), a long-running music festival first held in 1962, which has witnessed performances by many internationally famous musicians.

Main: View over Villa Pallavicino, set in lovely lakeside gardens

GARDENS ON THE LAKE

Lake Maggiore is an intense blue and spreads out over such a large expanse that it could almost be mistaken for the sea. Stresa is one of the loveliest and most historic towns by the lake, set on a shore bordered by luxuriant gardens. With its cascade of grand Art Nouveau hotels and Neo-Classical villas, it's no wonder that Stresa has been a much favored tourist destination since the end of the 19th century. It was here that Ernest Hemingway set several chapters of his 1929 novel *A Farewell to Arms*, but, before that, the town was a favorite destination for Stendhal, Dickens, and Byron, as well as the nobility of northern Italy, who built splendid villas here.

One of the most beautiful villas is Pallavicino, a stately residence in Neo-Classical style, developed from smaller buildings by the Marquis Ludovico Pallavicino in the 1860s. He also created the spacious gardens whose 242,000 sq yards (200,000 sq m) now feature flower-lined avenues, ancient trees, a botanic garden, and even a menagerie.

Left (left to right): Enchanting amphitheater on Isola Bella; elegant gardens of Villa Pallavicino in Stresa; view of Stresa on the shores of a choppy Lake Maggiore

Below (top to bottom): Aerial view of Isola dei Pescatori; peacock in the leafy gardens of Isola Madre

Not far from Stresa are the three Borromean islands, each with its own unmistakeable profile, adding a delightful touch of natural beauty and historic interest. The most famous is Isola Bella, a strip of rocky land where, during the 17th century, a lovely palace was built, surrounded by terraced gardens. The resulting Baroque wonderland, which takes up the whole of the island, was designed to give the island the appearance of a ship, and the dramatic impact is simply magical. Isola dei Pescatori is completely different in style. As its name (Fishermen's Island) suggests, it is a working island, with narrow streets, a small town square, and tall houses with long balconies used for drying fish. The largest of the islands, Isola Madre, is also the most natural, with its profusion of azaleas, camellias, rhododendrons, and wisteria. There is also a lush botanic garden in which peacocks, parrots, and pheasants roam freely, and a 17th-century palace built by the Borromeo princes.

These diverse islands are linked into a harmonious whole by Stresa, which also affords the chance of a bird's-eye view of them on a dazzling cable-car ride: yet another facet of its appeal.

BORROMEAN DIARY

Stresa, with its abundance of flowers, warm, soft colors, and beautiful landscapes, has been a popular vacation destination since the 19th century. Four days gives you time to find out why, by strolling its streets, visiting its villas with their lovely gardens, riding its cable car, and, most importantly, taking a lake ferry to its magical islands.

Four Lakeside Days

DAY 1

Spend your first day in Stresa, strolling along its lakeside promenade and admiring the views across the lake, which stretches north into Switzerland. After lunch, visit the Villa Pallavicino and explore its delightful gardens.

DAY 2

Take an early ferry to Isola Bella, where a tour of the palazzo takes you through a series of rooms decorated with canvases by famous Baroque painters, as well as fine furniture, sculptures, and Flemish tapestries. Spend time exploring the wonderful gardens, where white peacocks add to the magical aura. Head on to Isola dei Pescatori in time for a delightful lunch and wander through its quaint streets. Finally, take the ferry on to Isola Madre where, in addition to the fine botanic garden, it is worth visiting Palazzo Borromeo, which houses an unusual collection of puppets. Don't miss the last ferry home!

DAY 3

Today, board the Stresa-Mottarone cable car, which takes you up to the top of the mountain behind Stresa; during the 20-minute ride you can admire wonderful views over the lake. At the intermediate station of Alpino there is an alpine botanic garden with more lovely views. There are places to eat in Mottarone, and plenty of activities, from walks to sports like hang-gliding and mountain biking.

DAY 4

Spend the day in elegant little Arona, at the southern end of the lake. It is the home town of San Carlo Borromeo, a key figure in the Counter-Reformation. Just outside town stands a huge statue of the saint – at 115 ft (35 m) it is the world's second-largest bronze after the Statue of Liberty. Ascend to the top of it for marvelous lake views.

Dos and Don'ts

- ✓ Use the excellent ferry services for getting around the lake; the boats go to all the towns and islands. For information on routes and timetables, visit www.navigazionelaghi.it
- ✗ Don't hire one of the private boats offering transportation to the Borromean islands without first agreeing a price and a route.
- ✓ Try *magheritine*, delicious little sugar-sprinkled biscuits, a Stresa specialty.
- ✓ If you like sports, take advantage of the lake and its surroundings: there are plenty of golf courses and sailing schools that offer courses for different levels of ability.

Below: Botanic gardens at Villa Pallavicino

GETTING THERE
Pienza is in the Val d'Orcia, in central Tuscany. The nearest airports are at Perugia, 56 miles (90 km), and Florence, 78 miles (125 km).

GETTING AROUND
Explore Pienza on foot, leaving your car in one of the parking lots outside the town walls. The best way of exploring the countryside around Pienza is by car.

WEATHER
Clear fresh sunny days dominate the month, with average daytime temperatures of 75°F (24°C).

ACCOMMODATIONS
In the historic center, the elegant hotel Il Chiostro di Pienza is a former medieval monastery; doubles from US$165; www.relaisilchiostrodipienza.com

Also in the old town, Il Giardino Segreto has rooms and apartments decorated in traditional Tuscan style; doubles from US$75; tel. 0578-60452.

At the end of a spectacular avenue of cypresses leading up to the top of a hill, stands Relais La Saracina, a charming old farmhouse; doubles from US$315; www.lasaracina.it

EATING OUT
Sperone Nudo, in a 14th-century palazzo in the center of Pienza, serves traditional regional cuisine (dinner from US$35); www.speronenudo.it

In the delightful village of Monticchiello, with views of Pienza, Taverna di Moranda offers a fresh approach to classic Tuscan cuisine and ingredients (from US$62); www.tavernadimoranda.it

PRICE FOR TWO
US$275–440 per day including accommodations, meals, car rental, and admissions.

FURTHER INFORMATION
www.pienza.info; www.valdorcia.it

The Two Faces of Chianciano

Chianciano is a famous spa town thanks to its four springs which, although once enjoyed by the Etruscans and the Romans, were only really developed as thermal spas from the beginning of the 20th century. But the town also has an ancient core: the medieval quarter that occupies the upper part of the hill still has its ancient encircling walls as well as several fine buildings, including the collegiate of San Giovanni Battista and the Palazzo del Podestà.

Main: Handsome Renaissance town of Pienza, dominating the sunny Tuscan countryside

THE IDEAL CITY

PIENZA IS A TOWN THAT EXISTS BECAUSE OF A POPE'S DREAM. Enea Silvio Piccolomini, who became Pope Pius II, wished to build an "ideal city" according to Renaissance principles. To make his dream a reality, Piccolomini selected his own birthplace, then a fortified medieval village called Corsignano, for rebuilding, and charged Bernardo Gambarelli (better known as Rossellino), with the task of designing and building the new town center. Rossellino had collaborated with Leon Battista Alberti, one of the great architects of the age, in Florence, and had enlarged St. Peter's in Rome for Pope Nicholas V.

Building began in 1459, a year after the election of Pius II to the pontificate. Work proceeded rapidly and, by 1462, the monumental center of the town – with a piazza named after the pope himself – was already completed. Small but splendid, the piazza was built on a trapezoidal plan with squared paving, which emphasizes the proportions and balance of the design. Around the piazza stand the chief monuments of the town: the Duomo, Palazzo

Left (left to right): Pecorino di Pienza on display in a Pienza *formaggeria* (cheese shop); façade of Palazzo Piccolomini, a Renaissance masterpiece; elegant façade of Pienza's Duomo; *torta in balconata*, a local sweet made with nuts, raisins, almond milk, and dates

Below (top to bottom): Peaceful street in the heart of Pienza; rolling green countryside around Pienza

Piccolomini, Palazzo Borgia, and Palazzo Comunale. The hand of Rossellino, seen throughout Pienza, is especially noticeable in the Duomo, with its serene façade of travertine marble and its light interior, and in Palazzo Piccolomini, finished in rusticated stone.

But, rather than individual monuments, it is Pienza as a whole that expresses key Renaissance ideals: of the balance between life and government; of the desire to create conditions in which people might live and work together industriously and peacefully; of the conviction that, between man and nature, there should be continuity and harmony; and of the goal that architecture should form part of the natural setting without altering it, but complementing and completing it instead.

This is exactly what Pius II and Rossellino achieved at Pienza, where the town buildings are in perfect harmony with the landscape of the Val d'Orcia, one of the most beautiful valleys in the whole of Tuscany. Their "ideal city" nestles seamlessly into the surrounding hills, where the warm colors of clays and tufa mingle with sun-dappled, lush green vegetation.

RENAISSANCE DIARY

Pienza is a little jewel of the Renaissance in the heart of Tuscany, in a beautiful area that holds some of the richest art treasures in Italy. Over the course of three days you'll have time to wander Pienza's lovely streets and squares and visit some of the other delightful towns in the Val d'Orcia to discover the many pleasures they have to offer.

Three Days in the Val d'Orcia

DAY 1

Spend your first day getting to know Pienza. Start off in Piazza Pio II, home to the town's most important monuments, including the Duomo, with its restrained façade and light, three-aisled interior, which stands on a rocky spur marking the southern edge of the town. Palazzo Piccolomini is home to the still-furnished papal apartments, as well as a fine library and a hanging garden from which there are wide-ranging views over the valley.

DAY 2

Today, visit Montepulciano, about 8 miles (13 km) west. The heart of the town is Piazza Grande, where there are many lovely buildings including the 14th-century Palazzo Comunale, crowned with battlements. The town's most elegant street is Il Corso, lined with stately 16th-century residences. The Chiesa di San Biagio is a 16th-century masterpiece by Antonio da Sangallo the Elder.

DAY 3

Today, head 12 miles (20 km) southeast to Chianciano, then after a walk, a spa treatment, and lunch, continue for a farther 8 miles (13 km) to Chiusi, the ancient Etruscan town of Chamars. From its cathedral museum you can descend into the "Porsenna labyrinth," a series of tunnels leading to a great cistern. The archeological museum is also of interest; it has a good collection of Etruscan objects, and organizes visits to necropolises in the area, including the remarkable, frescoed Tomba della Scimmia (Tomb of the Monkey).

Dos and Don'ts

- ✓ Rent a bike and go for a ride in the Pienza hills. For more information, visit www.pienza.info
- ✓ Try one of the restorative health and beauty treatments on offer at the Chianciano spa, including massages, body wraps, and balneotherapy, or simply sip a glass of warm spring water.
- ✗ Don't expect to be able to see the Etruscan tombs of Chiusi without booking a guide. Visits are organized by the Museo Nazionale Etrusco (tel 0578 20177).
- ✓ Sample Pecorino di Pienza, a delicious local cheese.

Below: Diners in Pienza's Piazza Spagna

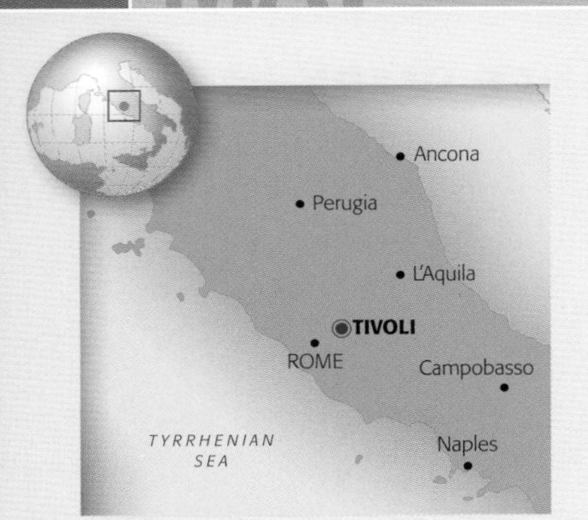

GETTING THERE
Tivoli lies 15 miles (24 km) from Rome's Ciampino airport, which is connected by bus and train to the center of Rome. Frequent trains run from Tiburtina station in Rome to Tivoli, which takes 1 hour.

GETTING AROUND
Buses link Tivoli, Hadrian's Villa, and Villa d'Este.

WEATHER
May in Lazio is pleasant and sunny, with average daytime temperatures around 75°F (24°C).

ACCOMMODATIONS
Palazzo Maggiore is a lovely 16th-century residence in the heart of Tivoli; doubles from US$124; www.palazzomaggiore.com

The hotel Torre Sant'Angelo is a magnificent castle that combines luxury with a venerable history: built on the ruins of a villa of Catullus, it was later an Olivetan monastery, and then a royal palace; doubles from US$220; www.hoteltorresangelo.it

EATING OUT
In the park of the Villa Gregoriana, with lovely views, the restaurant Il Ciocco serves good traditional cooking (dinner from US$35); www.ristoranteilciocco.com

The Sibilla restaurant, in old Tivoli, is set in an enviable position at the foot of two Roman temples, with views of the Villa Gregoriana waterfalls (from US$35); www.ristorantesibilla.com

PRICE FOR TWO
US$250–350 per day including accommodations, meals, and admission to the villas.

FURTHER INFORMATION
www.tibursuperbum.it

Water Music

One of the most extraordinary water features at Villa d'Este is the Fontana dell'Organo ("Fountain of the Organ"). This ornate 16th-century Baroque marvel contains a hydraulic musical organ in its central niche, the work of the Frenchman Claude Vernard. Vernard used a technique that may date from 1st-century AD Alexandria to use air and wind pressure to "play" the keys. The fountain was unused for over 100 years after it became fixed on one note, but has now been restored, and plays a theme composed by Liszt in its honor.

VILLA REFLECTIONS

Tivoli is set on the gentle slopes of the Tiburtine Hills, at a point where the River Aniene curves down through a rocky valley in a series of picturesque waterfalls. The setting provided a welcome retreat from the summer heat of Rome for its wealthier citizens and, in AD 118, it was chosen by Emperor Hadrian as the site for his magnificent new residence.

More a small town than a mere house, the villa took 20 years to complete, and the resulting sumptuous complex extended over an area of about 45 sq miles (115 sq km). Its grand buildings were richly furnished, and took full advantage of the beautiful natural setting and the copious water supplies. Hadrian's Villa bears the distinctive stamp of the "Philosopher Emperor." It was his wish to recreate here some of the many wonders he had seen on his numerous journeys to the imperial provinces. These included the Pecile,

Main: Teatro Marittimo at Hadrian's Villa

Above: One of the many fountains to be found in the gardens of Villa d'Este

Below: The Canopus, a colonnaded nymphaeum, one of the most famous sights at Hadrian's Villa

a grand portico surrounding a garden with a pool, inspired by the Stoa Poikile at the center of political and cultural life in Athens, Hadrian's favorite city. Here too is The Canopus, a nymphaeum in Egyptian style, replicating that on the banks of the Nile near Alexandria. The Terrace of Tempe is a great belvedere that dominates the valley which Hadrian named after one in Thessaly, northern Greece. But of all the beautiful spaces in the villa's grounds, the Teatro Marittimo is particularly charming. A circular building surrounded by a pool, it is accessible by means of little floating pontoons. This is a magical place of peace and seclusion and is thought to have been a private area of refuge for the emperor.

Following the fall of the Roman Empire, Tivoli's enchanting position continued to attract the Roman aristocracy, who built more sumptuous villas in the area. The loveliest of all is Villa d'Este, created in the second half of the 16th century for Cardinal Ippolito II d'Este, the son of Lucrezia Borgia. A princely villa, elegant and richly decorated, its splendor is nonetheless outshone by its gardens, with fountains, nymphs, water features, and grottoes creating fantastic "stage sets" of landscape and water.

WATER GARDENS DIARY

So close to Rome and yet so different in climate, character, and landscape, Tivoli makes a welcome change as much for the modern visitor as for the Roman citizens of the past. Three days is the perfect length of time in which to discover its charming villas and wander their gardens, as well as soaking in a Roman bath fit for an emperor.

Three Delightful Days

DAY 1

Devote your first day to visiting Hadrian's Villa, a short distance from Tivoli. The complex has all the elements of a complete town, with gardens, pools, fountains, nymphaea, baths, gymnasia, a racecourse, a stadium, theaters, and temples, and there is much to explore.

DAY 2

Spend the day in Tivoli itself. A popular vacation resort since antiquity (eminent citizens such as Horace, Cassius, and Quintilius Varus had villas here), it retains a lovely historic center rich in interesting monuments. The gardens of the Villa Gregoriana are especially fine. They were constructed in 1826, after a devastating flood of the River Aniene destroyed many buildings in the center of Tivoli. Pope Gregory XVI intervened to make the river course safer, diverting it through tunnels to create two fine new piazzas, a splendid waterfall, and the villa that bears his name. End the day with a swim and a massage at the luxurious Tivoli baths.

DAY 3

On your final day, visit Villa d'Este, which lies on the outskirts of the medieval town. The villa itself has marvelous vaulted, frescoed ceilings, but the highlight is its splendid gardens, which use water from the Aniene, conveyed here by impressive hydraulics, to create extraordinary water features. Particularly outstanding are Il Vialone, the first spectacular terrace area to which you descend from the villa, and the fountain Il Bicchierone (The Goblet), by Bernini.

Dos and Don'ts

- ✓ If you are in Tivoli on the first Sunday in May, don't miss the charming procession of the Madonna di Quintiriolo.
- ✓ Sample the local sheep's milk Pecorino cheese: its exquisite flavor is renowned throughout Italy.
- ✓ Indulge yourself at the Tivoli baths, whose sulfurous water was praised by the ancient Romans for its therapeutic properties.
- ✗ Don't bring a picnic to Villa d'Este: eating in the grounds is not allowed. There is, however, a delightful café where you can break for lunch during your exploration of the gardens.
- ✗ Don't drive to Hadrian's Villa: the parking lot is some distance from the villa. It is better to get there using one of the buses that run from the center of Tivoli.

Below: *Coda alla vaccinara* (oxtail), a typical dish of the region

JUNE

Where to Go: **June**

For Italian children, June marks the start of the summer vacation. For children and visitors alike this means the seaside: at a splendid beach like Varigotti, in Liguria, or a sandy cove such as those of Cala Gonone, in Sardinia. For some it may include the additional thrill of water sports – maybe windsurfing at Palau, in Sardinia, or diving in the clear waters off the little Sicilian island of Ustica. June is still too early for the mass rush to the sea, however, so this is a perfect time to enjoy warm sunshine and an uncrowded shoreline.

In June, the inland heights of Italy reveal a softer, welcoming side; the air is still fresh but the streams are running and pastures fill with flowers. An ideal introduction to the mountain way of life is the five museums built by Reinhold Messner along a route that winds among

FESTIVALS AND CULTURE

FLORENCE Sunset over Florence and the Arno River

RAVELLO
CAMPANIA

Wagner on the Amalfi Coast

The Ravello Festival celebrates the music of Richard Wagner, who composed Parsifal here. Concerts take place against the magnificent backdrop of the Amalfi coastline.

www.ravellofestival.com

GENZANO DI ROMA
LAZIO

A festival of flowers

The medieval streets along which the Corpus Christi procession travels are carpeted with beautiful floral compositions in an event called the Infiorata di Genzano.

www.infiorata.it

FABRIANO
LE MARCHE

A lively affair

Medieval Fabriano, long famed for its quality paper, comes alive during the San Giovanni Palio with parades, floral displays, and even a blacksmiths contest.

www.fabrianopalio.it/folklore.htm

"The festival is the perfect opportunity to discover all that this part of Florence has to offer."

TERMOLI
MOLISE

An ancient fishing settlement on the Adriatic coast

The old town of Termoli, built on a headland overlooking the sea, still has two working archaic fishing machines, called *trabucchi*.

www.termoli.net

FLORENCE
TUSCANY

Opera, ballet, and concerts at the Maggio Musicale Fiorentino

This early-summer festival of music and dance stands alongside Bayreuth and Salzburg as one of the most prestigious in Europe.

See pp154–5

UNFORGETTABLE JOURNEYS

URBINO View across the rooftops of this superb Renaissance town

CERVETERI
LAZIO

In search of ancient Etruscan civilization

Outside the town lie over 1,000 of the most breathtaking Etruscan necropolis tombs in Italy, on silent "streets" waiting to be explored.

See pp158–9

VIA CASSIA
TUSCANY

A drive through Tuscany

Tuscany's main highway, Via Cassia, passes through perhaps the most beautiful man-made landscape in the world, with medieval towns and farmland unchanged for centuries.

www.turismo.intoscana.it

URBINO
LE MARCHE

Revealing the Renaissance

Walk in the footsteps of the artist Raphael through this remarkably preserved crucible of culture, once the court of the Duke of Montefeltro, the archetypal Renaissance man.

See pp144–5

COLLIO
FRIULI-VENEZIA GIULIA

Take the "Wine and Cherry Trail"

The rolling hills of the Collio region are covered in vineyards that yield fine wines. Cormòns is the starting point for a range of memorable gastronomic pilgrimages.

See pp146–7

VILLA BARBARO
VENETO

A Palladian masterwork

Discover this elegant blend of country house and noble villa, set amid glorious parkland. Both house and grounds are full of delightful surprises.

See pp162–3

NATURAL WONDERS

VARIGOTTI Spectacular and unspoiled Baia dei Saraceni

VARIGOTTI
LIGURIA

Breathtaking beaches

The long curve of sandy beach at Varigotti, known as the Baia dei Saraceni, is possibly the most beautiful along this lovely stretch of the Ligurian Riviera.

See pp148–9

CRISSOLO
PIEDMONT

Where the river rises

Situated at the foot of Monviso, Crissolo is the departure point for excursions to Pian del Re, where a bubbling mountain stream is the source of the mighty Po River.

www.parcodelpocn.it

COGNE
VALLE D'AOSTA

A place called Paradise

A favorite vacation destination of the former Italian royal family, Cogne is ideal for nature-lovers, who can lose themselves in the beauty of the Parco del Gran Paradiso.

www.granparadiso.net

SANTA MARIA DI LEUCA
PUGLIA

At the meeting of the seas

Here on the uttermost tip of the "heel" of the Italian "boot," the Adriatic and Ionian seas meet.

See pp156–7

EGADI ISLANDS
SICILY

A natural paradise surrounded by crystal-clear sea

The waters of lovely Favignana and the other Egadi Islands, just off the coast of Sicily, teem with spectacular marine life.

See pp160–61

Previous page: *Procession of the Magi* by Benozzo Gozzoli (1459), housed in the Magi Chapel of Palazzo Medici-Riccardi, Florence

the splendid peaks of the Dolomites. In other places, the mountains give way to stunning lakes, and to gentler hills, blanketed by vineyards such as those of the Collio region. A drive along one of its wine routes is an excellent way of getting to know Italy and some of its hidden treasures, such as Villa Barbaro, Palladio's masterpiece in the green Veneto countryside that produces sparkling Prosecco wine.

It's not just the coast and countryside that merit a June visit. Italian cities are full of interest and activity, before the heat of summer settles on them: Urbino, with its Renaissance atmosphere; Caprarola, home to the sumptuous Villa Farnese; and Florence, which has an additional attraction in June – the Maggio Musicale Fiorentino, one of the most prestigious music festivals in the world.

LUXURY AND ROMANCE

CAPRAROLA View over the town from the terrace of Palazzo Farnese

"Sitting like a crown on top of a hill, the Renaissance Palazzo Farnese and its beautiful gardens dominate Caprarola."

CAPRAROLA
LAZIO

A regal residence

The dazzling Palazzo Farnese is set in lovely gardens whose statues, fountains, follies, grottoes, and secret gardens make them the perfect place for a romantic stroll.

See pp150–51

MONTE ISOLA
LOMBARDY

Island of enchantment

Set in Lago Iseo, Monte Isola is the largest lake island in Italy. Wonderfully picturesque, blessed with a mild climate, and car-free, it is the perfect spot for a romantic getaway.

www.monteisola.com

BAGNO DI ROMAGNA
EMILIA-ROMAGNA

Luxurious thermal spas

Indulge yourself with treatments at Bagno di Romagna's thermal baths, which make use of mineral-rich, warm spring waters appreciated as long ago as the Roman era.

www.bagnodiromagnaturismo.it

CORCIANO
UMBRIA

Romantic hideaway

Enclosed within 15th-century walls and surrounded by olive groves in the "green heart" of Italy, this is a tranquil and undiscovered town in whose palace you can stay.

www.bellaumbria.net/Corciano

LAKE COMO
LOMBARDY

Lakeside romance

Spend a romantic weekend by the lake that inspired composers, artists, and poets. The northern shores are wilder and less populated, offering visitors a more peaceful stay.

www.discovercomo.com

ACTIVE ADVENTURES

CASTEL FIRMIANO This fortress is part of the Messner Mountain Museums

ENTRACQUE
PIEDMONT

Flower-strewn alpine slopes between Italy and France

Entracque lies in the Parco delle Alpi Marittime. From here, hiking trails lead to enchanting lakes and spectacular mountain peaks.

www.parks.it/parco.alpi.marittime

PALAU
SARDINIA

Windsurfing paradise

The northern coast of Sardinia, with its clear seas and constant breezes, is an ideal destination for fans of windsurfing and many other water sports.

See pp164–5

USTICA
SICILY

Scuba dive the warm waters of the Mediterranean

The island of Ustica is the top of an extinct volcano to the north of Sicily. Home to a marine nature reserve, it offers exceptional scuba diving.

www.isole-sicilia.it

"This is a titanic project, into which the great man has thrown himself with his usual passion and iron determination."

MESSNER MOUNTAIN MUSEUMS
TRENTINO-ALTO ADIGE

In praise of the peaks

Learn all there is to know about mountains and climbers at five museums created by the great mountaineer Reinhold Messner.

See pp152–3

LAGO DI PIEDILUCO
UMBRIA

A haven for canoeists

Surrounded by dense woods of holm oak, the lake is a tranquil mirror, free of currents and so ideal for water sports, canoeing in particular. Be sure to test the lake's amazing echo.

http://piediluco.altervista.org

FAMILY GETAWAYS

CALA GONONE Tiny cove typical of the wonderful coastline

PARCO OLTREMARE
EMILIA-ROMAGNA

Theme park with a difference

Oltremare is a natural theme park, just outside Rimini, where rain forest and undersea habitats, as well as delightful dolphins, help children learn about nature and the environment.

www.parchi-divertimento.it

VERGEMOLI
TUSCANY

Explore the underground world of the Grotta del Vento

The "Cave of the Wind" is a magical place of bizarre rock formations, silent lakes, shimmering colors, and mysterious underground rivers.

www.grottadelvento.com

SAN BENEDETTO DEL TRONTO
LE MARCHE

Seaside family favorite

The long stretch of silvery sanded Blue Flag beach at San Benedetto del Tronto slopes very gently and is ideal for children.

www.sanbenedettodeltronto.it

CALA GONONE
SARDINIA

A marvelous stretch of Mediterranean coastline

Crystal-clear water and a coastline dotted with pretty coves and deep caves, Cala Gonone is also home to a colony of rare monk seals.

See pp142–3

"The jagged limestone coastline has many enchanting and secluded coves as well as deep caves, often opening out on to the water."

BOLSENA
LAZIO

A town filled with flowers

Lovely lakeside Bolsena is always a popular family resort, but during the Infiorata festival it is irresistible, its ancient streets carpeted in lovely pictures made of flowers.

www.bolsena-guida.it

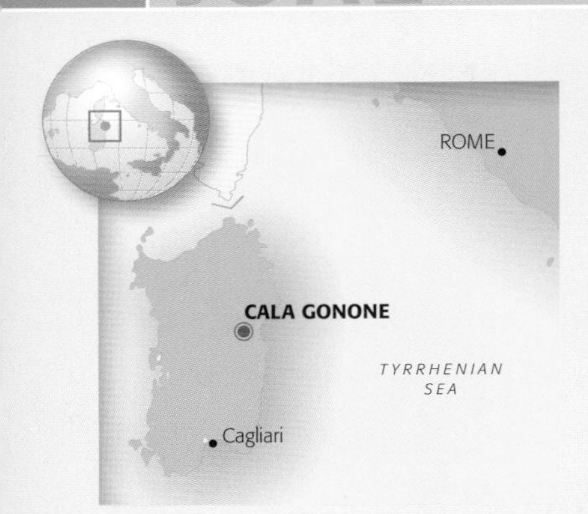

GETTING THERE
Cala Gonone, on the eastern Sardinian coast, is reached by road from Olbia (the nearest airport) in the north, via the SS125, which follows the coastline south as far as Cagliari.

GETTING AROUND
A car is best for exploring the coast and the interior, but you'll need to take a boat to some of the best coves in the area, or be prepared for a lengthy hike.

WEATHER
Summer has arrived in Sardinia, bringing hot, dry weather. The area is often affected by a strong north-west wind, known as the *maestrale*.

ACCOMMODATIONS
There are good hotels close to the beach with plenty of facilities: Hotel Smeraldo has double rooms B&B from US$110; www.hotelsmeraldo.com

For somewhere a little closer to the seafront, try the slightly larger Palmasera Village Resort; enjoy full-board accommodations from US$112–160 per person; www.palmaseravillage.com

EATING OUT
Expect seafood on the coast but do try local dishes from the interior, such as classic *porceddu* (spit-roasted pork). You should also try *culurgiones* (large ravioli) or *malloreddus* (a type of gnocchi). If you have room for dessert, try *seada* (fried cheese dumplings drizzled with honey) and finish with a glass of chilled *mirto* (myrtle-flavored liqueur).

PRICE FOR TWO
Around US$250–325 per day including meals and accommodations. Add about US$110 for a day's boat trip along the coast.

FURTHER INFORMATION
www.calagonone.com

The Taste of Sardinia

Probably introduced to the island with the arrival of the Spanish in the 15th century, the Cannonau grape survives the hot, dry climate because the vines trees are kept small and tightly packed. After being aged in oak barrels for at least a year, the red wine is full-bodied and robust. The co-operative at Dorgali makes an excellent Cannonau that goes well with the meat dishes of the area. Try it also with the famous Sardinian cheese, Pecorino, or the less well-known *taedda*, a creamy cheese made from sheep's and goat's milk – delicious spread on *carasau*, the crispy, thin Sardinian bread.

Above (top and bottom): Aerial view of the village of Dorgali; one of Sardinia's many Tombe dei Giganti (Tomb of Giants), Nuraghic burial grounds

Inset: A jeweler intent on working filigree gold, a Sardinian specialty

Far right: The hardy, dune-loving *soldanella di mare* (beach morning glory)

Below: Karst springs at Su Gologone

Main: The idyllic beach at Cala Gonone

SWIMMING WITH THE SEALS

Until the 19th century, Cala Gonone was just a small fishing village centered around a small harbor, but over the past 100 years it has grown into a notable tourist destination. The cause of the transformation was the 1,300-ft (400-m) tunnel built in 1860 through Monte Bardia, connecting Cala Gonone with Dorgali. It was along this dramatic winding road with wonderful views of the coast, with its white rocks, green, aromatic Mediterranean shrubs, and cool blue water, that the rest of the world happily made its way to Cala Gonone. Fortunately, this rapid growth has not ruined the village's historic center, which is well worth visiting for its attractive architecture, which includes traditional dark stone houses and a quaint little 17th-century church.

Although the number of visitors to the island has increased dramatically, development along the coast has been limited, keeping long stretches completely free of any human settlement, totally unspoiled, and often only accessible

The jagged limestone coastline has many enchanting and secluded coves as well as deep caves...

from the sea. The jagged limestone coastline has many enchanting and secluded coves as well as deep caves that open onto the water. These can be visited, thanks to the flotilla of boats that operates daily from Cala Gonone harbor. One of the largest and most attractive caves is the Grotta del Bue Marino. This is one of the last refuges for the monk seal – known in Sardinian as the sea ox *(bue marino)* – and is a cave system that extends back for an incredible 3 miles (5 km) into the depths of the rock.

But not all of the area's spectacular destinations are along the coast – head inland from Cala Gonone to see exhilarating sights such as the huge 125-ft (38-m) stalagmites at the Grotta di Ispinigoli, one of the largest cave systems in Italy. Then there are the *nuraghi* – mysterious prehistoric dwellings that are evidence of an ancient civilization that once existed in Sardinia. These stone monuments, built without mortar, make a truly impressive sight – there are around 40 near Cala Gonone. And finally, there is the majestic monolith of the Tomba dei Giganti (Tomb of Giants) at Dorgali, a large grave from the Nuraghic era, carved from a single block of granite.

BEACH-HOPPING DIARY

It is just about possible to do justice to the delights of the Cala Gonone coast in three days. Start with the beaches that are easily accessible by land, and then board a boat to visit the sea caves and secluded coves. Finally, spend a day touring the interior with its traditional villages, large cave systems, and fascinating ancient remains.

Three Days in Cala Gonone

DAY 1

If you don't feel like going anywhere, you can opt to stay on the beach in Cala Gonone, bordered by the quay. Almost joined to it, a little farther south, you'll find the long sandy beach of Palmasera, the largest on the coast and easily accessible from the coastal path on foot. In the afternoon, try driving a little way south, to Ziu Martine and Cala Fuili, two adjacent white-pebble beaches squeezed between cliffs. In the evening, relax by strolling around Cala Gonone and browsing in the little craft shops crowding Via La Marmora.

DAY 2

Today, take advantage of the many boats in the tiny harbor waiting to whisk you away along the coast. Visit the Grotta del Bue Marino and then take the boat on to Cala Luna: 2,300 ft (700 m) of beach, with a freshwater lake just behind, surrounded by oleanders that color the sand with their pink and red petals. To the north, the beach ends at a dramatic limestone spur that contains a deep cave system – experienced cavers with proper equipment might want to explore these.

DAY 3

Drive (or take a taxi) into the hinterland behind Cala Gonone. Dorgali isn't far away and has numerous craft workshops (particularly famous for their gold filigree jewelry). You'll need a car (4WD) to get to Tiscali and Serra Orrios to see the mysterious ruins left by the ancient Nuraghic civilization, which survived here until the 2nd century AD, or maybe you'd rather explore the marvelous Grotta di Ispinigoli, with its spectacular cascades of stalactites and stalagmites.

Dos and Don'ts

- ✗ Don't always go to the same beach, from Cala Gonone it's possible to try a different one each day.
- ✓ Always carry drinking water with you and, if necessary, food, as not all the beaches have café facilities.
- ✓ Go on a mini-cruise to explore the inlets of the Golfo di Orosei; excursions can be organized from the harbor and last a full day, often including lunch.
- ✓ Enjoy the Sagra del Pesce (Fish Festival) at the beginning of June in Cala Gonone – eat delicious fried fish cooked in an enormous frying pan measuring about 13 ft (4 m) across.

Below: Stalactites hanging from the roof of Grotta di Ispinigoli

GETTING THERE
Urbino is in northern Le Marche. The nearest international airport is at Rimini, 37 miles (60 km) away. From there, take freeway A14, leave at the Resero-Urbino exit, then follow the SP423 to Urbino.

GETTING AROUND
Leave your car in one of the parking lots by the city walls, such as Piazza del Mercatale.

WEATHER
Expect warm and pleasant weather, with average temperatures of 73°F (23°C).

ACCOMMODATIONS
The San Domenico, in front of the Palazzo Ducale, is an elegant hotel housed in a former 16th-century monastery, complete with cloister. Rooms from US$188; www.viphotels.it

Hotel Raphael is part of a 15th-century palazzo built by Valadier, close to Raphael's birthplace, and offers modern rooms with good city views; from US$110; www.albergoraffaello.com

Enjoy comfort and eco-sustainability at the Locanda della Valle Nuova, a farm in the hills around 20 minutes from Urbino. Doubles from US$150; www.vallenuova.it

EATING OUT
The Osteria Angolo Divino is the place to go for traditional regional cooking. Meals cost around US$48; www.angolodivino.com

Il Coppiere offers local dishes such as steak with truffles, from around US$35; tel. 0722 322 326.

PRICE FOR TWO
Around US$275 per day for meals and accommodations.

FURTHER INFORMATION
www.urbinoculturaturismo.it

Battista Sforza

The hairstyle is elegant, yet the profile of Battista Sforza, shown in this detail of a portrait by Piero della Francesca, is the embodiment of a strong and determined woman. Married to the duke of Urbino at 14, she gave birth to eight children and died in 1472, just 26 years old. Nevertheless, she still had time to support her husband as patron of the arts, and helped him to transform Urbino into one of Italy's most splendid Renaissance courts.

Above: Piazza della Repubblica, one of the busiest squares in Urbino; the Renaissance Chiesa di San Bernardino, Urbino
Main: The Loggia dei Torricini, part of the façade of the Palazzo Ducale in Urbino

BUILDING PERFECTION

WE CAN THANK FEDERICO DA MONTEFELTRO, famous warlord and duke of Urbino from 1444–82, and his wife Battista Sforza, for one of the most elegant towns built during the early Italian Renaissance, known as the *Quattrocento* (15th century). Urbino is as close as you can get to the "perfect city" imagined by Renaissance artists and captured on canvas in Piero della Francesca's celebrated *Ideal City*, now in the Palazzo Ducale in Urbino, which depicts airy spaces, elegant architecture, and spatial harmony. A passionate art-lover, Federico established a sophisticated court in Urbino, attracting poets, intellectuals, and, most notably, artists such as Piero della Francesca, Luciano Laurana, and Paolo Uccello.

The Urbino you see today is still the Urbino planned by Federico and completed by his son Guidobaldo, who founded its prestigious university in 1506. At the heart of the city is the architectural masterpiece, the Palazzo Ducale. Begun in 1444, the building was worked on by Luciano Laurana, who designed the western façade with its balconies stacked up on each other and its two slim towers. The western elevation was designed by Francesco di Giorgio Martini. Access to the palace is through the Corte d'Onore, designed by Laurana and an example of perfect harmonious proportions; from here you descend into the underground quarters, with stables, an ice house, and the kitchens. Then climb the dramatic staircase to the upper floor, once the palace apartments and now the Galleria Nazionale delle Marche (National Gallery of Le Marche) – it has an outstanding collection, including works by one of Urbino's most famous sons, Raffaello Sanzio (Raphael).

The Palazzo Ducale is Urbino's most outstanding monument, but the city itself is virtually an open-air museum, with marvelous buildings, wide streets, and open squares. More than anything, it offers visitors the chance to almost step back in time to the start of the Renaissance and explore a city where the humanist and rational ideals of the philosphers were set out in stone.

Urbino is as close as you can get to the "perfect city" imagined by Renaissance artists and captured on canvas by Piero della Francesca.

Inset: Room in Raphael's house in Urbino
Below (left and right): Fortezza Albornoz at the top of the hill overlooking the roofs of Urbino; *birbanti,* Le Marche biscuits made with pine nuts and lemon

RENAISSANCE DIARY

Urbino is where the philosophy of the Renaissance became manifest in the very buildings of the city. Today it is buzzing with students and tourists who are drawn by the splendid monuments, history, art, and atmosphere of a Renaissance city. Spend two days exploring the city and a day out in the surrounding countryside.

Three Urbane Days

DAY 1

The easiest route into the Old Town is via the spiral ramp at the fortified gate on Piazza Mercatale, the old site for the market. Head toward Piazza Rinascimento, the heart of the city, where the Palazzo Ducale stands, and devote the day to a visit to the palace and the excellent gallery within, home to one of the most important collections of Renaissance art. In the evening, enjoy a simple bowl of *passatelli* – strands of pasta made from breadcrumbs, parmesan cheese, and egg, and cooked in broth.

DAY 2

On your second day, now that you've seen some of his paintings, you should visit the 14th-century home of Raffaello Sanzio (Raphael) and the workshop of his father, Giovanni Santi, also an esteemed painter. On the first floor is a *Madonna with Child* attributed to the young Raphael. Urbino's cathedral is also worth a visit. It was first built in the 11th century, remodeled in the 15th and, following an earthquake, had its façade rebuilt in Neo-Classical form in the 19th century. For a lovely walk with marvelous views over the city, head for Fortezza Albornoz, at the eastern edge of town. In the evening, dine on game caught in the Le Marche countryside.

DAY 3

Visit the Chiesa di San Bernardino – the mausoleum built by Federico for the dukes of Montefeltro: it stands a little way from the center of Urbino, in a splendid panoramic position. Then drive to Urbania, the summer residence of the duke of Urbino. See the palace and cathedral, and explore the pretty medieval town, famous for its high-quality, handmade ceramics.

Dos and Don'ts

- ✓ Try the *casciotta* of Urbino, a young fresh cheese made from a mix of sheep's and goat's milk, then matured for a month.
- ✗ If you are looking for a quiet and restful stay, it would be best to avoid visiting on June 1, when the Festa di San Crescentino is held in honor of Urbino's patron saint. A grand procession is held in the center and it is a day of utter confusion in the narrow streets of the city.
- ✓ If you can, make sure you see one of the concerts during the town's summer jazz festival – it can be a great opportunity for jazz buffs to see some fantastic performers.

Below: The main courtyard at the Palazzo Ducale, Urbino

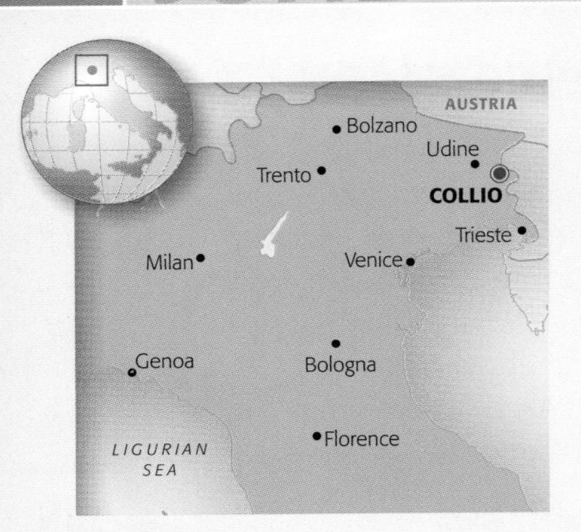

GETTING THERE
Collio is in southeastern Friuli-Venezia Giulia, close to the border with Slovenia. The airport Ronchi dei Legionari is around 12 miles (19 km) from Cormòns on the SS305.

GETTING AROUND
The best way of getting around is by car.

WEATHER
Warm but not stifling, with temperatures between 57°F and 79°F (14–26°C).

ACCOMMODATIONS
The Hotel Felcaro is an elegant villa surrounded by parkland. Rooms from US$150; www.hotelfelcaro.it

Set in the hills, among the Collio vineyards, the Villa Bianca can organize visits to local wineries and wine tastings. Rooms from US$68 (tel. 0481 60464).

The rustic farmhouse Al Poc da Subide is a comfortable and attractive *agriturismo* with rooms from US$90; www.alpocdasubide.com

EATING OUT
Central European influences can be seen in the robust Friuli cuisine of *brovada* (spiced pork sausage with pickled turnips); *frico* (potatoes with cheese); goulash served with polenta or dumplings; and the Slovenian *slikofri* (potato ravioli) – which should be washed down with Collio wines, naturally. Two good restaurants in Cormòns are Giardinetto (meals around US$55; tel. 0481 60257) and Cacciatore della Subida (meals around US$68; www.lasubida.it).

PRICE FOR TWO
US$235–315 per day for meals and accommodations.

FURTHER INFORMATION
www.cormons.info; www.turismofvg.it

A Gourmet's Delight

Cormòns is famed for its delicious cured ham. This delicacy should be hand-sliced with a knife and enjoyed without removing the fat, which makes the ham butter-soft. The ham comes from pigs raised on a controlled diet, but the real secret of the flavor lies in the curing of the meat by hand. The most skilled phase is the smoking of the ham using cherry, bay, and vine wood, and a mix of herbs, which give the meat its unmistakable aroma.

WHERE THE GRAPE IS KING

KNOWN AS "BRDA" IN SLOVENIAN and "Cuei" in the Friuli dialect, the 6 sq miles (16 sq km) of vineyards spread over the Italian hills on the border with Slovenia are simply Collio to the wine-loving community. Here, the production of fine wine has a tradition going back thousands of years. It is recorded that in the 3rd century AD the emperor Maximian, on his way to lay siege to Aquileia, crossed the Isonzo River on a bridge of barrels requisitioned from the farmers of Collio. However, it was in the mid-19th century that Collio wines found fame, thanks to Count Theodore Latour, who introduced grape varieties from France and Germany, amalgamating them with those historically grown in the area, such as Ribolla.

Collio is a wonder of nature. It combines the merits of a coastal zone – the Golfo di Trieste is not far away – with the hills and valleys of classic vine-growing terrain. This rare combination is why the

Main: The fertile vineyards of Collio flourishing under the June sun

Left (left and right): Part of the citadel walls at Gradisca; simple restaurant in the Collio area – also one of a chain of small workshops selling the local wine

Right: The spectacular Ponte del Diavolo (Bridge of the Devil) over the River Natisone in Cividale del Friuli

delicious local dishes include hare and venison, along with sea bass and little balls of cuttlefish. The white wines of the region – Müller-Thurgau, Pinot, Riesling, Tocai – are universally admired, while the reds – Cabernet, Merlot, and Collio Rosso – can stand in comparison with the best in the world.

However, although grapes are very important here, in terms of the economy, the local culture, and the landscape, they are not the only produce to flourish on the terrain. The road that crosses Collio is known as *La Strada del Vino e delle Ciliegie* (The Wine and Cherry Trail) and celebrates other produce of the region, creating a gastronomic pilgrimage through an irresistible patchwork of flavors, panoramas, and encounters. On the trail you'll pass the regional wine-making center, Cormòns, Queen of the Collio, as well as Capriva del Friuli, home to the elegant Castello di Spessa winery and Villa Russiz, which was instrumental in introducing French grape varieties to the area. A journey along this route is guaranteed to delight, as you enjoy the warm hospitality, exquisite foods, and local wines in pretty wine villages.

Above (top and bottom): The Castello di Spessa, dominating the green landscape of Capriva del Friuli; rows of barrels in the wine cellars of Castello di Spessa

Below (top and bottom): View from the Loggia dei Mercanti in Gradisca; Müller-Thurgau grapes, one of the most famous varieties of the region

VINEYARD DIARY

This hilly zone is naturally very attractive, with a landscape made up of small villages, woods, and vineyards. Four days is enough for a mini-tour of the Collio area starting at Cormòns and winding through the delightful countryside, visiting the quaint and ancient wine-producing towns along the way.

Four Days in the Hills

DAY 1

Start at charming Cormòns, a small town of pre-Roman origins, which experienced a period of splendor in the Carolingian epoch (8th–11th centuries), when it acquired its double town walls. The historic center is home to the Chiesa di Sant'Adalberto, which dates from the 13th century (although it was rebuilt in the Baroque era), and the Enoteca Regionale, or regional wine-tasting shop, dedicated to local wine production.

DAY 2

Take a day's tour along *La Strada del Vino e delle Ciliegie*, which unwinds through the hills of Collio, where the vines alternate with cherry trees (the cherries are ripe in June). The road goes past the pretty regional wine towns of Capriva del Friuli and Dolegna del Collio. As well as cherries and wines, enjoy the other local foods featured on the trail. Along the way, pause at Oslavia's shrine dedicated to the fallen of World War I, which contains the remains of nearly 60,000 soldiers who died in the battles at Gorizia.

DAY 3

Relax for a day in one of the *agriturismo* farms in the area, often built in *masi*, sturdy traditional rural houses. Here you'll be able to experience farming life close up and taste the warm Friulian hospitality and excellent rustic cuisine, yet still enjoy all the comforts of a hotel.

DAY 4

Explore Gradisca: the alleyways of its historic center, enclosed within walls with towers and 15th-century gates, still have a medieval feel. Many aristocratic residences were built here between 1650 and 1750, when the town flourished. Visit Enoteca La Serenissima, located in a 15th-century palazzo and the first wine-tasting shop in Italy – here you can try (and buy) all the best local wines. It is also a fine restaurant with a fabulous wine list.

Dos and Don'ts

- ⊗ Don't go unprepared: in summer Collio is very warm and mosquitoes and little bugs abound. Bring mosquito repellent.
- ✓ Buy a local and original souvenir – Friuli craftsmen are famous for their work with wrought iron.
- ✓ In Cormòns, it is worth visiting Vigna del Mondo (Vines of the World): a project in which grapes from around the world are made into Vino della Pace (Peace Wine), which is sent annually to heads of state around the world to promote peace.

Below: Aerial view of the town of Gradisca

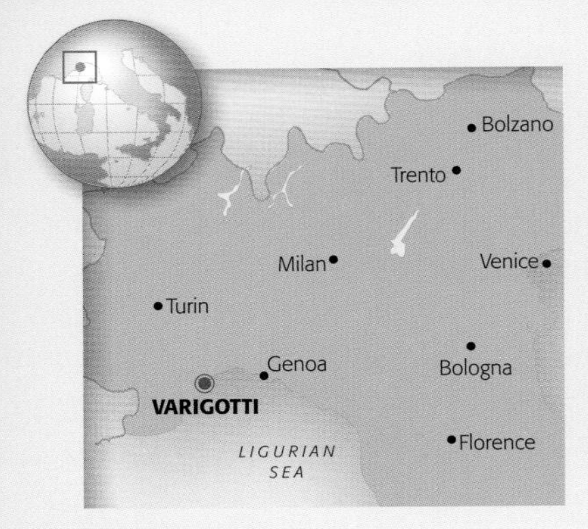

GETTING THERE
Varigotti is on the Ligurian Riviera, west of Genoa. From Genoa, the nearest international airport, take the A10 and exit at Spotorno. The nearest train station is Finale Ligure – around 3 miles (5 km) away. From there take a taxi or bus.

GETTING AROUND
The best way of exploring the area is to use the excellent bus network that links all the towns.

WEATHER
Warmth and sunshine are guaranteed. Breezes from the sea take the edge off the heat.

ACCOMMODATIONS
In Varigotti, the Hotel Miramare, with its own beach, offers comfortable doubles from US$245; www.hotelmiramarevarigotti.com

The elegant and modern 4-star Hotel Albatros has a spa and offers rooms from US$178; www.hotelalbatrosvarigotti.it

If you're looking for a camp site, try Terre Rosse, in the countryside around Noli. Pitches from US$5, plus US$9 per person; www.terrerossecamping.it

EATING OUT
In Varigotti, with a terrace overlooking the sea, the restaurant in the 5-star hotel Al Saraceno serves meals from US$82; varigotti.alsaracenogroup.com

For a family atmosphere and good food, try La Caravella; meals about US$35 (tel. 019 698 028); or *agriturismo* La Selva, with sea views, offering local dishes at US$35 (tel. 019 698 8320).

In Noli, la Scaletta takes a new look at traditional cuisine; meals around US$48 (tel. 019 748 754).

PRICE FOR TWO
US$125–370 per day including food and accommodations.

FURTHER INFORMATION
www.liguriapocket.eu/en/a/Riviera_of_Palms.htm

Main: Diver making a descent in the waters off Varigotti

PIRATE TREASURE

THE EVOCATIVE NAME BAIA DEI SARACENI (Bay of Saracens) harks back to the exploits of the Moorish pirates, who during the Middle Ages were in the habit of crossing the Mediterranean to carry out raids and hunt for ships, loot, and slaves. Seeing Varigotti and its lovely beach, one of the most sought-after spots on the Ligurian Riviera, it's hard to imagine that the peaceful harbor was once the object of savage pirate raids.

Today, the Baia dei Saraceni is the perfect destination for a seaside vacation. The beach is long, white, and sandy, and is easily accessible from the town. But there's more to this resort than just the beach: between the sea and the spectacular cliffs of the interior, the thin strip of shore measures a mere 650–985 ft (200–300 m) wide. Here, any development or building works have been restricted so that the original Ligurian fishermen's houses remain, still painted in vibrant shades of ochre, red, and yellow. Intelligent environmental policies have kept the sea clean, too,

The Bergeggi Reserve

The island of Bergeggi is a tiny place. At first glance it looks like a simple mound of rock, sparsely covered with shrubs, rising out of the blue sea in front of the little village of Bergeggi. On top of the uninhabited island there are ruins of various ancient military and religious buildings. However, the island and its surrounding sea is a delightful reserve for animal and plant species. The area is popular with divers for the varied marine life and interesting geology of the sea bed – limestone erosion has led to the development of many caves in the area.

JAN FEB MAR APR MAY JUN JUL AUG SEP OCT NOV DEC

Left (left to right): Houses on the seafront at Varigotti; detail of a typical Varigotti house, painted in warm colors; the magical Baia dei Saraceni

Right (left and right): Fishermen leaving the port of Noli on a fishing expedition; *taggiasca* olives, a typical crop in this fertile area

while also allowing it to be used for all kinds of water sports – from windsurfing and sailing, to snorkeling and diving – so that visitors can enjoy the beauty of the rich marine life. And if sport is not your thing, there is always fun to be had in just splashing about in the cooling waves after a spell on the warm sand. But, pleasant as it is, the Baia dei Saraceni is not the only beach at Varigotti worth visiting – extending west of the green Punta Crena headland, you'll find the largest beach in Liguria, another irresistible strip of soft sand, washed by the refreshing, clean sea.

And if you tire of such beauty, then simply travel a short way north along the coast to visit Noli, with its splendidly preserved medieval center. It may look tiny but, for 600 years between 1193 and 1797, the town was an independent republic, even building its own cathedral, the Chiesa di San Paragorio, a church that dates back to the 11th century. Tiny Noli once had an incredible 72 watchtowers, now only eight remain. But along with the town walls and imposing hilltop castle, they stand as reminders that not all visitors to this glorious coastline came with peaceful intentions.

DIVING DIARY

Despite being one of the most popular seaside destinations in Liguria, Varigotti has not been spoiled. It has retained its fishing-village charm and offers a great many diversions on its stunning white-sand beach. Spend a few days relaxing here before heading a short way north, up the coast for more of the same fabulous scenery and sea.

Six Days on the Ligurian Coast

DAYS 1–3

Spend a few days relaxing in and around Varigotti itself – you are on vacation after all. Enjoy the clear sea and the comforts of a beach with good facilities at Baia dei Saraceni. In the evening, go for a stroll through the delightful town to the fishing harbor with its pretty painted houses. Sample some of the excellent wines of the area, such as Pigato di Ortovero or Vermentino, accompanied by typical *taggiasca* olives.

Spare a day to take a walk along the clifftop coastal path from Varigotti to Capo Noli. On the way, stop off at Malpasso, a delightful beach surrounded by rocks, to spend some time on this peaceful part of the coastline. The route offers wonderful views and the chance to observe the local wildlife.

Maybe scuba diving or snorkeling is your passion – try the waters of Punta Crena by the cliffs where the sea rapidly reaches a depth of 66 ft (20 m) and is full of marine life.

DAYS 4–6

Enjoy a couple of days farther north in Noli, one of the best preserved medieval villages in Liguria, dominated by the ruins of the Castello di Monte Ursino. Enjoy a stroll in the historic center and don't miss the Chiesa di San Paragorio, a fine example of Ligurian Romanesque.

After swimming in the bay at Noli, try going a little farther along the coast to Spotorno. Its center still looks like an old fishing village, with seafront houses and castle ruins above. There's also a pleasant promenade along the seafront. At the far end of Spotorno lies the Isola di Bergeggi, where the island, the sea, and the facing cliffs are a nature reserve. It's a great place for diving, or take a boat trip along the coast to explore the many caves – some of which were inhabited in prehistoric times.

Dos and Don'ts

- ✓ Always carry plenty of drinking water with you, as some beaches don't have any facilities.
- ✗ Avoid taking a car: the beaches of Liguria can get crowded in summer – especially on weekends – so it can be hard to park.
- ✓ Do try *ravioli di boraggine* (herb-stuffed ravioli), which uses the delicate local herb borage in the filling.

Below: The Romanesque Chiesa di San Paragorio, Noli

GETTING THERE
Caprarola is in northern Lazio and is easily accessible from Rome and its airports. To reach Caprarola from Rome, take the Via Cassia (SS2) and then the Cassia Cimina road (SP1). There are also regular bus services.

GETTING AROUND
It is best to explore Caprarola on foot, but you will really need your own means of transportation for the surrounding area.

WEATHER
Expect sunny days with pleasant summer temperatures averaging around 77°F (25°C).

ACCOMMODATIONS
Casale del Barco is a romantic countryside B&B, with good views of Caprarola. Its pretty rooms have exposed stone walls and wooden beams, and start at US$82; www.casaledelbarco.com

Villa Antonelli, an 18th-century farmhouse set in the nature reserve of Lago di Vico, offers upscale hospitality with sauna, tennis courts, and swimming pool. Rooms with four-poster beds from US$205; www.villantonelli.com

EATING OUT
At Antica Trattoria del Borgo, in the center of Caprarola, you will find tasty traditional fare: typical regional salamis, roasts and game, homemade pasta, and a local specialty – roasted porcini mushrooms. Meals from US$40; www.anticatrattoriadelborgo.it

PRICE FOR TWO
US$210–295 per day including meals, accommodations, and entry to Palazzo Farnese.

FURTHER INFORMATION
www.caprarola.com

Civita Castellana

Just east of Caprarola, Civita Castellana has a fine medieval Duomo, Santa Maria Maggiore, notable for its portico decorated with vibrant mosaics. However, it is the imposing fort with an octagonal tower that dominates the town. The Rocca dei Borgia was built on a spur of rock at the foot of the Monti Cimini hills and is a prime example of 15th–16th-century military architecture. Architect Antonio da Sangallo the Elder created an impregnable fortress by adapting an exisiting medieval structure to make use of the cutting edge military technology of the time – firearms and cannons.

Above: View over Caprarola from the balcony of Palazzo Farnese; a detail from a fresco by Federico and Taddeo Zuccari in Palazzo Farnese
Main: The spectacular spiral staircase at Palazzo Farnese, Caprarola

RENAISSANCE MASTERPIECE

A TOWERING PENTAGONAL EDIFICE, SITTING LIKE A CROWN on the top of a hill, the Renaissance Palazzo Farnese and its beautiful gardens dominate the town of Caprarola. Originally intended for a fortress, the palazzo's five-sided foundations with corner bastions were the only elements retained from the design of Antonio da Sangallo (the Younger), drawn up at the start of the 16th century. When the project was resumed in 1559, the new architect, Jacopo Barozzi – known as Vignola – was commissioned to build not a fortification but an extravagant aristocratic villa. The result was the Palazzo Farnese, one of the most sumptuous of all Italian country residences. Vignola's designs went beyond the immediate vicinity of the palazzo: dramatic ramps sweep up to the villa, a great flight of steps has been carved into the hill, and an approach road carves a broad, straight line through the village. No longer required for defensive duties, the corner bastions have been transformed into peaceful terraces with far-ranging and panoramic views.

There are five floors inside the palazzo, containing two matching suites – summer quarters to the north and winter quarters to the west. At the heart of the building is a grand circular courtyard surrounded by a two-storied portico. The upper floor is reached from the courtyard via Vignola's magnificent spiral *Scala Regia* (Royal Stairs) – wide enough to ride a horse up. The rooms at the top of the palazzo are the most impressive, decorated with frescoes by artists of the Italian Mannerist movement (1520–80), from the Zuccari brothers to Jacopo Bertoja, from Giovanni de' Vecchi to Raffaellino da Reggio and Antonio Tempesta. The paintings cover such subjects as Greek mythology and biblical stories, and there's a fabulous map of the world.

Two bridges link the palazzo with the splendid Italian garden behind. This harmonious combination of delightful fountains, statues, parterres, follies, and grottoes leads on to a larger park, home to the little Palazzo del Piacere.

he upper floor is reached from the courtyard via Vignola's magnificent spiral *Scala Regia* (Royal Stairs) – wide enough to ride a horse up.

Inset: Copper worker practicing his traditional craft, Civita Castellana
Below: The southern façade of the Renaissance Palazzo Farnese, Caprarola; *acquacotta alle erbarelle* (soup with tomatoes, bread, and herbs), a local specialty

PENTAGON DIARY

One of Italy's best examples of a palatial Renaissance residence, the imposing Palazzo Farnese dominates the town of Caprarola from its hilltop. A weekend is enough time to look around the palace and see the town of Caprarola itself, as well as spending some time exploring the pristine lake and forest countryside nearby.

A Weekend in Caprarola

DAY 1

Spend your first day in Caprarola. Explore the town and the Chiesa di San Teresa del Carmelo before taking the dramatic approach road to the Palazzo Farnese. The straight road leads from the edge of town directly to the steps at the front of the main entrance.

Of the building's five floors, only the upper floor *(piano nobile)* is open to visitors – it is also where the most important works of art are kept. Access is through the central courtyard, up the spiral *Scala Regia*. This floor is divided into two splendid apartments decorated with sumptuous frescoes: those in the summer rooms are by Taddeo and Federico Zuccari, while the winter apartment features works by Bertoja, Raffaellino da Reggio, and Giovanni de' Vecchi. Don't miss the splendid gardens, with their fountains, statues, and grottoes.

DAY 2

Head for the Lago di Vico, a little lake a short distance from Caprarola. According to legend, it was Hercules who created the lake, by flinging his club to the ground. In actual fact, it is of volcanic origin and is now part of a protected nature preserve, traversed by paths and trails of varying difficulty. The lake is surrounded by a beautiful, dense, and ancient forest. There are plenty of waterbirds attracted to the lake and the woods are full of interesting flora and fauna.

For lunch, enjoy the Lazio hospitality and cuisine – perhaps some fish from nearby Lago di Vico, or rabbit and artichokes, all grown locally, and enjoyed with a glass of local Orvieto or Vignanello. If you have time, consider a trip to Civita Castellana to see its Duomo and mighty fort, as well as the town's coppersmiths, still working in ways that have changed little in hundreds of years.

Dos and Don'ts

- ✓ Make sure you spend time exploring the town of Caprarola, with its 16th-century churches.
- ✗ Don't be tempted to swim in Lago di Vico: the water is notorious for its dangerous sudden whirlpools.
- ✓ Make the most of the traditional agricultural fair, which takes place in Caprarola in June, and sample superb local produce.
- ✗ Don't gather or eat mushrooms in the area: it could be dangerous as there are many poisonous species.

Below: Lago di Vico, a paradise for nature-lovers

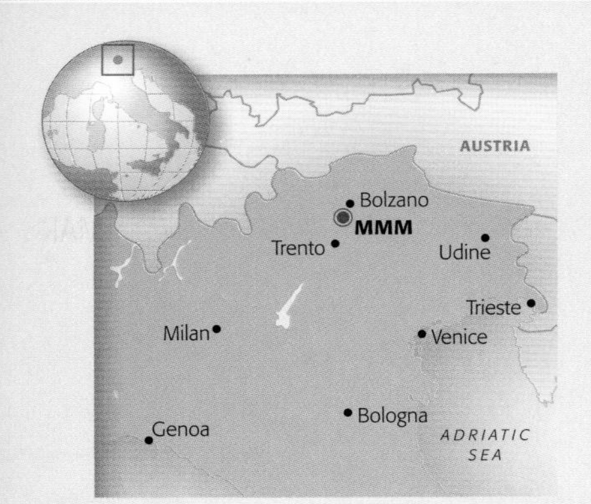

GETTING THERE
The five museums making up the Messner Mountain Museums (MMM) lie on a route that crosses a part of the Alpine range from west to east, from the peak of Ortles to the Dolomites. Start at the main museum in Castel Firmiano, not far from Bolzano (the nearest international airport is Verona); then turn toward the Val Venosta as far as Juval and from there head for Solda and the MMM in Ortles. Then, make your way to Il Ripa in Brunico and the final stage, the Dolomites at Cibiana di Cadore.

GETTING AROUND
It's best to undertake this route by car.

WEATHER
Bolzano has a typical summer climate in June, when temperatures may reach 86°F (30°C). Higher in the valley, the air becomes much cooler and temperatures fall noticeably.

ACCOMMODATIONS
Rural Hotel Sigmundskron is close to Castel Firmiano, with rooms from US$72; www.sigmundskron.com

On the road to Castel Juval, the Garni Brunner has doubles from US$68; www.garni-brunner.it

Rooms in the Dolomites mountain hut, on Monte Rite near the museum, are US$40; www.rifugiomonterite.it

The welcoming Hotel Andreashofer in Brunico has doubles from US$120; www.andreashofer.it

EATING OUT
Expect to pay around US$35 per head for a meal of local Alto Adige (South Tyrol) food.

PRICE FOR TWO
US$150–235 per day for food, accommodations, and entry to museums.

FURTHER INFORMATION
www.messner-mountain-museum.it

Reinhold Messner

Born in 1944 in Brixen, Italy, Reinhold Messner was the first person to climb all the "eight-thousanders" – the 14 peaks of the world higher than 26,247 ft (8,000 m). This was achieved without the use of oxygen or porters. Add to this, his crossing of the Antarctic by foot, and the traversing of the Gobi desert in 2004, at the age of 59, and you can see why the man enjoys such legendary status. His most recent exploit has been to set up the Messner Mountain Foundation (MMF) to support mountain peoples.

The "museum of the clouds" is the highest museum in Europe… in an old fort on Monte Rite with wide-ranging views of the most spectacular peaks in the Dolomites.

Top left: View of MMM Ortles, Solda

Left (left and right): *Torta di grano saraceno* (buckwheat cake) filled with blueberry jam, a local specialty; aerial view of the MMM at Castello di Brunico in Val Pusteria

Right (left and right): MMM Dolomites, at eye-level with the mountains; one of the inner courtyards at MMM Castel Juval

Main: Messner Mountain Museum of Firmiano
Inset: Bread, a feature of the cuisine of Trentino-Alto Adige

MOUNTAIN ADVENTURE

THE RELATIONSHIP BETWEEN MAN AND MOUNTAIN IS COMPLEX – a mixture of respect, fascination, and even fear – it's a relationship that mountaineer Reinhold Messner explores in his Messner Mountain Museums (MMM). This is a titanic project, into which the great man has thrown himself with his usual passion and iron determination. Like pieces of a giant jigsaw puzzle, the five different museums together create a complete and compelling portrait of the mountains.

The main museum, MMM Firmian, is housed in Castel Firmiano, an ancient residence near Bolzano. In a series of exhibitions, the museum describes meetings between man and mountain, confrontations in which man reflects upon and tests his own powers. Alongside areas dedicated to the history of the Alps and descriptions of the formation of the mountain chain, space is devoted to the religions that draw sustenance from such proximity. The spiritual dimension of the relationship between man and mountain is farther explored in the museum of Castello

Juval, situated on a ridge between the sunny Val Venosta and the gorge of Val Senales. Long fascinated by sacred mountains, such as Kailash in Tibet, Fujiyama in Japan, and Uluru (Ayers Rock) in Australia, Messner has constructed in one wing of the castle – his private residence – a display on the "mythology of mountains." The museum at Solda takes ice as its theme, where Messner describes the "fear of ice and of darkness" in an evocative underground space, built to resemble a crevasse in a glacier. MMM Ripa, which opened in 2010, is housed in the Castello di Brunico in Val Pusteria and is dedicated to the people who live in the mountains; it is meant to be a living museum, conceived as a place for meetings and exchanges between the local population and for visitors from other mountainous regions of the world. The final museum, MMM Dolomites, on the other hand, is a "museum of the clouds." The highest museum in Europe, it is dedicated to rock, the material of mountains, and sits at an altitude of 7,155 ft (2,180 m), in an old fort on Monte Rite with wide-ranging views of the most spectacular peaks in the Dolomites.

PEAK TO PEAK DIARY

A tour of Messner's five splendid Mountain Museums is a marvelous way of getting to know – and truly understand – the beauty of the mountains. Spend five days touring the area and you'll also get to appreciate the wonderful castles, friendly people, and enchanting landscapes that make the area such a magical attraction.

Five Days with Messner

DAY 1

Start at Castel Firmiano, first mentioned in the 10th century and the largest castle in the Alto Adige. The main Messner Mountain Museum (MMM), its huge exhibition includes pictures, sculptures, and memories of Messner's expeditions, and the history of the mountains. When creating the museum, a Neolithic grave was discovered containing a 6–7,000 year-old skeleton.

DAY 2

The second Messner Mountain Museum is in Juval at the heart of the Val Senales. The castle, perched like an eagle's eyrie on a rocky outcrop, dates back to the 13th century and was restored by Messner: it also includes a restaurant and a wine cellar.

DAY 3

The Museum of Ice is in Solda, a delightful little village that lies at the foot of the Ortles glacier. The Solda valley is a popular place, much visited in winter for the skiing and, in summer, for its many trails. There are many easy walks around the village. For something more energetic, pack a picnic and strike out into the hills.

DAY 4

The newest of the Mountain Museums is in the Castello di Brunico. It's the perfect reason for visiting the most important town in the Val Pusteria with its pretty center, today packed with shops and cafés, but still bearing traces of the old city-fortress at the foot of the castle. Enjoy a meal of speck with mushroom-flavored polenta, followed by the mountain staple of strudel.

DAY 5

The Dolomites Museum is on Monte Rite, between Pieve di Cadore and Cortina d'Ampezzo. Housed in an old ruined stronghold, it offers 360-degree views of the most spectacular peaks in the Dolomites.

Dos and Don'ts

- ✗ Don't go to the museum in Castel Firmiano if you have difficulty walking: the route is more like a hike, up and down from tower to tower, on fairly uneven ground.
- ✓ Do wear strong shoes and, in case the weather is poor, take an umbrella or waterproof coat with you, as parts of the museum are outdoors.
- ✗ The Juval Museum is open from Easter until the first Sunday in November, but you cannot visit when the Messner family is in residence; don't turn up without checking ahead.

Below: Pretty pink Alpine pennycress (*Thlaspi alpestre*)

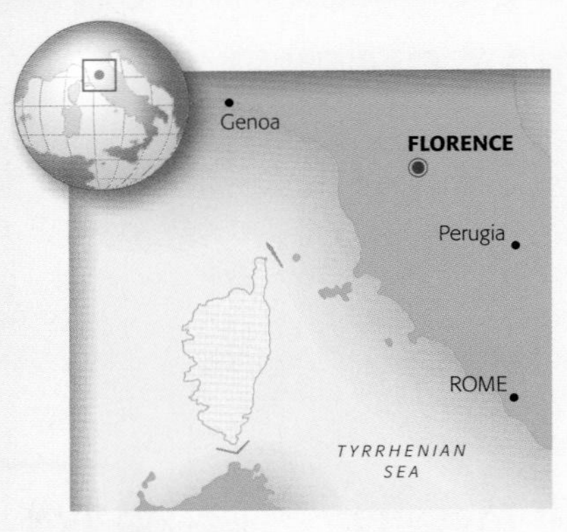

GETTING THERE
There is a shuttle bus every 30 minutes from Florence airport 3 miles (5 km) to the city center; a taxi costs around US$35. Trains and buses also run regularly between Santa Maria Novella station in Florence and Pisa airport.

GETTING AROUND
Florence is easily explored on foot.

WEATHER
It can get pretty hot here in summer, as the city is sheltered from cooling breezes – the temperature may reach as high as 95°F (35°C).

ACCOMMODATIONS
For a luxury experience, try the Hotel Lungarno. It has a collection of 20th-century paintings, and large windows that open on to the Arno River and the Ponte Vecchio – the view is superb. Rooms from US$475; www.lungarnohotels.com

The elegant B&B Il Salotto di Firenze is housed in a 19th-century palazzo in the historic center. Doubles from US$122; www.ilsalottodifirenze.it

EATING OUT
The upscale restaurant Guelfi e Ghibellini, part of the 18th-century Relais Santa Croce, offers a menu of traditional Tuscan dishes. Meals cost around US$95; www.relaissantacroce.com

Another restaurant that focuses on Tuscan cuisine is Il Latini, housed in the former stables of Palazzo Rucellai. Meals from US$55; www.illatini.com

PRICE FOR TWO
US$300–655 per day for food and accommodations.

FURTHER INFORMATION
www.firenzeturismo.it; www.maggiofiorentino.com

The Beautiful Game

On February 17, 1530, as the artillery of Charles V bombarded Florence, the besieged locals played a game of soccer on the banks of the Arno River to show their contempt for the enemy. To commemorate the match, a tournament of *calcio in livrea* (soccer in costume) is played in Florence at the end of June every year. Developed from an ancient Roman game, *calcio* is actually closer to rugby as the ball can be carried in the hands. Four teams (one for each of the quarters of Florence) of 27 players in historical dress take part in three fiercely fought matches.

CAPITAL OF CULTURE

LONG A LEADING PLAYER IN THE WORLD OF ITALIAN CULTURE, Florence plays host every year to *Maggio Musicale Fiorentino* (Musical May in Florence), one of the world's most prestigious festivals involving the great names in music and theater. The glittering series of operas, concerts, ballets, and spectacles lasts from May to June and has been hosted by the Teatro Comunale since 1933. This historic theater was built in 1862 in the western part of the city, not far from the Santo Spirito quarter, known as Oltrarno ("on the other side of the Arno River") by the Florentines because it is the only quarter of historic Florence on the Arno's left bank.

The festival is the perfect opportunity to discover all that this part of Florence has to offer. Close to the center of the city, Ponte Vecchio is the oldest bridge in Florence. Heading south across the bridge, in just a few steps you are transported from the bridge's cramped medieval atmosphere – its little workshops

Main: Symbol of the historic center of the city, the medieval Ponte Vecchio, Florence

all packed together – to the more expansive and aristocratic 16th-century Giardino di Boboli, a fine example of Italian Renaissance gardens. Other nearby monuments from the Renaissance period are Palazzo Pitti and the Basilica di Santa Maria del Santo Spirito. Palazzo Pitti, formerly a residence of the Medici family, is one of the most important galleries in Italy today. Santo Spirito was designed by the architect Brunelleschi, although the rather plain façade was not his design.

In the nearby Chiesa di Santa Maria del Carmine, you will find a clear example of the transition from the simple art of the Middle Ages to the three-dimensional compositions of the Renaissance. The sublime fresco cycle in the Cappella Brancacci (Brancacci chapel) was begun in 1425 by the artist Masolino, with many scenes painted by his pupil Masaccio, and completed in 1480 by Filippo Lippi. Their combined work forms an anthology of art in which it is possible to see the abandonment of late-Gothic forms and growing confidence with perspective – all within a few extraordinary years.

Above: Raphael's portrait of Agnolo Doni in the Galleria Palantina in Palazzo Pitti; a detail of the Cappella Brancacci fresco, inside the Chiesa di Santa Maria del Carmine

Below (left to right): Dance performance during the *Maggio Musicale Fiorentino*; Renaissance Palazzo Pitti, commissioned in 1458; sun setting over Florence, on the banks of the Arno River

MUSICAL DIARY

Florence played a pivotal role in the artistic, cultural, and intellectual revival that was the Renaissance, and has no equal in the world; today, it is a city that reveals its history everywhere you look. It is impossible to see everything in three days, so this tour concentrates on the Oltrarno or "other side of the Arno." *(see also pp12–13)*

Three Days of Great Art

DAY 1

Walk to the Oltrarno quarter across Ponte Vecchio, which spans the Arno River at its narrowest point, pausing to browse – but not buy – in the souvenir shops. Not far from the bridge stands Palazzo Pitti. Enter the museum and visit the Galleria Palatina (Palatine Gallery), home to one of the world's finest collections of art by Italian and European artists. Afterward, wander through the Giardino di Boboli, Florence's largest park. It is virtually an open-air museum, both for the many sculptures on display there and for its classic design and layout.

DAY 2

On your second day, farther explore the streets of the Santo Spirito quarter, which has always been a traditional home for craftsmen: wander the labyrinth of workshops and studios where objects of great beauty are crafted. Visit the Basilica di Santa Maria del Santo Spirito, whose perfectly proportioned, luminous interior reveals the hand of Brunelleschi. From here, head to the Chiesa di Santa Maria del Carmine, to see the fresco cycle in the Cappella Brancacci. In the evening, enjoy one of the *Maggio Musicale Fiorentino* shows.

DAY 3

For superb views over the city, climb up to the Forte del Belvedere above the city. Built behind Palazzo Pitti at the end of the 16th century, it is surrounded by an imposing pentagonal wall. In the afternoon, to avoid overdoing the sightseeing, spend some time just shopping and taking it easy. In the evening, enjoy some Tuscan cuisine – try *Tonno e fagioli* (tuna and bean salad) and *arista* (roast pork), followed by *bongo bongo* (chocolate profiteroles).

Dos and Don'ts

- ✓ Try a tender *bistecca alla fiorentina* (a thick T-bone steak), one of the city's authentic specialties.
- ✓ For something different, visit the Museo della Specola, not far from Palazzo Pitti. It's the oldest science museum in Europe and home to an extraordinary collection of wax models.
- ✗ Don't be tempted by the stalls around Ponte Vecchio: they often sell poor quality merchandise aimed at tourists. Go, instead, to the historic Florentine market of San Lorenzo. Even here, though, it is best to examine goods carefully and haggle.
- ✓ Book tickets for concerts and shows at the *Maggio Musicale*. Find out more information from www.maggiofiorentino.com

Below: Wagner's *Siegfried* performed at the *Maggio Musicale Fiorentino*

GETTING THERE
At the tip of Italy's "heel," in Puglia, Santa Maria di Leuca is served by Brindisi airport 75 miles (120 km); from here, take the SS613 to Lecce, the SS16 as far as Maglie, and the SS275 to Santa Maria di Leuca.

GETTING AROUND
A car is best for ease and convenience.

WEATHER
Summer is long and hot, but not muggy, because of the coastal position.

ACCOMMODATIONS
The pleasant-looking Grand Hotel l'Approdo has a diving school and looks out onto the marina. Rooms from US$110; www.hotelapprodo.com

The *agriturismo* Alcorico is an old farmhouse with an appealingly rustic atmosphere set among olive groves, five minutes from Santa Maria di Leuca. Doubles from US$95; www.agriturismoalcorico.com

EATING OUT
The restaurant in the Grand Hotel l'Approdo offers fresh fish and sublime sea views; meals around US$40.

The *agriturismo* Serine offers dishes from the peasant tradition of the Salento peninsula using top-quality homegrown ingredients. Meals cost around US$35; www.agriturismoserine.it

PRICE FOR TWO
You will need around US$205 per day for food and accommodations.

FURTHER INFORMATION
www.leuca.info; www.salento.it

The Beautiful City

Derived from the Greek for beautiful city *(kalé polis),* Gallipoli's name – not to be confused with the Turkish peninsula – is perfectly suited to this town on the Salentine coast, overlooking the Ionian sea. Built on a small island linked to the mainland by a stone bridge, Gallipoli's Old Town is a maze of narrow streets of tufa houses and old palazzi. The town is dominated by the massive bulk of the 16th-century castle and surrounded by walls, along which there is a path with panoramic views over a delightful, clean, and clear blue sea.

Above: Trulli houses on the Adriatic coast; fishermen landing their catch in Santa Maria di Leuca's harbor
Main: Naturally formed bathing pool among the rocks at Santa Maria di Leuca

BETWEEN TWO SEAS

SANTA MARIA DI LEUCA, OR SIMPLY LEUCA, lies at the very tip of the "heel" of the Italian boot, just where the waters of the Adriatic mingle with the waters of the Ionian sea – locals say that there's sometimes a line of two distinct colors at the point where the currents meet. The town is built along the foot of a long promontory topped by a church and a lighthouse, whose sweeping beam of light has assisted ships on their way from one sea to the other since 1866. The southerly location also means that this has always been a point of transit, a meeting place where different Mediterranean populations came into contact, resulting in a rich culture open to new influences. It is no coincidence that the legends say this was the first landing place on Italian soil not only for Aeneas, fleeing the destruction of Troy, but also for St. Peter, who arrived from Palestine much later to begin his evangelical work. The church is said to date from the era of St. Peter (although its current form dates from the 18th century) and was supposedly built on the site of a Roman temple of Minerva. The church's name, Santa Maria de Finibus Terrae (St. Mary at Land's End), is a reminder that this is a physical border, a clear line of demarcation, like the waters of the two seas.

The indented coastline is home to lovely sandy beaches as well as mysterious caves, carved out over millennia by the action of the waves.

And it's the sea that makes Leuca unique: transparent, crystalline, and stirred by currents which bring it alive, it is bordered by an indented coastline that is home to lovely sandy beaches as well as mysterious caves, carved out over millennia by the action of the waves. Head inside these caves and discover large cathedral-like caverns in which the water, illuminated by sunlight seeping through cracks between the rocks, takes on many different shades of color. These caves have been used since ancient times – some walls have Greek and Latin inscriptions while others bear evidence of Neolithic inhabitants. Today, they are the realm of scuba divers, keen to discover an underwater paradise rich in fish, corals, and rocks in all kinds of fantastic shapes and mysterious forms.

Inset: Grotta di Ciolo, a place of great fascination for divers and cavers
Below (left to right): Statue at the Chiesa di Santa Maria de Finibus Terrae; promenade on Santa Maria di Leuca's harbor; *frisedde*, a crisp local bread

CAVER'S DIARY

Santa Maria di Leuca lies on a fabulous stretch of Salento coast and is a much loved vacation spot in Puglia. Six days should be long enough to relax fully in this restful environment, where the sea crashes against the rocky shore carving out spectacular caves, and quiet green pine woods ring the whitewashed villages.

Six Days in Italy's Heel

DAYS 1–2

The first thing to do on arrival in Santa Maria di Leuca is to get into the cool sea. Don't waste time traveling, stay local to allow more time on the beach. In the evening, stroll to the lighthouse to watch the sunset: climb up to its terrace to see the two Salento seas, the Ionian and the Adriatic.

Go on a trip to one of the sea caves close to Santa Maria di Leuca. Two of the most beautiful, and easily reached by land, are Grotta la Porcinara, which has Greek and Latin inscriptions, and the Grotta del Diavolo, in which Neolithic remains were discovered.

DAYS 3–4

Leuca has interesting 19th-century villas along the promenade – look out for the Villa De Francesco-Licci, the Villa Daniele-Romasi, built in Moorish style, and the Villa Episcopo, which is reminiscent of a Chinese pagoda. Stop for a drink at a bar in the port and watch the fishermen returning home with their catch.

Drive out to the Grotta delle Veneri, near Parabita. This large natural cavern is where two female statuettes were found, dating from a period between 12,000 and 14,000 years ago and evidence of the worship of Dea Madre (Earth Mother), an ancient symbol of fertility.

DAYS 5–6

Take a trip northwest to the delightful town of Gallipoli. The Old Town is set on an island attached to a promontory, surrounded by harbors and dominated by the huge Castello Aragonese. Don't miss the vast Baroque Duomo with its great white façade.

Ponte del Ciolo, to the northeast, is a great place for divers. You can also visit some of the caves that are only accessible from the sea, such as the Grotta di Ciolo. The cliffs here are a favorite spot for people to jump off the rocks into the water and swim up to the caves.

Dos and Don'ts

- ✓ Make sure you have sunglasses, a hat, and good sun block: Puglia is very hot and sunny in summer.
- ✗ Don't go diving in the caves if you are inexperienced: even though they look enticing, the currents can be tricky.
- ✓ Travel by car: traveling around by train in these parts of Puglia can be slow and difficult.

Below: A Gallipoli alleyway

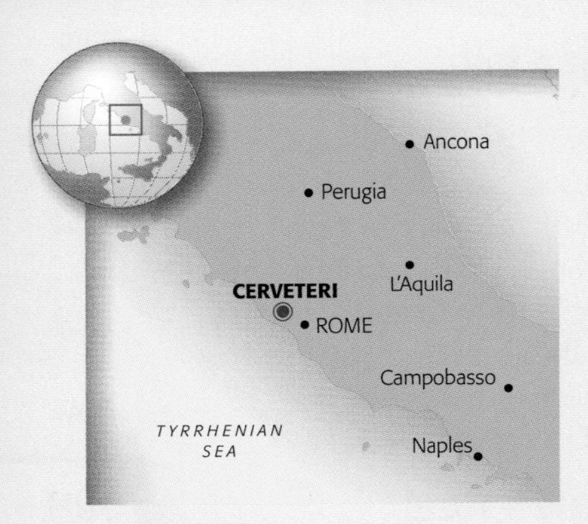

GETTING THERE
Cerveteri is around 25 miles (40 km) to the northwest of Rome and is easily reached from the capital or its airport (Fiumicino) by car, on the Via Aurelia (SS1) or the freeway A12 (exit Cerveteri-Ladispoli). Or you can take the bus.

GETTING AROUND
A bus service links Cerveteri with the Necropoli della Banditaccia 1 mile (2 km) away. It takes about 20 minutes to get there on foot. To explore the surrounding area, it is best to use a car.

WEATHER
Pleasantly summery, with average temperatures between 61°F and 79°F (16– 26°C).

ACCOMMODATIONS
Casa del Sole, a welcoming B&B in Cerveteri, has rooms from US$95; www.cerveteribreakfast.it

Isola di Rosa is a charming period residence with a health club, set in the hills a few minutes outside town. Doubles from US$135; www.isoladirosa.com

EATING OUT
At the Antica Locanda le Ginestre you can enjoy creative cooking based on fish dishes. Expect to pay around US$48–55 (tel. 06 994 0672).

For dining by the Lago di Bracciano, try Il Pescatore, which specializes in freshwater fish. Meals around US$40 (tel. 06 998 06013).

Fish is also the specialty at La Caletta, in Anguillara, with a seafront terrace overlooking a private beach. Meals around US$28–35 (www.la-caletta.com).

PRICE FOR TWO
Around US$245 per day for food, accommodations, and entry to the Necropoli della Banditaccia.

FURTHER INFORMATION
www.caere.it

A Perfect Lake

Such are the attractions of Lago di Bracciano that visitors return here time and again: they are drawn by the natural beauty of the landscape, its archeological and artistic heritage, and the sporting opportunities it offers. The lake is ideal for swimming, sailing, windsurfing, and even diving. Set among wooded hills, the three towns on its shores – Bracciano, Trevignano Romano, and Anguillara Sabazia – have Etruscan tombs, Renaissance castles, and Baroque buildings to explore, as well as wonderful restaurants serving fish from the lake.

Left: *Cinghiale in agrodolce alla romana* (sweet and sour wild boar)

Right (left to right): *Tomb of the Married Couple*, a masterpiece of Etruscan art from the Necropoli della Banditaccia; Anguillara overlooking Lago di Bracciano; waterfowl feeding as the sun sets on Lake Bracciano

Main: Tombs at the Necropoli della Banditaccia

CITIES OF THE DEAD

For two hundred years, between the 7th and 5th centuries BC, Etruscan Cerveteri, known then as Cisra, was one of the largest and most important towns in the Mediterranean. Over the next 200 hundred years, the city saw its influence diminish, just as Rome's star was rising, until in 273 BC it was totally absorbed into Rome's political orbit. Eclipsed by the feats of the Romans, the Etruscans remain relatively unknown to us. However, the well-preserved ruins at Cerveteri reveal significant insights into this ancient and sophisticated civilization.

Most of our knowledge of this mysterious people comes from their vast necropolises or cemeteries. The most important of these is the Necropoli della Banditaccia. This magnificent "city of the dead" extends over 1½ sq miles (4 sq km), and features around a thousand tombs in various styles and from different periods of Etruscan history, enabling us to understand a great deal more about their civilization, beliefs, and burial rituals. The oldest graves, which

Above: Palazzo Ruspoli in Cerveteri, now a museum of Etruscan artifacts

Below: Castello Orsini Odescalchi in Bracciano, one of the finest feudal residences in Europe

date from between the 9th and 8th centuries BC, take the form of a pit in which the ashes of the deceased were placed. Later the tombs became larger and more elaborate as the custom of cremation changed to one of burial. Circular underground chambers were cut into the rock and covered with a tumulus, or lined up as though in a street plan in "cube" form. The most interesting thing for archeologists about these tombs is that they are often modeled on the homes of the deceased, decorated with beautiful frescoes and filled with rich furnishings and objects of everyday use. The Tomb of the Reliefs is an underground tomb named after the fine painted stucco decorations on the walls, representing animals and domestic objects such as axes, ropes, fans, necklaces, and cups. Another example is the Tomb of Shields and Chairs, with six beds and pillows carved out of stone, as well as two chairs with curved backs and with a stool, on which votive terracotta statues were placed.

Wandering the silent "streets" of this burial ground and seeing these touching domestic items – testaments of love or respect – you can't help but feel moved by the noble and artistic Etruscan culture.

ETRUSCAN DIARY

Until the 5th century BC, Cerveteri was a powerful Etruscan city which made its fortune from trading. Only the huge necropolis remains to give us some idea about their advanced civilization. Five days is long enough to explore the Etruscan ruins as well as spend some time around the delightful Lago di Bracciano.

Five Days by the Lake

DAY 1

Start with a visit to the Necropoli della Banditaccia. The visitor route is a pleasant walk through what feels like an ancient ruined city, with main streets and side streets, along which the tombs are arranged as though following some gridded street plan.

DAY 2

Explore the historic center of Cerveteri, with its fortress, medieval quarter, and 16th-century Palazzo Ruspoli. This is home to the Museo Nazionale Cerite, with an assortment of objects from the nearby necropolises.

DAY 3

Enjoy a trip to Bracciano, mirrored in the waters of the lake of the same name. The town, a popular vacation destination, is dominated by the impressive bulk of Castello Orsini Odescalchi, a pentagonal fortress dating from the 15th century. The countryside around the lake is enchanting and it is a lovely area for walking.

DAY 4

Take a day trip to Anguillara, the most picturesque town on Lago di Bracciano. Built on a rocky spur pushing out into the lake, it shields an interesting historic center within its walls. From the terrace at the heart of the town there are lovely views over the lake; the scenery can also be enjoyed from the path around the town walls.

DAY 5

To learn still more about the Etruscans, visit the ancient city of Norchia, close to the pretty village of Vetralla, north of Cerveteri: it is an important Etruscan archeological site that features a necropolis set in a particularly scenic landscape.

Dos and Don'ts

- ⊗ Don't attempt to visit all the archeological sites of Cerveteri without checking the details first – some are not open to the public. For information, speak to the staff at the Necropoli della Banditaccia, the only site with regular opening hours.
- ✓ For information on trails and activities in the nature preserve of Lake Bracciano, visit www.parcobracciano.it
- ⊗ Don't miss the *Infiorata* in Cerveteri, a festival during the Feast of Corpus Domini, in May–June. Locals strew the streets with flowers, petals, and striking floral compositions.

Below: A "cube" tomb in the Necropoli della Banditaccia

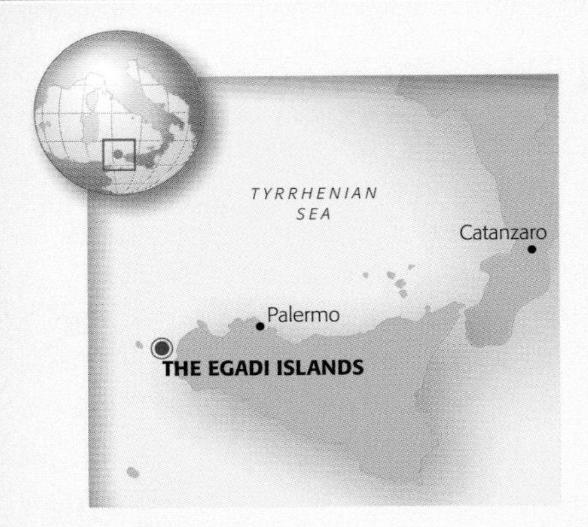

GETTING THERE
The Egadi Islands – Favignana, Levanzo, and Marettimo – lie just off the western coast of Sicily, close to Trapani. This town is served by Vincenzo Florio airport and by Palermo's airport. There are transfers to Trapani from both airports and ferry services from Trapani to the islands.

GETTING AROUND
Frequent ferries connect all the islands. Explore Favignana by mountain bike or scooter. Levanzo and Marettimo are criss-crossed by paths, making it enjoyable to discover them on foot. Boat trips are an essential part of any stay.

WEATHER
Expect a Mediterranean climate, with high summer temperatures, tempered by cooling sea breezes.

ACCOMMODATIONS
On Favignana, the small Hotel Aegusa, close to the harbor, has rooms from US$74; www.aegusahotel.it

The Hotel Egadi has a warm welcome for visitors. Doubles from US$88; www.albergoegadi.it

EATING OUT
The restaurant at the Hotel Egadi is renowned for its cooking – the menu, specializing in fish, offers traditional fare with a modern touch. Meals cost around US$68.

On Marettimo, dine at the innovative La Scaletta, where the menu is based on the daily catch – by reservation only. Meals cost from US$48–55 (tel. 0923 923 233).

PRICE FOR TWO
Around US$270 per day including meals and accommodations, ferry journeys, a trip to the Grotta del Genovese, and scooter rental.

FURTHER INFORMATION
www.egadi.com

Fishing Folk Tradition

Tuna fishing has always been important to these islands, so much so that it is even depicted in the Paleolithic drawings found in the Grotta del Genovese on the island of Levanzo. Today, the yearly *mattanza,* the traditional method of tuna fishing, still takes place, even now that, with so few tuna in the waters around the Egadi islands, it has almost turned into a folk ceremony. Conducted using age-old methods and accompanied by ancient songs of Arab origin, the *mattanza* is a bloody rite that belongs to a world somewhat distant from modern sensitivities.

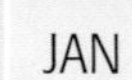

Above (left to right): The dome of La Chiesa Matrice, Favignana; tuna products from the *mattanza*; Egadi Island locals, keeping out of the sun
Main: The beautiful bay of Cala Rossa in Favignana, once a tufa quarry

THE FLOATING WORLD

SLIVERS OF MEDITERRANEAN PARADISE, the Egadi Islands are three tiny scraps of land, still wild for the most part and surrounded by crystal clear sea. Although the islands are only a short hop from Sicily, arriving here is like landing in a different world. The light is intense, reflecting off the white-painted houses and pale tufa rock, while the deep-blue, cloudless sky arcs overhead, fusing with the sparkling crystal sea on the horizon in a myriad shades of ultramarine.

Favignana, the largest of the islands, has a rugged and barren landscape. At the jagged coast, the thin soil has been scraped off to expose the tufa rock – the quarries have supplied stone to Sicily and north Africa for hundreds of years. The butterfly-shaped island is divided in two by a mountainous ridge – its highest point is Monte Santa Caterina, topped with a fort built by the Normans and extended in the 17th century by the Spanish. Forgotten about for centuries, Favignana's destiny is wrapped up in the blue sea that surrounds it and inevitably dictates the life of the islanders.

Traditionally, fishing and tuna are the main sources of the island's economy, but with fish stocks in decline, tourism is growing in importance. The surrounding sea is full of interest, washed by currents which leave the water beautifully clear and its treasures of corals and fish are revealed to visitors through boat trips and scuba diving.

Nearby lie the other two islands in the archipelago. Marettimo is the wildest and most unspoiled, partly because there are no cars on the island. It is, however, criss-crossed with walking trails to secluded coves that are ideal for bathing. Levanzo is the smallest island, renowned for its pebble beaches and the Grotta del Genovese. This cave houses an extraordinary archeological discovery – paintings dating back to the Paleolithic era, when the island was still joined to mainland Sicily, depicting men, animals, and fish, and possibly showing an ancient scene of tuna fishing.

The deep-blue cloudless
ky arcs overhead, fusing
vith the sparkling sea on
the horizon in a myriad
shades of ultramarine.

Inset: Tuna boats at Favignana
Below (left and right): A pebble beach on Levanzo; white houses ringing Levanzo's little harbor

TUNA FISHING DIARY

A nature preserve since 1992, Favignana and the Egadi Islands offer visitors an unspoiled maritime heritage and the enchantment of pristine, clear waters rich in marine life. A stay of three days allows a day on each island, although if you fall under the isles' magical spell, you just might wish to stay for longer.

Three Days in the Blue

DAY 1

Start off on the island of Favignana. Mostly flat – except for the peak of Monte Santa Caterina – it can be explored with ease by bicycle or scooter. A boat ride around the island from the harbor is also a must, giving you the chance to admire the glorious landscape of coves and clear sea. In the evening, enjoy the gastronomic specialties of the island such as couscous and, of course, tuna in one of its many forms: *bottarga* (dried and pressed tuna roe), *bresaola* (smoked and cured then sliced), or simply grilled as a steak.

DAY 2

Pack some supplies and take a boat to Levanzo; a number of paths lead from the harbor across the island. After a couple of hours' walk (or with less effort, by boat) you can reach the Grotta del Genovese and admire the incredible paintings, discovered in 1949. Going by boat also allows you to look down through the clear water, even to the sea bed.

DAY 3

Explore Marettimo, the wildest of the Egadi Islands. There are no cars and you'll need to bring supplies of water and something for a picnic. The island is riddled with paths leading through a harsh and barren limestone landscape to bays of extraordinary beauty. Look out for rare botanical species, the result of the island's isolation. The easiest way of getting to know the island, however, is to tour the coast by boat, and admire the cliffs, bays, and sea caves.

Dos and Don'ts

- ✓ If you enjoy fishing, organize a boat trip with local fishermen. The fishing trips can last up to two or three days, but will be an unforgettable experience. You can also organize shorter trips, should you wish.
- ✓ If you can, go diving in the waters of the Egadi Islands, as the views of the sea floor can be spectacular.
- ✗ Don't take part in night diving trips unless you are already an expert scuba diver.
- ✓ Book trips to the Grotta del Genovese in Levanzo in advance by telephoning 0923 924 032 or 339 741 8800. For the latest information, visit the website www.grottadelgenovese.it

Below: A traditional Marettimo house

GETTING THERE
Villa Barbaro is in Maser, in the eastern Veneto. Treviso is the nearest airport, 19 miles (31 km) away by car.

GETTING AROUND
A car is best for exploring this area of the Veneto.

WEATHER
June is a hot month inland, with daytime temperatures reaching over 86°F (30°C).

ACCOMMODATIONS
The Antica Locanda di Maser, with simple but comfortable rooms, is within walking distance of Villa Barbaro; doubles from US$75; www.locandadimaser.it

The elegant Hotel Villa Cipriani, once home to Robert Browning, stands in an enchanting position in the Asolo hills; doubles from US$482; www.ciprianiasolo.com

In Bassano del Grappa, the Bonotto Hotel Belvedere is an atmospheric hotel with a long history and elegant rooms; doubles from US$135; www.bonotto.it

EATING OUT
In Asolo, Cà Derton offers a modern take on traditional Veneto cuisine (dinner from US$55); www.caderton.com; Osteria La Trave (from US$34) also serves regional specialties; tel. 0423 952292.

In Bassano, the elegant Al Ponte has lovely riverside views and serves good regional cooking (from US$48); www.alpontedibassano.com

PRICE FOR TWO
US$245–655 per day, depending on your choice of hotel, but including accommodations, meals, car rental, and admission to the villa.

FURTHER INFORMATION
www.villadimaser.it

Asolo, City of Art and Culture

Asolo was first a Roman and then a Venetian possession. When, in 1489, Caterina Cornaro, widow of the king of Cyprus, abdicated in favor of Venice, she was given the fiefdom of Asolo, and the town became home to an elegant Renaissance court of humanists and men of letters. In later centuries it continued to attract writers and artists, among them poet Robert Browning, explorer and writer Freya Stark, and Italian stage actress Eleonora Duse, who is buried in the little cemetery of Sant'Anna.

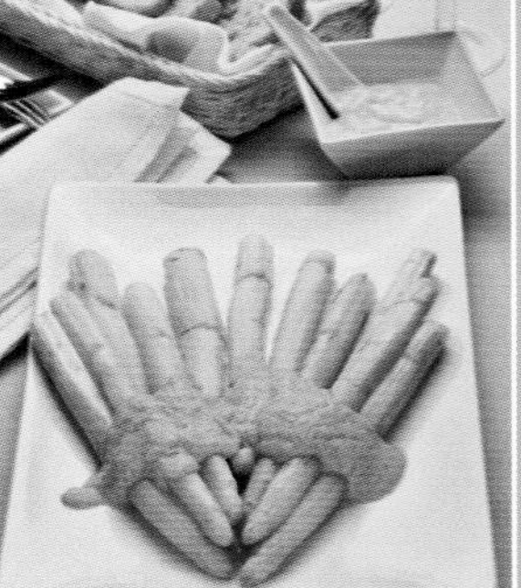

Left: White asparagus, a typical product of the region

Right (left to right): Interior of the Gispoteca Canoviana, a museum dedicated to the sculptor Canova, in Possagno; splendidly decorated doorway in Villa Barbaro; Ponte Vecchio at Bassano del Grappa; view of the Tempietto; Villa Barbaro's nymphaeum with its pool

Inset: Porticoes at Villa Barbaro, shaded from the hot summer sun

Main: Villa Barbaro's perfect Palladian main façade

PALLADIO'S LAST MASTERPIECE

THE VILLA BARBARO AT MASER is one of architect Andrea Palladio's finest creations. It was begun in 1550 on the site of an exisiting medieval house belonging to Andrea and Marcantonio Barbaro, both emiment figures in the Veneto Humanist culture. Palladio's design is of refined lightness, and succeeds in combining the needs of an elegant noble residence with those of a country house that continued to function as a working farm.

The front of the villa is impressive: the central portion is of Classical inspiration, with a pediment supported by columns reminiscent of Greek temples, flanked by two porticoed wings culminating in dovecotes, in a perfectly symmetrical design that emphasizes its architectural compactness. Behind the villa is a nymphaeum, some of whose figures are thought to have been carved by Marcantonio Barbaro himself. From its spring-water pool, thanks to an ingenious hydraulic system, water could be transported to the service quarters and then on to the garden.

Palladio's design is of refined lightness, and succeeds in combining the needs of an elegant noble residence with those of a country house.

TREVISO DIARY

Villa Barbaro is a particular gem among the villas of the Veneto, but the province of Treviso in which it lies is full of artistic and literary interest, and also has poignant reminders of the tragedies and heroics of both world wars. Over the course of three days you will have the chance to discover all three facets of this fascinating region.

Three Days of Contrasts

DAY 1

Allow a full day for visiting Villa Barbaro. Before you reach the villa, pause at the Tempietto, and then enjoy your first sight of the villa's façade. Inside, take your time studying little details in the splendid frescoed rooms. As well as the central room (the "crossing"), make sure you also see the rooms of Olympus, Bacchus and Conjugal Love, the Room of the Dog, and the Room of the Lamp. Then visit the gardens and, a short way from the villa, the Museum of Carriages, displaying elegant transportation from past centuries.

DAY 2

Visit Asolo, about 4 miles (7 km) west of Maser, a favorite destination for writers and artists in the 19th century. Its appeal is partly due to its delightful position, set in the cypress-covered foothills of the Dolomites, but also to the old heart of the town, centered around Piazza Maggiore, with its 14th-century cathedral and fortress, which offers lovely panoramic views over the countryside. From here, head north to Possagno, the birthplace of Canova, to see the striking temple he created for the town as well as his sculpture museum.

DAY 3

Today, drive the 19 miles (31 km) west to Bassano del Grappa. Despite much devastation of the city during World War II, it has retained one of the most interesting historic centers in the region. The chief highlight is the bridge, the Ponte Vecchio, originally designed by Palladio and the site of the Alpine troops' heroic resistance after the defeat of Caporetto. Ernest Hemingway was an ambulance driver in Bassano, and wrote part of *A Farewell to Arms* here.

Dos and Don'ts

- ✓ Make sure that the Villa Barbaro is open before setting out: it is closed several days a week. For details, check the website: www.villadimaser.it
- ✓ Sample the wines made in the cellars of Villa Barbaro, where they still use grapes from the vineyards around the villa, as they did in the era of Palladio.
- ✓ At Bassano del Grappa visit Villa Angarano. Although its original design by Palladio was modified by Baldassare Longhena, it is still well worth seeing.
- ✗ Don't overdo the grappa, a spirit distilled from the grape skins and pips left over after wine making. Its gentle fragrance is deceptive – it is very strong.

The internal layout of the villa is unusual. Its central block was intended as reception rooms and designed to look like a palazzo in itself, with a great cross-shaped salon from which other rooms lead off. The frescoes of Paolo Veronese make this salon unique. His paintings form part of the architecture, with *trompe l'oeil* doors, painted columns, and niches with statues, and even fantastic landscapes that blur the boundary between indoors and outside.

The hand of Palladio, who was greatly inspired by Classical models, can also be seen in the Tempietto which stands at the foot of the slope below the villa. This temple-church is one of the last works by the great architect. His genius is revealed once again in the innovative layout, which effortlessly combines a cylinder and a Greek cross and is surmounted by a dome inspired by Rome's Pantheon, supported by four massive pilasters.

Tradition has it that Palladio died at Maser in 1580, still working on the building. It survives today as a perfect summation of his masterly balance of architectural form with human needs.

Below: Fresco by Paolo Veronese inside Villa Barbaro

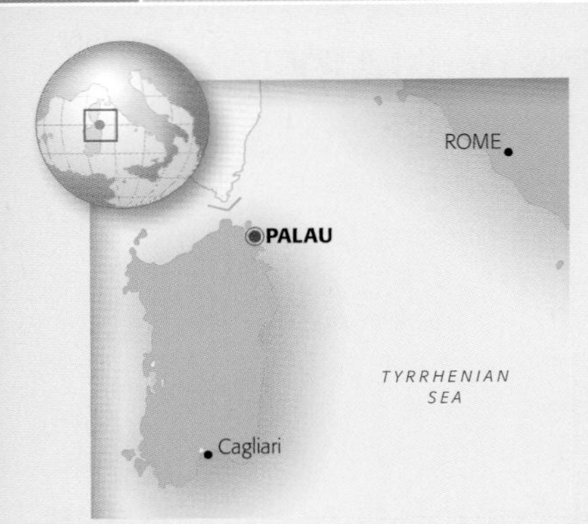

GETTING THERE
Palau lies in the north of Sardinia, with the Maddalena archipelago just offshore. Olbia airport is 25 miles (40 km) away. Take the SS125 for Palau and other towns on the eastern coast. A bus service runs from the airport to the town in summer.

GETTING AROUND
A car is necessary for exploring the area.

WEATHER
Pleasantly warm, with daytime temperatures averaging 82°F (28°C), but there is always a sea breeze. It can get relatively cool in the evenings.

ACCOMMODATIONS
Isola dei Gabbiani camp site is ideal for surfers: you can rent all the necessary gear and take lessons. Accommodations ranges from a pitch for your own tent (US$10, plus US$12 per person) to bungalows at US$80; www.isoladeigabbiani.it

Hotel Le Dune is close to the beaches of Isola dei Gabbiani and Porto Pollo, a short stroll from wind- and kitesurfing schools; doubles from US$150; www.hotelledune.it

EATING OUT
If you want to try the simple but flavorsome cooking of Gallura (such as *suppa coata*, a traditional peasant dish of durum wheat bread, meat broth, and Pecorino cheese), visit one of the many *agriturismo* farms (known here as *stazzi*) in the area, such as Saltara (dinner from US$35); www.agriturismosaltara.it

PRICE FOR TWO
US$175–315 per day for accommodations, food, and car rental, but not lessons or equipment rental.

FURTHER INFORMATION
www.palau.it

The Vermentino Grape

The grape variety Vermentino thrives in the maritime climate of Gallura. It arrived in Sardinia in the 14th century from Corsica, where it had been brought, in turn, from Spain. The wine produced from it is a dry yet soft white, with an intense perfume that evokes flowers and peaches. In Gallura this wine has now been awarded the status of DOCG (*denominazione di origine controllata e garantita*, or guaranteed denomination of origin). It is the perfect accompaniment to the region's fish dishes. Another delicious Gallura wine is Moscato di Tempio, a sweet and aromatic sparkling apéritif or dessert wine.

Above: Cork oak, typical of the island vegetation

Above right (left to right): Sardinian donkey; Aragonese tower of Santa Teresa di Gallura; windsurfer on the sands of Porto Pollo; Roccia dell'Orso (Bear Rock), a natural monument of wind-carved granite

Below (top to bottom): Sunset over Capo Testa, just to the north of Santa Teresa; the lovely beach and bay of Sciumara

Main: Windsurfers making the most of the brisk breezes offshore at Porto Pollo

ON THE CREST OF A WAVE

An emerald sea, a warm wind blowing, a coastline bordered by dune-fringed white beaches, sunbeams dancing across a sandy seabed through crystal clear water – all these create an idyllic setting for the spectacular twists and turns of the windsurfers' vividly colored sails. You could easily think that you're in the Caribbean, but you are not. This is the spectacular coastline of Isola dei Gabbiani (Island of Seagulls), near Palau in northern Sardinia.

Here, every year, from the beginning of summer, keen boarders and surfers converge from all over the world, professionals and beginners alike, all confident of finding the best possible conditions for practicing their favorite sport. The secret behind this is the particular, impossible-to-replicate weather patterns on both land and sea. This part of Sardinia's northeast coast is perfectly exposed to the Mediterranean winds known here as the *Tramontana* (north wind), the *Maestrale* (northwest wind), the *Ponente* (west wind), and the *Sirocco* (southwest wind), which

take seasonal turns to sweep undisturbed over perfect bays and beaches such as Porto Pollo, Porto Liscia, Porto Pozzo, Santa Teresa di Gallura, and the aforementioned Isola dei Gabbiani.

The latter is a particular favorite among boarders and surfers due to its geography. Despite its name, it is in fact a peninsula, linked to the coast by a narrow strip of sandy ground. The bays on either side of this have something to suit everyone, whatever that person's sport, style, or level of expertise, and whatever the weather. The west bay is characterized by a steady, light wind and constant wave movement, while the bay to the east, on which Porto Pollo lies, is more sheltered and offers smoother water but more blustery gusts of wind.

This image of a water sporting paradise is completed by the Isola dei Gabbiani itself, which is wholly devoted to a center for windsurfing and kitesurfing, with a camp site, vacation village and other facilities to cater for a surfer's every need. If the thrill of waves and water is what you seek, follow the example of those in the know and head for this beautiful corner of Sardinia.

WATER SPORTS DIARY

Palau is a town that lives by and for the sea. A paradise for water sports fans, it is also a perfect base from which to explore Gallura, one of the most fascinating parts of Sardinia. With five days at your disposal you can try out all the best beaches and a wide range of sports, as well as having time to relax on the sand and watch the experts at play.

Five Days of Sea Breezes

DAY 1

Spend the first day windsurfing. The best place for trying your hand at manoeuvres with the board is Porto Pollo, in a cove to the west of Palau: near here you will also find the legendary Isola dei Gabbiani, where surfing fans from all over the world congregate.

DAY 2

Pack a picnic and go for a walk to Capo d'Orso, which takes its name from a large granite rock whose form is reminiscent of a bear *(orso)*. Standing 400 ft (122 m) high, it overlooks one of the most beautiful stretches of the Sardinian coast. From the headland, walk down to the lovely Cala Capra cove, well sheltered from winds, where the transparent waters are perfect for snorkeling.

DAY 3

For another day of water and wind, head for Porto Pozzo, set at the end of a long, narrow cove west of Porto Pollo, offering modern facilities in a wild, unspoiled setting. As well as windsurfing, kitesurfing courses are taught here.

DAY 4

Today, visit Porto Raphael, one of the most beautiful villages on this lovely coast, with a charming little square facing the beach. There is a famous yacht club here that organizes prestigious regattas. After lunch, head to Cala di Trana for another chance to swim in a secluded cove.

DAY 5

Spend your last day in and around Santa Teresa di Gallura. The town was founded in 1808 by Vittorio Emanuele I of Savoy, who named it after his wife, Queen Teresa, and designed its street grid. Santa Teresa is set on a picturesque promontory popular with scuba divers: lessons and equipment rental are widely available. Alternatively, head down from the church square to the coral sands of Rena Bianca beach. Here, you can rent a pedalo or canoe to reach the many secluded coves scattered along the coast.

Dos and Don'ts

- ✓ Even if you are not a surfer, it is worth going along to Isola dei Gabbiani to admire the champions out on the waves.
- ✓ Try strawberry-tree honey; its slight bitterness goes well with *Pecorino sardo*, the Sardinian sheep's milk cheese.
- ✗ Don't set off without having booked a place to stay. The Sardinian coast is always busy in summer, so hotel rooms and even camp site pitches will be hard to find.

Below: Strawberry tree *(Arbutus unedo)*, used to make honey and jam

JULY

Where to Go: **July**

July is the height of summer and a busy time in the vacation season. It's also the month when some of Italy's most beautiful cities host major festivals, featuring superb music and some of the most illustrious names in international performance. At the start of the month, the Festival dei Due Mondi, in Spoleto, is already in full swing; next Perugia's piazzas ring to the sound of jazz; and then Ravenna puts on its festival of music and dance. If you'd rather hear the songs of birds, you'll appreciate the natural harmony of the wilderness of the Monti Sibillini, where you can find old towns like Sarnano. In July, the heat is on and the temperature is rising – so much so that many head for the mountains to find some cool, fresh air. For example, to the peaks of the Valle d'Aosta, with its

FESTIVALS AND CULTURE

RAVENNA Balinese dancing at the Ravenna Festival

RIVA DEL GARDA
Trentino-Alto Adige

A peaceful little town with a lovely lakeside promenade

On the banks of the lake from which it takes its name, Riva del Garda hosts a well-known classical music festival every year in July.

www.lagodigarda.it

RAVENNA
Emilia-Romagna

A harmony of music and art

The early Christian churches of Ravenna, decorated with fantastic Byzantine mosaics, are annually turned into extraordinary venues for a festival of music and dance.

See pp184–5

TORRE DEL LAGO PUCCINI
Tuscany

Home of Giacomo Puccini

Each summer, in its open-air theater by the lake, Torre del Lago hosts a festival to Puccini, the composer who lived and died here.

www.torredellago.com

"One need only hear a few notes of music for the mosaics to appear brought back to life."

PERUGIA
Umbria

Scene of one of Europe's major jazz festivals

In Perugia the piazzas, walls, and monuments of the old city echo with musical invention during the celebrated Umbria Jazz festival.

See pp176–7

SPOLETO
Umbria

Music and drama in a town with a medieval heart

A hillside town with a typically medieval appearance, Spoleto is a fabulous setting for this fascinating festival of music and theater.

See pp190–91

UNFORGETTABLE JOURNEYS

MARATEA The beautiful volcanic sand beach of Cersuta in Maratea

MARATEA
Basilicata

By a beautiful sea that is deep, clean, and full of life

Maratea is set on the coast in a magnificent geographical position, with a glorious sea on one side and rocky hills and cliffs on the other.

See pp178–9

THE CHIANTIGIANA
TUSCANY

A not-so-humble back road between Florence and Siena

By car or by bike, the Chiantigiana takes you through some stunning scenery, and passes right through the heart of the Chianti wine region.

www.sienaonline.com

THE VIA EMILIA
EMILIA-ROMAGNA

Down Emily Street

The Roman Via Emilia was a ruler-straight road running across northern Italy. You can follow it by train through some of the finest cities in Europe.

www.emiliaromagnaturismo.it

IDROVIA FERRARESE
EMILIA-ROMAGNA

Venice's Grand Canal isn't the only canal in Italy

The Ferrara waterway is navigable for 40 miles (65 km), linking the Po with the Adriatic and passing through the beautiful city of Ferrara.

www.adriacoast.com/eng-index.php

BRENTA CANAL
VENETO

Live a dream in Palladian villas owned by the aristocracy

Tour these noble residences by boat, stopping off at some, including Villa Foscari, built by Andrea Palladio in 1559 on the Brenta canal.

www.battellidelbrenta.it

NATURAL WONDERS

FÉNIS AND ISSOGNE The Valle d'Aosta, a perfect place for horseback-riding

CAPO GALLO-ISOLE DELLE FEMMINE
SICILY

Beauty in the bay of Palermo

This protected marine preserve safeguards a zone full of historical monuments and varied wildlife.

www.regione.sicilia.it/turismo/web_turismo/sicilia/index.htm

SAN VINCENZO
TUSCANY

Warm sand and blue sea on the Etruscan coast

San Vincenzo has outstanding beaches and splendid natural landscapes with Etruscan remains and quaint medieval villages.

www.costadeglietruschi.it

CORVARA
TRENTINO-ALTO ADIGE

Hikes into the Alta Val Badia

Corvara is the largest town in the Val Badia, in the heart of the pretty Dolomites. It's perfect as a departure point for exploring the wonderful valley landscape.

www.altabadia.it

"Snow-covered summits and deep pine woods form a majestic backdrop to Valle d'Aosta's many castles..."

PARCO NATURALE DEL MONT AVIC
VALLE D'AOSTA

Superb natural scenery of mountains, lakes, and forests

The park is in a secluded position dominated by the mountain peaks of Avic, Iberta, and Glacier.

www.montavic.it

FÉNIS AND ISSOGNE
VALLE D'AOSTA

Enjoy a trek on horseback among ancient castles

In a strategic position on the Italian and French border, Valle d'Aosta is known for the string of castles, built to keep watch along the valley.

See pp170–71

Previous page: View from Stromboli, one of the Aeolian Islands

sentinel-like castles, or to the peaks of the Dolomites in Merano, in Trentino-Alto Adige. Many prefer to head for the coast for the cooling breezes and refreshing sea: from Forte dei Marmi, in Tuscany, where the shady pine woods back on to the beaches, to Maratea, in Basilicata, where rugged, parched hills come to an abrupt halt at the jagged cliffs overlooking the soft blue sea; from Otranto in Puglia, where white houses huddle together on a jutting headland, to Lipari, in the Aeolian Islands, the perfect destination for fans of the underwater world. And, for those who'd rather stay on top of the water, for most of the time at least, there is the challenge of a breathtaking raft ride along the Lao River, in the wild setting of the Parco del Pollino, in Laino Borgo, Calabria.

LUXURY AND ROMANCE

OTRANTO Beautiful secluded cove at Porto Badisco

OTRANTO
PUGLIA

Journey to the easternmost point of Italy

With stunning blue seas and dazzling white walls, Otranto is a beautiful town with interesting cathedrals, castles, and catacombs.

See pp186–7

RONCIGLIONE
LAZIO

A quaint village with a pretty medieval center

Ronciglione is a short distance from the Lago di Vico, the best maintained of the Italian volcanic lakes, now a nature preserve.

www.prolocoronciglione.it

"Jutting into the sea at the most easterly point on the Italian peninsula, Otranto is a natural bridging point between East and West."

OFFIDA
LE MARCHE

Hunting for the old traditions in the Le Marche Apennines

A medieval village built on a rocky spur, Offida boasts a number of fine monuments, but is particularly known for the production of pillow lace.

www.turismoffida.it

STINTINO
SARDINIA

Enjoy a reviving plunge into crystal-clear water

La Pelosa is Stintino's magnificent beach, located at the northwestern end of Sardinia and overlooking the beautiful Golfo dell'Asinara.

www.stintino.net

VENOSA
BASILICATA

An old Lucanian town with extensive Roman ruins

An old town of Samnite origins, Venosa has fine archaeological ruins and a modern town built around the Castello Aragonese.

ww.initalytoday.com/basilicata

ACTIVE ADVENTURES

AEOLIAN ISLANDS A view of the island of Lipari at sunset

LAINO
CALABRIA

Rafting on a turbulent river in the Parco del Pollino

The River Lao gushes between deep rocky gorges and makes the ideal setting for canyoning, canoeing, rafting, and kayaking.

See pp188–9

PORTO CESAREO
PUGLIA

Swimming and snorkeling in a seaside paradise

Porto Cesareo is popular due to its beaches and offshore islands – a protected marine preserve.

www.parks.it/riserva.marina.porto.cesareo

AEOLIAN ISLANDS
SICILY

Diving and live volcanoes in the Aeolian Islands

North of the Sicilian coast, the Aeolian Islands form a fascinating volcanic archipelago with sea beds perfect for diving exploration.

See pp182–3

VAL DI FASSA
TRENTINO-ALTO ADIGE

Exploring the Marmolada

The Val di Fassa has popular resorts such as Moena and Canazei and is a great place for marvelous scenic walks and climbing up the Marmolada.

www.fassa.com

VAL PASSIRIA
TRENTINO-ALTO ADIGE

Cycling in the mountains

The Val Passiria has a number of bike trails of great natural beauty and interest: many start off from San Leonardo in Passiria, at the very heart of the valley.

www.valpassiria.it

FAMILY GETAWAYS

MERANO Heated pools in the luxurious thermal spa at Merano

LIGNANO SABBIADORO
FRIULI-VENEZIA GIULIA

A coastline of sandy beaches backed by shady pine woods

Lignano has a modern marina and around 5 miles (8 km) of fabulous beaches, perfect for families.

www.turismofvg.it

ROSETO DEGLI ABRUZZI
ABRUZZO

Blue Flag beaches and entertainment for all

Roseto is known for the perfume of its roses, its clean, safe beaches, and its lovely nearby hills.

www.rosetodegliabruzzi.com

"It's perfect for peaceful walks, calorie-busting mountain bike rides, or more sedate excursions on horseback."

SARNANO
LE MARCHE

A landscape dotted with thermal springs

On the slopes of the Sibillini mountains, Sarnano, with its preserved ancient center, has a famous thermal spa.

See pp174–5

FORTE DEI MARMI
TUSCANY

Coastal resort popular with the international jet set

Cool seas with stretches of sand backed by pine woods have made Forte dei Marmi one of the most fashionable destinations in Italy.

See pp172–3

MERANO
TRENTINO-ALTO ADIGE

Clean, healthy air and relaxing spas – blooming marvelous

A popular resort known for its mild climate, Merano is also famous for the lush botanical gardens of the Castello Trauttmansdorf.

See pp180–81

GETTING THERE
Fénis, Issogne, and the other castles of the region are in the southeastern part of Valle d'Aosta. Turin airport is 62 miles (100 km) from Fénis, just over 1 hour by car via the A5 freeway.

GETTING AROUND
You'll be on horseback, of course.

WEATHER
Summer in Valle d'Aosta brings lovely hot days with temperatures reaching 82°F (28°C).

ACCOMMODATIONS
In Fénis, Le Bonheur *agriturismo* is a farmhouse B&B offering riding lessons and a good restaurant; doubles from US$82; www.agriturismo-lebonheur.com/html

Lo Tatà B&B is in a former hayloft set in a pretty garden, near the castle in Fénis; doubles from US$76; www.lotata.it

EATING OUT
Locanda Al Maniero in Issogne serves a typical local menu (dinner from US$28). Specialties include *lardo d'Arnaud e mocetta* (bacon with cured mountain goat); www.ristorantealmaniero.it

In Verrès, the Da Pierre restaurant offers Valle d'Aosta cuisine with a French influence (from US$55) in a smart rustic setting; www.dapierre.it

PRICE FOR TWO
US$220 per day including accommodations, meals, admissions, and car rental. Add US$205–275 for each full day of riding.

FURTHER INFORMATION
www.regione.vda.it/turismo

Fontina Cheese

Fontina is a cheese redolent of fragrant mountain herbs. It is prepared using only milk from Valle d'Aosta cows that have been fed with hay from mountain pastures. Made since the 12th century, and renowned for its quality and flavor since that time, it is depicted in one of the late 15th-century frescoes in the Castello di Issogne. It is a symbol of the valley, of which the local people are justly proud, and features in many traditional recipes of the region, such as *fonduta*, a rich fondue-style dish made with milk, eggs, and butter, sometimes served with shaved white truffle.

HORSEBACK THROUGH HISTORY

VALLE D'AOSTA, A REGION OF TOWERING MOUNTAINS that soar above expanses of meadows to the azure sky, has for centuries kept a strict guard over its historical and natural riches. Its "sentinels" are its castles, 15 of them, which stretch up the valley from Bard to Saint-Pierre.

No two are the same: some have crenellated walls and sturdy fortifications, and their military origin is confirmed by still older lookout towers. Others, not so ancient, are also impressive fortresses, but they are of a ceremonial origin, having been built to celebrate the dynastic or military glories of days long gone by. Then there are those that were built at a time when a noble family was at the height of its prestige. This is the case with the most beautiful, and to this exclusive category belong Fénis and Issogne. Both were built in the 14th century, amid the pastures of the valley where there had once been important Roman villas.

Main: Ramparts of the magnificent Castello di Fénis

Left (left to right): Wooden a typical product of local craft King of France's bedroom in superbly preserved Castello c

Right: Courtyard of Castello with its "pomegranate tree" f

Far right (top to bottom): chapel ceiling at Castello di Is spiral staircase in the castle; r meandering through the gree of the valley

The Castello di Issogne is famous among art-lovers for its frescoes, attributed to Master Collinus who, towards the end of the 15th century, painted two cycles of pictures there: one depicting the tradesmen of the period (the apothecary, the delicatessen merchant, the baker), portrayed with a lively sense of humor; the other with a religious theme, rich in atmosphere and mysticism. Another artist also worked at Issogne under the name of Maestro di Wuillerine: he was responsible for the frescoes in the hall where Giorgio di Challant, the viscount during the castle's golden age, administered justice.

By contrast, it is the architecture that is striking at Fénis: no other castle in Valle d'Aosta has such a wealth of towers, battlements, balconies, galleries, staircases, and ramparts. It is an impressive legacy from the 15th century, when the castle hosted its own court.

Today, these venerable places can be visited on a range of treks organized by local riding schools. Such expeditions recall the spirit of travelers of the past, obliged to make arduous journeys from one castle to the next, but the 21st-century rider can follow in their hoofprints at a more leisurely pace.

Above: Battlements of the beautiful Castello di Saint-Pierre

JAN FEB MAR APR MAY JUN **JUL**

RIDER'S DIARY

Snow-covered summits and deep pine woods form a majestic backdrop to Valle d'Aosta's many castles, and to visit them on horseback is to travel back in time. A three-day visit is the ideal introduction, and not too tiring for the inexperienced rider, but you can easily extend your itinerary if you get the bug for history on horseback, as you surely will.

Three Days in the Saddle

DAY 1

Start your trek at Fénis with a visit to its Castello, which dominates the town. This is a jewel not only because of its architecture, which combines the austerity of a fortress with the elegance of a nobleman's residence (note the beautiful galleries in carved wood), but also because of the fine frescoes that adorn its walls. From here, ride westward to Castello di Quart, founded in the 11th century but added to over the ages to form a fascinating tumble of buildings perched on a rocky hillside. Return to Fénis for a dinner of delicious Valle d'Aosta produce.

DAY 2

Drive 19 miles (30 km) southeast to Arnad. Back in the saddle again it is a gentle ride to Castello di Issogne, where you can take a guided tour. Despite the massive and menacing appearance of the exterior, inside you will find an elegant Renaissance residence where a beautiful fountain, shaped like a pomegranate tree, adds a graceful touch to the courtyard, and magnificent fresco cycles adorn the walls. Dine in Issogne, Arnad, or Verrès before returning to Fénis.

DAY 3

Today, if you are settled in the saddle, ride east to the castles of Sarre and Saint-Pierre – a 32-mile (52-km) round trip. Sarre is a stately palace with an 18th-century exterior, while Saint-Pierre is a fairytale medieval castle housing a fascinating, if quirky, museum dedicated to the flora, fauna, and geology of the Valle d'Aosta.

Dos and Don'ts

- ✓ If you have time, it is well worth extending your trip to cover the whole circuit of the castles that dot the valley as far as Mont Blanc: their beautiful architecture and the splendid positions they occupy make this a memorable experience.
- ✓ Visit the Museo dell'Artigianato Valdostano (Museum of Valle d'Aosta Crafts), near Fénis, for an insight into the long and fascinating history of the local crafts that are still practiced in the valley today.
- ✓ Buy a typical Valle d'Aosta carved wooden item from one of the region's many talented woodworkers.
- ✗ Don't overdo it with Valle d'Aosta coffee. Drunk from a traditional *grolla* (a local wooden cup, round with several spouts), it is spiced up with lemon zest and sugar, and reinforced with a big shot of local brandy, which makes it a very heady beverage for the uninitiated.

AUG SEP OCT NOV DEC

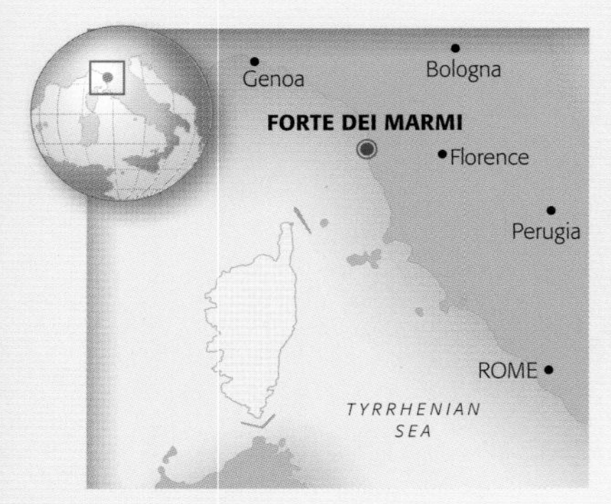

GETTING THERE
Forte dei Marmi is in Versilia, northern Tuscany. From Pisa, the nearest airport (25 miles/40 km), take the A12 freeway and leave at the Versilia junction – the journey takes just over half an hour. Or take the train to Forte dei Marmi station.

GETTING AROUND
The A12 freeway serves the whole of Versilia. There are also good train connections.

WEATHER
It will be hot (average maximum 84°F/29°C), although the sea makes the heat less oppressive.

ACCOMMODATIONS
The 4-star Hotel Negresco in Forte dei Marmi offers adjoining family rooms from US$462; www.hotelinegresco.com

The Hotel Eden in peaceful Cinquale is perfect for families and offers plenty of organized activities. Four-bed rooms from US$408; www.edenhotel.it

The Casa dei Pini in Viareggio is a welcoming B&B with a garden. A four-bed room costs US$42 per person; there's also a separate apartment with four beds from US$1,020 per week; www.bbviareggio.it

EATING OUT
For fresh fish and excellent local cuisine, try Lorenzo in Forte dei Marmi (around US$110; tel. 0584 89671); elegant Oca Bianca in Viareggio (around US$68; tel. 0584 388 477); or Bottega dei Piastroni di Pietrasanta (about US$28; tel. 0584 792 147).

PRICE FOR A FAMILY OF FOUR
From US$370 to US$870 per day. Sun loungers and beach umbrellas at one of the exclusive Forte dei Marmi beaches will cost about US$75 per day.

FURTHER INFORMATION
www.aptversilia.it; www.vacanzeinversilia.com

The Versiliana Festival

The Parco della Versiliana is the last vestige of a huge pine forest that once covered much of the coast. Each year during July and August, the park hosts the Versiliana Festival, offering a lively program of dance, theater, and exhibitions. "La Versiliana dei Piccoli" offers special entertainment for children such as creative games, fairy tales, and theater shows.

Above: Caffè Margherita in Viareggio, an example of Liberty architecture; a Forte dei Marmi street in bloom
Main: An exclusive beach at Forte dei Marmi

UNDER THE TUSCAN SUN

BEAUTIFUL BEACHES, BLUE SKIES, CLEAN WATER, and fragrant pine groves. What more could you want? Forte dei Marmi (Fort of Marble) in Versilia, the northwestern region of Tuscany, offers visitors more than just a standard seaside vacation. The resort is popular with families because of the many facilities the beaches have to offer visitors, such as restaurants, playgrounds, sports facilities, and safe bathing. The town was named after the fortress, built in 1788 by the Grand Duke of Tuscany Leopoldo I, and the marble extracted from the Apuan Alps and dispatched from its port. In the early years of the 20th century, Forte, as regular visitors call it, started to attract the international jet set to its attractive coastline, and began to transform itself into a summer gathering-point for the rich and famous. Forte dei Marmi quickly took to its new vocation as a hang out for the beau monde, and made good use of its natural beauty and the innate knack for hospitality characteristic of the Tuscans.

It was La Capannina, now one of the most famous and fashionable restaurants in the whole of Italy, that really started it all and put Forte dei Marmi on the map. In 1929, the resourceful innkeeper Achille Franceschi had the idea of setting up a cabin on the beach with a few little tables, a bar, and a wind-up gramophone. This soon became a favorite haunt of the rich and fashionable aristocracy who were staying in Forte. They in turn brought their friends along and soon there were beachfront clubs all along the coast, attracting the most famous stars of sports, music, and show business.

Today, evidence of those early glory days still remains. The Roma Imperiale district of town is studded with splendid villas built in the first half of the 20th century – the grandest of these being the Villa Agnelli, now a luxury hotel – designed by famous Italian architects such as Michelucci, Giò Ponti, and Pagano. The town feels supremely at ease with the rich and famous and is therefore accustomed to accommodating their tastes and demands, whether they are relaxing on the beach or mixing with other members of high society in the bars at night. But it is evident that the people of Forte have managed to retain their sense of humor while dealing with often demanding and capricious aristocrats and super-wealthy tourists. The town established the Museum of Satire and Caricature, solely dedicated to deflating the egos of the rich and powerful, in the fort at the fashionable center of town.

Below (left and right): The grand vacation villas set amid leafy gardens of Roma Imperiale, an upscale area of Forte dei Marmi; *zuppa di vongole* (clam soup), a popular local treat

Above: Badia di San Pietro (Abbey of St. Peter) at Camaiore

BEACH CLUB DIARY

Forte dei Marmi, with its cafés, smart shops, and well-tended bathing clubs, is one of Italy's most sophisticated destinations. But the safe, sandy, and clean beaches backed by shady pine groves are also excellent for families. A week allows plenty of time for relaxing on the beach as well as a few days exploring nearby areas of interest.

A Week in Versilia

DAYS 1–2

A visit to Forte dei Marmi must start with the fort, the oldest building in the town and home to the Museum of Satire and Caricature. The focal point of the town's most fashionable area, the fort is the place to be seen shopping, strolling, or enjoying an apéritif. Spend time relaxing with the family at one of the many pleasant beach establishments along the coast, sunbathing and swimming. Sporty types may enjoy a game of tennis or a round or two of golf.

DAYS 3–4

Rent some bikes and go for a gentle ride on the Versilia bicycle track, which runs from Forte dei Marmi to Viareggio. It follows the shoreline and is almost completely level, so it's perfect for children, too. Treat everyone to a cold drink or *gelato* (ice cream) when you get to Viareggio.

Head inland to Pietrasanta, near the marble quarries of the Apuan Alps – it has a prestigious training school for sculptors. Rocca di Sala looks over the village, which has retained its medieval aspect around the Piazza del Duomo.

DAYS 5–7

For your last few days divide your time between building sandcastles on the beach, walking in the shady pine groves of the Parco della Versiliana, and visiting interesting little villages nearby.

Explore pretty Camaiore, which still has the air of a small Tuscan village from times past, clustered around a fine Romanesque abbey.

Viareggio, along the coast, is also worth a day trip. It has a pleasant seafront promenade lined with elegant houses, leading to a pine grove, a large green area to the north of the town with ice-cream kiosks, bicycle rental, and children's playgrounds.

Dos and Don'ts

- ✓ Book your trip well in advance: Versilia is one of the most sought-after destinations for Italian families and is always popular in the summer.
- ✗ Don't ride on the Versilia cycle track during the busiest times of the day, as cars entering or exiting the bathing establishments will force you to keep stopping.
- ✓ Go to the twice-weekly market in Forte dei Marmi on Wednesday or Sunday. It is one of the best in the area.

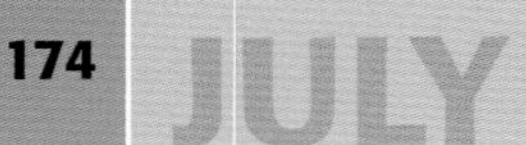

GETTING THERE
Sarnano is in Le Marche, not far from Macerata and the Sibilline Mountains. The nearest airport is Ancona. From here, take the A14 freeway and leave at the Macerata exit, then follow the SS77 and the SS78 to Sarnano.

GETTING AROUND
A car is best for visiting the towns around Sarnano.

WEATHER
Expect mainly warm summer days, but cooler temperatures in the evening.

ACCOMMODATIONS
Near Sarnano, the Casa Vacanza le Querce is ideal for families. It offers pleasant four-bed apartments from US$102 per day. The building is linked to the *agriturismo* of the same name, which has a riding school and a restaurant; www.lequerceagriturismo.com

Also close to Sarnano, the Quattro Stagioni camp site offers well-equipped pitches (around US$45 per day for 2 adults and 2 children) and bungalows (US$82 per day). It has a sports center with swimming pool; www.camping4stagioni.it

EATING OUT
The Vicolo di Sarnano restaurant serves typical Le Marche cuisine at reasonable prices. Meals cost about US$35 (tel. 0733 658 565).

In Camerino, Arte offers traditional dishes with a twist. Meals around US$40 (tel. 0737 633 558).

PRICE FOR A FAMILY OF FOUR
US$230–295 per day for meals and accommodations.

FURTHER INFORMATION
www.le-marche.com

Left (top to bottom): Alley in the center of Amandola; *ciauscolo*, a Le Marche salami that is smoked over juniper; the pretty hill town of Amandola

Right (left to right): The gardens at Terme di Sarnano, a renowned health resort; a stag in the Parco Nazionale dei Monti Sibillini; fields of sunflowers around Sarnano

Main: The hill town of Sarnano, a delightful spa resort

The University of Camerino

Although it had been operating since the 14th century, the University of Camerino was officially founded by Pope Benedict XII in 1727 with faculties of theology, law, medicine, and mathematics. It was nearly shut down during Napoleonic rule, but Pius VII reactivated it in 1816. Today, strengthened by a solid scientific and cultural tradition, the university has five faculties – Architecture, Pharmacy, Law, Veterinary medicine, and Science and Technology. The university and its students, who come from all over Italy, infuse life into this charming Le Marche village, rich in history and fine historic buildings.

THE GOOD LIFE

SARNANO, IN LE MARCHE, is renowned as one of the most beautiful villages in central Italy on account of its lovely hilltop location near the Sibilline Mountains and the well-preserved buildings at it ancient center, the Piazza Alta. These date back as far as 1265, the year when the village became a city-republic. Three fine churches – Santa Maria Assunta, Santa Maria di Piazza, and San Francesco (Italy's patron saint, who stayed briefly in these parts in 1214–15) – and three historic palaces – Palazzo del Podestà, Palazzo del Popolo, and Palazzo dei Priori – take you back to a medieval time that was marked by political ferment, but also famous for its achievements in the creative arts.

But along with marvelous stonework, the great charm of the village lies in the importance it attaches to the good things in life. There's the superb local cuisine, for example: a popular Sarnano dish is *vincisgrassi*, an oven-baked lasagne – a favorite with children. Another dish not to be missed is *ciauscolo*, a salami that is soft enough to

Above: Exterior detail of the Chiesa di San Venanzio at Camerino

HILL TOWN DIARY

Sarnano's charm resides in its authentic medieval atmosphere and exquisite hillside location, and the small spa town is proud of its heritage as an independent city-republic. Three days is enough time to enjoy Sarnano's generous hospitality and to explore other nearby towns and the Parco Nazionale dei Monti Sibillini.

Three Days in the Mountains

DAY 1

Get to know the delights of Sarnano and the magical spell cast over visitors by its narrow streets and flights of steps to quiet squares. Bask in the warm glow emanating from the red bricks used for every building and walk up to the Piazza Alta. Here, the grand palazzi and 13th-century church tell the history of the village as an independent city-republic and are worth the long climb up. Visit the splendid thermal baths – the waters are perfect for beauty treatments, and the spa offers facilities and entertainment for all ages.

DAY 2

Drive to Amandola, a little way south and a fine village of medieval origin. It has preserved some evocative architecture from the days when it was an important center of the wool industry. Today, Amandola is a popular starting-point for trekking and mountain bike rides in the Parco Nazionale dei Monti Sibillini, a huge forested mountainous area studded with abbeys and ancient villages. Take a picnic and spend the afternoon in the park, enjoying the mountain air.

DAY 3

Make a trip to Camerino, which has the special buzzy atmosphere of a university town with some 7,000 students – about as many as its inhabitants. Although nothing remains of the original Roman town, there are still plenty of historic buildings such as the Palazzo Ducale, Palazzo Arcivescovile, and Duomo. Be sure to look out for the marvelous view of the Sibilline Mountains from the belvedere of the fortress.

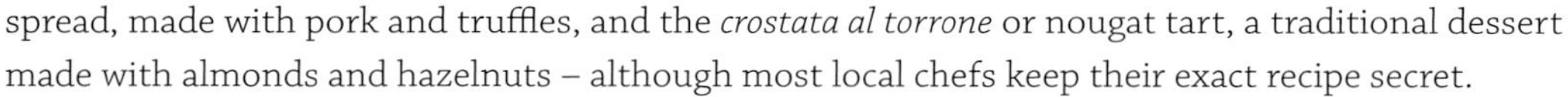

spread, made with pork and truffles, and the *crostata al torrone* or nougat tart, a traditional dessert made with almonds and hazelnuts – although most local chefs keep their exact recipe secret.

Once you've enjoyed the delicious cuisine, you might feel the need to look after your body a little. If you're looking to burn off some calories, Sarnano, at 1,768 ft (539 m) above sea level on the Apennine ridge, is the ideal place to indulge in some exercise. The countryside is wonderful, especially in summer, when the woods provide plenty of opportunities for adults and children alike to follow the pleasant leafy paths and explore the Parco Nazionale dei Monti Sibillini. The park is perfect for peaceful walks, calorie-busting mountain bike rides, or more sedate excursions on horseback – and keep an eye out for the chamois, deer, and birdlife. But it's not all hard work. Sarnano is the largest thermal spa in Le Marche and its spring water is rich in beneficial minerals. So, while the kids run around in the spa's gardens, soak your weary limbs in the relaxing thermal waters and let the skilled staff massage out any aches and pains from your muscles. And why not throw in a facial, too, while you're there.

Dos and Don'ts

- ✓ For information about walking routes, and flora and fauna in the Parco Nazionale dei Monti Sibillini, be sure to visit the *case del parco* (information offices) inside the park.
- ✗ Do not use public transportation to go to the Parco Nazionale dei Monti Sibillini – it is not very good. Go by car instead.
- ✓ Don't miss the Museo dei Martelli (Hammer Museum) in Sarnano. It has more than 500 exhibits of every size and material, from 40 countries representing 100 trades.
- ✗ Do not walk in the park without taking water and an accurate map of the paths.

FOUNTAIN OF YOUTH

THE ANCIENT WORLD OFTEN struggles to survive in modern cities; either "civilization" knocks it down and rebuilds something bigger and better, or it locks it up behind glass in a museum. But Perugia is different. The whole city is a museum, but one you can work in, wander around, sleep in, or eat and drink in, and, during the famous Umbria Jazz festival, dance or listen to great music in.

Visitors reach the city center on discreetly built escalators and elevators that whisk them up the steep hills. Two ancient gates, the Arco di Augusto (Arch of Augustus) and the Porta Marzia (Gate of Mars), dating back to the 3rd century BC, are reminders of the great Etruscan metropolis that once thrived here. At the very heart of the city is the 13th-century Fontana Maggiore, Perugia's most celebrated monument, decorated with bas-reliefs by Nicola and Giovanni Pisano that reveal the artistic flowering of the early Middle Ages. One of Italy's oldest universities was founded in Perugia in 1308, and today its students breathe fresh life into the old fabric of the city. The spiritual needs of the citizens were catered for at the

Main: The beautiful Fontana Maggiore in the city center, the work of Nicola and Giovanni Pisano

GETTING THERE
The international Sant'Egidio airport is 7 miles (11 km) from Perugia, the capital of Umbria. There is a shuttle bus service between the airport and the city center – a taxi will cost around US$35.

GETTING AROUND
Walk around the center, use public transportation (bus and *minimetrò*), or rent a scooter.

WEATHER
July is the hottest time of year, with temperatures around 86°F (30°C). The evenings are cooler.

ACCOMMODATIONS
The Hotel Giò Jazz Area is perfect for the Umbria Jazz festival. It has a music shop, a jazz library, and even an auditorium. Rooms from US$164; www.hotelgio.it

The Etruscan Eurohotel's theme is chocolate. Each room (costing from US$190) is named after a type of chocolate and filled with goodies; www.chocohotel.it

If you are after the tranquility of the countryside, but want to be within reach of the city center, try the San Felicissimo *agriturismo* with a garden and swimming pool – rooms from US$95; www.sanfelicissimo.net

Similarly, the *agriturismo* San Lorenzo della Rabatta is a fine medieval complex in the country. Doubles from US$110; www.sanlorenzodellarabatta.com

EATING OUT
In the historic center, Mi Cocco is a characteristic restaurant with modest prices – about US$28 (tel. 075 573 2511). Enjoy regional cuisine at the Antica Trattoria San Lorenzo in an intimate and elegant setting; meals about US$48 (tel. 075 572 1956).

PRICE FOR TWO
US$205–300 per day for meals and accommodations.

FURTHER INFORMATION
http://turismo.comune.perugia.it

Above: One of the city's subterranean passages

Below: Via dell'Acquedotto, one of the oldest streets in the city

Inset: Detail of *The Annunciation* by Perugino, displayed in the Galleria Nazionale dell'Umbria

Right of main (top and bottom): Cloister in the Basilica di San Domenico; chocolate, a traditional product of Perugia

City for Jazz Lovers

The Umbria Jazz festival, inaugurated in 1973, takes place every July in the heart of Perugia and is an unmissable date for all jazz fans. It is the most famous jazz festival in Europe, and worldwide is only surpassed by Montreal. Thousands of young and not-so-young people come to historic Perugia to hear the best international jazz musicians. It has become so successful that it has sparked the inauguration of another event, Umbria Jazz Winter, which takes place in Orvieto over New Year.

grand 14th-century cathedral of San Lorenzo and the churches of San Domenico and San Pietro. Magnificent buildings such as the Palazzo dei Priori and Palazzo del Capitano del Popolo, are examples of the later explosion of art and architecture that was the Italian Renaissance.

It was in 1973 that Perugia opened its cobbled streets and piazzas to musicians and became the home of Umbria Jazz, now a world famous festival. The finest jazz musicians perform here, and every summer jazz music rings out among the venerable buildings. Legendary artists such as Dizzy Gillespie, Ornette Coleman, Chet Baker, Bill Evans, and Sarah Vaughan have played and sung next to the very same walls and towers that have witnessed battles fought by knights in armor. Thousands of young people from all over the world come together and pack the squares around the Fontana Maggiore to play the guitar, chat, and generally have a good time, in between listening to concerts.

During the summer, Perugia's ancient walls and squares, remnants of a time long since past, provide the perfect setting for the modern sounds of jazz music and the hubbub of people enjoying themselves in this fine city. The past and the present exist together in perfect harmony.

Ornette Coleman, Chet Baker, and Sarah Vaughan have played next to walls that have witnessed battles fought by knights in armor.

Above: Locals and tourists resting in front of the Palazzo dei Priori

JAN FEB MAR APR MAY JUN **JUL**

JAZZ DIARY

Set in gentle countryside, Perugia is a city of art and ancient culture, the seat of an illustrious university, and the theater for Umbria Jazz, one of Europe's most important musical events. Spend a weekend in this atmospheric city, exploring by day a history that goes back to the Etruscans, and by night enjoying the music of world-class jazz performers.

A Weekend of Kisses

DAY 1

To reach the ancient heart of Perugia, save your legs and take the escalators from the Piazza dei Partigiani. Start with the Rocca Paolina. This was built by Pope Paul III after he put down the "salt war," a revolt in 1540 against papal power and taxes. The fort was built over the homes of the rebel leaders, creating an underground city. The restored fort provides a fascinating walk through the oldest parts of the city.

For lunch, perhaps order some salami, some *pane sciapo* – bread made without salt, a reminder of the town's refusal to pay salt taxes – and a glass of the local wine. Finish the meal off with a few of Perugia's famous chocolate *baci* or kisses.

In the evening, enjoy the lively atmosphere of the ancient center filled with jazz aficionados and revelers and listen to the melodic echoes of the music reverberating off the stone walls.

DAY 2

See some of the city's fine churches that are treasure chests of art. Visit San Domenico, a 14th-century church restored in the 17th century; San Pietro, rich in works by the best Renaissance painters; and the Duomo. The latter has beautiful frescoed walls in red and white marble, and an austere but harmonious interior.

Don't miss the Fontana Maggiore, the symbol of Perugia, in Piazza Grande. Nearby stands the Palazzo dei Priori, home to the fabulous Galleria Nazionale dell'Umbria.

If you're lucky, you might be able to get a ticket to see one of the headline jazz acts; if not, there are plenty of other excellent concerts to enjoy in Perugia.

Dos and Don'ts

- ✓ Try Perugia *baci* (kisses), the famous hazelnuts coated in chocolate, wrapped in a piece of paper with a love saying.
- ✗ Don't drive into Perugia. It's better to leave your car in the underground parking lot at Piazza dei Partigiani and reach the center by escalator, passing through the Rocca Paolina.
- ✓ Explore the small organic food market that takes place on the first Sunday of every month.
- ✗ Don't linger in the center too late in the evening if your hotel isn't nearby; the escalators close at 1am.
- ✓ Go to a concert at the Umbria Jazz festival. You will find all the information about the program on www.umbriajazz.com

AUG SEP OCT NOV DEC

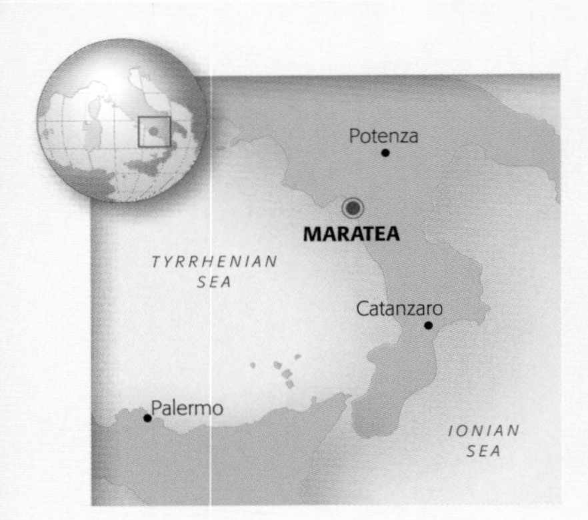

GETTING THERE
Maratea looks on to the Gulf of Policastro in Basilicata. The nearest international airports are Larnezia Terme (90 miles/150 km) and Naples Capodichino (140 miles/220 km). From the airports, it is best to travel to Maratea by car.

GETTING AROUND
There is a bus service linking places on the coast, but a car is the best way of exploring the surrounding countryside.

WEATHER
July is a hot and sunny month, with average maximum temperatures around 84°F (29°C).

ACCOMMODATIONS
Enjoy the luxurious atmosphere at the Locanda delle Donne Monache, an exclusive hotel in a restored 18th-century convent in Maratea. Rooms from US$155; www.locandamonache.com

La Torretta B&B in the hamlet of Cersuta is very welcoming, and ideal for a peaceful vacation. Rooms from US$68; www.beblatorretta.net

The luxury Santavenere Hotel, a few miles from Maratea, offers an unforgettable stay in a historic building sited on a cliff above the sea. Rooms from US$598; www.hotelsantavenere.eu

EATING OUT
Za' Mariuccia is a typical Basilicata restaurant by Maratea's harbor, with a terrace overlooking the sea; meals from US$40 (tel. 0973 876 163).

At the Taverna Rovita, local produce is creatively prepared; meals from US$48 (0973 876 588).

Enjoy smart dining at the Villa Cheta Elite. The menu combines innovative dishes with traditional cooking; meals from US$62; www.villacheta.it

PRICE FOR TWO
US$205–735 per day for meals and accommodations.

FURTHER INFORMATION
www.maratea.info

Natural Riches and Rags

South of Maratea, Praia a Mare sits on the volcanic rock of the Calabrian coast, its attractions clearly visible to the visitor. There is the long, gently curving beach with soft sand at its north end and fine pebbles in the south. Just offshore lies the rocky island, Dino, riddled with caves and buffeted by the sea, and so close to land it's almost touching. And on the coast, by the island, there is a medieval tower built to keep watch for Saracen pirates. Praia is also famous for its textiles and clothing production, on sale all over Calabria and Basilicata.

Above (left to right): Maratea's Torre Caina, one of the ancient towers of the Kingdom of Naples; typical Maratea ceramics; ruins above Maratea
Main: Delicate coral fans, small fish, and a scuba diver in the Tyrrhenian Sea

Above: The striking black lava beach at Cersuta, Maratea

PEARL OF THE TYRRHENIAN

Maratea owes its fame to its wonderful setting on the Gulf of Policastro. It enjoys a coastline that is a succession of steep cliffs and promontories high above a shoreline studded with magical inlets, tiny stretches of sand lapped by crystal clear waters, and limestone caves washed by the sea. There is an incredible contrast between the intense azure-blue of the sea and the green scrubby maquis that tumbles down the cliffs almost to the water, dotted here and there by huge flowering agaves. Naturally, the sea is the prime attraction here: water that is deep, clean, and full of life; water that offers scuba divers the excitement of a marine safari park where schools of multicolored fish dart about and rows of sea anemones and sea fans sway in arabesques.

But there is also much for the visitor to see inland: for example, the spacious subterranean Grotta delle Meraviglie di Marina di Maratea looks like an opulent palace with its great stalactites hanging down like curtains and huge stalagmite columns. It is clear from its layout, split into two centers, that Maratea is also a town with an interesting history. There's the upper part, Il Castello, a fortified citadel on the top of Monte Biagio, behind the present-day town; and down the hill, Maratea di Sotto (lower Maratea), founded around the 11th century after a boom in the population. Near Il Castello, the Santuario di San Biagio was founded between the 6th and the 7th centuries over an ancient temple of Minerva and restored several times over the years. Today, the area is dominated by the enormous Cristo Redentore (Christ the Redeemer) staute, over 69 ft (21 m) high and the second highest in the world after the one in Rio de Janeiro. Maratea di Sotto, by contrast, has closely packed medieval buildings surrounded by a maze of narrow streets and alleyways leading on to wider streets and pretty squares, almost every one home to one of Maratea's 44 churches.

A succession of steep cliffs and promontories high above a shoreline studded with magical inlets... and limestone caves washed by the sea.

Inset: Rivello, perched on the slopes of a hill
Below (left and right): Sailing boat in Maratea harbor; *salsiccia piccante*, a spicy pork sausage popular in Basilicata

COASTAL DIARY

It's not for nothing that Maratea is known as the "pearl of the Tyrrhenian Sea." It is set on rocky cliffs above stunning stretches of black or white sand. Along its coast, historic villages with pretty harbors perch on the edge of the shore close to marine depths rich in colorful underwater life. Spend three days here and you'll come to appreciate this gem of a town.

Three Days in Maratea

DAY 1

Spend the morning in Maratea, strolling around its pleasant little streets. Don't miss Chiesa di Santa Maria Maggiore, with its richly decorated Baroque interior, nor any of Maratea's other incredible churches. After lunch, take a stroll up to the top of Monte Biagio. Here you'll find the best place for viewing the Gulf of Policastro, near the statue of Christ the Redeemer. All around stand the ruined houses of the fortified town, Il Castello, huddled together as though in fear and protected by an inaccessible precipice on one side and walls and towers on the other. The town was deliberately sited in a depression – you cannot see the sea from its ancient center; but neither could the town be seen by Saracen pirates sailing by.

DAY 2

There is a range of options for boat trips available from Maratea's harbor, which will enable you to appreciate the wonderful coastal scenery. Take a cruise north 6 miles (10 km) to Acquafredda or south 3 miles (5 km) to to one of the sandy bays of Marina di Maratea – the black sand beaches are created from volcanic rock. Divers may wish to arrange scuba diving expeditions to discover the area's fabulous underwater marvels.

DAY 3

Visit the Grotta delle Meraviglie di Marina di Maratea, in Maratea Marina, and then continue to Rivello, a delightful inland village. Situated strategically on a ridge with very fine views, it was fought over by Catholics and Byzantines in the 10th century. With neither side able to gain control, the town was split into two communities – the lower part of town was occupied up to the 17th century by the Greek Orthodox community. Today, you can still see the vestiges of Byzantine-style architecture in the churches.

Dos and Don'ts

- ✓ Try the cold meats of Maratea: *lucanica salami* or, if you like spicy flavors, *soppressata* – dry-cured, uncooked salami made of coarsely ground pork and beef, and spices.
- ✓ Go and see a show at the Maratea Music Festival, held every year in summer, featuring big names in world music.
- ✗ Don't even think about scuba diving if you haven't taken a Professional Association of Diving Instructors (PADI) course.
- ✓ To reach Maratea, use the coastal road around the Gulf of Policastro; it is longer, but you will enjoy wonderful scenery.

GETTING THERE
Merano is in the heart of the Alto Adige and can be reached from Verona airport by transfer service. If you are coming by car, take the A22 freeway, leave at the Bolzano Sud exit and then take the Bolzano-Merano freeway.

GETTING AROUND
Merano is easily explored on foot. To visit the surrounding countryside, use the bus service.

WEATHER
July has fine warm days with high temperatures of 84°F (29°C). Evenings are nice and cool.

ACCOMMODATIONS
The elegant Hotel Ansitz Plantitscherhof offers a lot for both children and adults, including entertainers, pool activities, family cycling trips, and horse and carriage rides. Family suites for about US$368; www.plantitscherhof.com

Outside Merano, set among orchards, the rustic Auhof farmstead is perfect for a relaxing vacation. Four-bed rooms from US$110; www.auhof.it

EATING OUT
Good beer and hearty Alto Adige fare are on offer at Forsterbräu. You can dine there for US$28–35.

The Rauthof farmstead offers a marvelous view of the Merano valley and excellent traditional cooking based on fresh farm produce. Your children will love the apple, elderberry, and raspberry juices. Meals from US$35 (tel. 0473 244 741).

PRICE FOR A FAMILY OF FOUR
US$300–560 per day for meals, entrance fees, accommodations, and local travel.

FURTHER INFORMATION
www.meranodintorni.com; www.trauttmansdorff.it

THE PERFECT ENVIRONMENT

THERE CANNOT BE MANY PLACES YOU CAN FIND a Japanese garden, lines of desert cactuses, clumps of forest bamboo, a Chinese tea plant, a rice paddy, an array of aromatic plants, and the most northerly olive grove in Italy all growing together. But you will on a hill not far from Merano in the grand gardens surrounding Castel Trautmannsdorf, which takes its name from the historic family that has lived there since 1543. Within its walls you can still sense the presence of Princess Sisi, or Elisabeth of Bavaria, wife of Franz Joseph I Emperor of Austria, who spent time there with her daughters Gisela and Marie Valerie.

But even the stories of a glorious past aren't as impressive as the castle's botanic garden – home to a truly amazing collection of diverse species, from totally different climates. Yet, with a little attention and care, they seem to flourish in this stunning mountain environment. The gardens are

Main: The pretty, terraced Giardini di Castel Trautmannsdorf, Merano, South Tyrol

Castel Tirolo

A short way north of Merano, the 12th-century Castel Tirolo stands on a rocky spur overlooking a wide valley. It was the stronghold from where the Counts of Tyrol ruled over the region. The Counts increased their territory to become one of northern Italy's most powerful dynasties until 1363, when the region was annexed by the Habsburgs. A symbol of the area's former power, the castle still has the stern air of a medieval fortress, despite being decorated with some beautiful frescoes in the 14th century.

Left: Baths inside the Terme Merano, perfect for a relaxing soak

Right (left and right): Sauna in the Terme Merano; mountain bikers about to take on the hills

Far right (top and bottom): Smoked *speck*, mountain cheeses, and excellent local wines; the historic center of Merano beneath the mountains

arranged in 80 landscapes comprising four garden worlds – Forests of the World, Sun Gardens, Water Gardens, and South Tyrol Landscapes. Dotted around are 11 artist-designed pavilions and a viewing platform designed by architect Matteo Thun with stunning views of nearby Merano.

What worked for the plants also worked wonders for humans. The mild climate, fresh mountain atmosphere, and superb hospitality revitalized visitors to Merano who then insisted on coming back, turning the town into a tourist destination. Thus it became a popular resort, much loved by the nobility and the solid German bourgeoisie of the 19th and early 20th centuries – as reflected in the Germanic look of much of the town and the architecture of some of the grand houses.

But that's not all Merano has to offer. It now has a huge and luxurious spa center with relaxing and curative thermal baths, and some unique treatments. Immerse yourself in the local produce – try an apple massage, grape seed oil peel, or a cheese whey bath. Or, enjoy the Alto Adige hospitality and fruit, wines and cheeses in a more traditional way – during a delicious supper.

Above: The spectacular Tappeiner Promenade, Merano

WELLBEING DIARY

A vacation in Merano will bring on a state of wellbeing for the whole family due to the curative properties of the thermal baths, mountain views that fill the soul with life, and walks that fill the lungs with fresh air. Four days will allow you time to relax in the spa, enjoy some sightseeing, stretch your legs – and enjoy a wonderful stay.

Four Balanced Days

DAY 1

Spend the first day exploring the town. Head for the Corso della Libertà, which joins the two distinct areas of Merano: the late-medieval center, with its austere Gothic cathedral and Via Portici, lined with buildings with brightly painted façades; and the 19th-century Art Nouveau quarter. Merano also offers gastronomic delights such as *speck* (smoked bacon), which is great with one of the local wines such as Schiava, Lagrein, or the spicy Traminer.

DAY 2

Enjoy an active second day. You can try one of the many good walks in the woods near Merano. One of the best is the famous Tappeiner Promenade, which winds across the lower slopes of Monte Benedetto and offers delightful views of the town and the valley. Or, rent some bikes and test out your leg muscles – you can always just cycle along the flat valley floor.

DAY 3

Spend the morning in the thermal baths, enjoying health and beauty treatments as well as soothing soaks and saunas. The swimming pools are open to children, too, or make use of the babysitting service which will keep them occupied with games and activities. Take a drive to a farmhouse inn for a healthy lunch of spinach ravioli washed down by local apple or elderflower juice. In the afternoon, take a gentle stroll along the river on the famous Passeggiata d'Estate (Summer Walk).

DAY 4

Visit the Giardini di Castel Trautmannsdorf for a stroll among splendid plants from all over the world. Don't miss the special route devoted to the five senses, which will keep the kids amused. Then head on to Castel Tirolo, a fortress with a great view that is also a museum of Tyrolean history, next to a birds of prey center.

Dos and Don'ts

- ✓ Book visits to the thermal baths in advance: call 0473 252 000. For more information, visit www.termemerano.it
- ✗ Do not take your cell phone or camera into the baths: it is forbidden to use them inside the building.
- ✓ Try to attend one of the magical summer concerts in the Giardini di Castel Trautmannsdorf – part of *Serate ai Giardini* (Evenings in the Gardens); www.trautmannsdorf.com
- ✓ Buy the useful BusCard Merano: it gives you free travel on all buses that serve Merano and its surroundings.

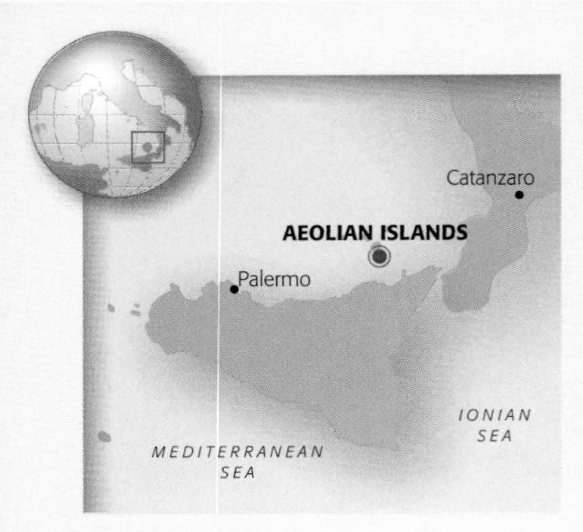

GETTING THERE
The Aeolian Islands, just north of Sicily, can be reached by sea from Milazzo. The nearest airports to Milazzo are Reggio Calabria (37 miles/60 km), and Catania (90 miles/145 km). Take the bus from Catania airport to Milazzo; buses from Reggio Calabria go to Messina, then take the train to Milazzo.

GETTING AROUND
Ferries and hydrofoils connect the islands of the archipelago. Rent a car or a scooter on the islands.

WEATHER
Summer is hot but tempered by sea breezes. Expect temperatures around 81°F (27°C).

ACCOMMODATIONS
For camping, Baia Unci on Lipari is next to the beach, a short walk from town. Pitches from US$10 per person, US$12 for the tent (www.baiaunci.com). Tre Pini on Salina is attractively sited in an olive grove. Pitches from US$12 per person, US$10 for the tent (www.trepini.com).

For a B&B, Diana Brown, in the center of Lipari, has doubles from US$82 (www.dianabrown.it). Da Francesco, a restaurant on Panarea, offers rooms for US$122 (www.dafrancescopanarea.com). On Alicudi, Casa Mulino has one-roomed apartments at US$115 (www.alicudicasamulino.it).

EATING OUT
Da Filippino's on Lipari serves the catch of the day from US$55 (tel. 090 981 1002). Porto Bello on Salina offers Aeolian dishes and sea views from US$48 (tel. 090 984 3125). In Filicudi, the Villa la Rosa serves local cuisine for US$35 (tel. 090 988 9965). On Stromboli, dine well at the Locanda del Barbablù, from US$55 (tel. 090 986 118).

PRICE FOR TWO
US$165–260 per day for meals and accommodations.

FURTHER INFORMATION
www.eoliando.it

Volcanic Rock

Strombolicchio is little more than a large upright rock in the middle of the sea, near the coast of Stromboli. It is all that remains of the first volcanic eruptions that took place between 160,000 and 300,000 years ago. A solitary lighthouse perches on the bare rock of the islet, but under the water its vertical walls are teeming with marine life: sea fans, coral, starfish, and seaweed attract silvery darting fish, much to the delight of scuba divers.

Above (left and right): Sunset over Lipari and the Aeolian Islands; fishing boats beside the harbor at Alicudi
Main: Bathers in the water by a pumice-stone quarry in Lipari

Above: Rocky cliffs at Pollara beach, Salina

BORN FROM FIRE

AN ARCHIPELAGO OF SEVEN VOLCANIC ISLANDS off the north coast of Sicily, the Aeolian Islands characterize the Mediterranean at its most primitive and elemental. Two of the islands, Stromboli and Vulcano, are home to active volcanoes that, occasionally glowing an angry red and belching out dark smoke, have fired the imaginations of the locals for thousands of years. Thus a wealth of myths abound about "the seven pearls of the Mediterranean." The islands get their name from Aeolus, the ancient Greek god of the winds who was said to live on Lipari, predicting the direction of the winds by observing the clouds of smoke streaming from the volcanoes – an important skill for the inhabitants of the archipelago, who have always been sailors and fishermen.

Each island offers an attraction and enjoyment peculiar to itself. Lipari is the "white mountain" because it is largely made out of volcanic pumice. On Vulcano, you must try bathing in one of the small natural hot mud lakes. Salina is an island of taste, famous for its sharp capers and sweet Malvasia wine. Panarea, the smallest, is the island for the young and fashionable. Alicudi and Filicudi are small, quiet, and beautiful in an isolated way, and Stromboli's sunsets are unique: you can watch the fiery glow of the volcano seemingly come to life as darkness descends.

What all the islands have in common is the sea and waters that are rich in colorful coral and marine life with no fear of humans. It's a diver's paradise – although serious aquanauts may not want to be distracted by all this beauty as they're actually scanning the depths intently for lost treasure. In ancient times, the Aeolian Islands provided a stopover for the traders who sailed the Mediterranean, and the sea floor often yields finds of amphorae, ceramics, coins, and even jewels. But regardless of the outcome of any dive you make, if you're visiting the islands, you can be sure that you've discovered the real Aeolian treasure.

Home to active volcanoes that, occasionally glowing an angry red and belching out smoke, have fired the imaginations of the locals for thousands of years.

Inset: Natural seawater swimming pool on Alicudi island
Below (left to right): Stromboli's glowing volcano; Greek-style architecture in Panarea; salted capers, a traditional product of Salina

RAINBOW DIARY

Prepare yourself for the array of colors on the islands: the white of the pumice-stone of Lipari, the red of Stromboli's glowing crater, and the green of Salina's woods. And everywhere there's black lava, a reminder of the volcanic origin of these seven rocky fragments scattered in the cobalt-blue sea between Calabria and Sicily. Six days is enough time to visit them all, if you wish.

Six Days with a Volcano

DAYS 1–2

A trip to the Aeolian Islands must start with Lipari, the largest island. Its center is noteworthy for the ancient cathedral and the castle, which today houses the Museo Archeologico Regionale Eoliano. Don't miss the beaches, from Canneto, a long stretch of pebbles, to the popular *Spiaggia Bianca* (White Beach) at Campobianco, with its pumice-stone quarries.

Go to Vulcano and climb up the Gran Cratere, the island's volcanic crater; or, for the less adventurous, as far as the Piano delle Fumarole, where you can enjoy a fine view over all the islands of the archipelago.

DAYS 3–4

Visit Salina, the greenest of the islands (and the only one to have natural freshwater springs). This island is famous not only for its beaches and its delicious sweet wine, but for the wild beauty of its hills – perfect for walking.

Next on your tour of the islands is Panarea, surrounded by rock stacks: it is the smallest of the archipelago and its whitewashed houses give it the look of a Greek island. Panarea is the most fashionable of the islands and is popular with the international yachting set.

DAYS 5–6

On the islands of Filicudi and Alicudi nature reigns supreme, especially on Alicudi, where there are no roads – perfect for those seeking peace. Both islands have great views and wonderful beaches with crystal-clear water.

Finally, to Stromboli, the most fascinating of the Aeolian Islands. It is famous for its volcanic activity and offers the unforgettable sight of volleys of lapilli (small volcanic stones) and blocks of lava tumbling down into the sea in a fiery cascade known as the *Sciara del Fuoco* (Stream of Fire). It is particularly exciting to take a boat trip at night to admire this wonderful spectacle from the sea.

Dos and Don'ts

- ☒ Don't try and stay the night on Vulcano, there's a constant strong smell of sulfur; better to go there just for the day.
- ☑ Go for a trek on the volcano in Stromboli. You can stop at the Punta Labronzo observatory and enjoy a magnificent view, or go right up to the summit (3,018 ft/920 m).
- ☑ For walks on the volcano in Stromboli, always go with a guide: it's always active and could be dangerous. Wear proper walking shoes or boots and take plenty of drinking water with you.

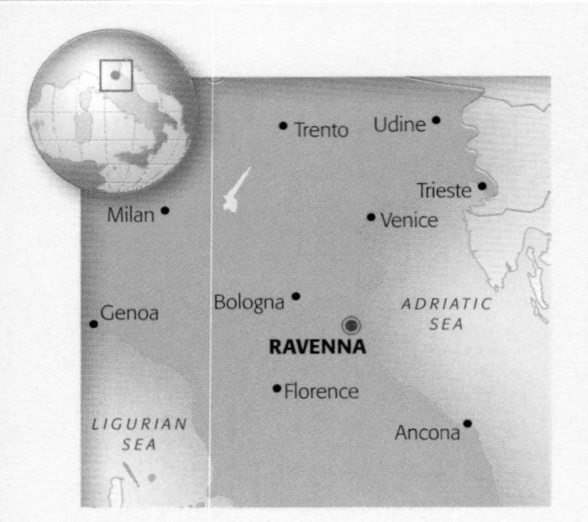

GETTING THERE
Ravenna is in Emilia-Romagna, not far from the Adriatic coast. The nearest major airport is at Rimini, 31 miles (50 km) away, and is linked by direct trains and buses. By car, take the SS16.

GETTING AROUND
Ravenna is easily explored on foot or by public transport. There is a good network of bike paths, too, and in summer, free bike rentals are available.

WEATHER
Expect fine, hot, and sometimes oppressive days with temperatures often in excess of 85°F (30°C).

ACCOMMODATIONS
Coffered ceilings and 15th-century frescoes are paired with modern conveniences at the Cappello; doubles from US$176; www.albergocappello.it

The smart Al Duomo B&B is a penthouse in the heart of the city center with panoramic views; doubles from US$95; www.alduomoravenna.com

At the gates of Ravenna, the Martelli *agriturismo* has welcoming, rustic bedrooms; doubles from US$90; www.agriturismomartelli.com

EATING OUT
La Gardela offers classic Romagna cuisine (dinner from US$35); tel. 0544 217147.

Ca' de Ven, in a historic palace in the city center, serves traditional recipes with a creative twist (from US$35); www.cadeven.it

At Bastione you can taste local wines accompanied by Romagna flat bread, cheeses, and desserts (from US$20); tel. 0544 218147.

PRICE FOR TWO
US$205–280 per day for accommodations, meals, and admissions, including a Ravenna "Visit Card".

FURTHER INFORMATION
www.turismo.ravenna.it

The *Pineta* of Classe

The *pineta*, or pine grove, in Classe is one of the last vestiges of the great forest that used to cover the entire Adriatic shoreline. It was famous in the past, when it was a source of highly prized timber. Today, much reduced in size, the *pineta* is a shady, green oasis of umbrella pines, holm-oaks, and Mediterranean shrubs. The Bevano River winds through it to reach the sea at the only intact natural river mouth on the Adriatic. Within the *pineta* is a network of paths that provides a welcome opportunity for pleasantly cool and refreshing walks in a stretch of the Romagna coast that remains unspoiled and undeveloped.

Above (left to right): Performance at the Ravenna festival; *passatelli in brodo* (pasta in broth), a Romagna specialty; Mausoleo di Teodorico
Main: Mosaics on the cupola of the Arian baptistry, showing the Apostles ringed around a centrepiece showing the Baptism of Christ

Above: Gateway in the fortress walls of the Rocca di Brancaleone

MIRACLES IN MOSAIC

THE GOLDEN EVENING LIGHT sets the tesserae of the Chiesa di San Vitale mosaics ablaze with shining splendor and casts mysterious shadows between its columns and wide arches. One need only hear a few notes of music for the mosaics to appear brought back to life. There is Theodora, with her enigmatic gaze and sumptuous apparel, surrounded by her court; facing her, the Emperor Justinian, her husband, with the bishop Maximian and his retinue; then Moses, Abraham, the Evangelists, angels, and prophets.

This miracle takes place every year in June and July thanks to the Ravenna Festival, one of the most prestigious musical events in Europe: a festival that makes the harmony of architecture and music its *raison d'être*, to the extent of transforming all the historic spaces of a city with a glorious past into the most ravishing theatrical backdrop to the performances.

Ravenna was the West's main political and cultural center in the centuries marked by the decline of the Roman Empire. And it is to this era that its most precious treasures belong: the Mausoleo di Galla Placida; the basilicas of San Vitale, Sant'Apollinare Nuovo, and Sant'Apollinare in Classe; the Neonian and Arian baptistries. Everywhere one is dazzled by the splendor of the interiors, decorated with mosaics that depict the tiniest detail – the pattern on a fabric, the sheen on intricate jewelry, the fleece of a sheep – in minute fragments of glass that refract the changing light.

One is dazzled by the splendor of the interiors, decorated with mosaics that depict the tiniest detail ... in minute fragments of glass.

The mosaics may be Ravenna's most potent attraction, but it has others: elegant streets that follow the winding route of the canals that once criss-crossed the city; the spacious Piazza del Popolo, packed with café tables at which the locals meet; the green spaces of the Rocca di Brancaeone gardens; the imposing mausoleum of Ostrogoth king Theodoric the Great; the tomb of Dante Alighieri, who died here in 1321; the remains of ancient houses with marble mosaic floors. All play their part in a city that offers a unique mélange of art, culture, and history.

Inset: Detail from the mosaics of Mausoleo di Galla Placidia
Below (left and right): Basilica di San Vitale; bicycles parked outside a café

BYZANTINE DIARY

The name Ravenna brings immediately to mind the mosaics that adorn the walls of its early Christian churches. They are incredible works of art that make up an ensemble unique in Italy, if not the world. In three days you can see the very best of them, and still have time to enjoy other facets of this delightful city, such as the vibrant festival that takes place here each summer.

Three Days of Marvels

DAY 1

Start by visiting Ravenna's two most important historic buildings, San Vitale and the nearby Galla Placidia. San Vitale's finest mosaics are concentrated in the presbytery. The exterior of the mausoleum dedicated to Placidia, wife of the Western Roman Emperor Constantuis III, is very austere, but the walls and vaulting within are entirely covered with mosaics, including a wonderful starry cupola. Then, go on to the Neonian baptistry to view its Baptism of Christ mosaics. On the way, make a detour to see the Domus dei Tappetti di Pietra ("House of Stone Carpets"), a Byzantine house with fine mosaic floors. Finally, pay your respects at the tomb of Dante.

DAY 2

Start the day at Sant'Apollinare Nuovo. Its beautiful mosaics, lining the walls of the aisle, depict two processions of virgins and martyrs. Have a picnic lunch in the leafy surroundings of the Rocca Brancaleone fortress, now a public park. After lunch, visit the Arian baptistry to compare its mosaics with the Neonian, then make your way to Theodoric's mausoleum with its impressive, monolithic 36-ft (11-m) wide dome.

DAY 3

Take a bus to Sant'Apollinare in Classe, a few miles outside Ravenna. Built as a basilica for the remains of the first bishop and patron saint of the city, it has a plain brick exterior in contrast to the splendor of the interior: three aisles flanked by 24 marble columns, leading toward the apse which is covered with some of the most glorious mosaics the city has to offer, the last ones created before Ravenna sank into the Dark Ages.

Dos and Don'ts

- ✓ Many of Ravenna's historic buildings are open to the public in the evenings in summer. Make the most of this opportunity to see the mosaics in a different and very romantic light.
- ✓ Buy a "Visit Card" pass, which gives admission to many of the city's most important sights.
- ✗ If you are in Ravenna on the third weekend of the month, don't miss the antiques market that takes place then.
- ✗ Don't bother to visit the beaches near Ravenna on the weekend; they will be extremely crowded.
- ✓ Take advantage of Ravenna's "free-to-hire" bicycle service. Collect a key from the main tourist office in Via Salara (or from some hotels) and then look for the bike racks around the town. Red bikes are for locals, yellow ones for tourists. Visit the website *(see opposite)* for more details.

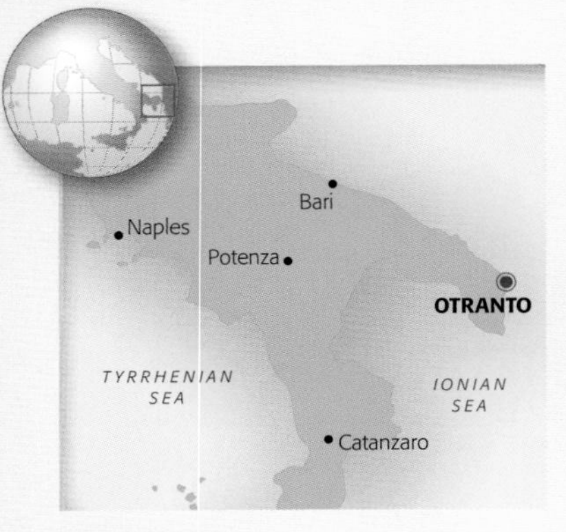

GETTING THERE
Otranto, on the east coast of the Salentine Peninsula, is the most easterly city of Italy. The nearest airport is Brindisi, 60 miles (90 km) away.

GETTING AROUND
You will need a car to get around the region.

WEATHER
July and August are the hottest months of the year, with daytime temperatures often exceeding 85°F (30°C); but the heat is tempered by sea breezes.

ACCOMMODATIONS
The 5-star Palazzo Papaleo is an ancient building in the heart of Otranto; its smart and comfortable rooms have frescoed ceilings; doubles from US$326; www.hotelpalazzopapaleo.com

The Masseria Montelauro is situated in peaceful countryside close to Otranto and the sea. It has a Mediterranean atmosphere and a lovely internal courtyard with fruit trees and a swimming pool; doubles from US$258; www.masseriamontelauro.it

EATING OUT
You can enjoy the specialties of Otranto cuisine (such as *taeddrha*, oven-baked layers of potatoes, vegetables, and mussels) in many restaurants, such as Da Sergio, in the historic center (dinner from US$40; tel. 0836 801408); the elegant Umberto 1972, with a garden (from US$40; 0836 803072); and Gattamorta farmhouse, just outside Otranto, which offers traditional cuisine with a fresh twist (from US$48; tel. 0836 817936).

PRICE FOR TWO
US$450 per day including accommodations, meals, and car rental.

FURTHER INFORMATION
www.comune.otranto.le.it

Market Day in Otranto

Otranto residents have an unmissable appointment every Wednesday: that is the day of the city's very lively street market. You can find everything here: delicious produce from the surrounding countryside, clothes, household goods, and even a flea market. Local crafts are represented too, such as ceramics and terracotta-ware, mosaics, basketry, and hand-loomed linen. It's great just to browse and enjoy the exciting smells and bright colors, while bargaining over prices is a very southern Italian custom that transforms shopping into an enjoyable skirmish.

CITY BETWEEN EAST AND WEST

EXTENDING OUT INTO THE SEA on the eastern edge of the Italian peninsula, Otranto has always been a natural meeting point between East and West. This made it a center of great strategic and commercial importance from the very earliest times, resulting in turbulent events that have shaped the city.

The history of Otranto began with the Greeks, who founded it, and continued with the Byzantines and the Normans, who turned it into the most important port in Salento, a place of departure for the Crusades and a center for trade and commerce. This prosperity was abruptly terminated by the Turks, who besieged and sacked Otranto in 1480 and slaughtered the 800 inhabitants who refused to abjure the Christian faith. This massacre is a milestone in the history of the city: the Chiesa di Santa Maria dei Martiri was built in the 17th century on the site of the slaughter, while the skulls of the martyrs line the walls of the Duomo. This is

Main: Port of Otranto viewed from the sea

one of the most celebrated historic buildings in southern Italy, with a magnificent Romanesque mosaic floor. Another response to the Turkish siege is the 15th-century castle, built by the Aragonese, with sturdy walls that still enclose the most ancient part of the town as a bastion against further attack. Its huge bulk has three circular towers and ramparts that, by the port, rise up from the sea, affording magnificent views. Within the walls, the historic center captivates visitors with its serried ranks of houses and many little churches, including the Chiesa di San Pietro with its precious Byzantine frescoes.

Otranto also enchants the visitor with its splendid shoreline alongside the intensely blue sea. This is a rugged coastline where rocky headlands and cliffs, plunging vertically into the water, alternate with small beaches and breathtaking little inlets. Many of these, such as Sapunerò, Mulino d'Acqua, and Imperia, cannot be reached from land. Below the waves, the seabed is sandy and scattered with rocks, gorges, and caves that are a paradise for scuba divers. One of the joys of Otranto is to leave its ancient harbor in a little boat and venture out onto waters that sparkle with every possible shade of blue.

Above: Massive towers of Castello di Otranto

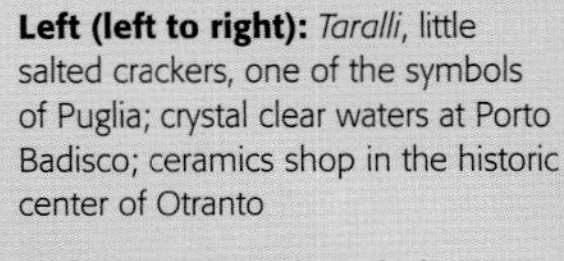

Left (left to right): *Taralli*, little salted crackers, one of the symbols of Puglia; crystal clear waters at Porto Badisco; ceramics shop in the historic center of Otranto

Right: Dramatic colors of a bauxite quarry not far from Otranto

SALENTINE DIARY

As well as its fascinating blend of Europe and the East, Otranto's charms include its crystal clear sea and secluded beaches, and the mighty Aragonese walls that enclose architectural jewels of rare beauty like a treasure chest. Over the course of three days you can sample a taste of all of these distinctive and contrasting pleasures.

Three Days at Europe's Edge

DAY 1

Devote your first day to a stroll around the historic center. The main street is the Corso Garibaldi, full of small shops. Don't miss the Duomo: its façade has a lovely rose window, there are splendid mosaics in the interior, and the crypt is a forest of columns. Chiesa San Pietro, with its Byzantine frescoes, and the romantic walk to the Pelasgi ramparts overlooking the port should also be on your agenda. There is no better way to unwind than over a meal in one of the town's restaurants, which serve exceptional local fish dishes.

DAY 2

Spend the day relaxing by the sea. The beaches of Punta Craulo, Conca Specchiulla (a cove surrounded by rocky walls), and Porto Badisco, which, according to legend, was where Aeneas landed when fleeing from Troy, are all easy to reach by road.

DAY 3

Drive or walk just 1 mile (2 km) out of town to the protected oasis of the lovely Laghi Alimini. These two sweet-water lakes, linked by a canal, are surrounded by reedy wetlands that are home to marsh orchids and Salentine heather as well as many types of water fowl and waders. There are bike- and footpaths throughout. The area also includes wonderful white sandy beaches. One of the most beautiful is Baia dei Turchi. This beach saw the landing of the besieging Turks, but today only lucky visitors tread its silky sands.

Dos and Don'ts

- ✓ Try *taralli*, the traditional salted crackers of Puglia, spiced with fennel or pepper; try dipping them in excellent extra-virgin Salentine olive oil, one of the best in Italy.
- ✓ Stroll a little way south of the town to visit the striking scenery of the abandoned bauxite quarry, with its dazzling red walls and emerald-green lakes.
- ✗ Don't visit the Laghi Alimini without insect repellent: the standing water attracts large swarms of mosquitoes.
- ✓ In the early evening, or on a Sunday, sit at a café table on the seafront and watch the world go by in the *struscio*, or "stroll" – the southern version of the traditional Italian social custom of *passeggiata*.

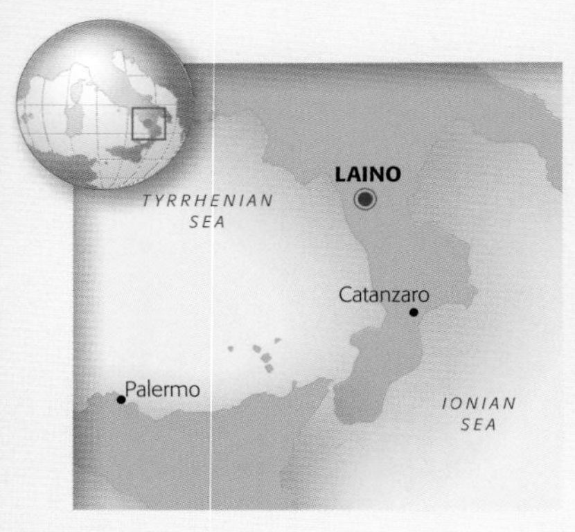

Above: Walkers exploring the wild gorge of Raganello; *maiale spadellato*, a delicious traditional pork dish
Main: White-water rafting on the turbulent waters of the Lao River

WHITE-WATER HEAVEN

SURROUNDED BY THE VERDANT HILLS and rugged mountains of the Parco Nazionale del Pollino, the Lao River is short but fed by rushing torrents. When it becomes enclosed by the steep, rocky walls of the spectacular Raganello gorge, the results are dramatic. This one simple fluke of nature is what makes nearby Laino Borgo one of the favorite destinations for lovers of white-water rafting, canyoning, and kayaking. The conditions that await them here are stunning: just after the town, the river gushes down into the deep canyon, full of cascades and rocks, racing along for around 4 miles (6 km) between rugged cliffs reaching 650 ft (200 m) high. It's an irresistible challenge to anyone who enjoys an adrenaline rush.

The history of Laino is bound up with that of its river: in ancient times the valley served as a caravan route through which merchandise from the Hellenistic Orient, unloaded at the Greek colonial port of Sybaris, was transported down to the Tyrrhenian coast. The town was a powerful trading center in the Greek era, when it minted its own coins, and again in the Byzantine era. Today it is divided into two distinct parts: Laino Castello, the original settlement, perched high on a hill; and the new Laino Borgo, which grew up in the valley after the devastating earthquake of 1982.

Naturally, it is in Laino Castello that one can see the most obvious reminders of the town's history, with houses clinging to the hillside and palaces whose stone portals bear their owners' noble coat of arms. However, much of it has now been abandoned, with many buildings still showing the evidence of earthquake damage, yet the old town still retains the atmosphere of its medieval past. At the top of the hill, the ruined feudal castle dominates the whole of the valley through which the Lao River cascades, between deep rock walls.

Laino Borgo, the meeting point for thrill-seekers, has a quite different aspect, set in the valley and crossed by the river. However, despite its comparative newness, and the increase in its population in recent decades, it has preserved the air of a community with ancient peasant traditions, including a great pride in its local crafts and music.

When you've had enough of watery thrills and spills, step back in time with a gentle walk to the sanctuary of the Madonna dello Spasimo, set amid lovely woodland and encircled by 15 small chapels, and an exploration of the Parco Nazionale del Pollino itself.

GETTING THERE
Laino is in the Parco Nazionale del Pollino, in northern Calabria. The nearest airport is Lamezia Terme, 110 miles (175 km) away. Take the A3 freeway and leave at the Laino Borgo exit.

GETTING AROUND
You will need a car to reach Laino Borgo and to travel around the Parco Nazionale del Pollino.

WEATHER
Laino, surrounded by mountains and rivers, enjoys a mild climate even in high summer. It is never oppressively hot.

ACCOMMODATIONS
The Al Verneto *agriturismo* B&B at Laino Borgo has comfortable, rustic rooms; doubles from US$82; www.alverneto.it

Masseria Campolerose is an *agriturismo* in the green surroundings of the national park; doubles from US$95; www.masseriacampolerose.it

EATING OUT
The restaurant at Masseria Campolerose offers local cuisine that reinterprets traditional country flavors (dinner from US$20). Among its specialties are tagliolini with goat's milk and grilled meats.

You will also find local specialties at the restaurant of the Chiar di Luna hotel in Laino Borgo (from US$35); www.hotelchiardiluna.it

PRICE FOR TWO
US$240 per day including accommodations, meals, and car rental. Add about US$135 for a half day of white-water rafting in the Lao gorges.

FURTHER INFORMATION
www.parks.it/parco.nazionale.pollino/Eindex.html
www.laino-borgo.net

Otters of the Pollino

The otter's natural habitat is in and around rivers and lakes in unpolluted and uninhabited areas; it feeds mainly on freshwater fish. In Italy, the otter is considered to be an endangered species, but at least one colony has found a safe haven and is thriving in the clear waters of the Lao River, in the Parco Nazionale del Pollino. This unspoiled area is also home to wildcats and Apennine wolves.

Below: View of Laino Castello on the slopes of the Pollino massif; canyoner tackling the rocks and torrents of the Raganello gorge

Above: Protected landscape of the Parco Nazionale del Pollino

POLLINO DIARY

Laino Borgo is an ideal base for a whole range of white-water adventures in the thrilling Raganello gorge. But it is also a town with ancient traditions, situated on the western edge of the Parco Nazionale del Pollino, a beautiful, wooded landscape full of wildlife and history. Three days getting to know this undiscovered corner of southern Italy will be time well spent.

Three Days in the Park

DAY 1

For a day of exciting water sports, you will find everything you need in Laino Borgo, from equipment rental to guides. Under the supervision of expert instructors, test yourself in a kayak trip through the Raganello gorge, starting downstream from the town, or tackle the Lao in a dingy, letting yourself be carried by the current down cascades and natural water-slides. If a hair-raising river trip is not your style, it is possible to follow the course of the gorge via footpaths on the riverbank, watching others tackling the torrents – a lot of fun in itself, and you get to stay dry.

DAY 2

Spend a relaxing morning exploring the old town of Laino Castello. Wander up its narrow streets to the castle on the hilltop, which has fine views. After lunch, head out of town about 2 miles (3 km) to the sanctuary of the Madonna dello Spasimo. It was built in the 16th century as a votive offering by a citizen of Laino who had returned safely from a pilgrimage to the Holy Land. Perhaps the most fascinating part of the sanctuary is the 15 small chapels dotted around the main shrine in a beautiful natural setting. Most are so small that only one person at a time can enter them.

DAY 3

Devote today to exploring the park, beginning at the Mormanno Visitor Center, about 6 miles (10 km) south of Laino. They can provide suggestions for walks on which you may see wildlife, including golden eagles and red deer. The park is famous for its Paleolithic era relics, too, such as the Grotta Ripara del Romito, a burial cave that has a fine carving of a prehistoric bull.

Dos and Don'ts

- ✓ For an original souvenir, buy a set of *zampogna* (bagpipes). These traditional instruments are made by local craftsmen and are an integral part of Calabrian Christmas festivities.
- ✓ Take with you suitable clothing for white-water rafting (scuba diving shoes or sneakers, swimsuit, and T-shirt) but don't worry about any other equipment, which will be supplied when you embark upon your trip.
- ✓ In summer, check on the traffic situation before traveling on the Salerno-Reggio Calabria A3 *autostrada*, the most important road in the area: there are often traffic jams.
- ✗ Canyoning, in which you negotiate the gorge on foot by scrambling, climbing, jumping, abseiling, and swimming, should not be attempted if you are not physically very fit: it is as demanding as it sounds.

GETTING THERE
Spoleto is in northern Umbria. The nearest airport is at Perugia, 37 miles (60 km) away, with good train and bus services to Spoleto.

GETTING AROUND
Spoleto is a pleasant town to explore on foot.

WEATHER
Average daytime temperatures can reach 84°F (29°C), falling at night to around 57°F (14°C).

ACCOMMODATIONS
The Palazzo Dragoni is a 16th-century building in the medieval quarter, with a view of the cathedral; doubles from US$170; www.palazzodragoni.it

Hotel Gattapone has fine views of the Ponte delle Torri; doubles from US$230; www.hotelgattapone.it

Eremo delle Grazie is an ancient hermitage on a hill overlooking Spoleto; doubles from US$258; www.eremodellegrazie.it

The Rivoli *agriturismo* B&B has a good restaurant, a swimming pool, and a riding school; doubles from US$92; www.agririvoli.it

EATING OUT
Tempio del Gusto gives authentic Umbrian flavors a touch of innovation (dinner from US$40); www.iltempiodelgusto.com

Il Tartufo interprets gastronomic tradition with originality (from US$55); www.ristoranteiltartufo.it

La Capanno serves Umbrian cuisine in a lovely garden (from US$48); www.ilcapannoristorante.it

PRICE FOR TWO
US$175–395 per day including accommodations and meals. Festival tickets cost from US$7 to US$272.

FURTHER INFORMATION
www.umbriatravel.com
www.festivaldispoleto.com

The Festival of Two Worlds

The Festival dei Due Mondi (Festival of Two Worlds) takes place in Spoleto each year from June to mid-July, culminating in a grand concert in the lovely setting of Piazza del Duomo. It was the brainchild of composer Gian Carlo Menotti, who dreamed of an international event (Europe and America being the "two worlds") that would celebrate all types of performance art – dance, opera, theater, and classical music – and make them accessible to ordinary people as well as to the cultural elite. It was launched in 1958 with a memorable performance of Verdi's *Macbeth*, directed by Luchino Visconti. Since then, many other distinguished international artists have performed or produced at the festival.

Above: Ancient stepped city streets; detail of a fresco by Filippo Lippi in the apse of the Duomo; Mascherone fountain, outside Rocca Albornoz
Main: Façade of Spoleto's 12th-century Duomo

Above: Spoleto's Roman theater, still in use today

A PINNACLE OF CULTURE

SPOLETO, WITHIN ITS WOODED SETTING, is one of the loveliest of the Umbrian hill-towns. Surrounded by a wall as early as the 4th century BC, it became a Roman colony in the following century. It later survived the barbarian invasions intact to become the heart of a powerful Lombard dukedom. As its importance increased, the town grew to the point of needing new and wider walls, which were built in 1296. It is that glorious era which Spoleto still evokes most strongly today, yet it also preserves numerous important vestiges of all the many facets of its past. This harmonious interweaving of different eras and different cultures helps give Spoleto its unique and fascinating atmosphere.

Small wonder, then, that a town with so much history and culture within its ancient walls should have spent over 50 summers hosting the Festival dei Due Mondi, a prestigious celebration of the performing arts that draws the great performers and directors of the world – from Rudolph Nureyev to Woody Allen – to delight thousands of cultural pilgrims year after year.

The harmonious interweaving of different eras and different cultures helps give Spoleto its unique and fascinating atmosphere.

The oldest part of the town is perched on the slopes of Sant'Elia. It's an uphill climb, but your efforts will be repaid by a panorama encompassing many wonderful historic buildings: San Gregorio Maggiore, with its massive campanile; the Casa Romana, once home to the mother of the emperor Vespasian; the Gothic Chiesa di San Nicolò; and the Roman theater, still in use today. Farther up the steep streets and steps are the lively Piazza del Mercato and handsome Piazza del Duomo. The latter fans out down to the cathedral, enhancing a façade that is one of the masterpieces of Umbrian Romanesque. At the town's highest point stands the Rocca Albornoz, a fortress built in 1359. Beyond it rise the vertiginous arches of the Ponte delle Torri (Bridge of Towers), which spans the abyss between the fortress and the forest of Monteluco. No wonder the visitors who come here for the arts are lured back again by the many other charms of this enduring town.

Inset: Ponte delle Torri, a magnificent 14th-century aqueduct
Below (left and right): Verdant landscape near Spoleto; *nociata*, a type of nougat, a local delicacy

FESTIVAL DIARY

With the main festival perfomances taking place in the evening, you can combine a weekend's cultural fix with a chance to get to know one of Umbria's most delightful walled cities. The streets will be bustling with other festival-goers, but it's easy to slip away from the crowds into lovely churches or across the magnificent aqueduct to peaceful countryside if you so choose.

A Cultural Weekend

DAY 1

Start your visit by exploring Spoleto's historic center. Don't miss the archbishops' palace, which houses an interesting museum and a courtyard that leads to the small Romanesque church of Sant'Eufemia (known for its metroneum, a segregated women's gallery). Pause to admire the Duomo, with its wonderful sculpted portal and a cycle of frescoes by Filippo Lippi in the apse.

In the afternoon, if you've a head for heights, walk across the Ponte delle Torri, with its breathtaking views, to the wooded hill of Monteluco and the pilgrim's church of San Pietro, with its splendid Romanesque carved façade. Return to town in time for dinner and a late-evening festival performance.

DAY 2

Today, venture outside Spoleto's ancient walls into the lower town, to see three more interesting medieval churches. San Paolo Inter Vineas ("among the vines," a name that reveals how it was built in open countryside), has exquisite 13th-century frescoes. The 12th-century Romanesque San Ponziano still has the 10th-century frescoed crypt of the original church. The most ancient of the three churches is the atmospheric 4th-century San Salvatore, built mainly with materials left over from the Roman era.

Return to the old town in time for lunch, then spend the afternoon browsing the workshops of Spoleto's talented artisans before an early-evening festival performance and an after-show supper.

Dos and Don'ts

- ✓ To make sure you get seats for the performances you want at the Festival dei Due Mondi, it is essential to book tickets in advance. Visit the official website for details *(see opposite)*.
- ✓ If you are here on the second Sunday of the month, look around the bustling street market for local crafts, antiques, and collectors' items. Or simply seek out the workshops of local craftsmen tucked away in Spoleto's little back streets.
- ✗ Don't try to visit the Rocca Albornoz without pre-booking (tel. 0743 223055) – it's worth seeing for its fine frescoes.
- ✓ Try some specialties of the local cuisine: *stringozzi* (long square pasta) with black truffles or meat *ragù*, and superb salamis whose recipes are based on centuries of tradition.

AUGUST

Where to Go: **August**

The roar of the crowd, the dust kicked up by hooves, the excitement of horses and riders jostling shoulder to shoulder for a few frenetic minutes: this is the most famous Palio in Italy – the Palio di Siena. This extraordinary race takes place on August 16 every year in one of the most beautiful medieval squares in the world. But if you're in the mood for performances, Italy has yet more to offer in August: for example, there's the opera season at the Arena in Verona, in the Veneto, or the Rossini Opera Festival that Pesaro holds every year in honor of its most famous son.

August also brings great opportunities to discover the long history of some splendid cities such as Tarquinia, in Lazio, with its marvelous Etruscan necropolises, or Siracusa, one of the oldest

FESTIVALS AND CULTURE

PESARO The glorious interior of the Rossini theater

PESARO
LE MARCHE

A celebration of Rossini by the seaside

An elegant and sunny city with long sandy beaches, Pesaro, the birthplace of Rossini, remembers the composer with a renowned music festival.

See pp204–5

NUORO
SARDINIA

Enjoy the spectacle of the Sagra del Redentore at Nuoro

At this religious folk festival, people come dressed in traditional costume from all over the island to one of Sardinia's major cultural centers.

www.discover-sardinia.com/regions

CORTONA
TUSCANY

The best Chianina steak

Every year on August 15 in Cortona they fire up a huge grill ready for the Festival of Beefsteak, and the air of this Etruscan city is filled with the sounds and smells of sizzling beef.

www.cortonaweb.net

CAGLI
LE MARCHE

An unusual Palio livens up summer in the town

Not far from the Adriatic coast, Cagli is a pretty historic town that comes alive in August with the traditional Palio, raced in costume.

www.cagliturismo.it

"In colorful silks, the jockeys jostle for position, poised bareback over their horses; waving flags flutter and then fall still."

SIENA
TUSCANY

Racing bareback in the most famous Palio in Italy

In a packed Piazza del Campo, Siena's Palio, raced by competing city wards, is the most important day of the year for the locals.

See pp210–11

UNFORGETTABLE JOURNEYS

REGGIA DI CASERTA Exquisite sculpture in the gardens

REGGIA DI CASERTA
CAMPANIA

A spectacular "Versailles" for the Bourbon kings of Naples

The palace of Caserta, built by the architect Vanvitelli, is a masterpiece surrounded by a splendid garden filled with fountains and sculptures.

See pp200–1

SANSEPOLCRO
TUSCANY

On the trail of art

Piero della Francesca, one of the greats of Italian art, worked throughout central Italy. Follow his paintings from Arezzo to Monterchi, and on to his birthplace of Sansepolcro.

www.sansepolcro-info.com

PAVIA
LOMBARDY

A notable city of art on the banks of the Ticino River

The university city of Pavia has a historic center and a Renaissance masterpiece of a monastery complex just outside.

See pp216–7

SORRENTO
CAMPANIA

The most beautiful walk in Italy

Trapped between an infinite blue sky and azure sea, you can see why they call the Amalfi coastal path the "Footpath of the Gods."

www.sorrentotourism.com/eng

PIEVE DI LIVINALLONGO
VENETO

The Great Dolomites Road

Pieve di Livinallongo sits halfway along a spectacular long drive between Bolzano and Cortina d'Ampezzo.

www.planetware.com/italy/pieve-di-livinallongo-i-vn-drlb.htm

NATURAL WONDERS

CABRAS The white sandy beach of Maimoni, lapped by an aquamarine sea

STROMBOLI
SICILY

A midnight climb to the center of the Earth

The black basalt volcano of Stromboli looks like a castle by day, but by night great red fireballs illuminate the sky.

www.messina-sicilia.it/english/

BELLAGIO
LOMBARDY

A picturesque lakeside town surrounded by forested hills

A celebrated vacation destination, Bellagio is famous simply for its perfect location – just where Lake Como divides into two.

www.bellagiolakecomo.com

PARCO REGIONALE DEL CONERO
LE MARCHE

A mountainous headland in the northern Adriatic

Thin white strips of secluded beach below lofty forest-covered cliffs – this is a regional park of great beauty.

www.parks.it/parco.conero

TREMITI ISLANDS
PUGLIA

Underwater caves, colorful corals, and sunken ships

Explore these rugged islands, protected by marine preserve status, with secluded coves and fragrant woods running to the water's edge.

www.isoletremitionline.it

"Summer is an excellent time to combine a nature trip with a relaxing stay by the sea."

CABRAS
SARDINIA

Unique wetlands area that attracts myriad waterbirds

The wild Cabras marshes are rich in ancient history and also attract flocks of pink flamingoes, ibises, and many other rare birds.

See pp198–9

Previous page: The colorful and fast-paced palio in Siena, Tuscany

ancient Greek colonies in Sicily. More recent history is on display at Caserta in Campania, where the kings of Naples tried to build their own Versailles, and in Pavia, where the Certosa, or Charterhouse, is a stunning Renaissance masterpiece.

For anyone in search of simple relaxation, there is Rimini, with its large sandy beaches and a huge range of entertainment. Or, for something a little more exciting, try sailing around the islands to the north of Sardinia, in an almost tropical sea, or improving your golf handicap on the fairways of Gressoney in Valle d'Aosta, against the spectacular backdrop of the snow-capped Alps. And bird watching fans are able to tick a few rare birds off their must-see list in the protected wetlands of Cabras, in Sardinia.

LUXURY AND ROMANCE

TARQUINIA A view of the mighty medieval walls of the city

ABANO TERME
VENETO

A spa town famous since the era of ancient Rome

This pleasant little town lies at the foot of the Colli Euganai, with countryside walks and spas offering therapeutic and beauty treatments.

www.italyheaven.co.uk/veneto

TARQUINIA
LAZIO

In the land of the dead

An ancient Etruscan city, Tarquinia is home to one of the largest necropolises in Italy. It also has a lovely historic center, full of medieval monuments.

See pp212–3

CERVO
LIGURIA

Great chamber music in a charming and rustic town

Set into the cliffs by the sea, Cervo is an interesting Ligurian town. In July and August, it is the delightful setting for a festival of chamber music.

www.cervo.com

SIRACUSA
SICILY

Two ancient Greek colonies

A city with a long and interesting history, Siracusa was formed by joining the original settlement on the island of Ortigia to Achradina, on the Sicilian mainland.

See pp214–5

VERONA
VENETO

Wonderful music in the city of Romeo and Juliet

Famous all over the world as the setting for the love between Romeo and Juliet, Verona hosts a special summer opera festival.

See pp196–7

ACTIVE ADVENTURES

MADDALENA ARCHIPELAGO Training yachts at Caprera

PONTINE ISLANDS
LAZIO

Dive in the clear waters of these delightful islands

The stunning Pontine Islands are famous for their wonderful beaches, great diving opportunities, and extraordinary Etruscan grottoes.

www.italyheaven.co.uk/lazio

PARCO REGIONALE DELL'AVETO
LIGURIA

Bird-watching in the Apennines

This preserve is an important area of natural beauty in the Apennines and home to more than 60 species of bird, including golden eagles.

www.parks.it/parco.aveto

"Sailors will enjoy the best conditions for learning to sail all year round – reliable winds, deep clear waters, and sheltered coves and bays."

MADDALENA ARCHIPELAGO
SARDINIA

Flying over the briny blue sea

The Maddalena archipelago enjoys the perfect wind conditions to make it a paradise for yachting enthusiasts – beginners welcome!

See pp208–9

TAORMINA
SICILY

Feel the thrill of paragliding over a beautiful coastline

Launch yourself into the air from the cliffs of Taormina over the deep blue sea for views of Mt. Etna.

www.gotaormina.com/en/sports/paragliding.html

ALAGNA VALSESIA
PIEDMONT

On the slopes of Monte Rosa

A variety of hiking routes leaves from Alagna, in the Parco Naturale Alta Valsesia, including one to a mountain hut, Capanna Regina Margherita, the highest in Europe.

www.alagna.it

FAMILY GETAWAYS

GRESSONEY A view of Lago Gover, with Monte Rosa in the background

"As a beginner, what ever your age, Gressoney-Saint-Jean will make for a memorable introduction to golf."

GRESSONEY
VALLE D'AOSTA

Golf at high altitude

At the Gressoney Golf Club, free lessons for beginners enable novices to improve at this challenging sport in astonishingly beautiful, natural surroundings.

See pp206–7

SILVI MARINA
ABRUZZO

Safe sea bathing on the sandy eastern coast

In this famous resort, known for its licorice production, enjoy the child-friendly sandy beaches.

www.abruzzo2000.com/abruzzo/teramo/silvi.htm

RIMINI
EMILIA-ROMAGNA

A beach resort with everything the visitor could need

With its wide, sandy beaches, amusement parks and fairgrounds, historic architecture, and nightclubs, Rimini has something for everyone.

See pp202–3

SPILIMBERGO
FRIULI-VENEZIA GIULIA

Travel back to the Middle Ages

Spilimbergo recreates the Middle Ages for the historical re-enactment of La Macia, when the town is full of people in costume and busy with medieval workshops.

www.turismofvg.it

MARINA DI CAMEROTA
CAMPANIA

Splash in the sea by the "Pearl of the Cilento"

Situated in the beautiful coastal area of the Parco del Cilento, Marina di Camerota is a superb resort with safe beaches, sea caves, and mountains.

www.parks.it/parco.nazionale.cilento

GETTING THERE
Verona is in the western Veneto. A shuttle bus service links the airport with the city, 7 miles (11 km) away.

GETTING AROUND
Verona is well served by public transportation.

WEATHER
August is hot in Verona, with an average daytime high of 82°F (28°C).

ACCOMMODATIONS
The Due Torri Hotel Baglioni is a 14th-century palace in the heart of the historic center; doubles from US$530 (a "musical package" of room plus reserved seats at the Arena is also available); www.baglionihotels.com

The Hotel Gabbia d'Oro is a small luxury hotel in an 18th-century residence with wood paneling, antiques, and art; doubles from US$482; www.hotelgabbiadoro.it

There are many B&Bs in the center and outskirts of Verona, including Residenza Carducci (doubles from US$95, www.residenzacarducci.com) and Arena Suite (doubles from US$68, www.arenasuite.it).

EATING OUT
Various restaurants serve the delicious local cuisine, including *bigoli* (thick whole wheat pasta), and *risotto all'Amarone* made with red wine. Among the best are Stueta (dinner from US$28), Via Stella (US$40), Al Calmiere (US$48) and Al Pompiere (US$55).

For a special dinner, try Il Desco, in a palace in the historic center (light menu: US$82; Veneto menu: US$130); www.ildesco.com

PRICE FOR TWO
US$200–665 for accommodations, meals, and Verona Card. A ticket for a performance at the Arena costs anything from US$20 to US$200.

FURTHER INFORMATION
www.tourism.verona.it

Opera Season at the Arena

In his memoirs, playwright Carlo Goldoni relates that he decided to give up law for the theater in 1734 after having attended a performance at the Verona Arena. But it is only since 1913 that the amphitheater has been used annually to host an opera season that is now the glory of Verona's summer. It was inaugurated with a superb performance of Verdi's *Aida* and, since then, the greatest singers have all appeared at the Arena – including Maria Callas (seen here with Aristotle Onassis), who made her debut here in 1947.

Main: Scene from *Aida*, performed at the Arena in Verona
Above (top to bottom): Detail of the San Zeno triptych, by Andrea Mantegna; exterior view of the Arena; cloister of San Zeno Maggiore; *gnocchi di patate* (potato dumplings), a typical Veronese dish

THE ROMANCE OF HISTORY

In a dazzling spectacle of light and sound, Verona's ancient elliptical amphitheater is filled with cascading music, spectacular lighting, magnificent sets, and, above all, the most beautiful voices of international opera. The magic of Verona's Arena casts its spell, night after night, in the performances of the Verona Opera Festival.

The building is not simply a potent symbol of the historic past of the city – it remains in use as a huge theater, just as it was in Roman times, when it was built for very different types of entertainment, including gladiatorial games, and an audience of up to 30,000 people, almost the whole population of Verona at the time. Today the Arena, with its impressive proportions, perfectly preserved shape, and the rosy hue of its stone terraces that have remained almost intact, is still stunning. It is Verona's best-known historic building and one of the icons of a city that is famous throughout the world as the setting of *Romeo and Juliet*, William Shakespeare's tragic tale of star-crossed lovers.

Above: The balcony cited as that of Juliet Capulet, high on the wall of Casa di Giulietta

Below: Aerial view of the Pietra bridge over the Adige River, the only surviving Roman bridge in the city

Above: Piazza della Signoria, with a statue of Dante in the center

VERONESE DIARY

Verona is above all a city that has preserved an outstanding artistic heritage, the legacy of a history that began in Roman times, when Verona was so important that it was nicknamed "Little Rome." In three days you can explore the many cultural and historical charms of the city, as well as enjoying at least one evening performance at the Arena.

Three Captivating Days

DAY 1

Start your exploration of Verona at the Arena, the Roman amphitheater built in the 1st century AD. From here, take the elegant Via Mazzini to Casa di Giulietta. Touch the statue of Juliet in the courtyard if you want to be lucky in love. Continue to the Piazza delle Erbe, site of the Roman Forum and now home to a picturesque market. After lunch, move on to the Piazza della Signoria to see the Renaissance Loggia del Consiglio and the Palazzo degli Scaligeri. End your tour at the Arche Scaligere.

DAY 2

Today, visit Verona's magnificent churches. Begin at the Duomo, built after the earthquake in 1117; it has a splendid Romanesque apse. Move on to the Chiesa di Sant'Anastasia, built in the 13th and 14th centuries, and then San Fermo Maggiore, formed from two churches: the lower one is Romanesque, the higher one Gothic. Finally visit the basilica of San Zeno Maggiore, a Romanesque masterpiece with a façade adorned with fine marble reliefs, a triptych by Mantegna, and the crypt that was reputedly the scene of the marriage of Romeo and Juliet. End the day with a performance at the Arena.

DAY 3

Visit Castelvecchio, and the Ponte Scaligero. This fortress and its bridge were built in the mid-14th century at the behest of Castelgrande II della Scala. The western part incorporates the palace, while the eastern section is defended by a wall. Today, the castle houses the Civico Museo d'Arte, one of the most important in northern Italy.

Opera-lovers may come to Verona for the festival's world-class performances in the Arena, but lovers cannot resist the appeal of Casa di Giulietta. Even if the story is not true, one cannot deny the romantic fascination that lingers in the memory of the scene played out upon its little balcony.

But Verona offers a great deal more as well. There is its network of streets, in a grid pattern that still follows the original Roman plan and creates an elegant and welcoming center; its lovely squares, such as Piazza delle Erbe, with its colorful market stalls and the beautiful palaces that encircle it; and Piazza dei Signori, with buildings that once constituted the heart of political power in the city. There are its churches, at once architectural masterworks and impressive legacies of the medieval period, such as San Zeno Maggiore and San Fermo Maggiore, and the extraordinary complex of Arche Scaligere, almost an anthology of Gothic sculpture, including the monumental tombs of Verona's once-powerful della Scala family. And then there are the elegant boutiques and fine restaurants, yet more delights to tempt you to a city that is one of the most beautiful in Italy.

Dos and Don'ts

- ✓ Buy an inexpensive Verona Card: valid for 3 days, it gives you free access to public transportation as well as the city's historic buildings and museums.
- ✓ Walk under the Arco della Costa that separates Piazza delle Erbe from Piazza della Signoria. Hanging from it for more than 1,000 years is the rib of a whale, which, according to legend, will fall only when a righteous person passes underneath the archway.
- ✗ If you are in Verona on the third Saturday of the month, don't miss the market of the Three As: artisanship, antiques, and art.
- ✗ Don't imitate those who have damaged Casa di Giulietta (Juliet's house) by scratching love messages on its walls, or attaching notes to it with chewing-gum.

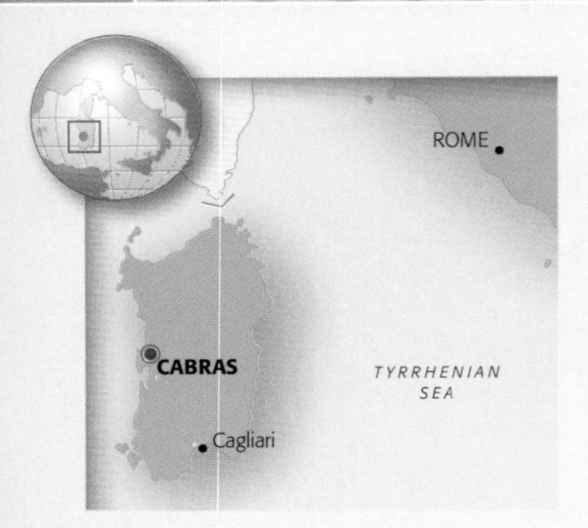

GETTING THERE
Cabras is a village in western Sardinia, a few miles from Oristano. The nearest airport is Cagliari, about 60 miles (100 km) away or 90 minutes by car. You can also fly to Alghero, about 80 miles (130 km) away, which is accessible on main roads.

GETTING AROUND
A car is very useful for getting around.

WEATHER
Most days will be hot and sunny. The evaporation of water from the lagoons cools the air and generates pleasant sea breezes.

ACCOMMODATIONS
Sa Cottilla is a pleasant, quiet B&B whose rooms look on to a courtyard. Rooms from US$82; www.sacotilla.it

Il Sinis *agriturismo*, near San Salvatore, offers spacious rooms with their own garden entrance from US$55 per person; www.agriturismoilsinis.it

The well-equipped Spinnaker camp site is in a pine grove by the sea and has holiday chalets (from US$85) and mobile homes (from US$102). A tent costs US$28 for two people; www.campingspinnaker.com

EATING OUT
There are many fish specialties such as *bottarga* (cured fish roe) and *merca* (air-cured mullet roe boiled and wrapped in marsh herbs). Don't miss grilled gilthead bream, sea bass, and eels from the Cabras lagoon. Two excellent restaurants are Sa Funtà in Cabras (about US$48) and Da Giovanni in Oristano (about US$40).

PRICE FOR TWO
US$150–230 per day for meals and accommodations.

FURTHER INFORMATION
www.oristanoturismo.it

Is Fassonis Regatta

Since ancient times, *is fassonis* – narrow rafts made from bulrushes – have been used on the Cabras lagoon. These boats are powered and steered by the boatman at the back using a pole. Said by some to date back to the Phoenicians, the rafts fell into disuse in the 1970s, but are still used in a race as the centerpiece of a festival on the first Sunday of August. Afterward there is a feast of grilled fish, washed down with Vernaccia wine.

THE KINGDOM OF WATER

The importance of water in defining the Sardinian town of Cabras should not be underestimated. First, there is the water that is the sea, stretches of the purest water in the Mediterranean lapping on 19 miles (31 km) of glorious, white-sand beaches. Second, there is the water that was an object of worship in ancient times – a spring in the village of Tharros, sacred since the prehistoric era, was used in ceremonies during the Punic era and is one of the most important archeological sites in Sardinia. And finally, there is the water that is the Cabras lagoon, one of the most interesting and unique natural habitats in Europe.

The lagoon is an enormous expanse of water, nearly 8 sq miles (21 sq km), but only 10 ft (3 m) deep at the most, the last vestige of the several thousand-year-old contest between the Mediterranean tides and the outpouring of the Tirso River, which has created a maze of inlets and stretches of brackish and

Main: Greater flamingoes on the lagoon at Cabras, an important wildlife preserve

Right (left to right): Fisherman's hut built of reeds among the dunes of Porto Suedda, near Cabras; the white sandy beach of Maimoni, near Is Arutas, lapped by an aquamarine sea; Cabras by the lagoon; air-cured mullet roe, a treasured specialty of the area

fresh water, lagoons, and lakes in the Sinis peninsula. Today, the Cabras lagoon is partly given over to fish farming and the production of *bottarga* (air-cured mullet roe) – reputed to be the best in Italy and a delicious first course, especially when washed down with the local Vernaccia di Oristano (a delicious almond-scented white wine matured in chestnut casks until it turns a deep amber-gold).

Perhaps the biggest attraction of the network of rivers, marshes, and lakes is the incredible bird life. Many of the fishermen's huts have been turned into hides for bird watchers. Here, you might see water-loving birds such as rare red-crested pochards, glossy ibises, flamingoes, and cormorants, while on the cliffs at the coast, the blue rock thrush, peregrine falcon, and herring gull all build their nests. And between the lagoon and the sea, herons, great bitterns, and mallards are regularly spotted. Summer is an excellent time to combine a nature vacation with a relaxing stay by the sea, but winter offers the unique spectacle of thousands of migrating birds using the lagoon as a resting point during their long journeys.

Above: View of Cabras from the top of one of the bridges over the marshes

WATERBIRD DIARY

The Cabras lagoon, which adjoins the Sinis peninsula, has been home to Neolithic peoples, Phoenicians, Carthaginians, Romans, Arabs, and the Spanish. Now its foreign inhabitants are more likely to be wading birds and a few tourists. Four days will give you a chance to appreciate both its history and its natural beauty.

Four Days in the Marshes

DAY 1

Spend the day taking a boat trip on the Cabras lagoon – it's perfect for bird watchers, fishing enthusiasts, and those who simply enjoy seeing the natural world. There are colonies of pink flamingoes in the shallow waters of the lagoon. Visit the Cabras Museo Archeologico Giovanni Marongiu and learn about the long history of the area. In the evening, dine with a view of the lagoon and enjoy a delicious meal of lake fish.

DAY 2

Relax for a day by the sea on the lovely beaches. The nearest is San Giovanni in Sinis (there's also a fine 5th-century church in the village); a little farther north lie the beaches of Maimoni and Is Arutas – the latter is famous for its bright, white quartz sand. Farther north still is the pristine beach of Is Arenas – 4 miles (7 km) of fine sandy dunes backed by a shady pine forest.

DAY 3

Visit the ruins of Tharros, one of the most important cities of the ancient Mediterranean. Founded by the Phoenicians in the 8th century BC, it occupies a splendid position on a stretch of land that divides the wide Gulf of Oristano from the open sea. Its fortunes declined in the 11th century, when the population, driven out by the raids of Saracen pirates, headed further inland, with many settling in Cabras.

DAY 4

On your last day, visit the little village of San Salvatore; its central square was used in the 1960s as the set for a spaghetti western. Near the village is a church, built on the site of a pagan temple devoted to the worship of water. In the 6th century, an underground sanctuary, or hypogeum, was built here. Return to the coast for another relaxing afternoon on the beach.

Dos and Don'ts

- ✓ Spend a morning or afternoon horseback-riding in the Sale Porcus oasis, north of Cabras; www.mandraedera.it.
- ✗ Don't swim at the beach of Is Arenas when it is windy – the sea currents can be dangerous.
- ✓ Visit the pretty Cantina Sociale in Oristano to learn about, and taste, the delicious local Vernaccia wine.

GETTING THERE
Caserta is in Campania, about 19 miles (31 km) north of Naples (the nearest airport). From here, take the A1 freeway, exiting at the Caserta Nord exit. Or you can take the train or bus – the stations are near the entrance to the royal palace.

GETTING AROUND
A car is best for day trips, although there is also a bus service.

WEATHER
In August the weather will be sunny and very hot.

ACCOMMODATIONS
Treat yourself to a room at the sumptuous Grand Hotel Vanvitelli for a decadent taste of a bygone era. Rooms from US$245; www.grandhotelvanvitelli.it

The Hotel Caserta Antica is in a peaceful position near the center of Casertavecchia. Family-run, it has a good atmosphere and is real value for money. Rooms from US$82; www.hotelcaserta-antica.it

The Locanda delle Trame, within walking distance of the palace, offers comfortable, modern rooms and a smart restaurant. Double rooms from US$135; www.locandadelletrame.it

EATING OUT
The restaurant Antica Hostaria Massa In Caserta has been delighting diners with excellent food since 1848. Meals from US$48 (tel. 0823 456 527).

Enjoy local cuisine at Mastrangelo, a monastery converted into a restaurant opposite Casertavecchia's cathedral. Meals from US$35 (tel. 0823 371 377).

PRICE FOR TWO
US$215–365 per day for meals, accommodations, and entrance to the palace (including the royal apartments, museum, and park).

FURTHER INFORMATION
www.reggiadicaserta.beniculturali.it

Buffalo Mozzarella

The buffalo, which originally comes from Asia and flourishes in humid marshy areas, has been bred in the countryside around Caserta for a very long time. Its milk has an unmistakeably different taste from that of other cattle – it's strong with a slight flavor of almonds. The buffalo milk is used to make mozzarella cheese, famous the world over. It is a fresh cheese with an ancient tradition and its name comes from the fact that in the final stage of production, the mixture is *mozzata* (divided) by hand to form the various shapes.

Above (left and right): View of the cathedral of San Michele, Casertavecchia, which dates back to the 12th century; the magnificent façade of the Reggia di Caserta

THE ITALIAN VERSAILLES

The numbers involved in creating the Reggia di Caserta (Royal Palace of Caserta) are simply mind boggling. The façade is 820 ft (250 m) wide; there are 1,200 rooms, 1,790 windows, and 34 staircases; and it took who knows how many workers 22 years to build using materials brought in from all over Campania and Tuscany, including Carrara marble and Follonica iron. The town of Caserta moved 6 miles (10 km) nearer to be a ready supply of labor, and the palace was probably the largest building constructed in Europe in the 18th century.

Inspired by the Palace of Versailles and the Royal Palace of Madrid, where he had grown up, Charles of Bourbon, the king of Naples, commissioned the great Neapolitan architect Luigi Vanvitelli to create one of the last great Baroque masterpieces. Neither saw it completed. Charles abdicated the throne in 1759 to become Charles III, king of Spain and Vanvitelli died a year before its completion in 1774. Undoubtedly one of the finest examples of Italian Baroque, the palace was built with five storys plus a basement, cleverly illuminated by daylight, for the kitchens, wine cellars, and workshops. The genius of Vanvitelli is revealed in the palace's simple but brilliant design: the huge rectangular building is divided into quarters with a courtyard in each. In the center, linking everything, is a large octagonal vestibule, possibly inspired by the Basilica di Santa Maria della Salute in Venice. The Royal Staircase has 116 steps, each one a single 20-ft (6-m) block of marble. The sumptuous interior of the palace is divided into eight apartments and visitors wander through a seemingly endless series of reception rooms and salons, each one more fabulous than the previous, decorated with original furnishings that still radiate their past glory.

The palace is complemented by the enormous park that opens up behind it; this was as important in Vanvitelli's plans as the palace itself. Here, too, the architect sought to upstage Versailles. There are natural-looking woods, a castle built for the young Bourbon princes, and vast water features, ponds, and fountains, culminating in a 260-ft (80-m) waterfall that finishes with a sculpture of Diana and Actaeon. This is an exquisite work of art, a spirited tableau of Diana bathing with her nymphs on one side as Actaeon is torn to pieces by his hounds on the other, the white forms brought to life among the ceaseless movement of the cascading water.

Main: The enormous gardens of the Reggia di Caserta
Below (left and right): Corinthian capital in the Basilica di Sant'Angelo in Formis; detail of the fountain of Venus and Adonis

Above: Diana bathing with her nymphs, Reggia di Caserta

PALACE DIARY

Before the construction of the Reggia di Caserta, there was nothing on the site but the hamlet of La Torre. With the palace's completion, Caserta became the seat of the court of one of Italy's most powerful royal houses until the Unification of Italy in 1871. Three days will give enough time to explore the palace, park, and some nearby villages.

Three Royal Days

DAY 1

Spend the first day touring the Reggia di Caserta. Admire the fabulous apartments, the sequence of 18th-century salons, and the spacious state reception rooms, and don't miss out on the gardens with their grand central axis formed by a series of statues, ponds, and fountains, ending with a stunning cascade. Nearby, you will also find the naturalistic English garden, perhaps the first of its kind to be created in Italy, adorned with fake ruins and statues from Pompeii.

DAY 2

Visit Casertavecchia, an ancient village, dating back to the 8th century, situated a short distance north from the newer settlement, created to help build the palace. Here, nestled against the mountains and overlooked by the ruins of an ancient fort, the alleyways, cobbled streets, and tufa houses will take you back to the Middle Ages. The village is dominated by the wonderful 12th-century cathedral, its cupola decorated with arabesque designs. Enjoy a taste of Campania with a lunch of mozzarella salad or pappardelle pasta with wild boar.

DAY 3

On your last day, take a trip to see the Benedictine Basilica di Sant'Angelo in the town of Formis, near Capua. Built on the ruins of a Roman temple dedicated to Diana, it is one of the greatest Romanesque buildings in Campania and its façade is graced by a five-arched portio decorated with a marvelous series of 11th-century frescoes. There are some more delicate frescoes inside the church.

Dos and Don'ts

- ✓ Bring along a picnic to enjoy in one of the designated areas in the palace gardens.
- ✓ When you pack, choose cool and comfortable clothes; Caserta is a long way from the sea and is generally very hot in summer.
- ✓ Go to one of the performances of the *Settembre al Borgo* (September in the Village) festival, which is held every year in Casertavecchia in late August or early September.
- ✗ Do not use public transportation to reach Casertavecchia; it is infrequent and not very reliable. If you don't have a car, plan to take a taxi.
- ✓ Bear in mind that the palace and its park are very large and that you'll need a complete day to see everything.

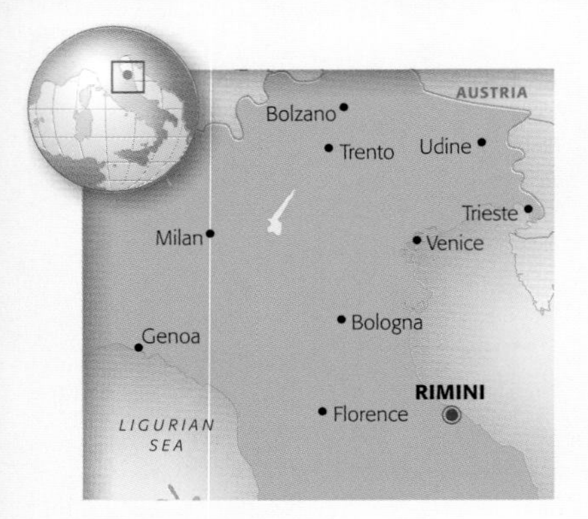

GETTING THERE
The airport of Rimini, the "queen" of the Romagna coast, is a short distance from the town center, and easily reached by taxi or bus no. 9 which runs every 30 minutes from the airport to the train station.

GETTING AROUND
Rimini and the coast are well-served by public buses. There is also a night service from bars and clubs outside town to the center. If using a car, the main roads are the A14 and the SS16.

WEATHER
It will be hot, but swimming and sea breezes will help to keep you and your family cool.

ACCOMMODATIONS
The Fra i Pini hotel is ideal for families, with lots of activities for kids, including beach games and trips to the nearby amusement parks. Family packages from US$1,350 per week B&B; www.hotelfraipini.it

The Camping Italia camp site is close to the center of town. It has a private beach, with a family zone and a young people's zone. Two adults with two children pay about US$40 per night for a tent, US$135 for a chalet; www.campingitaliarimini.it

At the Casa dei Mori *agriturismo* you can enjoy the peace of the countryside not far from from the center of Rimini. From US$162 a night for a family of four; www.casemori.it

EATING OUT
Enjoy Romagna cuisine at Al Grotta Rossa from US$35. Feast on the meat specialties at Il Quartino (US$28–42) or splash out on fish at the Marinelli da Vittorio restaurant (from US$55).

PRICE FOR A FAMILY OF FOUR
Expect to spend between US$230 and US$390 per day for meals and accommodations, plus US$28 for umbrella and sun bed rental; allow about US$135 for family entrance to an amusement park.

FURTHER INFORMATION
www.visit-rimini.com

Museum of Aviation

Kids of all ages – even the adult kind – will love the Parco Tematico e Museo dell'Aviazione. Covering almost 20 acres (8 ha) of wooded hillside, the museum contains a collection of nearly 50 full-size aircraft showing the history of aviation from World War II to the present day. There's also a museum of model aircraft, and a collection of the weaponry used against airplanes. In addition, there are displays of uniforms, mementos, and photographs relating to Italian military and civil aviation.

FUN FOR EVERYONE

BY DAY, CHILDREN PLAY ON WIDE SANDY BEACHES, swimmers splash in the shallows, pedaloes glide over the waves, and families relax in the shade of the beach umbrellas. At night, the Romagna seafront becomes the realm of nightclubbers, who flock here from all over the area. Starting with a few drinks at the beach bars, they parade up and down the seafront in all their glamorous finery until around 11pm, whereupon they set off for the clubs, often using the not-so-glamorous bus service.

Away from the beaches are Rimini's other family attractions – it has many amusement parks: Aquafàn is Europe's biggest aquatic park; Fiabilandia is great for children; Italia in Miniatura has models of Italy's historic buildings; Mirabilandia contains more than 30 attractions including the world's largest illuminated Ferris wheel; and the Rimini Dolphinarium is where these smart sea mammals entertain tourists.

Main: One of Rimini's wide, sandy beaches with rows of colorful umbrellas and sun beds

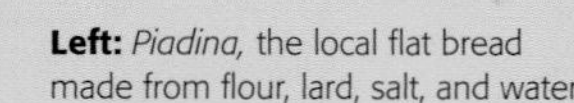

Left: *Piadina,* the local flat bread made from flour, lard, salt, and water

Right (left and right): The water park Aquafàn di Riccione; the Ponte di Tiberio, a testimony of Rimini's Roman past

Right of main (top to bottom): a vintage poster advertising Rimini's delights; the Piazza Tre Martiri, one of the most important landmarks in Rimini; well-equipped beach at Rimini, perfect for grown-ups and children alike

Few places in Italy can provide such a mix of activities to satisfy sun worshippers, thrill-seekers, shopaholics, clubbers, fashionistas, and, of course, families. It is precisely this ability to cater for diverse tastes and lifestyles that has made Rimini's fortune since the 19th century, when the shady pine groves and long sandy shore were discovered by the Romagna nobility.

And history-lovers aren't left out, either. The city was called Ariminum in Roman times and was an important staging post along the Roman road system. The craftsmanship of the Roman builders is displayed in the five-arched Ponte di Tiberio, still in use today, and the Arco di Augusto, the oldest surviving triumphal arch in Italy. Later, Rimini had a very prosperous period under the rule of the Malatesta dynasty. These *condottieri* (mercenary leaders or warlords) went on to construct some of the most interesting buildings in the historic center, such as Castel Sismondo, the now ruined 15th-century fortress, and the Tempio Malatestiano, designed by the great Renaissance architect Leon Battista Alberti and one of the earliest examples of a Neo-Classical church.

Above: Children's playground in Rimini

THEME PARK DIARY

Such are the many attractions of Rimini that everyone should be able to enjoy the vacation they want, whether their interest is clubbing, amusement parks, shopping, historical buildings, or simply relaxing on the beach. A week is plenty of time to do all this and more, such as enjoying the famous rich Emilia-Romagna food and drink.

A Week of Entertainment

DAYS 1-2

Enjoy a day relaxing on Rimini's great beaches. After dinner, walk around the center, enjoying the lively bars and admiring the town's beautiful historic buildings.

Go to Mirabilandia, to the north of Rimini, for a day of fun for both grown-ups and children alike in one of the biggest amusement parks in Italy.

DAYS 3-4

Visit Riccione, another famous beach resort on the Romagna Riviera. This town is also known for its villas set in magnificent parkland, and has been a spa resort since Roman times. After a day on the beach, it is worth trying the thermal treatments with mineral-rich spa water.

Spend a day splashing around at Aquafàn, near Riccione, one of the most famous aquatic parks in Europe, with slides and swimming pools to suit everybody's tastes.

DAYS 5-7

In between trips to the beach during the day, exploring Rimini, and visits to clubs in the evening, there are plenty of other things to do. Motorcycling fans shouldn't miss the Misano World Circuit in Misano Adriatico, home to some of the most important international competitions. Or, those with an interest in aviation might want to visit the Parco Tematico e Museo dell'Aviazione.

If you have young children, take them to Fiabilandia, an amusement park specially made for them. For something for everyone, try the Dolphinarium, which has a gallery of aquariums that recreate a range of river and marine environments – and dolphins, of course.

Nautical types can visit the Museo della Marineria (Navy Museum) in Cesenatico, with exhibits about the naval history of the Adriatic and models of traditional boats.

Dos and Don'ts

- ✓ Indulge your passion for motor sports by whizzing around in go-karts on the test track of the Misano World Circuit (open in summer from 6pm to midnight).
- ✗ Don't hunt for a free beach in Rimini: they are all equipped with facilities and you have to pay a daily charge to rent an umbrella and a deckchair or sunbed.
- ✓ Go to the street market that is held every Wednesday and Saturday morning in the center of Rimini.
- ✗ Don't book a hotel on the Rimini seafront if you want a peaceful stay: it is always crowded and noisy in the summer.

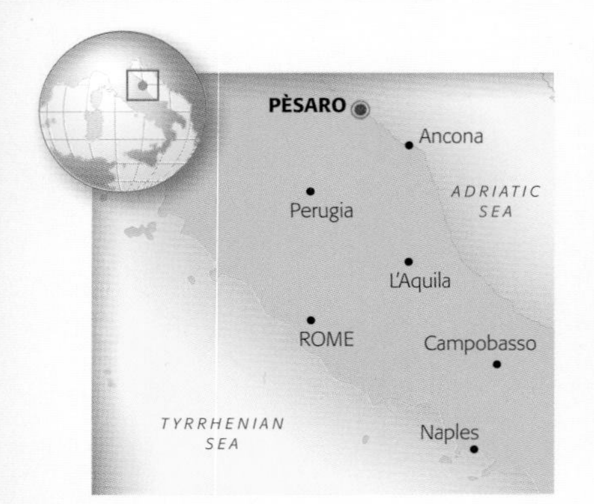

GETTING THERE
Pèsaro is in the northern part of Le Marche, on the Adriatic. Rimini airport is about 25 miles (40 km) away. From the airport, take the A14 freeway and leave at the Pèsaro–Urbino exit, or the SS16.

GETTING AROUND
The center of Pèsaro is closed to cars; get around on foot, by bike, and by public transportation. A car is best for exploring the surrounding areas.

WEATHER
It gets very hot in summer, with temperatures as high as 95°F (35°C).

ACCOMMODATIONS
The Villa Serena, an 18th-century residence, has kept its period charm and has a garden and swimming pool. Rooms from US$230; www.villa-serena.it

Close to Pèsaro and the sea, there's a peaceful and relaxing atmosphere at the Locanda di Villa Torraccia, a former look-out tower converted into a welcoming hotel. From US$135; www.villatorraccia.it

The Casa della Stella is a delightful and comfortable B&B in the countryside, with a view of the Rocca di Gradara. Doubles from US$95; www.casadellastella.it

EATING OUT
The Antica Osteria la Guercia is a historic restaurant in a 16th-century building. Dishes include *piadina* (flatbread) with *squacquerone* (soft cheese), and *maltagliati* (soup with garbazo beans and clams). Meals from US$28; www.osterialaguercia.it

The elegant Da Alceo restaurant has a fine terrace with a view of the sea, and serves excellent fish dishes. Meals from US$68; www.ristorantealceo.it

PRICE FOR TWO
US$215–355 per day for meals and accommodations. Tickets for the festival cost between US$14 and US$170 per concert.

FURTHER INFORMATION
www.turismo.pesarourbino.it

Pèsaro Harbor

Despite the industrial development of recent years, Pèsaro still has nooks and crannies where time seems to have stood still. One of these is the harbor, which seems more like a little fishing village than a big town harbor, with fishermen washing their nets and boats returning to port in the evening. This atmosphere extends to the fish market, with its distinctive boat-shaped main entrance, where the fishmongers give advice on what fish to buy and how to cook it.

Above (left to right): Aerial view of the beach at Pèsaro; Villa Ruggeri façade, a masterpiece of Italian Art Nouveau; the interior of the Teatro Rossini
Main: A scene from *Matilde di Shabran* during the Rossini Opera Festival

Above: Arnaldo Pomodoro's *Palla* in Piazzale della Libertà, Pèsaro

HOMAGE TO A COMPOSER

HE WROTE HIS FIRST OPERA, *Demetrio e Polibio*, when he was barely 14 years old and the last one when he was 40. Then followed 25 years of silence, interrupted only after the death of his father in 1839 by the composition of the last two sad movements of the *Stabat Mater*. This, in a few words, was the life of Gioachino Rossini, Pèsaro's most famous son. His artistic life was like one of his trademark crescendos. He started quietly and reached a peak between 1815 and 1823, when he created 20 operas. Then, wealth and fame assured, he concentrated on other forms of composition, before finishing on a high note with *Guillaume Tell* (1829) and retiring to his villa near Paris.

Every year, Pèsaro holds a festival in honor of Rossini, performing his masterpieces and reviving his less well-known operas. All this takes place in a town that has never forgotten its composer. The Conservatorio di Musica Rossini was created at his express wish and financed by a bequest from him – its 19th-century Auditorium Pedrotti has exceptional acoustics. The Teatro Rossini was inaugurated in 1816 with one of his operas, *La Gazza Ladra* (The Thieving Magpie). There is also a delightful museum in the house where Rossini was born, with playbills, press cuttings, portraits, and the spinet on which he practiced as a child.

His artistic life was like one of his trademark crescendos. He started quietly and reached a peak between 1815 and 1823, when he created 20 operas.

The Rossini Opera Festival is the perfect opportunity to get to know a town which is often overlooked by tourists, yet has a fine historic center. The Piazza del Popolo is dominated by the impressive 15th-century Palazzo Ducale; the Romanesque cathedral has recently uncovered an outstanding 6th-century mosaic floor; and the Rocca Costanza is a huge fortification that dates back to 1480. Pèsaro's more modern beachfront buzzes with life during the summer, with hotels, clubs, bars, and restaurants. Here, you might wish to live a little like the maestro and dine on the rich (and French) dish created in his honor – *tournedos Rossini* (steak with foie gras and truffles).

Inset: Playbills displayed in the Teatro Rossini, Pèsaro
Below (left and right): *Vongole alla pescatora* (fishermen's clams); the massive 15th-century fortification, Rocca Costanza

OPERATIC DIARY

Pèsaro presents an interesting historic center, a wonderful beach and lively seafront, as well as excellent restaurants and shops. What more could you ask for – one of Italy's most important musical events, the Rossini Opera Festival, of course. Four days will allow you to explore the town and the coast, and, most important of all, enjoy the musical extravaganzas of the maestro.

Four Days with Rossini

DAY 1

First of all, get to know the town. Start with the Piazza del Popolo in the center, with its large fountain and the elegant six-arch portico of the Palazzo Ducale. Admire the fabulous mosaics in the cathedral depicting Greek myths and scenes from the natural world; then proceed to the museum in Rossini's house and finally to the massive Rocca Costanza, with its cylindrical turrets and moat. Enjoy an evening drink and meal in the lively beach area.

DAY 2

Unwind by the sea, in the beachfront part of town – here you can see the Villa Ruggeri, the finest Liberty-style Art Nouveau villa in Le Marche. If you want wilder beaches with little rocky coves and expanses of sand, walk north along the beach. In the evening, stroll along the seafront past *Palla*, the bronze sculpture by Arnaldo Pomodoro, and enjoy a drink or two in a bar and a delicious meal beside the sea.

DAY 3

Take a short trip north along the coast to Villa Imperiale, an elegant example of a Renaissance summer residence. It owes its name to the Habsburg emperor Frederick III, who laid the first stone in 1470. The villa, made up of two buildings – the second one was added in 1530 – is surrounded by beautiful gardens and an extensive pine grove. Make sure you get back in time to get ready for the opera.

DAY 4

Head a short way inland to Gradara, a medieval walled village dominated by the spectacular Rocca di Gradara. The fortress is said to have been the setting for the tragic love of Paolo and Francesca, who were caught and killed by Francesca's husband and then immortalized in Dante's *Divine Comedy*. Take a walk around the harbor to see the fishing boats unloading their catch.

Dos and Don'ts

- ✓ For information about the Rossini Opera Festival and booking tickets, visit the official site: www.rossinioperafestival.it
- ✓ Book your visit to the Villa Imperiale at the IAT Centre in Pesaro (tel. 0721 30462).
- ✗ Don't take your car into the center of Pèsaro; it is closed to traffic. You can easily rent a bicycle, or simply tour on foot.
- ✓ Enjoy the sunset from the pier at Calata Caio Duilio, Pèsaro. There are also concerts there on Thursdays.

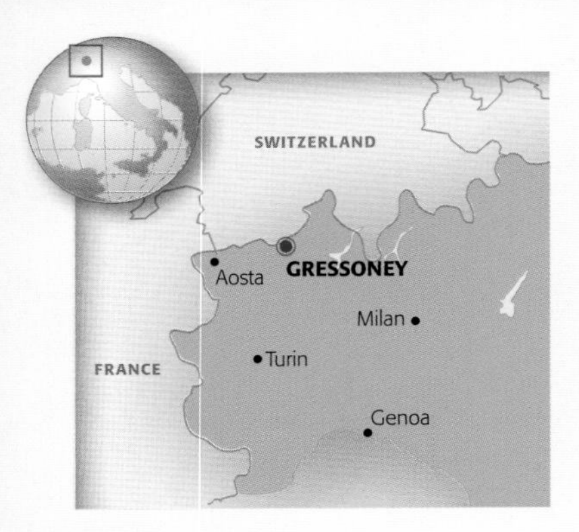

PUTT AMID THE PEAKS

THE MOUNTAIN VILLAGE of Gressoney nestles in a superb position at the foot of the Monte Rosa massif. Of its two parts, the upper one, Gressoney-La-Trinité, is situated at a height of 5,460 ft (1,664 m), making it one of the most popular winter sports resorts in Valle d'Aosta. However, together with the lower village of Gressoney-Saint-Jean (4,544 ft/1,385 m), it offers a wealth of summer leisure choices as well.

Among the many family-friendly options are mountain bike tracks and walking trails, but Gressoney has yet another activity for you to try that combines a gentle pace with high-altitude thrills and challenges – golf. Those who regard the game as little more than a leisurely, undemanding stroll will be amazed at how exciting it is when played so far above sea level, across the verdant slopes of Alpine meadows, amid pine forests, on a course dotted with many tricky (and natural) water hazards. But the real risk here is failing to follow the

Main: Golfers on the splendidly scenic fairway of the golf course at Gressoney

GETTING THERE
The Val di Gressoney is at the foot of Monte Rosa in the eastern Valle d'Aosta. A scheduled bus service runs from Turin airport, 50 miles (80 km) away, to Gressoney. By car, take the A5 to the Pont-Saint-Martin exit, then the SR44 to Gressoney.

GETTING AROUND
A car is useful, but there is a good local bus network.

WEATHER
Days are generally warm and sunny, but the valley's altitude means that it can turn cool or even cold, especially in the evenings.

ACCOMMODATIONS
Villa Fridau in Gressoney-Saint-Jean is a charming residence with every comfort, including a children's playroom, fitness center, and an excellent restaurant; family apartments from US$176; 18th-century hayloft suite from US$210; www.villafridau.com

The Romantik Hotel Jolanda Sport in Gressoney-La-Trinité has attractive, spacious rooms, a superb restaurant, and a spa with a swimming pool, as well as special deals for golfers; doubles from US$245; family suite from US$170 per person (all half-board; reductions for children); www.hoteljolandasport.com

EATING OUT
Gressoney-Saint-Jean has a number of excellent restaurants, including Il Braciere, serving rustic Alpine cuisine (dinner from US$42, tel. 0125 355 526) and the Nordkapp, offering gourmet dishes (from US$42; www.norkapprestaurant.com). Golfers can rest between holes at the Golf Restaurant, also in Saint-Jean (from US$28; tel. 349 179 0893).

PRICE FOR A FAMILY OF FOUR
US$380–515 per day including accommodations, meals, and local travel. Allow at least an extra US$68 per person for green fees and equipment rental for a round of golf.

FURTHER INFORMATION
www.gressoneymonterosa.it

The Walser People

As far back as the year 1000, small groups of peasants from the Swiss canton of Valais began to settle in the valleys around Monte Rosa. These are the Walser, and they have preserved their Germac dialect and culture to the present day. Their houses are easily recognizable. The supporting columns are stone, while the upper part of the house is wood, and the interiors make good use of the limited habitable space, with beds often built against a wall close to the warmth of the hearth.

Left: Turreted Castel Savoia, set amid Alpine botanical gardens

Right (left and right): Wooden bridge spanning a mountain cascade; view of Lago Gover, overlooked by Monte Rosa

Far right (top to bottom): Flower-bedecked balconies typical of the region; buckwheat dumplings, a traditional Gressoney dish; lovely Villa Margherita; chestnut-flour bread and polenta, two products of Valle d'Aosta

flight of the ball (and it will fly faster and longer in the thinner air) because the surrounding mountain and valley views are just too beautiful to resist, even for a golfer normally devoted to the game.

As a beginner, whatever your age, the golf club of Gressoney-Saint-Jean will make for a memorable introduction to the sport. It is a perfect practice course on which to swing your first strokes and learn from an expert instructor. For the more seasoned player, the 9-hole, 2,406-yd (2,200-m) par-68 course becomes more technically challenging with every hole. And the chalet-style club house is a welcoming spot for a break and refreshments on one of the most unusual courses you will ever play.

If you're after a little more adventure, Gressoney is the base for many demanding hikes and climbs, perhaps even to the summit of Gnifetti and its *rifugio* – at 11,965 ft (3,647 m) the highest refuge hut in Europe. There are breathtaking descents to be made amid the spray of whitewater rafting routes, or you could take to the skies on a paragliding flight. For anyone who likes the outdoor life, Gressoney has it all.

Above: View of rugged, snow-capped Monte Rosa

OUTDOOR DIARY

The Val di Gressoney follows the course of the River Lys, which rises in the snows of Monte Rosa. It is an ideal destination for everyone who loves Alpine activities, with the extra attraction of its fine golf course. If golf doesn't happen to be your game, you can easily spend five days with the family exploring this lovely region.

Five Days of Alpine Adventures

DAY 1 Begin your visit with a day of golf at the foot of Monte Rosa. If you are a beginner, start with some practical training; otherwise 9 spectacular holes await you. Later on, take a stroll around the village of Gressoney-Saint-Jean and see its typical Walser houses and the pleasant village center, including the delightful Villa Margherita, now Gressoney's town hall and well worth a visit.

DAY 2 Today, visit Castel Savoia in Gressoney-Saint-Jean, built at the end of the 19th century as a summer residence for Queen Margherita, wife of King Umberto I. The castle, set in pretty grounds, is reminiscent of a medieval manor house and has five delicate towers, each one unique. Take a tour of the elegantly furnished interior.

DAY 3 Today, take a walk to Alpenzu Grande, one of the few Walser villages where the features of life in the past are perfectly preserved: the mill, the village oven, the smithy, and the chapel. It is a steep but very beautiful walk from Gressoney-Saint-Jean, taking about 1 hour each way.

DAY 4 Use Gressoney-La-Trinité as your base for the day. From this typical mountain village, a variety of lovely walks run through woodlands. One of the best of these takes you to the source of the Lys in about 3 hours. Another runs to Lago Gabiet, set in a hollow at the foot of Monte Rosa.

DAY 5 If you have the family with you, take them to the Via Ferrata dei Bambini, just outside Gressoney-La-Trinité. This safe but exciting climbing route for children is equipped with harnesses, ropes, rails, and hand-holds, and is a great introduction to climbing for kids.

Dos and Don'ts

- ✓ Bring binoculars with you to take on mountain walks. Wildlife that you may see includes chamois, ibex, roe deer, marmots, and golden eagles.
- ✗ Don't visit Castel Savoia without booking the obligatory guided tour in advance. In summer the castle closes at 7pm and the last tour begins 30 minutes before that.
- ✓ Take a rainproof jacket and hat with you; there may be sudden cloudbursts, even in summer.
- ✓ If you prefer not to walk to Lago Gabiet, take the cable car from Staffal, a hamlet of Gressoney-La-Trinité.

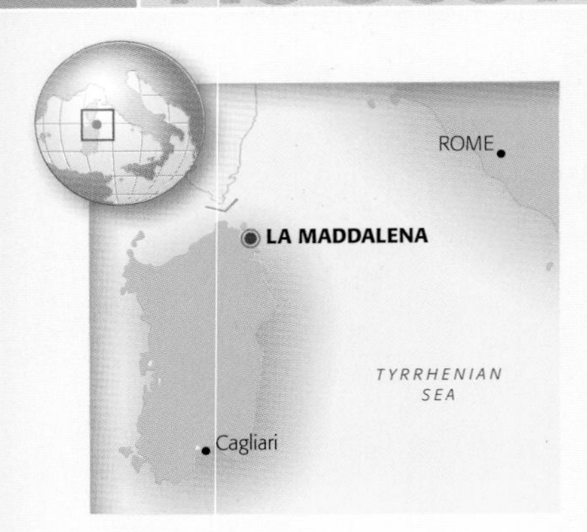

Above: Wonderful sunset over the Maddalena Archipelago; the sanctuary of Madonna dei Pescatori, Maddalena

WITH SAILS UNFURLED

Every Italian schoolchild knows that the island of Caprera was the last dwelling-place of Italian national hero Giuseppe Garibaldi, known as "the Hero of Two Worlds" for his military campaigns in South America and Europe. The island is a national monument and his house is now a small museum, with a simple grave in the garden. But the wild and rugged island of Caprera is also known by many from all over Europe as the home of the oldest sailing school in Italy and probably the greatest in the Mediterranean. Established in 1967 through an initiative of the Italian Naval League and the Italian Touring Club, Caprera's sailing school (Centro Velico Caprera) has trained more than 90,000 students, turning them into accomplished sailors or, as has often been the case, instructors for new generations of sailing enthusiasts.

Caprera and six more islands (Maddalena, Santo Stefano, Spargi, Budelli, Santa Maria, and Razzoli) and lesser islets form the Maddalena Archipelago, perfectly located for sailing and windsurfing. In these islands, the Mediterranean has grouped some of its choicest treasures, a myriad inlets, large and small, and dramatic rock formations backed by the sweet-smelling green shade of Mediterranean maquis. Pink is a key color here, from rosy sunrises and sunsets that bathe the islands in their warming glow to the pink granite cliffs at the north of Maddalena island, and Budelli island's famous *Spiaggia Rossa* "Pink Beach," created by millions of tiny pieces of coral and seen in Antonioni's 1964 film *Deserto Rosso*. The archipelago has been a marine nature preserve since 1994, so the waters are full of sea life. Divers will see schools of sharp-toothed silvery barracuda, playful dolphins, and bulky 3-ft (1-m) groupers against a backdrop of red, white, and purple gorgonians, vivid sea slugs, and colorful sponges. Sailors will enjoy the best conditions for learning to sail all year round – reliable winds, deep clear waters, and many sheltered coves and bays.

Garibaldi was not the only military leader to turn his eyes to the Maddalena Archipelago. Emperor Napoleon tried and failed to take the islands, and Admiral Horatio Nelson, one of the most famous and inspiring sailors of all time, recognized its strategic importance and spent a year here fitting out his ship *Victory* in 1804 in the lead up to the Trafalgar campaign.

Main: Yacht catching the wind off the coast of Caprera
Below (left and right): *Fregola,* a Sardinian pasta made from durum wheat; lighthouse on the tiny islet of Monaci, east of Caprera, warning passing boats of the sandbank and dangerous rocks

GETTING THERE
The Maddalena Archipelago is set at the northeast tip of Sardinia. The nearest port for the main town of La Maddalena is Palau, about 25 miles (40 km) from Olbia airport. From the airport you can go by car to Palau or, in summer, by bus.

GETTING AROUND
A car is useful for exploring Maddalena and Caprera – they are connected by a road bridge. There are many boat departures from Palau and Maddalena to the other islands in the archipelago.

WEATHER
The weather is hot and sunny, but there's always a breeze. Temperatures are pleasant in the evenings.

ACCOMMODATIONS
Close to the center of La Maddalena, the Petit Maison is an attractive B&B with a small garden. Rooms from US$130; www.petitmaison.net

The Abbatoggia campsite in the west of the island of Maddalena is a well-equipped complex by the sea. Two people sharing a tent will pay about US$28; www.campingabbatoggia.it

EATING OUT
Near the center of La Maddalena, La Grotta serves fish specialties (www.lagrotta.it), or try the Osteria da Liò, known for its apéritifs and fine cuisine (www.osterialio.com); meals at both from US$40.

In the north of La Maddalena, exclusive La Scogliera is a haunt of the rich and famous, set among the natural pink granite rocks of Cala Lunga. Meals from US$200; www.lascoglieraristorante.com

PRICE FOR TWO
US$150–250 per day for accommodations and meals. However, dining at La Scogliera can more than double this cost.

FURTHER INFORMATION
www.lamaddalena.com

Training for Sea Dogs

Wake early, eat breakfast, and take a lesson on dry land before setting out to sea for practical training until the evening. This is a typical day for students at the Centro Velico Caprera, one of the best sailing centers in the Mediterranean. It offers courses for all levels of ability from beginners to experienced ocean-going yachtsmen. As well as learning how to sail, students are taught to respect the power of the winds and sea, and the importance of looking after the environment around them.

Above: Boats at anchor in Maddalena's harbor

DIARY OF A SEA DOG

Seven rocky outcrops, sparsely covered by maquis, the Maddalena Archipelago is a sailor's paradise, with strong currents, sheltered coves, a constant wind, and one of the best sailing schools in Europe. Spend a week with the sea rolling beneath you and salt spray blowing in your face and you'll never be a landlubber again.

Seven Halcyon Days

DAYS 1–2

The largest island in the archipelago is Maddalena, with the only year-round inhabited center. Don't miss the opportunity to take a boat trip around the island and stop off at quiet coves to swim in the limpid sea.

If you feel like a walk, follow the path that runs around Maddalena island. Climb up to the San Vittorio fort for the best views of the archipelago. Or head west to Carlotta for breathtaking bays and the sanctuary of Madonna dei Pescatori, raised by a thankful sailor in 1800.

DAYS 3–4

Visit the Nino Lamboglia Museum of Naval Archeology, where you will see interesting finds from the Roman ship discovered near Spargi, which sank in the archipelago's waters around 120 BC. See, too, Chiesa di S. Maria Maddalena, which has two silver candlesticks, a cross, and a letter of thanks from Admiral Nelson from 1804.

Travel to Caprera, perhaps the most beautiful of the islands with delightful landscapes: wonderful beaches with sandy coves alternating with rocky escarpments.

DAYS 5–7

You cannot leave Caprera without visiting Garibaldi's museum, the Compendio Garibaldino. The Italian national hero spent the last years of his life in the villa and many of his possessions are on display.

Take a boat – or sail in your own, if you have one – to the unspoiled and pretty island of Santo Stefano. It is dominated by the bastion known as Napoleon's fort (he didn't build it, but used it in his attempt to capture the islands), built in the 18th century.

Sail around the archipelago's lesser islands and enjoy their rugged beauty. There are many bays where you can moor and enjoy a day of sea and sun.

Dos and Don'ts

- ✓ In Caprera, climb up to Monte Telaione (700 ft/215 m); from there you can enjoy excellent views of the whole island.
- ✗ Do not go scuba diving in the shallows of Bocche di Bonifacio, at the northern end of the archipelago, if you are a novice; the area is popular with scuba divers, but also very treacherous.
- ✓ Do take a class at the Caprera Sailing Centre – they run courses for everybody from beginners to experienced sailors; www.centrovelicocaprera.it
- ✗ Do not moor or swim at the pink coral sand beach of Budelli island. You may only visit the nature preserve with a guide.

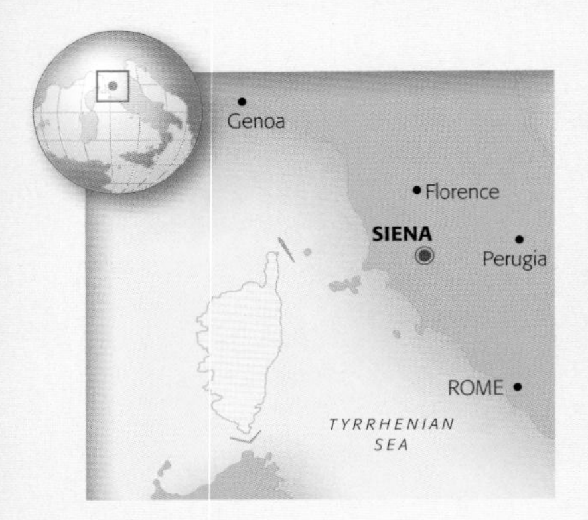

GETTING THERE
Siena is in the heart of Tuscany and can be reached by car from Florence, the nearest airport, via the Florence–Siena freeway, or by train or bus.

GETTING AROUND
Siena is easily explored on foot. The surroundings are served by a network of buses, but a car will give you more independence.

WEATHER
During the day it is hot – up to 88°F (31°C) – but the evenings are usually a bit cooler.

ACCOMMODATIONS
The Grand Hotel Continental, close to the Piazza del Campo, is housed in one of Siena's historic palazzi. Rooms from US$585; www.royaldemeure.com

The Palazzo Bruchi B&B is in a converted 18th-century residence. Doubles from US$135; www.palazzobruchi.it

The peaceful Certosa di Maggiano is located in a former 14th-century convent in beautiful countryside. Rooms from US$490; www.certosadimaggiano.com

Many *agriturismi* offer good-quality accommodations at reasonable prices, such as the delightful Marciano, with rooms from US$95 (www.agriturismomarciano.it). Or try La Cetina, a rustic *agriturismo* with a swimming pool; B&B from US$110 (www.lacetina.it).

EATING OUT
Da Enzo offers innovative cuisine and Tuscan specialties; meals from US$55 (tel. 0577 281 277).

Enjoy traditional dishes with a twist at the Osteria Le Logge; meals from US$68; www.giannibrunelli.it

The Capitano serves traditional Sienese dishes for about US$35–42 (tel. 0577 288 094).

PRICE FOR TWO
US$230–720 per day for meals and accommodations.

FURTHER INFORMATION
www.terresiena.it

Tuscany in a Bottle

Chianti is a ruby-red full-bodied wine that has been synonymous with Tuscany for centuries and has always accompanied generous servings of its richly flavored cuisine. It originates from the region north of Siena, a landscape of rolling hills and serried ranks of vines. This is the classic Tuscany, rolling hills threaded through by roads shaded by long rows of cypresses and dotted by grand farmhouses. Here, the gentle rhythm of life on the land seems barely to have changed over the centuries.

Main: Palio race in full flow in Piazza del Campo

THUNDER OF HOOVES

THE PIAZZA IS PACKED WITH A BUZZING CROWD; a line of perfectly conditioned horses froth, stamp, and quiver behind the starting rope; in colorful silks, the jockeys jostle for position, poised bareback over their horses; waving flags flutter and then fall still. The piazza falls silent in an air of expectancy. Suddenly, a cannon booms, the crowd goes crazy, and the race is on. There's a confused thunder of hooves spraying clouds of dust; a horse skitters, a jockey falls off, and, in a matter of seconds, the three circuits of the Piazzo del Campo are finished. But the cacophony of drums, trumpets, and cheers of the crowd continue in waves of uncontrollable enthusiasm.

This is Siena's Palio, a twice-yearly festival (July 2 and August 16) that has changed little since 1283, the first recorded occurrence. The whole city takes part in the festival, as each horse and rider represents a *contrada* or city ward. The festival lasts four days, with time trials and colorful costumed pageants by day, and banquets and boisterous

Above (top and bottom): The impressive complex of the Abbazia di Monte Oliveto Maggiore; cypresses on a ridge in the Crete Senesi, a hilly area south of Siena

Below: Panforte, a sweet, spicy mix of fruit, sugar, and nuts, also known as Siena cake

Above: The Palazzo Pubblico and Torre del Mangia in the Piazza del Campo, Siena

revelry by night. There's a steady build-up of excitement for the three days before the main race, the culmination of a year of preparations – the choosing of the jockeys, training of the horses, and commissioning of the *drappellone* (the prize for the winner, a silk banner painted by a famous artist).

The Piazza del Campo, where the Palio takes place, is one of the most beautiful squares in Italy: it is shaped like a shell, brick-paved, and divided into nine segments commemorating the Government of the Nine who ruled the city in the Middle Ages. Around the square, the medieval buildings seem to converge on the Palazzo Pubblico, beside the slender and elegant red-brick Torre del Mangia that rises to 290 ft (88 m). At the other end of the piazza is the Fonte Gaia, sculpted by Jacopo della Quercia in the first half of the 15th century (although the present fountain is a 19th-century copy) and fed by water from outside Siena via a system of tunnels and subterranean cisterns. A little farther on stands the Duomo di Siena, one of the most spectacular Gothic buildings in Italy, full of outstanding works of art and the highlight of a city that rejoices in its history like no other.

SIENESE DIARY

Siena is a glorious city with an extraordinary treasury of art, sculptures, frescoes, churches, and palazzi created by Italy's greatest masters of the Gothic and Renaissance. Spend three days exploring the city and enjoying the lively Palio atmosphere, then one day in the beautiful, calm, and green Crete Senesi countryside.

Four Days of the Palio

DAY 1

All visits to Siena must start with the Piazza del Campo – during the Palio it will be covered with tufa mud. Visit the municipal museum inside the Palazzo Pubblico to see frescoes by Simone Martini. If you're lucky, you may be able to see one of the Palio practice races. Dine a little away from the square as the prices will be lower and the restaurants less crowded.

DAY 2

Visit the Duomo di Siena – the building was to have been part of a larger religious complex, but this remained unfinished due to a plague in 1348. Only one nave was built, which today houses the Museo dell'Opera Metropolitana. Nearby is another masterpiece – the Baptistry (1325), graced by a font with bronze panels by Donatello and Jacopo della Quercia. Across the square is the Santa Maria della Scala, one of Europe's oldest hospitals, decorated with 15th-century frescoes.

DAY 3

For your last day in the city, you should see two more symbolic places in Siena: the high-rise Gothic Basilica di San Domenico, which has many precious paintings and the head of St. Catherine, and the Casa di Santa Caterina, the house where Siena's (and Italy's) great saint lived. Turned into a sanctuary in 1466, this has always been a destination for pilgrimages. If you haven't been able to get a ticket for the Palio, enjoy the nightlife and simply soak up the atmosphere and some Chianti.

DAY 4

Take a trip to the Abbazia di Monte Oliveto Maggiore, an abbey founded at the beginning of the 14th century by the Sienese nobleman Bernardo Tolomei. Enjoy the rolling, well-tended Crete Senesi countryside. Stop off along the way to enjoy of some of the great local food at a quiet, slow-paced *agriturismo*, seemingly a world away from the frenetic Palio atmosphere in the city of Siena.

Dos and Don'ts

- ✓ Attend the trial races for the Palio; you will get a better idea of the complicated dynamics of the race.
- ✗ Cars are not allowed in the city center, so wear comfortable shoes as you will have to walk everywhere!
- ✓ Visit the antiques market held in Siena every third Sunday of the month.

GETTING THERE
Tarquinia is in northern Lazio and easily reached from Rome's Fiumicino Airport, 60 miles (100 km) away. If you are coming by car, take the A12, then the SS1. Or, take the bus from the airport – one leaves almost every hour from Saxa Rubra station. If you travel by train to Tarquinia station, you will need to take the bus to the city center.

GETTING AROUND
Tarquinia can be explored on foot. To travel farther afield, use local transportation.

WEATHER
It is very warm in August with temperatures peaking around 84°F (29°C).

ACCOMMODATIONS
The Gran B&B Duomo in the historic center offers a smart and personalized setting with attention to detail. Doubles from US$82; www.granbandb.it

La Pecora Ladra is in the Lazio Maremma, not far from Tarquinia. It has rustic rooms furnished with impeccable taste, each one with a terrace. There's a swimming pool, Jacuzzi, and riding available. Rooms from US$245; www.lapecoraladra.com

EATING OUT
Re Tarquinio, in the medieval city center, offers well-flavored and sophisticated cuisine in a romantic ambience. Specialties include buckwheat noodles with porcini mushrooms, endive, pig's cheek, and Pecorino cheese. Meals from US$42; www.retarquinio.it

On the Tarquinia Lido, Velcamare has a terrace and a garden and serves creative regional cuisine. Meals cost about US$62; www.velcamare.com

PRICE FOR TWO
US$220–380 per day for meals, accommodations, and entrance to the necropolis and the museum.

FURTHER INFORMATION
www.ufficioturistico.comunetarquinia.it

Tarquinia's Salt Marshes

Theese pools, used for extracting salt intended for Rome, were dug in Tarquinia's salt marshes in 1805 on Pope Pius VII's orders. Commercially active until the 1980s, the marshes are now a nature preserve and home to flamingoes, egrets, herons, and oyster catchers, and the former salt pans are full of fish and crustaceans. You can still see the ruined tiny settlement where the salt workers used to live.

Above (left to right): Tarquinia's Roman aqueduct; a street in Tarquinia's historic center; marinated zucchini, a local delicacy
Main: Detail of the frescoes in the Leopardi tomb in the Necropoli di Monterozzi

Above: Tarquinia's ancient walls and fortifications

ETRUSCAN GLORY

TARQUINIA, IN THE HEART OF LAZIO, has enjoyed three previous incarnations: the Etruscan city of Tarchuna, the Roman colony of Gravisca, and the medieval city of Corneto. Each one has left traces behind, but the most remarkable remains are to be found in the Etruscan Necropoli di Monterozzi, occupying an area of nearly 3 sq miles (7.5 sq km) a little way outside the town. This city of the dead is home to some beautiful tombs of Etruscan aristocrats, who lived at a time when Tarquinia was powerful enough to hold sway over Rome – no fewer than three of the legendary Seven Kings of Rome (Tarquinius Priscus, Servius Tullius, and Tarquinius Superbus) were of Etruscan origin. There are around 200 chamber tombs in the necropolis, covered with beautiful frescoes depicting vibrant, colorful scenes. The purpose of the tombs, which were built to resemble Etruscan houses and were probably filled with domestic goods, was to surround the deceased with memories of their everyday life. The tombs were thus brightened up with paintings of parties, dancers, and musicians; in some tombs the walls display hunting or fishing scenes or contests between athletes, boxers, gladiators, and discus throwers. In short, the lifestyle of Tarquinian nobles 2,500 years ago is preserved in these tomb paintings, in pictures that speak to us not of death but of an existence full of fun and joie de vivre.

Neither Roman Gravisca nor medieval Corneto was built on top of the Etruscan city. The Romans, having subdued Italy, turned their thoughts to trade and established Gravisca by the sea, creating a major port to trade with Greece, and leaving behind many ruins; these include a religious complex with shrines and temples to Greek gods that were obviously good for business. Corneto, in perhaps more uncertain times, was established around a fortified hill and has kept its castle-like appearance, ringed by a circular city wall, from which its palaces, churches, and towers face out to sea. By the 12th century, Corneto was a strong and prosperous city and built the Chiesa Santa Maria di Castello, the town's largest Romanesque church. Other buildings such as the Palazzo Comunale, the Gothic churches, and the maze of small streets in the town center, were built later, during the days of the city-republics. Corneto became part of the Papal States in 1355 and was enriched by the addition of walled fortifications and the Renaissance Palazzo Vitelleschi, which often welcomed the popes of the time. Subsequent centuries also left their mark with Baroque churches and fountains and grand 19th-century residences, but perhaps no period has been as influential as that of the Etruscans who first chose to settle in this area. In 1922, the town of Corneto acknowledged its Etruscan heritage and changed its name to Tarquinia.

Below (left to right): Detail of a fresco in the Tori tomb in the Necropoli di Monterozzi; the courtyard of the Palazzo Vitelleschi, now the Museo Archeologico Nazionale di Tarquinia; an ornate Etruscan vase, one of the museum's exhibits

NECROPOLIS DIARY

The name Tarquinia immediately calls to mind the Etruscans and the testimony of their mysterious ancient civilization that we still have today, thanks to the tombs in the Necropoli di Monterozzi. But Tarquinia offers plenty more: four days will allow you to see the necropolis as well as Tarquinia's medieval center, archeological museum, Roman ruins, and beautiful beaches.

Four Etruscan Days

DAY 1

Spend the first day visiting Tarquinia's medieval center. Don't miss the fine Romanesque Chiesa Santa Maria di Castello, in the highest part of town, and the 13th-century Palazzo Comunale. Enjoy wandering through all the winding alleyways that suddenly open into spacious squares; then walk up to the ancient city walls above the rocky precipice and admire the sweeping panorama and the distant sparkling sea.

DAY 2

Spend the day at the Necropolis di Monterozzi, famous for its many frescoed tombs. Fourteen tombs are open to the public; visiting them is a truly exciting experience that takes you back 2,500 years in time. Return to Tarquinia for some savory Lazio cuisine – *carciofi alla giudea* (deep-fried artichokes), *spaghetti carbonara* (pasta with pancetta, Pecorino, and cream), and *saltimbocca* (veal and sage) – and the delicious local Tarquinia white wine.

DAY 3

Many of the finds from the necropolis and other archeological sites near Tarquinia are on display in the Museo Archeologico Nazionale di Tarquinia, in the fine Palazzo Vitelleschi. A visit there is a must, whether to see the museum's valuable collection of ceramics, items from everyday life, sarcophagi and frescoes from the tombs, or simply to admire the palace, a wonderful building constructed from 1436–39.

DAY 4

Finally, take a trip to Tarquinia Lido, a sandy beach backed by dunes, perfect for a relaxing day by the sea. If you want to maintain your record of visiting ancient sites, you can tour the ruins of what used to be Roman Gravisca. If not, just make the most of the cooling sea and don't forget to indulge in a nice seafood lunch.

Dos and Don'ts

- ✓ To reach the Necropoli di Monterozzi, take the bus from the Tarquinia tourist office – or walk; it is about 2 miles (3 km).
- ✗ Don't forget that in summer the Necropolis is closed on Mondays. If visiting in winter, check the opening hours.
- ✓ When you visit the necropolis, wear comfortable shoes and don't forget sunglasses and a hat.
- ✗ Don't miss the exciting night procession of boats and the fireworks that form part of the Ferragosto (August 15; Feast of the Assumption) festival at the Tarquinia Lido.

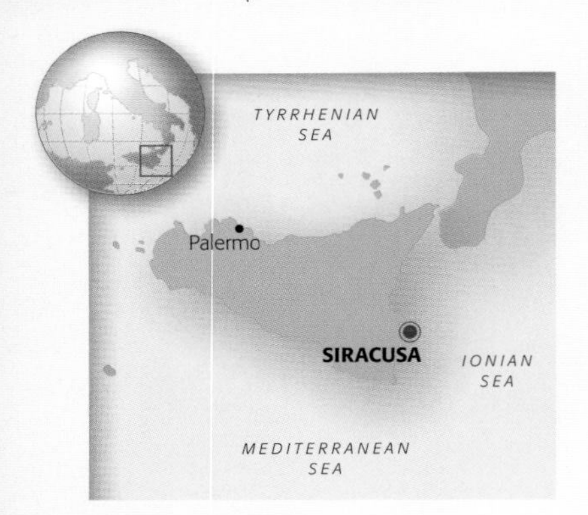

GETTING THERE
Siracusa, in southeastern Sicily, can be reached from Catania airport, about 37 miles (60 km) away, by taking the A18 freeway, then the SS114. Buses link Siracusa to Catania airport. Siracusa's ancient heart is the tiny islet of Ortygia, joined to the Sicilian mainland by the Umbertino Bridge.

GETTING AROUND
Get around the tiny island of Ortygia on foot; use public transportation to nearby places of interest.

WEATHER
It is generally very hot and dry in August, with peak temperatures around 90ºF (32ºC).

ACCOMMODATIONS
Some of Siracusa's best hotels are on Ortygia, the island seat of the Old Town *(Città Vecchia)*. The Grand Hotel Ortygia, on the seafront, has comfortable rooms from US$326 (www.grandhotels.it).

Alla Giudecca is a romantic hotel with old-world charm and four-poster beds. Rooms from US$122 (www.allagiudecca.it).

An exclusive stay awaits you at the Grand Hotel Villa Politi, with its spectacular cliff setting, great views, and pool. Rooms from US$285; www.villapoliti.com

EATING OUT
Central Le Baronie serves elegant cuisine. Meals from US$42; www.ristorantelebaronie.com

The Jonico Á Rutta e Ciauli restaurant offers typical Sicilian food in an Art Nouveau villa perched on a cliff. Meals cost around US$48 (tel. 0931 65540).

PRICE FOR TWO
US$260–460 per day for meals, accommodations, and entry to the museum and archeological park.

FURTHER INFORMATION
www.travelplan.it/siracusa_guide.htm

The Legend of Arethusa

In ancient times, the Fountain of Arethusa supplied water to the whole island of Ortygia; today, it is home to ducks, fish, and papyrus plants *(above)*, and is an obligatory destination for a romantic stroll. Greek myth tells that the god Alpheus fell in love with Arethusa, a nymph and companion of the goddess Artemis. Arethusa sought the help of Artemis, who turned her first into a cloud and then into a fountain on the island of Ortygia. Alpheus, however, turned into a river and crossed the sea to reach Arethusa and mingle his waters with hers.

THE GREATEST GREEK CITY

SIRACUSA IS A CITY BUILT IN LAYERS, where successive civilization has built their city on top of the previous one. And it has known many civilizations – the city's first incarnation was established by the Siculi, who settled on the island of Ortygia at least 3,000 years ago, well before the Greeks arrived in about 750 BC. The Greeks founded two colonies on this stretch of coast: Siracusa, on the island of Ortygia, still the historic and artistic center of the city, and Achradina, nearby on the Sicilian mainland, which became absorbed into Siracusa as the city grew.

After the Greeks came the Romans, then the Byzantines, and then the Saracens. A visit to the Duomo reveals this history: its wonderful Baroque façade was built in the early 18th century to replace the one destroyed by the earthquakes in 1542 and 1693, but inside you can see the traces of a Doric

Main: The illuminated seafront of Siracusa's Old Town on the island of Ortygia

Left: A stall of prickly pears at the Ortygia market

Right (left to right): The mighty walls of Castello Maniace on the Ionian Sea; stuffed peppers are a specialty of the island; Siracusa's Greek theater, one of the largest such theaters and still used to stage performances today

Right of main (above and below): Palazzo Vermexio, built in 1633 to house the Town Hall; intricate sculpture on the decorative façade of the Palazzo Impellizzeri in Siracusa

temple dedicated to Athena and also a Siculi temple built 300 years earlier. The Roman philosopher-statesman Cicero described the magnificent 5th-century BC Temple of Athena, saying that its doors were inlaid with gold and ivory and its roof, decorated with fine paintings was surmounted by a golden statue of the goddess, which served as a lighthouse to seafarers. He said it was a temple worthy of "the greatest Greek city of them all," one of the most powerful in the Mediterranean.

More evidence of the city's past glories are to be found in the Parco Archeologico della Neapolis, one of the best historical sites in Sicily, a short distance inland. The undoubted jewel of the park is the huge Greek theater, carved out of rock: proof that Siracusa was a major cultural center, attracting figures such as Aeschylus, who performed some of his tragedies here. There is also a Roman amphitheater, site of gladiatorial contests and horse-racing; but of particular interest are the latomias, a system of large quarries. Today, they are open and leafy, but in ancient times they were dark and damp pits where slaves and prisoners of war were forced to labor.

Above: Latomia del Paradiso, one of Siracusa's stone quarries

ARCHEOLOGICAL DIARY

One city, two distinct centers: Siracusa's urban structure mirrors its history, with the two Greek colonies founded in the 8th century BC a few miles from each other. Four days is enough time to see the sights of the city, enjoy the coastal delights, and also see the astonishing archeological excavations at Neapolis.

Four Days on Ortygia

DAY 1

Start with Ortygia and its Duomo: admire its fine Baroque façade, the combination of different eras in its interior, and the lovely square that it faces on to. To the north of the Duomo, there is a picturesque maze of alleyways around Piazza Archimede. This square, surrounded by many grand palazzi and with the lively sculptures of the Fontana di Artemide in the middle, is a meeting point for the city's inhabitants. Enjoy a coffee or a cool drink and simply watch the people walking past.

DAY 2

Set aside this day for a visit to the Parco Archeologico della Neapolis and enjoy these fantastic ruins set in leafy surroundings. Don't miss the Greek theater and the latomias, the notorious stone quarries. The best known of the quarries is the Latomia del Paradiso where you will find the "Ear of Dionysious," a cave famous for its acoustic amplification. In the evening, after all that walking, dine on fresh seafood in the center of Ortygia.

DAY 3

If you've had enough sightseeing, you could take a boat to one of the beaches along the coast, to enjoy the sea and sand. Or, if you're up for exploring more of the city, visit the catacombs of San Giovanni, used by early Christians to bury their dead. Built out of an existing Greek aqueduct, they're a labyrinth of tunnels deep underground.

DAY 4

To recap on all you've seen and learnt about Siracusa's ancient history, visit the excellent Museo Archeologico. It has an outstanding collection of sculptures from the excavations of the ancient Greek and Roman settlements. Try also to make time for a visit to Castello Maniace, built by Frederick II of Swabia in 1240, with fine sea views, and enjoy one more stroll around the old heart of the city.

Dos and Don'ts

- ✓ Go to the little Maniace Lido on the island of Ortygia or, a bit farther south, to the Arenella Lido beach to swim in the sea.
- ✓ Visit the open-air food market held in Ortygia every morning except Sundays – it's colorful, lively, and mouthwatering!
- ✓ See the Assunta regatta, a race between five *gozzi* (Ligurian fishing boats) that takes place every year on August 15.
- ✗ Don't stay out of doors in the middle of the day; Siracusa is very hot in August and it is better to cool off in a bar or restaurant.

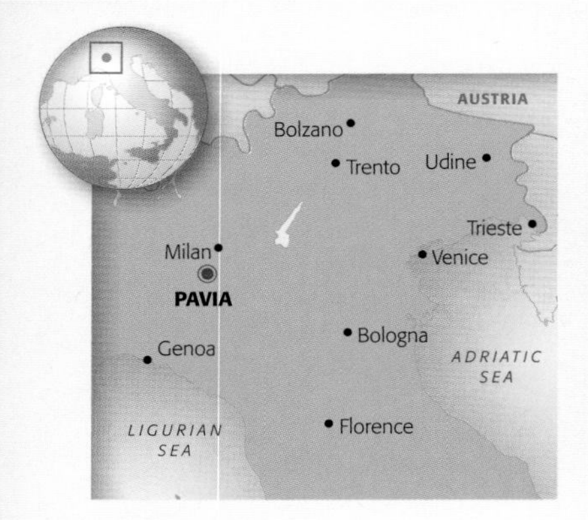

GETTING THERE
Pavia, in southwestern Lombardy, is on the Ticino River near its confluence with the Po. Milan's Linate Airport is the nearest airport; to get to Pavia from Milan, take the A4 freeway, leaving at the Berguardo/Pavia Nord exit; or you can reach Pavia by train or bus.

GETTING AROUND
Pavia is a small city, easily explored on foot. A frequent bus service connects it to Certosa.

WEATHER
In summer, the weather is hot and sometimes oppressive, but it is cooler in the evenings.

ACCOMMODATIONS
The smart and comfortable Hotel Moderno occupies a converted historic palace in the city center. Rooms from US$218; www.hotelmoderno.it

The Resort Cascina Scova, a short distance from the center in a pleasant park, offers a very relaxing and peaceful stay with a luxury spa and swimming pool. Rooms from US$218; www.cascinascova.it

EATING OUT
The Osteria alle Carceri in the historic center offers innovative versions of traditional cuisine; meals cost around US$35–42; www.osteriaallecarceri.it

Bardelli, in an Art Nouveau palace on the river, serves an elegant dinner from US$48; www.bardellipv.it

Outside town, in the nearby hills of Oltrepo, there are plenty of restaurants and *agriturismi* where you can enjoy local specialties at reasonable prices – around US$35–42. For example, Cascina Chiericoni (www.cascinachiericoni.it); the Melo Rosso (www.ilmelorosso.it); La Matellina, which also organizes riding trips (www.lamatellina.com); and Alla Costa, for a warm and welcoming atmosphere (www.agriturismolacosta.it).

PRICE FOR TWO
About US$340 per day for meals and accommodations.

FURTHER INFORMATION
www.italytravelescape.com/italian-towns

The Oltrepo Pavese

The Oltrepo Pavese, south of Pavia, is an expanse of rolling hills covered with venerable vineyards and dotted with villas, farms, and churches small and large. Here, thanks to the clay soil and temperate climate, vines have been cultivated since Roman times. The grapes have always produced fine wines, protected by the DOC mark (Denominazione di Origine Controllata or Registered Designation of Origin). The red wines include Bonarda and Barbera; the whites include Pinot Nero, Chardonnay, Riesling, and Muscatel, a classic sweet dessert wine.

Above (left to right): The elaborate façade of the Certosa di Pavia; *zuppa Pavese*, a local dish made with homemade bread, eggs cooked in hot broth, and Parmesan cheese; the grand staircase of Pavia University
Main: The two classic symbols of Pavia, the Duomo di Pavia and the Ponte Coperto (Covered Bridge) across the Ticino

Above: Equestrian statue in Pavia's main square, Piazza Duomo

A GLORIOUS PAST

BUILT ON THE TICINO, CLOSE TO THE PO, and with its own canal system, Pavia is characterized by water. The extensive system of canals were once major waterways connecting Pavia to other towns in Lombardy. Not by chance, therefore, is one of its symbols the magnificent Ponte Coperto – built in the 14th century, destroyed in World War II, and rebuilt a little farther downstream. Beyond the bridge lies the heart of Pavia, packed with architecture that reveals the city's history – as an important Roman town, as the capital of the Lombard kingdom, as the seat of one of the most prestigious universities in Europe, and as the center of one of Italy's most elegant Renaissance courts. Walk along the Strada Nuova, the city's main axis, and you'll find the buildings that bear witness to this past. To the north is the Castello Visconteo, a combination of mighty fortress and luxury residence. Then there's the university: medieval in origin but rebuilt and enlarged by Maria Theresa of Austria, it is composed of 15th-century and later Neo-Classical buildings. Farther south is the medieval center of Pavia, where you will find the Duomo, built in 1488 and housing works of art and architecture by Bramante and Leonardo da Vinci. There are also some magnificent Romanesque churches: San Pietro in Ciel d'Oro, simple and austere; the little San Teodoro, with its splendid apse and colonnaded crypt; and San Michele Maggiore, with its graceful sandstone façade.

But Pavia's most precious treasure is some distance outside the city: the Certosa, or Carthusian monastery, one of the most celebrated historic buildings of the Renaissance. Its construction started at the end of the 14th century and lasted for about two centuries, turning the Certosa into an anthology of Italian art. An impressive complex of white marble that stands out in the flat Pavia countryside, it has a stunningly beautiful carved façade. The walls of its bright interior are decorated with frescoes, while the monks' cells look on to its quiet cloisters.

Capital of the Lombard kingdom, seat of one of the most prestigious universities in Europe since the Middle Ages, center of an elegant Renaissance court.

Inset: Students in the library at the University of Pavia
Below (left to right): Detail of the Basilica di San Michele Maggiore; the small cloister of the Certosa di Pavia; a sluice gate on the Pavese canal

LOMBARD DIARY

Pavia is not a big or famous city, but it is home to many gems nevertheless. Its covered bridge rivals that of Florence and at one stage the city competed with Milan for supremacy in the north. However, its fortunes declined in the 16th century. Three days is enough time to see the city's historic buildings as well as the fabulous Certosa, 5 miles (8 km) outside town.

Three Days by the Canal

DAY 1

The best way of exploring the center of Pavia is to start with the covered bridge, which crosses the Ticino almost opposite the Strada Nuova. Walk along this lively street past its many shops to reach some of the city's most important historic buildings: the 15th-century Duomo with its audacious design – the octagonal dome was only built in 1884 – the university with its Neo-Classical anatomy theater, designed by Leopold Pollack, and the Castello Visconteo and its pretty courtyard with porticos, galleries, and clusters of windows topped by exquisite crenellations.

DAY 2

Discover Pavia's impressive Romanesque churches: San Michele, where the Lombard kings and, in 1155, Holy Roman emperor Frederick I Barbarossa were crowned; the small San Teodoro, decorated with ancient frescoes; and San Pietro in Ciel d'Oro, founded in the 7th century and rebuilt in the 12th, home to the sarcophagus containing the remains of St. Augustine. After a busy day exploring, finish off with supper in the center of town, perhaps dining on a rich, buttery risotto washed down with some excellent Oltrepo Pavese wine.

DAY 3

Visit the Carthusian Certosa di Pavia, founded in 1396 by Gian Galeazzo Visconti as a chapel and mausoleum for his family. The construction process went on until the mid-16th century and involved some of the most important Italian artists of the time, including Perugino, Bergognone, Guercino, and Procaccini. The magnificent façade, its top part not quite completed, is a sort of open-air sculpture museum, covered in hundreds of detailed statues and elegant bas-reliefs.

Dos and Don'ts

- ✓ Remember that the Certosa di Pavia is a place of worship: the monks ask visitors not only to dress appropriately but also to keep silent. The opening hours vary according to the time of year; in August they are 9–11am and 2:30–6pm.
- ✗ Don't go outside without taking insect repellent with you. The mosquitoes are prevalent at this time of year, owing to the many stretches of water in Pavia.
- ✓ If you like cycling, bear in mind that you can also reach the Certosa by bicycle, riding along the picturesque Pavese canal.

SEPTEMBER

Where to Go: **September**

Summer may be fading, but the days are still deliciously warm and the sunlight is golden. This is the right time to visit tourist hot spots that are swamped with visitors in high summer, such as chic little Capri, or the Costa Smeralda, Sardinia's stylish coast.

If something a little more unusual takes your fancy, you could try the climb up Mount Etna, through bizarre, lunar landscapes to the very mouth of the volcano, or head for the unspoiled nature of the Parco dei Monti Sibillini, admiring the landscape from above as you hang-glide, sharing the sky with eagles.

Unforgettable views are also to be had along Italy's cycling routes: passing some of the most beautiful peaks of the Dolomites; or bowling along through the Tuscan hills, whose rows of vines are

FESTIVALS AND CULTURE

MANTUA La Cittadella, an area of Mantua, mirrored in the Mincio River

MANTUA
LOMBARDY

Festival of books and writers

Festivaletterature transforms this fine Renaissance city into a vast and lively literary salon for five days each September, drawing readers and Nobel laureates alike.

See pp226–7

"A city of elegant beauty, rising up out of a lake: that is how Mantua first appears to visitors."

ASTI
PIEDMONT

Italy's oldest horse race

Italy's oldest Palio is run, not in Siena, but in the beautiful town of Asti. Horses race round the rose-red brick piazza against a colorful display of medieval pageantry.

www.italia.it/en/regions/piedmont

TURIN
PIEDMONT

The first capital of Italy

Seemingly austere and businesslike, Turin is a city full of art and culture, including museums without equal in Europe, and a program of over 80 concerts in its annual music festival.

See pp242–3

GREVE IN CHIANTI
TUSCANY

La Rassegna del Chianti

This festival, devoted to the region's famous wine, takes place in the Chianti hills. This is a chance to celebrate, taste, and buy, and there is music, dancing, and fireworks.

www.chiantiturismo.it

VENICE
VENETO

Historic regatta

Venice gets ready to party: this is the month of the dazzling Regata Storica as well as the Venice Film Festival, which attracts a host of international movie stars and celebrities.

See pp222–3

UNFORGETTABLE JOURNEYS

CAPRI The Piazzetta, the center of social life on the island

BARDOLINO
VENETO

Tour one of Italy's most famous wine regions

At the time of the grape harvest, this famous vineyard area on the shores of Lake Garda is a glorious sight, and a cycling tour is sheer pleasure.

www.promobardolino.com

CAPRI
CAMPANIA

In the footsteps of emperors

The "beautiful people" were not the first to discover and love Capri – the Roman emperors Augustus and Tiberius both had homes here. The hiking trails are spectacular.

See pp228–9

ROME
LAZIO

All roads lead from here

The Colosseum, the Forum, the Pantheon, and the Golden Milepost, from which all Roman roads began, date from when Rome was the most powerful empire in the world.

See pp236–7

MIRA
VENETO

Cruise along the Brenta canal

A boat trip from Venice to Mira is an unforgettable opportunity to see the hundreds of sumptuous villas that the Venetians built along the Brenta canal.

www.battellidelbrenta.it

OSTUNI
PUGLIA

The "Pearl of the Salento"

Ostuni is an unforgettable sight, with its tumble of dazzling whitewashed houses. It marks the start of the Via Appia, as well as an excellent wine route running as far as Brindisi.

See pp234–5

NATURAL WONDERS

MONTALCINO Gentle countryside of the Val d'Orcia

MAIORI
CAMPANIA

A window on to the sea

A popular resort on the Amalfi Coast, Maiori is set on a beautiful long stretch of beach. Nearby is the spectacular Grotta Pandone, a sea cave with intensely blue colors.

www.aziendaturismo-maiori.it

RISERVA NATURALE ABBADIA DI FIASTRA
LE MARCHE

Nature and history

This nature preserve covers a hilly, forested area rich in rare species, centered on a fine Cistercian abbey.

www.parks.it/riserva.statale.abbadia.fiastra

SERRALUNGA D'ALBA
PIEDMONT

Between the Alps and the plain of the Po

In the Langhe (whose name means "tongues of land"), razor-thin ridges reach out to sandy hills, towering fortress-like above an ocean of vines.

www.langhe.net

PARCO ALTA VALLE DI PESIO E TANARO
PIEDMONT

Back to nature

The Valle Pesio in the Ligurian Alps is the perfect place for expeditions on foot, bike, or horseback, with superb game fishing in the Pesio River.

www.vallepesio.it

MONTALCINO
TUSCANY

In the land of Brunello wine

The rolling, verdant hills of Val d'Orcia are the beautiful setting for the historic town of Montalcino, world famous for its delicious, ruby-red Brunello wine.

See pp230–31

Previous page: Children meeting an inquisitive dolphin at Genoa's aquarium

laden with grapes destined to become magnificent wines. Excellent wines, renowned since the Roman era, are also produced around Ostuni, far to the south in Puglia, a spectacular city whose white walls shimmer in the hot September sun.

Great cities of art also await you in September: Venice, buzzing with stars of the screen during its prestigious film festival; Turin, austere and businesslike, but revealing hidden treasures to those who seek them out; Genoa, whose vibrant port district has many delights to offer, including the largest aquarium in Italy; Mantua, which turns its lovely Renaissance center over to the world of books; and of course Rome, where the city's imperial past can be explored in peace now that the heat and the crowds have departed.

LUXURY AND ROMANCE

COSTA SMERALDA Lovely, unspoiled beach of Capriccioli

URBANIA
LE MARCHE

A city of peaceful charm

Not far from the beaches of the Adriatic Riviera, yet a world away, Urbania's charming historic center features a noble 13th-century palace.

www.le-marche.com/Marche/html/urbania.htm

TROPEA
CALABRIA

Sun, sea, and scenery

Tropea stands on a sandstone cliff on Calabria's Costa Viola. As well as beautiful beaches, the town boasts traces of ancient settlements within its well-preserved center.

www.prolocotropea.eu

COSTA SMERALDA
SARDINIA

A natural luxury

One of the most famous and spectacular stretches of coast in Italy, the Costa Smeralda is synonymous with no-expense-spared style and luxury.

See pp244–5

CASTELSARDO
SARDINIA

Spectacular setting on the Golfo dell'Asinara

The village, dominated by a great castle, is built on a promontory surrounded by crystal-clear sea. Sunset over the bay is unmissable.

www.sardegna.com/en/castelsardo

"The Costa Smeralda, which bewitched the Aga Khan in the 1960s, retains all its allure for today's visitors."

ERICE
SICILY

A town that has captured hearts for thousands of years

Ancient Erice has a Norman castle built over a temple dedicated to Venus, the Roman goddess of love. The views stretch all the way to Africa.

www.bestofsicily.com/erice.htm

ACTIVE ADVENTURES

CORTINA D'AMPEZZO Magnificent sunset over Lagazuoi

APRIGLIANO
CALABRIA

Horseback-riding in the Parco della Sila

Explore this spectacular natural park on horseback along lovely trails, starting from the stables at Aprigliano on the edge of the park.

www.parks.it/parco.nazionale.sila

MOUNT ETNA
SICILY

At the mouth of Mount Etna

Ascend the slopes of the highest and most important volcano in Italy, for one of the most magnificent and awe-inspiring views that you will ever see.

See pp224–5

CASTELLUCCIO DI NORCIA
UMBRIA

Take to the air amid the Apennine peaks

Castelluccio is famous for "free flight," in which you soar with the birds by hang- or paragliding.

See pp240–41

VILLENEUVE
VALLE D'AOSTA

Rafting on the Dora Baltea

Setting out by raft or canoe on the turbulent waters of the Dora Baltea River, against a backdrop of the mountains of Valle d'Aosta, is a supremely thrilling experience.

www.comune.villeneuve.ao.it

CORTINA D'AMPEZZO
VENETO

Mountain bike trails

Magnificent views of the Dolomites can be admired from the saddle, thanks to the widely varied 37 miles (60 km) of bike paths that make up the Lunga Via delle Dolomiti.

See pp232–3

FAMILY GETAWAYS

GENOA Visitors watching the graceful seals at the aquarium

PAESTUM
CAMPANIA

Impressive ancient temples

A popular seaside resort, Paestum is also the site of the ancient city of Poseidonia, still encircled by Greek walls and containing the ruins of several superb temples.

www.infopaestum.it

MURANO
VENETO

The magic of glass-blowing

Murano has many glass-blowers, and the whole family will be fascinated by the speed and danger of their art. As a bonus, the Lido's famous beaches are just a boat ride away.

www.murano.net

GENOA
LIGURIA

The largest aquarium in Italy

The Acquario di Genoa, in the city's lively, regenerated port, has over 12,000 sea creatures in its state-of-the-art tanks, and will enchant young and old alike.

See pp238–9

VALDOBBIADENE
VENETO

At harvest time, cycle the hills where Prosecco is made

The oldest wine route in Italy is a popular bike tour, with plenty for all the family to see and do, as well as wine-tasting for the grown-ups.

www.valdobbiadene.com

MAROSTICA
VENETO

A game of chess

An attractive walled town, Marostica is famous for the "living chess" matches, in historical dress, that take place here in even-numbered years.

www.italyheaven.co.uk/veneto/marostica.html

STARS ON THE WATERS

THE DELICATE LACEWORK of palace façades rising up from the water; the stillness of the *campielli*, little squares dominated by ancient churches; the graceful lines of bridges that span its historic canals – every corner of Venice has a surprise in store and is a joy to the eye.

In September the city also offers pomp and spectacle in the form of the Regata Storica, its historic regatta. The procession – a pageant of typical 16th-century gondolas led by the Bucintoro, a sumptuous galley like the one that carried the Venetian Doges – glides gracefully along the Grand Canal. But there are livelier events, too, in the form of hotly competitive gondola team races – cheered on by their crowds of supporters – at the end of which it seems as if all of Venice has taken to the canals by boat to join in the party and to enjoy the music and fireworks that round off the event.

Main: Dazzling parade of gondolas taking part in the historic regatta on Venice's Grand Canal

GETTING THERE
Marco Polo Airport is linked to the center of Venice by bus and taxi, which will get you to the city center in 20 minutes, and by waterbus, which takes 45 minutes.

GETTING AROUND
The historic center is easily explored on foot. Otherwise there are *vaporetti* waterbuses linking all the sights.

WEATHER
September is the best time to visit Venice, when the summer heat and humidity has abated and average daytime temperatures reach 75°F (24°C).

ACCOMMODATIONS
Treat yourself to an unforgettable experience at the Hotel Danieli, an icon of Venice; doubles from US$585; www.luxurycollection.com

On the Lido, the Hotel des Bains (doubles from US$1,075; www.desbains.hotelinvenice.com) and the Excelsior (doubles from US$1,210; www.hotelexcelsiorvenezia.com), are often the choices of the stars visiting the Venice Film Festival.

Much less expensive is the attractive and comfortable Do Pozzi, a few steps from Piazza San Marco; doubles from US$134; www.hoteldopozzi.it

EATING OUT
For a delicious meal (from US$28) of *cicheto* (appetizing small dishes of fish, seafood, cheese, and salami) and a glass of wine, try *bacari* (inns) such as Do Mori (tel. 041 522 5401) or l'Aciugheta (tel. 041 522 4292).

Da Romano on Burano (dinner from US$42; www.daromano.it) and Da Nane on the Lido (from US$68; tel. 041 527 9110) serve local cuisine.

PRICE FOR TWO
US$270–1,360 per day (depending on your choice of hotel) including accommodations, meals, and local travel.

FURTHER INFORMATION
www.turismovenezia.it

Punta della Dogana

A triangular spur of land at the tip of the island of Dorsoduro, the Punta della Dogana was the site of the Dogana del Mar, or customs house, of the former Venetian Republic. Today this 17th-century building, restored by the Japanese architect Tadao Ando, houses the Center of Contemporary Art. The 2008–09 conversion left the structure of the warehouses intact but inserted a dramatic concrete structure in the center of the complex, a striking juxtaposition of ancient and modern that perfectly expresses the gallery's ethos.

Left: Luxurious Hotel Ex one of the most fashiona places in Venice, viewed the waters of the Lido

Right: View of the Cam Sant'Angelo in the centr historic Sestiere di San M

Far right (top to botto *Spritz*, a Venetian apériti with Prosecco sparkling Campari, and soda; Bur typical multicolored hou gallery selling Murano's hand-blown glassware

These colorful and lively events have a cinematographic quality, but then the whole of Venice seems like one remarkable film set, an impression that is all the stronger during the Venice Film Festival. The oldest of its kind in the world (it was first staged in 1932), the festival is held on the Lido, a long sandy island that separates Venice's lagoon from the open sea, and whose tree-shaded avenues, overlooked by grand and elegant hotels, become a catwalk for world-famous actors and directors.

There are other islands in the lagoon, each with its own character. Burano is famous for its colorful houses and, in its little squares, women still make the fine lacework typical of the island. Murano has been a center of glass-working since 1291, when the workers moved here so that the fires that often broke out in their ovens would not threaten the city. Torcello, almost uninhabited, is different again: visitors come here for its wonderful historic buildings – the Basilica di Santa Maria Assunta and the Chiesa di Santa Fosca – and its tranquil atmosphere, a delightful contrast to the bustle, clamor, and excitement so typical of Venice's historic heart.

Above: George Clooney and Tilda Swinton arriving at the Venice Lido

PARTY DIARY

Venice puts on two big events in early September: the Venice Film Festival and, on the first Sunday of the month, the historic regatta. Both are spectacles not to be missed, especially with the backdrop of this beautiful city. In the space of four days you can visit all the sights, including the islands, join in the fun of the regatta, and still have time for some celebrity-spotting. *(See also pp44–5)*

Four Festive Days

DAY 1

Start your visit in Piazza San Marco, the heart of the city, surrounded by porticoes and dominated by the basilica and the Palazzo Ducale (Doges' Palace). Don't miss the interior of the basilica and its marvelous mosaics. Step behind the high altar to admire the Pala d'Oro (golden altar panel), a masterpiece of Byzantine goldsmiths' art, then climb up to the balcony for a view of the whole square. Enjoy a coffee or a cocktail at the 18th-century Café Florian, a haunt of Venetian intellectuals. After lunch, take a tour of the magnificent interior of the Palazzo Ducale, and walk across the famous Bridge of Sighs.

DAY 2

Visit the Lido to join the throngs of onlookers waiting for the celebrities to arrive at the Venice Film Festival. Pause for lunch at one of the grand hotels, such as the Hotel des Bains or the Excelsior. Later, take a boat along the Grand Canal, admiring the palaces that line its banks.

DAY 3

Spend the morning in the Galleria dell'Accademia, which holds a magnificent collection of Venetian art. In the afternoon, head for the island of Torcello to see its splendid churches. Toward evening, back in Venice, seek out a *bacaro*, a typical Venetian inn where you can have a glass of wine with a selection of delicious snacks.

DAY 4

Today take a boat trip around the lagoon's islands, spending some time on Murano to admire the master glass-workers at their craft, and perhaps buying an example to take home. Toward dusk, stop in Burano for a stroll around its charming little streets and squares.

Dos and Don'ts

- ✓ For information about screenings at the Venice Film Festival, and ticket purchases, visit the website www.labienniale.org
- ✗ In Piazza San Marco, don't accept an offer of a free trip to Murano. Tourists are generally steered toward shops that are trying to attract customers, and you will be subject to high-pressure sales pitches.
- ✓ Treat yourself to a ride in a gondola, but bear in mind that it will be expensive. Look at the tariffs displayed at the mooring places and agree a price with the gondolier in advance.
- ✓ Watch one of the many competitions that take place in the margins of the Regata Storica, after the procession. They always attract a lively crowd of spectators. For information, visit www.comune.venezia.it

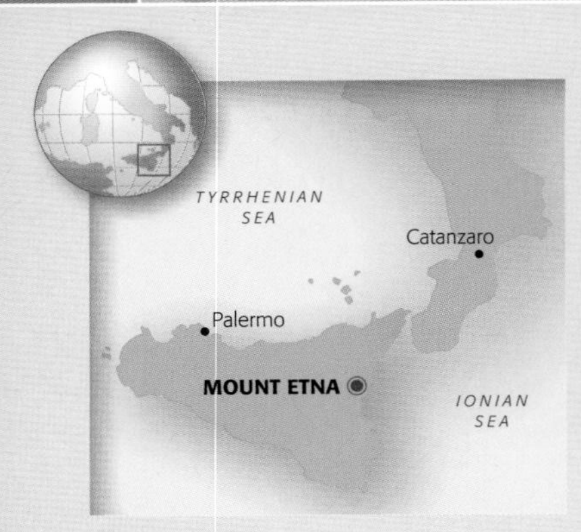

GETTING THERE
Catania airport is 19 miles (30 km) from Nicolosi, from where it is a farther 9 miles (15 km) to Zafferana Etnea or 6 miles (10 km) to Rifugio Sapienza, the main starting point for Etna treks.

GETTING AROUND
A car is the easiest way to reach Rifugio Sapienza, from where you can take an excursion that includes the Etna cable car and a guided jeep tour, and Zafferana Etnea, from where you can drive and then trek to the summit.

WEATHER
It is still hot in September, with daytime temperatures reaching 86°F (30°C). On Etna there can be rapid changes of temperature, so come prepared.

ACCOMMODATIONS
The Hotel Rifugio Sapienza has en-suite rooms in Alpine style; doubles from US$150, including breakfast; www.rifugiosapienza.com

In Nicolosi, La Giara B&B has attractive and spacious rooms; doubles from US$75; www.giara.it

In Zafferana Etnea there are two pleasant and welcoming B&Bs: the Giardino di Sara (doubles from US$82; www.giardinodisara.it) and the Poggio Felice (doubles from US$82; www.poggiofelicebeb.it).

EATING OUT
The restaurant at Rifugio Sapienza offers a good choice of local cuisine (dinner from US$35).

There is a good set menu for US$35 at La Rocca della Rosa, a 19th-century manor house in a charming garden in Zafferana Etnea; www.laroccadellarosa.it

PRICE FOR TWO
US$220 per day for accommodations, meals, and local travel. Add at least US$135 for a guided Etna excursion.

FURTHER INFORMATION
www.etnaonline.it

Parco Regional dell'Etna

An area of 220 sq miles (570 sq km) was designated in 1987 as a nature preserve for the protection of Mount Etna itself as well as its flora and fauna. The preserve includes the summit and the slopes of the volcano, which offers some spectacular sights: volcanic cones and black lava flows, but also abundant cultivated swathes of olives, citrus, and vines. You may be lucky enough to see golden eagles soaring on the thermals overhead, as well as falcons and herons, and wildcats, pine martens, and porcupines might be spotted.

Main: Volcanologists observing a spectacular eruption of Etna in 2002

THE KING OF VOLCANOES

STRONG LEGS, STAMINA, and a passion for unusual and exciting views: these are all great assets if you are visiting Europe's most spectacular volcanic zone, especially if you are starting from Zafferana Etnea. This pleasant village reclines on the eastern slopes of Mount Etna: a 10,900-ft (3,322-m) tall sometimes-sleeping giant, 28 miles (45 km) in diameter. The Sicilians call this monster by the almost affectionate name of Mongibello, a corruption of the Arabic *Jabal al-Burqan* or "mountain of mountains," dating from the medieval period of Arab rule over the island.

Experts say that Etna began to take shape some 600,000 years ago – a very long period of gestation that has had a striking impact on the appearance of this part of Sicily. Thousands of eruptions have been documented, from the one in the 7th century BC that triggered a tsunami in the Mediterranean to that of September 4, 2007, when the crater spewed forth a 1,300-ft (395-m) high fountain of lava.

Above: Wall of a house made entirely of lava in Zafferana Etnea

Above: Group of walkers heading for the crater

Below (top to bottom): Typical Sicilian dish of *lasagnette all'etnea* made with eggplant, anchovies, and peppers; pine marten in the nature preserve; baskets of marzipan displayed in a shop window

VOLCANOLOGIST'S DIARY

Etna, the highest volcano in Europe, rises majestically above the Sicilian countryside, solitary and proud. To do it justice, spend three days exploring and ascending the slopes to its craters. Each of these three trips has something unique to offer, and you will return from your visit with a sense of awe and respect for this mighty mountain.

Three Days on the Mount

DAY 1

From Rifugio Sapienza you can take an excursion via the cable car that starts from an altitude of 6,230 ft (1,900 m) and ascends to 8,200 ft (2,500 m). From here, a 4x4 jeep, with a guide, will transport you up to an observation point from which you can admire the central and southeastern craters, learn about them, and walk along lava flows created by past eruptions. You can do the same trip unaccompanied, if you prefer.

DAY 2

Devote the day to one of the many walks leaving from Zafferana Etnea that give you the opportunity to admire the majestic panorama of Etna's natural park. One of the best treks takes you to the deep narrow valley where the longest lava flow of the last century ran during the eruption of 1991–3. On your return, stroll around the village and stop for dinner in one of the local restaurants. In fall, many feature porcini mushrooms. Try *sciatore* – a delicious large cookie covered in chocolate – or a dessert that uses the local honey or marzipan.

DAY 3

Today, try the other way of discovering Etna: by train, in the little carriages of the Circumetnea, from Nicolosi. This railway line, which dates back to the beginning of the 20th century, runs right round the volcano and offers views of wooded slopes, dark lava flows, and summit craters. The most interesting part of the journey is between Riposto and Bronte, where the train's tracks cross impressive lava flows and run through vineyards and groves of citrus fruits.

Dos and Don'ts

- ⊗ When you are walking on the slopes of Etna, never leave the paths: the volcano is very steep and rugged and has many hidden precipices.
- ✓ For information about excursions organized by the Etna cable car company, visit www.funiviaetna.com
- ✓ For information on the timetable and route of the Circumetnea railway, visit www.circumetnea.it
- ✓ Check uphill walking itineraries in advance: some of them are steep and tiring and require a reasonable level of physical fitness.

Zafferana is one of the main starting points for a series of breathtaking ascents. From here you can drive 2,625 ft (800 m) upward, to the point where the lava finally halted after the most sensational eruption of the 20th century – it began on December 14, 1991 and lasted for 473 days. From this point you must continue on foot, ascending to 3,280 ft (1,000 m); here the view is dominated by the sight of the Val Calanna, once full of orchards, but now a shocking testimony to the volcano's power.

Also from Zafferana, a 9-mile (15-km) trek runs from the Pian del Vescovo (4,500 ft/1,372 m) via Rifugio Sapienza through beechwoods and broom as far as the Serra del Salifizio, from where there is a stunning view of the lava flows. Another option is to take the road for Monte Pomiciaro, arriving at a viewpoint from which you can see the mainland coast of Calabria across the sea. And finally, if you continue walking for a farther 40 minutes from here, across the Bove valley, you can look down into the crater and see the heart of the volcano with your own eyes. Are you ready?

GETTING THERE
Mantua is in southeast Lombardy. The closest international airport is Verona, 14 miles (22 km) away. By car, take the A22 freeway.

GETTING AROUND
Mantua's historic center is easy to explore on foot. Public transportation is fine for longer trips, but the best way to see Mantua is to rent a bicycle.

WEATHER
The weather in September is cooling down from summer, but still very pleasant, with average daytime temperatures around 75°F (24°C).

ACCOMMODATIONS
The small, quiet Broletto hotel is a 16th-century palace in the historic center; doubles from US$164; www.hotelbroletto.com

Rooms at the Rechigi are decorated with works of modern art and design; doubles from US$258; www.rechigi.com

Conte San Girolamo *agriturismo*, in a national park just outside Mantua, is a fascinating place dating back to the 18th century. Bicycles are available for the use of guests; doubles from US$108; www.agriturismo-sangirolamo.it

EATING OUT
Ristorante Cigno dei Martini adapts historic dishes of the Gonzaga dynasty, using exceptional local produce (dinner from US$60; tel. 0376 327101).

PRICE FOR TWO
US$300–450 per day including meals, local travel, accommodations, and admission fees.

FURTHER INFORMATION
www.turismo.mantova.it

A Passion for Books

Five days of literary gatherings, cultural events, poetry readings, plays, and concerts: this is the Festivaletteratura, held every September in Mantua, transforming the city into a vast and lively literary salon. Inaugurated in 1996, the festival grows in status every year. It now attracts poets, essayists, novelists, and critics of international renown, including Nobel Laureates such as Nadine Gordimer. Just as importantly, it also draws huge numbers of the reading public, who relish the idea of hearing their favorite writers speak, and even meeting them, in a relaxed and informal atmosphere.

Above (left to right): Gallery of the Teatro Olimpico at Sabbioneta; Mantua pumpkin, one of the region's most celebrated products; statue of Mercury, on the façade of Giulio Romano's house in Mantua
Main: Wonderful *trompe l'œil* ceiling of the Camera degli Sposi in the Palazzo Ducale, Mantua

Above: Citadel district of Mantua, reflected in the Mincio River

RENAISSANCE GRACE

A CITY OF ELEGANT BEAUTY, rising up out of a lake: that is how Mantua first appears to visitors. The city is, in fact, nestled in the curve made by three lakes, formed by the Mincio River, its splendid Renaissance buildings reflected in their rippling waters.

Mantua is the city of the Gonzaga dynasty, who ruled from the 14th to the 17th century, building it into one of the greatest centers of the Renaissance. It still reflects today the magnificence of its dukes: you need only visit the Palazzo Ducale, their former residence, to be immersed in the dazzling trappings of the court of one of Italy's most powerful dukedoms. The Palazzo Ducale is actually a complex of buildings, churches, courtyards, and gardens, and contains many remarkable works. Perhaps the finest of all is Renaissance painter Andrea Mantegna's *Camera degli Sposi*, or "Marriage Chamber" (1474), which features a cycle of frescoes that transforms the dark medieval heart of the Palazzo, originally a miltary fort, into an elegant, airy, light-filled pavilion with a marvelous *trompe l'œil* of an "oculus" skylight, from which angels and *putti* or cherubs gaze down upon you.

Mantua is not identified solely with its magnificent art treasures, however. It also captivates the visitor with its elegant ambience, lively streets and squares, and good shops, bars, and cafés, where you can relax in magnificent surroundings and watch the world go by.

Nearby Sabbioneta was built by Vespasiano Gonzaga as a center for art and culture, and planned according to Renaissance principles of an ideal city. Its fascination lies in its tranquil atmosphere, the classical proportions of its squares and palaces, its star-shaped city walls and the formal grid pattern of its streets. Like Mantua, it is a place of antique charm that wears its magnificence with grace.

A city of elegant beauty, rising up out of a lake: that is how Mantua first appears to visitors.

Inset: Bicycle in the Piazza dell'Erbe
Below (left and right): Ceiling in Mantua's Palazzo Ducale; view of Palazzo Te, Giulio Romano's austere masterpiece

HERITAGE DIARY

Exploring Mantua is like finding oneself in one of the magnificent courts of the Italian Renaissance. Along with nearby Sabbioneta, Mantua has been named a UNESCO World Heritage Site, and it is easy to see why. Three days allows time not only to get to know the compact historic heart of the city, but also to visit lovely Sabbioneta as well.

Three Days of Delights

DAY 1

To begin your visit, head for the Piazza Sordello, the heart of Mantua. Visit the Palazzo Ducale that looks on to the grandiose square, which incorporates works of amazing artistic beauty. After lunch, stroll around the streets in the center as far as the Piazza dell'Erbe, the site of a traditional market and surrounded by lovely buildings including the Romanesque Rotonda di San Lorenzo, one of the oldest churches in Mantua.

For dinner, try some specialties of Mantuan cuisine, such as *tortelli di zucca* (pasta stuffed with pumpkin), salami studded with fresh garlic, and *torta sbrisolona* (literally "crumbly cake" but actually a large, almond-flavored cookie).

DAY 2

Keep today free for a trail around the works of great architects of the Italian Renaissance: Leon Battista Alberti (visit the churches of Sant'Andrea and San Sebastiano) and Giulio Romano (magnificent Palazzo Te, the interior of the Duomo, and the house he designed for himself). Then carry on to leafy Piazza Virgiliana: named for the poet Virgil, one of Mantua's greatest sons. Before supper, join the locals in an early-evening stroll along the lake shore.

DAY 3

Take the bus to Sabbioneta to visit the town's own Palazzo Ducale and the Palazzo del Giardino, with its spectacular frescoed Galleria degli Antichi (Gallery of the Ancients), as well as Palladio's magnificent 16th-century Teatro Olimpico, Italy's oldest enclosed theater.

Dos and Don'ts

- ✓ Rent a bicycle and ride the length of the town's lake shore; it's a very pleasant path and offers romantic and unusual views of the town's historic buildings.
- ✓ If you are here on the third Sunday of the month, have a look around the antiques market in Piazza Virgiliana. It's an entertaining opportunity to rummage through the stalls in search of interesting curios.
- ✓ At certain times of year, including September, individual visitors must book in advance to visit the Camera degli Sposi. For information, visit www.mantovaducale.it/eng_info.htm
- ✗ Do not expect to see top authors or attend major events at the Festivaletteratura without booking the tickets in advance. For details, visit www.festivaletteratura.it

GETTING THERE
Capri is in the Gulf of Naples, off the Sorrentine peninsula. A shuttle bus runs from Naples airport to the port, from where there are regular ferries and hydrofoils to the island.

GETTING AROUND
Cars are not allowed in the center of Capri in September. The island has good public transport, or you can hire a moped. Marina Grande is linked to upper Capri town by a funicular railway.

WEATHER
Capri still has summery weather in September: the average daytime temperature is 79°F (26°C).

ACCOMMODATIONS
The elegant Casa Morgano is situated on the edge of Capri town in a wonderful position with stunning sea views and an infinity pool; doubles from US$340; www.casamorgano.com

The San Michele, a smart hotel in Anacapri, has lovely views of the sea and Monte Solaro; doubles from US$245; www.sanmichele-capri.com

EATING OUT
Da Gemma is one of the historic eating places in Capri, famous for its excellent pizzas (dinner from US$42); www.dagemma.it

La Capannina serves fabulous seafood (from US$68) and has a wine bar serving lighter meals; www.capannina-capri.com

PRICE FOR TWO
US$475 per day including accommodations, food, local travel, and beach facilities.

FURTHER INFORMATION
www.capri.net
www.capritourism.com

Anacapri's Settembrata

Each September, Anacapri, on the west side of the island, plays host to a remarkable festival. It's a competition between the island's four districts, which vie with each other to provide the finest gastronomic specialties, processions of allegorical floats, traditional costumes, folk dance, and music and puppet shows, and the streets of the village fill up with colorful stalls. The Settembrata is linked to the grape harvest and helps the villagers to keep their historic traditions alive, but visitors are more than welcome to join in the fun.

Main: Capri's Faraglioni rock stacks, rising from the clear blue sea

RHAPSODY IN BLUE

CAPRI, A TINY, ROCKY ISLAND, covering little over 4 sq miles (10 sq km), rises dramatically from a sea of constantly shifting shades of blue. With its steep, rocky cliff faces, secluded inlets, mysterious caves, and luxurious villas that are half-hidden in gardens permanently in bloom, your first view of Capri is guaranteed to be one that you will never forget. The first visitor to fall in love with Capri was Octavius (the future Roman emperor Augustus) in about 30 BC. Some years later, his successor Tiberius made the island his principal place of residence and built magnificent palaces such as the Villa Jovis, an imposing structure perched on a cliff that plunges straight down to the sea.

The sheer magic of the Capri coastline has always been one of its greatest lures. Among its most dazzling features are the Faraglioni, three rugged outcrops famous for their unique blue lizard, and the Grotta Azzurra, a huge cave flooded by the sea, which owes its intense blue color to sunlight filtering through a natural underwater "window" below its entrance.

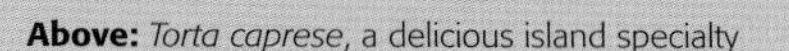

Above: *Torta caprese*, a delicious island specialty

Below: Via Krupp, the winding footpath linking Capri town with Marina Piccola and one of the most picturesque paths in the world

Above: Capri's Piazzetta, the island's social center

The sea may be Capri's greatest source of natural splendor, but it is by no means the island's only appeal to visitors. For those who enjoy celebrity-watching and designer goods, Capri town offers not only the café tables in the famous Piazzetta, but also bustling streets lined with luxury shops. Yet you need take only a few steps from here to find yourself gazing on unforgettable sea views from the Giardini Augusto, sumptuous terraced gardens dating from the 1930s and stocked with exotic island flora.

From Capri town, you can walk the spectacular Via Krupp, a path cut from the rock early in the 20th century, to Marina Piccola, a chic little resort that is home to Capri's most fashionable beach. More breathtaking panoramas unfold at every one of the myriad twists and turns en route. Verdant and secluded Anacapri is a starting point for several more rural walks, such as the Sentiero dei Fortini, a path linking the forts that once protected the western end of the island. This is an outstandingly beautiful route that winds its way through lush vegetation, yet is always in sight of the coast. Wherever you go and whatever you do on Capri, it is the siren song of that blue, blue sea that will keep calling you back.

CAPRESE DIARY

Capri has always attracted international celebrities, from Goethe to Gracie Fields, Jean-Paul Sartre to Jackie Kennedy, drawn here by its vibrant atmosphere and lovely scenery. Today its inimitable charm and rugged beauty continues to bewitch visitors and, over the course of five days, you are sure to fall in love with it as well.

Five Days of Sea and Sunshine

DAY 1 From Marina Grande to Capri town itself you could take the funicular railway, but a great alternative is the road that climbs up through orange groves and gardens. Once in the town, pause for a while at one of the bars in the Piazzetta, the island's open-air "salon." Then treat yourself to a shopping spree in Via Vittorio Emanuele and Via Camerelle, where you'll find the island's most famous shops, including Canfora, makers of the best Capri sandals.

DAY 2 Devote the morning to a boat trip around Capri, including the Faraglioni and the Grotta Azzurra. In the afternoon, walk out to the eastern cape to visit the Villa Jovis. Toward evening return to the village for an apéritif, a glass of Capri's excellent white wine.

DAY 3 In the morning, visit the Giardini Augusto. From here you can walk along the Via Krupp, high up above the sea, to Marina Piccola. Spend the afternoon on its lovely beach, and end the day with a seafood supper.

DAY 4 Walk via the Carthusian monastery of Certosa di San Giacomo to the Belvedere di Tragara Punto, passing many lovely villas en route. Stop for a swim and lunch at the foot of the Faraglioni, then continue to Arco Naturale to see the striking, red Modernist Villa Malaparte before making your way back to Capri town.

DAY 5 With charming Anacapri as your base, walk the Sentiero dei Fortini and take the cable car to the top of Monte Solaro. Several places in the village offer tastings of Capri's famous Limoncello, a lemon-based liqueur – try it and you're sure to take a bottle of this liquid sunshine home as a souvenir.

Dos and Don'ts

- ✗ Avoid visiting Capri on public holidays and weekends, when the island gets very crowded. Better to go midweek, when it's more peaceful.
- ✓ Give in to temptation and buy a pair of the classic Capri sandals – you'll be walking in the same shoes as Jackie Kennedy, Maria Callas, and Sophia Loren, among others.
- ✓ Try a slice (or two) of delicious *torta caprese*, a rich cake made of almonds and plain chocolate.

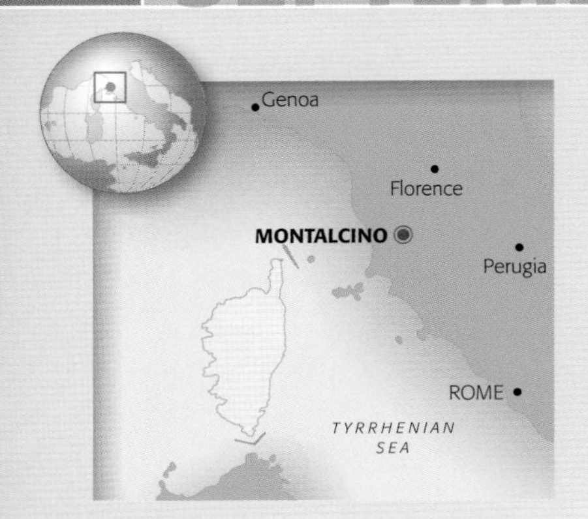

GETTING THERE
Montalcino is in the Val d'Orcia, in Tuscany. The nearest airports are Florence and Perugia. From either you can reach Montalcino by car in less than 2 hours.

GETTING AROUND
The most convenient way of getting around is by car.

WEATHER
The weather is still warm and sunny with daytime temperatures averaging 70°F (21°C).

ACCOMMODATIONS
The Porta Castellana B&B, in an old stone house, offers a hospitable welcome and a garden with a view; doubles from US$102; www.portacastellana.it

Vecchia Oliviera is in a converted olive oil factory, next to one of Montalcino's gateways, with smart, comfortable rooms, and a swimming pool; doubles from US$164; www.vecchiaoliviera.com

The Terme San Filippo hotel, near Castiglione d'Orcia, is an 18th-century palace in a thermal spa resort; doubles from US$144; www.termesanfilippo.com

EATING OUT
There are many restaurants in Montalcino where you can try the local cuisine (dinner from US$35), such as the Re di Macchia (tel. 0577 846116) and the Osteria d'Altri Tempi (tel. 0577 846087).

Just outside Montalcino, vineyard restaurants Fattoria dei Barbi (from US$42; www.fattoriadeibarbi.it) and Azienda Poggio Antico (from US$68; www.poggioantico.com) serve local dishes and their own fine wines.

PRICE FOR TWO
US$300 per day including accommodations, meals, and car rental.

FURTHER INFORMATION
www.prolocomontalcino.it

Brunello di Montalcino

One of Italy's most famous, finest, and most expensive wines, Brunello is ruby-red in color with an intense bouquet and flavors of red berries, chocolate, and leather. It is produced solely in the Montalcino area from Sangiovese grapes and is aged for at least five years, for most of that time in oak barrels. The region boasts other wines, which, though not as famous, are nevertheless worthy of note: they include Rosso di Montalcino, made from the same variety of vine but with a shorter maturing period, and sweet white Moscadello, perfect for accompanying dessert.

AMONG THE VINES OF BRUNELLO

A MEDIEVAL WALLED TOWN, perched on a hill, offering a breathtaking panorama as far as the eye can see of rolling countryside covered with vineyards – this is Montalcino, one of the great capitals of Italian wine. Toward evening, this gentle landscape of the Val d'Orcia can almost seem like a vast, calm sea, as the outlines become more hazy and the colors softly fade; and yet, when the all-important fall harvest time approaches, it may be bustling with activity long into the night.

Today the town owes its fame to the magnificent Brunello wine that is produced on the surrounding slopes, but in the past it was Montalcino's position on the Via Francigena, the main route between Rome and France, that gave it an important status. As a result, Montalcino developed as a fortified town (and one that has never been conquered) with huge defensive walls, dominating the valley. Within those

Main: Val d'Orcia viewed over the ancient rooftops of Montalcino

Left: Gentle, rolling coun of Val d'Orcia

Right: Ripening Sangiov vines around Montalcino

Far right (top to botto Glimpse of Montalcino's Duomo from an alleyway the historic centre; relaxi pavement café in Monta *finocchiona*, a local saus flavoured with red wine fennel seeds

walls is a maze of tiny medieval alleyways, leading to beautiful churches such as the 14th-century Sant'Agostino and San Francesco, or opening out into squares surrounded by porticoes, and climbing up to Montalcino's Fortezza. This is a substantial five-sided fortress, softened by slender corner towers that were built toward the end of the 14th century and incorporated part of the pre-existing walls.

Also evocative of the Middle Ages, and the journeys of monks and pilgrims across the Alps, is the nearby 11th-century Abazzia de Sant'Antimo, a fine example of Lombard–French Romanesque architecture said to have been founded on the site of a votive chapel built by Charlemagne.

Montalcino is at the heart of Val d'Orcia, a region whose landscape can be glimpsed in the background of so many pictures by the greatest Italian Renaissance painters. You can still see those vistas today, dotted with red-roofed hilltop villages, as you drive along roads flanked by cypresses and half-hidden among the vineyards. This is a timeless place, still filled with the beauty that caught the artists' eyes, to be savored slowly, with the same appreciation that you would give a glass of its magnificent red wine.

Above: Abbazia di Sant'Antimo, set in the green hills of Val d'Orcia

VINEYARD DIARY

Lovely Montalcino is worth a visit in itself, but it is also a gateway to the vineyards and historic villages of Val d'Orcia. With three days at your disposal you can sample all the delights of Montalcino as well as touring the local countryside. Vineyard tastings are an additional treat that only the designated driver will have to forego.

Three Days in Val d'Orcia

DAY 1

In the morning, explore Montalcino, wandering the maze of alleyways past artisans' workshops, cafés, and food shops selling gastronomic specialties (as well as Brunello wine, the area is famous for its cheeses, honey, and handmade cookies). Climb up to the fort to admire the view from its walls over the rolling hills of Val d'Orcia. After lunch, drive out to the Abbazia di Sant'Antimo: its austere contours stand out against the rolling hills, offering an unforgettable visual experience. On your return to Montalcino, sample the best of the region's wines, accompanied by tasting plates of local cheese, salami, and other produce, at one the town's *enotecas* (wine bars), such as the one in the fortress.

DAY 2

Today, drive the "Brunello Road" through the hills around Montalcino, stopping off at vineyards offering visits and tastings. As you drive north, the landscape changes and the wooded hills give way to the Sienese *crete*: rough hills with clay soil and bleak reddish ridges that give the area its characteristic "lunar" aspect. Well worth visiting is Buonconvento, one of the prettiest villages in Italy, with a perfectly preserved 14th-century historic center.

DAY 3

Drive out today to Castiglione d'Orcia, about 12 miles (20 km) southeast of Montalcino, a medieval village set in a splendid position among hills and vineyards. Look out for Rocca d'Orcia, just to the north of the village; this little hamlet is built around the impressive 12th-century fortress of Tentennano.

Dos and Don'ts

- ✓ Montalcino's "Honey Week" is held in September. If you are here for it you can taste a wide range of delicious local honeys, still produced using ancient traditional methods.
- ✓ To visit the cellars of Montalcino's Brunello winemakers, obtain a map of the vineyards free of charge at the Consorzio del Brunello in Montalcino.
- ✓ Bear in mind that, although entry to cellars is normally free, you must often pay for a tasting or may be expected to buy one or more bottles.
- ✗ When you do visit a cellar, don't touch the bottles and don't tap or knock against the barrels.

GETTING THERE
Cortina is in the heart of the eastern Dolomites. The nearest major airport is at Venice, 90 miles (145 km) away. By car, take the A27 freeway and leave at the Cadore/Dolomiti/Cortina exit, then take the SS51. There is also a bus service, but only at weekends.

GETTING AROUND
The best way of getting around is by car or bicycle, but the area also has an efficient and widespread network of buses and chair-lift facilities.

WEATHER
There are still clear, sunny days in September with average daytime temperatures around 64°F (18°C), falling sharply at higher altitudes.

ACCOMMODATIONS
To experience Cortina's fashionable and luxurious side, choose the elegant historic Hotel de la Poste, built in the 19th century as a stopping place for mail coaches; doubles from US$270; www.delaposte.it

Just outside Cortina, the Baita Fraina offers welcoming rooms in Alpine style, and a famous restaurant; doubles from US$120; www.baitafraina.it

For a stay in a mountain hut, the Son Forca has comfortable rooms and a good restaurant (doubles from US$54; 0436 861822); the Faloria has a terrace looking on to the Conca di Cortina and serves good local cuisine (doubles from US$120; tel. 0436 2737).

EATING OUT
An old Ampezzo hayloft has been transformed into a charming restaurant, the Toulà (dinner from US$68), with a wonderful view of the Dolomites; www.toula.it

The Meloncino al Camineto interprets local specialties with flair (from US$62) and has a terrace at the foot of the Tofane; tel. 0436 4432.

PRICE FOR TWO
US$245–460 per day, depending on your choice of hotel, including accommodations, meals, and car rental.

FURTHER INFORMATION
www.cortina.dolomiti.com
www.dolomiti.org

Sunset Over the Peaks

Red, orange, pink, violet, and finally a dark shape rising up against a starry sky – sunset in the Dolomites is an unforgettable sight, with infinite shades of color washing over the craggy summits in the slanting rays of the setting sun. Science may explain that these colors are produced by the particular chemical composition of the rocks (they are made, appropriately enough, of dolomite, a mixture of calcium carbonate and magnesium) but that does not make the sunset any less magical to the enchanted viewers that gather to watch this natural light-show.

Above (left to right): Freccia cable car approaching the summit of Tofana di Mezzo; chamois on slopes dappled with green lichen; view over Cortina d'Ampezzo
Main: Suspension bridge on the high-altitude Ivano Dibona path

Above: Lagazuoi mountain and hut, tinged with pink at sunset

JAN FEB MAR APR MAY JUN JUL AUG SEP OCT NOV DEC

PEARL OF THE DOLOMITES

THE AIR IS FRESH and sparkling-clear, the sun is shining, your bicycle is waiting, and you have binoculars for wildlife spotting and water and food supplies for when hunger strikes. You are in Cortina d'Ampezzo, in the heart of the Dolomites, a splendid stretch of the Alps with unique features that enabled it to gain UNESCO World Heritage status in 2009.

Nestled in a spectacular valley and surrounded by dramatic massifs such as the Tofane and the Cristallo, Cortina is a paradise for lovers of alpine sports: not only because of its ski stations, but also because of the opportunities to practice Nordic walking, climbing *via ferrata* (literally "iron roads," and equipped with cables, ladders, petons, and bridges), and mountaineering. But above all, once the snow has melted away, it is the ideal destination for those who enjoy mountain bike excursions, thanks to the Long Dolomites Path. This cycle path follows the route of the former Calalzo–Cortina railway, constructed in 1915 to help troop movements during World War I, and closed down in 1967. It is a spectacular route, around 37 miles (60 km) long, passing through some of the most amazing mountain scenery in the world: from the Tofane to the Marmarole, skirting the foot of Pelmo, Sorapis, and Antelao, where the jagged Dolomite pinnacles dramatically rise up out of thick pine forests. From Cortina, the cycle path winds its way gently through the Dolomiti d'Ampezzo nature preserve and offers detours that bring you to ancient churches, ruined castles, rustic mountain huts, and delightful hamlets.

For the seriously fit, there is a cycling tour of five *rifugi* (mountain huts) on a journey of 24 miles (39 km) with an altitude gain of 5,000 ft (1,500 m). There is also the "Great War" route that runs via the historic World War I trenches where Italian gun batteries were ranged against Austro-Hungarian emplacements.

Everything ready? Then off you go!

Nestling in a spectacular valley and surrounded by dramatic massifs... Cortina is a paradise for lovers of alpine sports.

Inset: Delicate flowers of the iconic alpine *Leontopodium alpinum*, better known as the Edelweiss
Below (left and right): Tre Croci pass, perfect for a gentle stoll amid mountain greenery; Pomagagnon, one of the most famous massifs in the Dolomites

OUTDOOR DIARY

Cortina has long been regarded as Italy's most fashionable ski resort, attracting the stylish international set since the early years of the 20th century, but it is synonymous with sports at all times of year, and you don't have to be a millionaire to enjoy it. Over four days you can try several of the best cycle and walking routes, through outstanding scenery, from your base at this chic resort.

Four Days Amid the Peaks

DAY 1

Go for a ride along the Dolomites cycle path. One of the most beautiful routes, 6 miles (10 km) long and quite easy, it takes you to the Fanes waterfalls along paths that in part go through the Dolomiti d'Ampezzo nature preserve. In the evening, take a stroll along the streets of Cortina and treat yourself in the shops of a town that is one of the fashion capitals of Italy.

DAY 2

If you want to test yourself with a more demanding route, follow the cycle path that allows you to explore the Tofane area and the Cinque Torri, visiting the World War I trenches on the summit. This route is 19 miles (30 km) long and the steep climb makes it arduous.

DAY 3

Today, visit lovely Lake Misurina, encircled by coniferous woodland, about 9 miles (15 km) northeast of Cortina. In its waters are reflected some of the finest Dolomite peaks, such as the Piz Popena and the unmistakable three summits of Lavaredo. To admire them more closely, head up to the Rifugio Auronzo. Return to Cortina via the Tre Croci pass, with the majestic Cristallo glacier as a backdrop.

DAY 4

Dedicate the day to an ascent of a *via ferrata* route. There are many of these "equipped" routes in the Cortina area, which permit you to reach places that would otherwise be the sole preserve of expert mountaineers. One of the most exciting is the Albino Strobel *via ferrata* that ascends the west slope of the Punta Fiames; from here you have an incomparable view over Cortina and the Boite valley.

Dos and Don'ts

- ✓ As you travel through the Dolomiti d'Ampezzo nature preserve, listen for woodpeckers and owls, and look out for golden eagles, vultures, marmots, ermines, hares, and, of course, agile chamois, of which there are 1,500 in the park.
- ✗ Don't attempt a *via ferrata* without an alpine guide, otherwise you may get into trouble.
- ✓ Take a trip on the Freccia nel Cielo ("Arrow of the Sky"), the cable car that takes you from the center of Cortina to the top of Tofana, an altitude of 10,466 ft (3,190 m).
- ✓ For more information about Cortina's cycle routes, visit www.dolomiti.org/dengl/Cortina/bike_resort/index.html

GETTING THERE
Ostuni is in Puglia, 25 miles (40 km) from the nearest airport, at Brindisi. From here you can reach Ostuni by car, via the SS379, or by train or bus.

GETTING AROUND
It is easy to explore Ostuni on foot, but a car is the best way of touring the surrounding countryside.

WEATHER
It is still hot at this time of year, with maximum daytime temperatures of 82°F (28°C).

ACCOMMODATIONS
La Sommità Relais, a 16th-century building in the center of Ostuni, offers chic modern decor and every luxury, including a spa; doubles from US$408; www.lasommita.it

The Nonna Isa B&B, a few steps from the center, is welcoming and pleasant, doubles from US$82; www.nonnaisa.it

Masseria Il Frantoio, an *agriturismo* in the Ostuni countryside, produces its own olive oil. It has a romantic courtyard and garden for candlelit dining; doubles from US$240; www.masseriailfrantoio.it

EATING OUT
Osteria del Tempo Perso, in a former bakery, serves regional cuisine (dinner from US$42) in a setting of rustic elegance; www.osteriadeltempoperso.com

Porta Nova, set in one of the towers of the city walls, offers creative dishes featuring local flavors (from US$54); www.ristoranteportanova.com

PRICE FOR TWO
US$245–570 per day (depending on your choice of hotel), including accommodations, meals, and car rental.

FURTHER INFORMATION
www.ostuni.com

Main: Breathtaking view of Ostuni's remarkable cityscape

The Appian Way of Wines

Reddish-hued soil, in vibrant contrast to the greens of olive groves and vineyards, marked out by dry-stone walls and dotted with the strange, conical-roofed *trulli* houses – this is the landscape around Ostuni, at the center of what the ancient Greeks called Enotria, or "land of wines." Ostuni is the starting-point of l'Appia dei Vini, a remarkable wine route that runs as far as Brindisi and takes in a wide range of wine-producing centers en route, a great way to enjoy the region as well as sampling its excellent wines.

PUGLIA'S WHITE CITY

La città bianca – "the white city" – Ostuni is the pearl of the Salento region. The region was occupied as long as 50,000 years ago by hunting peoples. Even they saw the strategic value of the three hills on which the town was later to be built, hills that still bear the three towers that dominate Ostuni's coat of arms. These towers date from the great era of the town's development, between the 11th and the 13th centuries, when Normans and Swabians expanded the area's olive-growing and Angevins fortified the city. Constrained by the walls, the town began to grow, in the only way it could. As a result Ostuni now has many multi-story buildings.

The whiteness of the town, which gives Ostuni its nickname, is due to the limewash applied to the external walls of houses. This has a twofold origin: in the Middle Ages the whitewash served to reflect the sun's rays and thus to let light into the alleyways and side-streets; in the 17th century, however, it had a darker purpose. The wash was applied to the

Left (left to right): Dancers in local costume perform the *pizzica pizzica*, a traditional Puglian dance; ancient olive tree in the countryside near Ostuni; craftsman weaving wicker baskets; beautiful Egnazia beach, a short way up the coast from Ostuni

Below (top and bottom): *Vincotto*, the mild vinegar of Puglia, served here over ice cream; narrow alleyway typical of Ostuni

Above: Ancient olive oil presses in the Masseria il Frantoio

walls in an attempt to disinfect them and protect against the plague that was raging through the region. Appropriately, Ostuni's symbol is the Baroque Colonna di Sant'Oronzo, standing over 70 ft (21 m) high, built in 1771 in honor of the saint who, according to tradition, protected the city from the disease.

The lovely cathedral, the Carmelite convent, and the remains of Castello Villanova all give the feeling that, here, each epoch has succeeded the former without ever disappearing entirely. The same is true of the farms or *masseria*, whose fortifications in times past were often required to repel incursions by the Saracens. There are about 300 *masseria* around Ostuni, each one with a special feature: Santa Caterina has a tall octagonal tower; Ottava, a small medieval church; Lo Spagnolo, a massive structure, opulent Baroque staircase, and look-out tower; Monticelli a Monte, a pressing room carved out of rock. In today's more peaceable times they continue, as they have done for centuries, to produce fine olives, oil, almonds, wine, and wheat. Whether you are roaming the countryside, or exploring the labyrinth of Ostuni's narrow streets, you cannot fail to feel the timeless quality of this part of Puglia.

SALENTINE DIARY

Ostuni shines out against the surrounding verdant landscape. Its hilltop center takes in a panorama that ranges over a hinterland rich in art and tradition to the turquoise shades of the distant sea. With four days at your disposal you can explore the town's history, culture, gastronomy, and nature – and even have time for a day at the seaside.

Four Days in La Città Bianca

DAY 1

Spend your first day exploring the town and being captivated by the maze of little streets in the medieval center that wend their way through the dazzlingly white houses. Don't miss the cathedral with its splendid façade, adorned with a large rose window. At dinner enjoy any of the numerous delicious local dishes, enhanced by the excellent olive oil produced in the region.

DAY 2

Visit the sanctuary of Sant'Oronzo with its frescoed crypt and the nearby sanctuary of San Biagio, carved out of rock, in a fine panoramic position. For lunch, head for one of the numerous *masseria* in the area. These former fortified farm estates today often offer *agriturismo* and have excellent restaurants. Spend the afternoon exploring the farms, sampling and buying local produce.

DAY 3

Treat yourself to a fantastic day by the sea on the Ostuni coast. Expanses of verdant Mediterranean maquis and sand dunes provide a backdrop to its perfect beaches, whose sandy coves are interspersed with stretches of rock. The Torre Guaceto nature preserve and marine park contains the last residues of the marshland that once covered the Brindisi coastline, and is home to turtles.

DAY 4

Today, head 6 miles (10 km) southwest to Ceglie Messapica, one of Puglia's most ancient towns, surrounded by massive stone city walls in a countryside dotted with *trulli*. Ceglie is the acknowledged gastronomic capital of the Alto Salento region, so take the opportunity to try the local cuisine in one of its many fine restaurants.

Dos and Don'ts

- ✓ If you are in Ostuni on the second Sunday of the month, explore the Zaccaredde antiques market that takes place around the Villa Comunale.
- ✗ Don't attempt to get to the farms of the Ostuni countryside by public transportation: you will need a car to reach them.
- ✓ Always take drinking water with you when you go out: there are periods of water shortage in summer and there may be rationing or cuts at certain times of day.
- ✓ Buy olive oil produced in the traditional presses that are still used in the region; you can visit the mills, see the presses used to process the olives, and taste the oil.

GETTING THERE
Rome's main airport is Fiumicino. A shuttle train takes 30 minutes to reach the central Termini railway station.

GETTING AROUND
Rome is a wonderful city to explore on foot, but there is also a good bus system. The best way to get to Ostia Antica is by train.

WEATHER
September is still a summer month in Rome, with daytime temperatures reaching 81°F (27°C).

ACCOMMODATIONS
The Forum hotel, in a former convent, has a wonderful view of the Roman Forum and Trajan's Markets. The roof garden includes a smart restaurant; doubles from US$394; www.hotelforum.com

The Lancelot is a charming, family-run 3-star hotel not far from the Colosseum; doubles from US$252; www.lancelothotel.com

The Pantheon View B&B is in an excellent position, although the view of the monument is actually slightly restricted; doubles from US$150; www.pantheonview.it

EATING OUT
The oldest restaurant in Rome, La Campana, was founded in the 16th century just a few steps from the Pantheon. It serves traditional Roman cuisine (dinner from US$48) such as artichokes, oxtail, and pasta with fresh anchovies; www.ristorantelacampana.com

The San Teodoro is in the heart of imperial Rome, between the Forum and the Palatino; it serves excellent cuisine (from US$68) in smart surroundings, including a lovely summer garden; www.st-teodoro.it

PRICE FOR TWO
US$310–555 per person for accommodations, meals, and local travel, including the Roma&Più Pass.

FURTHER INFORMATION
www.turismoroma.it

The Golden Milepost

This was one of the most important sites in imperial Rome, but today all that is left is a block of marble decorated with a bas-relief. The Golden Milepost, a column of marble covered with bronze, was erected in 20 BC by the emperor Augustus. It was considered the starting point for every Roman road, and was inscribed with the number of miles between Rome and all the main cities of the empire, in order to emphasize that Rome was the true *caput mundi* – head of the world.

Above (left and right): Grotesque theatrical mask in the ruins of Ostia Antica; view of the interior of the Colosseum

HEART OF THE EMPIRE

PART THEATER, PART STADIUM, an arena in which men faced fierce wild animals and gladiators dueled to the death – in short, the Colosseum of Rome. Originally known as the Flavian Amphitheater, it was renamed in the Middle Ages in acknowledgement both of its exceptional size and of the Colossus of Nero, a vast bronze statue of the emperor that once towered nearby.

The construction of the Colosseum began in AD 72 under the emperor Vespasian, the first of the Flavian emperors. The work took eight years, and Vespasian did not see its completion. It could seat 50,000 spectators around an arena 280 ft (85 m) long and nearly 180 ft (55 m) wide. Colossal indeed, yet still not the largest in Rome at the time: that was the Circo Massimo ("Great Circus"), which could hold 200,000 spectators. It was Vespasian's son, the emperor Titus, who inaugurated the finished Colosseum, in AD 80, with 100 consecutive days of games. It ceased to be used for such events around the 6th century and, since then, has been a cemetery and a fortress; sacked for its precious blocks of travertine marble and damaged by earthquakes.

The Colosseum was constructed above an artificial lake facing the imperial Forum, a magnificent collection of monumental squares. Their construction had started more than a century earlier in 46 BC, when Julius Caesar decided to build, in his own name (and, perhaps uniquely, at his own expense), a huge, colonnaded square next to the old Forum that had always been the heart of the city. Other emperors, in turn, had followed suit. In AD 2, Octavian created another monumental square, the Forum of Augustus, dominated by the Temple of Mars the Avenger commemorating Julius Caesar's bloody end at the hands of the conspirators who assassinated him. This temple was surrounded by a high wall to keep at a distance the plebeians and the poor living in the nearby quarter of Suburra. Later emperors Nerva and Trajan built their own fora nearby. The addition of the Colosseum to this grouping completed an ensemble that encapsulates the awesome power of the empire at its height.

But, for the visitor of today, it is the Colosseum that undoubtedly remains the most eloquent symbol of the pride of imperial Rome, just as Vespasian would have wished.

Main: Ruins of the Forum, one of the oldest sites in the whole of Rome
Below (left to right): Detail of the exquisite bas reliefs on Trajan's Column; *carciofi alla matticella* (artichokes baked with oil, garlic, and mint), a Roman specialty; façade and campanile of the early Christian basilica of Santa Maria in Cosmedin

Above: Constantine's Arch, a magnificent feat of commemorative architecture

JAN FEB MAR APR MAY JUN JUL AUG SEP

ROMAN DIARY

They say that "a lifetime is not enough" to explore Rome: there are so many wonderful places to see here, each of them speaking of a different moment the city's history. With just four days you must be selective, so begin by getting to know the oldest parts of Rome, dating from when it was the heart of a vast empire. *(See also pp28-9 and pp288-9)*

Four Imperial Days

DAY 1

Start at the Colosseum, one of Rome's greatest monuments. From here, head for Constantine's Arch, built by the emperor who put an end to the persecution of Christians; then continue to the Palatine Hill where, according to legend, Romulus founded the city. The area is covered with the ruins of the emperor Domitian's residences: the Domus Augustana, his private residence, and the Domus Flavia, the imperial palace. Go back up the Via dei Fori Imperiali to the Roman Forum, the ancient center of the civil and religious life of the city. The Forum is crossed by the Via Sacra, where there is an array of temples and, at the end of it, the Arch of Septimus Severus. Don't miss Trajan's Column, decorated with a spiral bas relief.

DAY 2

In the morning, visit the Pantheon, the best preserved of the buildings of ancient Rome. Built by the emperor Hadrian, it is topped by a cupola shaped in a perfect hemisphere, one of the greatest masterpieces of Roman architecture. Spend the afternoon in the Capitoline Museum, which has a superb collection of ancient sculptures. Just to the south is the basilica of Santa Maria in Cosmedin, famous for its "Mouth of Truth."

DAY 3

Start the day at the ruins of the Baths of Caracalla. They were so large they could hold 1,600 people at one time. A short stroll from the baths will take you to the remains of the Circo Massimo, where there were up to 24 chariot races each day during the reign of Caligula. The Baths and the Circo are now part of a huge green open space in the heart of Rome.

DAY 4

Today, get a real feeling of how the city looked in the Roman era by visiting Ostia Antica, Rome's former port, about 20 miles (30 km) southwest of the city. Here you can still clearly see the grid pattern of the streets and the well-preserved ruins of a great many buildings: houses, shops, baths, and temples.

OCT NOV DEC

Dos and Don'ts

- ✗ Be careful if you are asked a question as you put your hand in the Bocca della Verità (Mouth of Truth), a 1st-century marble carving in the portico of the basilica of Santa Maria in Cosmedin – it is said that it will bite off a liar's hand.
- ✓ Try to see a performance at RomaEuropa, a festival of modern music and drama held in September. For information, visit the website at: www.romaeuropa.net
- ✓ Buy a Roma&Più Pass. Valid for three days it includes all public transportation and gives free entry to the first two museums or sites that you visit, reduced entrance fees to all other sites, and other reductions. For details, visit: www.romapass.it

GETTING THERE
Genoa is the capital of Liguria. Its international airport is only 4 miles (6 km) from the city center and is linked by a bus service that runs every hour to the central Principe station.

GETTING AROUND
The best way to explore Genoa is on foot, but there is also a good bus network. Lifts and funicular railways connect the city center to the scenic hill areas.

WEATHER
September brings clear, sunny days with average highs of 75°F (24°C), but cooler evenings.

ACCOMMODATIONS
The small family Hotel Balbi is set in a historic palace; family rooms from US$135; www.hotelbalbigenova.it

The elegant, modern Hotel NH Marina overlooks the old port, near the Aquarium; two linked rooms from US$486; www.nh-hotels.it

The Agnello d'Oro is a quiet hotel offering packages that include entry to the aquarium; family rooms from US$162; www.hotelagnellodoro.it

EATING OUT
The wood oven at the Sà Pesta restaurant is used to bake bread and savory tarts; the kitchen offers classic dishes such as *trofie* pasta with pesto (dinner from US$35); 010 246 8336.

Da Maria is an institution in Genoa and serves divine local dishes (under US$28); tel. 010 581080.

At Antica Osteria del Bai, dine on elegant cuisine in a 15th-century fortress (from US$55); www.osteriadelbai.it

PRICE FOR A FAMILY OF FOUR
US$340–690 for accommodations, meals, and local travel. Add about US$160 for a visit to AcquarioVillage.

FURTHER INFORMATION
www.genova-turismo.it

Piano on the Port

Genoa has been a sea port since the 5th century BC, but the 20th century saw traffic decrease to the point where its harbor was barely in use. All this changed in the run-up to 1992, the 500th anniversary of the discovery of America by Christopher Columbus (long thought to be Genoese). It was decided to revive the area in celebration of the city's seafaring hero, and the project was entrusted to another Genoese, architect Renzo Piano. The result is a huge complex that comprises both restored and enhanced old buildings and dramatic new ones, creating an attraction for tourists that has become a pivotal part of the city.

TREASURE OF THE SEAS

HAVE YOU EVER COME FACE TO FACE WITH a 6-ft (1.8-m) green moray eel? It would be a fearsome encounter in the tropical Atlantic ocean. Or a four-eyed fish that can see above and below the water at the same time? Try the swampy parts of South America. How about a brittle star, whose long, pale arms twirl elegantly toward its prey? If you've dived the icy waters of the South Atlantic or Antarctica, perhaps.

All these strange sea creatures, and many more, can also been seen in safety and comfort at the Acquario di Genova, the largest aquarium in Italy. It was opened in 1992 in the old harbor area, which has been regenerated as a splendid "Piazza on the Mediterranean." The aquarium offers an entrancing display for children of all ages, with 70 tanks holding over 12,000 aquatic creatures, putting them in close contact with some of the most elusive and unusual animals in the natural world. The most popular

Main: Penguins take gracefully to the water at Genoa's superb aquarium

are the residents of the five largest tanks: dolphins, sharks, seals, penguins, and turtles. It is a thrilling experience, thanks to the walk-through passageways, to see a shark circling above your head, its gaping jaws full of pointed teeth. And it's not all "look but don't touch" – young children will love the "petting pool" where they can stroke the velvety skin of friendly stingrays.

The old port area offers many other family-fun experiences. The Biosphere holds a tropical forest where you can see plants and animals, including hummingbirds and scarlet ibis, at close quarters. The Città dei Bambini e dei Ragazzi ("City of Children and Kids") has lots of interactive game stations at which to learn about science and technology. For budding explorers there's the Museo Nazionale dell'Antardide (on the Antarctic) or the Museo del Mare – and the pier for boat trips. For a final thrill, take a ride up in the Bigo – a strange, futuristic crane-lift that whisks you up to a height of 130 ft (40 m) for a view of Genoa that Christopher Columbus could only have dreamed about.

Above: Renzo Piano's Biosphere, containing a lush tropical forest

Above: Elegant façades of Baroque palaces on Via Garibaldi

Below (left to right): Spectacular jellyfish in the Acquario di Genova; boat on display at the Museo del Mare; visitors watching the dolphins at the aquarium; *Recco focaccia* bread, flavored with cheese, a delicious Ligurian specialty

WATERSIDE DIARY

Genoa's destiny was always linked to the sea and, thanks to a superb regeneration, today the port is once again the city's bustling hub, though not with cargo and ships so much as with thousands of tourists every year. Three days is the perfect length of time for a family visit: there's plenty to keep the kids happy – and the grown-ups, as well.

Three Exciting Days

DAY 1

Devote most of the day to the aquarium, a memorable experience for the whole family. Within its 107,000 sq ft (10,000 sq m) space you will see some 600 different animal species. When you emerge from its undersea world, move on to the Biosphere, a splendid steel and glass structure poised over the water. Inside is a delicate ecosystem in which plants and animals from the rain forest flourish.

DAY 2

In the morning, visit Città dei Bambini e dei Ragazzi, also in the port area. Opened in 1997, this is a great center where play and experiments put the fun into learning about science and technology. After lunch, take in the Maritime or the Antarctic museum before strolling the short distance from the old port to the San Giorgio Palace, where Marco Polo was held prisoner and dictated his Travels; from here you can wander the *carrugi*, the alleyways in the most ancient part of Genoa, to reach San Lorenzo, Genoa's Gothic cathedral.

DAY 3

In the morning visit the Via Garibaldi; here, in the ancient Strada Nuova, you can admire 14 splendid palaces in the space of a few hundred yards. They were built between the mid-16th and the early 18th century, when this was the residential area for large Genoese families, and many of them contain museums. Palazzos Bianco and Rosso hold the city's finest art collections. End the day back in the harbor, ready to take a trip up in the Bigo at twilight, to see the lights of the city come on below.

Dos and Don'ts

✓ Buy an AcquarioVillage pass, a single entry ticket that gives you admittance to the aquarium, the Bigo, the Biosphere, the Museo del Mare, and the Città dei Bambini e dei Ragazzi. It can be used over several days and costs around US$48 for adults and US$35 for children under 12.

✓ To avoid waiting, book in advance for your visit to the Acquario di Genova, which is always busy. You can do this online by visiting: www.acquariodigenova.it

✗ Don't take flash photos or use video cameras with lighting in the aquarium. This is forbidden, as is dropping things into the tanks, feeding the animals, and banging on the tank windows.

GETTING THERE
Castelluccio di Norcia, in southeastern Umbria, is served by the airports of Perugia and Ancona, both of which are about a 2-hour drive from Castelluccio.

GETTING AROUND
A car is needed to get around the area, but Castelluccio also offers other possibilities for more active local travel, such as walking and horseback-riding.

WEATHER
September is still a summer month in this part of Italy, but temperatures in Castelluccio are lower due to its altitude; average daytime temperatures reach around 63°F (17°C), with clear, sunny days.

ACCOMMODATIONS
Taverna Castelluccio is a small hotel, simple and welcoming, with a good restaurant; doubles from US$88; www.tavernacastelluccio.it

La Valle delle Aquile, a countryside *agriturismo*, is a farmhouse with lovely apartments; doubles from US$80; www.lavalledelleaquile.com

EATING OUT
Locanda de' Senari *agriturismo* in Castelluccio serves classic Umbrian dishes (dinner from US$35) using home-grown ingredients; www.agriturismosenari.it

The Granaro del Monte, in Norcia, has been in existence for 150 years. Specialties include tagliatelle with wild boar, filet steak with truffles, lentil dishes, and ricotta tart (from US$48); www.bianconi.com

PRICE FOR TWO
US$245 per day for accommodations, meals, and car rental. Add a minimum of US$680 per person for a basic course in paragliding or hang-gliding.

FURTHER INFORMATION
www.castellucciodinorcia.it

The Heart of Norcia

An ancient town set on a verdant plain in the midst of the Apennines, Norcia is encircled by city walls in the shape of a heart. It is the birthplace of St. Benedict, patron saint of Europe, and has a basilica dedicated to him, built on the site of the house where he was born. The cured meats and salami made here from wild boar and pork are so renowned that *norcineria* is the Italian name for all such products. Black truffles, lentils, and sheep's milk cheese are the other local specialties.

Above (left and right): View of the Castelluccio di Norcia plateau and the Apennines; ancient street in the historic center of the village of Castelluccio

SOARING WITH EAGLES

THE JAGGED OUTLINE of Castelluccio, perched on a hill in the Umbrian Apennines at 4,760 ft (1,450 m) above sea level, appears on the horizon. A little way beyond it is the impressive bulk of Monte Vettore. Far away, you can see the greens and blues of the Parco Nazionale dei Monti Sibillini with its lakes, woods, and limestone hollows set among steep hills. Any minute now, perhaps, a peregrine falcon or a golden eagle will fly past and look at you in amazement – after all, you are sharing the sky with him.

Since 1976 Castelluccia di Norcia has hosted a national school for paragliding and other forms of "free flight," which is now famous throughout Europe. It welcomes beginners and the experienced alike and offers its students help from expert instructors as well as the latest, safest equipment. It is no surprise that many northern European flying schools send their students here to perfect their skills. In the beginning, its courses were focused primarily on hang-gliding, which, at that time, was the only way of taking off from a hillside. Today, by contrast, the skies above Castelluccio are filled with people paragliding, hang-gliding, paramotoring (paragliding with an auxiliary motor), and taking courses to qualify for paragliding or hang-gliding in tandem.

The natural conditions here are perfect for every type of free-flight activity: the plains of Castelluccio are surrounded by a circle of mountains that generate constant winds and perfect thermals for ascent. The effect is enhanced by the hollows created by a former Apennine lake that dried up over the centuries, leaving three huge depressions, or dolines, in the landscape.

From above, the view is spectacular: the three hollows that form the plains of Castelluccio stretch out below you, vivid in fall shades of red, gold, and brown. You will see walkers and riders crossing their vast expanses, and rafters negotiating their rivers (you won't see, but they are there, underground, speleologists exploring the karst caves). You'll see plenty of sheep, too: there are around 4,000 of them, against a human population of about 190. At the heart of the plains is the lovely village of Castelluccio, its walls painted with white graffiti slogans, a curious ancient custom. The views from its terraces are almost as fine as from the air – better still, they can be enjoyed with a glass of wine and a gastronomic meal, perfect at the end of an active day.

Main: Paraglider preparing for flight, with the village of Castelluccio in the background
Below (left and right): *Corallina*, a typical salami from Norcia; horseback-riding in the countryside between Castelluccio and Norcia

Above: View of Castelluccio perched on its hilltop

HIGH PLAINS DIARY

For such a tiny village, set in the middle of vast expanses of empty plain, Castelluccio has a big reputation. It is internationally renowned as a center for outdoor activities, and is bustling with sporty visitors all year round. There are so many exciting things to try that six days will fly by as you explore the countryside by land and air.

Six Adventurous Days

DAY 1

On your first morning, place yourself in the hands of an expert, and try a tourist flight in tandem with an instructor. This is an exhilarating experience, requiring no skills or training, that will introduce you not only to the joys of being airborn but also to the lovely landscape around Castelluccio. If you want to learn to hang- or paraglide for yourself, you will need to book a five-day course.

DAY 2

Plan a hike to discover the plains of Castelluccio at ground level. There is a wide range of short walks, more demanding routes, and hill-climbing in the area. Pack a picnic, and binoculars for bird-spotting.

DAY 3

Spend the day in Norcia, visiting the town's beautiful ancient monuments and sampling as many of its gourmet specialties as your appetite and wallet allow.

DAY 4

Today visit Serravalle, a few miles from Castelluccio and Norcia, to try rafting on the Corno River. You can descend in a rubber dinghy, canoe, or kayak, admiring the lovely scenery of the Valnerina as you go.

DAY 5

Go horseback-riding on the plateau. There are itineraries to suit all levels of experience – or you could start with a beginner's lesson if you are a novice.

DAY 6

Visit the Abbazzia di Sant'Eutizio in Piedivalle, a lovely complex on the wooded slopes of Monte Moricone. The abbey dates back to the 12th century and was an important political and cultural center in the Middle Ages.

Dos and Don'ts

- ✓ For more information on free-flight courses run by the school in Castelluccio, visit: www.flycastelluccio.com
- ✓ For information on horseback-riding trips, ranging from an hour's gentle trot to a full day's trek out onto the plains, visit: www.escursioniacavallo.it
- ✗ There is no need to take special equipment with you for a flying course: the school will provide everything you need.

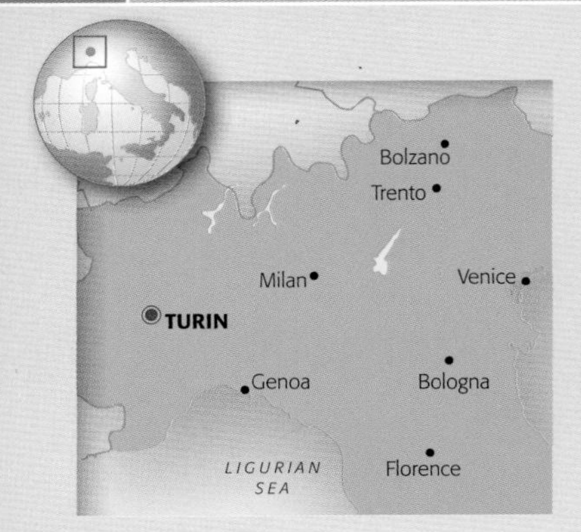

GETTING THERE
The capital of Piedmont, Turin is served by Caselle international airport, which is connected to the city by a regular bus service, departing every half-hour.

GETTING AROUND
The city has an excellent public transportation system for getting around and for tourist activities (boat trips on the Po, historic trams, City Sightseeing buses).

WEATHER
There are frequent sunny days and pleasant temperatures averaging around 73°F (23°C).

ACCOMMODATIONS
The smart Art Hotel Boston in the city center is decorated with valuable works of contemporary art and the stunning rooms are individually designed. From US$150; www.hotelbostontorino.it

The B&B Ai Savoia is in an 18th-century historic residence with bedrooms decorated in period style from US$108; www.aisavoia.it

The B&B Alla Buona Stella, also in a historic palace, is cozy and welcoming. Rooms from US$135; www.allabuonastella.it

EATING OUT
There are many restaurants where you can enjoy Piedmontese cuisine such as *agnolotti al plin* (tiny ravioli), *risotto al Barolo* (risotto with wine), *bonet* (chocolate terrine), and *panna cotta* (a creamy pudding). Try Capannina (about US$48; tel. 011 545 405); Bue Rosso (US$42; tel. 011 819 1393); C'era una Volta (US$42; tel. 011 655 498) and Vallée (US$55; tel. 011 812 1788).

PRICE FOR TWO
You will spend about US$285 per day on meals, accommodations, and the Torino+Piemonte Card.

FURTHER INFORMATION
www.turismotorino.org

Il Grande Torino

The name "Superga" brings back memories of a great tragedy to all Italian soccer fans, and especially those from Turin. On May 4, 1949, the airplane bringing back the legendary Grande Torino team (they won the Italian Championship five years running) from Lisbon crashed into the side of a hill near the Basilica di Superga. Everyone on board perished, including several journalists and the flight crew. Today, there is a Museo del Grande Torino commemorating the disaster and containing memorabilia from the team.

Main: Piazza San Carlo, with the almost symmetrical churches of Santa Cristina (left) and San Carlo, and the equestrian statue of Emanuele Filiberto

AN ARISTOCRATIC CAPITAL

TURIN IS INFUSED WITH THE STYLE AND SPIRIT of the Savoy, the royal dynasty that had its capital here between 1563 and 1864. Yet the city conceals a Roman heart – the central area is located on what was a Roman military camp, later the colony of Augusta Taurinorum. The Palazzo Madama, on Piazza Castello, was where the Fibellona Gate stood in Roman times, and the nearby Piazza Palazzo was the site of the former Roman forum. The Savoyards also followed the Romans in grouping all the important government buildings together.

But it is predominantly the Savoy exuberance and majesty that has left its mark on the center of Turin. In order to get a flavor of this, you only need to go to Piazza San Carlo, the "drawing-room" of the city, enclosed on one side by twin churches, and dominated by the equestrian monument of Emanuele Filiberto of Savoy. Around the square are gathered some of the most representative buildings: the Palazzo Carignano, designed in the 17th

Left (left to right): Chocolate terrine Asti-style, called *bonet;* a classical music concert during the MITO SettembreMusica; painting by Nicola De Maria, *Testa dell'artista cosmico pittore e cantante* (Head of the artist, cosmic painter, and singer); Castello del Valentino, set in a park of the same name

Below (top and bottom): Egyptian statues in Turin's excellent Museo Egizio; Mole Antonelliana, home to the Museo Nazionale del Cinema

Above: The cupola of the Basilica di Superga

century by Guarino Guarini, is a fine example of Piedmontese Baroque. We also owe to Guarini the grandiose Palazzo dell'Accademia, which today houses the city's outstanding Museo Egizio: the most important Egyptian museum after the one in Cairo. A short walk away along the porticoed Via Po stands the Mole Antonelliana. Reaching a height of 550 ft (168 m), it was built as a synagogue by the architect Alessandro Antonelli for Turin's Jewish community to celebrate the granting of freedom of worship to non-Catholics. Work began in 1863 and was finished only at the beginning of the 20th century. The Mole was never used as a synagogue; since 2000 it has housed the Museo Nazionale del Cinema (National Museum of Cinema).

But art and architecture are not Turin's only cultural strengths – in September, it temporarily forgets its rivalry with the other major northern city, Milan, and collaborates in an exciting music festival, MITO SettembreMusica. Both cities fill with the sounds of talented musicians from all over the world, performing a wide range of musical genres, from opera to jazz to avant-garde.

SAVOY DIARY

Despite recent rapid economic growth that has made it one of Italy's major industrial centers, Turin has preserved its historic center. Four days is enough time to see the city's main sites and also to enjoy excursions outside the city to see the Basilica di Superga and the Palazzina di Caccia di Stupinigi.

Four Days by the Po River

DAY 1

A tour of Turin must start near the historic Po River. At the Piazza Vittorio Veneto, the largest square in Europe, admire the circular Chiesa di Gran Madre di Dio on the opposite bank. From here, continue to the Mole Antonelliana, home to the Museo Nazionale del Cinema; take the elevator to the top, from where there are views over the whole city. Then make a stop for a cup of rich hot chocolate in one of the nearby historic bars.

DAY 2

On your second day, head for Piazza Castello. Around this square are some of Turin's most important buildings: the Palazzo Reale, the Chiesa di San Lorenzo, and the Duomo. From the square, you can wander down Via Roma and Via Garibaldi, the shopping streets – an opportunity to treat yourself to something special. Keep the afternoon free for a visit to the Museo Egizio (Egyptian Museum), which has some 30,000 exhibits covering 5,000 years of history.

DAY 3

Travel to the edge of the city for a walk around Parco del Valentino, an extensive green area stretched along the Po River that was created in the mid-19th century – it has an impressive castle and a medieval town quarter with a fort. Then visit the fantastic domed Basilica di Superga, built in 1731 on a hill outside Turin and containing the grand Savoy tombs inside.

DAY 4

Don't miss the astonishing Palazzina di Caccia di Stupinigi, a Rococo masterpiece in a lovely park a short distance outside Turin. It was built in 1729 as a hunting lodge for Vittorio Amedeo II and was turned into a sumptuous royal palace, maintaining its original cruciform plan. In the evening, try to get tickets to a concert for the MITO SettembreMusica, a festival featuring all types of music held across the city during September.

Dos and Don'ts

- ✓ Try *gianduiotti*, the famous Turin chocolates named after Gianduia, the city's stock Commedia dell'Arte character.
- ✗ Stay aware of your wallet, watch, and camera: as in lots of tourist centers, pickpockets target crowded places.
- ✓ Buy a Torino+Piemonte Card. It gives admission to over 160 attractions and free access to public transportation including the elevator at the Mole Antonelliana, the shuttle service to Veneraria Reale, and boats on the Po. A 3-day card costs US$30.

GETTING THERE
The Costa Smeralda, or Emerald Coast, is a short but marvelous stretch of coastline in northeast Sardinia. From Olbia airport, Porto Cervo is about 40 minutes by car on main or minor roads. There is also a bus service between the airport and Porto Cervo.

GETTING AROUND
The best ways to get around are by car or bike. Boat trips are also a delightful way to explore the coast.

WEATHER
September is still summery, with maximum daytime temperatures around 81°F (27°C), but cooler evenings.

ACCOMMODATIONS
Cala di Volpe is one of the best and most exclusive resort hotels on the Costa Smeralda. Designed by Jacques Couëlle to resemble an old fishing village, it is a maze of arches, passages, and pastel-colored turrets. The elegant furnishings are in rustic style, with hand-crafted Sardinian furniture and fittings; doubles from US$1,215; www.starwoodhotels.com

The exclusive Pitrizza hotel, blending perfectly with its natural surroundings, offers a stay of discreet luxury and impeccable service. The saltwater swimming pool, carved out of granite, offers a superb view of the sea; doubles from US$1,290; www.starwoodhotels.com

EATING OUT
Il Pescatore has a terrace looking on to the old Porto Cervo marina. As the name ("the fisherman") suggests, fresh fish is a specialty (dinner from US$108); tel. 0789 931 624).

For a more informal lunch or dinner, head to Gastronomia Belvedere, offering yet more superb fish cuisine (from US$42); tel. 0789 96501.

PRICE FOR TWO
US$1,360 per day including accommodations, meals, and local travel: the cost will be much lower if you choose less expensive hotels.

FURTHER INFORMATION
www.portocervo.net
www.quicostasmeralda.it

A Sailor's Paradise

Porto Cervo is set around a natural cove whose name derives from its antler-like headlands (*cervo* means "deer"). It has two harbors: the old one, built in the 1960s, and the new one, construction of which started 20 years ago – with moorings for over 700 boats, it is one of the largest and best-equipped harbors in the Mediterranean. Its Yacht Club organizes some of the most important and exciting regattas in the world.

Above (left and right): Tombe dei Giganti at Arzachena; fresh fish, a key ingredient in Sardinian cuisine
Main: Aerial view of part of the Costa Smeralda, showing Capriccioli and, in the background, Cala di Volpe

Above: Rocky headland typical of the lovely Costa Smeralda coastline

COSTA BEYOND COMPARE

IT TOOK A PRINCE –the Aga Khan Karim – to create Porto Cervo, the queen of Sardinian holiday destinations, out of almost nothing. It was in the 1960s that he realized the potential of this bay, called Poltu Celvu (Stag Harbor) in the local Gallura dialect because the coastline looks like the antlers of a stag. The Aga Khan's architects, famous names such as Luigi Vietti, Michele Busiri, and Jacques Coüelle, chose to abide by traditional Sardinian architectural styles, as far as possible, to achieve a perfect harmony with the surrounding landscape and the local culture. This pattern was later replicated along large stretches of Sardinia's northeastern coast.

Today, Porto Cervo seems as if it has been here for ever, with its charming little squares – Piazzetta delle Chiacchiere and Sottopiazza – and its maze of narrow village streets. Look closer and you'll see that they are lined with shops bearing the most exclusive designer names, stylish nightclubs, and fine restaurants, but the effect is subtle, as befits a resort designed by royalty.

Toward evening, yachts return from secret coves along the coast: this is the time to sip an *apperitivo*, or enjoy sunset colors from on high at the Chiesa di Stella Maris.

Every summer, Porto Cervo's harbor becomes an almost obligatory destination for the international jet set, from Hollywood stars to oil sheikhs. You could find yourself mingling with them toward the evening, when their yachts return from secret coves along the coast: this is the time to sip an *apperitivo*, or enjoy sunset colors from on high at the Chiesa di Stella Maris (Star of the Sea).

The Aga Khan may have devised Porto Cervo out of almost nothing, but the "almost" is important: it was nature, not man, that created the stunning beaches along this stretch of coast, from Portisco to Rena Bianca (whose name means "white sands") to Razza Juncu – a series of wonderfully romantic rocky little beaches that are best reached from the sea. One of the loveliest is Liscia Ruja, a sickle of pinkish sand that is the Costa's longest beach. It's here that the partygoers of Porto Cervo's buzzing nightlife end up in the morning, and who can blame them?

Inset: The Chiesa di Stella Maris, the striking modern church of Porto Cervo
Below (left and right): Place name and the symbol of the Costa Smeralda, engraved on a granite block; typical architecture of delightful Porto Cervo

EMERALD COAST DIARY

The Costa Smeralda, which bewitched the Aga Khan in the 1960s, has retained all its allure for today's visitors, rich or poor. Spend your four days basking in the beauty of green and azure waters and long white beaches whose sandy coves are sheltered by verdant dunes, and chill out in the luxury of chic restaurants and bars where you can discreetly star-spot to your heart's content.

Four Days With the Jet Set

DAY 1
After a dip in Porto Cervo's splendid turquoise sea, take a stroll through the village. The route from the Piazzetta delle Chiacchiere to the Sottopiazza is a succession of alleyways and arcades lined with designer shops, so take your time. Then continue to the old marina, where you can admire some of the most beautiful yachts in the world. To round off your day, there is a difficult (but enjoyable) choice to be made from among the many fashionable restaurants and bars that line the harbor.

DAY 2
It is almost obligatory to spend a day by the sea when you are on the Costa Smeralda. There are many beaches within easy reach of Porto Cervo, by car, bike, or on foot. Or rent a boat to take you to a little cove that can be reached only from the sea. Alternatively, golf enthusiasts can test themselves by playing at the Pevero Golf Club, one of the most famous courses in Italy.

DAY 3
Head for Porto Rotondo, another pretty resort about 9 miles (15 km) down the Costa Smeralda from Porto Cervo. On the way, pause at lovely Capricciola and Cala de Volpe. Like Porto Cervo, Porto Rotondo attracts the cream of high society: hence the numbers of prestigious shops in the narrow streets and luxury yachts in the harbor.

DAY 4
If you feel the need for quiet reflection, far from fashionable attractions, head inland a little way to Arzachena, set in an area rich in archeological remains. Visit the Tombe dei Giganti (Tombs of the Giants), Sardinia's most famous and best-preserved examples of the Nuraghic civilization *(see also p65)* which inhabited the island from the Bronze Age to the 2nd century AD.

Dos and Don'ts

- ✓ Go on a boat trip with snorkeling facilities, or simply rent a boat and explore for yourself, if you have snorkeling gear. The rocky coastline teems with fascinating sea life, and the waters are clear and warm.
- ✗ Do not stay in Porto Cervo itself if your budget is limited: hotel prices are very high, even in low season.
- ✓ If you wish to visit any of the small islands opposite Porto Cervo, check which ones are open to visitors. They form part of the protected Parco Nazionale Arcipelago di Maddalena. For information, visit: www.lamaddalenapark.it

OCTOBER

Where to Go: **October**

October is a month of magical fall colors: in forests burnished with glorious tones of red and yellow, and in skies which now take on delicate hues. Admire this natural splendor in the Colli Euganei, the hilly area of the Veneto hinterland, where you can explore old towns such as Este, cradle of one of the dynasties that helped to create the concept of the city-state, which played such an important part in the Italian Renaissance. Other cities have equally fascinating histories: Trieste, the former Adriatic port of the Habsburg Empire; Viterbo, an ancient papal seat once greater than Rome, and a place where history was made; San Gimignano whose towers were symbols of medieval power and wealth; and Naples, capital of a kingdom that was one of the most important in Italy for hundreds of years.

FESTIVALS AND CULTURE

NAPLES View over magnificent Castel Nuovo and the port

NAPLES
CAMPANIA

Discover art treasures among the alleyways of Naples

Take a tour of the historic center of Naples, seeking out the many facets of a city rich in history and imbued with a unique atmosphere.

See pp250–51

CREMONA
LOMBARDY

Sweet celebrations

Cremona introduced nougat into Italy, and celebrates this with its lively Festa del Torrone.

www.italytravelescape.com/general_information_about_cremona.htm

SAN VINCENZO AL VOLTURNO
MOLISE

Ancient traditions

Close to Castel San Vincenzo stand the atmospheric ruins of a medieval abbey. The current monastery nearby keeps alive many traditional skills, typical of a region known for its fine handicrafts.

See pp254–5

STRASSOLDO
FRIULI-VENEZIA GIULIA

Steeped in history

Twice a year the castle of Strassoldo, nestled within a beautiful village, throws open its gates. Local artists and craftspeople fill the ancient rooms with their work.

www.castellodistrassoldo.it

CALCI
TUSCANY

Traditional food festival

This charming village, set in woods and olive groves, is the place to be in October when its annual chestnut festival takes place, with plenty of food and drink to sample.

www.comune.calci.pi.it

UNFORGETTABLE JOURNEYS

THE COLLI EUGANEI Santuario Giubilare delle Sette Chiese at Monselice

VITERBO
LAZIO

Ancient center

Viterbo was a medieval seat of the papacy, and is at the center of a region with many historic sites as well as some superb "wild spas" in the surrounding countryside.

See pp264–5

VARESE
LOMBARDY

In the footsteps of pilgrims

Varese is the starting point for a pilgrimage route up the Sacro Monte with its lovely chapels. By day there are fine views of Lake Maggiore, but the trail is very atmospheric by night.

www.vareselandoftourism.it

CODRONGIANOS
SARDINIA

Spectacular Pisan churches in the heart of Sardinia

Sardinia's beautiful Romanesque churches, surrounded by the spectacular landscape of the island, are the focus for a truly memorable day of exploration.

See pp260–61

"The alternating bands of white and black give the building a sophistication that is an astonishing contrast with the barren wilderness in which it stands."

TRENTO & ROVERETO
TRENTINO-ALTO ADIGE

Capitals of modern and contemporary art

Trento and Rovereto both have lovely historic buildings but are also home to MART, a fine museum of modern and contemporary art.

See pp256–7

THE COLLI EUGANEI
VENETO

A tour through the gentle hills of the Colli Euganei

Seek out the lovely towns of the Este family, a powerful Renaissance dynasty, set among rolling hills suffused with warm fall tones.

See pp252–3

NATURAL WONDERS

TAVOLARA A spectacular and beautiful island

RITTEN
TRENTINO-ALTO ADIGE

Pyramids in Italy

The world's longest cable car ride takes you to the Ritten plateau where the Erdyramids, thousands of thin clay spires, rise from the ground like earthen stalagmites.

www.ritten.com/erdpyramids.htm

BAIA DI IERANTO
CAMPANIA

Breathtaking bay

There can be few more spectacular panoramas than that of the bay of Ieranto, on the southern tip of the Sorrento peninsula, a magical place enclosing a curve of emerald sea.

www.santagatasuiduegolfi.it

CAMPOCATINO
TUSCANY

Mountains of marble

From this shepherds' village, high in the Alpi Apuane, follow the ridge to Tambura to discover a landscape of dazzling white marble – the quarries chosen by Michelangelo.

www.ingarfagnana.com

TAVOLARA
SARDINIA

Underwater paradise

This tiny island off the Sardinian coast has many marvelous spots for scuba diving and snorkeling, with coral, sponges, anemones, and giant clams to be seen.

See pp272–3

"A majestic massif that slopes down towards the sea and features high, steep cliffs, at the base of which the waves have carved out deep and mysterious caves."

BOLGHERI
TUSCANY

Wildlife haven

The magnificent sand dunes, cypress groves, and wetlands of Bolgheri are a wildlife preserve of international importance.

www.toscanatoscana.it/eng/bolgheri.htm

Previous page: Piazza Unitá d'Italia in Trieste, on a bright October day

Smaller towns have their own stories to tell: Alberobello, in Puglia, whose traditional white, conical-roofed houses, built in dry stone, could easily be demolished to avoid taxation; Codrongianos, where the sunbaked Sardinian countryside hides Romanesque churches in pure Pisan style, evidence of that empire's influence at the time; or the towns and villages of the Colli Euganei, treasure houses of fine art.

October is a month with much to offer the sports enthusiast. For example, at Tavolara, on the eastern coast of Sardinia, you can go diving in a still-warm sea; in the Val di Vara, the river is at just the right height for a thrilling whitewater rafting trip; and, in Trieste, any sailor will want a place in a small boat to take part in the events of La Barcolana, one of Europe's most spectacular sailing regattas.

LUXURY AND ROMANCE

SAN GIMIGNANO View of the medieval town and its towers

SANTA CATERINA DEL SASSO
LOMBARDY

Monastery on Lake Maggiore

Arrive by boat at this beautiful place to see how it appears suspended over the water, its walls partly hewn into the rock.

www.sgr.info/tourism/maggiore/caterina.htm

VELLETRI
LAZIO

In the land of Castelli Romani

One of the most charming towns in the Castelli Romani area, a region dotted with volcanic lakes of great beauty, Velletri is perfect for quiet exploration in the fall sunshine.

www.comune.velletri.rm.it

BOBBIO
EMILIA-ROMAGNA

Medieval majesty

The fine early medieval town of Bobbio is set on the Trebbia River in a valley described by Ernest Hemingway as the most beautiful in the world.

www.comune.bobbio.pc.it

SAN GIMIGNANO
TUSCANY

A medieval Manhattan

Its many towers give this town an unmistakable, fairytale profile. Its narrow streets may be crowded in summer, but in October it is a peaceful and romantic place to stay.

See pp268–9

"There were once at least 72 towers rising up high above San Gimignano's city walls, in its finest era."

MONFORTE D'ALBA
PIEDMONT

The finest food and wine in the land

In the heart of the Barolo region, the medieval town of Monforte d'Alba is a gourmet's paradise where truffles perfume the fall air.

www.piemontefeel.com

ACTIVE ADVENTURES

SAN GIUSEPPE JATO The colors of the Sicilian countryside in the fall

VAL DI VARA
LIGURIA

Kayaking down the Vara

Tackle the challenging white waters of the Vara torrent as it courses through *borghi rotondi* (round villages), such as Varese Ligure.

www.turismoprovincia.laspezia.it/en/destinations/val-di-vara

SAN GIUSEPPE JATO
SICILY

Superb river and lake fishing

This little town in western Sicily is the starting point for fly and spin fishing trips to the many rivers, lakes, and reservoirs set amid the beautiful countryside of the Conca dOro.

See pp262–3

PANTELLERIA
SICILY

Warm seas surround Italy's southernmost island

Snorkeling, diving, sailing: Pantelleria, the "almost African" island to the south of Sicily, is the perfect autumn destination for lovers of water sports.

www.pantelleria.it

ASIAGO
VENETO

Bungee jumping from one of the highest bridges in Europe

A popular tourist destination in summer and in winter, Asiago also offers the chance for braver visitors to bungee jump off a bridge.

www.bungy.it

VEGLIO
PIEDMONT

Take to the trees

Make your way through the forest, high in the air, via rope bridges, ladders, and swings, at this adventure park with a difference in the Valle di Mossa.

See pp266–7

FAMILY GETAWAYS

TRIESTE Lovely marina of Sestiere, along the coast from Trieste

TRIESTE
FRIULI-VENEZIA GIULIA

Celebrate the sea and sailing at La Barcolana

Thousands of sailing boats, little and large, throng the waters off the coast of the Adriatic port of Trieste during the annual regatta of La Barcolana.

See pp258–9

MORBEGNO
LOMBARDY

Something for everyone

Morbegno is the gateway to the Valtellina, offering hiking, riding, and cycling trips; whitewater rafting and canyoning; lovely flora and fauna; spas, good food, and fine wines.

www.portedivaltellina.it

ALBEROBELLO
PUGLIA

In the village of the *trulli*

Alberobello is a village entirely composed of *trulli*, typical Pugliese dry-stone houses, with conical roofs and dazzling white walls – a stay in one is a magical experience.

See pp270–71

LAMPEDUSA
SICILY

A safe haven for turtles

The lovely, unspoiled island of Lampedusa is one of the few sites in the Mediterranean where the loggerhead sea turtle (*Caretta caretta*) can lay its eggs in safety.

www.lampedusa.it

BOMARZO
LAZIO

Renaissance rock monsters

Wander through the magnificent gardens of the 16th-century Parco dei Mostri, catching glimpses of rock-carved creatures amid overgrown temples and theaters.

www.bomarzo.net

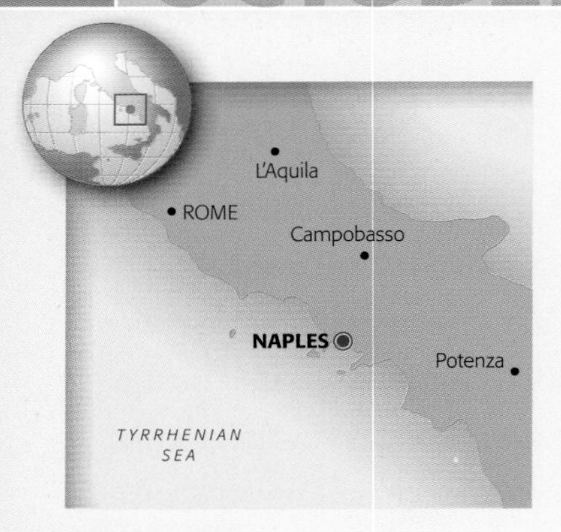

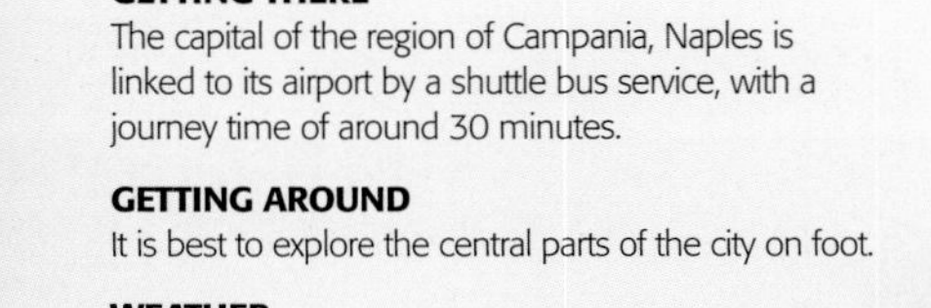

GETTING THERE
The capital of the region of Campania, Naples is linked to its airport by a shuttle bus service, with a journey time of around 30 minutes.

GETTING AROUND
It is best to explore the central parts of the city on foot.

WEATHER
The average maximum daytime temperature is 72°F (22°C), with frequent sunny days.

ACCOMMODATIONS
In the historic center, the Romeo is a designer hotel offering all modern comforts, pared-down elegance, and a spa; doubles from US$248; www.romeohotel.it

The Chiaja Hotel de Charme is in a refurbished 18th-century residence a short stroll from Piazza del Plebiscito; doubles from US$135; www.hotelchiaia.it

Also in the Chiaia quarter is the comfortable and welcoming B&B Cappella Vecchia 11; doubles from US$102; www.cappellavecchia11.it

EATING OUT
Dora is one of the best fish restaurants in Naples (dinner from US$62), tel. 081 680519.

For a really superb pizza, visit Da Michele, where five generations of master pizza-makers have been serving delighted customers since 1870 (from US$20); www.damichele.net

Classic Neapolitan cooking (from US$28) is served at Cantina di Via Sapienza; tel. 081 459078.

PRICE FOR TWO
US$245–395 per day including accommodations, meals, car rental, and Campania Artecard.

FURTHER INFORMATION
www.inaples.it

CITY OF DAZZLING CONTRASTS

When Naples was the capital of one of the most important kingdoms in Italy, as it was from 1282 until 1861, its heart was Piazza del Plebiscito. This monumental square is framed by a wide arc of Neo-Classical columns, flanking the church of San Francesco di Paola, and, on its eastern side, stands the Palazzo Reale, residence of the Neapolitan kings and a potent symbol of their former power.

Piazza del Plebiscito marks a definite change in the urban pattern of the center of the city: on one side are monuments that testify to the Viceroyal and Bourbon history of Naples; on the other lies the dense network of alleyways and streets that is the Quartieri Spagnoli, or Spanish Quarter. This is a district of crowded, low buildings, draped washing lines, and crumbling courtyards, yet it nonetheless also displays traces of ancient splendors. Naples's many such contrasts invite exploration.

Main: View of stately Piazza del Plebiscito and Chiesa di San Francesco di Paola, one of Naples's most splendid churches

Palazzo Reale

Designed in the 17th century by Domenico Fontana, the Palazzo Reale (Royal Palace) has been modified over the centuries to adapt to changing times, but the façade, 587-ft (169-m) long and decorated with statues of the kings of Naples, the main courtyard, and parts of the interior retain their original form. An imposing staircase leads to the royal apartments, a series of sumptuous rooms with some of their original furnishings, as well as the delightful little court theater and the Cappella Reale (Royal Chapel), with an altar of gilded bronze inlaid with precious stones.

Left (top to bottom): Two Neapolitan icons of Italian cinema: the actors Totò (right) and Peppino De Filippo; bust of San Gennaro in the Duomo; lines of washing hung out to dry across the narrow streets of Quartieri Spagnoli

Right (left to right): Stalls selling carved statues for nativity scenes; monks in conversation in the cloister of the Chiesa di Santa Chiara; *sfogliatelle* (puff pastries filled with cream or ricotta cheese), in a Neapolitan coffee house

Via Chiaia and Via Toledo (which the Neapolitans call Via Roma) are elegant shopping streets, lined with façades bearing the most illustrious names in Italian fashion, the most famous *pasticcerie* (pastry shops), and the most stylish bars. The nearby Maschio Angioino, by contrast, is an imposing waterside castle evocative of the time when Naples was the seat of a splendid Renaissance court.

Spaccanapoli, the long street that slices through the city from east to west, is the heart of the oldest, most picturesque and chaotic area of the city. Here you will find lovely churches and ancient palazzi which, although often sorely in need of restoration, may still contain a magnificent noble staircase, a splendid carved doorway, or a courtyard enclosed by a harmonious loggia.

And there is yet another Naples: a city of culture, lively with concerts and theater performances, home to some of Italy's most important museums filled with treasures from what was once one of the most flourishing regions of Magna Graecia and the Roman Empire.

Naples may at first seem a diamond in the rough, but its many dazzling facets soon shine through.

Above: View of Maschio Angioino, also known as Castel Nuovo

NAPOLI DIARY

Naples is a city of contrasts: its crowded streets are full of life and color, its ancient monuments and museums tranquil places of culture and beauty. It is a city crying out to be explored and, with five days at your disposal, you can enjoy all its many charms as you slowly wander the ancient streets. *(See also pp102–3)*

Five Days of Treasures

DAY 1 Start your day in Piazza del Plebiscito and, after visiting the Palazzo Reale and San Francesco di Paola, look in at the nearby Teatro San Carlo before heading off to shop in Via Roma. Pause at Pintauro for the best *sfogliatelle* in Naples, or at the Gran Caffè Gambrinus for excellent coffee in an elegant turn-of-the-century setting.

DAY 2 Tour the Maschio Angioino, the castle built in 1284 and rebuilt in the 15th century. Be sure to see the dungeons and the excavations, as well as the paintings and sculptures in the Museo Civico here.

DAY 3 Devote most of the day to the Museo Archeologico Nazionale, one of the most important museums in Europe, where finds from excavations from Campania, including Pompeii *(see pp76–7)* and Herculaneum *(see pp24–5)*, are displayed. From here go to the Duomo, which holds the remains of San Gennaro, patron saint of Naples.

DAY 4 Walk along Via San Biagio dei Librai, one section of Spaccanapoli, to feel part of bustling Neapolitan street life. Turn into Via San Gregorio Armeno, famous for its artisan workshops, where the traditional statues that feature in Neapolitan nativity scenes have been made for centuries.

DAY 5 Head for Piazza del Gesù, where the Chiesa di Santa Chiara stands, with its famous cloister decorated with majolica tiles in lovely floral designs. Visit the nearby chapel of San Severo. Its beautiful statue of Veiled Christ is a masterpiece of shroud depiction, the fabric convincingly draped around the face and body.

Dos and Don'ts

- ✓ Buy a Campania Artecard: this all-inclusive ticket covers entrance to many museums and use of public transportation.
- ✓ For a lasting souvenir, choose a nativity statue from the famous craft workshops in Via San Gregorio Armeno.
- ✓ Try to see a performance at the Teatro San Carlo. For more information, visit: www.teatrosancarlo.it
- ✗ Don't wear flamboyant or precious jewelry or an expensive watch in the streets of Naples: they may be snatched. It is also wise not to carry too much cash.

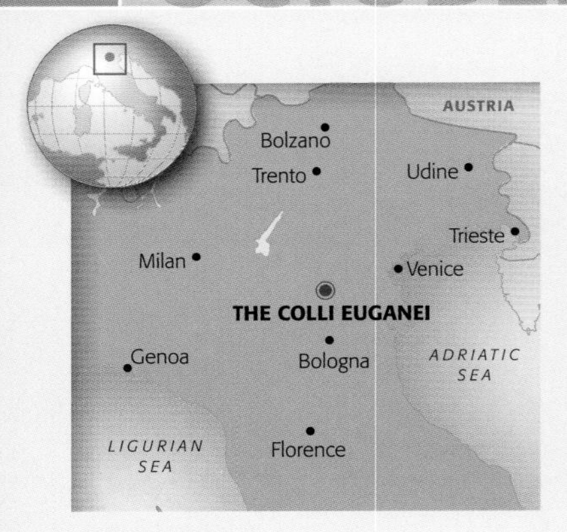

GETTING THERE
The Colli Euganei are in the Veneto region of northern Italy. The closest airport is Venice, from where it takes around 1 hour to reach Este by car.

GETTING AROUND
You will need a car to explore the Colli Euganei.

WEATHER
Summer is turning to fall, but daytime temperatures still reach a pleasant 64°F (18°C).

ACCOMMODATIONS
There are numerous excellent and hospitable B&Bs in Este (doubles from US$68), including Il Poeta (www.bbpoeta.it) and Annamaria (www.bandbannamaria.it).

Il Ca' Rocca, just outside Monselice, offers rural charm and modern comfort, plus gardens and a pool; doubles from US$108; www.carocca.it

The luxurious Abano Grand Hotel has an excellent spa with thermal pools, gym, health and beauty treatments; doubles from US$380; www.abanograndhotel.it

EATING OUT
Excellent regional home cooking (dinner from US$42) is served at Il Gambero di Este; tel. 0429 3157.

Traditional dishes and specials based on truffles and wild mushrooms (from US$55) can be sampled at the Torre di Monselice; tel. 0429 73752.

At elegant Casa Vecia di Abano Terme you can dine on grilled meats and game (from US$55) in the lovely garden; tel. 0498 600138.

PRICE FOR TWO
US$245–475 per day including accommodations, meals, and car rental.

FURTHER INFORMATION
www.collieuganei.biz

Festa della Giuggiola

The *giuggiola* (jujube) is a fruit the size of an olive, which the Romans brought back from north Africa. You will spot the intense red of its berries on local trees. When the fruit is mature, its skin becomes wrinkly and the pulp sweet, its flavor reminiscent of a ripe date. The town of Arquà Petrarca dedicates an annual festival to the fruit, with music, dance, displays, and processions in historical costume. It takes place on the first two Sundays in October and provides an opportunity to taste a range of products based on the fruit: jams, syrups, and the famous *brodo di giuggiole* (literally, "jujube broth"), a traditional Veneto liqueur.

Above (left and right): Panoramic view of the Colli Euganei and the Veneto plain; dramatic Castello di Monselice

GREEN HILLS OF HISTORY

Millions of years ago, a chain of volcanoes was responsible for the creation of the Colli Euganei, a succession of rounded hills that suddenly interrupt the monotony of the Veneto plain, ruffling the horizon with their characteristic green outline. Today there is no volcanic activity, the only active traces of that time being the thermal spas with which the area is richly supplied. All that is left of the volcanoes themselves is this line of gentle hills, garlanded with long rows of vines and swathed in red in the fall, shaded with dark patches of woodland and dotted with the bright walls of castles and towns built upon their slopes.

These towns are astonishingly rich in history. Este, for example, was the birthplace of one of the most powerful dynasties in Italy – the Este family – which was destined for a significant role as the ruling elite of Ferrara, Modena, and Reggio Emilia. Este is a delightful settlement, gathered around a castle built in the 14th century over the ruins of an earlier fortification. It is an imposing building, with a keep that watches over the entire town, encircled by powerful, battlemented walls forming a broad polygon punctuated by 12 towers. Este's red-hued fortifications stand out against the surrounding green hills, making the town's profile unmistakeable and testifying to the power of the Este family down the centuries. Este is not the only town surrounded by a ring of walls in this gently rolling countryside. Nearby Montagnana, on a hilltop, is encircled by a spectacular crown of battlements. These fortifications have survived miraculously intact over the centuries and are among the best preserved in Europe. They stand as a reminder of the Middle Ages, when the region was the setting for bitter battles between rival dynasties.

The towns and abbeys of the Colli Euganei are treasure houses of fine art and traditional culture, but there is more. In the spas, which make good use of the hot mineral water springs exploited since the Roman era, visitors can try a wide range of beauty, health, and relaxation treatments, as well as testing the curative properties of the water. The landscape in fall – rich in shades of red and gold – is a lovely setting for long walks or bicycle rides on quiet paths, many of which run through vineyards where you can sample the new wine. Today, the peaceful landscape of the Colli Euganei is a secret paradise just waiting to be discovered.

Main: View of the Canale Bisatto flowing between the old buildings of Este
Below (left and right): *Castrato alla veneta*, a local mutton stew; view of the Santuario Giubilare delle Sette Chiese at Monselice

Above: Aerial view of Este, with the Colli Euganei in the background

HILLSIDE DIARY

The lovely landscape of the Colli Euganei is especially beautiful in the fall, cloaked in magical colors. The weather is still warm and the historic villages, monuments, and spas are more peaceful now than in high summer. It is well worth allowing plenty of time to seek out and enjoy this region's hidden treasures – six days is ideal.

Six Tranquil Days

DAY 1

Devote your first day to Este. Begin your tour at the castle, and then move on to the Museo Nazionale Atestino, which holds an interesting array of objects from ancient Ateste, as the town was originally known. After lunch in the heart of the village, be sure to visit the convent of Santa Maria della Consolazione, which has a 15th-century cloister and a splendid mosaic from the Roman era.

DAY 2

Spend the day in Monselice. Once a proud, fortified city, it is dominated by its magnificent Castello. Climb the path, lined by six chapels, to the Chiesa di San Giorgio: together they form the Giubilare delle Sette Chiese ("seven churches"). Among other must-see places here are the 13th-century Duomo and the splendid Ca' Marcello, a castle dating from the 14th century.

DAY 3

Pay a visit to Montagnana, set among rolling green hills. The village is notable for its intact walls, fortified by 24 towers, that entirely surround the old center of the village. Here you'll find the lovely 16th-century Duomo, while outside the walls stands the handsome Villa Pisani, the work of Andrea Palladio.

DAY 4–6

Treat yourself to a day at the Abano Terme spa: you can choose from a wide variety of health or beauty treatments.

Today, take a tour along the Colli Euganei *Strada dei Vini* (Wine Road), calling in at the hillside vineyards and cellars open for wine tastings.

Visit Arquà Petrarca, where the great Italian lyric poet Petrarch chose to spend his final years; his former home is frescoed with scenes inspired by his poetry. If you time your visit right, you will also be here to enjoy the lively Festa della Giuggiola and buy some jujube produce.

Dos and Don'ts

- ✗ Don't drive at too fast a pace along the hillside roads; take your time and appreciate the gorgeous landscape.
- ✓ Rent a mountain bike to explore the many trails among the hills; the views alone make it well worth the effort.
- ✓ Buy a hand-painted ceramic vase, a typical craft in this area of the Veneto.

GETTING THERE
The abbey of San Vincenzo al Volturno lies in western Molise. The nearest airport is Naples, about 1 1/2 hours away by car. From the airport take the A1 freeway, exit at Caianello, and continue on A-roads.

GETTING AROUND
It is best to rent a car to get around the countryside.

WEATHER
Fall tinges the landscape with warm colors; the days are often clear with mild temperatures.

ACCOMMODATIONS
Near Castel San Vincenzo and the abbey, the *agriturismo* Il Casale di San Lorenzo offers comfortable independent apartments and a good restaurant. Doubles from US$35 per person for B&B; www.ilcasaledisanlorenzo.it

Antica Dimora 191 is in the center of Isernia, in a palazzo dating from the end of the 19th century. Rooms, furnished with period furniture, start from US$95; www.anticadimora191.com

Azienda Acquasalsa is surrounded by the lush countryside of Agnone: the stone buildings have been restored with great taste and are comfortably equipped. Rooms from US$40 per person, for B&B; www.acquasalsa.it

EATING OUT
At Cantina dell'Eremo in Castel San Vincenzo you can sample local cuisine including fresh pasta, soups, and lamb, from US$34 (tel. 0865 952 043). In Isernia try the food at Pantagruel, using traditional Molise produce. Meals cost about US$28–35 (tel. 0865 2126).

PRICE FOR TWO
Budget for around US$230 per day for food and accommodations, and two or three days' car rental.

FURTHER INFORMATION
www.sanvincenzoabbey.org

Campitello Matese

The road up to the village is long, tortuous, and winding. At the top, however, an extraordinary landscape opens up, with the plain below and the Abruzzi mountains in the distance. From Campitello Matese, a resort with ski slopes and ski-lifts, the ascent to the heights of Monte Miletto is extremely rewarding – you can go by chairlift or on foot (walking takes around an hour). From the top, you can see as far as the Majella and the Gran Sasso, the highest and most impressive peaks in the Apennines.

In 1832, a peasant discovered the barrel-vaulted Crypt of Epifanio, in the shape of a Greek cross and decorated with exquisite frescoes.

Main: San Vincenzo al Volturno, seen through the Portico dei Pellegrini
Inset: The Volturno River in the Parco Nazionale d'Abruzzo
Above: Central nave in the abbey of San Vincenzo al Volturno

ANCIENT SPIRITUALITY

ALTHOUGH ONLY A FEW PARTS OF THE ANCIENT MONASTIC COMPLEX remain standing, San Vincenzo al Volturno is still striking in its grandeur, reminding visitors of a time when it was one of the most powerful Benedictine monasteries in southern Italy. Its history is known thanks to an exceptional document, the *Chronicon Vulturnense*, an illuminated manuscript drawn up in around 1130, which describes the life of the building chronologically. In 731 three noblemen from Benevento: Paldo, Taso, and Ato, visited the abbey of Farfa – a Benedictine monastery in the region of Lazio – and the abbot at the time suggested that they should found a monastery near Volturno. On their return, the three men honored the request and the monastery was built and prospered. Somehow, the monks became embroiled in political quarrels between two powerful Germanic tribes, the Franks, who controlled northern Italy, and the Lombards, established in the south. In the resulting power struggle, the then Lombard abbot Potone was forced to

Left (left to right): Bell in the papal foundry of Campane Marinelli; alleyway in the heart of Isernia; the village of Castel San Vincenzo; the remains of the ancient Basilica di San Vincenzo al Volturno

Right: Distinctive "tear-shaped" *caciocavallo* cheese from Agnone

Above: The Fontana della Fraterna in Isernia

swear allegiance to the Frankish king. However, these were just minor problems compared to what was to come in the late 9th century when marauding Arabs sacked the monastery.

In the 11th century, San Vincenzo al Volturno was moved to a more secure site on the right bank of the Volturno River, but entered a long period of decline. Abandoned for centuries and plundered for building materials, the monastery has nonetheless yielded up some priceless treasures over the years. The first great discovery was in 1832 when a peasant uncovered the barrel-vaulted Crypt of Epifanio. In the shape of a Greek cross and decorated with frescoes of exquisite craftsmanship, it was properly excavated a century or so later, revealing an extraordinary complex in terms of its scale and richness of decoration. The oldest part of the abbey is composed of two churches with assorted monastic rooms: the refectory, the kitchens, the lavatorium (the communal baths for the monks), the cloister, and offices. The most recent wing, which dates from the beginning of the 12th century, suffered severe damage in the course of World War II and unfortunately has been significantly modified.

MONASTIC DIARY

San Vincenzo al Volturno lies close to Castel San Vincenzo, the largest Molise town in the Parco Nazionale d'Abruzzo, an area that protects a wide range of flora and fauna. Four days is enough time to see the ancient abbey and explore an area seldom visited by tourists, an unspoiled wilderness and one of the last European preserves of the brown bear and wolf.

Four Days in the Parco d'Abruzzo

DAY 1

Visit the monastery of San Vincenzo al Volturno. Don't miss the excavations of the oldest part, and in particular the crypts of Epifanio and Giosuè, which contain precious frescoes. Explore nearby Castel San Vincenzo, set in a picturesque position above the artificial lake of Volturno and an ideal place to stop for a lunch of *sagne e fagioli,* a local bean and pasta dish.

DAY 2

Spend a day walking in the wilds of the Parco Nazionale d'Abruzzo: there is a visitor center and museum at Castel San Vincenzo devoted to Apennine wildlife. Pack a picnic and take one of the many recommended excursions. One of the most striking is the trail leading to the lake near the village, starting from Monte della Rocchetta, where the Volturno River rises.

DAY 3

Drive to Isernia, a town that dates back to pre-Roman times with a pleasant historic center around Piazza Celestino V, site of the medieval Fontana della Fraterna. Look out for the elderly ladies working at *tombolo,* a traditional lace craft, outside their houses.

For a change of scenery, drive on to the ski resort of Campitello Matese for some mountain activity and views of the snow-topped Apennines.

DAY 4

Tour Agnone, famous for the manufacture of bells. The town is surrounded by thick woods and is home to a pretty parish church dedicated to Sant'Emidio, which contains splendid 19th-century sculptures by Giovanni Dupré and his daughter Amalia. The Museo Internazionale della Campana (International Bell Museum) is also worth a visit, next to the papal bell foundry Marinelli, one of the oldest in the world.

Dos and Don'ts

- ✓ Consult the website www.parcoabruzzo.it or a visitor center for information concerning trails and walks in the park. Don't go walking in the Parco Nazionale d'Abruzzo without a good map.
- ✓ If you are in search of souvenirs, Agnone is famous for its bells and its goldsmiths' workshops, and Isernia is known for its lace.
- ✗ Don't drop in unexpected to San Vincenzo al Volturno. You must make a reservation several weeks ahead in writing: www.sanvincenzoabbey.org
- ✓ Buy some of the products of the area scented with local truffles (the cheeses are delicious).

GETTING THERE
The nearest airport to both Trento and Rovereto is at Verona. To reach the two towns – they are less than 19 miles (30 km) apart – follow the A22 to the Brenner pass (the main axis) by car, or take the train.

GETTING AROUND
The town centers can be visited on foot or by using public transportation.

WEATHER
Expect mild temperatures around 66°F (19°C), although it can be chilly in the evenings.

ACCOMMODATIONS
In Trento's historic center, the Accademia, a restored palazzo, has comfortable well-equipped rooms from US$217 (www.accademiahotel.it). Also in the town center, the B&B Elisa is elegant and welcoming with doubles at US$102 (www.bbelisa.com).

In Rovereto, the modern Nerocubo is a designer hotel with character, and a rich collection of modern art. Rooms from US$133 (www.nerocubohotel.it).

The friendly Hotel Rovereto offers good service and nice rooms from US$155 (www.hotelrovereto.it).

EATING OUT
In Trento, the charming 18th-century *stube* (beer cellar) Osteria Le Due Spade offers imaginative local cooking with a tasting menu at US$60 (www.leduespade.com). At Il Volt, sample excellent Trentino cooking for about US$35 (tel. 0461 983 776).

In Rovereto, elegant cuisine is prepared at the centrally located Il Doge; meals from US$55 (tel. 0464 486 737). At Il Novecento (in Hotel Rovereto), you can dine on Trento and Mantova cooking from around US$48.

PRICE FOR TWO
US$245–365 per day for meals, accommodations, and a Trento Card.

FURTHER INFORMATION
www.apt.trento.it; www.visitrovereto.it

The Wines of Trentino

In Trentino, vineyards cloak the valley floors and the lower slopes of the mountains, thriving on the ancient terraces. These hills produce some of the most prized wines in Italy, such as Trentodoc, among the most sought-after Italian sparkling wines. Other wines include the perfumed Nosiola, which gets its name from its distinctive hazelnut *(nocciola)* aroma, and the great Trentino red wines, Marzemino and Teroldego, perfect with cheeses or the robust meat dishes characteristic of the flavorful local cuisine.

Above (left to right): South Tyrolean *canederli* (dumplings) made with cheese and served with leeks and tomatoes; the house-museum of Futurist artist Fortunato Depero; view of Rovereto beside the River Adige
Main: Cupola above the piazza of Rovereto's MART gallery

Above: Palazzo delle Albere in Trento, home to MART, a modern art gallery

BACK TO THE FUTURE

FOUNDED BY THE ROMANS IN 23 BC, Trento still bears the imprint of its origins in its orderly grid of main streets. The town's strategic position in a major Alpine pass made it an important staging post for armies traveling between Italy and Germany and this is what persuaded the king of Germany and Holy Roman Emperor, Conrad II, to create the Bishopric of Trentino in the 11th century, to be governed by a loyal and sympathetic prince-bishop. For 800 years, prince-bishops ruled the town which, profiting from its connections and location, gradually accumulated the impressive collection of splendid buildings that can still be seen in the center today.

The town was centered around the Piazza Duomo, once the site of a cemetery in which San Vigilio, its patron saint, was buried – the splendid cathedral whose left flank forms one side of the square is dedicated to him. In 1545, the cathedral was the setting for the Council of Trent, one of the Catholic Church's most important councils and its response to the groundswell of Protestant reform. Leading off Piazza Duomo are Trento's most elegant streets, lined with palazzi whose exteriors are decorated with beautiful frescoes that have earned the town the name of "painted city." These streets and buildings date in part from the era of Bernardo Clesio, prince-bishop between 1514 and 1539, who attracted many skillful architects and artists to work in the town. The Castello del Buonconsiglio is a fortress built in the 13th century to control the road to Germany. In the 15th century, the Torre dell'Aquila (Eagle Tower) was added to the castle and decorated with a beautiful cycle of frescoes. Bernardo Clesio then added the Magno Palazzo, a grand Renaissance residence, to the fortress and created a building that combines both military and luxurious residential functions. It is a fine addition to the town's historic center.

However, a stay in Trento is incomplete without a visit to MART, the gallery of modern art of Rovereto and Trento. Part of the museum is in the Palazzo delle Albere, an impressive 16th-century villa-fortress, but the main museum site is at Rovereto, 19 miles (30 km) from Trento, in an area once famous only for its wines but, today, getting a reputation for its contemporary art. The gallery contains a very fine collection of masterpieces from the 1920s to the present day, as well as often holding important temporary exhibitions. The structure built to house the artworks – the work of the Swiss architect Mario Botta – is also magnificent. The most striking element of the building is its huge glass cupola, which floods the museum with light on sunny days.

Below (left to right): Detail from *Ciclo dei Mesi* (Cycle of the Months), frescoes in the Torre dell'Aquila in the Castello del Buonconsiglio in Trento; the sign of the venerable restaurant Al Vo, the oldest tavern in Trento; the imposing fortifications of the Castello del Buonconsiglio

TYROLEAN DIARY

Trento has an impressive historic center with a cathedral and castle, gentrified by aristocratic palazzi that line its elegant streets. Four days will give you time to explore the town, along with its (and Rovereto's) other attractions: gorgeous Alpine countryside, great hospitality, and a fine museum of contemporary art.

Four Days of Art in the Alps

DAY 1

Start off in Trento at the Piazza del Duomo, with its 18th-century Baroque Fontana di Nettuno in the center and the Cazuffi houses, their façades decorated with frescoes, on the northern side. The piazza is also home to the lovely Romanesque Duomo. Attached to the cathedral is the Castelletto, a medieval fortified building with a slim tower, the Torre di San Romedio. Explore the adjacent streets, lined with the most beautiful palazzi.

DAY 2

Visit the grand Castello del Buonconsiglio – don't miss the Venetian-Gothic loggia, with wonderful views; the elegant arcade is graced with frescoes by Renaissance painter Romanino. Another must-see sight is the Torre dell'Aquila with its *Ciclo dei Mesi* (Cycle of the Months), a fine example of Gothic painting. Afterward, enjoy a plate of Alpine cheeses and ham with a glass of delicious local wine in one of the *osteria* (taverns) in the center of town.

DAY 3

Visit the Palazzo delle Albere, a 16th-century residence that is now a branch of MART, the museum of modern and contemporary art. In the afternoon, pack a picnic and pick up some maps for walking trails from the tourist office – simply hop on a bus to one of the smaller Alpine towns or lakes. After your exertions, spend the evening at some of the wine cellars in the town, which offer the chance to try excellent wines and Trentino grappas.

DAY 4

For your last day head over to Rovereto to visit the other branch of MART, where the gallery's Futurist collection is displayed. Afterward, go for a stroll in the historic center of this lively little town – its pretty medieval quarter is dominated by a castle. Don't miss the house-museum of the painter Fortunato Depero, which was designed by the artist himself. There are bicycle rental shops around Trento so you may like to ride to Rovereto and back.

Dos and Don'ts

- ✓ Buy the Trento Card: there are two types, valid for 24 or 48 hours respectively, which give you free entry to various museums and wine cellars, and travel on public transportation.
- ✓ Take the Trento-Sardagna cable car to the Parco delle Poze for a magnificent view over the town.
- ✗ Don't go on a wine tasting tour if you have to drive later.
- ✓ For information on the opening hours of MART, and on the temporary exhibitions, consult the website www.mart.trento.it

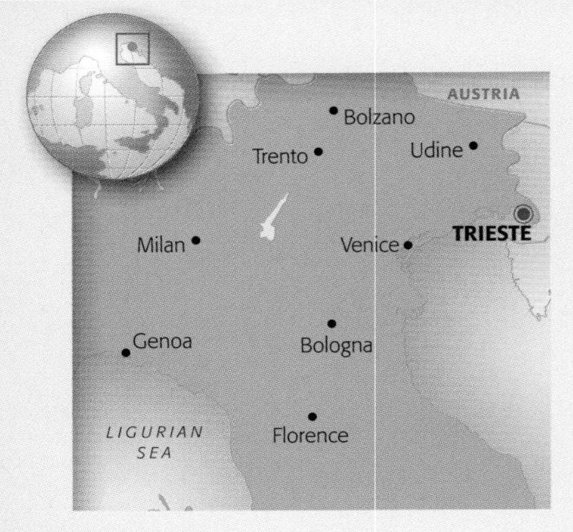

GETTING THERE
Located in the far southeast of Friuli-Venezia Giulia, Trieste lies on the gulf of the same name, on the border with Slovenia. The city is served by Ronchi dei Legionari Airport, from where a shuttle bus service runs to the city center, taking around 1 hour.

GETTING AROUND
Trieste has an efficient public transportation network.

WEATHER
October in Trieste brings frequent sunny days, with maximum temperatures of around 64°F (18°C).

ACCOMMODATIONS
The friendly B&B Crispi is in the center of town; family rooms from US$135; tel. 0346 966 5499.

Hotel Riviera & Maximilian's has views over the Golfo di Trieste and Castello di Miramare; family rooms from US$352; www.hotelrivieraemaximilian.com

EATING OUT
There are plenty of restaurants specializing in fresh fish, including elegant Al Faro, with good sea views (dinner from US$55; tel. 040 410 092); La Lampara, where you can try *brodetto alla triestina* (Trieste fish soup) and *polenta e sardoni in saor* (polenta with piquant sardines); (from US$48; tel. 040 220 352); or Scabar, famous for its outstanding seafood (from US$55; www.scabar.it).

For something a bit different, try Suban, where the food shows Hungarian, Viennese, and Slovenian influences (from US$55; www.suban.it).

PRICE FOR A FAMILY OF FOUR
US$355–435 per day including accommodations, meals, and the "T for You Card."

FURTHER INFORMATION
www.triesteturismo.net
www.trieste-tourism.com

The Risiera di San Sabba

The Risiera di San Sabba, a former rice mill in the industrial zone to the south of Trieste, has a tragic history. From 1943–45 it was used by the Nazis and the Fascists as Italy's only concentration camp. Initially established as a transit camp for detainees destined for Auschwitz, it soon became a death camp in its own right, at which thousands of members of the city's Jewish community, and other prisoners, met their deaths. It is now a National Monument and a deeply moving museum of remembrance.

Main: Trieste's famous boat race, watched over by the city's lighthouse, the Faro della Vittoria

SPECTACULAR REGATTA

THE SAILS OUT ON THE WATER seem to go on for ever, their white wings fluttering, performing gentle arabesques over the waves. This is the sight that greets you at La Barcolana, one of the biggest regattas in the world, which takes place each October at Barcola, on the edge of Trieste. The boats are of every shape and size – any kind of boat, as long as it has sails, can take part in the event, and nearly 2,000 are here to take up the challenge.

The course is a rough quadrilateral around 16 nautical miles (30 km) in length, with the farthest marker buoy actually in Slovenian waters. The competitors come from multiple, diverse backgrounds, brought together by their passion for the sea and for sailing. For most of them, the appeal of the regatta lies not so much in the competition itself but rather in the possibility of sailing side-by-side with professional yachtsmen and women and with some "giants of the sea" – boats built by designers of international fame, using cutting-edge techniques and materials.

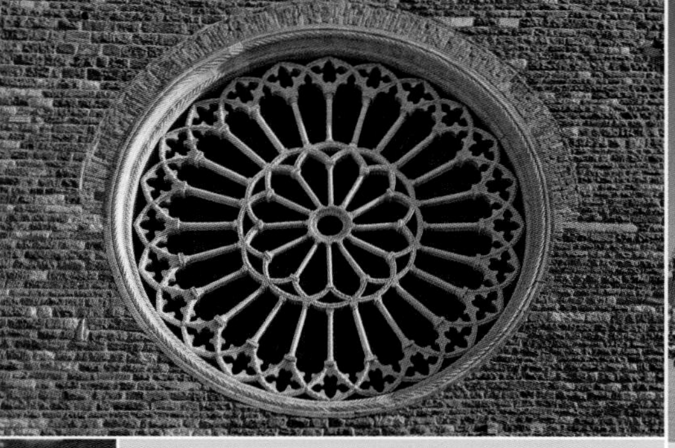

Above: Façade of Palazzo Luogotenenza, in Piazza dell'Unità d'Italia

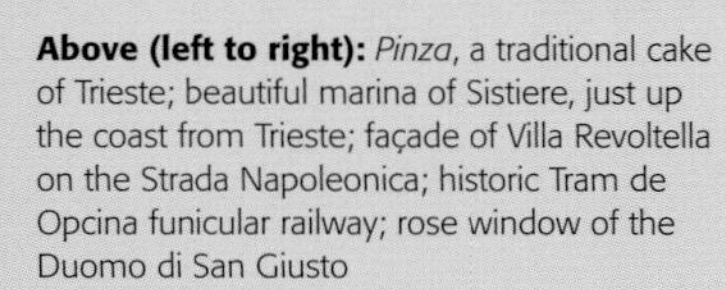

Above (left to right): *Pinza*, a traditional cake of Trieste; beautiful marina of Sistiere, just up the coast from Trieste; façade of Villa Revoltella on the Strada Napoleonica; historic Tram de Opcina funicular railway; rose window of the Duomo di San Giusto

Below: Elegant Castello di Miramare, perched above the clear waters of a marine preserve

At 10am on the dot, on the second Sunday of October, all the boats line up for the start, and it doesn't really matter if, in the evening, with the maximum time allowed having elapsed, quite a few stragglers are yet to pass the finish line. A day of thrills and entertainment has been had by everyone, sailors and spectators, and perhaps especially by the lucky ones who have wangled a space on a friend's boat in exchange for a bottle of good wine to be drunk on its return.

Trieste is the backdrop to this lively festival, a historic border city stretched out along the shore on Italy's extreme eastern edge, where a kaleidoscope of traditions create an atmosphere that is simply unique. The monument that best symbolizes this fusion between the cultures of Eastern and Western Europe is Castello di Miramare, from which a cannon shot signals the start of the race. Built in the 1850s by Archduke Maximilian of Habsburg, brother of the Austrian emperor Franz Joseph and governor of the Lombardo-Veneto region, it dominates a headland of particular beauty. To see it from the sea, especially from a boat in La Barcolana, is an unforgettable experience.

LA BARCOLANA DIARY

Set against the curve of a karst plateau, the shape of Trieste is like a stadium for sailing, giving the whole city good views over La Barcolana. The week leading up to the race is a time of general festivity, when there is even more than usual to see and do. Spend four days getting to know the city, with the regatta as your grand finale.

Four Days on the Gulf

DAY 1

Begin with a stroll in Trieste's "drawing room" – Piazza dell'Unità d'Italia – a fine, wide space open to the sea. Pause for a cappucino at the historic Caffè degli Specchi, then move on to explore the tranquil quarter of Teresiano, built in Neo-Classical style under the Habsburgs around the handsome Canal Grande. In the afternoon, take bus 8 or 10 from the central train station out to the Risiera di San Sabba.

DAY 2

Today take the Tram de Opcina, a funicular railway that runs from the center of the city to the Strada Napoleonica. A promenade much loved by the people of Trieste, it offers enchanting views over the entire city. In the afternoon, visit the 19th-century chalet-style Villa Revoltella, set in spectacular gardens.

DAY 3

Spend the day in San Giusto, the ancient heart of the city, set on a hill. Trieste's cathedral, of the same name, is here, with fine 13th-century Venetian-style mosaics. Here too is Castello di San Giusto, an ancient fortress which is home to the Lapidario Tergestino, a collection of Roman mosaics, sculptures, and bas-reliefs. Beside the castle are the ruins of a Roman court of law.

DAY 4

If you don't have a place on a boat, arrive early at Castello di Miramare for the spectacular start of La Barcolana. Besides the magnificent gardens, it is worth exploring the sumptuously furnished interior. The visitor center here also has exhibitions on the Miramare marine reserve below the castle. Stay to watch the winning boats return during the afternoon.

Dos and Don'ts

- ✓ For all the information you need on La Barcolana events and schedules, visit: www.barcolana.it
- ✓ Return to Piazza dell'Unità d'Italia each evening before La Barcolana for free live concerts and additional, smaller races and regattas, and to see the boats moored along the quays.
- ✓ Buy the "T for You Card," which gives free admission to museums as well as free travel on public transportation.
- ✗ Don't use an umbrella if the cold Trieste wind known as the *Bora* is blowing: it will be a waste of effort. Instead, make sure you have a good rain- and windproof coat.

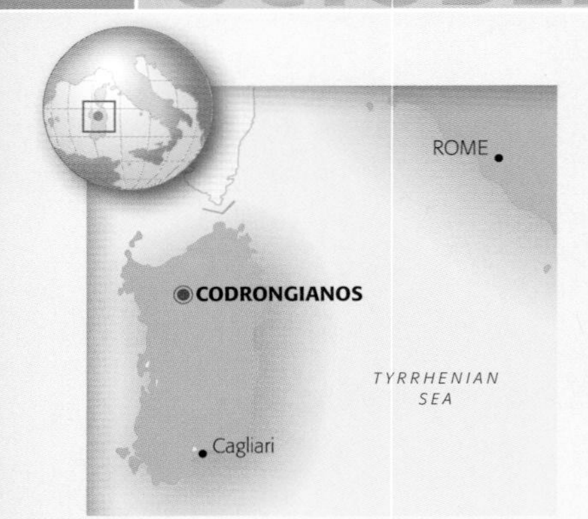

GETTING THERE
Codrongianos is situated in the interior of northern Sardinia, southeast of Sassari. The airport at Alghero is less than 31 miles (50 km) from Codrongianos.

GETTING AROUND
The best way of getting around the area is by car.

WEATHER
Expect frequent clear and sunny days, with moderately warm temperatures up to about 72°F (22°C). It can be quite cool in the evenings.

ACCOMMODATIONS
Guests at the small and pleasant Hotel Funtanarena, set among the green hills of Codrongianos, will find a warm welcome. Doubles from US$128; www.funtanarena.it

Near Porto Torres, the *agriturismo* Cuile de Molino offers excellent regional cooking and quiet, countryside hospitality from US$34 per person for bed and breakfast; www.cuiledemolino.it

EATING OUT
To sample a typical menu, from antipasto to *mirto* (after-dinner myrtle liqueur), go to the *agriturismo* Da Piero, near Codrongianos. Meals around US$42; www.agriturismofiori.com

Dine in elegant surroundings, overlooking the sea at Al Galeone in Porto Torres. It serves good fish dishes and grilled meats, as well as traditional Sardinian cuisine. Meals from US$42; www.ilgaleone.com

PRICE FOR TWO
You will spend around US$215 per day on meals and accommodations.

FURTHER INFORMATION
www.sardegnaturismo.it

Sardinian Myrtle

Cultivated all over Sardinia, and in particular in the north of the island, myrtle (*Myrtus communis*) is a shrub that produces small dark red or bluish-black berries. These are used to produce a liqueur that is obtained by macerating the berries in alcohol for several days (this is how it acquires its purple color) or alternatively macerating the shoots (in which case, the color will be white and pale green). The resulting liquid is filtered and a sugar syrup added. An aromatic liqueur emerges, best served ice-cold.

Above (left and right): Raised prehistoric altar at the archeological site of Monte d'Accoddi; *cossa prena* (stuffed leg of lamb with tomato sauce)
Main: Basilica della Santissima Trinità di Saccargia, built in stripes of black basalt and white limestone

ROMANESQUE SARDINIA

UNDER A CLEAR BLUE SKY TYPICAL OF NORTHERN SARDINIA, among rugged hills cloaked unevenly with aromatic Mediterranean shrubbery, not far from the village of Codrongianos, stands a genuine marvel: the Basilica della Santissima Trinità di Saccargia. Upon approaching the building, the visitor's initial reaction is almost one of disbelief. Its simple design displays an austere Romanesque magnificence. The powerful chromatic effect created by the alternating bands of white and black, limestone and basalt, and its imposing statuesque quality, give the building a sophistication and modernity that is an astonishing contrast with the barren and sparse wilderness in which it stands.

According to legend, the building has its origins in a journey made through the area by an aristocratic couple who enjoyed the generous hospitality of the local Camaldolese monks. Upon their return home, the couple prayed to the Madonna for a son. When the child was born, the pair thanked the monks by donating money for a grand new church, which was built and consecrated on October 5, 1116. Architects and master craftsmen were summoned from Pisa for the construction of the building. It was again skilled Pisan craftsmen who, a few years later, renewed the façade, added the bell tower, extended the interior, and built the walls. Inside, the nave – 95 ft (29 m) long and 20 ft (6 m) wide – opens out into two elegant chapels. In the central apse, luminous frescoes revealing Byzantine influence catch the eye, rare examples of 13th-century Sardinian painting. The church, infused with spirituality, is an invitation to meditation and is still visited by numerous pilgrims today. Although it was abandoned in the 16th century, it is largely intact in its original beauty.

Of the monastery of the Camaldolese monks, at one time a thriving religious complex, only a few poignant and crumbling ruins remain; but even these are a spectacle that visitors are unlikely to ignore.

'he alternating bands of vhite and black give the uilding a sophistication nd modernity that is an stonishing contrast with he barren wilderness in which it stands.

Inset: Decorative detail of the Basilica della Santissima Trinità di Saccargia
Below (left and right): The colorful and aromatic wild shrubs of the island; the extraordinary granite-dotted landscape of Sardinia's interior

Above: Wild horse in the Sardinian Mediterranean *macchia*

MACCHIA DIARY

Four days exploring Sardinia's interior will reveal the island's rich bounty: you'll find rugged *macchia*-covered hills dotted with granite boulders; dense, shady woodland; and lush green meadows. Among these natural riches there are Neolithic burial grounds, medieval watchtowers, and an architectural heritage of medieval churches.

Four Days Among the Myrtle

DAY 1

Visit the Basilica della Santissima Trinità di Saccargia, near Codrongianos, one of the most significant Romanesque churches in Italy. Typically Tuscan in its alternating bands of light and dark stone, the façade is beautiful, tall, and harmonious, preceded by a large arcaded portico flanked by a slender bell tower. The interior has a single nave, and contains a cycle of beautiful 13th-century Byzantine-influenced frescoes.

DAY 2

Not far from Platamona, to the north of Codrongianos, lies the Chiesa di San Michele, a lovely example of Sardinian Romanesque. Head back south inland to the archeological complex of Monte d'Accoddi, which dates back to the 3rd millennium BC. It is famous for its megalithic ziggurat-styled altar, used for propitiatory rites devoted to the fertility of the land. Return via Sassari, where you can do some souvenir shopping. In the evening, enjoy traditional Sardinian cuisine such as pork roasted over hot charcoal with aromatic herbs, and a glass of strong Cannonau wine.

DAY 3

Head north to the coast again to visit Porto Torres and the Basilica di San Gavino, the oldest example of Pisan-influenced Romanesque architecture in Sardinia. The church, built between 1030 and 1080, has an unusual feature in that it has two apses facing each other. Explore the town's Roman remains, then head along the coast to spend the afternoon at one of the beautiful local beaches.

DAY 4

To the south of Codrongianos visit Ardara, where the 11th-century Romanesque church of Santa Maria del Regno stands, with its characteristic façade in dark stone. Continue in an easterly direction to the fertile plain of Ozieri, where the church of Sant'Antioco di Bisarcio stands out: isolated on a rocky spur, its construction began in the 11th century. The building successfully combines Romanesque-Pisan architecture with French influences.

Dos and Don'ts

- ✓ Think about buying a rug or tapestry from Sassari – these are still handcrafted using ancient wooden looms.
- ✓ Visit the beach of Platamona, east of Porto Torres, which is backed by a pine forest and is ideal for a picnic.
- ✗ Don't drive fast: the roads in Sardinia's interior are not well maintained – drive carefully at low speeds.
- ✓ If you are looking for a souvenir, you could buy something made of cork. Grown locally, it is part of an ancient craft tradition.

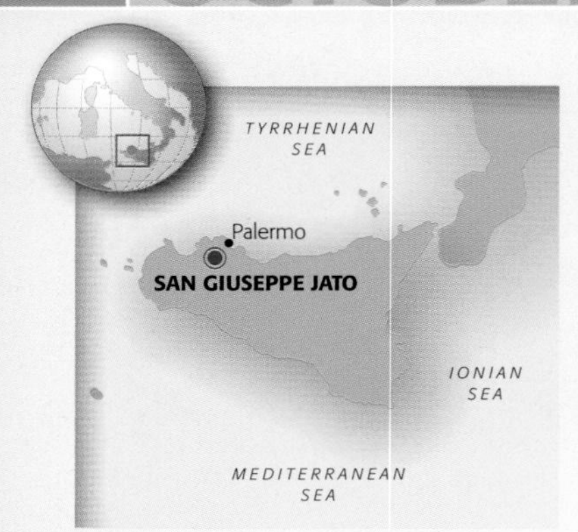

GETTING THERE
San Giuseppe Jato is about 19 miles (30 km) south of Palermo, the nearest airport. It can be reached by car from the airport via the SS624.

GETTING AROUND
The best way of getting around the countryside near San Giuseppe Jato is by car.

WEATHER
Expect pleasant maximum temperatures of around 73°F (23°C) during the day.

ACCOMMODATIONS
The Casale del Principe *agriturismo*, in the heart of the peaceful Jato valley, has great historic charm: first it was a 16th-century look-out tower, then an 18th-century convent, and finally a farm. Double rooms from US$135; www.casaledelprincipe.it

Enjoy simple, comfortable rooms at the Sant'Agata *agriturismo* near Lago di Piana degli Albanesi. B&B from US$108 (US$162 for half board); www.agriturismosantagata.pa.it

EATING OUT
Many restaurants and *agriturismi* offer local dishes such as pasta with sardines and mountain fennel, fresh pasta with *astrattu* (sun-dried tomatoes), or *lu bruciuluni*, a thick slice of meat rolled up with various types of stuffing. Two good places to eat are the Masseria Rosella (www.masseria-rossella.com) and the Masseria La Chiusa (www.masserialachiusa.it): a meal will cost you about US$42 (both places also offer accommodations).

PRICE FOR TWO
About US$245 per day for meals and accommodations.

FURTHER INFORMATION
www.palermotourism.com

Sicilian Carts

A simple wooden cart is transformed into something truly special by colorful decorations depicting the knights of old or religious scenes. You can see these traditional carts in many parts of Sicily, but especially inland from Palermo during village festivals, when they parade through the streets pulled by horses in elaborate harnesses. These splendid cart decorations are painted by highly skilled craftsmen, who manage to interpret traditional themes with a uniquely personal touch.

AN ANGLER'S PARADISE

Sicily's countryside is generally harsh and drought-ridden, but the Jato valley is a happy and verdant exception. Separated from the flat lands around Palermo – the famous Conca d'Oro or Golden Shell – by hills whose most prominent feature is Monte Jato (2,762 ft/842 m), the valley has always been fertile and prosperous thanks to its rivers. The most important of these is the Jato River (a name that crops up frequently in these parts), which is fed by water from the rivers Cannavera, Rizzolo, and Chiusa and, after a long and obstacle-ridden course, which includes filling up the artificial Lago Poma, flows into the sea near Castellammare del Golfo. On its way toward the sea, as it reaches flatter ground, the river slows, widens, and curves like a mighty snake. Along its green and fertile banks, clumps of trees form small shady spinneys that offer shelter, while below, the sparkling clean

Main: View of Lago Pomo, set in beautiful countryside

Far right (top to bottom): Historic center of Castellammare del Golfo; countryside around Castellammare del Golfo; horses on one of the area's many stud farms

Left: Terracotta urn, traditionally used for olive oil or wine, now an attractive planter

Right (left to right): Delicious *arancini con burro*, balls of buttery rice filled with soft cheese; ducks on Lago Poma; farming in the countryside

water rolls and spins on inexorably toward the sea. These pleasant conditions are ideal for anglers to indulge in their sport; there's plenty of large fish to be caught, and local angling clubs whose members can advise, guide, and even instruct visitors who come to fish.

But what makes the area unique is the way that the farming culture has managed to work together with nature in an environmentally friendly way to everyone's benefit. The farms scattered over the district and, in particular, the splendid watermills along the Jato River – some dating back to the 12th century – testify to this: from the Principe mill, with its pointed-arch aqueduct and impressive iron pulleys, to the Chiusa and the Quarto Mulino, where the flow of water is cleverly divided in two and powers wheat-grinding machinery on one side and pasta-making machinery on the other. It's a tribute to the ingenuity of man, letting nature do all the hard work and keeping the environment just as it was, with the only emissions being flour and pasta. Just delicious!

Above: Ancient stone walls of a country farm

FISHING DIARY

San Giuseppe Jato is situated in one of Sicily's most fertile areas, enriched by the waters of the river that flows through it. The river also fills two large lakes, making it the ideal place to go fishing. Five days will give you time to catch some fish, go walking in the countryside, and visit the coast.

Five Days in the Valley

DAY 1
Go fishing at Lago Poma, not far from San Giuseppe Jato – the pretty lake is filled with delicious perch. Or, if you prefer bird-watching, take a trip to the Lipu del Lago oasis, frequented by local and migrating waterbirds. If you haven't caught any fish, relax with an evening meal of pasta with Sicilian sausages and a glass of red wine.

DAY 2
Visit the ruins of the ancient city at San Giuseppe Jato. Inhabited since prehistoric times, in 1246 it was bold enough to rebel against Frederick II, who then destroyed it and deported its inhabitants to Puglia. Once you've enjoyed the history, admire the scenery of the glorious river valley and mountains.

DAY 3
Fishing enthusiasts can spend the morning at the lake at Piana degli Albanesi, a short way from San Giuseppe Jato. In the afternoon, visit San Cipirello, a village near San Giuseppe Jato, to tour its wine cellars. Buy some of the full-bodied local wine to wash down a fish supper, caught by yourself if you've been lucky.

DAY 4
Walk the Watermill Route along the riverbank past the Gambascio mill, the Jato mill (the oldest in the valley), the pretty Principe mill, built in 1800 by the prince of Camporeale, and the Provvidenza mill. After leaving the river, you'll come to Dammusi, a former Jesuits' house converted into a summer residence in the 18th century by Prince Beccadelli and now a farm.

DAY 5
Today, head north to Castellammare del Golfo. Wander around the historic center with its great fortress and then spend some time on the sandy beach. Enjoy lunch in a shady restaurant overlooking the sea, then either return to the beach or take a boat trip out into the gulf.

Dos and Don'ts

- ✗ Don't swim in the Jato River: it can be dangerous because of strong currents, especially after rain.
- ✓ Always take a good large-scale map with you on walks as the paths are not always well marked.
- ✓ Visit the country market that is held in San Cipirello every Saturday – it's just next to San Giuseppe Jato; you can buy local crafts and also the excellent wines of the region.
- ✓ For bird-watching, choose binoculars that are not too heavy but with good magnification – something like 8 x 40.

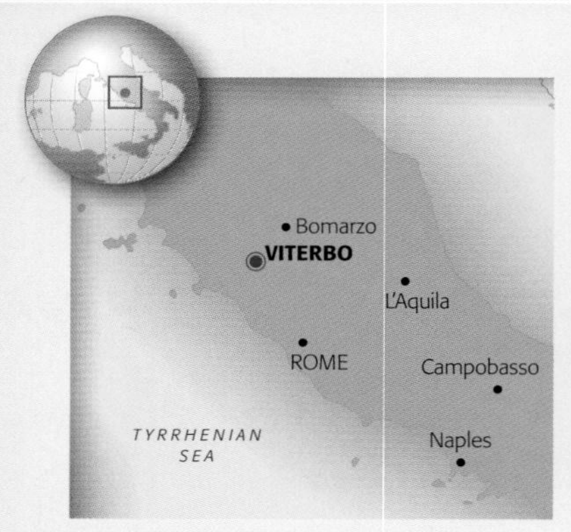

GETTING THERE
Viterbo is about 62 miles (100 km) north of Rome's Fiumicino Airport. By car, take the E80 and SS675, a journey of about two hours.

GETTING AROUND
The only sensible way of exploring the narrow streets of the historic center is on foot. You will need a car for the day trip and to visit any of the "wild spas."

WEATHER
The days are still pleasantly clear and warm, with a maximum temperature of 68°F (20°C).

ACCOMMODATIONS
The Mini Palace, a few steps from the historic center, is a modern, 4-star hotel with all amenities; doubles from US$135; www.minipalacehotel.com

The B&B dei Papi, a historic residence in the town center, offers a great combination of contemporary design and old-world ambience; doubles from US$122; www.bbdeipapi.it

EATING OUT
La Torre restaurant and wine bar is in the former stables of the Palazzo Mercanti, near the medieval city walls. It offers traditional fare with a creative twist (dinner from US$55); www.enotecalatorrevt.com

Trattoria Richiastro serves dishes with a medieval flavor (from US$42) in a lovely 13th-century residence; tel. 0761 228 009.

PRICE FOR TWO
US$275–410 per day including accommodations, meals, and car rental.

FURTHER INFORMATION
www.viterboonline.com

Monsters in the Garden

Bomarzo's Bosco Sacro garden was the brainchild of *condottore* Vicino Orsini. He commissioned architect Pirro Ligorio to create a fantastic park in the grounds of the family castle, in memory of his wife Giulia Farnese. Completed in 1552, it gradually fell into ruins and lay almost forgotten until the 1970s. Now carefully restored, and known locally as the Parco dei Mostri (Park of Monsters) it is a delight to explore, revealing arcane symbols and stone creatures such as dragons, sea monsters, and sphinxes. What was it for? An inscription reads: "Just to Lighten the Heart."

Above (left to right): Civita di Bagnoregio, perched on its spur of volcanic rock; fishing boats on the shore of Lago Bolsena; a view of the small town of Bolsena; spaghetti with cheese and black pepper, a simple dish typical of Lazio

Below (top and bottom): *Pollo alla Borgia*, a specialty of Viterbo, with a sauce of pine nuts, anchovies, and capers; Piazza delle Erbe, the historic heart of Viterbo

Main: Architectural detail of Viterbo's Palazzo dei Papi, decorated with lions, a symbol of the town

STEEPED IN HISTORY

A MASSIVE CITY WALL, triangular in shape, surrounds the historic center of Viterbo, testament to a period when the town was a seat of the papacy, at a crossroads of cultures and with a population that, in the 13th century, exceeded that of Rome. Today, 800 years later, Viterbo is still redolent of the time when popes Alexander VI and Clement IV ruled from here. It was in Viterbo that the 1271 Conclave was held for over 33 months until the election of Gregory X.

The Palazzo dei Papi witnessed many such great events, which influenced the history of the town and even Italy as a whole. It is a magnificent Gothic residence, built between 1255 and 1267, set in a square that was formerly the religious heart of the town. Also in this square is the Duomo di San Lorenzo, built in austere Romanesque form and then restored in Gothic style with the addition of the elegant campanile. The center of civilian life in Viterbo is, however, the Piazza del Plebiscito, a wide space dominated by the Palazzo dei Priori. The construction of this impressive building started in the

Above: Impressive walls of Viterbo's historic center

JAN FEB MAR APR MAY JUN JUL AUG SEP **OCT** NOV DEC

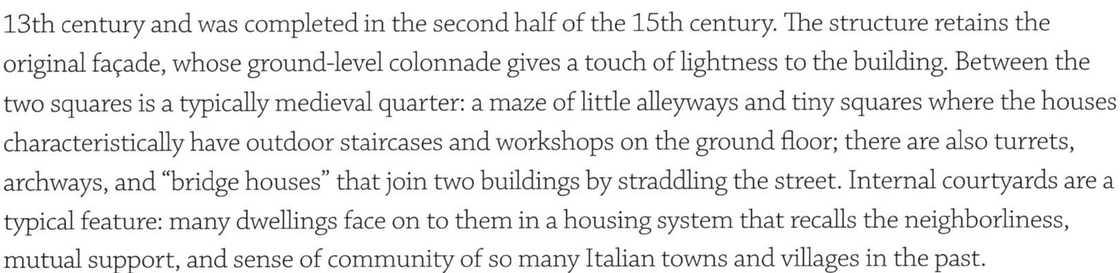

13th century and was completed in the second half of the 15th century. The structure retains the original façade, whose ground-level colonnade gives a touch of lightness to the building. Between the two squares is a typically medieval quarter: a maze of little alleyways and tiny squares where the houses characteristically have outdoor staircases and workshops on the ground floor; there are also turrets, archways, and "bridge houses" that join two buildings by straddling the street. Internal courtyards are a typical feature: many dwellings face on to them in a housing system that recalls the neighborliness, mutual support, and sense of community of so many Italian towns and villages in the past.

While Viterbo attracts countless visitors to experience the charms of an unspoiled medieval town, it is the spa waters from springs in the area that draw yet more tourists every year. Renowned since ancient times and used for a range of cures, in places the warm water flows out freely, creating delightful "wild spa" pools in which people bathe even in winter. Whether it is history or healing waters that bring you to Viterbo, you will leave feeling refreshed and restored by this welcoming and very special town.

MEDIEVAL DIARY

To visit Viterbo is to step back into the past; it has the typical warmth of provincial Italy, ancient traditions remain part of daily life, and friendliness is undiminished. With four days at your disposal you can get to know the town and its people, spend a day at its historic baths, and still have time to visit some gems of the surrounding region.

Four Days in the Past

DAY 1

Start your visit to Viterbo in Piazza San Lorenzo, seeing the cathedral, next to its slender 14th-century campanile, and the Palazzo dei Papi. Admire the elegant loggia that completes the fine façade and be sure to see the Sala del Conclave, where at least five popes were elected. The town's commercial center extends along elegant Via Cavour and Corso Italia, where you can finish your day with a stroll, some shopping, and an *apperitivo*.

DAY 2

Head for the typically 13th-century San Pellegrino quarter, looking in at the many little antique shops that line its narrow lanes. Pause to admire the Piazza del Plebiscito; the Palazzo dei Priori looks on to this square and it is worth entering to see the magnificent frescoes that adorn its rooms. Then go to the Santa Maria Nuova church, one of the oldest in Viterbo and full of wonderful frescoes and paintings.

DAY 3

Spend the day relaxing in Viterbo's spas. The official Terme dei Papi, built on former Roman baths, offers numerous treatments; or there are the "wild spas" in the countryside, such as Bagnaccio, Palliano, Carletti, and Bulicame, mentioned in Dante's *Inferno*.

DAY 4

Devote the day to a driving tour of the countryside north of Viterbo. Visit Bolsena, which looks on to the beautiful lake of the same name. It occupies a wide volcanic crater and is the largest of its kind in Italy. From here, continue on to Civita di Bagnoregio, one of the finest historic villages in Italy, perched on a spur of volcanic rock. As you head back toward Viterbo, be sure not to miss a visit to Bomarzo's Parco dei Monstri.

Dos and Don'ts

- ✓ For tempting pictures of Viterbo's thermal spas, visit www.termediviterbo.it (in Italian only).
- ✓ Spend an evening at one of the musical events of the Aug–Oct Viterbo Festival Barocco: it attracts musicians of international repute with a series of Baroque concerts (www.provincia.vt.it/barocco).
- ✓ Take a boat trip on Lago Bolsena; you can hire a dinghy or a traditional lake boat without a special license.
- ✗ Don't wear your best shoes on your visit to Civita di Bagnoregio. It is quite a walk across the bridge and up to the old town, so walking boots or sneakers are more suitable.

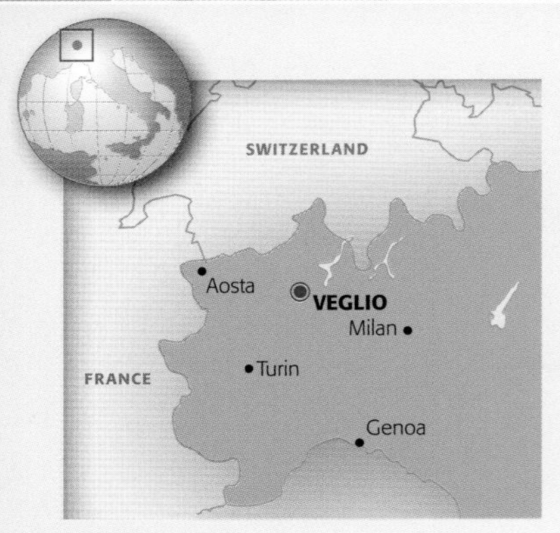

GETTING THERE
Veglio, in the Valle di Mosso of northern Piedmont, can be reached in a couple of hours by car from the two nearest airports, Milan–Malpensa and Turin–Caselle, both about 37 miles (60 km) away.

GETTING AROUND
You will need a car to get to Veglio and around the Valle di Mosso.

WEATHER
Daytime temperatures may reach 68°F (20°C) in the valley, but it will be colder at higher altitudes.

ACCOMMODATIONS
La Baitanella B&B, near the Parco Avventura and the bungee jumping center, is a converted 19th-century mountain hut, warm and welcoming with good views; doubles from US$95; tel. 015 748 158.

The Ianua Coeli *agriturismo* in Biella offers simple but comfortable accommodations; family apartments from US$135; www.ianuacoeli.biella.com

EATING OUT
There are plenty of restaurants near the park offering regional cooking (dinner from US$35): Locanda Casa Nostra serves hearty pasta and meat dishes (www.casanostralocanda.it); the specialty at Il Castagneto is pizza with *macagn* cheese and porcini mushrooms (www.ilcastagneto.org); at Locanda Argimonia, try the local *bagna càuda*, a warm dip served with fresh vegetables as an appetizer (tel. 349 702 2351); and Angolo di Giò is a typical mountain restaurant offering traditional hot-stone cooking (tel. 015 748 0019).

PRICE FOR A FAMILY OF FOUR
US$410 per day including accommodations, meals, and car rental. Add US$22 per person for entry to the park and US$122 per person for a bungee jump.

FURTHER INFORMATION
http://veglio.parcoavventura.it
www.valledimosso.it

Holy Mountains

The Sacro Monte di Varallo was founded in 1481 by Bernardino Caimi, a Franciscan friar. It unfolds in a series of 44 chapels along the ridge of a rocky spur overlooking the village of Varallo, ending at the Basilica dell'Assunta. It is one of several such pilgrim routes in Piedmont, marked by religious statues and sanctuaries that faithfully reproduced buildings of the Holy Land at a time when pilgrimages were too dangerous to undertake because Palestine was occupied by the Turks.

AERIAL ESCAPADES

As a child, did you ever imagine yourself in a forest, swinging from branch to branch high above the ground like Tarzan? Well, it's now an adventure sport in its own right, and whatever your age. you can make a childhood dream a reality in specially equipped adventure parks. One of the best in which to take to the treetops is the Parco Avventura Veglio, a dense woodland area whose trees, reaching 65 ft (20 m) high, have all sorts of secret routes hidden within their foliage. Among the branches, at every level, there are ladders large and small, cable bridges, nets, wires, pulleys... in short, everything you need to complete a thrilling and challenging route around the park without ever setting foot on the ground.

Sound easy? Well imagine yourself swooping along in midair hanging from a pulley; crossing a wire stretched between two tree trunks like a tightrope walker; teetering over a slender gangplank; or crawling along a horizontal ladder between flexible hawsers that bounce at every step. Beneath you is a void; around you, a forest canopy vibrant with warm fall colors. But dare you pause to enjoy it?

Main: Intrepid visitors to the Parco Avventura Veglio tackling a bridge of suspended cables

Naturally it is all perfectly safe. You'll be instructed in the use of carabiners, the clever devices that keep you firmly attached to the cables as you move around the park, and fitted with a safety harness, helmet, and sturdy gloves. There are seven different routes of varying difficulty for adults and children. The most challenging is the Red Route, open only to those who are over 15 and in good physical shape. Otherwise the sky's the limit for a thrilling experience that will test your agility, reactions, balance, concentration, courage, coordination, and teamwork.

The park is situated in the Valle di Mosso, a delightful region of rolling hills and woodland, with the unmistakable outline of Monte Rosa in the distance. The valley is at the heart of the most important textile district in Italy, yet has managed to preserve its appearance and traditions unspoiled. Among these is the profusion of lovely sanctuaries, chapels, and basilicas that were built as sites of pilgrimage, with life-size statues of the saints and elements of medieval Jerusalem in their architecture. If you can tear the kids, or yourself, away from Veglio's high-adrenaline thrills, there are even more uplifting pleasures to be discovered in its hills and forests.

Above: San Giovanni Battista in Biella, a Romanesque masterpiece

Far left (top to bottom): *Bagna càuda*, a typical fall delicacy of the region, made with garlic, oil, and anchovies; climbing a net in the adventure park; view of the monumental steps and entrance portal of the sanctuary at the top of the Sacro Monte di Oropa

Above (top and bottom): Lush beech woods typical of the region; the marmot, a shy inhabitant of the local countryside

Below: Making the leap in a bungee jump

OUTDOOR DIARY

Veglio's first impression as a small, quiet village lost in the Piedmont countryside conceals some thrilling opportunities for outstanding open-air fun that the whole family will enjoy. Three days gives you time to test your mettle on high, and also take in some of the more tranquil historic and natural sights that the region has to offer.

Three Adventurous Days

DAY 1

Select the route in the Parco Avventura that is most suitable for you and your family: there's a choice of courses in ascending order of difficulty. Each one offers different equipped routes that allow you to "walk" a certain distance above the ground, but always under the supervision of the well-trained staff. If you are in need of a rest, pause on the summit of the hill to admire the superb panorama over the wooded valley, with Monte Rosa on the horizon.

DAY 2

Take a break after the thrills of the Parco Avventura. The Valle di Mosso offers some lovely walks, one of the most exciting of which takes you on a 4-hour hike through thick woods to the sanctuaries of Banchette and Mazzucco. Alternatively, drive north to walk the route of the Sacro Monte di Varallo, or south to the lovely town of Biella, in an area famous for its traditional transhumance (seasonal movement of livestock) routes, and visit the Sacro Monte di Oropa and the nearby magnificent botanical gardens.

DAY 3

Time for more adventures. Veglio is where the first bungee-jumping center in Italy was opened in 1994. Participants leap from a spectacular bridge known as the Colossus because of its dramatic size: 500 ft (152 m) high and 1,150 ft (350 m) long. This is the place to come for an unforgettable rush of adrenaline as you throw yourself into the void in complete safety.

Dos and Don'ts

- ✓ The Parco Avventura Veglio is open every Sunday in October; for more information, visit the website *(see opposite)*.
- ✓ When you visit the park, wear athletic clothing and sturdy walking shoes; if you wear glasses, use a length of cord to secure them and, if you have long hair, tie it back.
- ✗ Under-18s are not allowed to visit the adventure park on their own; they must be accompanied by an adult. Children under 6 years old must be accompanied by an instructor on any route, so do not forget to notify the park in advance. The Red Route is not open to people under 59 inches (150 cm) tall.
- ✓ You will find information about the Bungee Centre at the website www.bungee.it

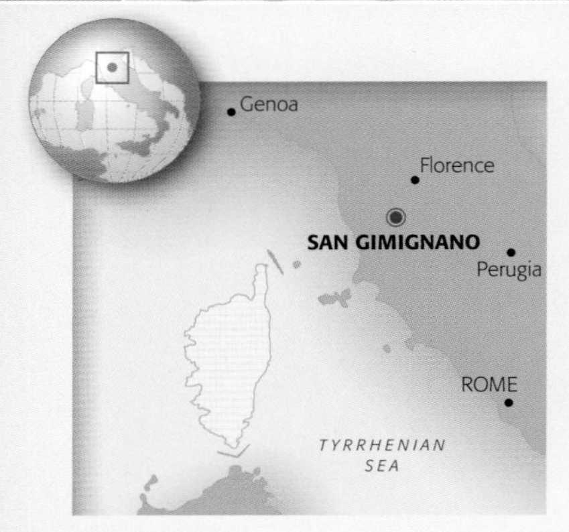

GETTING THERE
San Gimignano, in central Tuscany, is easily reached by car from Florence, the nearest airport, in about an hour. Take the Florence–Siena freeway, leaving at the Poggibonsi Nord exit, then follow the signs to San Gimignano. There are also many buses from Florence.

GETTING AROUND
The historic center within the city walls is closed to traffic and is pleasant to explore on foot.

WEATHER
The weather is mild, with frequent sunny days and average maximum temperatures around 70ºF (21ºC).

ACCOMMODATIONS
There are two comfortable hotels in the town center, in the historic Piazza della Cisterna: the former palazzo Leon Bianco has spacious and well-furnished rooms from US$115 per night; www.leonbianco.com

The Cisterna, a 13th-century residence, has Florentine-style rooms from US$120; www.hotelcisterna.it

Set in an olive grove in the countryside, the Villa San Paolo is a spa hotel offering a wide range of treatments; doubles from US$160; www.villasanpaolo.it

EATING OUT
There are many places in town where you can enjoy delicious Tuscan cuisine, such as Mangiatoia (about US$48, tel. 0577 941 528), Osteria del Carcere (about US$42, tel. 0577 941 905), and the smart Dorando (about US$68; www.ristorantedorando.it).

Outside the city walls, the romantic and elegant restaurant Relais La Collegiata, originally the church of a 16th-century convent, enjoys a magnificent view of the towers of San Gimignano. Meals cost about US$95; www.lacollegiata.it

PRICE FOR TWO
About US$300 per day for meals and accommodations.

FURTHER INFORMATION
www.sangimignano.net

Vernaccia and Saffron

San Gimignano is famous not only as a town of art and culture, but also as the native land of one of Italy's most renowned wines: Vernaccia. This wine has been appreciated since the earliest times – in 1296 the town authorities put a tax on its export, which had a negative effect on trade. Another typical product of the region is saffron, a highly valued spice and, in the Middle Ages, the most expensive one in the world. In 1228, San Gimignano was able to pay off a large debt partly in gold and partly in saffron.

Main: The amazing towers of San Gimignano

THE CITY OF BEAUTIFUL TOWERS

There were once at least 72 towers rising up high above San Gimignano's city walls, in its finest era. They were built to symbolize the power of the most important families in the Middle Ages and are still the pride and joy of the town, which attached such importance to its looks that it passed a law in 1282 forbidding the demolition of any buildings unless more beautiful ones were erected in their place. Today, only 15 of the 72 towers remain standing, but, even so, they are so spectacular that San Gimignano is known as "the city of beautiful towers."

This very special "medieval Manhattan" came into existence between the 11th and 12th centuries close to the Via Francigena, one of the main roads in the Middle Ages, well-traveled by pilgrims from all over Europe heading for Rome. In the 13th century, San Gimignano embellished itself with splendid architecture and built mighty city walls as protection. Inside these walls, the narrow streets spread out uphill, flanked by golden stone medieval houses. These

Above: Well-preserved residence in the historic center

Above (left to right): The narrow streets of San Gimignano's historic center; San Gimignano's statue keeps a serene watch over the town; San Gimignano seen from below; craftsman modeling a clay vase; the Chiesa di Santa Maria in Cellole, one of the oldest churches in the region

Below: The Piazza della Cisterna centered on a 13th-century well in San Gimignano

are streets to get lost in, to wander aimlessly, admiring the buildings. Explore the narrow alleyways until you reach the heart of the town, marked by two main squares – the Piazza della Cisterna and the Piazza Duomo – where you will find San Gimignano's most important buildings. In the Middle Ages, the Piazza della Cisterna, surrounded by ancient palazzi and tower-houses, was where markets and town festivals were staged – it still has the original herringbone pattern pavement and the well after which it's named. The second square is dominated by two buildings, the Collegiata, a very fine Romanesque church with a magnificent flight of steps, and the Palazzo del Popolo, the seat of lay power in the medieval town. Yet these buildings are themselves dominated by the two towers that symbolize San Gimignano: the oldest, known as "Rognosa," which rises up by the Palazzo del Popolo, and the tallest, Torre Grossa. Climbing the long flight of steps to the top of Grossa is tiring, but your efforts will be amply rewarded by the views of the town, looking over the tops of the other towers to the gently rolling hills and the distant horizon.

HILL TOWN DIARY

Popular with tourists, San Gimignano is one of the best preserved medieval towns in Italy. Its towers make it instantly recognizable, but the art treasures held within its walls are just as remarkable. Although it's small there's enough art, architecture, and fine food and wine to keep you busy for about three days.

Three Days Among the Towers

DAY 1

Enter San Gimignano via the San Giovanni gate, which opens on to the urban stretch of the ancient Via Francigena; from here, walk up to the town center, admiring the old buildings that surround it. At the Piazza della Cisterna, explore the medieval palazzi and impressive residences around the well.

Enjoy lunch – perhaps some cured meats and vegetable dishes and a glass or two of Vernaccia. Spend the afternoon just wandering among the winding alleyways, and buy some souvenirs.

DAY 2

Today, head for the Piazza del Duomo and visit the Romanesque Collegiata, the most important church in San Gimignano, which contains some remarkable 14th- and 15th-century frescoes. Don't miss the nearby Palazzo del Popolo, which houses a sumptuous picture gallery. To see the gentle Tuscan landscape from above, climb up the Torre Grossa, nearly 180 ft (55 m) high.

Visit the Montestaffoli fortress, which dates back to the 14th century and was built into the older city walls. Today, only one of its towers remains standing, affording fine views of the town. In the nearby Villa della Rocca is the Wine Museum, which allows visitors to taste excellent Vernaccia in the wine bar inside the museum.

DAY 3

Don't miss the Chiesa di Sant'Agostino in the northern part of the town – a Romanesque church with a cherished cycle of 15th-century frescoes. After lunch, take a trip to see the Chiesa di Santa Maria in Cellole, a few miles north of San Gimignano – the ancient church has a fine font made of travertine marble. Finish your stay with a dinner of traditional food, such as pork with saffron potatoes, and yet more delicious Vernaccia.

Dos and Don'ts

- ✓ Go on a tour of wine cellars in the area, where you can taste the excellent locally produced wines.
- ✓ Buy a piece of ceramic pottery, hand-painted by one of the many craftsmen in San Gimignano.
- ✗ Don't bring your car into the town center – it is closed to traffic. Leave it in the parking lot near the San Giovanni gate.
- ✓ Give a tip to the custodian of the Chiesa di Santa Maria in Cellole – you'll have to ask him to open up the church.

GETTING THERE
Alberobello is in central Puglia, in the southern part of the Murge – a great limestone plateau. It is served by the international airports of Bari and Brindisi and is about 1 ½ hours by car from each of them.

GETTING AROUND
A car is essential for getting around independently.

WEATHER
Expect pleasant temperatures of up to 72°F (22°C), and frequent sunny days.

ACCOMMODATIONS
Consider staying in a stone *trullo*. The Trullidea Resort, in the center of Alberobello, has larger *trulli*, suitable for families, from US$150; www.trullidea.it

The Trulli San Leonardo, a 15-minute walk from Alberobello, has authentic *trulli* and a swimming pool with slides. A four-bed *trullo* costs from US$164; www.trullisanleonardo.it

For a delightful farm stay, the Masseria Madonna dell'Arco in Martina Franca has apartments from US$164; www.masseriamadonnadellarco.it

Or, try the Masseria Aprile in Locorotondo, with apartments from US$120; www.masseriaaprile.it

EATING OUT
In Alberobello, the Aratro in a converted *trullo* offers traditional dishes from US$28 (www.ristorantearatro.it); the Poeta Contadino is both rustic and elegant, with meals from US$68 (www.ilpoetacontadino.it); and the Peschiera di Monopoli offers excellent fish cuisine from US$68 (tel. 080 801 066).

PRICE FOR A FAMILY OF FOUR
About US$380 per day for accommodations and meals, with an extra US$80 for a visit to the caves.

FURTHER INFORMATION
www.italyheaven.co.uk/puglia/alberobello.html

The Fasano Safari Park

Italy's largest safari park is located in Fasano and covers an area of more than 346 acres (140 ha). Mostly covered with Mediterranean maquis, the park contains about 200 different species, with the bigger animals living in large, open enclosures. You need to go on a safari around this part of the zoo by car. In the other parts of the park, you can explore on foot and using the park's little train, the Metrozoo. There are also theme parks, a monkey house, and a dolphinarium, and much more besides.

Above (left and right): Colorful boats in Monopoli harbor; the white houses of Monopoli, a town established by the Greeks

A FAIRY-TALE VILLAGE

A COLLECTION OF WHITEWASHED DWELLINGS topped by cones, two-thirds the size of normal houses, often fused together in clumps to form an organic complex: these are the famous *trulli* of Alberobello, a village in the heart of Puglia. There is something otherworldly about the *trulli,* as though they were not built for human habitation. Their size, similarity, and close-packed nature recall the constructions of the insect world. And like beehives and ants' nests, their simple geometric shape actually conceals great architectural skills – these dry-stone houses were originally built without mortar.

A *trullo* usually consists of a series of square rooms with domed ceilings, which lead off the central room where the family gathers for meals. This room often has a built-in overhead mezzanine that serves as a larder or as a child's bedroom. As the owner's family grows, extra rooms can be added to the main structure. From the outside, the grey limestone domes display a range of embellishments – the pinnacles are made in a variety of shapes and the tiles are often painted with traditional Christian, magic, pagan, or Jewish symbols.

Trulli are not exclusive to Alberobello: they are typical of the Murge, where you find the most ancient ones – some dating back to prehistoric times. What makes Alberobello unique is the sheer concentration of *trulli* – there are nearly 1,500 of them along the little streets, all looking the same but each one having its own individual features. How did so many come to be in the same place? To find the answer, you must go back to a time when the counts of Conversano ruled the heavily wooded region. In the 15th century, shepherds and peasants started to settle in what is now Alberobello and turned the countryside into profitable farmland. Since the new settlement required taxes to be paid, the counts only permitted the farmers to build dry-stone houses, so that they could easily be dismantled in the event of a royal inspection. In 1797, after a request from the put-upon people of Alberobello, King Ferdinand IV of Bourbon issued a royal decree granting freedom to the village. At last, the *trulli* could be made permanent, thus creating this extraordinary fairy-tale spectacle, appreciated by visitors hundreds of years later.

Main: A *trullo* in Alberobello, an architectural symbol of the region
Below (left to right): A regional specialty, *lanache alla barese (*fettucine with mussels); a shady *trullo* garden in Alberobello; a traditional weaving loom, still used in Puglia to make fabric

Above: View from the Chiesa di Madre di San Giorgio, Locorotondo

TRULLI DIARY

Alberobello is a magical place, to be enjoyed by simply wandering its charming streets and letting yourself be guided by instinct and curiosity. Six days will allow you and your family to explore the southern part of the Murge, spend time at lovely sandy beaches, and appreciate some of the area's remarkable natural and artistic treasures.

Six Days in the Murge

DAYS 1–2

First, enjoy the best view of Alberobello, from the Belvedere Trulli in the Piazza del Popolo, then head for the center of the village. There are two main districts with *trulli*: the Rione Monti and the Aia Piccola. Look out for the Sovrano *trullo*, famous for its two storys.

Make a trip to nearby Martina Franca, whose medieval heart was developed in the 14th century. Today, it still has a fine historic center, with magnificent Baroque palazzi and the sumptuous Palazzo Ducale.

DAYS 3–4

Visit Locorotondo: the village gets its name from its road system of concentric circles and it has a fine historic quarter packed with pretty, whitewashed houses. Among these dwellings you will also find the 18th-century Chiesa di Madre di San Giorgio.

Take the family to Monopoli – not only is it a picturesque port with some beautiful historic buildings, but it also has some delightful sandy beaches to the south, within walking distance of the center. Enjoy a beach picnic or dine on seafood freshly caught in local waters.

DAYS 5–6

Enjoy another trip to the coast and also take in some culture – there's an archeological park at Egnazia and a museum with some fine sculptures. This Roman city grew up along the route of the Via Traiana; it was devastated in AD 545 by the Ostrogoths and finally abandoned in the 9th century. Just north of here are some lovely sandy beaches.

Don't miss out on a visit to the Castellana caves, north of Alberobello, with spectacular calcareous and crystal stalagmites and stalactites shaped over thousands of years into an extraordinary variety of magical shapes and colors. The huge caves extend for 2 miles (3 km).

Dos and Don'ts

- ✓ For information on the opening hours and exploring the Castellana caves, visit www.grottedicastellana.it
- ✗ Don't visit the Castellana caves without taking a cagoule with you: the caves are very damp inside, although the temperature is constant at 59ºF (15ºC).
- ✓ Buy one of the amusing terracotta whistles made by local craftsmen – children love them.
- ✗ Don't be put off by the *trulli* that have been turned into tacky souvenir shops in Alberobello; head instead for the Aia Piccola district, where most of the *trulli* are occupied by families.

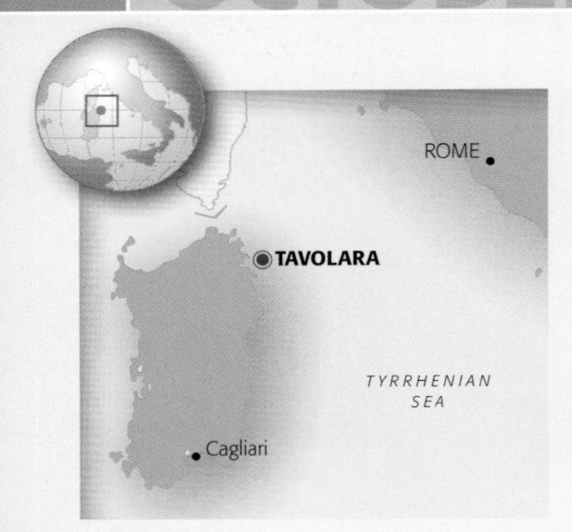

GETTING THERE
The island of Tavolara is northeast of Sardinia and reached by ferry from Loiri Porto San Paolo. The nearest airport is Olbia and from there you can reach Loiri Porto San Paolo by taking the SS125. It takes just 10 minutes for the ferry to reach the harbor of Spalmatore di Terra.

GETTING AROUND
The only way of getting around is by sea: by renting a boat or relying on the scuba diving centers.

WEATHER
Pleasant, with maximum temperatures of about 72°F (22°C) and plenty of sunny days.

ACCOMMODATIONS
Loiri Porto San Paolo, on Sardinia, is the starting point for excursions and dives around the island of Tavolara. The Castello di Tavolara hotel is a few steps from the beach and the harbor, and offers a welcoming and pleasant stay. Rooms from US$102; www.hotelcastelloditavolara.com

For those who prefer to camp, the Tavolara camp site (www.camping-tavolara.it) is well equipped and offers a range of accommodations: tent pitches (US$11.50 per person), trailers (US$42 for two people), and mobile homes (US$48 for two).

EATING OUT
The two restaurants on Tavolara island are Da Tonino (tel. 0789 58570) and La Corona (tel. 0789 36695). Both overlook the sea and offer top fish cuisine. Meals cost about US$48.

In Loiri Porto San Paolo, try dining at Il Sole – enjoy excellent local cuisine and seafood for about US$48 (tel. 0789 40582).

PRICE FOR TWO
US$165–245 per day for accommodations and meals. Allow at least US$55 per person for a guided dive.

FURTHER INFORMATION
www.amptavolara.it

A Protected Sea

Off the northeast coast of Sardinia, the Tavolara–Punta Coda Cavallo area is a marine preserve that includes about 50 miles (80 km) of coastline and a large expanse of sea. It's of great scientific interest to naturalists with spectacular gorgonians, colorful coral and sponges, and a wide variety of marine animals and fish such as lobsters, sea bream, and groupers. Diving is permitted in parts of the preserve, although underwater activity involving contact with the seabed and anchorage of boats is completely forbidden.

Main: The view from Loiri Porto San Paolo with the island of Tavolara in the distance

THE RUGGED ISLAND

A STRING OF ROCKS AND ISLETS LIE SCATTERED ACROSS THE SEA like a precious necklace stretched from Tavolara to Sardinia, a reminder that, in the distant Paleolithic period, it was not an island but a promontory into the sea. This is a sea that for millennia has formed a delightful natural paradise just off Sardinia's eastern coast, graced by beautifully clean and transparent waters. Tavolara rises steeply from the waves like a great sea monster with a massive mountain ridge for a spine. The island, rectangular in shape, flattens out at its extremities into two narrow spits of land: the Spalmatore di Fuori to the east, now a NATO military base; and the Spalmatore di Terra, extending toward the mainland, a long isthmus of white sand that becomes thinner and thinner as it pushes into the sea, and curls around a tiny harbor and a few settlements. The island, which today forms part of a huge marine nature preserve with the nearby islets of Molara and Molaretto and a stretch of the eastern Sardinian coast, is a

Above: Tavolara seen from one of the beaches of Loiri Porto San Paolo

Above (left to right): The island of Tavolara in all its beauty; Tavolara beach, with maquis vegetation and crystal-clear sea; shoals of colorful fish in the sea around Tavolara; a Sardinian-style seafood salad; a wild goat on the rocks on Tavolara

Below: A group of scuba divers in the sea near Loiri Porto San Paolo

favorite destination for scuba divers. The jagged cliffs that run around the island are riddled with deep and mysterious caves, hollowed out over the centuries by the ceaseless waves. These cliffs, plunging vertically for nearly 70 ft (21 m) into pristine waters, provide a welcome home to the numerous forms of marine life that inhabit the cracks of the rocky walls, and create a remarkable spectacle. On the seabed, the sandy floor is thickly covered with the soft fronds of sea plants, waving in the shifting currents and forming part of a very rich eco-system.

Tavolara also enchants those who are not interested in scuba diving. The pinkish-white sandy beaches fringing the rocky promontory look on to a sea whose colors constantly shift from turquoise to purple to deep blue. There are more visual delights for those who venture into the island's interior, walking on switchback paths that slowly wind up the steep slopes of the mountain among the rocks and Mediterranean maquis. At the top, your efforts are amply repaid by the view that opens up over the whole of the coast and beyond to Corsica. Beneath you, the water is so clear that you can see the sun beams dance across the seafloor, while on the horizon, the sea magically twinkles and sparkles.

SCUBA DIARY

Diving in Tavolara is a unique experience, in a sea that is unspoiled and full of marine life. The island also offers a remarkable landscape, to be appreciated by walking the paths that climb the slopes of the rugged, hilly massif. Seven days will give you the opportunity to explore both land and sea in this area, and have some time to relax.

Seven Days in Tavolara

DAYS 1–2

For your first day, head underwater just off Tavolara at Tedja Liscia, where the rocky walls plunge into the sea: it's known for its jackfish, lobsters, red starfish, yellow sea fans, and sponges.

Today, scale the heights of Punta del Cannone, the highest point on the island. The last section is demanding and should only be tackled by experienced climbers, but you can still enjoy fine views from lower down.

DAYS 3–5

Try cave-diving at Carabottino – an exciting system of caves linked by wide tunnels that wind underwater and offer the spectacle of a wide variety of fish.

Have another dry day and walk up to Punta La Mandria, the island's second summit; it is easily reached and there is a splendid view of Molara from the top, which is also a great spot to enjoy a picnic. Spend the afternoon on the beach. Take a boat trip to the Grotta del Papa, a cave accessible from the sea that contains Neolithic cave paintings. In the evening, enjoy a seafood dinner on the island and watch the sun's slow and rosy setting.

DAYS 6–7

There's still plenty more diving to be enjoyed – try a challenging deep dive to the Secca del Papa, with snapper and red and yellow sea fans, or an easier dive to Secca del Fico, known for grouper and colored sponges.

Non-divers can explore the coast. Head south to Porta Taverna for another fine sandy beach, which is backed by a lagoon that sometimes has flamingoes. If you crave shops and cafés, head north to Olbia – you'll pass some nice beaches on the way.

Dos and Don'ts

- ✓ It is advisable to dive with a guide even if you have some experience scuba diving.
- ✗ Don't climb the Punta del Cannone without proper equipment; the last stretch includes Grade 3 climbing and should be done with ropes and slings.
- ✓ You need permission from the Parco Naturale Marino for the dive at Secca del Papa; for information, visit www.amptavolara.it
- ✗ Don't approach the eastern side of the island: it's a military zone. Access from sea and land and sailing within 1,640 ft (500 m) of the shore is forbidden.

NOVEMBER

Where to Go: November

The misty days of November bring about just the right conditions for ripening the much-prized white truffle, whose perfume pervades the town of Alba, in Piedmont. Even now the climate in the south of Italy is still mild, perfect for visiting some beautiful and interesting outdoor sights, such as the great Doric temple of Segesta, set in lovely Sicilian countryside; the marvelous Roman mosaics of Villa del Casale in Piazza Armerina, also in the heart of Sicily; or Pisa's dazzling Piazza dei Miracoli, with the iconic Leaning Tower as its focal point and far less crowds than in the summer.

To bask in a timeless elegance, head to the Italian lakes, tinged with an air of wistful melancholy in November: to tranquil, other-worldly Lake Orta, in Piedmont, or the romantic Villa Balbianello on

FESTIVALS AND CULTURE

PISA Old Pisan houses seen from the fortress bridge

MARANELLO
EMILIA-ROMAGNA

Home of the prancing horse

The Galleria Ferrari in Maranello displays the amazing cars, engines, and trophies that make up the history of Ferrari, a name synonymous in Italy with Formula 1.

See pp286–7

VIGEVANO
LOMBARDY

Leonardo's traces

Leonardo da Vinci lived and worked at the Sforza court here in the late 1490s. Evidence of his work can be seen around the town, in its buildings as well as in a permanent exhibition.

www.lacittaideale.org

RECANATI
LE MARCHE

Town of poetry

A small, picturesque town, Recanati is the birthplace of the great 19th-century poet Giacomo Leopardi, who described it in many poems.

www.le-marche.com/Marche/html/recanati.htm

SEGESTA
SICILY

Temple in the Trapani hills

An ancient city of Magna Graecia, Segesta has several important ruins including one of the most perfectly preserved Greek temples, which stands alone in an enchanting landscape.

See pp294–5

PISA
TUSCANY

Miraculous beauty

Piazza dei Miracoli, the monumental heart of Pisa, with its Leaning Tower, Duomo, Baptistry, and nearby Camposanto, is one of the most splendid open spaces in the world.

See pp298–9

UNFORGETTABLE JOURNEYS

PIAZZA ARMERINA View of the historic center

MATERA
BASILICATA

Cave-dwellers' city

Explore the Sassi of Matera, a district riddled with troglodyte caves inhabited since prehistoric times. The atmosphere and setting are quite remarkable.

See pp284–5

VIA CLODIA
LAZIO

Etruscan experience

Via Clodia runs through the ancient Etruscan heartland. Discover cities that were already old when Rome was still a collection of mud huts.

www.elegantetruria.com/itlaye.htm

ALTAMURA
PUGLIA

Journey back in time

From the attractive town of Altamura you can seek out dinosaur footprints, ancient tombs and the site of the discovery of 400,000-year-old Altamura Man.

www.altamura.cchnet.it

PIAZZA ARMERINA
SICILY

Imperial splendor

Close to beautiful Piazza Armerina lies an impressive Roman villa that dates from the time of imperial Rome, lavishly decorated with extraordinarily well-preserved floor mosaics.

See pp280–81

SELLA RONDA
TRENTINO-ALTO ADIGE

A circuit for skiers

The Sella Ronda is a circular ski route around the Sella massif in the heart of the Dolomites. It's 16 miles (26 km) long, so you'll need to set out early.

www.sella-ronda.info

NATURAL WONDERS

LAKE ORTA Sunset over the lake and its encircling mountains

"A path rises, through pine and beech woods, to the top of the promontory where you'll find a perfect spot for quiet contemplation on the harmony of nature and art."

PARCO REGIONALE DELLE MADONIE
SICILY

Natural marvel

Covering the slopes of the Madonie massif, the Madonie regional park has a breathtaking range of Sicilian flora and fauna.

www.parks.it/parco.madonie/Eindex.html

LAKE ORTA
PIEDMONT

Nature and art in harmony

Take a little boat out on the limpid waters of Lake Orta, a secluded and beautiful lake. At its center is the tiny island of San Giulio, with a lovely Romanesque church.

See pp296–7

PARCO NATURALE DELLA REGIONE DEL BEIGUA
LIGURIA

Spectacular views

Follow ancient mule tracks with spectacular sea views and some of the best bird-watching in Italy.

www.parcobeigua.it

SERRE
CAMPANIA

A treat for bird-watchers

A reservoir in the Campania hinterland forms the heart of a wetland oasis that is a haven for overwintering wildfowl. Otters can be seen here, as well.

www.comune.serre.sa.it

CASTIGLIONE DELLA PESCAIA
TUSCANY

Ancient marshlands

Near Castiglione della Pescaia lies the nature preserve of Diaccia Botrona, a wetlands and reedbed area home to flamingoes and other waterbirds.

www.castiglionepescaia.it

Previous page: Dramatic view of Matera, with its famous "sassi" cave dwellings

Lake Como, where Anakin wooed Padmé in *Star Wars II*.

If, on the other hand, you are in the mood for some real-life dolce vita and the buzz of fashionable society, nothing could be better than a trip to the country's vibrant capital, Rome. It is not just full of historic monuments to admire, but also home to some of Italy's most glamorous shopping streets.

For thrills of a different kind, Formula 1 fans will want to visit Emilia and Maranello, the home of Ferrari, where you can get behind the wheel of a race simulator and pretend to be Fernando Alonso. Or, for first-hand exhilaration, descend into the Grotte di Frasassi, a vast cave system in Le Marche, where, over the centuries, water has created extraordinary patterns of lace in stone.

LUXURY AND ROMANCE

ROME View across the glorious Piazza Navona

CASTELL'ARQUATO
EMILIA-ROMAGNA

Medieval town of music

The birthplace of Giacomo Puccini is an impossibly lovely and atmospheric medieval hill-town dominated by the castle that gave it its name.

www.borghitalia.it/html/borgo_en.php?codice_borgo=386

ROME
LAZIO

Shopping heaven

Take some time off from antiquity to enjoy Rome's fabulous shops. For chic boutiques, explore the area behind Piazza Navona; for designer names, visit Via dei Condotti.

See pp288–9

LENNO
LOMBARDY

Romantic lakeside villa

The Villa Balbianello at Lenno is perhaps one of the most romantic spots on beautiful Lake Como. Its gardens, with wonderful views, were used for love scenes in *Star Wars II*.

See pp282–3

SAN MARINO
SAN MARINO

A republic in miniature

The microstate of San Marino is the oldest in the world. Its setting and its beautiful historic center give the feeling of stepping into a fairytale.

www.sanmarinosite.com

PRÉ-SAINT-DIDIER
VALLE D'AOSTA

Fabulous alpine spa

Known to the Romans, the thermal springs of Pré-Saint-Didier are now the focus of state-of-the-art pools, waterfalls, and a wide range of luxurious treatments.

www.termedipre.it

ACTIVE ADVENTURES

GENGA & THE GROTTE DI FRASASSI River-hewn landscape

OPI
ABRUZZO

Game-fishing on the Sangro

Set on the banks of the River Sangro, in the Abruzzo national park, Opi is ideal for lovers of game-fishing, who will find plenty of leaping trout in the sparkling, rushing waters.

www.opionline.it

MUGELLO
TUSCANY

Cycling wooded valleys

A couple of miles from Florence, this richly wooded valley, scattered with old villages, offers a range of cycling trails with cozy, welcoming accommodations along the way.

http://turismo.mugello.toscana.it

"There are passageways and halls of rock, giant alabaster stalactites, and calm pools colored by crystal deposits."

GENGA & THE GROTTE DI FRASASSI
LE MARCHE

Underground marvels

Descend into a breathtaking abyss at one of the most famous and impressive cave systems in Italy on a fascinating guided tour.

See pp278–9

PARCO SASSO SIMONE & SIMONCELLO
LE MARCHE

On horseback in the hills

This lovely natural park has a number of horseback-riding trails, enabling you to explore a hidden corner of Italy.

www.parks.it/parco.sasso.simone.simoncello

ANTEY-SAINT-ANDRÉ
VALLE D'AOSTA

Choose your sport

At Antey-Saint-André it is possible to try every kind of outdoor sport, from paragliding to horseback-riding, and free climbing to rafting.

www.montecervino.it/sezione.asp?idsezione=6&lang=ENG

FAMILY GETAWAYS

ALBA Countryside of Le Langhe, luxuriant even in November

SULMONA
ABRUZZO

Confetti you can eat

Sulmona is famous for its sugared almonds (Confetti di Sulmona), which are made in hundreds of colors and formed into designs such as flower petals.

www.sulmona.org/index.en.php

FONTANELLATO
EMILIA-ROMAGNA

Land of fairytale castles

With its battlemented walls rising from the still waters of a moat, and its lavish interior, one half expects to glimpse knights and ladies at the fortress of Rocca Sanvitale.

See pp292–3

CARLOFORTE
SARDINIA

A hidden treasure

Charming Carloforte is a bustling, old-fashioned fishing port on the island of San Pietro. With its tiny, sandy beaches and hidden coves, it's a great family winter getaway.

www.sardegnaturismo.it

"In misty fall, the town's charm is linked to an unmistakeable musty aroma that fills the streets, leaking out of every restaurant and delicatessen."

VAL GARDENA
TRENTINO-ALTO ADIGE/SUTIROL

You can ski as well!

Val Gardena has long been a family-friendly ski resort. The area boasts sleigh rides, ice skating, and bowling alongside its many excellent pistes.

www.val-gardena.com/en/kids/page37.html

ALBA
PIEDMONT

White diamonds

Alba, capital of the white truffle, is the focus of a famous annual festival with lively events as well as chances to taste and buy the rare and pricy "white diamonds."

See pp290–91

GETTING THERE
Genga and the Grotte di Frasassi are in the heart of Le Marche. Ancona is the nearest airport, just over half an hour away by car on the SS76.

GETTING AROUND
The best way of exploring the area is by car.

WEATHER
Cool, but not too cold, with mean maximum temperatures of around 52°F (11°C).

ACCOMMODATIONS
The 3-star Hotel Le Grotte, situated between Genga and the caves, is comfortable and has modern bedrooms and a swimming pool. Rooms from US$132; www.hotellegrotte.it

The Locanda Palazzo near Arcevia is an interesting country house-inn, converted from an ancient manor and surrounded by greenery. Enjoy rustic elegance from US$115 per night; www.locandapalazzo.com

Le Betulle *agriturismo* is near Avacelli, one of Arcevia's magnificent fortresses. It offers simple, welcoming rooms at US$110 per night; www.agrituristlebetulle.com

EATING OUT
Da Maria restaurant in Genga offers specialties of fresh pasta with mushrooms or truffles, lamb served hot from the grill, and rabbit roasted inside a suckling pig. Meals from US$35 (tel. 0732 90014).

The Pinocchio restaurant in the historic center of Arcevia serves delicious cuisine at moderate prices; meals from US$28; www.pinocchioristorante.com

PRICE FOR TWO
About US$230 per day for accommodations and meals. Add US$20–60 per person for cave tours.

FURTHER INFORMATION
www.frasassi.com

The Temple of Valadier

This temple, built by Giuseppe Valadier at the behest of Pope Leo XII, is situated in a natural cave on the road leading into the heart of Genga's historic center. It is an astonishing Neo-Classical octagonal chapel, constructed from blocks of fine travertine excavated from a quarry near the cave. It contains Canova's *Virgin and Child* (actually a copy – the original is in the care of the parish of Genga).

Above (left and right): The rock formation Foro degli Occhialoni (Hole of the Goggles), a window on to the ravine below, in the Parco Naturale Regionale Gola della Rossa e di Frasassi; Gola del Furlo (the Furlo Pass), in the Riserva Naturale Statale Gola del Furlo

NATURE THE ARCHITECT

LEGEND HAS IT THAT A SWEET ITALIAN MAIDEN and a tough Germanic warrior, seeking shelter many centuries ago, founded the village of Genga and Castello Petroso, the castle whose massive presense towers over the village 40 miles (65 km) from Ancona. History may have conferred colorful and mythical origins on Genga, but the village also has a natural heritage that will delight the traveler, now as in the past, with its abundant wonders.

In 1971, a group of speleologists discovered by chance a massive system of caves, crystalline lakes, gorges, fissures, and spectacular rock formations that extends over nearly 12 miles (19 km), creating a magical underground world. Today, starting from an entry point close to the 11th-century Abbazia di San Vittore alle Chiuse, formerly the site of Roman baths, visitors can explore a myriad of fantastic subterranean sites: the Cave of the Moustaches, the Midday Cave, and the Cave of the Great Wind. There are passageways and halls of rock, giant alabaster stalactites, and calm pools colored by crystal deposits. Deep below the surface of the earth, the silence is broken only by the incessant drip, drip, dripping of water that has created the caverns and their calcareous deposits over many, many thousands of years. Then, when you've had enough of this dark underworld, climb up to see the impressive 2-mile (3-km) Frasassi ravine, cut out of the soft rock by the River Sentino.

Going underground in these parts is not the only way to appreciate the richness of nature's bounty. The caves are located in the Parco Naturale Regionale Gola della Rossa e di Frasassi, the vibrant green heart of Le Marche. This pristine area of river-cut gorges, ancient woodlands, and gentle mountains provides protection to much flora and fauna and presents an unspoiled environment to the visitor. Eagles and falcons soar in the skies above; wolves, wild boars, and deer roam through the oak and beech forests; and the cave-riddled limestone gorges are the perfect night roost for many species of bats. There are walking trails throughout the park and with just a bit of effort you can climb the slopes of Monte Picco (2,200 ft/671 m) and be sure of an unparalleled view of the valley, while just a short distance away lies Lago Fossi, an oasis of peace and calm, and the perfect location for a picnic.

Main: Stalagmites and stalactites inside the cave known as the Ancona Abyss
Below (left and right): A local specialty, *agnello alla cacciatora* (hunter's lamb); view of Arcevia

Above: The fortress-like Abbazia di San Vittore alle Chiuse

CAVER'S DIARY

The natural magic of the area is not just confined to the Grotte di Frasassi, it can also be seen in the countryside nearby. Three days is enough time to see Genga and the Frasassi caves and also to explore the surrounding national park, dotted with medieval villages built around churches that radiate the spirituality of times gone by.

Three Days in the Park

DAY 1

Genga, the nearest village to the Grotte di Frasassi, is a delightful medieval settlement with ancient walls, surrounded by dense woodland. Book your visit to the caves – there's a range of tours available – but before venturing into the magic of the underground world, savor Genga's tranquil atmosphere by visiting the village museum and the Temple of Valadier. Then spend the afternoon exploring the caves. Afterwards, relax with a chilled glass of Verdicchio, a fragrant white wine produced in the hills, and a few slices of *ciauscolo*, the soft salami that is also typical of the region.

DAY 2

There's a lot to see in the surrounding area: San Vittore with its Roman bridge, Castello Petroso and the great Abbazia di San Vittore alle Chiuse, one of the greatest examples of Romanesque architecture in Le Marche. Explore Pierosara Sassoferrato, an intact medieval corner of the province with a towering fort and historic church; visit, too, the hermitage of Fonte Avellana, one of the largest medieval monastic settlements in Italy, founded in AD 980. Here, you can still see the scriptorium where beautiful illuminated manuscripts were produced, the library, and the spartan monks' cells.

DAY 3

From Genga, pack a picnic and follow one of the walking trails into the Parco Naturale Regionale Gola della Rossa e di Frasassi – there's a visitor information center in the village. Climb up to the Foro degli Occhialoni, walk around Lago Fossi or follow any one of many trails. Afterward, for more of the same, head north to the Riserva Naturale Statale Gola del Furlo, or if you want to see more of Le Marche's history, consider a visit to Arcevia, with its 15th-century walls and medieval forts, or Pergola, to admire the fabulous Roman Cartoceto bronzes, an equestrian group from the 1st century BC.

Dos and Don'ts

- ✓ You'll need an adventurous spirit to visit the caves: the temperature inside is some 18°F (10°C) colder than outside (take a sweater) and the ground is uneven in many places.
- ✗ During the visit, don't touch the walls of the caves, especially the calcareous concretions: it is prohibited!
- ✓ Pay attention to what the guide says – visits to the caves are always led by professionals and there are several tours or itineraries, lasting between 70 minutes and 3 hours.

GETTING THERE
Piazza Armerina is in the heart of Sicily, 22 miles (35 km) from Enna. There is a bus service from Catania, the nearest airport (if taking the train, get off at Dittaino and then take a bus). If you rent a car, take the A19 freeway to the Dittaino exit, then continue on main roads.

GETTING AROUND
To reach the Villa Romana del Casale, go by taxi or rented car (better for getting around independently), since the bus service between the town and the villa is suspended in winter.

WEATHER
Even in November, the weather is never very cold; mean maximum temperatures around 59°F (15°C).

ACCOMMODATIONS
The Suite d'Autore is a designer hotel overlooking the Piazza Duomo. Each suite is decorated in a artistic theme. From US$;135 www.suitedautore.it

Outside town and overlooking the surrounding hills, the Gigliotto *agriturismo* is set in a restored 14th-century monastery. There are 14 tastefully furnished bedrooms arranged around a courtyard. Enjoy the swimming pool, garden, and nearby riding school. Doubles from US$108; www.gigliotto.com

EATING OUT
You will find good, traditional food at the Centrale da Totò. Meals around US$35 (tel. 0935 680 153).

Outside town, enjoy intriguing cuisine at the Autore Al Fogher in a cozy and elegant ambience for about US$54 (www.alfogher.net), or dine for around US$40 at the excellent Gigliotto farmhouse *(see above)*.

PRICE FOR TWO
You will spend about US$275 per day on meals, accommodations, and a visit to Villa Romana del Casale.

FURTHER INFORMATION
www.bestofsicily.com/armerina.htm

Above: Piazza Armerina at night

Below (top to bottom): The ruins of Villa Romana del Casale, a key attraction of the area; the Ponte San Francesco, decorated with beautiful ceramics, connects two of the three hills on which Caltagirone stands; a traditional dish of vermicelli with anchovies, almonds, and sun-dried tomatoes

Main picture: *Two Lovers*, a detail of the colorful mosaics in the Villa Romana del Casale

Stairway to Heaven

Famous for its ceramics production, Caltagirone, like many other towns in southeastern Sicily, was destroyed by the 1693 earthquake, then rebuilt in Baroque style making use of the local colorful majolica. Be sure to see the grand flight of steps that leads up to the Chiesa di Santa Maria del Monte at the highest point of the old town: the 142 different steps are clad in hand-painted majolica and overlooked by a ceramics workshop where you can see the craftsmen at work.

AT HOME WITH THE ROMANS

WILD ANIMALS BEING PURSUED BY HUNTERS, bikini-clad athletes participating in sports, Ulysses getting the better of the cyclops Polyphemus, and Hercules slaying fearsome monsters – these are just a few of the scenes in the fabulous mosaics at the Villa Romana del Casale, a wonderful Roman residence a few miles from Piazza Armerina. In the heart of Sicily, set within a wooded valley, it is an imposing villa – some claim that it belonged to Maximian, co-emperor with Diocletian between AD 286 and 305 – whose floors are home to the largest and richest collection of Roman mosaics in Italy, covering an area of over 4,000 sq yds (3,500 sq m). The beautiful floor decorations are undoubtedly North African in origin and reveal many aspects of daily Roman life in a charming, natural, and lively way.

The villa was built in the early 4th century AD and consists of four main clusters of interconnected buildings. It was abandoned around AD 1000 and covered by a landslide in the 12th century that buried it under more than

Above: Piazza Armerina's historic center, topped by the cathedral

MOSAIC DIARY

The Roman Villa Romana del Casale is one of the most fascinating sites in Italy. It was discovered at the end of the 19th century and the excavations continue to this day. Three days is enough time to see the villa and Piazza Armerina, as well as Morgantina for its Greek ruins, and Caltagirone for its Baroque architecture and ceramics.

Three Days in the Heart of Sicily

DAY 1

Head straight for the Villa Romana del Casale, 3 miles (5 km) from Piazza Armerina, and spend the morning exploring this wonderful complex. The tour winds along walkways that are positioned to enable you to admire the mosaics, kept under Perspex structures to protect them from atmospheric pollution.

In the afternoon, explore Piazza Armerina. The town, which is situated in the heart of one of Sicily's most fertile areas, has a fine 18th-century cathedral that stands out majestically on the top of a hill, and the ruins of a 14th-century Aragonese castle. Enjoy a nice seafood pasta supper with a bottle of local wine.

DAY 2

Visit Morgantina, an important archeological site to the east of Piazza Armerina. An agora, the center of religious and civil life in ancient Greek cities, was brought to light here and it also has a market and theater in an excellent state of conservation.

On the way back, visit the Aidone archeological museum. Many interesting finds from the Morgantina excavations are exhibited here, including a bust of Persephone from the 3rd century BC.

DAY 3

Make a trip to Caltagirone – once the site of a Saracen fortress, the mountain town was destroyed by an earthquake in 1693. Completely rebuilt, it is best known for its Scalinata di Santa Maria del Monte, a great series of steps that has been decorated with colorful ceramic tiles. There are pottery workshops and even a pottery museum, which tells the history of the craft. There are also many splendid Baroque churches to see in town.

Dos and Don'ts

- ✗ Don't arrive at the Villa Romana del Casale after 9:30am if you want to avoid lines at the ticket office. Alternatively, schedule your visit for the lunch hour between 1pm and 2pm.
- ✓ When you visit the villa, take drinking water with you – even in fall, the Perspex covering that protects the mosaics means it can be very hot in there.
- ✗ Don't go to the Villa Romana del Casale if you have difficulty walking and need a wheelchair: the walkways in the villa are regrettably not accessible to wheelchairs.
- ✓ Buy some of the fine ceramic objects from Caltagirone – they make excellent souvenirs of the area.

10 ft (3 m) of earth. This thick layer of mud helped preserve the villa and its colorful mosaics for centuries until excavations in the mid-20th century brought their splendor to light once more.

Visiting the villa, you'll enter the grand atrium, a large porticoed courtyard with a fountain in the center that was reached through a triple-arched doorway. It is here that you can appreciate the monumental size of the complex. On one side you'll find the thermal baths, with rooms for different temperature pools, and, straight ahead, the large latrine built in a recess (a sign of the importance of the household at a time when latrines were certainly not the norm), as well as the gymnasium; on the other side you come to the peristyle or colonnade, the hub where all the parts of the villa converge. From the peristyle, you will pass to the reception area, which has the magnificent Corridor of the Great Hunt, the apsed basilica, clad in marble, and many private apartments.

But despite the grandeur of the villa complex, it is surely the vibrant polychrome mosaics whose dynamism, attention to detail, and fluid execution will stay with you forever.

GETTING THERE
Lenno is on the western branch of Lake Como, less than 19 miles (31 km) northeast of Como. From Milan, the nearest airport, you can reach Lenno by car, train, or bus in about 1½ hours.

GETTING AROUND
You access the Villa Balbianello by boat from Lenno. There is a good ferry service from Como to Lenno.

WEATHER
Lenno has a very mild climate, even in the winter.

ACCOMMODATIONS
The Albergo Terminus in Como, looking on to the lake, is in a restored Art Nouveau palazzo and has preserved all its aristocratic charm. Rooms from US$250; www.lake-como-hotel-terminus.com

The Darsena is a small historic hotel in Tremezzo, in a great location right by the lake. Enjoy comfortable rooms from US$135; www.centrohotelslagocomo.it

EATING OUT
If you would like to taste lake specialties at reasonable prices, try the simple and welcoming Santo Stefano restaurant. Specials include *missoltini* (lake shad, grilled and served with vinegar) and ravioli stuffed with fish from the lake. Meals cost around US$35; www.santostefano.too.it

You can have an elegant and romantic dinner at the Navedano di Como, probably the only hothouse restaurant in Italy. When you enter the 19th-century building you are immediately immersed in a magical atmosphere among the fragrant flowers, plants, and elegant furnishings. Their creative cuisine is also very special. Meals cost around US$68; www.ristorantenavedano.it

PRICE FOR TWO
You will spend about US$355 per day on meals, accommodations, and entry to the villas.

FURTHER INFORMATION
www.lagodicomo.com

The Silk Museum

Como, a 2,000-year-old Roman town, has long been a center of silk production. The secret of silk was smuggled out of China in the 6th century to the Middle East. Six hundred years later the expertise came to southern Italy. Today, you can follow this history in the Museo Didattico della Seta (Silk Museum): it has nearly 10,000 sq ft (930 sq m) of exhibition space where an old silk mill has been recreated. You can also see the stages of the processing: from the breeding of the silkworms, to the silk-throwing and the weaving, dyeing, and printing of the fabrics.

ROMANTICISM BY THE LAKE

An emerald-green garden with stone balustrades, looking out over a stretch of cobalt-blue lake and, in the distance, a range of mountains that change from white to gray to green and then blue. This is the glorious landscape that saw interplanetary love blossom between Amidala, queen of Naboo, and the Jedi knight Anakin Skywalker in Episode II of the *Star Wars* movie saga. George Lucas may be a magician with the special effects but he had no need of digital technology to create this other-worldy marvel: he found it in the garden of the Villa Balbianello, in one of the most evocative corners of Lake Como.

The villa is built on the very tip of a promontory that extends into the lake. The thickly wooded hill behind the villa hides the nearby town and, with the two bays on each side, creates an atmosphere of splendid isolation. The views are further enhanced by the fine loggia that is open on two sides, one of Balbianello's special features. This architectural treasure came into existence at the end of the 18th century thanks to Cardinal Angelo Maria Durini, a man of letters and refined tastes, and a patron of the

Main: Villa Balbianello and its luxuriant garden by the calm waters of Lake Como

arts who wanted to realize his dream of a sumptuous and secluded place to which he could retire. The villa was constructed over a former Franciscan monastery – retaining the church's two bell-towers in its design – becoming a complex with two elegant residences, a chapel, a small harbor on the lake shore, and the fine loggia. All this is surrounded by a delightful terraced garden that follows the rocky shoreline of the promontory and farther embellishes the beauty of the lake.

With the exterior and layout of the villa complex established, it was up to its last private owner, the 20th-century mountain climber, explorer and traveler Guido Monzino, to make a significant contribution to the interior of the villa. To him we owe not only the internal furnishings, with wonderful 18th-century items of mainly French and English provenance, but also the arrangement of his personal collections and records of his expeditions, with collections of Chinese, African, and pre-Columbian art – interesting items from a long time ago, from countries far, far away...

Above (top and bottom): Villa d'Este in Cernobbio, built in the 16th century and today a luxury hotel; baked perch with herbs, a local delicacy

Below: Statue- and tree-lined path in the garden at the Villa Balbianello, Lenno

Above: Canova's *Cupid and Psyche* at the Villa Carlotta in Tremezzo

VILLA DIARY

Villa Balbianello looks on to Lake Como, an enchanting place with echoes of the era when the Milanese aristocracy built grand holiday villas here. Many of these are still standing today, sheltering among the trees along the fringes of the intensely blue lake. Three days is enough time to see the best villas and the main town of Como.

Three Days by Lake Como

DAY 1

Go for a stroll in the village of Lenno, nestling by a little bay in the lake. It has a beautiful 11th-century church, restored in the 16th century, with a baptistry nearby. From here head for the grand Villa Balbianello. Don't miss the view of the lake from the balcony and allow a few hours to explore the rooms, in particular the Expeditions Museum, which has memorabilia from Guido Monzino's travels. Walk around the gardens and enjoy the wonderful views from the trails. Finish the day with a meal of lake fish and a locally brewed beer looking over the water.

DAY 2

Take a boat to Tremezzo, one of the most romantic places on the lake, and visit Villa Carlotta. The villa is named after Princess Carlotta of Prussia, who was given it as a gift in 1843. Built at the close of the 17th century, the villa was enriched by valuable works of art, including sculptures by Antonio Canova, still on display inside the villa. But the main attraction is the fabulous garden, which is divided into two parts: an Italian garden designed in the 18th century and an English one, laid out by the princess herself. Afterward, take the boat across to Bellagio for a stroll around the cobbled streets of this pretty town and enjoy an evening drink.

DAY 3

Take a trip to Como, situated at the southern end of the lake. It's a lively town, full of fine shops, a silk museum, and great architecture – next to the impressive Gothic Duomo is the Broletto, the former town hall. Don't miss the walk to the Tempio Voltiano, a romantic shrine that Como dedicated to Alessandro Volta, inventor of the first reliable battery. Continue on along the shore to the Neo-Classical Villa dell'Olmo with beautiful formal gardens and wild parkland.

Dos and Don'ts

- ✓ Visit the Villa Balbianello in early November; it closes between November 15 and March.
- ✗ There is no need for a car: the road along the lake is narrow and winding and is slow-moving through lakeside towns. Traveling by boat is much better.
- ✓ To reach Villa Balbianello, take the ferry from Lenno or Sala Comacina; on the weekend you can also walk along the gravel road that starts off from Lenno's lake shore.
- ✓ Buy a silk scarf, blouse, or tie: Como is world-famous for its silk weaving – it's good quality at reasonable prices.

GETTING THERE
Matera is in eastern Basilicata. The nearest international airport is at Bari, about 37 miles (60 km) away; you can get from the airport to Matera in just over an hour by car.

GETTING AROUND
A car is the best method of getting around.

WEATHER
Even in November, average temperatures peak around 59ºF (15ºC), or higher on sunny days.

ACCOMMODATIONS
The Hotel Sant'Angelo, among the *sassi*, has atmospheric rooms carved out of the rock, and breathtaking views from its terraces; doubles from US$135; www.hotelsantangelosassi.it

The Caveoso Hotel, also in the heart of the *sassi*, offers stylish hospitality and rock-cut rooms from US$102; www.caveosohotel.com

Tempa Bianca, an 18th-century country house and horse stud farm in Materano, has welcoming rooms and a good restaurant. From US$48 per person for B&B; www.tempabianca.com

EATING OUT
Don Matteo is a smart restaurant, set in a former cave, offering creative cuisine for about US$68; www.donmatteoristorante.com

The Lucana is welcoming and informal with specialties from around US$42; tel. 0835 336 117.

At the Casino del Diavolo, enjoy dishes such as *favetta* (fava bean purée) and *orecchiette con funghi cardoncelli* (pasta with wild mushrooms). Meals from around US$35; tel. 0835 261 986.

PRICE FOR TWO
US$245 per day for food and accommodations.

FURTHER INFORMATION
www.sassiweb.it

Montescaglioso

It sounds unwelcoming, yet Montescaglioso (Scaly Mountain), a short way south of Matera, has probably been inhabited since as far back as 1000 BC. Today, it is known for the Abbazia di San Michele Arcangelo. The origin of the abbey is unclear, but it probably dates to the 5th century, although earliest written records date it to AD 1078. It was rebuilt at the end of the 15th century and flourished until 1784, when the monks moved to Lecce. There are two very beautiful cloisters with highly prized frescoes, and a fine library and chapterhouse.

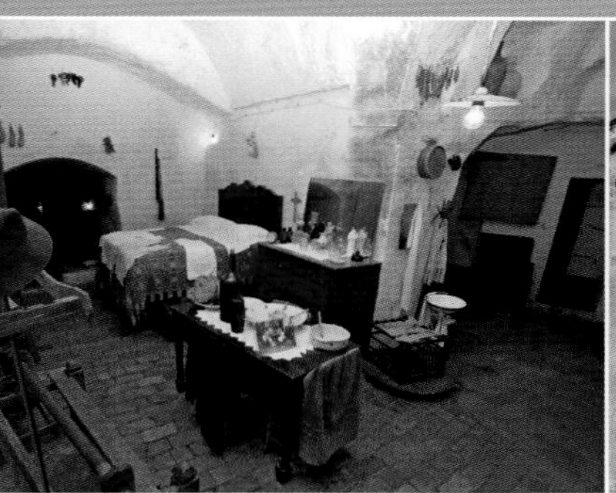

Main: Matera's Sassi district, now a UNESCO World Heritage Site, topped by the Duomo's bell tower
Above (left to right): Interior of one of the *sassi*; rose window of Matera's 13th-century Romanesque Duomo; view of the Sassi district

Above: View of the arid countryside around Matera

AMONG THE CAVEMEN

KNOWN AS THE "CITY OF STONE," Matera is famous for its dwellings – known as *sassi* (stones) – carved out of the volcanic tufa with amazing skill, connected by alleyways and stacked higgledy-piggledy one on top of another in apparent disarray. However, there was method in this madness – the dwellings are arranged in groups around a well, which was used by several families. The light filters in at unexpected angles and, thanks to the cooling properties of the stone, which functions as an air conditioner, the temperature inside is a constant 59°F (15°C). The roofs of the caves were often used as kitchen gardens, with complicated irrigation systems. This sophisticated ecosystem is undoubtedly impressive, but what is most astonishing is that this phenomenon has been in existence since the Paleolithic era (some of the finds date back at least 10,000 years). Matera's *sassi* were defined as official districts in 1204, and, with few changes, they were inhabited until the 1970s, when the residents were moved to new homes because of the lack of facilities. Now declared a UNESCO World Heritage Site as one of the best examples of cave settlements in the Mediterranean, many of the *sassi* have been redeveloped into boutique hotels, joined together to form stylish homes, and even returned to their original state as interesting anthropological museums.

The location of the *sassi* is an attractive one – they extend into two almost parallel valleys, divided by the rocky spur of Matera Old Town (Civita). This meant it was an easy place to defend, and therefore attracted settlers. The volcanic rock was easily carved and allowed constant improvements to be made over the years: the Palombaro Lungo, one of the largest cisterns in Matera, has parts that were built 3,000 years ago and others that go back only to the 18th century.

And there is more. Hidden in the volcanic rock you may also glimpse a monastery, with monks' cells clustered around the church, here and there are rock-cut churches and even a Byzantine basilica. The interiors of these surprising buildings are ablaze with brightly colored frescoes of religious portraiture and symbolism. It is hardly surprising that the area was used as a location for films chronicling the birth of a secret underground sect – Christianity. Pier Paolo Pasolini's *The Gospel According to St. Matthew* and Mel Gibson's *The Passion of Christ* were both filmed here.

And while some were tunnelling down into the soft rock, others were building upward, in an ongoing dialogue between cave and bell tower. In contrast to the hidden cave churches, Matera's Civita is proudly topped by its 13th-century Romanesque Duomo and 170-ft (52-m) bell tower.

Below (left to right): Matera bread, famous since the 15th century and said to be the best in Italy; the ancient uninhabited village of Craco, 40km from Matera; Chiesa di San Domenico, a 13th-century masterpiece

UNDERGROUND DIARY

Matera is said to be one of the oldest towns in the world and is surely one of the most remarkable. The dwellings, or *sassi*, carved out of rock, form a unique sand-colored landscape, shaped over many centuries. Spend three days in Matera to explore the ancient cave-dwelling districts, the more recent – but still very old – Matera Civita, rock-cut churches, and Montescaglioso.

Three Days in Matera

DAY 1

Start your tour of Matera at Piazza Vittorio Veneto, from where you can enjoy a wonderful view. Admire the urban plan of the *sassi*, divided into two districts: the Sasso Barisano and Sasso Caveoso. They are both remarkable and worth exploring simply by strolling through the narrow streets, without a definite objective. The cave districts are studded with rocky churches, which are not to be missed; they are very old (built between the 8th and the 13th centuries) and decorated with beautiful frescoes. The most important ones are San Pietro Caveos, Santa Maria d'Idris, and Santa Lucia delle Malve.

DAY 2

Visit modern Matera: again start from the Piazza Vittorio Veneto for a stroll around the town's churches and palaces. Visit the 13th-century Duomo with its fine Romanesque façade. The 13th-century Chiesa di San Domenico, renovated in 1744, is also worth a visit. For lunch, enjoy a simple bruschetta with tomato, red onion, and basil or try a pasta dish with a fiery chili sauce.

Next, head for the archeological park outside Matera. Here the landscape is arid and sparsely covered with vegetation, but it has an ancient heritage of exceptional value – around 160 rock churches, many decorated with fine medieval frescoes, prehistoric tombs, and cisterns carved out of the rock.

DAY 3

Today, make the short trip south to Montescaglioso. On the way you can see the surrounding countryside. Once there, climb up to the abbey and enjoy a walk along the Matera Gravina – a limestone gorge that is home to plenty of wildlife and plants. Enjoy a long walk, safe in the knowledge that you'll be sampling more of the simple but often spicy Basilicata cuisine, washed down with the excellent local wine, in the evening.

Dos and Don'ts

- ✓ Arrange for a guide to show you round the rock churches in the archeological park. For information, visit www.parcomurgia.it
- ✗ Don't take dogs or other pets with you when you visit the park; they will not be admitted.
- ✓ Buy a papier-mâché souvenir – it's a traditional local craft.

GETTING THERE
Maranello is in Emilia-Romagna, about 12 miles (19 km) or 30 minutes' drive from Modena (the nearest airports are Bologna and Parma). There is a bus service between Modena and Maranello.

GETTING AROUND
The best way to get around the countryside is by car.

WEATHER
Expect maximum average temperatures to reach around 54°F (12°C) at this time of year.

ACCOMMODATIONS
For the ultimate auto experience, try the 4-star Ferrari-themed Maranello Village. A double room will cost US$115; www.maranellovillage.com

If you are looking for a small, peaceful hotel just outside Maranello, you will love the Locanda del Mulino. Rooms from US$95; www.locandadelmulino.com

EATING OUT
In Maranello, the Cavallino restaurant, opposite the famous Ferrari car factory and owned by them, is an unmissable stopping point for car enthusiasts. Enjoy traditional Emilia-Romagna cuisine from US$48; www.ristorante-cavallino.it

The Osteria dei Girasoli in Sassuolo offers inspiring modern cuisine made with local produce for around US$48; www.osteriadeigirasoli.com

Near Fiorano, the Volta delle Rondini *agriturismo* serves genuine local cuisine, with meals about US$42; www.lavoltadeirondini.it

PRICE FOR TWO
You will spend about US$250 for meals, accommodations, and entry to the Galleria Ferrari.

FURTHER INFORMATION
www.galleria.ferrari.com; www.maranello.it

The Prancing Horse

A black horse prancing on a yellow background above the letters SF (Scuderia Ferrari); at the top, three stripes in the colors of the Italian flag: this is the world-famous Ferrari logo. However, its origin is not so well known: the horse is the emblem that was displayed on the airplanes of Francesco Baracca, an Italian aviation ace who died during World War I. In 1923, the mother of the aviator suggested to Enzo Ferrari, then an Alfa Romeo racing driver, that he could use it as an emblem for his cars. From then on, the Prancing Horse was used as the symbol of his prestigious motor-racing stable.

THE LEGEND OF THE HORSE

FERRARI IS THE MOST FAMOUS motor racing stable in the world. In the 1920s, Grand Prix racing driver Enzo Ferrari drove for Alfa Romeo, and then in the 1930s managed the development of their racing cars, before establishing his own company, Ferrari, in Maranello at the heart of Modena in 1943.

Ever since then, Maranello has been one of the automobile capitals of the world and, as befits a true capital, proudly signals its status with many monuments to Enzo Ferrari and the Prancing Horse. These monuments include the factory buildings and Ferrari workshops designed by great architects, such as Massimiliano Fuksas, Renzo Piano, and Jean Nouvel. But the finest monument of all is the Galleria Ferrari, where past and present blend together and reach out into the future. The gallery was inaugurated in 1990, is managed directly by Ferrari, and attracts 200,000 visitors every year, offering

Main: Renzo Piano's futuristic Galleria del Vento (Wind Tunnel)

Left: Ferrari Monza 750 in the Galleria Ferrari in Maranello, home to many Ferrari products

Right (left to right): Mud cones in the Riserva Naturale Regionale delle Salse di Nirano; *nocino*, a sticky brown liqueur made from walnuts; the Palazzo Ducale, one of Sassuolo's most important historic buildings

an unforgettable insight into the heart of the Ferrari legend. The models exhibited relate the story of Ferrari racing, from the 125S car that won the first Ferrari race in 1947 – the definitive classic racing car – to the F2005, the 51st vehicle built for the Formula 1 world championship.

Next, visitors can appreciate the Ferrari's road cars, the dream of every car enthusiast, arranged in a chronology from the 1948 166 Inter to the 2006 599 GTB Fiorano, a work of art that can travel at 190 mph (305 kph). The gallery also puts on important exhibitions on themes such as the recent "Ferrari and America," which marked 60 years of the Italian firm's presence in the American market.

Showing just how much the Ferrari factory has become a Maranello fixture, the gallery offers its visitors numerous special offers with hotels, restaurants, and museums in the area. It is an excellent opportunity to round off a visit by trying out Modena's famous gastronomy of ham, balsamic vinegar, great cheeses, Vignola cherries, Lambrusco wine, and *nocino*, a sweet walnut liqueur.

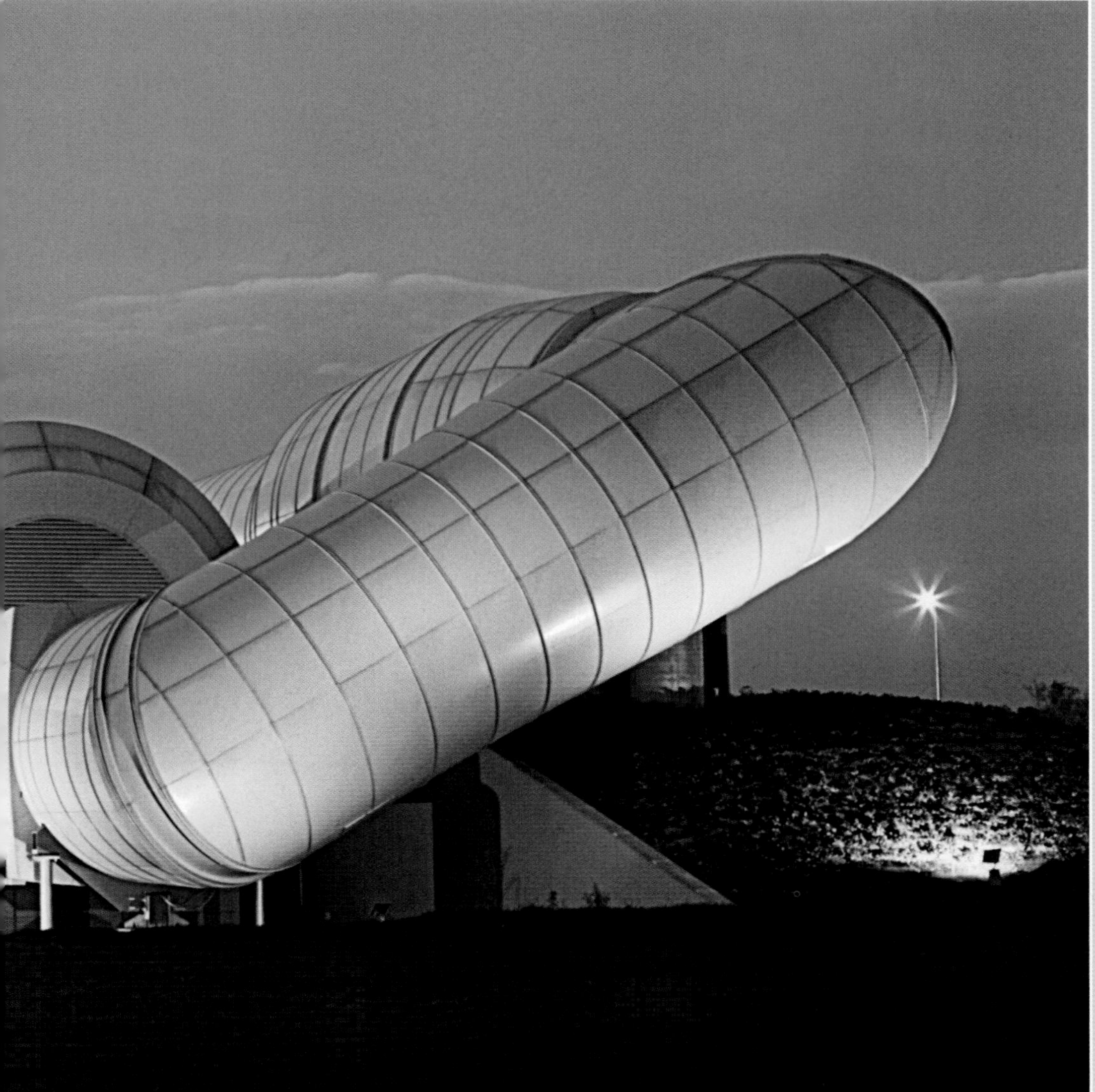

Above: The red factory chimney of the Ferrari works

AUTOMOTIVE DIARY

Maranello means Ferrari, Formula 1, and fast cars. During four days, visitors can see the museum dedicated to these legendary automobiles and then go on an artistic and gastronomic tour of Modena *(see also pp96–7)*, visiting the towns and villages of Fiorano, Sassuolo, and Montegibbio, home to historic castles, museums, and palaces.

Four Days of Ferrari

DAY 1

Enjoy a day at the Galleria Ferrari, Maranello. After admiring the motoring memorabilia – cars, trophies, and engines – treat yourself to a fine dinner based on local produce such as *zampone* (stuffed pigs trotter) or maybe a cheesy risotto dressed with Modena's famous vinegar; as a digestif, try a glass of *nocino*, a delicious local liqueur made from young walnuts.

DAY 2

Make a visit to nearby Fiorano: the hamlet is dominated by the sanctuary of the Beata Vergine del Castello, built in 1634 to house the picture of the Virgin painted on the portal of the old castle. Just outside the village is the Castello Spezzano, which has a ceramics museum with displays of local ceramics. For dinner, enjoy tortellini, little pasta parcels filled with prosciutto and Parmesan, washed down with a glass of lightly sparkling Lambrusco.

DAY 3

Head for Sassuolo and its magnificent Palazzo Ducale, built in 1634 at the behest of Francesco I d'Este, the Duke of Modena. The palazzo has elaborately furnished rooms decorated with glorious frescoes and is surrounded by splendid parkland, perfect for a leisurely stroll, with a Baroque fishpond and a chapel.

DAY 4

On your last day, visit Montegibbio, dominated by a large 14th-century castle (although there is evidence that a fort has stood here since the 10th century). The interior has an elliptical courtyard surrounded by various buildings such as the keep, the 17th-century church, and the residential palace, also lavishly decorated with frescoes. Afterward, enjoy a walk among the lunar landscapes of the Riserva Naturale Regionale delle Salse di Nirano, where tiny volcanoes burp up sulfurous mud.

Dos and Don'ts

- ✓ While you're in the area, buy something ceramic – Fiorano and Sassuolo are famous for their beautifully decorated pottery.
- ✗ Don't book a hotel outside Sassuolo's historic center; it's a very industrialized area and not very attractive.
- ✓ Admire the exterior of the Galleria del Vento (Wind Tunnel) – you're not allowed to go in – where they aerodynamically test the cars. Designed by Renzo Piano, it was completed in 1997.

GETTING THERE
Leonardo da Vinci (Fiumicino) is the capital's main airport. The Leonardo Express train service will take you to Rome's Termini train station in 30 minutes. There are plenty of shuttle buses between the airport and the capital, or you can take a taxi.

GETTING AROUND
Explore Rome on foot, using public transportation for longer distances or when you're tired.

WEATHER
Still quite mild, with maximum temperatures averaging around 61°F (16°C).

ACCOMMODATIONS
The historic 5-star Hotel Hassler is at the top of the Spanish Steps, overlooking the shopping streets. Very luxurious, it has smart restaurants and an exclusive spa. From US$475; www.hotelhassler.com

The Art Hotel in Via Marguta, a few steps from the Piazza di Spagna, was converted from a former school, creating a special place with hi-tech furnishings alongside works of art and design. Rooms from US$394; www.hotelart.it

EATING OUT
Imàgo Hassler has a covered terrace with a fine view over the city and elegant and imaginative cuisine. Meals from US$95; www.imagorestaurant.com

Casina Valadier, in the Villa Borghese, is ideal for a romantic lunch or dinner with a great view of the city. Meals from US$62; www.casinavaladier.it

Penna d'Oca, a few steps from the Piazza del Popolo, is a smart and welcoming restaurant offering creative cuisine and meals from US$68 (tel. 06 320 898).

PRICE FOR TWO
About US$640 per day for meals, accommodations, and the Roma&Più Pass Transport; allow a little more if staying at the exclusive Hotel Hassler.

FURTHER INFORMATION
www.turismoroma.it

The Rome Ghetto

There have been Jewish communities in Rome since the 2nd century BC, but it was only in 1555 that Pope Paul IV decided to confine them in a walled-in district, opposite the Isola Tiberina. It remains a Jewish quarter to this day, as is testified by its food shops and kosher restaurants, and extends around the Via Portico di Ottavia, the road to the central synagogue. Here, too, you will find the Jewish Museum of Rome, which tells the story of the city's Jewish community and organizes guided tours within the ghetto walls.

Main: The famous Spanish Steps and Trinità dei Monti, a symbol of Rome
Above (left and right): The Museo dell'Ara Pacis displaying the altar built by Augustus in 9 BC; the famous twin churches of Santa Maria in Montesanto (left) and Santa Maria dei Miracoli, in the Piazza del Popolo

ROMAN HOLIDAY

Despite the name, Via del Babuino (Baboon Street) has nothing to do with baboons. In 1581, a rich local merchant built a public fountain and decorated it with a statue of a reclining Silenus, a half-man, half-goat spirit of the springs from Greek mythology. Thinking it ugly, the witty locals immediately re-baptized the statue "er Babuino," and the name stuck. Today, the street is synonymous with upscale shopping, and forms a straight line from the showy Piazza di Spagna at the foot of the Spanish Steps to the refined Piazza del Popolo. Like the neighboring streets, Via del Babuino is a glittering expanse of shop windows that sparkle with the most famous names in fashion and jewelry. Next to the fashion shops you'll find exclusive art galleries – in streets such as Via Margutta – that have preserved an out-of-town atmosphere with hidden gardens and leafy pergolas. Artists are attracted to the area and display their work here from time to time. These streets, which once provided the backdrop for unforgettable movie scenes – including Audrey Hepburn and Gregory Peck's Vespa ride in *Roman Holiday* – are today synonymous with luxury and high society.

And yet, as in all parts of Rome, you need only divert your gaze from the tempting shop windows for a moment to discover something remarkable. For example, the Chiesa di Santa Maria del Popolo, in the square of the same name. This early Renaissance church contains some of Rome's finest art treasures: the frescoes of Pinturicchio and Bramante, a chapel designed by Raphael and completed by Bernini, and two large paintings by Caravaggio. Head to the river to find the Museo dell'Ara Pacis, home to one of ancient Rome's most important monuments. The altar was built to commemorate the consolidation of the empire and an end to war under Augustus and is decorated with exquisitely delicate friezes and bas-reliefs. The nearby Mausoleum of Augustus, commissioned by the emperor as a tomb for himself and his family, is actually a very romantic place despite the many despoliations it has suffered over the centuries. The area is an example of the extraordinary interweaving of ancient and modern that adds to Rome's charm and makes it one of the most fascinating cities in the world.

Below (left to right): A favorite Roman dish, *Vignarola*, a mixture of artichokes, fava beans, and peas; poster for *Roman Holiday*, one of the movies that helped to crystallize the idea of Rome as a romantic city; the cupola of the Cappella Chigi, with mosaics depicting the *Creation of the World* by Raphael, inside the Chiesa di Santa Maria del Popolo

Above: The celebrated Piazza Navona

CAPITAL DIARY

Streets that are centers of fashion, wonderful architecture, and historic buildings filled with priceless works of art – Rome has it all. It would take weeks to see everything that this extraordinary city has to offer, but five days is just enough to see a few interesting Roman, medieval, and Renaissance sights. *(See also pp28–9 and pp236–7)*

Five Days in the Eternal City

DAY 1

Start at the Piazza del Popolo and visit the Chiesa di Santa Maria del Popolo. One chapel was decorated by Pinturicchio for the della Rovere dynasty, the Cappella Chigi was designed by Raphael and completed by Bernini, and two paintings in the Capella Cerasi are by Caravaggio. Afterward, stroll down Via del Babuino and soak up the atmosphere of one of Rome's finest shopping streets.

DAY 2

Head for the Pincian Hill and explore the Villa Medici, a 16th-century villa surrounded by a magnificent garden. Stroll along to the terraces with panoramas of the city. Enjoy lunch in nearby Villa Borghese, then walk to the church known as Trinità dei Monti and down its famous Spanish Steps to Piazza di Spagna.

DAY 3

Continue from where you left off the day before at the Piazza Augusto Imperatore and see the Ara Pacis and the nearby Mausoleum of Augustus. Continue into Via Condotti – another famous shopping street – and stop off at the Caffè Greco, a famous rendezvous for Roman artists and intellectuals, for a coffee or something stronger.

DAY 4

Cross over the Tiber River, and stroll around Trastevere, one of Rome's most picturesque quarters, full of bars and restaurants. The church of Santa Maria in Trastevere has some fine 12th-century mosaics. In the evening, join in with the locals at the Piazza Santa Maria, one of the centers of Rome nightlife.

DAY 5

Spend the day at the Porta Portese street market, the largest and most famous in Rome, held every Sunday morning. You will find everything there from antique furniture to shoes, from stamps to kitchen utensils. Take a break at midday and enjoy a thin-crust Roman pizza beside the river, then wander slowly back to your hotel.

Dos and Don'ts

- ✓ Take a boat trip on the Tiber – it's an interesting and different way of seeing the city.
- ✗ At the Porta Portese street market, don't pay the display prices: haggling is expected.
- ✓ Buy a three-day Roma&Più Pass Transport: it gives free travel on public transportation and free entry to two museums or sites, as well as reduced entrance fees to all other sites. For more information, visit www.romapass.it

GETTING THERE
Alba is in the southern part of Piedmont. From Turin, the nearest airport, you can reach Alba by car in just over an hour by taking the A6 freeway, leaving at the Bra exit, and following the signs to your destination. There are also frequent trains and buses from Turin.

GETTING AROUND
Use a car for getting around the countryside independently.

WEATHER
Fall may be chilly but you'll be kept warm by the great local wines and truffle-flavored cuisine.

ACCOMMODATIONS
The Cascina Baràc hotel near Alba, in verdant surroundings, offers a first-rate rural stay. Four-bed apartments from US$258; www.barac.it

The Bricco dei Cogni is an elegant manor house with a panoramic position among the Langhe vineyards. Four-bed rooms from US$204; www.briccodeicogni.it

EATING OUT
In the heart of Alba there are two restaurants in one historic building: La Piola, on the ground floor, offers traditional fare in an informal atmosphere with superb local wines; and the elegant Piazza Duomo on the first floor, which offers inspiring, top-quality cuisine. Meals cost between US$54 and US$ 95; www.piazzaduomoalba.it

The Locanda del Pilone, an old farmhouse near Alba surrounded by vineyards, offers dinners that combine tradition and innovation for around US$82; www.locandadelpilone.com

PRICE FOR A FAMILY OF FOUR
About US$350 per day for meals and accommodations.

FURTHER INFORMATION
www.langheroero.it; www.fieradeltartufo.org

The Truffle

The white truffle, or *trifola* as it is called in Alba, is usually eaten raw, sliced very thinly, with simple dishes that bring out its flavor. Light brown in color, with firm, compact flesh marked by very fine streaks, its price – always on the high side – varies from one season to the next according to whether the weather has been dry, which favors growth, or wet, which slows it down. Specially trained dogs are often used for tracking down this "white diamond" and every truffle-hunter has their favorite secret hunting ground.

Left: Towers and town hall of Alba

Right (left to right): The famous wine town, Barolo, surrounded by vineyards; the medieval castle of Grinzane Cavour, now a museum of local products; misty view of the rural village of Govone

Main: A glorious sunset over the quiet town of Alba
Above (top to bottom): Grand ballroom at the Castello di Govone; the snow-capped Monviso rising above historic Alba; Villa La Favorita, a wine-producing fruit farm in Alba

HOME OF THE TRUFFLE

As far as the eye can see there is wave after wave of hills. On the horizon they form ethereal and indistinct silhouettes, while those nearby are cloaked in close-knit rows of vines, flaming red and yellow at this time of year. Here and there the line of hills is broken by deep, thickly wooded valleys; on top of distant ridges, small villages stand out against the sky, while large *masseria* (farmhouses) break up the studied geometry of the vineyards. These are the hills of the Langhe, an area of Piedmont with wines that are prized throughout the world: Dolcetto, Nebbiolo, Barolo, Grignolino. And at its heart sits Alba, in a hollow along the bank of the Tanaro.

Alba is an attractive little town with a rich history – its buildings are brick-red in color and its center is studded with medieval towers. But Alba is not really famous for its history or architecture. In the misty fall, the town's charm is linked to an unmistakable musty aroma that fills the streets, leaking out of every restaurant and

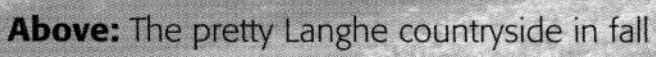
Above: The pretty Langhe countryside in fall

delicatessen. Alba is renowned for its fabulous white truffles. This aromatic treat is the queen of Piedmontese gastronomy and grows abundantly in the Langhe among the oaks, lime trees, poplars, and willows. Every fall, in one of Italy's most important gastronomic events, Alba dedicates a festival to this expensive delicacy, which attracts gourmets from all over the world.

Of course, Alba also has plenty of artistic and architectural merits – there's the Palazzo Comunale with its 14th-century frescoes, the Chiesa di San Domenico with its fine Gothic façade, the Romanesque Duomo with its Gothic campanile, and the Baroque Chiesa di Santa Maria Maddalena, built in the 18th century. These historic buildings are grouped in a few historic streets lined with boutiques and wine bars. Spend some time shopping here, then sit outside at a café and enjoy a glass of fine wine while watching the evening *passeggiata*.

FALL DIARY

The white truffle is undoubtedly the star in Alba, but don't forget the Barolo wine and, for dessert, the delicious chocolates of Ferrero, whose factory is nearby. In November, as the hills blaze with fall colors, Alba holds its world-famous truffle festival. Five days is enough time for you to explore the local countryside and towns and appreciate their fabulous food and wine.

Five Days in the Langhe

DAY 1

Explore the historic center of Alba – once known for its 100 towers, of which only four remain. For lunch, walk down the main street, Via Vittorio Emanuele (known locally as Via Maestra), and enjoy an apéritif and light lunch at an outside table. In the afternoon, head for the Palazzo dei Congressi, which in the fall becomes a truffle temple. Thankful for your small lunch, enjoy wine and food tastings, and, of course, the famous truffle.

DAY 2

The quiet roads of the Langhe countryside are perfect for family hikes or cycle rides. Wherever you go, you will find wine cellars offering tastings and sometimes excellent simple food to perfectly complement the wine.

DAY 3

Head for Grinzane Cavour, whose castle stands atop a hill covered with vineyards and has an ethnographic museum as well as a regional Piedmontese wine cellar. Inside, you'll find a delightful section dedicated to local wine and gastronomy, with displays of kitchen equipment, an 18th-century distillery, and a cooper's workshop.

DAY 4

Visit the village of Govone, dominated by a fine 18th-century castle that used to be the summer residence of the Savoyards. Toward the end of November it becomes a Christmas village, holding all sorts of events, including a Christmas film festival.

DAY 5

You must visit Barolo, famous throughout the world for its full-bodied wine. The village is characterized by two castles, one of which houses another important regional wine cellar. Enjoy a meal of delicious local foods and, of course, some of the dark red Barolo wine.

Dos and Don'ts

- ✓ Treat yourself to a truffle. They are very expensive, but the fabulous musky flavor is out of this world!
- ✗ Do not eat your truffle with fancy dishes; all you need to bring out the flavor is a fried egg or a simple plate of *tagliolini* pasta.
- ✓ Do visit the world truffle auction – it is held in the castle of Grinzane Cavour at the beginning of November.
- ✓ Visit www.christmasfilmfestival.it for detailed information on Govone's festival programme (Italian only).

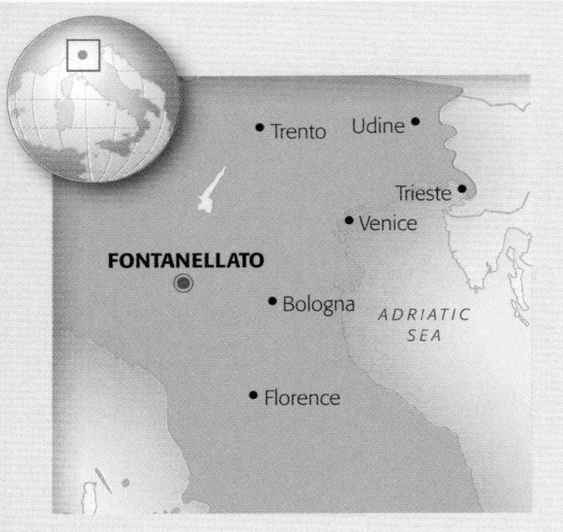

GETTING THERE
Fontanellato is in the north of Emilia-Romagna, about 12 miles (19 km) northwest of Parma, the nearest airport. From Parma, you can reach Fontanellato by car, taking the SS9 then the SP11, or by bus.

GETTING AROUND
The area has a good network of buses, but it is easier to tour the surrounding countryside in a car.

WEATHER
Expect maximum temperatures around 50ºF (10ºC), with a good few pleasant sunny days.

ACCOMMODATIONS
La Cascina is a B&B in a rural farmhouse near Fontanellato, offering informal hospitality. Four-bed rooms from US$150; www.hotellacascina.com

There is an old-world atmosphere at the Locanda del Lupo in Soragna, with suites featuring four-poster beds at US$245; www.locandadellupo.com

In the countryside around San Secondo Parmense, the B&B Dalla Nonna Maria offers a warm welcome. The spacious attic room is ideal for families. About US$95–108 per day; www.bbnonnamaria.it

EATING OUT
There are numerous restaurants in the area that serve delicious local specialties such as *culatello* (the best Parma ham), herb tortelli (a type of ravioli) with Parmesan, and *zabaglione* (a light custard). Try the elegant Due Foscari in Busseto (about US$55; www.iduefoscari.it), the welcoming Osteria Ardenga near Soragna (about US$42–55; www.osteriardenga.it), or the smart Al Vèdel in Colorno (from US$42; www.poderecadassa.it).

PRICE FOR A FAMILY OF FOUR
About US$355–440 for meals, accommodations, and entrance to the main historic buildings.

FURTHER INFORMATION
www.comune.fontanellato.pr.it/turismo; http://turismo.parma.it

Parmesan Cheese Museum

The Parma area is famous for its gastronomic products, acknowledged worldwide as Italian delicacies. One of the most valued of these is the "King of Cheeses," *Parmigiano reggiano*, named after the two towns Parma and Reggio Emilia, in the center of the production area. A museum has been created in a former cheese factory in Soragna explaining the history, myths, and manufacture of this extraordinary product, with displays of historic tools. A visit also includes a delicious tasting of Parmesan.

THE PAINTED FORTRESSES

As you approach from one of the numerous narrow streets that lead to Fontanellato's main piazza, suddenly the fortress comes into view, and the effect is impressive. The massive bulk of the Rocca Sanvitale, a harmonious collection of towers, turrets, and battlements surrounded by a wide, carp-filled moat, looks somewhat out of place in this pretty square of chocolate-box houses.

Built for military purposes in the 15th century, the fortress was also used as a noble residence and the castle perfectly performed these two functions for centuries. The exterior is large, dark, and forbidding, and it exudes an air of impregnability in accordance with the best military tradition. But once you have crossed the drawbridge and entered within the walls, the courtyard reveals details, such as the double portico and bright terracotta tiles, that recall the Renaissance tradition. This impression

Main: Detail of the fresco by Parmigianino in the Diana and Actaeon room of Rocca Sanvitale in Fontanellato

is emphasized by the interior decor: the wonderfully proportioned halls are adorned with portraits, furnishings, and colorful frescoes, such as in the rooms decorated by Parmigianino in 1523, where a delicate trompe l'oeil recreates an angel-filled pergola in the vaulting, while the myth of Actaeon, the hunter turned by the goddess Diana into a stag, is skilfully depicted in the lunettes. It's an exquisite relic of a period of aristocratic civilization that left a fine heritage in central Italy.

Fontanellato's impressive fortress is not the only one in the area. Emilia-Romagna has many fine castles and princely villas that for centuries provided patronage to the greatest intellectuals and artists of the age. One of the most impressive of these is the Reggia di Colorno, a 14th-century fortress that was transformed three centuries later into such an elegant palace that the dukes of Parma chose it for their summer residence. It was renovated once more in the mid-18th century, creating a sumptuous and elegant "little Versailles," famous for its rich heritage of art and furnishings. Then, in the 19th century, its park was turned into an English garden.

Above: Gardens of the Reggia di Colorno

PARMA DIARY

A land of culture and cuisine, the area around Parma is studded with castles and princely residences that are remarkable for their incredible architecture and artistic treasures. During a five-day stay, you and your family will be able to see a different town every day, each with its own spectacular art-filled fortress.

Five Days Among the Castles

DAY 1

Explore Fontanellato and its fantastic fortress. Inside, look out for the room with frescoes by Parmigianino and the Optical Room, created in the 19th century in one of the towers, where the square outside is reflected using a series of lenses. The village center has typical porticoed streets and is a pleasant place for a stroll and a coffee.

DAY 2

Head for nearby Soragna and visit its 14th-century fortress, turned into a princely residence in the 16th century. Visit, too, the 1855 synagogue and the Jewish Museum, both reminders of the large Jewish community that thrived in the Parma area from the 15th century onward. And don't miss the Parmesan Cheese Museum.

DAY 3

Today, visit Busseto, home of Giuseppe Verdi and a 13th–14th-century fortress that had one wing converted into the elegant Teatro Verdi in the 19th century. Enjoy a lunch of local hams and cheeses, followed by pasta. You'll appreciate why the cuisine of Emilia-Romagna is one of the most highly thought of in Italy. In the afternoon, visit the nearby village of Roncole where you can see the modest house where Verdi was born.

DAY 4

Visit the Castello di Roccabianca, built between 1450 and 1465 at the behest of Pier Maria Rossi as a present for his beloved, Bianca Pellegrini. It has a wonderful cycle of frescoes inspired by Boccaccio's *Decameron*, and holds tastings of local liqueurs and hams.

DAY 5

A short distance north of Parma stands the Reggia di Colorno, built at the beginning of the 17th century on the site of a pre-existing fortress. This fantastic residence has the air of a royal palace and its magnificent park was turned into an English garden in the 19th century.

Dos and Don'ts

- ✓ You can only visit Fontanellato's Rocca Sanvitale on a guided tour. For information, visit www.comune.fontanellato.pr.it
- ✗ Don't travel early in the morning or toward evening – in the fall you may encounter thick fog.
- ✓ Visit the producers of Parmesan to see the cheeses being made before trying (and perhaps buying) them.
- ✗ Visiting hours are limited in November for the Reggia di Colorno, and by tour only. For tours in English, you'll need to book; visit www.castellidelducato.it for more information.

Above (top to bottom): Rocca Sanvitale, Fontanellato, complete with fish-filled moat; the 15th-century Castello di Roccabianca; statue of Giuseppe Verdi in Busseto's piazza named after the great composer

Below: Staircase in the 14th-century Rocca di Soragna

GETTING THERE
Segesta is in northwestern Sicily. The area is served by two international airports, Trapani and Palermo. It takes about half an hour to reach Segesta from either airport by car via the A29.

GETTING AROUND
The best way of following the itinerary is by car.

WEATHER
In the fall, Sicily offers mild temperatures and plenty of sunny days.

ACCOMMODATIONS
The Baglio Pocoroba hotel, not far from the Segesta archeological site, is a former farm set in the countryside and offering a peaceful stay. From US$48 per person for B&B; www.pocoroba.it

In Castellammare del Golfo, the Hotel Al Madarig (The Stairs) – the town's ancient Arabic name – is centrally located and looks on to the sea. Doubles from US$130; www.almadarig.com

Also in the center of Castellammare, the 4-star Cetarium is smart and very comfortable. Double rooms from US$114; www.hotelcetarium.it

EATING OUT
L'Approdo in Castellammare serves fine seafood (about US$42; www.lapprodo.org). The Tenuta Plaia restaurant near Scopello by the gates of the Riserva dello Zingaro offers good local cuisine for about US$42; www.plaiavini.com

PRICE FOR TWO
You will spend about US$245 per day for meals, accommodations, and entry to the Segesta excavations and the Zingaro preserve.

FURTHER INFORMATION
www.bestofsicily.com/segesta.htm

Sicily's Biggest Tuna Fishery

On the northwest coast of Sicily, the village of Scopello grew up around an 18th-century fort and became one of the biggest centers for the fishing and processing of tuna in Sicily. There are references to tuna fishing around Scopello going back as far as the early 13th century. Today, the tuna fishery sits in a tiny cove amid picturesque rock stacks and has fallen into disuse, but everything – the equipment, boats, even the fishermen's houses – has remained as it was, a poignant reminder of a fishing culture that has now all but disappeared.

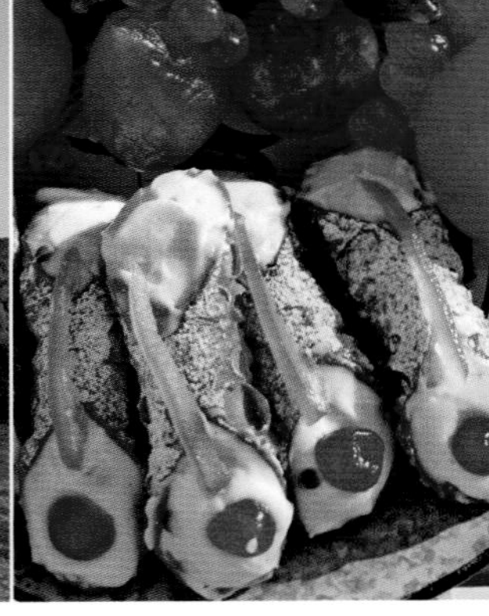

Above (left and right): The Doric temple at Segesta, one of the best preserved Greek temples anywhere in the world; a Sicilian dessert, *cannoli* are tubes of pastry filled with sweetened ricotta cheese and decorated with candied fruit

THE SINGING STONES

IT IS SAID THAT ON CERTAIN DAYS the wind, whistling through the great stone columns of the Segesta temple, produces a mysterious soft tone like an organ. It may be just a myth, conjured up by the romantic atmosphere of the place: a virtually complete Doric temple with 36 mighty columns built in the 5th century BC, standing alone on a hill in enchanting countryside. A short but steep walk up to the 1,300-ft (400-m) summit of Monte Barbaro leads to a dramatic open amphitheater, set on a plateau with stunning views over the valleys below. Nearby Segesta was an ancient city that, according to the eminent Greek historian Thucydides, was founded by exiles from Troy. The Roman poet Virgil, in his famous epic, *The Aeneid,* recounts that the city was founded by Aeneas in person. Archeologists, however, think that Segesta was founded by the Elymians who, as in the Trojan legend, migrated to the area from Asia Minor around the 12th century BC.

The temple, solemn and impressive as it is, still presents a few mysteries for archeologists: why is there no trace of the roof, and where is the altar room where the rites were carried out? The generally accepted answer is that the temple was never actually finished – war with Selinunte, the Greek colony on the southern coast of Sicily, prevented the completion of the temple – even though it was Selinunte that was destroyed in the conflict in 409 BC, following the involvement of the powerful Carthaginians from North Africa. Just over a century later, Segesta was destroyed by Agatocle, the Tyrant of Syracuse, but rose again under the Romans and continued even after its sacking by the Vandals at the end of the 5th century. Recent archeological finds have brought to light the remains of an Arab and medieval Segesta, with the ruins of a 12th-century mosque next to a Norman castle and a church. But by the end of the 13th century, the city had been totally deserted.

The nearest town is Calatafimi, just a few minutes away, which developed around a Byzantine fortification during the Moorish occupation of the area, when it was known as Kalat-al-fimi. From the 14th, century the town was under feudal rule until, in 1860, Garibaldi's 1,089 troops overthrew the Bourbons here – a crucial step in the unification of Italy and commemorated in the hilltop Monumento Ossario in Colle Pianto Romano. A little distance to the north lies the beautiful port of Castellammare del Golfo and, just next to it, the small fishing village of Scopello, gateway to the pristine Reserva dello Zingaro.

Main: View between the massive Doric columns of the Greek temple in Segesta
Below (left and right): Fertile farmland near the archeological site at Segesta; an unspoiled and secluded cove in the Reserva dello Zingaro

Above: The amazing view from the Greek theater at Segesta

JAN FEB MAR APR MAY JUN JUL AUG SEP OCT **NOV** DEC

TEMPLE DIARY

Segesta is perched on the summit of Monte Barbaro and was one of the most powerful cities of pre-Roman Sicily. Its most important historic buildings, the Doric temple and the theater, date back to that era and make it one of the most famous archeological sites on the island. Use your three days to explore Segesta and also to visit the coast to the north.

Three Magical Days

DAY 1

To experience Segesta's magic to the fullest extent, head first of all for the Doric temple, which stands alone in a romantic landscape, impressive and beautiful even in its incomplete state. Then visit the theater, built on the northern slope of the mountain and constructed from blocks of local limestone. Sadly, the stage has been destroyed, but instead you can appreciate the amazing panorama. Near the theater is the archeological site, which has yielded some interesting remains. These have made it possible to reconstruct the entire history of the city, from prehistoric times to the Middle Ages. Pay a visit to Calatafimi for lunch and an afternoon stroll – the town has several interesting churches with frescoes.

DAY 2

Pack a picnic and head north to the Reserva dello Zingaro, reached via the small village of Scopello. The preserve protects a large stretch of Sicily's northwestern coast. Park the car and enter the preserve through a tunnel, then explore the area on winding footpaths through a fairy tale landscape of azure sea fringed by small coves and sandy beaches. It will probably be too cold to swim – unless you are pretty hardy – but you should be able to find a sheltered spot for a picnic. The shoreline is covered with arid-loving plants and vegetation such as lentisk, broom, dwarf palms, and olive trees.

DAY 3

For another wonderful look at the Sicilian seaside, visit Castellammare del Golfo. Here, you will be enchanted by the sight of the Mediterranean maquis that grows right up to the houses and the glorious sandy beaches on either side of the promontory dominated by its medieval castle. In town, you'll be able to enjoy a meal, perhaps some lovely fresh seafood, in a restaurant overlooking the sea.

Dos and Don'ts

- ✓ Check in advance on the opening hours of the archeological sites in Segesta: they vary according to the time of year.
- ✗ Don't pick flowers or plants in the Zingaro preserve, or fish in its waters – these activities are prohibited.
- ✗ Don't take your dog (or other domestic animal) into the Zingaro preserve: they are not allowed in, even on a lead.

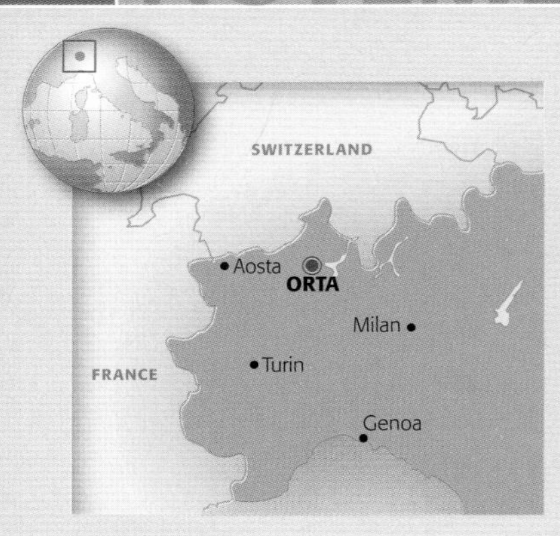

GETTING THERE
Orta San Giulio lies on the eastern shore of Lake Orta in northern Piedmont. The nearest airport is Milan Malpensa, 25 miles (40 km) away. By car, take the A26 freeway to the Arona exit, then follow main roads to your destination.

GETTING AROUND
You can use your car to get around independently, but the area also has a good bus network, and frequent boats and ferries link the various sights along the lake.

WEATHER
The average maximum daytime temperature is 52°F (11°C); higher on sunny days, which are frequent.

ACCOMMODATIONS
The Contrada dei Mont, in Orta's historic center, has been converted from an 18th-century nobleman's house. Rooms have stone walls and exposed beams; doubles from US$150; www.lacontradadeimonti.it

Villa Crespi is a very special place to stay. Built in 1879, in sumptuous and eccentric Moorish style, it is surrounded by a large garden sloping down to the lake; doubles from US$340; www.hotelvillacrespi.it

The Albergo Sacro Monte is situated at the entrance to the Sacro Monte di Orta, surrounded by parkland; doubles from US$102; www.sacromontealbergo.it

EATING OUT
The superb restaurant of Villa Crespi offers haute cuisine with innovative touches (dinner from US$102).

L'Ustaria Cà dal Ratt, bordering Lake Orta, serves imaginative reinventions of local specialties, as well as superb fish dishes (from US$42); www.lustaria.it

PRICE FOR TWO
US$215–450 including accommodations, meals, and local travel.

FURTHER INFORMATION
www.lagodorta-cusio.com

Woodland Harvest

In the fall, the woods around Lake Orta are ablaze with red and yellow foliage, a welcome sight as winter approaches. It's an idyllic setting in which to join with the locals as they take part in the seasonal ritual of foraging for chestnuts, formerly a mainstay of the peasant diet, and wild mushrooms. In Piedmont the superb funghi is strictly protected and you need a permit to gather mushrooms, which may not be worth buying for a short visit. But, anyway, it's still a perfect excuse for getting out into these beautiful woodlands.

Main: Jetty pointing the way to the convent of Mater Ecclesiae on the island of San Giulio
Above (top to bottom): Mater Ecclesiae, reflected in the waters of Lake Orta; chapels on Sacro Monte di Orta; hill of della Motta, leading to Chiesa di Santa Maria Assunta; sunset over Lake Orta

A PLACE OF CONTEMPLATION

A QUIET AND PEACEFUL AMBIENCE, lush natural surroundings, exquisite buildings tucked away down narrow cobbled streets, romantic little restaurants, small shops selling local produce... all these and more are part of the welcome offered by Orta San Giulio to those who visit its secluded setting on a peninsula extending into Lake Orta. The village combines quaint medieval houses with fine Baroque buildings, decorated with loggias and balconies. Piazza Motta is its "drawing room," enclosed on three sides by elegant porticoes. Its fourth side is the lake shore itself, which offers a wonderful view over to the tiny island of San Giulio.

Just 1,320 ft (400 m) of limpid water separates the island from the village of Orta, yet San Giulio is quite different in character. Its pretty houses, gardens, and orchards are dominated by the Basilica di San Giulio, one of the largest Romanesque buildings in the region. Next to it is the campanile, embellished with double and triple lancet windows.

Above: *Ecce Homo,* in a chapel on the Sacro Monte di Varallo

LAKELAND DIARY

Lake Orta is small but irresistible. In fact, it's impossible not to fall in love with it, as so many visitors have found out over the years. Flanked by two holy mountains, and with an island that's a veritable treasure house of art and history, it is a peaceful and timeless place that merits three relaxing days of exploration. You will come away refreshed and uplifted.

Three Tranquil Days

DAY 1

Spend your first day in the village of Orta San Giulio, exploring its narrow cobbled streets, discovering its ancient palaces, and peeping in the windows of its little shops. Stop for a cappuccino in Piazza Motta, the "salon" of the village, with an expanse of café tables stretching almost to the water's edge. In the square, admire the 16th-century Palazzo della Comunità and then make the climb up to the Chiesa di Santa Maria Assunta. After lunch, take a boat over to the island of San Giulio to visit its medieval basilica, stroll its charming streets, and simply enjoy its peaceful atmosphere and splendid views.

DAY 2

If the weather is fine, first shop for a picnic to take with you on a trip up the Sacro Monte di Orta. You can easily spend the day meandering the winding paths through the wooded natural park in which it is set, visiting each chapel and statue on the 1-mile (1.5-km), gently ascending route, and pausing for breathtaking glimpses of the lake as you go. Be sure to return before dusk.

DAY 3

Today, drive 25 miles (40 km) around the southern end of Lake Orta and up into the hills above its western shore to visit Varallo, in Valsesia. This is the oldest Sacro Monte in Italy, founded in 1491 by the Franciscan monk Bernardino Caimi *(see p266)*. The drive itself is lovely, and the Sacro Monte inspiring. In the afternoon, make your way back to Orta for a last afternoon basking in its tranquil beauty and enjoying an *apperitivo* in Piazza Motta as the sun sets over the hills across the water.

Tradition has it that Julius of Novara arrived on the island in 390 and founded the basilica after driving away dragons and snakes. The present church was built soon after the year 1000 and, despite various alterations in subsequent centuries, has kept its charm intact. The island can be explored on foot along a street that forms a complete circle, with lovely glimpses of hidden gardens and moorings reserved for the private boats belonging to the houses facing the lake.

What truly makes Orta San Giulio a spiritual center, however, is the Sacro Monte just behind it. It forms part of the circuit of Piedmontese "holy mountains" *(see p266)* that offer a pilgrimage in miniature, evoking sites in the Holy Land with chapels on a well-marked route. The Sacro Monte di Orta is made up of 20 chapels, built in three distinct periods between 1590 and 1788, whose special feature is the cycle of frescoes and statues that represent episodes in the life of St. Francis. They are dotted along a path that rises, through pine and beech woods, to the top of the promontory where, as with all of Orta, you'll find a perfect spot for quiet contemplation of the harmony of nature and art.

Dos and Don'ts

- ✓ If it's a warm, sunny day, as is often the case even in early November, have a picnic on top of the Sacro Monte: from here there is a sweeping view over the whole lake.
- ✗ Don't bring your car into Orta San Giulio itself; leave it in one of the large parking lots at the edge of the village.
- ✓ Browse the village's vintage jewelry shops; there are always treasures to be discovered.
- ✓ If you want to find out about obtaining a fungi permit (called a *tesserino*), contact the town hall at: municipio@comune.ortasangiulio.no.it

GETTING THERE
Pisa is in western Tuscany. From its Galileo Galilei Airport, just outside the city, trains run to Centrale station, and frequent shuttle buses connect the airport to points right across the city center.

GETTING AROUND
Best explored on foot and by public transportation.

WEATHER
Pisa's position just 7 miles (12 km) from the sea gives it a temperate climate. In November the maximum daytime temperature can reach 61°F (16°C).

ACCOMMODATIONS
The luxurious Relais dell'Orologio, in the heart of Pisa, is a converted 14th-century tower-house; doubles from US$475; www.hotelrelaisorologio.com

The Royal Hotel Victoria has a delightful 19th-century ambience; doubles from US$135; www.royalvictoria.it

The attractive Delle Tre Donzelle B&B has lovely river views; doubles from US$94; www.delletredonzelle.it

EATING OUT
In many Pisan restaurants, for about US$42 you can sample delicious local cuisine from *zuppa pisana* (bean and vegetable soup) to *torta coi bischeri* (chocolate, dried fruit, and pine nut tart). Try Il Campano, in a 13th-century tower-house (tel. 050 580 585); Osteria dei Cavalieri (www.osteriacavalieri.pisa.it); or Antica Trattoria da Bruno (www.anticatrattoriadabruno.com).

PRICE FOR TWO
US$250–630 per day including accommodations, meals, and a visit to the Campo dei Miracoli, including an ascent of the Leaning Tower.

FURTHER INFORMATION
www.pisaturismo.it

A MIRACLE IN MARBLE

FROM AN ARCHITECTURAL ERROR arose the most famous tower in the world, the Leaning Tower of Pisa, built in the 12th century upon the soft clay soil of a place now known as the Campo dei Miracoli, or Field of Miracles. And miracles are certainly brought to mind by the four wonderful buildings that share this grassy space, decorated with slender columns and adorned with exquisite bas-reliefs and statuary, their white marble standing out against the verdure.

Built within not much more than a century of each other, these masterpieces of the Campo dei Miracoli harmonize extraordinarily well, and testify to the time when Pisa was a wealthy and powerful maritime republic as well as a cultural center of huge importance that attracted the greatest artists of the day. It is to these artists and craftsmen that we owe the magnificent Duomo, begun in 1064 and clad in alternate black and white marble, a characteristic Romanesque style in Pisa; the Baptistry, started in 1153, a grand circular building with wonderful sculptural decorations; the Camposanto,

Main: View of Pisa's Duomo and Leaning Tower, set in the Campo dei Miracoli

Leaning Legacy

Pisa's famous tower had begun to lean even before it was completed: the ground subsided as soon as the third story was added in 1178. Construction was halted in 1185 and restarted only in 1275. By the end of the 13th century the tilt from the vertical had already reached 35 in (90 cm). In 1992, when it was nearly 9 ft 10 in (3 m), work began to consolidate the foundations and the tower was closed, reopening in 2001. The current tilt is about 12 ft 10 in (3.9 m), or an angle of 3.9 degrees from the vertical.

which contains earth from Golgotha, brought back by Pisans returning from a crusade in 1203; and the unmistakable form of the Campanile (bell tower), better known as the Torre Pendente, or Leaning Tower: seven storys of slender colonnades, begun in 1173 but not completed for over 175 years.

The Campo dei Miracoli may be a concentration of sublime architectural and artistic works, but there are many other historic buildings in Pisa, too, confirming the city as one of the supreme examples of Italian art. The Piazza dei Cavalieri was redesigned at the behest of the Medicis (the rulers of Pisa from 1406) by Giorgio Vasari, who reworked its features with typical 16th-century panache. The Scuola Normale Superiore, the prestigious institution founded by Napoleon in 1810, now has its seat in this magnificent square. The Lungarni, or streets along the Arno River, are lined with historic palazzi and are today the most romantic place in Pisa for the *passeggiata*, or evening stroll. Pisa's ancient university is the place where Galileo, the city's most famous son, gave his lectures; its botanical garden was designed by Cosimo de Medici. As well as all these, there are the outstanding museums, glorious churches, quiet side streets, and friendly restaurants. By all means view Pisa from on high in the Leaning Tower, but be sure to get to know it at street level, too.

Far left (top to bottom): *Cenci*, fried biscuits made with orange zest, sweet white wine, eggs, flour, and sugar; lofty cupola of the Baptistry; detail of the façade of Palazzo della Carovana in Piazza dei Cavalieri, seat of Pisa's Scuola Normale Superiore

Above (top and bottom): Torre Guelfa in the Cittadella Vecchia; architectural detail of the Palazzo dell'Orologio

Below: Internal courtyard of the monumental Camposanto

Above: Pisan houses, viewed from a bridge over the Arno River

ARCHITECTURAL DIARY

Pisa is an ancient city, whose origins go back to the Etruscans. Its most splendid era was the time when it was a powerful maritime city, but it continued to flourish during the Renaissance under the rule of the Medici. Over three days you can trace this rich history as you explore its ancient streets in the mild winter sunshine.

Three Days of Miracles

DAY 1

Dedicate your first day to the Campo dei Miracoli. Admire the façade of the Duomo with its elegant loggias and pause to study its fine side door. Inside, don't miss the magnificent carved pulpit and have a look especially at the chandelier: it is said to have inspired Galileo's discoveries concerning the oscillations of a pendulum. Move on to the Baptistry, Romanesque in design and rich in 13th-century sculptural ornamentation. Climb the Leaning Tower and conclude your tour with the Camposanto (cemetery) on the northern side.

DAY 2

Visit Pisa's Renaissance quarter, including the Piazza dei Cavalieri. Among the many fine buildings here is the Palazzo dell'Orologio, which incorporates the Torre della Fame where Ugolino della Gherardesca, accused of treason, starved to death along with his children in 1208 (the episode is described in Dante's *Inferno*). Around lunchtime, move on to the Cittadella Vecchia, the oldest part of the city. Finish your walk with a *passeggiatta* along the banks of the Arno River.

DAY 3

Spend the day discovering Pisa's lovely churches: the Gothic Santa Maria della Spina, on the Arno, is named (and spikily decorated) for its relic of a thorn from the crown of Christ on the cross; San Michele in Borgo is a superb example of the transition from Romanesque to Gothic; Santa Caterina has a marvelously opulent façade and works by Pisano within; and San Sepolcro has an unusual octagonal ground plan. As you walk from one church to the next, you'll come upon even more delights of Pisan architecture and life.

Dos and Don'ts

- ✓ Buy your tickets for the historic buildings of the Campo in the Museo dell'Opera del Duomo; that way you will avoid long lines.
- ✗ Don't be taken in by the sales pitch of the hawkers in the Campo dei Miracoli: enjoy the spectacle of this magnificent place and take no notice of them.
- ✗ Don't plan to visit the tower with young children: under-8s are not admitted.
- ✓ Look around the food market in the Piazza delle Vettovaglie: it is held every day under an elegant 16th-century portico in the medieval heart of the city and gives you a chance to try many famous local specialties.

DECEMBER

Where to Go: **December**

Christmas is eagerly anticipated in Italy, and not just by the children. You can while away the days of Advent in the magical atmosphere of the Christmas market of Bolzano; or at that of Bressano, launched by Father Christmas himself; or at the traditional Milanese fair of Obei Obei! held on December 7, the feast day of Sant'Ambrogio, patron saint of the city.

Other Italian towns and villages are the setting for traditional Christmas events, as well, from the taking of myrrh from the tomb of St. Nicholas at Bari, to the deeply moving *presepe vivente* (living nativities), involving the adults, children, and animals of villages such as Pietrelcina and Guardialfiera. There are other celebrations in December, too, including that of the new olive oil at Paciano in Perugia.

FESTIVALS AND CULTURE

PISTOIA Façade of the Ospedale del Ceppo, decorated by della Robbia

UNFORGETTABLE JOURNEYS

THE CAMPI FLEGREI View of Pozzuoli set on a lava outcrop

NATURAL WONDERS

VIESTE Spectacular rock formation of the Architello

BARGA
TUSCANY

A Tuscan Mary and Joseph

Barga, one of Tuscany's loveliest towns, becomes Bethlehem as two townsfolk, dressed as Mary and Joseph, walk its streets seeking shelter for the night.

www.barganews.com

PORDENONE
FRIULI-VENEZIA GIULIA

Subterranean celebration

Not far from Pordenone are the magical caves of the Grotte Verdi di Pradis, where local cavers meet each Christmas for a special Mass.

www.showcaves.com/english/it/caves/Verdi.html

THE CAMPI FLEGREI
CAMPANIA

Place of myths and legends

The Campi Flegrei, near Naples, is a volcanic region with a lake that the ancients thought was the gateway to Hades through which the Sybil guided Aeneas.

See pp306–7

UDINE
FRIULI-VENEZIA GIULIA

Cultural crossroads

Near the borders of Slovenia and Austria, Udine, the capital of Friuli, is a city of diverse art and culture. It has its own language and a history going back to Neolithic times.

See pp316–7

THE CASENTINO
TUSCANY

One of Italy's last great forests

The vast woodlands of the Casentino offer opportunities to track down wolves, wild boar, and roe deer, and spot the majestic golden eagle.

www.casentino.it

CAGLIARI
SARDINIA

Cagliari's Christmas offerings

Sardinia's elegant capital hosts one of Italy's finest Christmas markets. Local delicacies such as *turrone* (nougat) and strawberry honey jostle for space with colorful woven rugs and hand-painted pottery.

www.sardegnaturismo.it

"An infernal landscape of gray mud that boils, steams, and hisses sulfurous gases just like the Hades that the Sybil knew."

PRATO NEVOSO
PIEDMONT

The magic of the Alpi Marittimi

At Prato Nevoso, high up the Alpi Marittimi, you can ski by moonlight, amid lovely mountains sihouetted against a starry sky.

www.scuolascipratonevoso.it/eng/lascuola.htm

PACIANO
UMBRIA

Celebrating the new olive oil

The charming hill village of Paciano, surrounded by its medieval walls, hosts a lively olive oil festival with tastings and local gastronomy.

www.comune.paciano.pg.it

BARI
PUGLIA

A place of pilgrimage

Home to the relics of St. Nicholas, Bari is visited by Russian pilgrims on his feast day, December 6, when a vial of myrrh is extracted from his tomb.

www.stnicholascenter.org

PACHINO
SICILY

Wine road of Sicily

The wine route from Pachino to Avola runs through black-soiled land with a hot microclimate that produces powerful, delicious wines.

www.stradadelvaldinoto.it

VIESTE
PUGLIA

Sea-sculpted coastline

At the tip of the Gargano headland, the coast around Vieste is carved into bizarre and mythic forms by the action of the sea on soft limestone.

See pp322–3

PISTOIA
TUSCANY

An elegant medieval city of art

Pistoia has a lovely historic center enclosed within 14th-century walls, with fine palazzos and splendid churches full of fine works of art, with examples by Pisano and della Robbia.

See pp310–11

CHAMOIS
VALLE D'AOSTA

Leave the world behind

Chamois is the last commune in Italy with no road access. Follow mule tracks to the village for views of the Matterhorn, Europe's most spectacular mountain.

www.comune.chamois.ao.it

MONTEVECCHIO
SARDINIA

A coast of greens and blues

Montevecchio lies at the heart of the Costa Verde, its coastline rugged with cliffs and caves and dotted with ruined mines where Sardinia's wild deer now roam in peace.

www.lacostaverde.it

RODDI
CAMPANIA

On the hunt for Italy's "white diamonds"

In the woods around Roddi, join a *trifolau* (truffle hunter) and his dog in a midnight search for the rare and valuable white truffle.

www.universitadeicanidatartufo.it

Previous page: Beautiful interior of La Scala opera house in Milan

Even in midwinter a mild, gentle climate awaits you in the south, so you can still explore the countryside of Campania, where the cave of the Sibyl awaits you at Cumae; the mystical rock formations on the Vieste coast of Puglia; or the wine routes of Sicily.

For outdoor sports fans, December is the month when facilities in the main ski resorts open, so you might finish the year by taking to the pistes of Val Senales, Prato Nevoso, or Prato Spilla. And if the snow is late, never mind: there is always the Parco del Matese in Campania, a paradise for free climbing, or the fast-flowing current of Sicily's Alcantara River for white-water rafting. If that all sounds a little chilly, why not immerse yourself in one of Italy's many spas, so beloved of the Romans, for a warm and indulgent Christmas treat.

LUXURY AND ROMANCE

BOLZANO Handsome Castello di Bolzano, once home to Thun ceramics

"Its situation, off the beaten tourist track, makes Ascoli Piceno a destination for connoisseurs of architecture, culture, and good living."

ASCOLI PICENO
LE MARCHE

Elegant town of pale marble

Beautiful Ascoli is centered around the noble Piazza del Popolo, where its citizens gather to meet and chat over a coffee or a glass of the region's excellent wines.

See pp314–5

ACQUI TERME
PIEDMONT

Gastronomy and health

Indulge in the cuisine and fine wines of the region, then refresh and revive yourself with health and beauty treatments at the superb thermal spas of Acqui.

www.termediacqui.it

SATURNIA
TUSCANY

Hot springs in ancient lands

At the foot of Saturnia, one of Italy's oldest towns, hot mineral springs gush through pure white travertine rocks. Several nearby spas harness the healing waters.

www.termedisaturnia.it

TODI
UMBRIA

One of the glories of Umbria

Todi's magnificent medieval Old Town is the place to try some of Umbria's finest winter cuisine, with game such as pigeon and boar, truffles, and wild mushrooms featuring on many menus.

See pp320–21

BOLZANO
TRENTINO-ALTO ADIGE

Magical Christmas market

Bolzano puts on a sparkling show with one of Italy's loveliest Christmas markets. There's no better way of getting into the spirit of the Italian Christmas.

See pp324–5

ACTIVE ADVENTURES

VAL SENALES Maso Corto, a ski resort in the heart of Val Senales

CAMPO IMPERATORE
ABRUZZO

On the slopes of Gran Sasso

Reachable by cable car, Campo Imperatore is one of Italy's oldest ski resorts, set amid a lovely region known as "Little Tibet." Walking and cross-country ski trails abound.

www.campoimperatore.net

PARCO DEL MATESE
CAMPANIA

Something for everyone

Free climbing and caving, hang- and paragliding, cycling, hiking, fishing, and much more: the Matese has every kind of sport available.

See pp308–9

GOLE DELL'ALCANTARA
SICILY

Tackling the torrent

The spectacular gorges of the slopes of Etna, through which the Alcantara River flows, are popular with fans of white-water rafting, canyoning, and other challenging sports.

See pp312–3

LINGUAGLOSSA
SICILY

Snowshoes on the volcano

Below you is the sea; above you rise great clouds of steam. Scaling Mount Etna on snowshoes is one of Italy's most surreal winter sports.

www.gotaormina.com/en/sports/skiing.html

VAL SENALES
TRENTINO-ALTO ADIGE

Snow and sunshine in a high Tyrolean valley

Dedicated skiers stay at the highest mountain hotel in Europe, and even novices will love one of the best-equipped snowparks in Italy.

See pp318–9

FAMILY GETAWAYS

MILAN Room in the Theater Museum of La Scala opera house

PIETRELCINA
CAMPANIA

A living nativity in the streets of this revered village

The birthplace of Padre Pio, the deeply venerated priest, Pietrelcina is also famous for the *presepe vivente* that takes place in late December.

www.cappuccinipietrelcina.com

PRATO SPILLA
EMILIA-ROMAGNA

Family ski resort

Set high in the Parma Apennines, Prato Spilla is an environmentally friendly, small ski resort offering a wide range of sports and facilities for all the family, and a warm welcome.

www.pratospilla.pr.it

MILAN
LOMBARDY

Christmas in the city

In Milan, the Christmas season kicks off on December 7 with the Fiera degli Obei Obei street fair and the glittering first night of the opera season at La Scala.

See pp304–05

GUARDIALFIERA
MOLISE

A moving tradition

The oldest part of the village of Guardialfiera is the setting for a charming *presepe vivente*, or living nativity, in which over 150 local people play a role.

www.guardialfieraonline.it

"This is the date when the Christmas tree and crib appear in Milanese homes, but a festive atmosphere pervades the whole city."

BRESSANONE
TRENTINO-ALTO ADIGE

Advent and onwards

Advent in Bressanone begins with the procession of St. Nicholas through the streets, handing out sweets to children, and continues with the lively and charming Christmas market.

www.brixen.org

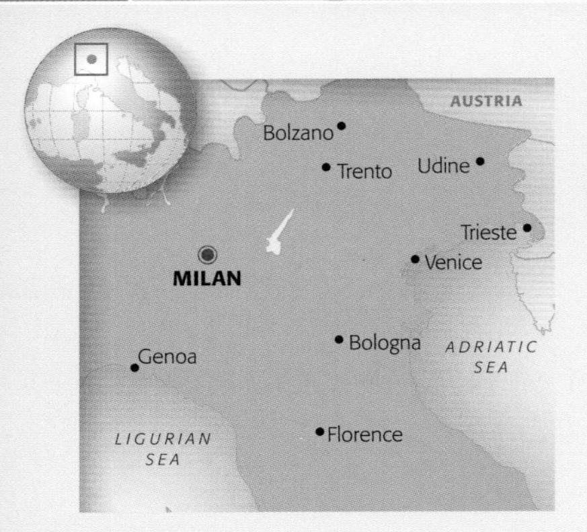

GETTING THERE
Milan, the capital of Lombardy, has two airports: Linate (4 miles/6 km) and Malpensa (30 miles/ 50 km). A shuttle bus runs from Linate to the center; Malpensa has bus and train links.

GETTING AROUND
The city is well served by public transportation and the center is easy to explore on foot.

WEATHER
Milan can be very cold in December, with average daytime highs of only 43°F (6°C) but snow gives the city a magical atmosphere.

ACCOMMODATIONS
The elegant Hotel Manin is in a quiet position facing the public gardens of Porta Venezia; family suites from US$340; www.hotelmanin.it

The-Place Luxury Suite Apartments, scattered around the city center, offer every luxury and convenience, including babysitting (by prior reservation) and breakfast; apartments from US$300; www.the-place.it

EATING OUT
Milan, like any other big city, has restaurants and cafés to suit every taste and pocket. La Dogana del Buongusto is an *enoteca* serving creative cuisine (dinner from US$48; tel. 02 894 23797); Zucca e Melone offers refined Lombardy cooking at good prices (from US$42; tel. 02 894 55850); Arrow's specializes in seafood (from US$55; tel. 02 341 533); Ribot serves grills and classic Tuscan dishes (from US$55; tel. 02 3921 0657); and Giannino presents top-flight Milanese cuisine in a lovely *belle époque* setting (about US$68, tel. 02 6698 6998).

PRICE FOR A FAMILY OF FOUR
US$570 per day including accommodations, meals, local travel, and admissions.

FURTHER INFORMATION
http://ciaomilano.it

Teatro alla Scala

The opera house of La Scala, as it is known, opened in 1778. Its façade is unremarkable; in contrast to its horseshoe-shaped interior, which boasts a stage that even today is one of the largest in Italy and has extraordinary acoustic properties. It is these acoustics, together with the unrivaled importance of Milan as an artistic and cultural center, that have enshrined the Teatro alla Scala as a true temple of opera.

OH BEAUTIFUL!

OH BEI! OH BEI! That was the cry once used by Milanese street vendors to attract the attention of passersby at a fair that has ushered in the Christmas season in Milan since 1288. It's thought that the phrase derives from the exclamation: "O bella!" (Oh beautiful!). Drawn by the shouts of street hawkers, the sound of singing, and the delicious scents in the air, you'll find yourself lost in a mass of stalls, surrounded by locals greeting friends at every turn. For in Milan, at the beginning of December, it seems that everyone is at the Fiera degli Obei Obei, originally held near the basilica of Sant'Ambrogio, patron saint of Milan, whose feast day falls on December 7.

Traditionally this is the date when the Christmas tree and crib appear in Milanese homes, but a festive atmosphere pervades the whole city: in shop window decorations; festoons of Christmas

Main: View of the Piazza della Scala and the famous opera house

lights brightening the streets; shoppers dashing by laden with lavishly gift-wrapped parcels; and restaurants packed with diners exchanging good wishes. The date also sees the city stage one of the most fashionable and sought-after events in Italy: the launch of the opera season at La Scala, attended by the great and the good of Italian culture and society.

It may be difficult to obtain a ticket for the opening night of La Scala, but December is the perfect time to discover Milan: wandering its quiet residential streets, peeking in at hidden courtyards in elegant palaces, and looking up to see pretty rooftop terraced gardens. Then there are its churches – not just the marvelous Duomo but the jewel-box that is Santa Maria delle Grazie. This 15th-century church has a rather special painting on its convent's refectory wall – Leonardo's *Last Supper*. Away from the summer crowds, you can appreciate it in peace.

This astonishing city is always a place of contrasts, but never more so than at this time of year. These are magical days in Milan, when the whole city dresses up for the party.

Above: Ornate room in La Scala's theater museum

Below (top and bottom): Panettone, a typical Italian Christmas cake, studded with dried and candied fruits; exterior of Chiesa di Santa Maria delle Grazie, home to Leonardo's *Last Supper*

Above: Rear of the Teatro alla Scala, restored by the architect Mario Botta

MILANESE DIARY

Milan is an exciting city all year round, and in the run up to Christmas it's impossible not to join in the fun. But there are quiet spots to enjoy as well, if you want a break from the party atmosphere. Over four days you can take in all the fun of the Fiera as well as Milan's tranquil side, both familiar and undiscovered. *(See also pp56–7)*

Four Magical Days

DAY 1

You'll want to spend most of the day at the Fiera delgi Obei Obei, rummaging among the stalls, sipping mulled wine, and just enjoying the festive atmosphere. When you have had enough of the crowds, step into the lovely Romanesque Chiesa di Sant'Ambrogio, whose finely crafted golden altar dates back to the year 835.

DAY 2

In the morning, stroll along Corso Magenta, lined with the elegant palazzi of the Milanese nobility, until you reach the Chiesa di Santa Maria delle Grazie, whose apse is particularly beautiful. Take a break for lunch before you move on to what you've really come here to see – Leonardo da Vinci's *Last Supper*, which is in the convent, accessed from the church square.

DAY 3

Today, visit the Teatro alla Scala; you may not be able to go inside, but the adjacent museum has one of the finest theatrical collections in the world. At lunchtime, stroll over to the Galleria Vittorio Emanuele II. This spectacular, glass-and-iron domed 19th-century arcade is lined with stylish shops, chic bars, and restaurants.

DAY 4

Head for Corso Venezia, flanked by impressive Neo-Classical buildings and facing the public gardens. In the Villa Reale, a late 18th-century Neo-Classical building, the Civico Museo d'Arte Contemporanea has an outstanding collection of art from the 19th century to the present day, including a marvelous collection of Post-Impressionist paintings. After lunch, walk on to the superbly restored Acquario Civico di Milan, whose lovely Art Nouveau building now holds 36 state-of-the-art aquaria and open pools.

Dos and Don'ts

- ✓ Opera-lovers determined to try for a ticket to a performance at La Scala should visit www.teatroallascala.org
- ✓ Take the children to a play at the Teatro Gerolamo, home to one of the most important marionette companies in Italy. For details, visit www.marionettecolla.org (Italian only).
- ✗ Do not try to see Leonardo's *Last Supper* without booking in advance. You could wait for a long time in the cold, and even then you might not get in. Visit www.cenacolovinciano.net

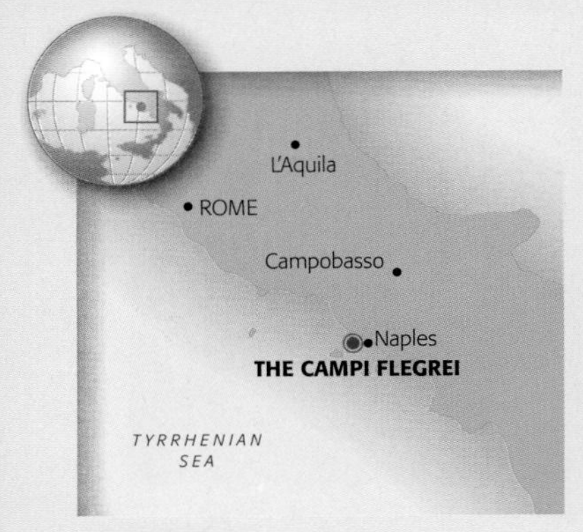

GETTING THERE
The Campi Flegrei are situated just west of Naples in Campania. From Naples' Capodicino Airport, 15 miles (24 km) away, trains on the Ferrovia Cumanarail and Ferrovia Circumflegrea lines, and the Metro, run to Pozzuoli, the main town of the Campi Flegrei.

GETTING AROUND
Use the good public transportation network that links Pozzuoli, the Campi Flegrei, and other sites.

WEATHER
Winter is mild here, with an average maximum daytime temperature of 57°F (14°C).

ACCOMMODATIONS
The modern Hotel Solfatara is set in a fine position on the Bay of Pozzuoli, in the heart of the Campi Flegrei; doubles from US$82; www.hotelsolfatara.it

The stylish Batis hotel, with a good restaurant, is a renovated 19th-century building near the excavations at Baia; doubles from US$95; www.batis.it

EATING OUT
In central Pozzuoli, Il Tarantino offers traditional local dishes (dinner from US$82), with freshly caught fish a specialty; www.trattoriadaltarantino.it/tarantino.htm

Tradition and innovation are combined in the fine cuisine at the Abraxas, a welcoming *osteria* in Pozzuoli (from US$35); www.abraxasosteria.it

PRICE FOR TWO
US$245 per day including accommodations, meals, local travel, and admission to the Campi Flegrei sites.

FURTHER INFORMATION
www.infocampiflegrei.it

Casina Vanvitelliana

In the 18th century, Lago Fusaro, an expanse of water separated from the sea by a long spit of sand, became a fishing and shooting reserve for the Bourbon kings of Naples. They commissioned architect Luigi Vanvitelli to build a shooting lodge on a small island in the lake. Completed in 1792 by Luigi's son Carlo Vanvitelli, the result is an elegant, octagonal, pagoda-like villa, harmonious in its geometry and luminous against the deep blue water, connected to the shore by a long wooden bridge. It continues to enchant visitors today, as it did its famous guests in the past, who included Mozart and Rossini.

Above (left and right): View of Pozzuoli, perched on a lava outcrop; remains of the temple of Jove, situated on the highest terrace of Monte di Cuma

FIELDS OF FIRE

A LONG, STRAIGHT PASSAGE stretches out before you. Its trapezoidal walls close in over your head. The only illumination is from crevices that let in dramatic shafts of light. And, at the end, is a pitch-dark, vaulted room – but dare you enter? This, according to legend, is the Antro della Sibilla – the grotto of the Cumaean Sibyl, the prophetess who guided Aeneas into Hades to visit his dead father. It makes little difference to know that the passage was probably part of a network of underground routes created for military purposes: you still half expect to hear a whispered prophecy emanating from the mysterious darkness at the end of the passage.

The Antro della Sibilla is in Cumae, the first colony founded by the Greeks on the Italian mainland, in an area known as the Campi Flegrei (the Flegrean Fields). This is a region with conspicuous evidence of volcanic activity, as its name suggests (*flegraios* means "burning" or "fiery" in Greek), and it has inspired a many myths. Here, a clash took place between the gods and the Titans; here, too, in Lago del Averno, was the entrance to Hades used by Aeneas. The lake's name derives from the Greek for "birdless," because there was a time when the sulfurous gases bubbling from its surface caused birds flying over it to fall dead from the sky. Small wonder it seemed to the ancients like the mouth of hell. However, this did not deter the Romans from creating a system of canals at the end of the first century BC, linking the lake to the sea.

The main town of the Campi Flegrei is Pozzuoli. One of the most important ports in Roman times, it retains a large, well-preserved amphitheater where you can still see the cages for the wild animals, as well as the machinery used to take them into the arena to fight with gladiators. The town has long been affected by a phenomenon known as bradyseism – the gradual uplift or descent of the earth's crust. It is actually possible to "read" this in the marks of sea molluscs up to 23 ft (7 m) high on the marble columns of Pozzuoli's ancient market. Since 1968 alone, earthquakes have caused the town to rise over 11 ft (3.5 m).

Other parts of the Campi Flegrei continue to display lively volcanic activity: you need only visit Solfatara, a semi-extinct volcano, to be immersed in an infernal landscape of gray mud that boils, steams, and hisses sulfurous gases just like the Hades that the Sybil knew.

Main: Dramatic corridor of the Antro della Sibilla at Cumae
Below (left and right): Oranges grown in the fertile volcanic soil of the Campi Flegrei; fishermen on the attractive harbor at Pozzuoli

Above: Dramatic skies over the deserted beach of Miseno

ARCHEOLOGY DIARY

A rough landscape, marked and shaped by volcanic eruptions, yet favored by nature and the sea, the Campi Flegrei's long history has left behind evocative testimonies in what are some of the most interesting archeological sites in Italy. Over four days it is possible to take your time exploring this fascinating and little-known region.

Four Days in the Ancient Past

DAY 1

Begin your day in Pozzuoli, visiting the ruins of the *macellum*, the ancient market, to see the traces of molluscs on its columns marking what was once sea level. Move on to the Grand Amphitheater, one of the largest in Italy, which could hold 40,000 spectators. After lunch, visit Solfatara (its name comes from "sulpha terra" – land of sulfur), on the edge of town, to enjoy the excitement of a close encounter with a volcanic crater.

DAY 2

Walk west around the bay to Baia, famous since Roman times for its warm, healing springs. The archeological site here contains numerous buildings constructed between the 2nd and the 1st centuries BC, on various levels that step down toward the sea. Don't miss the Aragonese castle in the village: it has a fine view of the bay and houses the noteworthy archeological museum of the Campi Flegrei. If you want to pause for a quick snack, try *casatiello*, a delicious rustic cake, perhaps washed down with a glass of Falanghina wine.

DAY 3

Like Baia, Bacoli was a popular resort in Roman times. The reservoirs here supplied water to the military port of Miseno, which was the headquarters of the imperial navy's fleet. These can still be seen today, including the *Piscina mirabile*, a vast, almost cathedral-like vaulted and pillared space hewn out of the tufa cliff.

DAY 4

Today, visit the archeological site of Cumae, including the awe-inspiring Antro della Sibilla, the remains of the city walls, and two temples, dedicated to Apollo and Jove. From the terraces of Monte di Cuma there are splendid views of Lago del Averno.

Dos and Don'ts

- ✗ Don't wear obviously valuable jewelry and keep other possessions safely tucked away when going around the sites of the Campi Flegrei; pickpockets and thieves could take advantage while you are distracted.
- ✓ Buy one good-value ticket that gives entry to all the archeological sites of the Campi Flegrei. Purchase it online and even print it out yourself by visiting www.pierreci.it
- ✓ You can visit the Casina Vanvitelliana on Sundays; for more information, see www.casinavanvitelliana.it (Italian only).

GETTING THERE
Parco del Matese is in northern Campania. The nearest airport is Naples, about 53 miles (85 km) away. By car, take the A1 freeway to the Caserta Nord exit and then follow the signs to Caizzo/ Piedimonte Matese. Trains and buses also connect Naples to Piedimonte and other places in the park.

GETTING AROUND
The most convenient way of getting around is by car.

WEATHER
The weather in the park varies from mild to very cold, depending on the altitude.

ACCOMMODATIONS
Albergo Penza, in the center of Piedimonte Matese, offers a warm welcome; doubles from US$82; tel. 0823 543 181.

There are many *agriturismi* in the park, including Le Pastene (doubles from US$42; tel. 0823 784 397); L'Antica Quercia (doubles from US$82; www.antica-quercia.it); and La Roccia (doubles from US$68; www.agriturismolaroccia.net).

EATING OUT
The region's simple, well-flavored dishes include *capretto alla cacciatora* (kid with rosemary and garlic) and *agnello cacio e ova* (lamb stew with cheese and eggs). To sample them (dinner from US$35), try Giardino degli Ulivi in Piedimonte Matese (tel. 0823 911 208) or Bacco e Bivacco in San Potito Sannitico (www.baccoebivacco.it).

PRICE FOR TWO
US$230 per day including accommodations, meals, and car rental.

FURTHER INFORMATION
www.parks.it/parco.matese

Roccamonfina

The charming village of Roccamonfina, set amid chestnut forests, is clustered on the slopes of an old volcano, now extinct, whose crater can still be seen. Some of world's oldest fossilized footprints have been found in the lava here. The sanctuary of Santa Maria dei Lattani, a 15th-century complex with a graceful cloister, adds to the attractiveness of the village. Its statue of the Virgin Mary, in painted stone, dates back to the 11th century. According to tradition, it was found in a cave by a shepherd in the 15th century.

UNCHARTED NATURE

IT CAN'T BE SAID that the people of the Monte Matese region have had an easy life over the centuries. When the Roman general and dictator Lucio Cornelio Silla conquered the region in the 2nd century BC, he deported many of its inhabitants to north Africa and Spain. In the 6th century, Saracen pirates made incursions into the area, razing villages to the ground. And in October 1943, US Army troops battled for five whole days to drive out Nazi forces. This checkered history has made the Matese people a hardy breed, a trait that's well suited to their environment, and what a wonderful environment it is.

Parco del Matese is an area that is not well known to tourists. Utterly unspoiled, it has plenty to offer visitors, whatever their interests. If you love nature, you will be in your element. Lago Matese is an important wintering place for thousands of wild birds, and the Matese massif, its luxuriant summer

Main: Lago Matese and the Matese massif, under a light dusting of snow

Left: Aerial view of the town of Cerreto Sannita, at the entrance of Parco del Matese

Right (left and right): *Panzarotti sanniti* (little pastries filled with cheese, sausage, and eggs) are a local specialty; anglers on the banks of Lago Matese

greenery now white with snow, has countless wonderful walks and treks to enjoy. It is perfect, too, if you like a vacation full of activities. The cave of San Michele Arcangelo, lived in by prehistoric peoples and used for worship by the Lombards since the 6th century, is just one in a zone where potholing is a hugely popular activity. Caves such as the Cul di Bove and Pozzo della Neve require great courage and even greater experience, but there are myriad other caves where the novice can attempt a first descent. You can climb upward, too, on free-climbing walls that range from easy to the most challenging. There are opportunities, as well, for hang-gliding, parascending, mountain biking, and the demanding team sport of "Airsoft," in which the woods and hills of the Matese become the terrain for very realistic battle games.

Combine a wonderful natural setting, spectacular wildlife, and outdoor adventures with villages rich in cultural, artistic, architectural, and historical heritage; add a fine culinary tradition and a warm welcome, and you have Parco del Matese, a region that truly does have something for everyone.

Above (top and bottom): Hang-glider above the Parco del Matese; façade of the Collegiata di San Martino in Cerreto Sannita

Below: Narrow street in the historic center of Piedimonte Matese

Above: Lago Matese, crowded with wintering waterfowl

OUTDOOR DIARY

There are many reasons for visiting Parco del Matese: its wild natural beauty and the great opportunities for outdoor sporting activities and nature-watching; but also the historical and cultural heritage of its ancient villages. To fully appreciate the diverse appeal of this little-known region, allow six days – you won't find them wasted.

Six Diverse Days

DAY 1 Explore the caves of the Matese. Parco del Matese offers various guided itineraries, some for expert cavers and others for beginners. Among the most exciting are the Lete caves, full of stalactites and stalagmites.

DAY 2 Visit Sant'Angelo di Alife, which has a range of practice walls on which you can try free climbing under the guidance of an instructor. In the afternoon, explore this historic little town, visiting the Roman ruins and the grotto of San Michele Arcangelo.

DAY 3 Today, go walking in the park. The Matese has an extensive network of well-marked paths. One of the most exciting hikes takes you from Lago Matese to the summit of Monte Miletto. Allow at least half a day for the 9-mile (15-km) return trek.

DAY 4 Spend a relaxing day in ancient Piedimonte Matese. Take the opportunity to sample and buy some of the local specialties, particularly the region's excellent cheeses, including *caciotte*, *pecorino*, and *caciocavalli*.

DAY 5 Visit the Oasi Le Mortine, a wildlife sanctuary set in an oxbow of the Volturno River, with nature trails and hides from which to view the plentiful birdlife.

DAY 6 Cerreto Sannita, at the entrance to the park, is well worth a visit. Destroyed by an earthquake in 1688, it was rebuilt according to new town planning ideals, with wide streets in a grid pattern and fine Baroque buildings such as the Collegiata di San Martino.

Dos and Don'ts

- ☒ Don't venture into any cave without an expert local guide. Even the simplest one can turn out to be dangerous, especially after rain.
- ☑ Be sure to bring a good pair of binoculars for visits to Lago Matese and Oasi Le Mortine. The number of bird species to be seen there in the winter is quite remarkable.
- ☑ Buy a ceramic vase made by the craftsmen of Cerreto Sannita, typically with blue patterns on a pale background.
- ☑ To experience a magical Christmas moment, see the Living Nativity scene enacted every year in Piedimonte Matese.

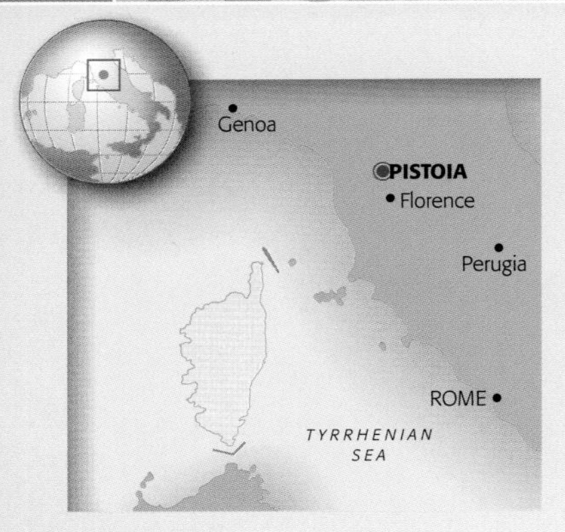

GETTING THERE
Pistoia is in northern Tuscany, about 30 miles (50 km) northwest of Florence airport, from which there are easy road, rail, and bus links.

GETTING AROUND
It is best to explore the historic center on foot. You can get to Montecatini easily by bus, train, or car.

WEATHER
The maximum daytime temperature in December is around 50°F (10°C).

ACCOMMODATIONS
The Puccini is one of the most prestigious palazzos in the historic center: it was the famous composer's birthplace; doubles from US$ US$; www.puccini.tv

Villa Giorgia stands on a hilltop from which there are lovely views over nearby Pistoia. The farmhouse retains all its ancient rustic charm, complemented by the restrained, modern elegance of the interior; doubles from US$218; www.villa-giorgia.com

La Tenuta di Pieve a Celle is an exclusive residence in the Pistoia countryside, with elegant rooms and a pool. It serves its own organic produce; doubles from US$150; www.tenutadipieveacelle.it

EATING OUT
In the heart of the old town, *osteria* La BotteGaia offers traditional Tuscan dishes with a modern twist (dinner from US$42). Try the delicious Pistoia pasta with duck, or a tart of fresh porcini mushrooms. Their homemade produce can be bought from the adjacent shop; www.labottegaia.it

At Baldovino you can sample good local cooking with some innovative touches (from US$35); tel. 0573 21591.

PRICE FOR TWO
Around US$300 per day including meals, accommodations, and local travel.

FURTHER INFORMATION
www.pistoiaturismo.it

The Waters of Montecatini

The spa waters of Montecatini Terme have been highly valued since antiquity, but it was in the late 18th century, when the fashion for spas became widespread in Europe, that the town became a famous location for treatments and cures. Its streets are lined with gorgeous buildings of the period. The lovely medieval town of Montecatini Alto, reached by a historic funicular train, has a peaceful atmosphere, and lovely vistas can be enjoyed from the path along the line of the old walls.

TREASURE OF THE MIDDLE AGES

THE CATHEDRAL OF PISTOIA alone would make this a city worth visiting. Built on soft and graceful lines, with slender columns forming an elegant loggia, it has three orders of arcading, two colors of marble creating elegant geometric effects, and there is a wonderful bas relief by Andrea della Robbia embellishing its portico, much as an elegant woman would discreetly wear a precious jewel. Pistoia is often unjustly omitted from major tourist itineraries, yet it has treasures for those who seek it out. Its noble Romanesque buildings have stories to tell of battles between the Guelphs and the Ghibellines, and there are Renaissance traces, too, from the era in which it was governed by the Medici.

Pistoia's medieval layout is centered around Piazza del Duomo, the exact center of the ancient town. Around the square, as well as the cathedral, flanked by its bell tower, stand a baptistry from the

Main: Detail of the 14th-century entrance to the baptistry of San Giovanni in Corte, in Piazza del Duomo

14th century, clad in multicolored marble, and Palazzo dei Vescovi and Palazzo del Comune. Twice a week a colorful market takes place here, as it has for centuries. Not far away is another marvel: the Ospedale del Ceppo. Begun at the end of the 13th century to offer assistance to the needy, it was embellished in the 16th century by an arcade decorated with a terracotta frieze, a genuine masterpiece of the Renaissance in the delicate plasticity of the modeled figures. Giovanni della Robbia was one of the artists responsible. A little farther on is the Chiesa di Sant'Andrea, a prototype of the Pistoia Romanesque style. Inside, the succession of graceful arches supported by slim columns highlights the beautiful pulpit carved by Giovanni Pisano. Farther on again is the colorful church of San Giovanni Fuorcivitas, with its striking bands of white and green marble. Its interior is embellished by many extraordinary masterpieces. However, it is the nearby Cappella del Tau, a simple rectangular space decorated with a 14th-century fresco cycle by Niccolò di Tommaso, which is perhaps the most rare and precious jewel of this lovely and little-known city.

Above: Ospedale del Ceppo, with decoration by Giovanni della Robbia

Above (top and bottom): *Scarpaccia dolce di zucchine* (courgette tart) a local delicacy; carvings on the pulpit of Chiesa di Sant'Andrea, by Giovanni Pisano

Below (top and bottom): Chiesa di Sant'Andrea; Romanesque façade of the cathedral of San Zeno

MEDIEVAL DIARY

An elegance both refined and discreet that seems to envelop and charm you: this sums up Pistoia. Enclosed within 14th-century walls, its medieval streets and unevenly shaped piazzas are home to prestigious palazzos and splendid churches, rich with works of art. Three days of delightful discoveries await you as you explore.

Three Magnificent Days

DAY 1

The heart of Pistoia is Piazza del Duomo, surrounded by some of the most important monuments in the city, including the octagonal baptistry of San Giovanni in Corte. Inside the cathedral itself is the superb altar of San Jacopo, a magnificent example of the Gothic silversmith's art. Move on to Palazzo dei Vescovi to visit the Museo Capitolare di San Zeno, in which the cathedral's rich treasury is displayed. Spend the afternoon in charming Montecatini Alto, a little way southeast of Pistoia.

DAY 2

Begin the day with a visit to Chiesa di Sant'Andrea, with a famous pulpit by Giovanni Pisano, and the Chiesa di San Bartolomeo in Pantano, both fine examples of Pistoia Romanesque architecture. After lunch, stroll on to the Ospedale del Ceppo. The façade of this former hospital is embellished with a 16th-century portico that includes a splendid frieze in colored terracotta illustrating the misericordia (the seven works of mercy) alternating with the cardinal and theological virtues. Within the building is a fascinating museum of surgical instruments.

DAY 3

Another Romanesque masterpiece in Pistoia is the church of San Giovanni Fuorcivitas; be sure to see the holy water stoup sculpted by Giovanni Pisano and the pulpit, the work of a pupil of Nicola Pisano. The final stop on your visit should be the nearby Cappella del Tau, which owes its name to that letter of the Greek alphabet, worn on the cloaks of monks belonging to the order of St, Anthony. This little chapel is entirely covered in a marvelous cycle of 14th-century frescoes.

Dos and Don'ts

- ✓ Visit Pistoia's Giardino Zoologico. This large zoo is home to more than 600 creatures, including mammals, birds, reptiles, and amphibians, and is dedicated to biodiversity conservation.
- ✗ Don't plan on visiting any of Pistoia's churches in the afternoon without checking opening times first: some will be closed and others have very reduced opening hours.
- ✓ Have a browse around the markets of Pistoia. The largest takes place on Wednesdays and Saturdays in Piazza del Duomo, but on other days the food market in Piazza della Sala is both picturesque and appetizing.

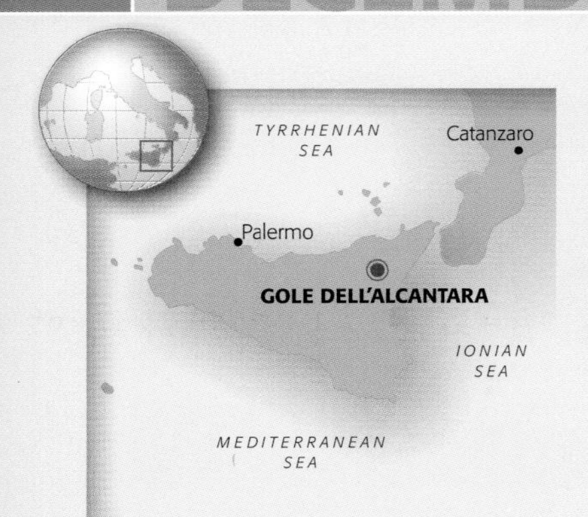

GETTING THERE
The Gole dell'Alcantara are in northeast Sicily, about 40 miles (65 km) from the nearest airport at Catania. By car, take the A18 freeway, exit Giardini Naxos, and continue on the SS185 to the gorges.

GETTING AROUND
You will need your own means of transportation.

WEATHER
Mild daytime temperatures reaching 63°F (17°C) are the norm for December in Sicily.

ACCOMMODATIONS
Terralcantara offers visitors three different, welcoming places to stay. Il Borgo is a converted manor house on a hill; doubles from US$68. La Casa delle Monache has elegant rooms and a good restaurant; doubles from US$68. Il Poggio is a renovated farmhouse with fine views; doubles from US$82; www.terralcantara.it

In Randazzo, B&B Ai Tre Parchi offers warm hospitality and attractive rooms; doubles from US$82; www.aitreparchibb.it

EATING OUT
The *agriturismo* Ghiritina has menus including unlimited pizza (from US$22); www.bbghiritina.it

La Dispensa dell'Etna in Castiglioni serves regional cuisine (from US$35); www.ladispensadelletna.eu

Ristorante Veneziano in Randazzo serves traditional dishes using local produce (from US$42). Try the porcini mushroom *carpaccio* or pasta with pistachio cream; www.ristoranteveneziano.it

PRICE FOR TWO
US$300 per day including accommodations, meals, and car rental.

FURTHER INFORMATION
www.parcoalcantara.it
www.terralcantara.it

The Abbazia di Maniace

The abbey of Maniace stands in a small wooded valley between Randazzo and Bronte . Built in the 12th century as a modest monastery by the Norman king Ruggero, it was dedicated to the Byzantine General Maniace, who had defeated the Saracens on this spot. When it later became a Benedictine abbey its buildings were embellished with towers and fortifications. In 1799, it was given by the king of Naples to Horatio Nelson, in gratitude for his assistance in suppressing a revolt in Naples. From that time onward, his descendants were allowed to use the title of dukes of Bronte, a privilege that was only repealed in 1981.

Main: Canyoner abseiling down into the Gole dell'Alcantara
Above (left to right): View of the Valle di Alcantara; ricotta cheese tart, a specialty of the region; one of the valley's ancient churches

Above: Tackling the challenging waters of the Gole dell'Alcantara

A WILD AND ROCKY RIDE

THOUSANDS OF YEARS AGO the tranquil Alcantara River basin was changed beyond recognition when an eruption of Mount Etna sent a huge flow of magma coursing over it. Cooled swiftly by the river, the lava split and crystallized and, over the centuries, the force of water has eroded the cracks into rugged gorges, 82 ft (25 m) deep and between 16 ft (5 m) and a mere 6 ft (2 m) wide, punctuated by unexpected columns of basalt and rocks in grotesque and bizarre formations. It is at Fondaco Motta that the most awe-inspiring gorge of the Valle di Alcantara begins, over 3.75 miles (6 km) long and passable for half of that length.

The gorges can be visited from the top or from the base, with fascinating, winding routes to follow on horseback or on foot. However, you can also explore the gorges from within, trying out one of the many aquatic sports available here. Rafting, for example, offers a breathtaking ride downstream through cascading waves, flanked by the dark rock walls that flash past in a blur of speed. And if that's given you the taste for adventure, there are opportunities for other means of travel, such as "hydrospeed" (the term for individual rafting) and kayaking, in which your tenacity and courage is put to the test in a truly thrilling way.

If, on the other hand, you want to stay dry (or at least fairly dry), yet still get down into the heart of the gorges, you can rent a pair of waders and give river trekking a try. You can follow the course of the Alcantara right by the river's edge, tackling the twin challenges of rock and water. There are trails of varying difficulty, and the sense of satisfaction is immense. For the very fit, there are also canyoning excursions. And novices needn't worry: the instructors that accompany you are highly experienced in meeting the challenges of the gorges. They'll be on hand to make sure you have a safe but exhilarating experience.

You can follow the course of the Alcantara right by the river's edge, tackling the twin challenges of rock and water.

Inset: Dark, sheer basalt walls of the Gole dell'Alcantara
Below (left and right): Lago Biviere, overlooked by Mount Etna; view of the historic center of Randazzo

RIVER DIARY

The gorges of the Alcantara River are a must for thrill seekers, but are a rewarding experience, too, for anyone who loves an unspoiled, untamed natural enviroment. With five days at your disposal you can choose to explore the gorges by various means, but also get to know the Valle di Alcantara as a whole – its culture and history, its food, its wildlife, and its people.

Five Days in the Valley

DAY 1
Spend the day in the Alcantara gorges: experience the excitement of descending the river at high speed, or more gently, but no less thrillingly, on foot. Afterward, reward yourself with some of the delicious local sweets, such as ricotta tart, *cannoli* (cream-filled pastries), and *mastrazzoli al miele* (honey cookies).

DAY 2
Today, get to know the Alcantara area from another perspective, on horseback. There are two riding trails in the Parco Naturale dell'Alcantara: one winds its way around its three towns; the other is a mountain trek.

DAY 3
The region has a range of food and wine trails, such as the wine road that runs from Castiglione di Sicilia to Randazzo, the area where Etna DOC wine is produced. There are some very good wineries along the route, so spend the day visiting, sampling, and buying from them.

DAY 4
Visit Randazzo, one of the most interesting towns in the Etna area. Almost entirely built from lava, it retains its medieval appearance. Its three churches correspond to the three communities that live there: Cattedrale di Santa Maria for Catholics; Chiesa di San Nicolò for Greek Orthodox; and Chiesa di San Martino for Lombards.

DAY 5
Spend the day on a tour around Lago Biviere, in the Parco Naturale dei Nebrodi. Covering around 45 acres (18 ha), it is the most important upland wetlands zone for wildlife in Sicily and you'll see a wide variety of wintering waterfowl. The tour route passes through dense woods to hill tops, offering panoramic viewing points over the surrounding valleys and the sea in the distance.

Dos and Don'ts

- ⊗ Don't venture into the Alcantara gorges alone. Always consult one of the park's specialist guides.
- ✓ Buy an example of the lovely embroidery made in the area, whose patterns and techniques reflect an ancient tradition.
- ✓ Sample local wine, olive oil, and other typical regional produce direct from the growers. For more information, visit www.terralcantara.it

GETTING THERE
Ascoli Piceno is in the south of Le Marche. The nearest airport is at Pescara, 42 miles (68 km) away. Take the A14 freeway, exit San Benedetto del Tronto, and follow the main road to Ascoli.

GETTING AROUND
You will need a car to get around, but the town center is easy and pleasant to explore on foot.

WEATHER
Temperatures hover near freezing in December, but the town has a charm all of its own when blanketed in snow.

ACCOMMODATIONS
Palazzo Guiderocchi is a gorgeous historic building just a short stroll from Piazza del Popolo; doubles from US$94; www.palazzoguiderocchi.com

Set in the hills close to the town, Villa Cicchi is a lovely 16th-century *agriturismo*; doubles from US$150; www.villacicchi.it

EATING OUT
Specialties of the town include *olive ascolane* and *fritto all'ascolana*, deep-fried lamb and seasonal vegetables served with "fried cream."

Traditional and sophisticated dishes can be tried at Le Scuderie (dinner from US$42); www.ristorantelescuderie.it

Ristorante Del Corso specializes in fish and seafood (from US$55); tel. 0736 256 760.

PRICE FOR TWO
US$300 including accommodations, meals, car rental, and a museum admissions card.

FURTHER INFORMATION
www.comune.ascolipiceno.it

Acquaviva Picena

This perfectly preserved village is set among the Le Marche hills, 12 miles (20 km) northeast of Ascoli Piceno. Access is through a 15th-century gate. At the summit of the village is a 14th-century fortress, once home to the dukes of Acquaviva, which now contains a museum of ancient weapons. The village still upholds the artisan tradition of weaving with reeds and rushes; there is even a small museum dedicated to *pagliarole*, baskets of woven straw (*paglia*).

MASTERPIECE IN MARBLE

An elegant piazza, lined with arcades and loggias and enclosed on one side by the grouped apses of Chiesa di San Francesco – this is Piazza del Popolo, in the heart of Ascoli Piceno. The town is characterized by the abundance of travertine marble, which has been used not only in the construction of buildings, but also for the paving. Travertine is a pale stone, quarried in the area, that has been used since antiquity for the town's important monuments, giving Ascoli its uniquely luminous appearance. From the Roman era to the Middle Ages and the Renaissance, you can see examples of the stone in use just by walking through the elegant, preserved historic center.

In Piazza del Popolo, a meeting place for the people of Ascoli, there are important traces of the town's history: in Palazzo dei Capitani del Popolo, the ancient seat of local government, overlooked by a

Main: View of Ascoli Piceno, as sunset tints the buildings of its historic center

Left: Cloisters of the convent of San Francesco in Amandola

Right (left and right): Historic Caffè Meletti; baptistry of San Giovanni, in Piazza Arringo

Far right (top to bottom): Elegant Piazza del Popolo; one of two stone lions guarding the central door of Ascoli's Chiesa di San Francesco; central nave in the Duomo di Ascoli Piceno, dedicated to Sant'Emidio

battlemented medieval tower; in Chiesa di San Francesco, whose slender Gothic form takes up one of the shorter sides of the piazza, with its decorative apses and carved doorways; in the Loggia dei Mercanti, built in the 16th century by the powerful Corporazione della Lana (the wool guild); and in the 62-arched colonnade, each column different from the next. Nearby Piazza Arringo, too, takes you back in time to the Middle Ages. Here stands the Palazzo Comunale, made up of two buildings joined together in the 17th and 18th centuries, as well as the town's handsome Duomo. In this cathedral you can follow the development of architectural styles, from its Romanesque crypt to its Renaissance façade, while the nearby octagonal baptistry is pure Gothic. Then there are Ascoli's lovely medieval towers: of its original estimated 200, around 50 remain standing, some of them complete and others incorporated into later buildings.

These monuments, built in the town's signature fine white marble, combine to make Ascoli an extraordinary center of art, and it is one that offers warmth and cordiality as well as culture.

Above: *Olive ascolane*, olives stuffed with meat, rolled in breadcrumbs, and fried

TRAVERTINE DIARY

More ancient than Rome, Ascoli Piceno was founded by the Piceni tribe, led to the site, so legend says, by a woodpecker (*picchio*). Its location, off the beaten tourist track, makes it an ideal destination for any connoisseur of architecture, culture, and good living. With three days to spend in and around Ascoli, you can enjoy them all.

Three Cultural Days

DAY 1

Begin your visit at Piazza del Popolo, to admire its colonnade and historic buildings. Pause for a cappuccino at Caffè Meletti, decorated in original Art Nouveau style. Then move on to Piazza Arringo, the oldest square in the town, embellished by twin fountains decorated with dolphins and sea horses. Visit the Duomo, with its beautiful 16th-century façade and, inside, a polyptych by Carlo Crivelli, dated 1473, and the baptistry, with its circular basin for full-immersion baptism. Afer lunch, pay a visit to the Pinacoteca Civica (art gallery), in Palazzo Comunale.

DAY 2

Today, drive northwest to the medieval walled town of Amandola, home to numerous artisan workshops that restore antique furniture. After lunch, drive east to Acquaviva Picena with its fine fortress and charming narrow streets. Return to Ascoli Piceno in time for an *apperitivo* of delicious *olive ascolane* with a glass of Rosso Piceno, one of the excellent local wines.

DAY 3

In the morning, go to Via Soderini to admire the Torre Ercolani, one of the most beautiful of the town's many towers. Alongside is a Lombard palazzo dating from the 12th century. Cross Ponte Augusto over the River Tronto; built in the 1st century BC, the bridge has an original passageway in its interior. Spend the rest of the day exploring the town, pausing at Chiesa di San Vincenzo e Atanasio, its façade decorated with 64 panels once covered with frescoes, whose ancient crypt was built over a spring said to cure leprosy.

Dos and Don'ts

- ✓ Visit the Christmas market that takes place each December in Ascoli Piceno; you can find charming original Christmas decorations and attractive handicrafts.
- ✓ If you are passionate about music, consider buying a violin. Musical instrument-making is an ancient tradition here.
- ✗ Don't drive into the center of Ascoli Piceno. Many streets are closed to traffic, and it can be difficult to keep your bearings on the narrow one-way streets.
- ✓ Buy an all-inclusive ticket to visit Ascoli Piceno's museums; you can find all the information you need online, on the website www.ascolimusei.it

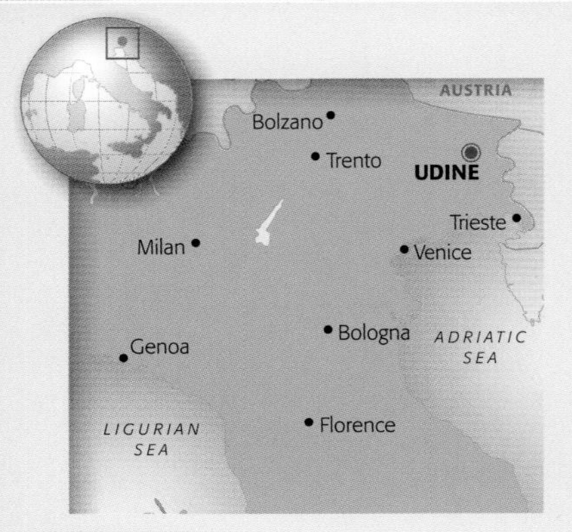

GETTING THERE
Udine is in eastern Friuli-Venezia Giulia. The nearest airport is Trieste's Ronchi dei Legionari, 25 miles (40 km) away, linked to Udine by a bus service. By car, take the A4, then the A23, exiting at Udine.

GETTING AROUND
It is best to explore the historic center on foot.

WEATHER
The average maximum daytime temperature in December is 46°F (8°C).

ACCOMMODATIONS
In a building dating from the 15th century, converted into a hotel in the 1800s, the elegant and central Astoria Hotel Italia is a city landmark; doubles from US$164; www.hotelastoria.udine.it

The B&B Dimora Montegnacco is housed in a palazzo in the heart of the historic center; doubles from US$75; www.dimoramontegnacco.it

EATING OUT
In the historic center, try good regional cooking at Vecchio Stallo (dinner from US$42); tel. 0432 21296.

Also in the center, Vitello d'Oro serves superb fish and seafood (from US$68); www.vitellodoro.com

At Trattoria Agli Amici, on the edge of Udine, the cooking is of the highest standard – individual and exquisite (from US$68; 8-course tasting menu, US$95); www.agliamici.it

PRICE FOR TWO
US$240–325 including accommodations, meals, admissions, and local travel.

FURTHER INFORMATION
www.turismofvg.it

Left: Aerial view of the historic center of Udine, showing the castle perched on its central hill

Right (left and right): Street stall in the historic center displaying dozens of *scarpez*, typical Friulian shoes; lion of St. Mark, the symbol of Venice, seen from the Loggia del Lionello in Piazza della Libertà

Main: Night view of Piazza della Libertà and the Loggia di San Giovanni, seen from the Loggia del Lionello

CITY OF CHARACTER AND CHARM

UDINE, THE ANCIENT CAPITAL of Friuli, and now its major modern city, is set on a plain around a dramatic, man-made hill built, according to legend, by Attila the Hun so that he could admire from on high the blazing city of Aquileia, which he himself had set on fire.

Just 12 miles (20 km) from Slovenia and 25 miles (40 km) from Austria, the city occupies a highly strategic position at a crossroads for trade and culture, which has resulted in a wealth of fine historic buildings and artistic treasures. Its castle, for example, has been a dominant feature of the city almost as far back as Roman times; within its walls is one of the oldest and most splendid parliament rooms in Europe. Facing the magnificent central Piazza della Libertà is the harmonious Loggia del Lionello, and the Loggia and Tempietto di San Giovanni, both dating from the 16th century and built by a flourishing commercial bourgeoisie, full of zest for culture and society. It was

Prosciutto di San Daniele

San Daniele del Friuli, a short distance from Udine, is the birthplace of one of Italy's most renowned gastronomic products: a *prosciutto* (cured ham) that has been produced here since the Middle Ages. The process involves just three ingredients – leg of pork, sea salt, and the San Daniele air – but it is a complex one, lasting over a year. The resulting ham is shaped like a guitar, the meat almost rosy in hue and with a mouthwatering aroma and flavor.

Above: Fountain in Piazza Matteotti, built by Giovanni da Udine in 1534

Above: Main portal of the Duomo di Udine, surmounted by a 14th-century arch decorated with a scene of the Redemption

Below: Façade of a historic palazzo facing onto Piazza Matteotti

into this pleasant and prosperous community that the artist Giambattista Tiepolo arrived in 1726, to be showered with praise and commissions by its ruling elite. He would return in later life to paint again in the city that so enjoyed his work, leaving a legacy of paintings and frescoes that almost rivals those of his native Venice and other major European cities. Today, art remains a passion in Udine: its Galleria d'Arte Moderna is one of the major Italian galleries of modern art.

The people of Udine have always aimed high, a quality reflected in the cathedral bell tower. The plan was to build it tall enough for a crowning statue of the Madonna to be able to "speak," on the same level, to the angel atop the castle (which, being on a hill, had a natural advantage). However, it proved impossible to find the huge quantity of building materials needed, and the tower achieved only the modest height we see today. This is typical of Udine, a place of charm and curiosities, passions and pragmatism. With its character, culture, and many green spaces, it is always high on the list of the best places to live in Italy. No wonder its citizens are so cheerful in their welcome.

FRIULIAN DIARY

Udine has a Renaissance core from which elegant streets radiate, lined with palazzi in Venetian and Art Nouveau styles. There is so much to see and do within the city itself, with its lovely architecture, fine museums and galleries, beautiful green open spaces, and hospitable *osterias*, that three days will fly by before you know it.

Three Days of Art and Culture

DAY 1

Begin your visit in Udine's most important square, Piazza della Libertà. The feature that immediately catches the eye is the Loggia del Lionello, with its elegant motif of pink and white bands. The goldsmith Nicolò Lionello designed its Venetian-Gothic shape. On the opposite side stands the 16th-century portico of San Giovanni, which incorporates the older clock tower, the Torre dell'Orologio. From the piazza, go through the Arco Bollani, which was designed by Andrea Palladio, to arrive at the 16th-century castle, at one time the residence of Venetian governors and today home to an excellent art gallery that includes works by Tiepolo and Caravaggio. Before it stands Santa Maria del Castello, with its 18th-century archangel and a lovely Renaissance façade.

DAY 2

Start the day with a visit to the Duomo, which has a lovely 14th-century doorway and is flanked by an octagonal bell tower in German-Gothic style. The interior, reworked in the 18th century, contains several works by Tiepolo, while traces of the Middle Ages can be seen in the Cappella di San Nicolò and the baptistry. Do not miss the Oratorio della Purità, adorned with another fresco by Tiepolo. In the afternoon, visit the Museo Diocesano in the Palazzo Vescovile for yet more marvelous Tiepolo frescoes.

DAY 3

Spend the morning at Gamud, Udine's modern gallery of art, which has works by Italian artists from the middle of the 19th century to the present day. While away the afternoon exploring Udine's lovely streets and squares, and its many appealing little shops.

Dos and Don'ts

- ✓ Udine's soccer team, Udinese Calcio, is hugely popular with the locals. Visit the team store on Via Mercato Vecchia for a distinctive black-and-white scarf and you'll be warmly welcomed wherever you go.
- ✗ Don't be surprised if you are hailed with a cheery *"Mandi!"* – it is the Friulian dialect's equivalent of *"Ciao!"*
- ✓ Browse around the traditional Christmas market for unique gifts or just to revel in the festive atmosphere.
- ✗ Don't try to visit Udine's museums on a Tuesday: they are closed (unlike those elsewhere in Italy, which close on Mondays).

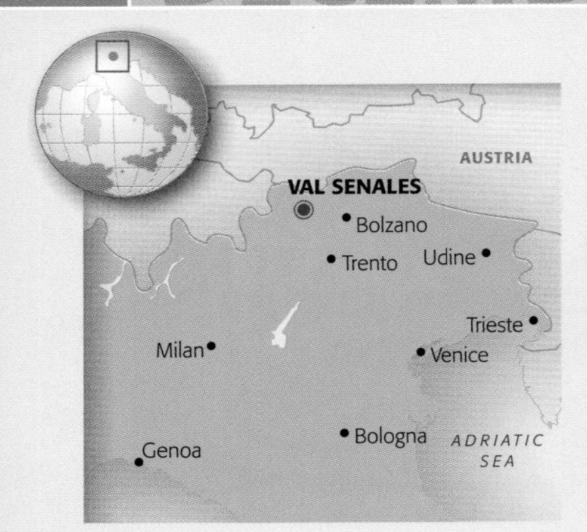

GETTING THERE
Val Senales is in western Trentino-Alto Adige. The nearest airport is Bolzano, 34 miles (55 km) away. Take the SS38 to Naturno, then follow local signs.

GETTING AROUND
You can travel around the valley by car or make use of the extensive network of buses.

WEATHER
Heavy snowfalls alternate with gloriously sunny days, perfect conditions for a skiing holiday.

ACCOMMODATIONS
For the most dedicated of skiers, the dream place to stay is the Berghotel Grawand above Maso Corto, the highest mountain hotel in Europe. Reached by cable car, it has a pool, sauna, and panoramic restaurant; doubles from US$150 half board; www.grawand.com

The old farm of Oberniederhof, in Madonna di Senales, has a comfortable apartment in Alpine style; from US$95; www.oberniederhof.com

EATING OUT
Several restaurants in Val Senales, such as the Croce d'Oro in Madonna di Senales (dinner from US$42; www.goldenes-kreuz.com), take part in the initiative "Eating as in Ötzi's day," serving dishes made with ingredients that the ice man would have known. Try aromatic bread made from just-milled grain, salad of lentils, and wild herbs or nettle soup.

PRICE FOR TWO
US$365 per day for accommodations, meals, lift ticket, and local travel.

FURTHER INFORMATION
www.valsenales.com

Ötzi the Ice Man

Discovered in 1991, at an altitude of over 9,840 ft (3,000 m) in the Similaun glacier, Ötzi is the mummified corpse of a man who lived 5,300 years ago. Thanks to the freezing conditions, he was in an excellent state of preservation, and was found together with his clothing and items of equipment. He met his end on one of the glacier's more inaccessible paths, shot by an arrow. Today, Ötzi's home is the Museo Archeologico in Bolzano *(see p325)*, where he is kept in a refrigerated chamber, with walls coated in ice tiles, at 21°F (-6°C) and at close to 100 percent humidity.

Above: Mountains around Val Senales after a heavy fall of snow

Far right (top to bottom): White partridge, often seen in winter; Black Forest gâteau, typical of local Germanic-influenced cuisine; Gletscherbahn cable car, heading for the summit of Monte Grawand; youngster enjoying the snow on a simple toboggan

Below: Haflinger, the small mountain horse long bred in the region

Main: Skiers on the slopes of Val Senales, about to set off after a fresh snowfall

PEAKS OF PERFECTION

In Val Senales, thanks to its altitude and direct access to a glacier, it is possible to ski all year around. However, in the run-up to Christmas the quaint Tyrolean villages of the region take on a festive air, with traditional customs, music, and decorations, that is warm and welcoming after a long day on the slopes.

The 13 skilifts are ultra-modern and serve 15 pistes of every type, suited to every level of skier. Are you a novice and in need of a beginner's slope? There are gentle pistes and expert instructors to get you started and build your confidence. Are you an expert skier? Challenging black runs await. There's plenty to keep the cross-country skier happy, too, with four pistes, the longest of which runs for 6 miles (10 km). And, for more modern sports such as snowboarding and freestyle, there are the 142,000 sq yards (120,000 sq m) of the glacier snowpark. Here the pistes, created and tended using the most advanced technology, offer something for every level of ability. There's a

Above: Maso Corto ski resort in the heart of Val Senales

TYROLEAN DIARY

With its 22 miles (35km) of high-altitude pistes and its exceptional snowpark – one of the best-equipped in the Alps – Val Senales is, not surprisingly, one of this region's most popular ski resorts. Nonetheless, with six days at your disposal, you'll have plenty of opportunities to get away on your own into the tranquil beauty of the peaks.

Six Days on the Slopes

DAY 1 On your first morning, take the Gletscherbahn cable car that leaves from Maso Corto, at an altitude of 6562 ft (2,000 m), and takes only six minutes to reach Monte Grawand at 10,500 ft (3,200 m). At this height the panorama of peaks and glaciers leaves most visitors open-mouthed. Various trails lead from the glacier, including the Schmugglerabfahrt run, which descends 3,937 ft (1,200 m) over the course of 5 miles (8 km).

DAY 2 Devote the day to snowboarding at the superb snowpark in Val Senales. Take a lesson if you are a novice – if you are an experienced boarder just let rip and have fun.

DAY 3 For a more relaxing day, take the Lazaun chairlift, also from Maso Corto; from the mountain station at the top there is a track for cross-country skiing and one for tobogganing. But if you are feeling tired, you can just stay put, enjoy the sunshine, and have a delicious Tyrolean meal at the Alpine hut restaurant by the chairlift.

DAY 4 Spend the day improving your ski carving technique – the Val Senales ski school offers courses or individual lessons, and the wide pistes here are ideal.

DAY 5 Take the free ski bus to the little village of Lana, where there is a cable car that acends Monte San Vigilio to a less well-known ski area, with four lifts and 3 miles (5 km) of runs through lovely scenery.

DAY 6 If you are an experienced mountain skier, you can go on a trail that begins at the cable car of Maso Corto, and goes as far as Giogo di Tisa, where the mummified body of Ötzi was found. Alternatively, spend your final day enjoying your favorite pistes for one last time.

Dos and Don'ts

- ✓ Check the latest meteorological conditions prior to leaving for the snowpark: if visibility is poor or snow is falling heavily, it could be closed.
- ✗ Don't set out for the place where Ötzi was found if you are not a highly proficient Alpine skier.
- ✓ If you have small children, take them to the Pinocchio nursery, close to the valley station of the cable car: they will have fun, and you will, too.

half-pipe as well as easy, medium, and pro line courses, and plenty of instructors are on hand – all passionate boarders themselves – keen to help you progress from one level to the next.

Val Senales is not just about challenges, however; here the art of hospitality is taken to great heights, and there are plenty of activities for the non-skier. Guided snowshoe hikes are run, or you can take to the trails on horseback; there is an ice rink and an indoor swimming pool; there are toboggan runs and climbing routes; and in the evening there are many cozy bars and restaurants, music, and seasonal activities. All this makes Val Senales a great place for families, too. There are facilities specifically designed to cater for children, as well as winter day nurseries to keep the kids entertained while mom and dad take to the slopes with complete peace of mind.

Val Senales really does offer something for everyone, and its friendly Tyrolean welcome makes you feel immediately at home amid the marvelous setting of its snowy peaks and clear blue skies.

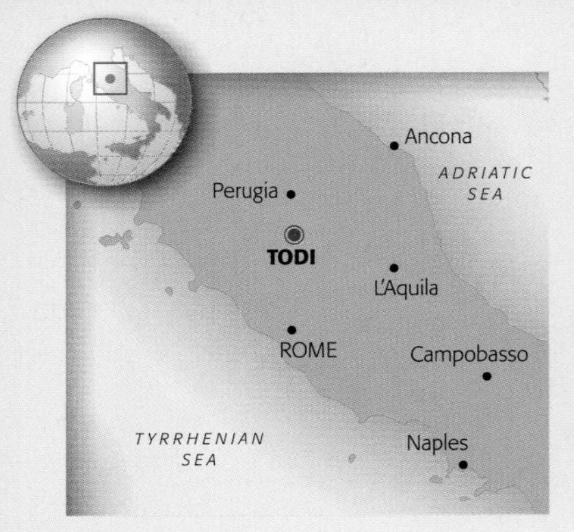

GETTING THERE
Situated in central-southern Umbria, Todi is around 25 miles (40 km) south of Perugia, the nearest airport. By car, follow the SS3-bis, or use the bus and train links.

GETTING AROUND
The center of Todi can be explored on foot.

WEATHER
Average daytime temperatures reach 48°F (9°C), or more on sunny days.

ACCOMMODATIONS
San Lorenzo Tre is a 17th-century residence in the historic center of Todi, which has kept all its old-world charm; doubles from US$150; www.sanlorenzo3.it

A former 12th-century convent on the edge of town, the elegant Hotel Bramante has its own health club; doubles from US$190; www.hotelbramante.it

The Relais Todini is a 14th-century manor house in the hills of Todi, now a luxury hotel and spa offering a warm welcome, luxury furnishings, and impeccable service. The restaurant serves the best of Umbrian cooking; doubles from US$218; www.relaistodini.com

EATING OUT
Ristorante Umbria offers local specialties (dinner from US$55) such as *zuppa di farro* (spelt soup), *palomba alla ghiotta* (pigeon), and dishes based on mushrooms and truffles; www.todi.net/umbria

Jacopone, a charming restaurant in the historic center, serves excellent meat dishes including wild boar with truffles (from US$42); www.todi.net/jacopone

PRICE FOR TWO
US$275–365 including accommodations, meals, admissions, and car rental.

FURTHER INFORMATION
http://todionline.it

An Oasis of Nature

The Tiber River (il Tevere in Italian) rises in the Emilian Apennines and then continues its course through the valleys of Umbria, across the area around Todi. It is here that the river presents its most charming aspects: surrounded by luxuriant vegetation, it flows placidly through green valleys and forms the lovely Lago di Alviano. This unspoiled oasis, an important staging post for migrating birds, is at the heart of an area of great environmental, historical, and cultural interest, protected by its status as the Oasi Naturalistica di Alviano.

Above: 14th-century Rocca di Todi, the highest point of the town; lovely Chiesa di Santa Maria della Consolazione

WALLS WITHIN WALLS

THE TOWN OF TODI developed in concentric layers, with encircling walls that moved outward as the centuries went by. It is possible to trace its development like the rings in a tree trunk: from the original Umbro-Etruscan center; on to the Roman era, which saw the expansion of the town onto two hills just outside the original walls; and then to the so-called "new" city, which dates from the Middle Ages, the era of the town's greatest splendor.

Not much remains to be seen of Todi's Roman era, but the *nicchioni* are still there. This series of recesses, set in a load-bearing wall, was designed to support an elevated street, no longer visible, in Piazza del Mercato Vecchio. There are also nine enormous cisterns, cut deep into the hill beneath Piazza del Popolo; an impressive feat of engineering now open to the public.

But it was in the Middle Ages that the town acquired its definitive appearance. Its four quarters were surrounded by a ring of fortifications, with seven access gates, which climb upward toward Piazza del Popolo. The square, built above the cisterns and on the site of the ancient Roman forum, was constructed in order to link the two hilltops on which Todi stood. For this reason it is surprisingly level, in a town that is otherwise all slopes and steps. This spot may have been the heart of Todi since Roman times, but it looks entirely medieval, flanked by three palatial seats of power – Palazzo dei Priori, Palazzo del Popolo, and Palazzo del Capitano – and one side of the cathedral, set in a raised position, with an imposing staircase leading up to it. The rest of the historic center is also medieval for the most part, full of narrow twisting streets and noble buildings, including the lovely Chiesa di San Fortunato, built in 1292, with a magnificent sculpted doorway in its unfinished façade.

The Renaissance bequeathed one true masterpiece to Todi, the Chiesa di Santa Maria della Consolazione. Built outside the town walls, according to tradition, it is the work of Donato Bramante. The church, begun in 1508 and finished a century later, is a landmark in the panorama of the town: pale and square, surmounted by a large dome, its classical proportions are in perfect harmony with lovely Todi and the beautiful countryside around it.

Main: View of the ancient and beautiful town of Todi
Below (left to right): Bronze statue of Jacopone da Todi, the Italian priest and poet; vaulted covered alleyway in the medieval heart of Todi; dish of *porchetta* (roast pork), a specialty found throughout this part of central Italy

Above: View over the elegant Piazza del Popolo

ARCHITECTURE DIARY

A powerful city in the Middle Ages, Todi has, as well as its fine Piazza del Popolo, many other monuments and palazzos worthy of note, scattered around the steep streets of a town much loved by visitors. Devote two days to its many delights, then spend a day in the surrounding countryside seeing more of this lovely region.

Three Days of History

DAY 1

Start your visit in Piazza del Popolo; visit the cathedral, linked to the piazza by 29 travertine marble steps and embellished by a magnificent rose window and a 16th-century wooden door. Also, look at the medieval palazzos surrounding the square; of particular interest is Palazzo del Popolo, one of the oldest public buildings in Italy. After lunch, a visit to the Roman cisterns, which lie underneath the piazza, is an unmissable experience.

DAY 2

In the morning, stroll along Via Mazzini as far as the Chiesa di San Fortunato, which dates from the end of the 13th century; take time to explore the town's medieval streets. Then go to Piazza del Mercato Vecchio to admire the *nicchioni,* four huge Roman arches built to support a street that passed above the piazza at one time. Later, visit the Tempio di San Fortunato to see the tomb of the saint Jacopone da Todi, then leave by the nearby Porta Liberta and walk downhill to the splendid Renaissance church of Santa Maria della Consolazione. Inside, in the main apse, is a 15th-century fresco of the *Madonna of Consolation*, to whom the church is dedicated.

DAY 3

Spend the day on a pleasant circular drive. First, travel southwest past the Lago di Corbara, then south through the beautiful Parco Fluviale del Tevere to the Oasi Naturalistica di Alviano. From here, head southeast, then northward, to the delightful spa resort town of Acquasparta. Sample its curative mineral waters before heading back north to Todi in time for dinner.

Dos and Don'ts

- ✓ To visit the Roman cisterns, you must apply to the Museo Pinacoteca in Todi: tel. 075 894 4148.
- ✗ Don't expect to bathe at the Terme dell'Amerino in Acquasparta – the water is for drinking only.
- ✓ If you have time, head a little way farther south of Acquasparta to see the fine Roman ruins at Carsulae.
- ✓ The Oasi Naturalistica di Alviano is open on Sundays only, from September to May. During your visit, be sure to keep to the marked paths, and be as quiet as possible, in order not to disturb the abundant wildlife.

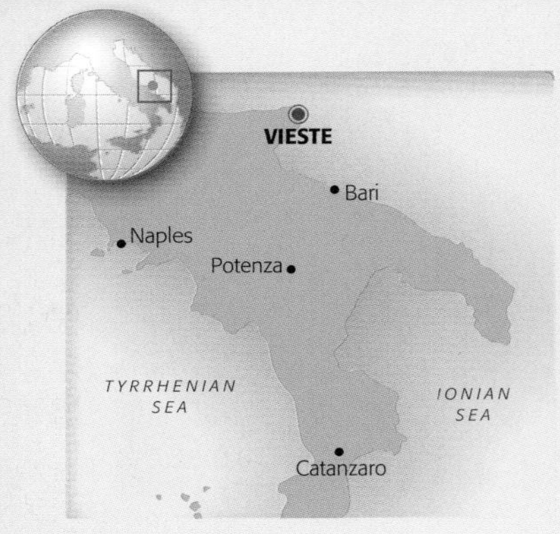

GETTING THERE
Vieste is in northern Puglia, at the tip of the Gargano headland. The nearest airport is at Bari, 112 miles (180 km) away, about 2 hours 30 minutes by car.

GETTING AROUND
You will need a car to get to and around Vieste.

WEATHER
Vieste enjoys a particularly mild climate, even in December, with an average maximum daytime temperature of 57°F (14°C).

ACCOMMODATIONS
Hotel Punta San Francesco, in the historic center of Vieste, has simple but comfortable rooms; doubles from US$82; www.hotelpuntasanfrancesco.it

The B&B Rocca sul Mare is in part of a medieval monastery and stands in a splendid position on the seafront; doubles from US$68; www.roccasulmare.it

EATING OUT
At Ristorante San Michele you can try regional specialties including fresh pastas such as *orecchiette* and *strascinati*, stuffed mussels, and grilled fish (dinner from US$35); tel. 0884 708 143)

Enoteca Vesta serves excellent Pugliese cuisine (try the *troccoli con i ceci*, pasta with garbanzo beans), accompanied by a wide range of wines (from US$35). The interior is charming, carved out of a natural cave; www.enotecavesta.it

PRICE FOR TWO
US$300 per day including accommodations, meals, and car rental.

FURTHER INFORMATION
www.vieste.it
www.gargano.ws

The Living Nativity

Every December the story of the nativity is brought to life in the heart of Rignano Garganico, the smallest village of the Parco Nazionale del Gargano, with around 400 local people taking part. As well as the classic elements and characters of any nativity play, a bygone way of life is charmingly evoked, with villagers enacting roles ranging from the washerwoman to the seamstress, the basket-maker to the blacksmith and, of course, the innkeeper.

Main: Baia delle Zagare, one of the loveliest beaches on the Gargano headland
Above (left to right): Pugliese olive grove; ancient fishing apparatus known as a *trabucco*; *marzotica*, a local type of ricotta cheese

Above: View of Vieste, perched on its rocky outcrop

LEGENDS IN LIMESTONE

WHICH CAN WIN, in the battle between land and sea? Perhaps neither, and the Gargano headland is a good demonstration of that. Formed from limestone, unlike the rest of the Adriatic coast, here the onslaught of waves and gales has been subdued and tempered by the soft terrain, which it has in turn etched and shaped into often quite astonishing forms.

Splendid old Vieste, the most northerly town on the headland, is built on a rocky point that juts out almost determinedly into the sea. Just to the south, the beach of Pizzomunno opens out, a long sandy strip where the deep blue sea looks unexpectedly peaceful in winter. This beach is the site of a poignant local legend. The story goes that a young fisherman, Pizzomunno, was loved equally by the sirens, who admired his skills in piloting his boat through the waves, and by a village girl, called Cristalda, who was poor but exceptionally beautiful. Full of jealousy, the sirens lured Cristalda into the sea to drown and poor Pizzomunno, stunned with pain, turned to stone on the sand. The monolith, 82 ft (25 m) high, seems to stand guard over nearby Vieste, as it waits eternally for the sea to give back what it once so cruelly stole. Legend says that she returns to him just once every 100 years.

Here, the onslaught of the waves and gales has been subdued and tempered by the soft terrain, which it has in turn etched and shaped into often quite astonishing forms.

This is a coastline full of mystery and myth, and countless stories have been spun about the great "doorway" of Architiello and the grottoes that punctuate the limestone cliffs. Then there are the Tremiti islands off the headland's northern coast. It was on the largest, San Domino, that the ancient Greek hero Diomedes is said to have spent his last years. The goddess Venus turned his men into seabirds who, on his death, were heard to sing in mourning. Those birds are still here today – their Latin name is *diomedea* but they are better known as Cory's shearwater, and their plaintive, human-sounding calls add yet another layer to the magical aura that imbues this very special place.

Inset: Limestone stack at Pizzomunno
Below: Architiello, a spectacular rock arch at the entrance to the bay of San Felice, near Vieste; lighthouse of Pugnochiuso

GARGANO DIARY

Vieste is a handsome town, with a medieval quarter of white houses perched on the cliffs, clear waters, and marvelous grottoes accessible by sea. It is the ideal point of departure for tours of the Gargano and along the wonderful coastline and, with four days at your disposal, you will have time for several such leisurely excursions.

Four Days on the Headland

DAY 1

Spend the day getting to know Vieste, with its historic center of bright white houses in sharp and lovely contrast to the intense blue of the sea. Stroll around the streets and climb as far as Punta San Francesco, where there is a castle of Norman origin. In 1554, this was the scene of one of the bloodiest episodes in the history of Vieste: the slaughter of thousands of local citizens by the pirate Dragut Raïs, on the rock known as Chianca Amara ("bitter stone"), not far from the beautiful Apulian-Romanesque cathedral.

DAY 2

In the morning, visit the beach of Pizzomunno. It is glorious even in winter, with its magnificent monolith rising from the golden sand. After lunch, stop in at Vieste's curious Museo Malacologico, which displays shells from all over the world.

DAY 3

Today, drive out to Pugnochiuso, enjoying the views which open up at each bend in the coastal road. Among the most beautiful sights is the Vallone del Vignaiolo, a valley that extends as far as the Adriatic and culminates in a beach of fine white sand, and Baia delle Zagare, a bay studded with lighthouses.

DAY 4

Make an excursion to the Parco Nazionale del Gargano. There are several walking trails through the park, organized by expert guides. One of the most famous is the walk leading to various *masserie*, ancient rural farmhouses typical of the area. If you don't want to walk, there are guided pony treks through the park that you can do instead.

Dos and Don'ts

- ✗ Don't drive too fast: the coast road around the Gargano twists and turns. Not only will you be safer, you'll also be able to appreciate the magnificent landscape more fully.
- ✓ If the sun is shining, make the most of the mild weather with a picnic on the beach.
- ✓ Buy some olive oil from the Gargano, one of the most famous areas in Italy for top-quality oil.
- ✓ For pictures and video of the Living Nativity, see the website: www.preseperignano.com (Italian only).

GETTING THERE
Bolzano is the gateway to the Alto Adige (South Tyrol). In winter, flights operate to its Dolomiti airport from various European countries. The closest major airport is Verona, about 93 miles (150 km) away, with good road and rail links.

GETTING AROUND
Bolzano and its environs are served by an efficient and extensive network of public transportation.

WEATHER
There are plenty of ways of keeping warm in the cold days leading up to Christmas; and the city is even more enchanting when it snows, as it may well do.

ACCOMMODATIONS
Centrally located but in a quiet position, Hotel Greif is a perfect blend of art (each room is decorated by a different artist), history (it dates back to the Middle Ages), and modern comfort; doubles from US$245; www.greif.it

In the center of Bolzano, the Park-Hotel Mondschein-Luna has elegant rooms with four-poster beds; doubles from US$228; www.hotel-luna.it

EATING OUT
Top-quality cooking in elegant surroundings is offered by the restaurant of the Hotel Laurin (dinner from US$54); http://hotel.laurin.it

Bolzano's Ca' de Bezzi has been serving food for over 600 years and offers a range of delicious local dishes (from US$35); www.batzen.it

PRICE FOR TWO
US$380 per day including accommodations, meals, and the Museumobil Card.

FURTHER INFORMATION
www.bolzano-bozen.it

Thun Figurines

Thun *angeli laudantes* (singing angels) are one of the emblems of Christmas in Bolzano. They sprang from the creative imaginations of a local couple, Count Otmar Thun and his wife Lene, who, in 1950, because of their passion for ceramics, opened a craft workshop in the cellar of their castle on the edge of Bolzano. Since then, the Thun company has become world famous, and today, as well as their delightful little figurines, decorated with tremendous care, they offer many other ceramic products, each one different but at the same time unmistakeably "Thun."

Left: Houses with *erker* bay windows in the historic center of Bolzano

Right (left and right): Traditional *pandolce* of Bolzano, made with dried and candied fruits, liqueur, and spices; central Piazza Walthers, site of the city's famous Christmas market

Main: The lively Christmas market of Bolzano, known locally as the Bozner Christkindlmarkt

CHRISTMAS CELEBRATIONS

First of all you hear the music – Christmas carols floating through the air. Then comes the scents of cinnamon, spruce wood, roast chestnuts, and *vin brûlé* (mulled wine). Then you see the lights from Christmas decorations twinkling on market stalls and glittering on buildings. This is the Christmas market in Bolzano, a fusion of Austrian and Italian traditions. Piazza Walther is filled for the duration of Advent with the typical wooden cabins of Christkindlmarkt, one of the most important events in the city's calendar and the perfect way to get in the mood for Christmas celebrations.

The event also offers you the chance to get to know this beautiful, unusual city, whose historic center shares features with both Italian and Austrian cities: its streets bordered by porticoes; palazzos with frescoed façades; and churches with evocative features, such as the cathedral, whose roof is decorated with a motif of diamonds formed by green, black, and ochre tiles, in the Alpine tradition. Piazza Walther, built for Maximilian of Bavaria in 1808, is the heart of the historic

Above: Castel Sant'Antonio, site of the first Thun ceramics factory

Above: Via dei Portici, one of Bolzano's attractive arcaded streets

Below: Decorative tile-work on the roof of the cathedral of Bolzano, dedicated to Maria Assunta

center, but the streets surrounding the square are considerably older. Via degli Argentieri, for example, follows the line of ancient walls that were demolished in the 13th century. Piazza delle Erbe, enlivened daily by the hustle and bustle of an excellent food market, owes its curious curved shape to the fact that it, too, lies along that route. It leads on to Via dei Portici, the main focus of commercial life in Bolzano, which also dates from the 13th century and is lined with houses that often feature *erker* – pretty, many-sided bay windows – protruding from the façades.

There is another Bolzano, too, which merits exploration – a modern city, curious and open to artistic ideas both from Italy and Europe as a whole. This is the Bolzano that came up with innovative projects such as the Museion, a new museum of modern and contemporary art. Far from just a picture gallery, it is built to a futuristic design with great walls of glass that, after dark, are transformed into gigantic screens on which vast, specially commissioned works can be projected. It's a piece of modern magic amid a city in celebration of its past, and a heady addition to Bolzano's appealing cultural melting pot.

CHRISTKINDL DIARY

Bolzano is a bilingual city, a harmonious blend of two different characters – Italian and Austrian – that is reflected in its artistic and cultural life. Spend four days getting to know and appreciate this diversity as you explore Bolzano old and new. Best of all, you are here for its Christmas market, when the whole city takes on a magical air.

Four Festive Days

DAY 1

You can't help but begin your visit at the Christmas market in Piazza Walther, browsing stalls laden with handicrafts and Christmas decorations. Sample the typical cakes such as apple strudel and *zelten*, a rich Christmas cake made with candied fruit. Later, visit the Gothic cathedral, flanked by a 16th-century bell tower. Look out for the pulpit, decorated with lizards and with cherubs holding stonemasons' tools, and visit the splendid treasury museum in the base of the tower.

DAY 2

Today, explore the city: start off at the Chiesa dei Domenicani, where you can admire a chapel entirely covered in frescoes of the Giotto school. In Piazza delle Erbe, browse the stalls in what is the most "Mediterranean" corner of Bolzano. After lunch, visit the Museion, as much of interest for its building as for the collections and exhibitions on show.

DAY 3

In the morning, visit the Museo Archeologico dell'Alto Adige. The star here is Ötzi, the perfectly preserved body of a man who lived 5,300 years ago. Discovered in the Similaun glacier at Val Venosta in 1991, Ötzi is now on show here, in a specially refrigerated chamber *(see p318)*. Spend the afternoon browsing around the streets of the city center, lined with elegant shops.

DAY 4

Today visit Gries, once an independent town, but now absorbed into Bolzano. In the 19th century it was a popular health resort, and some lovely *belle époque* architecture remains. There is also a handsome Benedictine abbey complex, founded in 1406.

Dos and Don'ts

- ✓ For information on exhibitions and events at the Museion, consult the website: www.museion.it
- ✓ If you can tear youself away from Bolzano, visit the upland plateau region of Renon. You can get there quickly from the center of town by cable car, and continue on the narrow-gauge railway from Soprabolzano to Collalbo.
- ✗ Don't knock back too much of the *vin brûlé*. Sweet and spicy, it may taste innocuous enough, but can be very strong.
- ✓ Buy the Museumobil Card. It gives free travel on all public transportation, as well as admission to a range of museums.

Tourism and the Environment

NATURE IN ITALY

The geography of Italy is astonishingly varied. There are high mountains, rolling hills, upland plateaus, plains, volcanoes, and caves; rugged headlands and sandy coves, islands, lakes, and rivers. In fact, virtually every kind of natural environment can be found here, to an extent that has few equals in the world. And although it is true that, for many tourists, the main attraction of Italy is the extraordinary beauty of its coastline, an equal number choose the enchanting loveliness of the countryside.

In many regions, such as the Cinque Terre, the countryside around Siena, the Lucanian Apennines, and the Alpine valleys, the Italian landscape is mercifully unspoiled, with features that are truly timeless. With 24 national parks and 140 regional parks, together with a good number of state and regional preserves and protected marine preserves, a considerable proportion of Italian territory is environmentally safeguarded. A complete database is available on the website www.parks.it with links to all such protected areas and information on visits and excursions, accommodations, and leisure options. Each park has its own regulations, which should be followed out of respect for nature and to prevent harm to its ecosystem.

AGRITURISMI (VACATION FARMS)

One of the best ways of immersing yourself in the Italian countryside is by choosing an *agriturismo* vacation. This means staying on a farm that has diversified from agriculture, and has converted buildings for residential use. The word for "farmhouse" varies according to the region (it might be *casale*, *cascina*, *masseria*, or *baglio*) but, whatever the name, they all provide a holiday far away from frenetic city life. They often have a swimming pool and may offer a range of activities (such as horseback riding, hiking, tennis, or mountain biking) and the chance to buy farm produce, such as wine, olive oil, or honey. A selection of *agriturismi* can be found at www.agriturismo.org.uk

ECO-VACATIONS

There are various eco-vacation options available in Italy. These can be organized independently, perhaps by applying to park authorities *(see above)* or by consulting the website www.ecoturismo-italia.it (not all sections are available in English), which promotes travel as an activity compatible with environmental sustainability, using tourism to help care for the environment and foster appreciation of local cultures. Look, too, at the website of the Associazione Italiana Turismo Responsabile (www.aitr.org), a non-profit organization that works to promote responsible tourism. Other websites that provide a directory of ecologically sound tour options to Italy include www.responsibletravel.com and www.ecotourdirectorycom

Above (left to right): Grande Albergo in Sestri Levante, one of the most luxurious hotels on the Ligurian coast; Palazzo Vecchio in Piazza della Signoria, Florence; visitors to the Colosseum in Rome taking a well-earned rest; underground train on the M3 line of the Milan metro **Below left:** Typical Italian countryside *agriturismo*

TRAVEL INFORMATION

TRAVELING IN ITALY should present no particular difficulties. Tourism is, in general, well-established, and visitors are almost invariably warmly welcomed and well catered-for. Nevertheless, a certain amount of planning is advisable in order to avoid problems, be prepared for the unexpected, save time and money, and help ensure that you make the most of a trip to this beautiful country.

Health

US Department of State http://travel.state.gov/travel/tips

No specific vaccinations are required in order to visit Italy. Standards of hygiene and medical care are generally good throughout the country.

The main risk is probably excessive heat in the summer months, especially in urban areas, where temperatures can reach, or even exceed, 105°F (40°C), with high levels of humidity. Wear light, breathable clothing and a sun hat with a wide brim, and carry a bottle of water with you. When possible, do as the Italians do, and avoid going out in the middle of the day. Another summer problem, in towns and cities and also anywhere close to standing water, is mosquitoes. A good insect repellent will be enough to keep them at bay.

If necessary, pharmacies will supply first aid and can dispense over-the-counter medicines without the need for a doctor's prescription. Pharmacies can be found all over the country and are easily identified by the sign of a green cross. They are usually open Monday to Friday from 8:30 or 9am to 12:30 or 1pm and then again from 3:30 or 4pm to 7:30 or 8pm, as well as on Saturday morning. Some are open all day *(orario continuato)* and there are also 24-hour pharmacies in many locations, usually in well-populated areas. When a pharmacy is closed there will be a notice in the window giving the names and addresses of others in the area, which open on a rota basis. In a medical emergency, dial 118 to be put through to the Pronto Soccorso (Emergency Service), which will provide assistance over the phone and send an ambulance if necessary, taking the patient to the nearest appropriate hospital, by helicopter if circumstances dictate.

Citizens of the United States and other countries not part of the European Union are strongly advised to take out comprehensive travel and medical insurance.

Citizens of the EU, as well as those of Iceland, Liechtenstein, Norway, and Sweden, in possession of a European Health Insurance Card (EHIC) who need medical attention can use services provided by the Servizio Sanitario Nazionale (Italian National Health Service). The EHIC entitles the holder to state-provided medical treatment; be aware that, in most instances, you will have to pay initially, complete a claims form and await reimbursement upon your return home. The payment of prescription charges remains the responsibility of the patient.

Personal Security

Emergency police number Tel. 113

Italy is a comparatively safe country for travelers, and crimes of violence are extremely rare. However, in large cities especially, keep a close guard on your possessions when traveling on public transportation, sightseeing, or when on the beach. Never leave your belongings unattended, or visible in a rental car. Take photocopies of your passport and any other important documents: carry the copies with you, leaving the originals safely in your accommodations. Lost or stolen items must be reported as soon as possible at the nearest police station, and a copy of the report *(denuncia)* obtained. If you lose your passport or identity card, apply to your nearest consulate or embassy with a copy of the *denuncia*. Block stolen credit cards immediately by contacting your home bank.

FOR YOUR SAFETY

- Don't carry any valuables in a backpack over your shoulder.
- Don't leave belongings unattended, especially on beaches or when using public transportation.
- Photocopy and keep safe your passport, travel tickets, and any other important documents; carry the copies with you.
- Don't carry all of your money with you, and especially not all in one place.
- Be aware of potential pickpocket scams on crowded public transportation or at major tourist attractions.
- At night, avoid areas around train stations, and isolated or poorly lit roads.

Insurance

Travel Insurance www.worldtravelcenter.com

As well as health insurance to cover medical costs, all travelers are advised to take out a comprehensive insurance package. An insurance policy, purchased in advance from your home country, should cover inconvenience resulting from flight delays, loss of or damage to baggage, the theft of belongings or documents, accidents (and personal liability in such a case), legal assistance and advice, and (in the case that you are not otherwise insured) complete medical cover.

Drivers from the US and other non-EU countries must obtain a certificate of international insurance (Green Card, or *Carta Verde* in Italian). If, however, you do not fulfil the criteria for a Green Card, a temporary policy can be acquired at the international border (valid for at least 15 days but not more than six months) or you can take out insurance with a company certified in Italy. If you are picking up a car on arrival in Italy, it is advisable to check the terms and conditions of the car rental company's insurance policy online at home before you book, in order to be sure that you are fully covered for all eventualities.

Citizens of the EU, Andorra, and of Croatia, Iceland, Liechtenstein, Norway, and Switzerland, can drive a car in Italy using the RCA cover (certificate of third-party insurance) valid in their own country.

Passports and Visas

Visa information http://italy.visahq.com

Citizens of the US, Canada, Australia, and New Zealand, as well as EU nationals, do not need a visa for stays of less than three months. Most EU visitors need only a valid identity document, but visitors from the UK, Ireland, Denmark, and Sweden must have a passport. For almost everyone else, a visa as well as a valid passport are required, giving the name of your destination and the length of your stay. Visas can be obtained from Italian consulates in your country of origin, and are usually issued 90 days after submitting an application; you must specify the reason for your visit. Visitors staying in hotels or similar accommodations will be automatically registered with the police; anyone staying privately is required to register with the police within eight days of arrival in Italy.

Money

Travelex www.travelex.com

As well as Italy, Austria, Belgium, Cyprus, Finland, France, Germany, Greece, Ireland, Luxembourg, Malta, the Netherlands, Portugal, Slovakia, Slovenia, and Spain have adopted the euro (€) as their currency. Citizens of other nations should apply to their own bank to exchange their local currency for euros or to purchase travelers' checks. Check exchange rates carefully before you travel.

In Italy, exchange commission rates can vary widely. Tourist resorts have bureaux de change, as do major arrival points such as airports and stations. However, they often charge a higher rate of commission than the banks. To get immediate access to cash, make use of an ATM (Automated Teller Machine, known in Italy as a *bancomat*). These can be found outside many banks (changing money at an Italian bank counter can be a very time-consuming process). Most have instructions in several languages. You will need to key in your PIN number.

The easiest way to make purchases or other payments, such as hotel bills, is with a credit card: the overwhelming majority of commercial outlets accept the main international cards, such as American Express, MasterCard, and Visa. You may have more difficulty in paying by credit card in more out-of-the-way regions, especially in the south of the country, where tourists are less common, or in small family-run restaurants and shops, where you may need to use cash.

DIRECTORY OF USEFUL CONTACTS

GENERAL INFORMATION

ENIT
www.italiantourism.com
The official tourist board website of Italy.

Italian Tourism
www.italia.it
Online "showcase" about all aspects of Italy.

UNESCO
www.unesco.org
List and information on UNESCO World Heritage sites in Italy.

Venere
www.venere.com/hotels/italy
Useful for booking hotels, B&Bs, and *agriturismo* farm holidays.

SUSTAINABLE TOURISM

Aitr Associazione Italiana Turismo Responsabile
www.aitr.org
Italian association dedicated to promoting ethical tourism.

LIPU
www.lipu.it
Website of the Italian League for the Protection of Birds (Lega Italiana per la Protezione degli Uccelli, or Lipu), which organizes nature trips and countryside hikes (Italian only).

Panda
www.fattoriedelpanda.net
Website linked to the Italian branch of the World Wildlife Fund, with eco-friendly accommodation in WWF and other natural parks in almost every region of Italy.

Parks.it
www.parks.it
Information (including maps and opening times) on all the Italian parks and preserves.

Responsible Travel
www.responsibletravel.com
Website specializing in ecotourism and socially responsible holidays.

HEALTH

European Union
www.ec.europa.eu
The European Commission website with current health alerts and information.

US Department of State
http://travel.state.gov
Website giving current US Government health advice and information, with a section on Italy.

WHO
www.euro.who.int
The website of the World Health Organization with information on Italy's healthcare system.

PERSONAL SAFETY

Carabinieri
www.carabinieri.it
All essential information for contacting local police, the *carabinieri*. Tel. 112.

Fire Service
www.vigilfuoco.it
The official website for the Italian Fire Service *(Vigili del Fuoco)* (Italian only). Tel. 113.

State Police
www.poliziadistato.it
List of all the Italian state police headquarters, with telephone numbers. Tel. 113.

INSURANCE

Europ Assistance
www.europ-assistance.com
Private breakdown assistance in Italy and elsewhere.

Mondial Assistance
www.mondial-assistance.com
Assistance and travel insurance services.

PASSPORTS AND VISAS

Visa HQ
http://italy.visahq.com/
Information on passports and visas for visitors to Italy, searchable by country of origin.

EMBASSIES AND CONSULATES

Australia
www.italy.embassy.gov.au

Canada
www.canada.it

United Kingdom
ukinitaly.fco.gov.uk

United States
italy.usembassy.gov

MONEY

Travelex
www.travelex.com
Online currency purchase.

GETTING AROUND

Airports
www.aeroporti.com
List of all Italian airports with relevant links (Italian only).

Ferries
www.ferriesonline.com
Ferry and hydrofoil timetables for Italy and its islands.

Freewats
www.autostrade.it
Information on routes, tolls, and construction on the Italian freeway network.

Railways
www.ferroviedellostato.it
Timetables, ticket prices, and booking service for the Italian railway network.

INTERNET

Internet Train
www.internettrain.it
A chain of Internet cafés, quite widespread throughout Italy.

Jiwire
www.jiwire.com
List of free WiFi hot spots.

TELEPHONES

Telecom Italia
www.telecomitalia.com
Italy's national telecom company.

Below: Train passing close to the Castello di Torremuzza, not far from Motta d'Affermo, Sicily

WHAT TO PACK

Depending on the time of year and the region that you are visiting, what you should pack will vary markedly. However, there are some key points that apply where and when ever you go. The Italians are a notoriously style-conscious nation, to whom being well-dressed is a matter of course. If you are dressed scruffily when shopping or dining, you may feel somewhat out of place. Even more importantly, both men and women should dress appropriately for visits to places of worship. Sometimes there is a notice at the entrance indicating the etiquette to follow, but, as a rule, a woman should cover bare shoulders and possibly her hair (carry a light shawl for this purpose) and, ideally, wear an over-the-knee skirt, while a man should wear pants, not shorts.

Generally speaking, in summer you will need light, breathable clothes in linen or cotton (but be prepared for ironing), including t-shirts and shorts with pockets, and comfortable walking sandals. Include some light clothes that cover your legs and arms, to ward off mosquitoes in the evenings, but pack insect repellent as well. Other indispensable items are a hat with a wide brim and good UV-screening sunglasses, whether you are going to the coast or the mountains. The same applies to a high SPF sunscreen and a total sunblock for lips and noses – as necessary for a ski trip in winter as for a beach trip in summer. And don't forget your swimwear.

In winter, the best plan is to dress in layers. Temperatures may be very low outside, but Italians tend to keep the heat turned up high indoors, so you will need to be able to shed a few items. Especially in the north of the country you should be prepared for rain, either with a sturdy telescopic umbrella or a waterproof jacket, and weatherproof footwear.

It's a good idea to carry a first aid kit with you. If you take medicines for any chronic condition, bring a copy of your prescription with you in case you lose or run out of anything. Bring all your usual toiletries as you may not be able to buy, say, your favorite shampoo.

If you are going on an adventure trip or to an out-of-the-way area, it's best to bring a multi-size sink/bath plug and a small flashlight with you.

Italian voltage is 220v, so bring at least one plug adaptor. However, it is increasingly common to find a hairdryer in your hotel room. Finally, don't forget to pack chargers for cameras, cell phones, and other electric devices.

Internet

Jiwire www.jiwire.com

The Internet has become a key tool for organizing travel, not just in the planning phase, but also when you are on vacation. It is increasingly the case that you will need (or at least want) access to the web to check timetables, book accommodation, or simply find out about what is happening in the place where you will be staying. More and more hotels are providing a PC in a public area, on which guests can check their mail, surf for information, update their social network profile, or upload photos. Some hotels offer WiFi in bedrooms for guests traveling with their own laptop. Check if there is a charge for these services.

Another solution is to seek out an Internet café, but, apart from in larger cities, you may experience some difficulty finding one near to where you are staying, unless you are in a university area or close to a large station. Consult the list of Internet cafés on the website www.cafe.ecs.net. In airports and at major train stations, and in increasing numbers of public places including a well-known burger chain, WiFi hot spots (free or paid) can be found.

Cell Phones

GSM World www.gsmworld.com

Italians were among the earliest and most enthusiastic adopters of the cell phone, and there is good coverage in almost every region. Check before you travel that Italian GSM frequencies are compatible with those of your provider, and take a look at their tariffs to avoid any unpleasant surprises on your bill. If you know you will need to make quite a few phone calls while abroad, consider buying a SIM card from an Italian operator, to use the local network and save money, making sure in advance that the your handset has been "unlocked."

Alternatively, there are plenty of public telephone booths in Italy. Few still accept coins so you will need to buy an international prepaid card (*carta* or *scheda telefonica*). These are available from tobacconists, post offices, newsagents, and some bars.

Post Offices

Posteitaliane www.poste.it/en

Post offices and some tobacconists weigh and price letters and sell stamps. Local post offices open from 8:25am–1:50pm on weekdays, and from 8:25am–noon on Saturday. Main post offices are open all day from 8:25am–7pm. Letters and cards to Europe cost the same as post sent within Italy, but will be more to other countries. For mail within Europe allow 3 working days for delivery, 5–7 to North America.

Photography

Photobucket http://photobucket.com
Image Shack http://imageshack.us

If you have a digital camera, you will have no problem buying memory cards or equipment for your camera (lenses, subaqua cases, tripods, etc). To make sure that your precious memories are safe, and to free up space on your memory card, it's worth joining a free online media-hosting site such as Photobucket or Imageshack, to which you can upload pictures and video as you travel. Alternatively, most camera shops will download your pictures and movies onto a CD or DVD. If you use a traditional camera, you may not find it easy to buy film or equipment, so bring all that you need with you.

While there are no restrictions on taking photos outdoors (other than of military installations), it is not always permissable to take pictures inside churches, museums, or archaeological sites: a notice at the entrance will give details of any restrictions, and should be obeyed.

Getting Around

Airports www.aeroporti.com
Ferries www.ferriesonline.com
Freeways www.autostrade.it
State Railways www.ferroviedellostato.it

Thanks to the topography of the country, the Italian transport system is reasonably well developed.

Italy is well served by airports, especially in the central-north. The main international hubs are Rome Fiumicino, and Milan Malpensa, but other busy airports include Milan Linate and Rome Ciampino, as well as Bergamo, Bologna, Catania, Naples, Palermo, Pisa, and Venice. During the summer season, smaller airports near the major tourist resorts are also very busy. Your travel agent or internet research will help you to work out the most economical flights, possibly with a stopover in one of the main European hubs if you are traveling from a non-EU country.

Traveling by train can also prove to be a comfortable (if slower) way of reaching Italy. You can book train travel right across Europe in one transaction on the RailEurope website (www.raileurope.com). Italy's efficient national railway network is run by Ferrovie dello Stato. The coach company Eurolines (www.eurolines.com) also runs services to Italy from most other European countries.

Car rental can be arranged at airports and train stations, but it's best and cheaper to do this in advance, online.

You will have to travel via alpine passes and mountain tunnels if you approach Italy from the north by car. The designation of freeways consists of the letter A followed by a number (A1, A12, A22), and most are toll roads, so there may be congestion at toll booths at busy times of the year and on weekends. Secondary roads are either Nazionale (N) or Strade Statale (SS), and their condition varies widely.

The most important national ports are Brindisi, Genoa, Naples, Palermo, and Venice. The islands can be reached by ferries from the main ports, or by internal flights.

The Weather in Italy

The elongated form of the Italian peninsula, which stretches far into the Mediterranean sea, means that Italy experiences a wide variety of climates, strongly influenced by its mountain ranges and by proximity to the sea. Latitude determines the distinct differences in climate and weather between the north and the south of the country, but in the interior, even in the far south, a more continental climate prevails. The entire Alpine range in the north experiences the inevitable long, cold, and snowy winters, while summers are generally cool and often showery; mid-season is usually very pleasant, and spring and fall also see plenty of mild and sunny days.

The Po Valley, in Emilia-Romagna, is where extremes of climate are most strongly felt: its long, bitter winters contrast markedly with hot and humid summers. Here, too, spring and fall are the best seasons for temperate days, ideal for visiting the many cities of art for which the region is well known.

In Central Italy, especially in those areas close to the coast, climatic extremes are much less pronounced, and the weather is mild for much of the year. Nonetheless, winters can still be very cold, especially along the Apennine chain – the "spine" of Italy – where the highest peaks are snow-capped for much of the winter and make an excellent (and usually less crowded) alternative to the Alps for winter sports enthusiasts.

Southern Italy has a warm climate all year round. Lovely springs and falls provide a foil to blistering summer heat; in winter it is rare for the temperature to drop below freezing, except at high altitudes far from the sea, where winters can be chilly and snow is not unusual. Sicily and Sardinia experience the most Mediterranean climate, with long, sunny summers and mild winters that see blue skies interspersed with rain.

Summer can bring sudden thunderstorms, fierce but usually of short duration, along the entire length of the peninsula. They can even be a welcome relief from the heat, freshening the air and brightening the countryside.

In summary, fall and spring are the best seasons for visiting Italy's cities, inland regions, and the southern coast, while summer is ideal for northern coastal regions and Alpine hikes, and winter for snowy sports or a touch of southern sun.

Above: Summer sunset over the beach at Alassio in Liguria; Gothic church of San Vigilio in Colfosco, against the snowy backdrop of the Monte Sella mountains

Climate Charts

These show average quarterly maximum and minimum temperatures; average daily hours of sunshine; and average quarterly rainfall in the main Italian cities.

MILAN

	Dec-Feb	Mar-May	Jun-Aug	Sep-Nov
°F (max)	43	63	83	63
°F (min)	30	45	61	48
Sunshine	2 hours	6 hours	9 hours	4 hours
Rainfall	2.4 in	3.4 in	2.9 in	3.5 in

FLORENCE

	Dec-Feb	Mar-May	Jun-Aug	Sep-Nov
°F (max)	52	66	86	70
°F (min)	36	46	61	50
Sunshine	3 hours	6 hours	9 hours	4 hours
Rainfall	2.9 in	2.9 in	2.2 in	3.6 in

ROME

	Dec-Feb	Mar-May	Jun-Aug	Sep-Nov
°F (max)	55	66	84	72
°F (min)	39	46	63	52
Sunshine	4 hours	7 hours	10 hours	6 hours
Rainfall	3.2 in	2.4 in	1.2 in	3.8 in

NAPLES

	Dec-Feb	Mar-May	Jun-Aug	Sep-Nov
°F (max)	55	66	82	72
°F (min)	39	48	62	54
Sunshine	4 hours	6 hours	10 hours	6 hours
Rainfall	43 in	2.8 in	1.3 in	4.9 in

JANUARY – APRIL

VENICE Elaborately costumed participants in Carnevale

JANUARY

Festa di San Silverstro/ Capodanno
Rome and countrywide
December 31–January 1
The arrival of the new year is enthusiastically celebrated in the streets of the capital, centered around Piazza del Popolo.
www.comune.roma.it

La Fòcara
Novoli (near Lecce), Puglia
January 16–17
A gigantic bonfire of bundles of vine branches burns all night in honor of Novoli's patron saint, Antonio Abate.
www.focara.it

Fiera di Sant'Orso
Aosta, Valle d'Aosta
January 30–31
Valle d'Aosta's traditional crafts fair.
www.fierasantorso.it

FEBRUARY

Sagra delle Mandorlo in Fiore
Agrigento, Sicily
End January–early February
A festival of folklore, music, and dance to celebrate the blossoming of the region's almond trees.
www.mandorloinfiore.net

Festa di Sant'Agata
Catania, Sicily
February 3–5
A solemn but colorful and popular festival in honor of the Catania martyr; this is the third most well attended Christian religious festival in the world.
www.sicilyweb.com/santagata

Carnevale
Venice, Friuli-Venezia Giulia
February–March
One of the most famous carnivals in the world, the Venice Carnevale is celebrated throughout the city's streets, which fill with crowds of revelers wearing the beautiful traditional masks, street theater, parades, music, and dance.
www.carnevale.venezia.it

MARCH

La Sartiglia
Oristano, Sardinia
February–March
The ancient *corsa all'anello* (in which riders joust at a suspended ring) is part of a tournament of horseback races and events.
www.sartiglia.info

Capodanno Fiorentino
Florence, Tuscany
Sunday after March 25
A colorful historical procession captures the spirit of the old Florentine new year, on the day of the Annunciation.
www.firenzeturismo.it

Giornate di Primavera
Throughout Italy
March–April
Over one spring weekend, the FAI (Italy's equivalent of the US's National Register of Historic Places) opens hundreds of buildings and to the public free of charge.
www.fondoambiente.it/en

APRIL

Settimana Santa
Taranto, Puglia
March–April
Taranto's Holy Week processions on Maundy Thursday and Good Friday are profoundly moving.
www.holyweektaranto.com

Scoppio del Carro
Florence, Tuscany
Easter Sunday
Literally "the Explosion of the Cart," this spectacular pyrotechnic expression of Holy Fire takes place outside Florence's Duomo.
www.duomofirenze.it

Trento Film Festival
Trento, Trentino Alto-Adige
April–May
An international film festival dedicated to mountains, climbing, exploration, and the environment. Besides screenings, there are performances, themed exhibitions, and conferences.
www.trentofestival.it

MAY – AUGUST

SIENA Horses raring to go at the start of the Palio

MAY

Maggio Musicale Fiorentino
Florence, Tuscany
May–June
An international festival of music, ballet, and theater.
www.maggiofiorentino.com

Festa di San Nicola
Bari, Puglia
May 7–9
A picturesque evening procession to the sea carrying the statue of St. Nicholas, culminating in fireworks.
www.basilicasannicola.it

Festa dei Ceri
Gubbio, Umbria
May 15
A demanding uphill team race through the streets of Gubbio, with gigantic "candle" *(ceri)* pedestals carried aloft.
www.ceri.it

JUNE

La Biennale di Venezia
Venice, Friuli-Venezia Giulia
June–November
This is one of the principal events in world culture, devoted to art (in odd years) and architecture (in even years). The Venice Film Festival (which takes place annually in Aug–Sep) is part of the event.
www.labiennale.org

Opera Festival
Verona, Friuli-Venezia Giulia
June–August
World-class operas are staged in the magnificent setting of the Arena, Verona's superb Roman amphitheater.
www.arena.it

Festival dei Due Mondi
Spoleto, Umbria
End June–mid-July
This prestigious international festival of opera, dance, classical music, and drama takes place in lovely, medieval Spoleto.
www.festivaldispoleto.com

JULY

Umbria Jazz
Perugia, Umbria
Mid-July
The most important jazz event in Italy, with performances by world-famous artists.
www.umbriajazz.com

La Versiliana
Marina di Pietrasanta, Tuscany
July–August
Theater performances, cultural events, and art exhibitions, including events for children.
www.laversilianafestival.it

Festa del Redentore
Venice, Friuli-Venezia Giulia
Third weekend
Since 1577, a spectacular festival of thanksgiving has been held on the Grand Canal, to give thanks for the city's liberation from the plague. Fireworks, regattas, and other events form one of the most traditional and authentic Venetian celebrations.
www.comune.venezia.it

AUGUST

Rossini Opera Festival
Pesaro, Le Marche
Mid-August
Opera festival dedicated to celebrating the works of the Pesaro-born composer Gioachino Rossini.
www.rossinioperafestival.it

Palio di Siena
Siena, Tuscany
July 2 and August 16
A centuries-old challenge, this world famous horse race takes place in Piazza del Campo, with riders from the different quarters of Siena competing.
www.ilpalio.org

La Notte della Taranta
Melpignano, Puglia
End August
A grand concert to conclude the lengthy festival of Salentine *pizzica* (Salento folk music).
www.lanottedellataranta.it

SEPTEMBER – DECEMBER

MILAN Elegant foyer of La Scala opera house

SEPTEMBER

Trasporto della Macchina di Santa Rosa
Viterbo, Lazio
September 3
A gigantic illuminated structure, bearing a statue of Santa Rosa, is carried through the town, borne aloft by *facchini* ("porters") chosen for their strength.
www.viterboonline.com

Festivaletteratura
Mantua, Lombardy
First two weeks
International literary festival with a program of readings, cultural events, and performances.
www.festivaletteratura.it

MITO SettembreMusica
Milan and Turin
Mid-September
With performances ranging from classical music to contemporary sounds, this major music festival is held in prestigious locations in Milan and Turin.
www.mitosettembremusica.it

OCTOBER

La Barcolana
Trieste, Friuli-Venezia Giulia
Second Sunday
A spectacular regatta that sees the participation of hundreds of sailing boats of all sizes, plus other races and events.
www.barcolana.it

Festival Internazionale del Film di Rome
Rome, Lazio
Mid-October
After Venice, this is the most important film festival in Italy, featuring major world premieres.
www.romacinemafest.it

Fiera Internazionale del Tartufo Bianco
Alba, Piedmont
October–November
A gastronomic fair devoted to the rare and expensive white truffle – the "white gold" of Piedmont.
www.fieradeltartufo.org

NOVEMBER

Festival dei Popoli
Florence, Tuscany
First week
International festival dedicated to cultural and social documentary film, with lectures, discussions, and workshops.
www.festivaldeipopoli.org

Roma Jazz Festival
Rome, Lazio
Throughout November
This major event dedicated to jazz is an important date in the European music calendar.
www.romajazzfestival.it

Romaeuropa Festival
Rome, Lazio
September–December
Three months of events: visual arts, music, dance, and theater, featuring innovative works by emerging new artists.
www.kadmusarts.com/festivals/3895.html

DECEMBER

Inaugurazione della Stagione, La Scala
Milan, Lombardy
December 7
Opening night of the new season at Milan's famous La Scala opera house is a glittering, star-studded occasion for which tickets are highly sought-after.
www.teatroallascala.org

Mercatino di Natale
Bolzano, Trentino Alto-Adige
December
One of the most atmospheric Christmas markets in Italy.
www.bolzano.net

Presepi Viventi
Various locations
December–January
In the Christmas period, nativity scenes are set up throughout Italy, but the most famous and moving are the traditional Living Nativities in which local people play all the roles.
www.presepevivente.it (Italian only)

Index

Page numbers in **bold** indicate main references

A

B

C

Picture Credits

The publisher would like to thank the following individuals, companies, and picture libraries for permission to reproduce their photographs:

Key: t – top; b – below; c – center; f – far; l – left; r – right.

Area vacanze Valli Tures e Aurina: 93c; / FeRe: 93bl; / Klausberg: 93br; / W. Lucker: 93tl; / H Seeber: 93tc, 93tr, 93bc.
Archivio Geo Mondadori, Milano: 69cr, 170fbl, 233tl, 290fbl; / Adriano Bacchella: 206fbl, 207br; / Gianluca Boetti: 171ftr; / Ghigo Roli: 233ftl.
Archivio Maggio Musicale Fiorentino: 155br.
Archivio Parco Nazionale Arcipelago Toscano: 106-107t, 106tl, 106tr, 106cl, 106fbl, 107fbr.
Associazione Strada del Franciacorta, Erbusco: 129br.
Associazione Turistica Val Senales: 318-319c, 318tl, 319ftr, 319bcr.
Alessandra Chemollo, Venezia: 222bl.
Atp Friuli: 146-147c, 147bl;
Bruno Balestrini, Milano: 288tl.
Simona Bartolena, Milano: 70bl, 270fbl.
Bergamo Jazz/Luciano Rossetti: 104tr.
Cameraphoto, Venezia: 34-35.
Canevaworld Resort: 114bl.
Marta Carenzi, Milano: 306bl, 306br.
Charbonnier Mongolfiere: 38-39c.
Comune di Rignano Garganico: 322bl.
Comunità Montana Valle Vigezzo (VB): 66tl, 67br.
Consorzio Turistico Valtellina Terziere Superiore: Ivan Previsdomini: 98tl.
Conti Sertoli Salis, Tirano: 98fbl.
© Contrasto, Milano / Davide Lanzilao: 223ftr.
Costa Edutainment/Merlofotografia: 238-239c, 238bl, 238br, 239tr, 239br.
© Cuboimages: Richard Ashworth: 108-109c; / Adriano Bacchella: 50-51c, 51br, 97fbr, 127tl, 148tr, 148bl, 149tl, 152tl, 161c, 294tr, 318cl; / Stefano Beccio: 267tr; / Claudio Beduschi: 15bl, 50br, 51bc, 88bl, 127br, 148tc, 210bl, 289ftr; / Michele Bella: 56fbl, 96bl, 129tcr, 135br, 145tl, 177ftr, 185br, 217c, 231cr, 290bl; / Bluered: 16tr, 16c, 18tl, 20cl, 20bc, 20-21bc, 31bl, 43tr, 44br, 46fbl, 47bc, 48bc, 58br, 66br, 69bl, 73bl, 78bc, 78br, 79bl, 81tl, 81c, 83br, 89br, 90fbl, 94br, 97tr, 100-101c, 101br, 104bl, 104tl, 116bl, 117tr, 123bl, 127c, 127bl, 129tr, 130br, 131bc, 142bl, 145c, 151br, 153fbr, 157br, 157cbl, 162fbl, 170bl, 174fbl, 175tr, 183tl, 187tr, 189tr, 191bl, 201tr, 205tl, 216c, 217tr, 217bl, 227ftl, 229c, 231ftr, 231bl, 233br, 236tl, 240bl, 252br, 258br, 262fbl, 278tr, 280fbl, 280ctl, 286br, 291tc, 292bl, 294tl, 314bc, 315bl, 315cr, 315br, 320fbl, 324-32c, 325tc; / Marco Bianchi: 006-007, 218-219; / Caterina Bruzzone: 78fbl, 94-95c, 148tl; / Edy Buttarelli: 57tr, 44tr, 128bl, 172tr, 223bl, 293ctr;/ Alberto Campanile: 15c, 92bl, 146br, 232c, 233ftr, 253c, 257bc, 257br, 318bl;/ Enrico Caracciolo: 23bl, 32fbl, 33tr, 33fbr, 92-93c, 131c, 188tl, 188br, 261tr; / Anania Carri: 82bc, 201c, 205tr, 205c, 208tr, 232bl, 322tr; / Marco Casiraghi: 17br, 142tl, 142-143c, 143fbr, 164tl, 164-165c, 165tr, 198bl, 209tr, 260c, 261bl, 272tc, 290-291t, 291tl; / Angelo Cavalli: 268tl; / Anne Conway: 147tcr, 316tr, 317tc, 317bc, 320bc; / Dionisolemma: 54br, 55br, 157tr, 178bl, 189c, 234-235c, 270bc, 283tr; / Andrea Durazzi: 26-27c, 151bl, 151tl, 213tl, 264bl; / Eyeubiquitus: 203tcr; / Lee Frost / Robert Harding: 44bl; / Enrico Fumagalli: 99bl, 123ftr, 136-137c, 165tl, 205ftr, 223br, 278bl, 278br, 279tr, 280-281c, 314-315c, 314br, 315ftr; / Alfio Garozzo: 16tl, 22c, 22bl, 23tl, 40bc, 40br, 46-47c, 54tr, 54fbr, 109tl, 116-117c, 117c, 123br, 157tl, 204bl, 214bl, 262bl, 264tr, 264cr, 264bl, 270tl, 280tl, 281tr, 293cb, 294bl, 295c, 295tr, 312c, 313tr, 313c, 313bl; / Alfio Giannotti: 13br, 58tl, 73br, 102tl, 102cl, 164c, 188bl, 200tr, 250fbl, 250br, 251tr, 285ftl, 285tr; / Gimmi: 13tc, 13bc, 33tl, 42fbl, 49br, 50bl, 53bc, 72-73c, 73c, 100tl, 100bl, 124bl, 134tl, 154fbl, 172tl, 174-175c, 213ftl, 213ftr, 213bc, 213br, 231tr, 233tr, 233bl, 237tr, 254tl, 258tr, 310bl, 311bcr, 311ftr; / Robert Harding: 24-25c, 25bl, 29br, 32tl, 51c, 78-79c, 130-131c, 134-135c, 136fbl, 211c, 223tr, 223cr, 264tr, 225br; / Gavin Hellier: 115br; / Norma Joseph: 271c; / Elio Lombardo: 23tr, 28br, 29bl, 135bc, 237c, 264fbl / Riccardo Lombardo: 16fbl, 47cr, 47bl, 52-53c, 53fbl, 54br, 90bl, 94fbl, 116tl, 134tr, 160c, 161tl, 161tc, 161tr, 161br, 263ftr, 313tl, 313br; / Dario Mainetti: 127tr;/ Mauritius: 30c, 32tc, 64tl, 64cl, 77bl, 81bc, 126c, 148-149c, 183bl, 196-197c, 222-223c, 243bc;/ Federico Meneghetti: 16-17c, 16cl, 16bc, 16br, 17bl, 17bc, 19tl, 19br, 42-43c, 43bl, 48tl, 58fbl, 68bc, 72bl, 73bc, 82-83c, 83cr, 83bl, 83bfr 123c, 147br, 147tcr, 162-163bc, 172bl, 173tr, 171br, 172bc, 175bc, 203tfr, 206-207c, 234tc, 234tr, 234bl, 235tr, 235tl, 245tr, 252tl, 252tr, 253tr, 258tc, 261tl, 278tl, 286bc, 307tr, 309tr, 313ftr, 316tl, 317tl, 324bl, 325tl, 325tr; / Giorgio Mesturini: 50fbl, 51t, 94bl, 120tl, 120bl, 143tr, 161bc, 164tr, 208tl, 208br, 272tl, 272tr, 272bl, 272-273c, 273tc, 273tr, 273br; / Nicolò Minerbi: 116tr, 186fbl; / Bruno Morandi: 64-65bc; / Francesca Morgera: 263br; / Oliviero Olivieri / Robert Harding: 161bl, 261br; / Paroli Galperti: 79c, 88-89c, 143br, 147bc, 293ftr; / Claudio Penna: 32-33c, 291tr; / Luca Picciau: 120-121c, 164bl; / Roy Rainford / Robert Harding: 77bc; / Walter Rawlings/Robert Harding: 77c; / Cesare Re: 58bl, 66tr, 94cl, 207ftr, 217br; / R&DValterza: 106-107c, 174cl, 266bl, 322tcl, 322br, 322tl; / Paolo Reda: 57br, 230bl; / Ghigo Roli: 21bc, 39bl, 39fbr, 69bc, 121br, 157c, 191tr, 270tr, 271tr, 261c, 320tr, 321tr;/ Ellen Rooney: 79br; / Ellen Rooney / Robert Harding: 229tr; / Umberto Ronchetti: 130fbl, 186br; / Mauro Ruffini: 207tr, 207bcr, 242-243c; / Vittorio Sciosa: 64bfl, 117fbr, 156bl, 228bl, 250cl, 251bl, 270br, 280cbl; /Enzo Signorelli: 16bl, 31tl, 31br, 31tc, 40bl, 47bfr, 54tl, 59br, 94tl, 95br, 108-109tc, 109br, 174tl, 174bl, 179tl, 179ftr, 179bl, 200br, 214-215c, 214bc, 214br, 240tl, 255tr, 262br, 307c, 312bl; / Marco Simonini: 30bl, 31tr, 175bl, 199tr, 199bl, 199br, 256bl, 257tr, 257ftr, 319tr; / Enrico Spanu: 198bc, 198br, 208bl; / Patrizia Spinelli: 43br; / Angelo Todini: 32bl, 42bl, 46br, 182c, 191tl, 191ftr, 296-297c, 324tl, 325bc; / Nico Tondini: 155bl; / Stefano Venturini: 38tl, 38bc; / Vincent: 304-305c; / John Warburton-Lee: 26tl, 31c, 45c, 173c, 262-263c, 268tr, 319br; / Damiano Zanderighi: 287tr; / Walter Zerla: 19c, 23bc, 53bl, 97br, 117br, 130bl, 131bl, 131br, 134bl, 135tc, 149br, 164tc, 224bl, 269tl, 269tr, 268tc, 269cr, 296tcl, 296bl;
© Corbis/Atlantide Phototravel: 58-59c, 58bc; / Grand Tour: 228-229c; / WWD/Condé Nast: 56bl; / Hein Van den Heuvel/: 64-65c.
Archivio Mondadori Electa: 8-9, 12 bl, 12 bc, 12br, 18c, 20tl, 23c, 28-29c, 28bl, 29t, 31bc, 32tr, 32tr, 40tl, 42br, 51bl, 64bl, 65br, 68-69c, 72fbl, 72br, 74-75c, 76bl, 76c, 77tr, 78bl, 101tr, 103cr, 104bc, 106bl, 123tc, 127bc, 131tc, 135tr, 137br, 138-139c, 144bl, 145bc, 149tr, 151tr, 151bc, 155tr, 155cr, 158tl, 159fbr, 162bl, 172br, 177tr, 179br, 184c, 185tr, 185ftr, 185bl, 188tr, 191tc, 196 bl, 197tc, 200fbl, 205bl, 207tcr, 211tc, 211bc, 213tr, 217ftl, 217tl, 227tl, 227bl, 227br, 229tc, 231br, 236tr, 236bl, 236b, 239bl, 242tr, 242tl, 251br, 252bl, 255tc, 257ftl, 257bl, 264cl, 265tc, 266tl, 268bl, 278bc, 283cr, 285bl, 288tl, 288bl, 292-293c, 296fbl, 305cr, 308br, 311tr, 319tcr, 324tr; /Sergio Anelli: 19tr, 57fbr, 68bl, 69br, 74tl, 74cl, 75cr, 75fbr, 90-91c, 122c, 123bc; 196tcl, 196bcl, 197tr, 197bc, 305br; / Archivio dell'Arte Luciano Pedicini: 24bl; / Graziano Arici: 44tc, 44bc, 56-57c; / Arte e Colore: 102bl; /Luigi Baldin: 162br; / Bruno Balestrini: 49c, / Remo Bardazzi: 43cr, 43bc; / Michele Bella: 96cl, 91br; / Osvaldo Bohm: 45br; / Fabrizio Carraro: 238fbl , 243tl, 243tr, 288tr; 24br, 103tr, 104tc, 104br, 125tr, 258tr, 258bl, 258tc/Marco Covi: 002-003; 18-19c, 19cr, 19fbr, 163tr, 163br, 163bl, 163fbr; / Favarato: 54bl, 81tc, 146bl, 165br, 191br, 240bc; / Foglia: 77tc, 77br / Fotomoderna: 145tr, 145bl; / 162-163c; / Roland Halbe: 304bl, 305ftr; / Katia Kissov : 273tl; / Federico Magi: 18bl, 21br, 23tc, 65fbr, 68fbl, 71br, 83tr, 108bl, 157cbr, 186bl, 208bc, 235tc, 258tl, 316bl, 320br, 322tcr; / Paolo Manusardi: 176tl; / Riccardo Marcialis: 18bl, 245tc; / Paolo Monti: 145br; / Diego Motto: 227tr, 227ftr; / Prima Press: 19br, 48br, 66bc, 120fbl, 225ctr, 261tc, 262bc, 270bl, 280bl; / Antonio Quattrone: 123tl, 226c; / Marco Ravenna: 19bc, 41c, 215tfr, 215cr, 215br, 293tr; / Giovanni Ricci: 300-301; 305tr; / Lucio Rossi – Polis: 239cr; / Daniel Teggi: 46bc, 183br, 287bl; / Thelma & Louise: 53br, 77tl, 215bl, 313tc; / Arnaldo Vescovo: 41br, 46bl, 47tr, 47br, 060-061, 084-085, 70tl, 70tr, 70bc, 70br, 71c, 91tr, 91cr, 91fbr, 154-155c, 154br, 176bl, 177cr, 192-193, 211tr, 236br, 288-289c, 288cl, 288bl, 288fbl, 289tr, 289cr, 289br, 289tr.
Ente Giardini Botanici Villa Taranto: 89bl, 89bc.
Ente Grotte di Frasassi: 279c.
Ente Turismo Alba, Bra, Langhe, Roero: 290cl.
Ente Turismo Merano e dintorni: 180fbl, 181ftr, 181tr, 181rc, 181br.
Ente Turismo Modena: 96fbl.
Ente Turistico della Valle d'Aosta: 206br, 207bl.
FAI - Fondo Ambiente Italiano © Giorgio Majno: 283br.
Festivaletteratura: 226bl.
Gardaland, Castelnuovo del Garda: 114c, 115tl, 115c, 115bl, 115bc.
© Getty Images, Milano: 198-199c, 224-225c; / Popperfoto: 242bl.
© Granataimages: 38fbl, 54-55c, 67c, 196fbl, 250bl; / Alamy: 186-187c, 202-203c.
Andrea Jemolo, Roma: 150c, 289c.
Maria Elisa Le Donne: 235br.
Fabrizio Lovera, Torino: 234tl.
© Marka: Giulio Andreini 210-211c. Bilderbox age fotostock: 18fbl. Danilo Donadoni: 321c. Max Galli: 230br. SuperStock: 286bl. Vidler Steve: 1.
Mart-Museo di Arte Moderna e Contemporanea di Trento e Rovereto: 256c, 257tl.
Mondadori Syndication: 38cl, 40tr, 88br, 95bl, 96tl, 98br, 104tcl, 108fbl, 117tl, 177br, 185tc, 202bl.
Maurizio Montanari/Archivio Ravenna Festival: 185tl.
Luca Mozzati, Milano: 288br.
© NEW IMAGE: Giuseppe Carfagna 16bc, 19tr, 20-21c, 23br, 25tr, 25fbr, 66bl, 68br, 80c, 81tr, 81bl, 81br, 82bl, 100tr, 100fbl, 100-101t, 108cl, 123tr, 133tl, 142cl, 150s, 151c, 154bl, 158tr, 158bl, 159tl, 159cr, 159br, 160bl, 162bc, 174br, 179ftl, 179tr, 179c, 183tc, 184bl, 188bc, 200tl, 205bc, 203tr, 217bc, 250tl, 269tc, 282bl, 288fbl, 306tl, 306tr, 306fbl, 309bl, 315tr; / M. Di Marco: 75tr; / R. Fabriani: 99br.
Luigi Nifosì: 274-275.
Olycom/Stockfood Italia: 142fbl.
Parco della Villa Pallavicino, Stresa: 132tr.
Parco Tematico Aviazione: 202fbl.
Parcoavventura: 266cl, 267br.
Luciano Pedicini, Napoli: 250-251c.
Pila S.P.A.: 27fbr.
Pro Loco di Arquà Petrarca: 252fbl.
Pro Loco, Sondalo: 98bl.
Antonio Quattrone, Firenze: 12fbl, 13fbr, 196tl.
Rabatti & Domingie, Firenze: 13bl.
© REALY EASY STAR: © Franco Banfi: 178c; / © Franco Barbagallo: 108tr; / © Claudio Beduschi: 15bl; / © Enrico Bottino: 90tl, 322c; / © Antonio Capone: 24fbl, 200bl; 254-255c, 254tr, 254cl, 254bl, 254fbl, 255tl, 284c, 308-309c, 308fbl, 308bl, 309ftr, 309cr, 309br; / ©Riccardo Carnovalini: 124tr; / © Santi Coco: 294bc; / © Claudio Concina: 240tr, 129bcr, 285br; / © Giuseppe Corte: 158-159c; / © Orazio Cristaldi: 186-187bc, 187br; / © Duilio Fiorille: 16tl; / © Gemma Giusta: 183tr; © Fabio Iorio: 285tl; © Alberto Maisto: 164fbl, 244bl, 245bl, 260bl; / © Giuseppe Masci: 322c, 322bl; / © Marco Moretti: 182bl; / © Guido Orlando: 54bl, 294br; / © Adriano Penco: 55bl, 183c; / Lara Pessina: 159tr; / © Res: 83bc, 185c, 190bl, 268-269c; / © Francesca Sciarra: 183bc, 225ftr; / © Antonio Sollazzo: 54cl; / © Pasquale Sorrentino: 25bc; / © Toni Spagone: 16bl, 16br, 19bl, 25cr, 20bl, 38bl, 39bc, 39br, 55bc, 88bc, 103fbr, 104bl, 124tl, 125c, 128-129c, 129fbr, 132-133c, 133br, 133fbr, 136bl, 152-153c, 156c, 157bl, 170-171c, 170br, 171tr, 171cr, 171bl, 180-181c, 191c, 203bcr, 203br, 206bl, 245tl, 240br, 241tr, 254tc, 264-265c, 264tl, 265tl, 265tr, 266fbl, 267ftr, 283ftr, 284bl, 285ftr, 285bc, 287br, 290-291c, 290tl, 290tc, 293br, 296tl, 296bcl, 296tr, 314bl, 320tl, 320bl; / © Egidio Trainito: 244c, 245c, 245br; © Tullio Valente: 48tr, 48bfl, 124-125c, 125tl, 125br, 146bc, 147bcr, 258-259c, 258tl, 316-317c, 317tr; / © Renato Valterza: 225cbr, 267cr.
Redazione web della città di Torino: 242tc.
Regione Autonoma Valle d'Aosta, Assessorato Turismo, Sport, Commercio e Trasporti, Ufficio Promozione e Pubblicità: 26fbl.
Rhaetische Bahn By-line: swiss-image.ch: 99fbr; / Peter Donatsch: 98bc, 98-99c.
Daniele Robotti: 27tr, 27tc.
Rossini Opera Festival/Amati Bacciardi: 204c.
RPBW ph. Stefano Goldberg: 286-287c.
Luigi Rubino: 215tr.
© Scala, Firenze: 12-13c, 135tl, 310-311c, 311tcr, 311br; / Su concessione del Ministero per i Beni e le Attività Culturali: 212c, 213bl.
Scenari Srl – Andrea Lazzarini Editore – Stresa (VB): 133cr, 132tl.
Sonia Servida, Milano: 59bl, 136tl, 144c.
Settimane Musicali di Stresa e del Lago Maggiore: 132bl.
SIME: Cogoli Franco 96-97c; /Giovanni Simeone: 102-103c; /Ripani Massimo: 241c; / Serrano Anna: 176-177c.
Sole di Vetro: 27br, 115tc, 217ftr, 282-283c.
Georg Tappeiner: 152cl, 152bl, 152fbl, 153br.
Tappeiner Spa: 152br, 153bl.
Terme Merano/Georg Tappeiner: 180-181bc; / Gionata Xerra: 180bl.
©TIPS: Antique Research Centre 80bl; / Claudio Beduschi: 266-267c; / Bildagentur: 230-231c; / Marcello Pedone: 190c; / Guido Alberto Rossi: 5, 110-111, 166-167, 205ftl, 246-247; / Mark Edward Smith: 48bl, 222br; / Tips Italia 54fbl, 104c, 202bc, 225tr, 209c; / Francesco Tommasinelli: 126l; / Topfoto: 227c.
Ufficio Territoriale di informazione turistica dell'Oltrepò Pavese: 216bl.
Umbria Jazz Festival: 176fbl.
Arnaldo Vescovo, Roma: 29fbr.
Webphoto, Roma: 288bc.

Jacket images
Front: **Alamy Images:** Funky Travel/Paul Williams fbl. **Getty Images:** Iconica/Eric Meola br; The Image Bank/Jorg Greuel fbl; Photographer's Choice/Dirk von Mallinkrodt fbr; Taxi/Ulf Sjostedt (main). Back: **4Corners Images:** SIME/Cogoli Franco b; **Corbis:** Robert Harding World Imagery/Bruno Morandi ca; **Getty Images:** Slow Images cb; **Photolibrary:** Tips Italia/Danielle Nicoli t. Spine: **4Corners Images:** SIME/Gusso Luca b.**Getty Images:** Photographer's Choice/Harald Sud t. Back Flap: courtesy of **Curtis Brown Limited** t.

For Mondadori

Senior Editor:
Claudia Vassallo

Editorial:
Elisa Checchi, Nicoletta Geminiani, Rino Parlapiano, Elena Pullé

Design Coordinator:
Chiara Forte

Design:
Giorgio Gardel

Picture Research Coordinator:
Simona Bartolena

Picture Research:
Marta Carenzi, Valentina Minucciani, Sonia Servida

Technical Coordinator:
Rosella Lazzarotto

Quality Control:
Giancarlo Berti

Maps:
Marco Zanella